GEORGE FENICH | KRISTIN MALEK

MEETINGS, EXPOSITIONS, EVENTS & CONVENTIONS

AN INTRODUCTION TO THE INDUSTRY

Sixth Edition

Kendall Hunt
publishing company

Kendall Hunt

publishing company

www.kendallhunt.com
Send all inquiries to:
4050 Westmark Drive
Dubuque, IA 52004-1840

CONTENTS

CHAPTER 5: EXHIBITIONS AND TRADE SHOWS 159

CHAPTER 6: SERVICE CONTRACTORS 195

CHAPTER 7: DESTINATION MANAGEMENT COMPANIES 223

CHAPTER 10: LEGAL ISSUES IN THE MEEC INDUSTRY   333

CHAPTER 15: INTERNATIONAL ASPECTS IN MEEC 517

PREFACE

The meetings, expositions, events, and conventions (MEEC, pronounced like *geese*) industry continues to grow and garner increasing attention from the hospitality industry, colleges and universities, and communities. This book gives a broad overview of this industry and is thus an introduction. This book is not meant to provide a hands-on or step-by-step method for handling gatherings in the MEEC industry. The latter is addressed in two books by Fenich: *Planning and Management of Meetings, Expositions, Events, and Conventions* and *Production and Logistics in Meetings, Expositions, Events, and Conventions*. Both of these books are based on and align with the Meeting and Business Event Competency Standards (MBECS).

This book is being produced at this time for a number of reasons. One is the continued growth of this industry; in spite of the ebbs and flows of the economy, the MEEC segment of the hospitality industry remains resilient. Communities continue to build or expand MEEC venues unabatedly, and the private sector has also become a player in convention center construction and operation. People still find a need for face-to-face meetings. The MEEC industry appears to be on a growth curve and is of interest to many people.

Also, college faculties have indicated a need for a book such as this. The authors have been teaching introductory MEEC courses for many years and have found that they are having to continually supplement existing books to make them both current and more complete in addressing the various segments of the MEEC industry. This book concept originated at a meeting of the Convention Special Interest Group at the International Council on Hotel, Restaurant, and Institutional Education (ICHRIE) Convention in 2001 when the need for a new text was discussed. The members of this group all noted the need, and Fenich volunteered to spearhead an effort to put together a new book using faculty and industry experts to write various chapters. This book is a culmination of that effort. The result is a text where some of the best and most notable people in the MEEC industry have made contributions.

The approach to deciding on topics was unusual. Rather than have a list of topics or chapters based on people's willingness to contribute, a more scientific method was used. Fenich began by reviewing existing books, both theoretical and practical, to ascertain which topics to cover. Topics that appeared in more than one text were compiled into a list. Then a number of meetings were held with educators, and the relative importance of topics was discussed, which led to the development of a comprehensive list of topics. This list was sent to educators and practitioners, who were asked to rank the importance of each topic as critically important, important, or not important. Results were used to pare down the list, and an iterative voting procedure (Delphi technique) was used to reach the decision as to the topics to include in the book. This sixth edition not only has updated material and statistics but also has relied on feedback from adopters and reviewers to make improvements to the previous edition.

It should be noted that this industry is referred to in many ways: "Meetings and Events," "Events," "Meeting Planning," and others. A very common acronym, and one used extensively in Asia, is "MICE," which stands for "Meetings, Incentives, Conventions, Events" and is pronounced as the plural of mouse. That acronym was purposely *not* chosen for the title of this text. The reason is that most programs of study deal with the Incentives or Incentive Travel very little, if at all. Furthermore, the Incentive Travel segment has evolved significantly in the past few years moving away from trips that were strictly for pleasure (as a reward for performance) and much more into trips that have notable education and training components. Thus, they are now much more like sales training meetings, motivational meetings, or team building exercises, but only on a more grandiose scale. Thus, this book deals with meetings, expositions, events, and conventions.

NEW IN THIS EDITION

- The inclusion of an in-depth analysis and discussion on the impacts of COVID-19 on all of the sectors operating within the MEEC industry
- All chapters and data have been updated
- Many new images
- The chapter on technology has been significantly rewritten and updated
- The chapter discussing international aspects of MEEC includes additional regions of the globe with an active and growing presence of the MEEC industry
- The glossary has been expanded to include all key terms found in the chapters
- A new co-editor to the textbook has been added, and teaching materials have been completely updated

Meetings, Expositions, Events, and Conventions should be of interest to practitioners, educators, students, and the general public. It is the most up-to-date book on the MEEC industry and will provide users with an overview of the industry; it is also comprehensive and covers a wider range of MEEC topics than any other book currently available. It can easily serve as the basis for an introductory college course on the subject or for orientation sessions for new employees in the industry. It should meet the needs of anyone interested in knowing more about the MEEC industry.

George G. Fenich, PhD and Kristin Malek, PhD

ACKNOWLEDGMENTS

I would like to thank Kathryn Hashimoto for her unabated support, patience, and encouragement; the chapter contributors for their work and insights; and students everywhere for their interest in the MEEC industry. Also, thank you to the educators in the MEEC field for helping develop the concept for this book and for continuing support through adoptions of this text. The contributors are:

PART 1: INTRODUCTION

Chapter 1: Introduction to the Meetings, Expositions, Events, and Conventions Industry

Amy Calvert
Chief Executive Officer
Events Industry Council
Washington, District of Columbia

Mariela McIlwraith
Vice President of Sustainability and Industry Advancement
Events Industry Council
Washington, District of Columbia

Chapter 2: Meeting, Expositions, Events, and Convention Organizers

Kristin Malek, PhD, CMP, CED, DES, CHE
Event Management Extension Specialist and Assistant Professor in HRTM
University of Nebraska—Lincoln
Lincoln, Nebraska

PART 2: KEY PLAYERS

Chapter 3: Destination Marketing Organizations (DMOs)

Jonathon Day, PhD
Associate Professor and Graduate Program Director
School of Hospitality and Tourism Management
Purdue University
West Lafayette, Indiana

Chapter 4: Meeting and Convention Venues

Lisa Young, PhD
Associate Professor
DePaul University
Chicago, Illinois

Juan Mendez
Instructor
DePaul University
Chicago, Illinois

Chapter 5: Exhibitions

Marsha Flanagan, MEd
Vice President, Learning Experiences
International Association of Exhibitions and Events
Dallas, Texas

Chapter 6: Service Contractors

Sandy Biback, CMP Emeritus, CMM
Imagination+ Meeting Planners, Inc.
Toronto, Canada

Chapter 7: Destination Management Companies

Alan Fyall, PhD
Associate Dean Academic Affairs
Visit Orlando Endowed Chair of Tourism Marketing
Rosen College of Hospitality Management

University of Central Florida
Orlando, Florida

Steve Brinkman, MEd
Instructor
Rosen College of Hospitality Management
University of Central Florida
Orlando, Florida

CHAPTER 8: SPECIAL EVENTS MANAGEMENT

David L Smiley, MS, PGA
Indiana University Bloomington
School of Public Health, RPTS
Bloomington, Indiana

PART 3: IMPORTANT ELEMENTS IN MEETING, EXPOSITION, EVENT, AND CONVENTION PLANNING

CHAPTER 9: FOOD AND BEVERAGE

George G. Fenich, Ph.D.
Professor
School of Hospitality Leadership
East Carolina University
Greenville, N.C.

Kristin Malek, PhD, CMP, CED, DES, CHE
Event Management Extension Specialist and Assistant Professor
Hospitality, Restaurant, and Tourism Management program
University of Nebraska
Lincoln, N.E.

CHAPTER 10: LEGAL ISSUES IN MEETINGS AND EVENTS

Tyra Warner, PhD, JD, CMP
Department Chair and Assistant Professor
Hospitality, Tourism, and Culinary Arts at College of Coastal Georgia
College of Coastal Georgia
St. Simons Island, Georgia

Chapter 11: Technology

Jim Spellos
Meeting U
Bayside, New York

Chapter 12: Sustainable Meetings and Events

Michelle Millar, PhD
Associate Professor
School of Management | Department of Hospitality Management
University of San Francisco
San Francisco, California

Chapter 13: Planning Meetings and Events and
Chapter 14: Producing Meetings and Events

Amanda Cecil, PhD, CMP
Associate Professor
Indiana University
School of Physical Education and Tourism Management (PETM)
Department of Tourism, Conventions, and Event Management (TCEM)
Indianapolis, Indiana

Erica Shonkwiler, MBA
Lecturer
Department of Tourism, Event, and Sport Management
Indiana University (IUPUI).
Indianapolis, Indiana

Chapter 15: International Aspects in MEEC

Mady Keup
Retired
SKEMA Business School
France

Chapter 16: Putting It All Together

M. T. Hickman, CMP, CPECP
Lead Faculty
Hospitality, Exhibitions, and Event Management
Dallas College—Richland Campus Hospitality
Dallas, Texas

George G. Fenich, PhD, is a professor in the School of Hospitality Leadership at East Carolina University. Dr. Fenich worked in the hospitality industry for 15 years before joining academe. He teaches and researches in the area of conventions and meetings, has written over 70 academic articles, a dozen textbooks, and has presented at over 150 conferences—including the International Council on Hotel Restaurant and Institutional Education; the Destination Marketing Association International; the Association for Convention Operations Management; the International Association of Assembly Managers; AHTMM in Istanbul, Taipei, and Mauritius; the International Conference on Meetings and Events held in Shanghai China; and the Professional Convention Management Association. He is on the editorial board of six academic journals—including editor-in-chief for the *Journal of Convention and Event Tourism*. He is also the principal of the consulting firm Fenich & Associates, LLC.

Kristin Malek, PhD, CMP, CED, DES, CHE is an event management extension specialist and assistant professor in the Hospitality, Restaurant, and Tourism Management program at the University of Nebraska. Dr. Malek worked in the hospitality industry for over 10 years before joining academe and still remains active with industry groups and consulting. She teaches and researches in the area of meetings and events with a focus on engagement, co-creation, and ROI. She has been named as a Top 20 Meeting Industry Trendsetter by *Meetings Today Magazine* (2016) and has been recognized as an Emerging Leader of the Year by PCMA (2018). She has achieved designations as a Certified Meeting Professional (CMP), Certified Event Designer (CED), Digital Event Strategist (DES), and Certified Hospitality Educator (CHE).

CHAPTER 1

INTRODUCTION TO THE MEETINGS, EXPOSITIONS, EVENTS, AND CONVENTIONS INDUSTRY (MEEC)

© r.classen/Shutterstock.com

CONVENTIONS AND TRADE SHOWS ARE A SIGNIFICANT ELEMENT OF THE MEEC INDUSTRY

CHAPTER OBJECTIVES

- Define the foundational concepts relating to the meetings, exhibitions, events, and conventions industry.
- Create context of the global events industry's role as part of the tourism and hospitality ecosystem.
- Inform the history, scope, scale, and economic impact of the events industry.
- Articulate the ways in which standards, certifications, best practices, codes of conduct, assessment of risk as well as ethical practices are important factors in the events industry.
- Share and highlight career definitions and opportunities for the meeting and events professional.
- Outline current and ongoing trends in the MEEC industry.

The meetings and events industry is a complex and multi-faceted business and the professionals who support the planning and execution of events must bring a diverse set of skills and knowledge to the job.

WHAT IS THE MEETINGS, EXPOSITIONS, EVENTS, AND CONVENTIONS INDUSTRY?

The **meetings, expositions, events, and convention (MEEC)** industry is large and touches virtually every aspect of the hospitality industry. MEEC includes business sectors such as travel and hospitality, convention and visitors' bureaus, corporate meeting planning, event venues, technology services providers, and more. The types of events that are part of the industry include: sporting events such as the Olympic, Paralympic Games, and Superbowl; social events like family reunions and weddings; corporate events such as sales meetings, product launches, and strategic planning meetings; and business events, often referred to as meetings, incentives, conventions, and exhibitions (MICE).

The meetings and events industry is complex and multi-faceted. The professionals who support the planning and execution of events must bring a diverse set of skills and knowledge to the job. They must understand the foundational ways in-person, digital, and hybrid (combining in-person and digital elements) events support organizational strategy, drive business outcomes, support human capital. They must also understand the direct and indirect economic impact that events have on the communities they serve and how to measure and communicate these impacts.

The Olympic and Paralympic Games are an example of one of the many aspects of the MEEC industry. Note that the 2020 Olympic and Paralympic Games, scheduled to take place in Tokyo, Japan, have been rescheduled to 2021 due to the COVID-19 pandemic.

© JPstocker/Shutterstock.com

The MEEC industry is built upon partnerships and collaboration between all facets of the industry and supply chain. This commitment to collaboration is needed to achieve event success and return on investment (ROI) for the participant, the host organization, and the event partners. Events need to convey a commitment to creating welcoming environments through empathy, customization, and a commitment to building community and value.

In 2018, the Events Industry Council (EIC) released commissioned findings on the global economic significance of business events that was conducted by Oxford Economics. This is the most recent extensive report globally. Key findings of the report include:

DIRECT IMPACTS OF GLOBAL BUSINESS EVENTS (2017)

- **Number of participants**: Business events involved more than 1.5 billion participants across more than 180 countries.
- **Direct spending (business sales)**: Business events generated more than $1.07 trillion of direct spending, representing spending to plan and produce business events, business events-related travel, and other direct spending, such as spending by exhibitors.
- **Direct GDP (gross domestic product) and employment:** Business events supported 10.3 million direct jobs globally and generated $621.4 billion of direct GDP.
- **Average spending per participant**: On average, $704 was spent per business event participant.
- **Top countries**: The top 50 countries accounted for $1.03 trillion of business events direct spending, representing 96% of the global total.
- **Prior country-level studies**: Previous country-level analyses of business events activity accounted for almost two-thirds of the estimated global total, providing a solid research foundation.

TOTAL IMPACTS OF GLOBAL BUSINESS EVENTS (2017)

After accounting for indirect and induced impacts, business events supported a total global economic impact in 2017 of:

- $2.5 trillion of output (business sales)
- 26 million jobs
- $1.5 trillion of GDP (representing contribution to global gross domestic product)
- The business events sector directly generated more output (business sales) than many large global sectors, including consumer electronics and computers and office equipment.
- The $1.5 trillion of total GDP supported by global business events would rank the sector as the 13th largest economy globally, larger than the economies of countries such as Australia, Spain, Mexico, Indonesia, and Saudi Arabia. Based on its $621.4 billion direct GDP impact, the business events sector would rank as the 22nd largest economy globally.

The full report, along with regional fact sheets can be found on the EIC website at www.eventscouncil.org

INDUSTRY TERMINOLOGY AND PRACTICE

We have always, generically, referred to gatherings of two or more people as a "**meeting**." This term could encompass meetings that are also called "conventions," "congresses," "symposia," some of which could have tens of thousands of people in attendance. If one adds displays of materials or products to a meeting, the meeting then has an **exposition** or **exhibition** (trade show) component. Together, a meeting that has a trade show component is called a **convention**. When sporting, social, or life cycle activities are added, then a generic term that encompasses them all is "events." An even broader and more generic is the term "gathering."

One must be conscious of how your stakeholders or target audience will interpret the name that is applied to a specific gathering. To provide greater clarity, it is important to define the scope of these generic terms when referencing impact data. As an example for the EIC Global Economic Significance Study, the following definition was added for the business events included in the study: "A gathering of 10 or more participants for a minimum of 4 hours in a contracted venue. This includes business events, but excludes social, educational (formal educational activities at primary, secondary, and university level education), and recreational activities, as well as consumer exhibitions."

The following list of terms is important for anyone involved in the MEEC industry to know. The terms were developed by the terminology panel of the Accepted Practices Exchange (APEX), an initiative of the EIC, and are a small sample of the thousands of words that apply to this industry. The complete glossary of terms used in the MEEC industry can be found online at www.eventscouncil.org. The terms and other material from the EIC are used throughout this book and with their permission.

Meeting: An event where the primary activity of the participants is to attend educational and/or business sessions, participate in discussions, social functions, or attend other organized events. There is no exhibit component.

Exposition: A large public show, exhibit, or trade show. These events focus primarily on business-to-consumer (B2C) relationships. *Primarily used in North America*

Exhibition: An event at which products, services, or promotional materials are displayed to attendees visiting exhibits on the show floor. These events focus primarily on business-to-business (B2B) relationships. Related terms: trade fair, trade show.

Event: An organized occasion such as a meeting, convention, exhibition, special event, gala dinner, etc. An event is often composed of several different yet related functions.

Convention: Gathering of delegates, representatives, and members of a membership or industry organization convened for a common purpose. Common features include educational sessions, committee meetings, social functions, and meetings to conduct the governance business of the organization. Conventions are typically recurring events with specific, established timing. Related terms: congress, conference.

Trade Show: An exhibition of products and/or services held for members of a common or related industry. Not open to the public. Related terms: exhibition.

Seminar: (1) Lecture and dialogue allowing participants to share experiences in a particular field under the guidance of an expert discussion leader. (2) A meeting or series of meetings of a small group of specialists with different skills who have a specific common interest and come together for training or learning purposes.

Workshop: (1) Meeting of several persons for intensive discussion. The workshop concept has been developed to compensate for diverging views in a particular discipline or on a particular subject. (2) Informal and public session of free discussion organized to take place between formal plenary sessions or commissions of a congress or of a conference, either on a subject chosen by the participants themselves or else on a special problem suggested by the organizers. (3) Training session in which participants, often through exercises, develop skills and knowledge in a given field.

Conference: (1) Participatory meeting designed for discussion, fact-finding, problem solving, and consultation. (2) An event used by any organization to meet and exchange views, convey a message, open a debate, or give publicity to some area of opinion on a specific issue. No tradition, continuity, or timing is required to convene a conference. Conferences are usually of short duration with specific objectives, and are generally on a smaller scale than congresses or conventions. Related terms: congress, convention.

Clinic: Workshop-type educational experience where participants learn by doing.

Break-Out Sessions: Small group sessions, panels, workshops, or presentations, offered concurrently within an event. Break-out sessions occur apart from the general session.

Assembly: (1) A general or formal meeting of an organization attended by representatives of its members for the purpose of deciding legislative direction, policy matters, holding elections, or conducting governance business of the organization. Consequently, an assembly usually observes certain rules of procedure for its meetings; generally prescribed in its Articles & By-laws. (2) The process of erecting display component parts into a complete exhibit.

Congress: (1) The regular coming together of large groups of individuals, generally to discuss a particular subject. A congress will often last several days and have several simultaneous sessions. The length of time between congresses is usually annual, although some are on a less frequent basis. Most international or world congresses are the latter type; national congresses are more frequently held annually. (2) European term for convention. Related terms: conference, convention. *Primarily used in Europe.*

Forum: Open discussion with audience, panel, and moderator. A meeting or part of a meeting set aside for an open discussion by recognized participants on subjects of public interest.

Symposium: A meeting of a number of experts in a particular field, at which papers are presented and discussed by specialists on particular subjects with a view to making recommendations concerning the problems under discussion.

Institute: In-depth instructional meeting providing intensive education on a particular subject.

Lecture: Informative and educational presentation to an audience.

Panel Discussion: Instructional technique using a group of people chosen to discuss a topic in the presence of an audience, or for a virtual event, such as a webinar.

Social Event: (1) An event with the purpose of facilitating networking among attendees, (2) Lifecycle celebration (e.g. a wedding, bar/bat mitzvah, anniversary, birthday, etc.).

THE ORGANIZATIONAL STRUCTURE OF THE TOURISM AND HOSPITALITY INDUSTRY: IN SUPPORT OF THE GLOBAL BUSINESS EVENTS INDUSTRY AND HOW MEEC FITS IN

The tourism and hospitality industry is multifaceted. The framework offered below is meant to help provide a basic understanding of the industry and is not intended to be an all-inclusive inventory. MEEC professionals rely on partners to support the successful outcomes of each event. To understand how MEEC is connected to the hospitality and service industry, one must understand the key segments of the tourism and hospitality industry itself.

There are **four major** segments of the tourism and hospitality industry: lodging, food and beverage, transportation and travel, and tourism and recreation.

LODGING

The lodging segment consists of all types of places where travelers may spend the night. These can include hotels, conference centers, resorts, motels, bed-and-breakfasts, AirBnB accommodations, and college dormitories. The important characteristics of this segment are that they are available to the public and charge a fee for usage.

FOOD AND BEVERAGE

As the name would indicate, this segment contains two sub-segments: food service operations and beverage operations. Food service operations can include the following: table service facilities that can be further broken down by price (high, medium, and low), by type of service (i.e. luxury, quick service), or by cuisine (i.e. American, East Asian, Italian). Food service also embraces other types of operations including caterers and institutional operations (i.e. hospitals, schools, nursing homes). Beverage operations can also be broken down by price or type of service. This includes whether they serve alcoholic beverages or not.

TRANSPORTATION AND TRAVEL

This segment includes any means or modality that people use to get from one place to another, which includes walking. The better-known elements include air, water, and ground transportation.

- *Air transportation:* This sub-segment includes regularly scheduled airline carriers such as Delta or American as well as charter air service that can involve jets, propeller aircraft, and helicopters.

- *Water transportation:* This sub-segment includes cruise ships, paddle wheelers, charter operations, ferries, and water taxis. Cruise ships are a significant element since they not only provide transportation but lodging, food and beverage, entertainment, and meeting facilities.
- *Ground transportation:* This sub-segment includes private automobiles, taxis, limousines, ride-share services, jitneys, buses, trains, cog railways, cable cars, monorails, horse-drawn vehicles, and even elephants and camels.

TOURISM AND RECREATION

This segment of the hospitality and tourism industry includes anything that attracts people to a destination. It includes natural and person-made attractions, and entertainment.

- *Natural attractions:* This sub-segment includes national parks, mountains, seashores, lakes, forests, swamps, and rivers.
- *Person-made attractions:* This sub-segment consists of things made or constructed by human beings, including buildings such as monuments, museums, theme parks, zoos, and aquariums.
- *Entertainment:* This includes anything that provides entertainment value for a guest such as movie theaters, playhouses, orchestras, bands, and festivals.

There are many overlaps between the categories: A hotel may be an attraction in itself, such as the Broadmoor Resort in Colorado Springs. Hotels often have food and beverage outlets, attractions, and entertainment. Furthermore, some of the businesses mentioned above cater to tourists, meeting-goers, and local residents alike.

Understanding the interactions and complexities of the hospitality and tourism industry helps explain why it is difficult to determine the size and scope of these industries. Until the late 1990s, the U.S. government, using its North American Industry Classification System (NAICS) codes, did not even track many elements of these industries. Because travel and tourism is not a single industry producing a single product, it cannot be measured in its true form by a singular NAICS code. Travel and Tourism Satellite Accounts (TTSAs) are a relatively new economic statistical method to measure more accurately the impact of the travel and tourism industries on the U.S. economy. Similarly, meetings and events cannot be measured by a single industry measure. The **EIC** undertakes a research project every three to four years to measure the economic significance of the meetings and events industry.

HISTORY OF THE INDUSTRY

Gatherings, meetings, events, and conventions (of sorts) have been a part of people's lives since the earliest recorded history. Archeologists have found primitive ruins from ancient cultures that were used as meeting areas where citizens would gather to discuss common interests, such as government, war, hunting, or tribal celebrations. Once humans developed permanent settlements, each town or village had a public meeting area, often called a town square, where residents could meet, talk, and celebrate. Under the leadership of Alexander the Great, over half a million-people traveled to what was then Ephesus (now Turkey) to see exhibitions that included acrobats, magicians, animal trainers, and jugglers. In Rome, the Forum was a type of organized meeting to discuss politics and decide the fate of the country. Ancient Rome had the Colosseum, which was the site of major sporting events such as gladiatorial contests. Think about it—someone had to organize them! Using excellent roadways, the Romans were able to establish trade markets to entice people to visit their cities. In Old England, there are stories of King Arthur's Round Table, another example of a meeting to discuss the trials and tribulations of the day. Religious gatherings of various faiths and pilgrimages to Mecca are examples of ancient religious meetings and festivals. The Olympics began as an ancient sporting event that was organized as similar events are today. World's Fairs and Expositions are still another piece of the MEEC industry.

© Todamo/Shutterstock.com

Vancouver Convention Centre

The First Continental Congress in Philadelphia is an example of a "formal meeting," in this case, to decide the governance of the 13 colonies. Political conventions have a long history in the United States and are part of the MEEC industry. Americans have also created festivals and celebrations of every sort. Mardi Gras in New Orleans and events like this are also a part of the MEEC industry.

Today, structures supporting the MEEC industry are integral parts of major cities. It is a well-known fact that in order to be considered a *world class city,* a community must have a convention center and a stadium/arena for sports and events. All of the largest cities have these venues, including New York City, Washington DC, Barcelona, Chicago, London, Moscow, Pretoria, and Hong Kong. These public facilities attract out-of-town attendees for conventions and events and are an important economic driver for the community.

In spite of the long history of meetings, meeting planning as a recognized profession is a more recent development. The development of the first academic meeting planning program in the U.S. was approved by the state of Colorado in September of 1976 and was implemented by Metropolitan State College (now University) in Denver. This initiative was closely followed by the meeting planning program at Northeastern Oklahoma University in Tahlequah. In 1979, Patti Shock started the hotel convention service management and meeting planning classes at Georgia State University (GSU). In 1983, trade show classes were added with the financial support of the National Association of Exposition Managers (NAEM) (now the International Association of Exhibitions and Events—IAEE) and IAFE (International Association of Fairs and Expositions). Today, there are almost 700 academic programs worldwide and over 150 in the U.S. alone that have programs around the MEEC industry.

One factor that contributed to the rapid development of both industry education and academic programs during the 1980s was the development and implementation of the Certified Meeting Professional (CMP) examination and designation by the Convention Liaison Council (now the EIC). This certification gives both status and credence to the person who achieves it. Additional certificate programs have followed. Industry certifications and certificates offered by EIC member organizations include:

- American Hotel and Lodging Educational Institute Certified Hotel Administrator (CHA) and Certified Hospitality Facilities Executive (CHFE)
- American Society of Association Executives Certified Association Executive (CAE)

- Association of Collegiate Conference and Events Directors—International Collegiate Conference and Events Professional Certification (CCEP) and One-Stop Shop Certification
- Association for Destination Management Executives Destination Management Certified Professional (DMCP)
- Destinations International Certified Destination Management Executive (CDME)
- Events Industry Council's CMP and CMP-HC program
- Hotel Sales and Marketing Association International Certified Hospitality Revenue Management Executive (CRME), Certified Hospitality Digital Marketer (CHDM), Certified in Hospitality Business Acumen (CHBA)
- International Association of Exhibitions and Events Certified in Exhibition Management (CEM)
- International Association of Venue Managers Certified Venue Executive (CVE) and Certified Venue Professional (CVP)
- International Live Events Association Certified Special Events Professional (CSEP)
- Meeting Professionals International Certificate in Meeting Management (CMM)
- National Association for Catering & Events Certified Professional in Catering and Events (CPCE)
- National Speakers Association Certified Speaking Professional (CSP)
- Professional Convention Management Association Digital Évent Strategist Certification (DES)
- Religious Conference Management Association Certified Faith-Based Meeting Professional (CFMP)
- Society for Incentive Travel Excellence Certified Incentive Specialist (CIS) and Certified Incentive Travel Professional (CITP)
- Society of Government Meeting Professionals Certified Government Meeting Professional (CGMP)

The organization now known as the Event Industry Council was founded in New York in 1949 by four organizations: the American Society of Association Executives (ASAE), the American Hotel and Motel Association (now the American Hotel Lodging Association), the Hotel (now Hospitality) Sales and Marketing Association International (HSMAI), and the International Association of Convention and Visitor Bureaus (IACVB) (now Destinations International). The EIC is a cross-industry effort and has led its constituent organizations in the professionalizing of the industry through certification, establishing best practices, and education (Figure 1).

AMC Institute
American Hotel & Lodging Association (AH&LA)
ASAE & The Center for Association Leadership (ASAE & The Center)
Association of Collegiate Conference and Events Directors-International (ACCED-I)
Association of Destination Management Executives International (ADMEI)
Convention Sales Professionals International (CSPI)
Corporate Event Marketing Association (CEMA)
Destinations International
Event Service Professionals Association (ESPA)
Exhibition Services & Contractors Association (ESCA)

Federacion De Entidades Organiz adoras De Congresos Y Afines De America Latina (COCAL)
Financial & Insurance Conference Professionals (FICP)
Hospitality Sales & Marketing Association International (HSMAI)
IACC
Incentive Research Foundation
International Association of Exhibitions & Events (IAEE)
International Association of Professional Congress Organisers (IAPCO)
International Association of Speakers Bureaus (IASB)
International Association of Venue Managers (IAVM)
International Congress and Convention Association (ICCA)
International Exhibition Logistics Association (IELA)

International Live Events Association (ILEA)
Meeting Professionals International (MPI)
National Association for Catering and Events (NACE)
National Coalition of Black Meeting Professionals (NCBMP)
National Speakers Association (NSA)
Professional Convention Management Association (PCMA)
Religious Conference Management Association (RCMA)
Society for Incentive Travel Excellence (SITE)
Society of Government Meeting Professionals (SGMP)
Society of Independent Show Organizers (SISO)
Southern African Association for the Conference Industry (SAACI)
U.S. Travel Association (U.S. Travel)

FIGURE 1:
Events Industry Council Member Organizations

In 1895, the basis of today's convention and visitor bureaus (CVBs)—also called destination marketing organizations (DMO)—was put forth when journalist Milton Carmichael wrote in *The Detroit Journal* that local businessmen get together to promote the city as a convention destination and represent the city and its many hotels to bid for that business. Shortly thereafter, the Detroit Convention and Businessmen's League was conceived to do just that. Carmichael was the head of the group that later evolved into the Detroit Metro CVB that is now labeled *VisitDetroit*.

The role of CVBs has changed over time. As in Detroit, most began by trying to attract only conventions and business meetings to their community. Later, they realized leisure visitors were an important source of business and added the "V" for visitors to their name. Today, virtually every city in the United States and Canada, and many cities throughout the world, has a CVB, DMO, or convention and visitors' association (CVA). The CVBs, DMOs, and CVAs are membership organizations that help promote tourism, meetings, and related business for their cities. In some international destinations, the CVB is a division of the government. Many CVBs have now evolved to not only market but help develop and manage tourism in their destinations. In this text, the terms CVB and DMO are synonymous and interchangeable.

EVOLUTION AND MATURATION OF THE MEEC INDUSTRY

(The following section is adapted from the textbook: *Planning and Management of Meetings, Expositions, Events, and Conventions* 1st Edition by Fenich)

Similar to other industries, such as law and accounting, as an industry evolves and matures, there is an increasing need to formalize a set of competency standards to which professionals must adhere. Until recently no common set of knowledge, skills, and abilities (KSAs) existed for events professionals. It is important to note that the global business events industry continues to evolve and adapt and transform our industry and event professionals need to be on a continuous learning journey to ensure the relevance of their skills and experiences.

This dearth of standards changed in 2011 with the development of several competency standards, all building off a common platform—the Meetings and Business Events Competency Standards (**MBECS**), the Canadian Human Resources Council Competency Standards, and the CMP International Standards. While all slightly different for their individual purposes, they all contain similar "DNA"—a similar set of knowledge, skills, and ability statements required of meetings and events professionals at the different levels of position or purpose. Each will be addressed in separate sections of this chapter along with correlating resources available to the professional through certifications and industry associations.

MBECS

Using the MBECS as an example, the standards are divided into 12 domains or blocks with 33 skills and almost 100 sub-skills or sub-segments. The domains and skills are listed in the enclosed figure.

A. STRATEGIC PLANNING
    1. Manage Strategic Plan for Meeting or Event
    2. Develop Sustainability Plan for Meeting or Event
    3. Measure Value of Meeting or Business Event

B. PROJECT MANAGEMENT
    4. Plan Meeting or Event
    5. Manage Meeting or Event Project

C. RISK MANAGEMENT
    6. Manage Risk Management Plan

D. FINANCIAL MANAGEMENT
    7. Develop Financial Resources
    8. Manage Budget
    9. Manage Monetary Transactions

E. ADMINISTRATION
    10. Perform Administrative Tasks

F. HUMAN RESOURCES
    11. Manage Human Resource Plan
    12. Acquire Staff and Volunteers
    13. Train Staff and Volunteers
    14. Manage Workforce Relations

G. STAKEHOLDER MANAGEMENT
    15. Manage Stakeholder Relationships

H. MEETING OR EVENT DESIGN
    16. Design Program
    17. Engage Speakers and Performers
    18. Coordinate Food and Beverage
    19. Design Environment
    20. Manage Technical Production
    21. Develop Plan for Managing Movement of People

I. SITE MANAGEMENT
    22. Select Site
    23. Design Site Layout
    24. Manage Meeting or Event Site
    25. Manage On-site Communications

J. MARKETING
    26. Manage Marketing Plan
    27. Manage Marketing Materials
    28. Manage Meeting or Event Merchandise
    29. Promote Meeting or Event
    30. Contribute to Public Relations Activities
    31. Manage Sales Activities

K. PROFESSIONALISM
    32. Exhibit Professional Behavior

L. COMMUNICATIONS
    33. Conduct Business Communications

CMP INTERNATIONAL STANDARDS

The **CMP International Standards (CMP-IS)** define the **CMP** Exam leading to the CMP credential. The development of these common standards marks a milestone in the MEEC industry. The standards synopsized above represent the first time that the base of knowledge in the meetings/events industry has been codified. This has been a great advancement for the meeting planning profession, the individuals who work in the industry, as well as academics, students, and individuals who train the next generation of professionals. The CMP International Standards are divided into 9 domains or blocks with 28 skills and almost 100 sub-skills. The domains and skills are listed in the enclosed figure.

The CMP program was launched in 1985 to enhance the knowledge and performance of meeting professionals, promote the status and credibility of the meeting profession, and advance uniform standards of practice. Today, the CMP credential is recognized globally as the badge of excellence in the events industry. The qualifications for certification are based on professional experience, education, and a rigorous exam.

BENEFITS OF CMP CERTIFICATION

According to a recent industry study conducted by PCMA, meeting planners who hold the CMP earn (on average) more than $10,000 annually than their non-certified counterparts. CMP certification is the mark of excellence in comprehensive events management. Certification opens the door to better and more opportunities. Client expectations for meetings are higher than ever and recruiters and prospective employers recognize CMP certification in our growing industry.

CREATED BY AND FOR MEETING PROFESSIONALS

The CMP exam was developed and is maintained by meeting professionals from all over the world who volunteer their time to ensure that the program reflects the best practices in the meeting management field. More than 11,000 meeting professionals in 55 countries around the globe hold the CMP designation. This unique community represents every sector of the industry—from corporations and associations to government and institutional organizations.

The CMP program aims to increase the professionalism of meeting management professionals in all sectors of the industry by:

- Identifying a comprehensive body of knowledge in the meeting management profession.
- Promoting industry standards, practices, and ethics.
- Stimulating the advancement of the art and science of meeting management.
- Increasing the value of CMPs to their employers.
- Maximizing the value received from the products and services provided by CMPs.

The CMP-HC subspecialty

The CMP healthcare subspecialty (CMP-HC) program was launched in 2014 to address the needs of a growing segment of CMPs who manage the production of meetings in the healthcare industry. The CMP-HC is a subspecialty of the CMP. Those seeking this certification must first pass the CMP exam. The CMP-HC credential was designed to validate CMPs who have demonstrated a superior understanding and mastery of the specific regulations, laws, and best practices that must be followed when conducting a healthcare-focused meeting.

DOMAIN A: STRATEGIC PLANNING

- SKILL 1 Create Strategic Plan for Meeting or Event
- SKILL 2 Develop Sustainability Plan for Meeting or Event
- SKILL 3 Develop Business Continuity or Long-Term Viability Plan of Meeting or Event

DOMAIN B: PROJECT MANAGEMENT

- SKILL 4 Plan Meeting or Event Project
- SKILL 5 Manage Meeting or Event Project

DOMAIN C: RISK MANAGEMENT

- SKILL 6 Manage Risk Management Plan

DOMAIN D: FINANCIAL MANAGEMENT

- SKILL 7 Manage Event Funding and Financial Resources
- SKILL 8 Manage Budget
- SKILL 9 Manage Monetary Transactions

DOMAIN E: HUMAN RESOURCES

- SKILL 10 Recruit Staff and Volunteers
- SKILL 11 Train Staff and Volunteers

DOMAIN F: STAKEHOLDER MANAGEMENT

- SKILL 12 Manage Stakeholder Relationships

DOMAIN G: MEETING OR EVENT DESIGN

- SKILL 13 Develop Program
- SKILL 14 Engage Speakers and Performers
- SKILL 15 Coordinate Food and Beverage Services
- SKILL 16 Design Environment
- SKILL 17 Manage Audiovisual and Technical Production
- SKILL 18 Develop Plan for Managing Movement of Attendees

DOMAIN H: SITE MANAGEMENT

- SKILL 19 Select Site
- SKILL 20 Design Site Layout
- SKILL 21 Manage Meeting or Event Site
- SKILL 22 Manage On-site Communications

DOMAIN I: MARKETING

- SKILL 23 Manage Marketing Plan
- SKILL 24 Create and Manage Marketing Materials
- SKILL 25 Create and Manage Meeting or Event Merchandise
- SKILL 26 Promote Meeting or Event
- SKILL 27 Contribute to Public Relations Activities
- SKILL 28 Manage Meeting-Related Sales Activities

USE OF THE MBECS AND CMP INTERNATIONAL STANDARDS

USES FOR MEETINGS/EVENTS PROFESSIONALS

These competencies represent all the KSAs an event professional needs to acquire, and be proficient in, during the course of their career. Industry professionals can perform a personal "skills assessment" of these standards and skills at which they are adept and those that they are not. The resulting "gap analysis" can help guide their professional and personal development. MBECS and the CMP International Standards can also help plot career paths. Being able to provide an assessment that shows a broad mastery of the subject will enhance employability and mobility across sectors and countries. This also allows an industry professional to promote the attainment of this knowledge and associated skills to employers or clients.

Standards are of great value to employers and managers. The standards can aid in the development of job descriptions and job specifications. This leads to improvements in determining workforce requirements and producing worker solicitations. The standards can also help in developing a sequence of training for employees as well as a basis for performance assessment and feedback.

USES FOR THE ACADEMIC COMMUNITY

These standards provide the internationally accepted basis for developing courses of study and their requisite content. It is up to a given program or institution to determine how the content is delivered: in meetings/events specific courses, in business courses, in general education, or a combination. The significant advantage of using a standard like MBECS or the CMP International Standards is that they are not prescriptive: one size does not fit all. Existing programs can "benchmark" themselves against the standards with resulting global recognition. These standards also provide a platform for dealing with governmental authorities and accrediting bodies. Using MBECS, a program can show the relevance of their course offerings and justify the content based on an international body of knowledge. Students can use the standards to develop their educational pathways and to validate their "employability" to recruiters. They could also use the standards to determine which educational programs best meet their learning needs. For academics, the standards can help delineate areas or topics in the meetings/events world that need research.

USES FOR ASSOCIATIONS

First and foremost, standards provide recognition of the knowledge, skills, and abilities required by the industry. This can then help guide the development of program content and delivery that is consistent with international standards. They can also be used by the members of an association to determine their educational or professional development needs and how the association can best fulfill those needs.

IN SUPPORT OF THE INDUSTRY

EVENTS INDUSTRY COUNCIL'S APEX ACCEPTED PRACTICES EXCHANGE COMMISSION

Throughout this book, you will hear about the EIC (formerly the Convention Industry Council) and its **APEX**.

The EIC is at the forefront of efforts to advance the meeting, incentive, convention, and exhibition industry. It represents a broad cross-section of the industry with more than 30 meetings and events-related associations as members, representing more than 103,500 individuals as well as more than 19,000 firms and properties involved in the industry. Formed in 1949, the council provides a forum for member organizations to advance the industry. The council facilitates this by enabling the exchange of information among members through the development of programs to promote professionalism within the industry and by educating the public on the industry's profound economic impact. By its nature, the council provides an impartial and inclusive forum for the APEX initiative and the development of accepted practices for the industry.

APEX brings together stakeholders in the development and implementation of industry-wide accepted practices to create and enhance efficiencies as well as solve common problems and address industry issues. APEX also creates resources and tools to address these issues, such as education, white papers, and sample documents.

Some of the results of accepted practices implementation include:

- Time and cost savings
- Eased communication and sharing of data
- Enhanced customer service
- Streamlined systems and processes
- Less duplication of efforts and increased operational efficiencies
- Better educated and more professional employees
- Solving common issues and problems

CMP CODE OF ETHICS

The EIC has published the CMP Code of Ethics. It is available here with permission for your reference.

The CMP Code of Ethics establishes basic standards of values and conduct for CMP applicants and to CMPs. This Code applies only to CMPs.

As a recipient of the CMP designation by the Events Industry Council ("Certificant"), a CMP must pledge to:

- Maintain exemplary standards of professional conduct at all times.
- Actively model and encourage the integration of ethics into all aspects of the performance of my duties.
- Perform my responsibilities in accordance with the laws and regulations of the local, state, or national governments under which I reside.
- Maintain the confidentiality of all privileged information, including the identity or personal information of other CMP candidates and the contents of the CMP examination, except when required to do so by law or by court order.
- Never use my position for undue personal gain and to promptly disclose to appropriate parties all potential and actual conflicts of interest.
- Communicate all relevant information to my employer in a truthful and accurate manner in order to facilitate the execution of my fiduciary responsibilities.
- Not use the CMP designation or service mark in any way other than that which is authorized by the EIC, and to immediately cease using the designation should I fail to maintain the requirements of the CMP certification or for any other reason have my certification revoked, including payment of required fees.
- To abide by all policies and procedures of the CMP program as outlined in the CMP Handbook or those that may be set by the CMP Governance Commission in the future.
- To be truthful in all information provided to the EIC in all applications and recertification applications at all times.

Any action of a Certificant or applicant that compromises the reliability of the certification process may be subject to the process described by the Procedures.

CAREERS IN AND AROUND THE MEEC INDUSTRY

The MEEC industry is a vibrant, dynamic, and exciting part of the travel, tourism, and hospitality industry.

Some of the most important aspects of working in MEEC are strategic planning and visioning, business acumen (financial and people management, legalities and risk management, sales and marketing, ethics, risk management, safety and security, and duty of care), execution of ideas into concepts, and knowledge of adult learning techniques. In addition to knowledge and ability for preparing and delivering virtual and face-to-face meetings, industry professionals must know more about sustainability, social impact, and technology for meetings and events.

A wedding planner is a career in MEEC

Many careers in MEEC involve multiple aspects of the tourism and hospitality industry. For example, someone who works in convention or group sales in a facility must interface with, be knowledgeable about, and manage people who work with guest rooms, front desk, food and beverage, catering, and all of the meeting facilities. EIC members are actively developing tools and resources to support the careers and wellness of our workforce.

AMERICAN HOTEL AND LODGING ASSOCIATION (AHLA) CAREER DEVELOPMENT RESOURCES

AHLA's resources, supported by the AHLA Foundation, include:

- Apprenticeship and empowering youth programs
- Debt-free college program
- Career center
- Career development program

AMERICAN SOCIETY OF ASSOCIATION EXECUTIVES (ASAE) ASSOCIATION CAREER HQ

ASAE's Career headquarter site includes:

- Job summaries and salaries

- Coaching, mentoring, and other services
- Article, webinar, and video collections
- Resources for employers

ASSOCIATION OF COLLEGIATE CONFERENCE AND EVENTS DIRECTORS—INTERNATIONAL (ACCED-I) CAREER CENTER

ACCED-I's Career Center resources include:

- Resume tips and review
- Interviewing recommendations
- Resources for networking in the digital world
- Career advancement and coaching

ASSOCIATION MANAGEMENT COMPANY (AMC) INSTITUTE TALENT CENTER

AMCI's Talent Center resources include:

- AMC career paths
- Job seeker resources
- A day in the life video series
- Association Management Company 101

FINANCIAL & INSURANCE CONFERENCE PROFESSIONALS (FICP) MENTORSHIP PROGRAMME

FICP's mentorship program resources include:

- FICP Hospitality partner mentorship program webinar
- Mentor and mentee interest form

HOSPITALITY SALES & MARKETING ASSOCIATION INTERNATIONAL (HSMAI)

HSMAI's Foundation offers an interviewing resource guide including:

- Insights for interviews: hospitality sales
- Insights for interviews: hospitality revenue management
- Insights for interviews: hospitality digital marketing

IACC scholarships and internships

IACC offers the following programs:

- Student scholarships
- Global internships
- Job opportunities

Incentive Research Foundation (IRF)

Research reports from IRF include:

- Wellness in meetings and incentives travel study
- Solving the wellness engagement challenge using mobile apps

International Association of Exhibitions and Events (IAEE) Career Center

IAEE's Career Center resources include:

- Job search tools
- Employer/recruiter resources
- Getting started in exhibitions and events
- Professional development resources

International Association of Venue Managers (IAVM) Career and Learning Resources

IAVM's resources include:

- Career center
- Mentor program
- College partnership program
- Job shadowing program

Meeting Professionals International (MPI) Resources

MPI's Wellbeing Resources include:

- A free whitepaper on quarantine survival strategies
- Tips for self-care from the World Health Organization
- A list of regional and national crisis hotlines
- Resources for financial, mental, and physical well-being

PROFESSIONAL CONVENTION MANAGEMENT ASSOCIATION (PCMA) RECOVERY DISCOVERY

PCMA's Recovery Discovery campaign includes:

- COVID-19 Recovery Dashboard
- Accelerating Reskilling PCMA Foundation Donation Campaign
- Business Events Compass: Insights and Strategies for the Next Normal
- Convening Asia Pacific Global Recovery Forum, 10 November 2020

SOCIETY OF INCENTIVE TRAVEL EXCELLENCE (SITE)

SITE's Career Center includes:

- Resume and interviewing recommendations
- Career advancement and digital networking resources

EXAMPLES OF ROLES WITH THE GLOBAL BUSINESS EVENT INDUSTRY AND ORGANIZATIONS THAT SUPPORT THESE SUBSPECIALTIES:

Business Events Strategist/Meeting Professional: Organizes meetings and other gatherings for companies, corporations, and associations. These gatherings can include a small board of directors meeting, a stockholders meeting, new product introductions and training, educational seminars, and regional or national conventions. Corporate Meeting/Event Planners fall into this category.

Exhibition Manager: organizes and manages trade shows.

Sales Executives/Hotel or Conference Center Sales: The majority of sales and convention or catering services positions in hotels and conference centers deal with groups, and MEEC covers most of those groups.

Food and Beverage Manager/Restaurant Sales: While most people think of restaurants attracting walk-in clientele, many rely heavily on the MEEC industry for business. Food and beverage (F&B) venues employ a significant number of people on their group sales staff. In New Orleans, Arnaud's and Emeril's, for example, have group or convention sales teams.

Entertainment/Sporting Venue Sales & Services: Although these places primarily attract individual patrons, most also devote much time and effort to selling, providing space for, and producing events for groups. These off-site venues are often good alternatives for experiential learning.

Destination Management Professional: Destination Management Companies (**DMCs**) function as the "local experts" for companies and associations in organizing gatherings and events, arranging, and supervising transportation, and securing entertainers. People employed for DMCs usually work in either sales or production.

Hotel Operations: Hotels are one of the primary locations where MEEC events are held, using ballrooms, meeting rooms, breakout rooms, and so on, for their gatherings along with sleeping rooms and F&B for their attendees. The hotel departments that deal with the MEEC industry are sales, catering, and convention services.

Convention Centers/Facilities Management: These venues include dedicated facilities such as McCormick Place in Chicago, the Jacob K. Javits Convention Center in New York, the Congress Center Messe in Frankfurt Germany, and the Canton Fair in Guangzhou, China—the world's biggest.

Venue Management/Multipurpose Venues: The venues include arenas like the Superdome in New Orleans or the Astrodome in Houston. With these venues, careers are often found in either sales or operations.

Exposition Services Contractors: If you like to build things or have thought about being an engineer or architect, you should consider being an exposition services contractor (ESC). ESCs design and erect the booths, backdrops, staging, and so on for exhibitions, meetings, and conventions. The decorations and backdrops for your school prom may have been done by an ESC. Again, career paths exist in sales and production and increasingly in design of sustainable products and services.

Convention and Visitor Bureaus (CVBs) Destination Marketing Organizations (DMOs): CVBs serve to represent a wide range of MEEC companies and to market the destination to business and leisure travelers. CVBs have many departments and careers, including convention sales, tourism sales, housing bureaus, convention services, marketing, research, and member services.

Special Events Professional: These event professionals specialize in organizing events such as galas and award ceremonies. They are highly creative and often design unique experiences for their clients. They may be hired by other event professionals to design a special event within a larger program, such as an awards ceremony within an annual conference.

Housing Specialists and Site Selection Specialists: A housing bureau coordinates group reservations and manages hotel rooming blocks on behalf of the event organizers. Site selection specialists source hotels and venues for events, including managing the requests for proposals (RFPs) and negotiate and facilitate contracts on behalf of their clients. Career opportunities in these areas include reservation agents and site selection associates.

Virtual & Digital Event Strategist: These event professionals specialize in designing and executing events that include virtual or digital elements. Careers include production specialists, digital platform specialists, developers, and graphic designers. As more in-person events include hybrid elements, having skills in this area are beneficial for all event professionals.

Key Event Stakeholder Groups: It is often said that MEEC is a "relationship industry," that is, one built on who you know and with whom you do business. As in many industries, we depend on those we know to help us learn and grow and to provide accurate information. These relationships are built over time and always with the understanding that first and foremost, ethical business practices will be the most important aspect of how we relate.

Think for just a moment about all the individuals and businesses involved in the execution of a single meeting or event. They could include the following:

The Meeting Sponsor

- Association or corporation sponsor; Marketing Leadership
- Staff specialists in departments that include marketing, governance and government affairs, education/professional development/training, membership, information technology, and accreditation
- Meeting professional
- Executive director or chief executive officer
- Administrative and logistical support and others who staff call centers, copy materials, process registrations, manage human resources, control purchasing, and more
- Volunteer Leadership, Board of directors, Committees
- Strategic Partners & Sponsors

The Facility

- Owners
- Executive staff, including but not limited to: general manager, revenue manager, resident or hotel manager, directors of sales, marketing, convention services, catering, housekeeping, engineering, maintenance, purchasing, human resources, food and beverage, front office operations, sustainability, social responsibility, and security.
- The thousands of other full- and part-time, year-round, and seasonal staff: groundskeepers, animal handlers, housekeepers, food servers (for banquets, room service, or outlets), maintenance, security, and engineering.

The Destination

- CVB/DMO (president, directors of sales, marketing, convention services, membership, registration, social responsibility, and all support staff)
- Restaurants
- Attractions
- Off-site venues
- Theaters (movie and legitimate)
- Copy and printing companies
- Transportation (buses, airport shuttles, taxicabs, limousines)
- Airport concessions
- Doctors, medical personnel, and emergency workers
- Pharmacies
- Florists
- Destination management companies
- Audiovisual suppliers
- General services contractors
- Specialty services contractors
- Dry cleaners and tailors
- City, county, and state employees
- IT division and telecommunications department

All Others Who Provide Services for Meetings

- Talent (entertainers, disc jockeys, bands, magicians)
- Education (speakers, trainers, facilitators)
- Sound and lighting
- Transportation (air, rail, car, boat, and travel agencies)

- Printing
- Shipping
- Promotional products
- Off-property food and beverage
- Translators for those who speak American Sign Language and other languages
- Americans with Disabilities Act equipment
- Carpentry
- National sales (hotels, conference centers)
- "Third-party" or independent meeting planners

Even the president of the United States and Congress impact our industry by determining trade regulations, travel restrictions, security issues, who needs a visa and whether or not our country goes to war.

Is there anyone who does not have some influence on the meetings and events industry? A case can be made that every person has an impact, in some way, on each and every meeting—even those meetings of two or three that take place in an office or restaurant. Take a few minutes and add to the jobs or functions above that might affect a meeting. Then think again. Also, create a career pathway for at least one of the careers noted above.

WHICH CAREER IS RIGHT FOR YOU?

The following are some of the career planning questions you might ask yourself to determine if this may be the right profession for you:

- Do you like to plan work or social events, or adjust your day, down to the last detail, ensuring everything is locked in?
- Do you have and regularly update a date book or Outlook calendar that includes everything you need to do for weeks or even months into the future?
- Have any of the activities or skills outlined in this chapter struck a chord, and made you say, "this sounds like me" or "I have that ability or strength" and I want to be part of that?
- Do you ask good questions, rarely taking anything as a given? Do you think about contingencies or what if "x" happened? How would I adjust?

If you answered "yes" to some of these questions, you may just have the aptitude to be a good meeting/event professional.

TRENDS IN 2020

In 2020 meetings and events are not just face-to-face gatherings for the sole purpose of exchanging business information. Rather, they are enriching, one-of-a-kind experiences where attendees create community engagement and drive brand awareness and loyalty.

In this section, we will focus on the following key areas: the impact of COVID-19, the transforming role of technology, content and community, the pivot from event logistics to event strategists, and sustainability and social impact.

THE IMPACT OF COVID-19

EVENTS INDUSTRY COUNCIL'S APEX COVID-19 BUSINESS RECOVERY TASK FORCE AND PRINCIPLES FOR RECOVERY

As we publish this textbook edition, it is important to note that COVID-19 has created unprecedent disruption and job loss. This impact will be felt for some time. There is sector job loss in the millions, decreased travel, canceled and postponed meetings and events, and closed businesses and closed borders across the global events ecosystem. These will have a long-lasting impact on economic recovery worldwide and as a result we set on a course for recovery that will require a commitment to unity, adaptations, and transformation. In response to the global pandemic, the EIC, a global federation of more than 30-member organizations, formed the APEX COVID-19 Business Recovery Task Force. The task force's work groups are focused on aggregating and curating accepted practices across the events ecosystem and providing a framework for recovery and resilience as the industry adapts to its most significant disruption. Importantly, the work from the task force is grounded in principles for recovery that are based on the Sustainable Development Goals. This guidance is intended to be global in nature. The work will continue to evolve through regional workshops led by task force members to ensure it is either applicable or customized to each region (Figure 2).

SUSTAINABLE DEVELOPMENT GOALS

We are approaching the aggregation and development of the tools, resources and guidance for the APEX COVID-19 Business Recovery Task Force guided by key principles to support our industry's recovery. Global business events support the recovery of all industries and organisations worldwide by fostering human connections and building communities. The principles that we have identifie d ign to the Sustainable Development Goals and are as follows:

 1   Recovery will require a *global citizenship mindset and open coordination* between all stakeholders.

2   A successful event experience requires that the participating communities have a strong *sense of well-being*.

 3   Recognition that health is prioritised, and that access to *safe livelihoods* is deeply intertwined with physical, mental and economic health.

 4   Global *protocols, training and communication* are needed to secure the health of workers and event participants.

 5   Support is needed to *upskill our workforce* to leverage and optimise the use of safety, design and technology practices.

 6   An intentional commitment to *sustainability, equity and social impact* is essential for an effet ive r ecovery.

FIGURE 2: Events Industry Council Principles for Recovery

Changes to Event Protocols and Design in Response to COVID-19

Event professionals have had a long-standing commitment to health and safety. Prior to the COVID-19 pandemic, many cleaning and sanitization practices by hotels, venues, and other service providers were completed below the line of visibility, meaning that they were done at times when guests or attendees were not in the area. In response to COVID-19, the frequency, visibility, and communication of cleaning and sanitization practices has increased. Event organizers are collaborating closely with their supplier partners to develop protocols that support social distancing and leverage technology to provide digital options for event participation.

Increase in Advocacy for the Events Industry's Workforce

The need to advocate on behalf of our industry's workforce has never been more important than what we are experiencing due to COVID-19. As a result, coordinated efforts and campaigns have been developed to encourage our industry to speak with a unified voice to emphasize to governments around the world about the importance of supporting our industry. This will not only benefit our industry today; it supports all industries that depend on the power of human connections to accelerate the global economic recovery.

TRANSFORMING ROLE OF TECHNOLOGY

Increased Technology Use for Engagement

Technology use in the events industry continues to evolve from production technology to human-centered engagement technology. Great care is being taken to develop exceptional experiences for event participants by leveraging technology to drive engagement with event content, facilitate networking, and amaze participants through creative and inspiring design. Event professionals are also taking into consideration the "second screen", the personal devices that event attendees carry to provide far more than a simple schedule at a glance. These can also integrate location-based wayfinding in a trade show, encourage connections with exhibitors and sponsors through gamification, and provide extended learning opportunities.

The Transition to Omni-Channel Events

Before COVID-19, meeting and event professionals would often refer to events as in-person, digital/virtual, or hybrid: combining elements of both. More recently, we are seeing a move to describing events as being omni-channel, where participants can seamlessly transition between in-person or digital experiences. This approach is beneficial during times of uncertainty and designing the experience with this approach in mind helps to encourage participation. As a result of this, event venues will likely need to continue to expand wireless internet capabilities and security.

Data Security, Trust, and Responsibility

Meeting and event professionals collect data from participants through registration processes, travel reservations, and integrations of event apps with social media platforms. With the rise of new technologies being used in events, such as facial recognition software, event professionals need to take measures to ensure data security and compliance with all applicable regulations. Given that data privacy and security regulations vary by jurisdiction, event professionals need to consider the regulations that apply not only to where an event is being held, but also in all the jurisdictions from where participants reside. This is not only important from a legal compliance aspect, but also for building trust with your event stakeholders.

CONTENT AND COMMUNITY

An important shift in the past decade has been toward community-led content development. This means that it is no longer simply the event organizers, speakers, and facilitators that are determining the content and marketing for an event. This is increasingly a role that is being filled by event participants. More specifically, social media engagement during an event provides crowdsourced context for the information shared by presenters. This form of participation also helps create a community, as well as helps the event to connect with the social networks of their participants.

PIVOT FROM EVENT LOGISTICS TO EVENT STRATEGISTS

Meeting and event professionals are also continuing to increase their value to their organizations by serving as event strategists in addition to being well versed in logistics. This important shift means that event professionals and their supplier partners are focusing on the organization's strategic objectives and designing experiences and services that support these goals.

SUSTAINABILITY AND SOCIAL IMPACT

The Sustainable Development Goals are an important framework for event professionals. They provide guidance on how we can support the achievement of our goals through socially and environmentally responsible practices. The EIC Sustainable Event Standards provide specific guidance for event organizers and suppliers to improve their sustainability impacts.

The EIC Sustainable Event Standards are a collection of standards that assess events and industry suppliers on a wide range of sustainability criteria in support of environmental and social responsibility. There are seven different standards representing different sectors of the industry: event organizer, accommodations, A/V and production, destination, exhibitions, food and beverage, and venue.

Event organiser

Accommodations

Audio Visual & Production

Destination

Exhibitions

Food & Beverage

Venue

SUSTAINABILITY

Sustainability in the events industry has greatly evolved in the past 10 years, and there is still considerable opportunity for us to improve. Focus areas for event professionals include evolving to a circular economy approach for materials, managing environmental impacts of food choices and food waste, and accelerating toward carbon neutrality.

DIVERSITY, EQUITY, INCLUSION, AND ACCESSIBILITY

As an industry, we strive to create environments that are welcoming for all. While designing inclusive events is neither new nor a trend, it is included here as a priority area for event design. Event professionals are becoming better able to understand how their unconscious bias affects the way they design events and event marketing and are actively rethinking how an event's elements can be designed to encourage diversity, equity, inclusion, and accessibility. This is also a focus area in the development of meaningful and equitable career pathways in our industry.

SOCIAL IMPACT

Events are also being increasingly designed and recognized for their social impact. While you may first think of this as including a community service project, the social impact that events can have on a community can be much broader. For example, events have a social impact on a community by creating jobs, and opportunities to learn and make new connections. Many venues are also supporting their communities as emergency evacuation centers or temporary hospitals during a crisis.

CASE STUDY A DAY IN THE LIFE: NATURAL PRODUCTS EXPO EAST

ABOUT NATURAL PRODUCTS EXPO EAST

Natural Products Expo East is a business-to-business (B2B) trade show that connects manufacturers with all channels of distribution that sell products in the natural, organic, and healthy products industry. The growth, success, and production of the show is in large part due to the various partners involved. Over the years, the partners that came

© Shutterstock.com

together in Baltimore collaborated and worked through countless obstacles that arose from slow growth and transformation. As a result, the attendee and exhibitor experiences enhanced year after year, and our unique, resilient event industry family grew and strengthened.

EVENT IMPACTS

Natural Products Expo East was held in Baltimore over 20 times from 1991 to 2019, making it one of the longest running annual conventions Baltimore has had the privilege to host. The Expo grew steadily over the years until it was the largest convention in the city each year, with over 29,000 attendees in 2019. An event of that size is incredibly beneficial to a destination in many ways and in 2019 the Natural Products Expo East had over $17 million in direct economic impact and supported 4,983 jobs in Baltimore city.

While the economic impacts of a convention of that size are huge, Natural Products Expo East also left a lasting impact on the community through their sustainable practices and community givebacks. These included:

- Nearly 56,000 pounds of food were donated to the Maryland Food Bank. The USDA measures the average meal as 1.2 pounds, so this is equal to nearly 46,628 meals that were donated!
- Over 9,000 pounds of furniture and other items were donated to local non-profits Second Chance and the Loading Dock
- There was a year over year increase of 204% for overall compost totals. This was mainly due to a robust onsite trash sorting program throughout the duration of the show.
- Nearly 750 pounds of food were donated to local farm partner, Carriage House Farms.
- There was a year over year increase of 120% for the diversion of plastic wrap. A total of 11 plastic bales were recycled.
- 40 bales of cardboard and over 750 pallets were also captured and recycled.

Natural Products Expo East also left many lasting impacts on the community through various givebacks throughout the event. A great example of this is how they were able to engage attendees by weaving community givebacks into the fun of their outdoor party on the final evening. As attendees gathered to let loose and dance to Blues Traveler in front of the iconic Baltimore Orioles Camden Yards baseball stadium at the Hilton Baltimore, the price of admission was to pack up a backpack for donation. Show organizers partnered with the Living Classrooms Foundation in Baltimore to donate over 500 Under Armour backpacks filled with healthy food and drink for kids in the community. The product was donated by the exhibitors on the show floor and packed into backpacks by the attendees. It was an amazing way to engage attendees and leave an impact on the community.

A Day in the Life of Event Professionals During Natural Products Expo East

Lacey Gautier, Natural Products Group Show Director at New Hope Network (a division of Informa Markets and Brian Rubin, Vice President Operations at Informa Markets

The sun is rising over the Inner Harbor as we all walk over to the Convention Center, excited by the show branding and paying close attention to the hustle and activations outside the building.

We meet with the various show teams (operations, sponsorship, registration, sales, housing, client services, floor managers), security leads, building operations teams, catering, Visit Baltimore and the General Services Contractor (GSC) to walk through the day, review what was done overnight and what's still to come. Was the 23,000 square yards of carpet placed and nearly 6,000 pieces of furniture delivered to their respective locations? Has the show management and sponsorship freight been delivered? Is the Sales Office equipped to handle 1,000+ onsite booth re-sign appointments for next year's show?

Meetings break and security heads out to check on the posts of nearly 100 security and Baltimore Police officers, while the show teams disperse to check on the multitude of areas including the conference rooms, trade show floor, registration tents, an area being transformed into a concert venue on Eutaw Street, and the many sponsored areas and activations featured throughout the convention center and host hotels.

The show floor is buzzing with activity. Over 1,500 exhibitors are setting up and displaying over 2.1 million pounds of freight. Some of them are in hallways and lobby spaces that we worked with the convention center staff and our GSC to convert into non-traditional exhibit spaces so we could continue to grow the event and expand our presence in Baltimore. Utilizing this additional space was a collaborative effort to do what we in the event industry do best…make it work! How do we get freight to these areas, lay electrical, provide hand and dish washing space, protect the carpet and areas that are traditionally not used for the heavy traffic and machinery of a tradeshow floor, create a safe and secure perimeter and access points without doors? It took a lot of effort and collaboration from many different departments, but it is turning out to be awesome.

One last walk through with the fire marshall to ensure the show floor aisles and exits are clear, and all our structures and exhibitors booths are up to code, and we are ready to open the doors to 29,000 attendees.

Doors are open and the show is in full swing. The show teams are now shifting gears to the afternoon events and tomorrow night's concert featuring the Revivalists. One snag, the band comes into a sold-out city a day earlier than expected and the Housing team is quickly scrambling to find them hotel rooms for the night. Additionally, the weather forecast is not looking great, so we are pivoting to ensure we have a rain plan for the outdoor concert. The BCC, our production team, and our neighboring partner, the Hilton Baltimore, quickly meet to discuss this and work to free up some ballroom space in case of weather.

We all file into the afternoon Production meeting where each group: A/V, Security, Catering, Traffic Control, Sponsorship, Press, Operations, Registration, Sales, Floor Management, Cleaning, and Building Leadership each go through the morning, address concerns, work through issues. Can we really shut down city traffic on Sharp Street to allow Personally Owned Vehicles to drop off show supplies? Can we erect a 40' × 80' clear tent over Eutaw Street to keep the concert outside with views of Camden Yards? How does the weather affect our outside registration and building access plans? How significantly did the presidential motorcade impact our sponsored food truck locations? And then we all disperse with our various action items as we execute the evening's events and prepare for the exhilarating week ahead.

Olivia Puglisi, Director of Convention Services at Visit Baltimore

It is 8:00 a.m. on the first day of the show and Olivia arrives at her office. After a quick check of her emails to ensure she is caught up on anything that happened overnight, she heads directly to the Convention Center. As she walks the few blocks to the center, she observes the attendees of the Expo leaving their hotels and heading to the convention center. She pops into one or two hotel lobbies to check on the welcome signage in place at the front desk and other public spaces. The hotels have worked hard to include special touches that are important to the attendees, like organic creamer and compostable cups at the coffee shop as well as fun and engaging lobby activations such as local wineries providing tastings beside check in and a DJ in the bar alongside healthy grab and go breakfast items!

Back outside, Olivia confirms that the welcome banners outside of the center are in place to welcome the convention attendees to Baltimore. She swings by the outdoor registration tents and checks in with the Baltimore Police Officers patrolling the perimeter of the building watching the reg tent, helping with traffic control for exhibitor load in and general crowd control.

Arriving inside the building, Olivia is always impressed at how the Convention Center staff and show organizers transform the space and collaborate to maximize booth space in a non-conventional way. What are normally registration lobbies are filled with new product showcases! A quick check in with her counterpart, Ali, the Convention Services Manager at the convention center, brings her up to speed on the morning's happenings and she makes a note to check up on a few things.

Her next stop is to see OnPeak, the housing manager for Expo East, at the housing desk. There she learns about any issues or happenings that took place overnight at the convention hotels. Olivia makes a few calls to her hotel partners to check on the status of some guest relocations and next steps to set the situation right. She will follow up with OnPeak to let them know as soon as issues have been resolved.

Seeking out Lacey, Brian, or one of their team is the next item on her agenda. She wants to check in with them to see how exhibitors are doing before the show floor opens, check on the route for the 5K the next day and see if there are any tasks that need her attention from a city perspective.

Olivia sends an email to all the convention hotels to check in with them, ask about any anticipated relocation situations for the week or other issues to head off and remind them of important details and notes from a housing standpoint, or from show staff. She wants to be notified first of any potential problems so that she can partner with the hotel to solve the issue and present a united solution to Brian and Lacey. Olivia also checks in with the headquarter hotel and other venues in the city who are hosting events for the show.

In the afternoon she grabs Aurelia, the Sr. Director of Sales at Visit Baltimore, brings her up to speed on the day and heads back over to the center to be part of the daily staff meeting with the Expo team, decorators, and full BCC team. She learns of updates, concerns and solutions that happened that day as well as plans for the evening and next day. Following the meeting, Olivia touches base with Lacey and team to follow up on traffic concerns due to the Orioles game, hotel issues and any other questions related to the city.

That evening Olivia stops by the evening event being held outside on the Hilton lawn. She checks in with the Director of events at the hotel to get updates on the events that took place at the hotel that day and plans for the evening. There was concern about weather earlier in the day and the hotel was able to work with Lacey and her team on various back up plans, but luckily none were needed, and the party is in full swing.

Alexia "Ali" Testa, Convention Services Manager, Baltimore Convention Center

It is opening day at Natural Products Expo East, and Ali Testa arrives at the convention center at 6:30 am. She begins her day by meeting with the show organizers, as well as with the fire marshal and public safety and the general services contractor (GSC). She then does a walkthrough of the exhibit hall to ensure that all exhibitors are following fire marshal codes and that all waste, freight, and forklifts are off the show floor for the safety of attendees and exhibitors.

After the show opens at 9:30 am, Ali stays in regular contact with the show organizers, public safety, building services, and client services, as well as with the BCC's partners for communications and internet, A/V, general services contractor and food and beverage provider. This is important for her to be able to coordinate the response to any issues that may arise during the day.

Mid-afternoon, she participates in a full-team daily meeting, where they discuss any items needing attention, attendance numbers, food and beverage notes, trash, and waste diversion weights. For the event, all trash is sorted to meet sustainability goals for the event. Cardboard bailing happens throughout the event, with a resulting three to four trailers full of cardboard sent to recycling.

Later, she meets the Convention Services Manager that will be onsite for the remainder of the day to go over any key priorities.

At 4:30 pm, the show closes, and lights in the hall go to half lighting levels to conserve energy and indicate the end of the day. Once the exhibit hall floor is cleared of attendees, the BCC team makes adjustments throughout the show floor for any additional exhibitors arriving, new freight being dropped off, or cleanup.

After the show closes, evening activities begin on the Outdoor Terrace. At the end of the reception, the food and beverage team sorts leftover items to identify which food items are suitable for donation, and which should be composted.

Following the end of the show, Ali works with the General Services Contractor to donate event materials. Furniture is donated to Second Chance, building materials to The Loading Dock, and food to the Maryland Food Bank. Donations, recycling, energy use data is then compiled to be included in the post event sustainability report.

SUMMARY

The success of the industry to individuals who currently work in or who choose to work in MEEC depends on what we do now and how we anticipate and plan for the future. Those who choose to stay in or join this industry must have critical thinking skills and the willingness to consider the impact of all local and worldwide events on one's own meetings and events.

Event professionals should strive to have a keen awareness of their audiences to create and build lasting connections.

Adult learning techniques will continue to shift to adapt to consumer behavior and to leverage different formats and environments that offer relevance to each participant. We have been given a moment through the impact of COVID-19 to revisit our foundational values and to create a road map more commitment to these values of equity inclusion sustainability to ensure a relevant and vibrant future. Global Business events will be a catalyst to the global economic recovery, and we will strive thru our resilience to be better valued and understood as an industry. This is indeed a moment of opportunity for our industry and those seeking to join our industry should be inspired by the path before us and the opportunity to make a difference.

Those who succeed in meetings and events will, in the future, need to be curious, informed, and customer focused. They will be planning experiences, not just meetings.

In this chapter, you have been introduced to the world of MEEC as an acronym for the global events industry, key certifications representing international standards, key trends in 2020 as well as sample of career pathways and organization in existence to support the journey. As we have seen, MEEC is multifaceted and exciting, and offers diverse career opportunities. MEEC is also very large and incorporates many facets of the hospitality industry. It has tremendous economic impact. You are now prepared to continue with the remaining chapters in this book. They provide more details about the concepts and practices of MEEC that this first chapter only touches on.

Face-to-face meetings will continue because there is a need for human interaction. These meetings and events will succeed because they are enhanced by virtual audiences who add to the energy and diversity prior to, during, and after the meeting or event. (Think Twitter and the hashtags being used now for meetings; envision even greater involvement in the future.)

You have thus far decided to read this text and to learn about this dynamic industry. YOU are the future; you bring to it your experiences and insights. Observe, learn, and take action to keep MEEC moving forward.

KEY WORDS AND TERMS

For definitions, see https://insights.eventscouncil.org/Industry-glossary

APEX	exposition
BEO	KSAs
conference	MBECS
convention	MEEC
CSM	meeting
DMC	MPI
Events Industry Council	sales and marketing
exhibition	

REVIEW AND DISCUSSION QUESTIONS

1. What are meetings?

2. Describe some events from the past that were "meetings."

3. Describe some current aspects of MEEC industry jobs.

4. Who attends meetings?

5. What can be accomplished by convening or attending a meeting?

6. What are key jobs in a facility (hotel, resort, conference center) that contribute to the successful outcome of a meeting?

7. What is the EIC?

8. What is APEX, and what is its impact?

9. What is the impact of meetings on the global economy?

10. What is MBECS?

11. What are the EIC Principles for Recovery?

12. Create your own career pathway in the MEEC Industry.

13. Create a list of situations in the MEEC industry where ethics would come into play.

CHAPTER CONTRIBUTORS

Amy Calvert, Chief Executive Officer (CEO) of the Events Industry Council.

Mariela McIlwraith, Vice President of Sustainability and Industry Advancement of the Events Industry Council.

The EIC is a federation of more than 30 associations in the meetings, conventions, events, and exhibitions industry. The council administers the CMP credential, develops best practices through its APEX Initiative, promotes sustainable and socially responsible meeting practices through its Center for Sustainability and Social Impact, and conducts research on the economic impact of meetings and events.

PREVIOUS EDITION CHAPTER CONTRIBUTORS

Joan L. Eisenstodt, president of Washington, DC-based Eisenstodt Associates, LLC.

Kathryn Hashimoto, Ph.D., faculty member in the School of Hospitality Leadership at East Carolina University

Karen Kotowski, CAE, CMP, former Chief Executive Officer of the Events Industry Council

CHAPTER 2

MEETING, EXHIBITION, EVENT, AND CONVENTION ORGANIZERS AND SPONSORS

© UfaBizPhoto/Shutterstock.com

CHAPTER OBJECTIVES

- Understand the major types of organizations that hold gatherings and differentiate the types of meetings and the planning required for each.
- Identify the associations that support the professional development of those responsible for producing gatherings.
- Outline the major trends facing MEEC organizers and sponsors.

This chapter focuses on explaining the entities that organize and sponsor different types of gatherings. Each of these segments holds gatherings to satisfy their unique needs and target attendee population. Whether the organization is a nonprofit association or a corporation, a government agency or a private company that produces exhibitions, it has goals that may require a MEEC gathering to commemorate an event. The purpose of this chapter is to identify who these organizing/sponsoring organizations are, the types of gatherings they hold, how much time on average they have to plan their events, who their attendees are, and how they build attendance. Additionally, the people who play a major role in producing these gatherings are identified as well as the professional associations who provide them with support and professional development.

WHO HOLDS GATHERINGS?

The three most significant entities that organize and sponsor MEEC gatherings are (1) corporations, (2) associations, and (3) the government. Other organizations who arrange gatherings are also discussed in this chapter.

CORPORATIONS

Although there are numerous kinds of corporations, for the purposes of this chapter the term **corporations** will refer to legally chartered enterprises that conduct business on behalf of their owners with the purpose of making a profit and increasing its value. This can be further subdivided into public and private corporations. Public corporations sell stock on the open market and have a board of directors who oversee the affairs of the corporation on behalf of the shareholders (or owners) who elected them. Private corporations have the same fundamental purposes as public corporations, but their stock is not sold on the open market.

Virtually all businesses have needs that require them to plan and execute gatherings. Publicly held companies have a legal requirement to hold an annual shareholders meeting. Many companies hold press conferences or a ribbon-cutting ceremony. Organizations also have continuing needs to train personnel in matters of company policy and procedures and to further develop new policies and procedures to improve their effectiveness. Client groups may be brought together to capture their opinions in a focus group or to introduce them to a new product or service. Incentive meetings are held to reward top producers within a corporation. Executive retreats may be held to improve communication or to develop long-term business plans. Gatherings are also held to honor employees (for promotion or retirement), to celebrate holidays, and to build overall morale within the organization. Companies could also entertain clients in VIP areas at concerts or major sporting events such as the U.S. Open or the Super Bowl.

Many corporate meetings are booked as needed, typically less than 6 months before the meeting will take place. When a corporation decides to hold a gathering, it determines what the budget will be, where the gathering will be held, and who will attend. Since the corporation typically pays for all expenses associated with attending the meeting, the corporation is in complete control. The decision to hold a corporate meeting is typically made by persons in positions of key responsibility within the corporate hierarchy. Officers and senior managers in the sales and marketing area may call for a meeting of their regional sales managers to develop sales strategies for new product lines, or senior financial managers and controllers may call a meeting of their dispersed staffs to discuss budgets for next year. Most of the attendees of a corporate gathering or event are members of the corporate family and/or persons who have a close business relationship with the company. Attendance by corporate personnel is usually mandatory.

While attendance at corporate meetings may be mandatory for most attendees, marketing is still needed. The purpose of the meeting should be carefully crafted and company websites should be updated with relevant information regarding the meeting to include its theme and objectives. While invitations might not be formally sent, notices about the meeting and RSVP registration websites will most likely be created for the meeting. It is important that the company use internal marketing to create excitement prior to the meeting so attendees arrive eager to learn, listen, and enjoy their time out of the office. Even though it may be a "command performance", this does not lessen the need to make the meeting informative, productive, and enjoyable for those attending.

Corporate meetings can be as diverse as corporations themselves. Paying special attention to your details, embracing the corporate culture, and knowing your objectives can result in a successful corporate meeting.

Types of Corporate Gatherings and Events—Their Purposes and Objectives

Corporate meetings range from small VIP board of directors' meetings to large sales meetings, customer incentive meetings, and lower-tiered staff training meetings. One common thread between them is that they are always paid for (hosted) by the corporation. The funds come from a department or individual budget within the corporation.

The meeting objectives will typically include motivation, training, camaraderie, brainstorming, and reviewing goals. There is usually an emphasis on the social events at a corporate meeting. Although perceived as recreation, the opportunity for networking between departments and across various levels at non-meeting functions could potentially impact future corporate decisions. Social events should be strategically planned to ensure that the proper people are sitting together at dinner or assigned to the same foursome at the golf outing.

Corporations have a variety of needs that can be satisfied by scheduling a gathering. What follows should not be viewed as a comprehensive list, but rather as an overview of the variety of gatherings sponsored by corporations.

Stockholder meetings

Voting shareholders of a corporation are invited to attend the company's stockholders meeting. This is an annual meeting that has historically been held in the city where the company is headquartered, although many companies now rotate between different locations to be more accessible to all stockholders. Attendees are presented with reports on the state of the corporation and can vote on issues of corporate significance. While most stockholders do not attend this meeting, they do participate in the governance of the corporation by filing a "proxy statement" in which they identify how they want their shares voted.

Management meetings

There are numerous reasons for a company to hold management meetings. Every major division of a corporation may have a need to bring its decision makers and other important personnel together to develop plans, review performance, or improve their processes. While some of these meetings may occur on a scheduled basis, others may be called spontaneously to solve problems and address situations that require immediate attention.

Board meetings

The board of directors is a specific type of management meeting held by the governing body of a corporation. They typically meet several times a year, usually in the city where the corporation is located. While a board meeting may be held in the corporate headquarters, these meetings may require lodging, dinners, and related activities that are often held at local hotels and other types of venues.

Training meetings

As companies undergo change, it may be necessary to hold training meetings to keep managers and key employees up-to-date on improved methods of job performance or to gain skills needed to operate new systems and equipment. Companies may also use training meetings to introduce new managers to corporate procedures and culture. Some of these meetings may be held on a regularly scheduled basis while others may be held when conditions dictate.

Sales training and product launches

Sales training and product launches are one specific type of training meeting. These events are often held to upgrade the performance of the sales staff, distributors, and retailers, and to introduce new products and services to distribution networks and the general public. These events are designed to educate and motivate those who have a significant impact on the success of the corporation.

© Gorodenkoff/Shutterstock.com

Professional and technical training

Professional technical training is another specific type of training meeting. These meetings may be held to bring managers and others up-to-date on issues relevant to their role within the company and to enhance the knowledge of their service providers. For example, a company may have a meeting of its unit and regional controllers to discuss changes in tax law and company policies.

Incentive trips

Many corporations offer **incentive trips** to reward their top performers based on certain criteria. At these meetings, there is a large amount of time spent on "fun" activities that the employees see as rewarding them for a job well done, such as a golf tournament, sightseeing tours, and outdoor adventures. Those winning these trips may be employees, distributors, and/or customers. Companies may bring together these top performers with their corporate leadership to create a more synergistic organization. While these trips are often to exciting and glamorous destinations, organizations are increasingly scheduling specific activities for the participants to increase collaboration with each other and provide an added value to the sponsoring corporation. According to the 2019 Incentive Travel Industry Index, 84% of companies utilize non-cash incentives to retain and engage employees with 40% specifying they use travel rewards. With a shifting generational workforce, it has been found that travel is among the most popular and fastest-growing strategies for motivating employees. Over 65% of firms worldwide stated that they planned to expand their current incentive travel programs.

Public shows

Public shows (also called consumer shows) are gatherings where businesses sell their products directly to the general public. This is often in the form of tradeshows where exhibitors display their products that the locals will have an interest in and would be excited to attend. This is the reason they are called "public shows." Examples of these types of events are boat shows, car shows, winter sport shows, and art shows. There is normally a fee for each attendee to get into the event. Corporations that sell the types of "goods" on display at a public show own and sponsor these events. To attract the public to attend, the organizers use social media, local radio and television stations, newspapers, and many times local billboards to announce the event. Depending on the show topic, an emerging trend is for specific exhibitors to offer some scheduled entertainment and/or educational sessions within their booths to drive attendance and increase awareness of their products or services.

DEPARTMENT AND/OR INDIVIDUAL RESPONSIBLE FOR ORGANIZING AND PLANNING

Corporate planners have always had a variety of positions, titles, and backgrounds. Many of the people who plan corporate meetings have responsibilities beyond, or in addition to, the planning of meetings. Prior to COVID-19, corporate planners spent about three-quarters of their time planning meetings with about half of these meeting planners having job titles that specified meeting planner/convention management. With adjusting budgets, changes in corporate hierarchies, and shifting of job responsibilities throughout COVID-19, it will be interesting to see how this may or may not change in the next 5 years.

At smaller corporations, it is typical that a single person will take on a variety of duties, therefore a specific "Meetings and Events Department" may not exist. Most professionals who plan meetings within smaller corporations tend to work in the departments that hold the meetings (sales and marketing, human resources, or finance) and have assumed meeting planning responsibility at the request of their supervisors. For larger corporations, like Microsoft, Coca-Cola, Exxon-Mobile, and Cisco, meeting planning departments are stand-alone units as these organizations may have hundreds of large and small meetings throughout the year.

Many corporate meeting planners join professional associations to support their continued learning and development. This provides opportunities for increased networking, learning what is on the cutting edge of their profession, and allows them the opportunity to establish a name within their organizations and field. The associations that they most often join include Meeting Professionals International (MPI), Professional Convention Management Association (PCMA), Society for Incentive Travel Excellence (SITE), and Corporate Event Marketing Association (CEMA) (Table 1).

United States	Europe	Asia Pacific
1. Orlando	1. London	1. Singapore
2. Las Vegas	2. Berlin	2. Bangkok
3. Chicago	3. Barcelona	3. Hong Kong
4. Atlanta	4. Paris	4. Kuala Lumpur
5. Dallas	5. Amsterdam	5. Shanghai

TABLE 1. Top cities that hosted meetings in 2019

ASSOCIATIONS

In the United States, over 300,000 association meetings and events occur each year that are attended by over 60 million people. This is a segment of the industry that cannot be ignored. The term **association** is defined as a group of people organized for certain common purposes, whether that be for professional, industry, educational, scientific, or social reasons. This definition of the word is true in MEEC as well. Gatherings such as annual **conventions**, topical conferences, world congresses, and topical workshops and seminars are held for the benefit of the association's membership. Internally, meetings need to be held for the betterment of the association, such as board of directors' meetings, committee meetings, and leadership development workshops. Many associations have an affiliated exhibition held in conjunction with their annual convention, at which products or services of interest to the attendees are displayed by various vendors. Besides providing value to the members of the association and potential recognition for the association, these gatherings also generate a significant revenue stream for the organization.

Associations offer their members opportunities to enhance their professional development at conferences, seminars, and workshops. These events may combine structured educational sessions with informal networking events, such as receptions, golf tournaments, and dinners. Associations encourage their members to become involved so that meetings *for* members are planned with input *from* members. The meeting planner works with member committees from the initial planning stage through the final production of the event. Committee members can suggest program topics and speakers that their colleagues will resonate with. Local committee members may suggest local venues for social events, tourist attractions and tours, entertainment options, and golf courses for a conference tournament. Member assistance is a value-added and integral part of the planning that helps ensure an event's appeal and success.

Association meetings, especially conventions, can range from several hundred to tens of thousands of attendees. Two-thirds of conventions are held in conjunction with a trade show or exhibit. The average convention has over 250 exhibitors and requires over 50,000 square feet of exhibit space. This size issue can eliminate many smaller cities and venues from being selected as the location for these events. This limited availability of size-appropriate venues can create increased demand by larger associations for big cities and venues that can accommodate their meetings/events. It also creates increased competition among the larger destinations to capture larger associations' business. This business means big dollars to cities and venues and can have a significant economic impact on the city as a whole. To adjust to these supply and demand factors, larger associations typically book their major gatherings 5 to 10 years, or even more, ahead of the scheduled date to ensure that they have the space needed for their event. Small associations have a broader selection of locations including regional, or second tier, cities that can accommodate their gatherings and therefore require less lead time to secure needed accommodations and facilities. However, unlike corporations, almost all associations regardless of size still tend to book their meeting locations at least 1 year before the meeting date.

The decision-making process for association meetings is rather complex and goes through several distinct stages. Once it is decided that a meeting will be held (usually by the board of directors or as stated in the association's constitution or bylaws), the objectives of the meeting are established first. No planning of any meeting should begin until these objectives are established. The next step is to decide on the location where the meeting will be held. Some organizations rotate their meetings through their geographic regions, thereby dispersing hosting opportunities and responsibilities throughout their total membership. The specific city to host the meeting is sometimes decided by the association's board of directors and at other times is dictated by the executive director based on site visit feedback by the association's internal meeting planner or by an external contract meeting management provider. This report will give a summary of reasons why a destination is being recommended: hotel prices, convention center prices, available **air lift** (number of daily flights and quantity of seats) into the city, weather expected at the time of the meeting, availability of hotel rooms, cost per attendee to visit the city, history of the meeting being held in the same city in the past, labor rates, and overall ease of doing business in that particular city.

Once the choice has been narrowed down to one specific city, the meeting planner (based on site visits and inspections) will locate a venue. This will be based on the availability on the desired dates and what venue is well suited to the needs of the meeting. Typically, the meeting planner makes the recommendation to the association's board and leadership and, if approved, negotiates the financial and meeting details with the facility. This results in a contract that is eventually signed by both the venue and the association's senior staff person (usually the executive director or chief financial officer).

Association events are a source of revenue for associations. The greater the number of paid attendees, the greater the revenue, and the more lucrative the event is to the association. However, since members must pay registration fees and spend additional funds for travel and lodging, the association must provide programs that its members will find too valuable to miss.

TYPES OF ASSOCIATIONS

As defined by the leading association for association planners, the Professional Convention Management Association (PCMA) has segmented the association category into four types: professional, medical or health, trade, and SMERF.

Professional

An association where membership comprises persons from the same industry. Membership exists at the individual level and each person is responsible for paying his/her own membership dues. According to *PCMA Convene Magazine's* 29th Annual Meetings Market Survey (2020), professional associations comprise 48% of all associations.

Medical or health

An association where membership comprises persons specifically from a medical or health area. While this is still a "professional" field, this field is segmented due to its large influence and strict requirements. According to *PCMA*, this segment encompasses 21% of all associations.

Trade

An association where membership comprises organizations from the same industry. Membership exists at the company level and individuals employed by the member company become members by extension. According to *PCMA*, this segment encompasses 19% of all associations.

SMERFs

This term refers to small associations with members who join for **S**ocial, **M**ilitary, **E**ducational, **R**eligious, and **F**raternal reasons. Educational groups could include universities, for-profit education groups, or high schools. Fraternal groups could include Kiwanis, Elks, or University fraternities and sororities. Persons attending these meetings tend to pay their own expenses; accordingly, this category tends to be very price-sensitive. According to *PCMA*, this segment encompasses 7% of all associations.

© Anton Gvozdikov/Shutterstock.com

Any of these association segments can take place at a local, state, regional, national, or international level, which is dictated by where the association members are located. Additionally, in the United States, any of these categories can have a special tax-exempt status granted by the Internal Revenue Service. Although tax-exempt associations do not have a profit motive, these associations need to be run efficiently and must have their revenues exceed expenses. Since all revenues are used to support the mission of the organization, excess funds (like profits in the corporate world) are allowed to stay with the organization, tax-free. On average, associations derive one-third of their annual operating revenues from excess revenue (profits) derived from their annual meeting/convention.

TYPES OF ASSOCIATION GATHERINGS AND EVENTS— THEIR PURPOSES AND OBJECTIVES

Conventions

According to the accepted practices exchange (APEX), a **convention** is a gathering of an industry organization convened for a common purpose. Association-related conventions tend to be annual and common features include educational sessions, committee meetings, social functions, and meetings to conduct the governance business of the organization. Many conventions have an exhibition (or trade show), which may be a major source of revenue for the association. Exhibitors pay to participate in these events because these events offer them an opportunity to showcase their products and services to a well-targeted group of potential buyers at a much lower cost than making individual sales trips to meet with the association members individually. Conventions are supported, in-part, by sponsors: companies or entities that will benefit from exposure to attendees at the convention.

Regional conferences

Organizations with a regional structure often schedule one or more events each year to bring together members who are in the same geographic area. They might also hold specific regional social gatherings at the larger annual convention.

Board meetings

The association's board of directors typically meets several times a year to provide collective advice and direction to the association. These meetings are usually the smallest association meetings held and provide updates on the operations of the association and conference-planning efforts. Traditionally, these have been held face-to-face.

Committee meetings

Many association committees will hold their own smaller meetings to discuss the affairs related to their purpose (e.g., government relations, convention host committee, national conference program committee, and publications committee). Depending on the committee, these are oftentimes conference calls.

Training meetings and educational seminars

Associations often offer their members opportunities to upgrade their professional skills and knowledge through meetings targeting specific topics. Many professions require continuing education (e.g., continuing medical education for different medical specialties). Members will earn **continuing education units (CEU)** by attending training meetings. Some associations offer training meetings to develop the leadership potential of the association's elected national and regional officers. Seminars offered could be led by experts that allow the participants to share their views and experiences with each other.

MARKETING AND ATTENDANCE

One major difference between association and corporate gatherings is that attendance at association meetings is voluntary, not mandatory. Since attendance at association meetings is voluntary, the meetings must offer appealing programs to draw members to the events. Another difference is that many of the attendees are personally responsible for their own registration cost, transportation, hotel, and related expenses. In some instances, employers may fund the attendance of employees at industry and professional association events that are work related and are seen as having an educational value for the employee.

The marketing of association meetings is critical to their success. All association marketing should begin with an understanding of who the members are and their needs. This focus should be brought into the development of all meetings. In today's business world, and especially with the normalization of online meetings due to COVID-19, attendees may be reluctant to spend too much time out of the office in order to attend a meeting. It is the association's job to plan a robust program that entices the attendee and gives them a true and valuable reason to travel to a meeting. Many attendees must prove the value of the meeting to their boss to get permission to attend. Good marketing material is crucial to demonstrate this value.

If the meeting provides genuine opportunities for the members to satisfy their needs, the promotional aspect of marketing the meeting becomes much less intense. Since the primary group of attendees are members of the association, the key elements of marketing include providing advance notification of the date and location of the upcoming meeting along with information about the planned content, speakers, and special activities. Later, detailed registration information and a preliminary program will need to be provided.

The vehicle for communicating this information to the members has traditionally been through direct mail and notices or advertisements in the association newsletter and magazine. This has changed as technology and cost considerations have moved many associations toward the use of electronic media to communicate with their members. There has been a rapid growth in the use of e-mails and social media to promote a meeting and directs recipients to visit the association's website to seek out details. Promoting and marketing the following year's meeting or convention at the current year's event is also recommended so that attendees can block these dates on their calendars and generates positive excitement 1 year in advance.

To expand the number of attendees at the gathering, many associations send promotional materials and notices to nonmembers who have been targeted as sharing an interest in the meeting's purpose. Since the nonmember fee to attend the meeting is usually higher than the member fee, this effort, if successful, could result in attracting new members to the organization and can raise additional revenue for the association.

DEPARTMENT AND/OR INDIVIDUAL RESPONSIBLE FOR ORGANIZING AND PLANNING

In associations, typically the event planner is an internal paid employee, a member committee led by an executive director, or outsourced to an association management company. This is often determined by the size of the association. Nearly two-thirds of association planners have earned an undergraduate degree with approximately 20% having obtained a post-grad degree.

Association meeting planners join professional associations in greater numbers than their corporate counterparts. There are over twenty associations for meeting planners in specific industries that can be seen on the Event Industry Council website under member organizations. The most well-recognized across industries is the Professional Convention Management Association (PCMA), the American Society of Association Executives (ASAE), and Meeting Professionals International (MPI). There are also many local organizations of meeting planners that provide support and professional development opportunities.

	Corporation	Association	Government
Definition	Legally chartered enterprises that conduct business on behalf of their owners with the purpose of making a profit and increasing its value	A group of people organized for certain common purposes, whether that be for professional, industry, educational, scientific, or social reasons	Subdivisions of federal, state, or local government
Purpose	Training, team building, and incentives	Primarily educational and networking with some having trade show components	Primarily training and educational
Decision Makers	Centralized (typically leaders in the corporate hierarchy)	Decentralized (oftentimes committee decision)	Managers who decide to have the meeting and fund it from their departmental budget

TABLE 2. Comparison

Attendees	Members of the corporation or have a close business relationship with the company	Members of, or people interested in, that particular industry	Government employees and, depending on the event, the general public
Spouse Attendance	Rare	Common	Rare
Attendance	Mandatory	Voluntary	Mandatory for personnel; voluntary for public
Size	Varies by company; typically less than ten to one thousand	Several hundred to tens of thousands	Varies by event
Marketing	Minimal; invitation or notice to all attendees	Crucial; often mailers, magazines, and electronically	Internally similar to corporate, when public is invited similar to association
Location and Site Selection	Convenience, service, and security are valued	Seek attractive locations to help build attendance, amenities and nearby attractions are important	Convenience, service, and security are valued
Lead Time	Less than six months	Large associations—Five to 10 years or more; smaller associations—minimum one year	Less than three to four months
Payment	Corporation pays for everything	Attendee pays for travel, hotel, and registration; registration and sponsorships cover cost of the conference	Funding is awarded through the legislative process; department allocates meeting budget
Planner	Corporate planner, most likely a part of someone's job, could be any department in the company	Association planner and board or outsourced to association management company	Similar to corporate planners who are spread throughout the agency, will outsource an independent planner if outside of their internal capabilities
Professional Associations	Meeting Professional International (MPI), Professional Convention Management Association (PCMA), Society of Incentive and Travel Executives (SITE), and the Association of Insurance and Financial Services Conference Planners	Professional Convention Management Association (PCMA), the American Society of Association Executives (ASAE), Meeting Professionals International (MPI), the Center for Association Leadership, and the Religious Conference Management Association	Society of Government Meeting Professionals (SGMP), Professional Convention Management Association (PCMA), and Meeting Professionals International (MPI). If responsible for organizing exhibitions—International Association of Exhibitions and Events (IAEE).

TABLE 2. Comparison (continued)

GOVERNMENT

Government entities at all levels hold gatherings as they have continuing needs to communicate and interact with many constituent bodies. These meetings may involve the attendance of world leaders, with large groups of protestors and supporters, or a small group of elected local officials holding a legislative retreat. Different from corporate and association meetings, government meetings are subject to various rules and regulations. Since it would not be realistic to include information specific to each of the 190+ countries in the world, the information in this section will look at general information that applies to the inherent job responsibilities of government meeting planners. Specific links and statistics will focus on the United States.

Managers at government agencies are typically those who identify the need to hold a meeting and have the responsibility to provide funding through their departmental budget process or to locate other sources of funding. Meetings, like other parts of an agency's budget, are mostly dependent on funding provided through the legislative process. Accordingly, as political interest in an agency's mission grows or diminishes, the budget will increase or decrease, as will its ability to sponsor gatherings. As seen in recent years, public backlash and policies by the U.S. government can impact off-site meetings and attendance by employees of government agencies. This has also happened in the past, but due to the nearly instantaneous accessibility of information via media outlets, these occurrences are advertised more in the mainstream media.

Government meetings have characteristics typical of both corporate and association meetings. The purpose of many government meetings is the training of government workers. On the federal level, many of these meetings are replicated in several areas of the country to minimize travel expenses for the employees of an agency's branch offices. Other government meetings may involve both agency employees and those in the general public who may have an interest in the topic of the meeting. Meetings such as those to discuss prescription drug proposals or the future of social security are likely to go "on the road" to gather input from the public. Attendance by employees at government meetings would generally be mandatory, while attendance by the general public would be voluntary. Mandatory attendance by government employees requires only that sufficient notice be provided so that participants can adjust their schedules in order to attend. Attracting voluntary attendees may require additional promotion.

There has been some movement by government agencies to hold meetings online. In addition to the goal of reducing costs, other restrictions make government meetings more restrictive. In the United States, facilities where federal meetings are held must be able to accommodate persons with certain physical limitations, as per the Americans with Disabilities Act, and they must meet fire safety certifications. Additionally, the federal government, and many state governments, have established **per diem rates** that set limits on the amount of money a government attendee can spend per day for lodging and meals. Since the list of per diem rate tables is so extensive, it is recommended that those in need of the current federal domestic per diem rates go to the General Services Administration website at http://www.gsa.gov/. Both of these facts have also contributed to the acceptance of online programming.

© Pavel L Photo and Video/Shutterstock.com

FINANCIAL RULES AND REGULATIONS

Government meetings are distinct from association and corporate meetings because they are bound by government regulations and operating policies that may not apply to other types of meetings. Since most government activities are paid for by taxpayer money, there are strict financial rules and regulations that government meetings must abide by.

First, rates for hotel rooms. To save the government money, the government sets per diem rates for lodging (and meals and other incidental expenses) for travelers for all locations in the continental United States. In most cities, these set rates are below those charged to conference groups. Additionally, government meetings are restricted because they can only be held in properties that comply with the Hotel Motel Fire Safety Act of 1990. Once you find a hotel that agrees to your terms and rates, hotel contracts are then not considered "official" by the government. A hotel contract may be attached to the paperwork submitted to the procurement official, but in all cases, the government contract—not that of private sector—is the prevailing authority. Funds *must* be approved before the service is rendered, not after. In addition, the government *must* be able to cancel a contract without damages if funding for an event is withdrawn, if there are furloughs or closures of government facilities, or if other government actions make it inadvisable to hold the meeting.

Federal procurement policies also distinguish the government meeting. Bids for meeting supplies and services must be obtained from *at least* three vendors for most purchases. Additionally, the meeting planners usually are not the people who commit federal funds so it is vital to determine who actually has the authority to commit funds and sign contracts on behalf of the government.

SECURITY

There is no segment of the MEEC industry more attuned to safety and security than the government segment. In the United States, those organizing government meetings must work on a regular basis with the Department of Homeland Security since many of their attendees are high-profile leaders. Although this list is in no way comprehensive, the following are some suggestions for implementing security:

- Plan and prepare
- Refine the pre-convention meeting to emphasize security issues
- Be sure there is coordination of all parties involved
- Establish a security team and its decision makers
- Provide education on security for attendees
- Be proactive rather than reactive
- Stay informed and alert to incidents

Since government meetings frequently bring together representatives from the Uniformed Services and non–Department of Defense agencies, the meetings are often labeled as classified. If a meeting is classified, it might have to be held in a "secure" facility, whether a government building or a public facility secured by trained personnel.

DEPARTMENT AND/OR INDIVIDUAL RESPONSIBLE FOR ORGANIZING AND PLANNING

Government-sponsored meetings are far more complicated than most private-sector conferences because if they are assigned to a person internally, they are often planned by people who are not full-time meeting planners. They may be budget analysts, public affairs officers, scientists, secretaries, or administrative officers. If the department is large enough to have their own meeting planner, then government meeting planners resemble their corporate counterparts.

Due to lack of internal expertise, many government agencies hire meeting management companies or independent meeting planners to handle meetings that fall beyond their internal capabilities. In the Washington, DC area, there are several meeting planning companies that specialize in managing government meetings. There are very strict guidelines within the government as to what a government meeting planner can provide to the attendees in terms of food and beverage and outside activities. It is imperative that the government meeting planner study these regulations and be prepared at any time to go through a financial audit at the conclusion of the meeting.

Meeting planners who work for the government and/or independent meeting management companies are also likely to join associations to support their professional development. This focus on continuing education is especially critical in the government (and health) segments since regulations change often. These organizations will help the government meeting planner learn and understand the strict guidelines and financial/sponsorship rules described earlier. These associations include the Society of Government Meeting Professionals (SGMP) and its local or regional chapters, the Professional Convention Management Association (PCMA), and Meeting Professionals International (MPI). Those who have responsibility for organizing exhibitions are likely to join the International Association of Exhibitions and Events (IAEE).

OTHER ORGANIZATIONS ARRANGING GATHERINGS

POLITICAL ORGANIZATIONS

Aside from their subject matter, political events do not differ much from non-political events with the main differences being in security, press, and venue management. Political events could include major conventions, special events such as inaugurations, trade shows, fundraising events, and local events. Oftentimes conventions tend to be significantly larger than non-political conventions that can create challenges for crowd control. Since attendees are highly passionate about their cause, and political speakers can be very polarizing, specialized security agencies are utilized and disruptive guests are handled in a much harsher fashion, which could even result in formalized legal action. Press should be expected at these types of events and given dedicated space, such as press boxes, press risers, and room for multiple cameras.

Labor Unions

The labor union market has seen a steep decline in private sector union membership from going from 24.3% in 1973 to approximately 5%. In 2019, the highest rates of union membership were in the public sector (police officers, teachers, etc.). Despite this shift, there are still over 60 unions, representing over 14 million people, in the United States that hold meetings regularly, such as the Carpenters, Decorators, Electricians, Riggers, Stagehands, and Teamster Unions. Union meetings are typically held every other year and are only held at unionized properties and tend to be large since it is attended by all members. Oftentimes prominent political speakers are featured in the meeting. The national conventions typically have sponsored functions, social programs, high spouse attendance, and high per-person expenditures.

In 2019, approval for labor unions reached a 50-year high and had the largest gains from workers ages 34 and under. Unions were featured prominently throughout COVID-19 over safety concerns on behalf of their members and workers. This shift in perspective and various activities aside, it remains to be seen whether union membership will continue to decrease over the next decade.

ENTITIES THAT HELP ORGANIZE GATHERINGS

In addition to internal meeting planners, there are other types of organizations that are key players in aiding corporations, associations, government, and other entities in producing their meetings and events. These include exhibition management companies, association management companies, meeting management companies and independent meeting managers.

EXHIBITION MANAGEMENT COMPANIES

Exhibition management companies are in the business of owning and managing trade shows and expositions. These companies both develop and produce shows that profit their companies as well as produce events for a sponsoring corporation, association, or government client. While trade shows and public shows are both events at which products and services are displayed for potential buyers, the **trade show** (or **exhibition**) is generally not open to the public and the market is well defined by the trade or profession. Alternatively,

public shows (or **expositions**) are open to the public and usually charge an admission fee. Depending on the nature of the exposition, the attendees vary greatly and are basically defined by their interests and geographic proximity to the show location.

The companies who operate these exhibitions are profit-making enterprises that have found areas of economic interest that attract either the general public (e.g., auto, boat, home, or garden show) or members of a specific industry (e.g., high-technology, communications, networking) depending on the purpose and type of show. Exhibitions provide the opportunity for face-to-face marketing. The owners and senior managers of company-owned shows decide where, when, and how often they will produce their shows. This decision is typically driven by a profit motive; offering too many shows could lead to a cannibalization of the market, whereas offering too few shows creates an opportunity for the competition to enter the market with their own show. Larger exhibition management companies manage several exhibitions within a given year. They will divide their staff by the various shows so that their time can be dedicated to getting to know the event, growing it, marketing it, and eventually producing it on site. If an exhibition management company is smaller, all staff members most likely will work as one team on the exhibition. The main association that supports the exhibition management industry for the production side of the business is the IAEE. Other related associations include the Exhibit Designers and Producers Association, the Exposition Services and Contractors Association, and the Healthcare Convention and Exhibitor Association.

Some associations hire **exhibition management companies** to manage all or part of their exhibitions. For their efforts, the companies are paid for the services they provide. Among the top 10 largest exhibition management companies are Reed Exhibitions and Emerald Expositions. Their shows serve a wide variety of industries, domestically and globally, including aerospace, art and entertainment, electronics, hospitality, security, sport and health, and travel. Other exhibition management companies include International Gem and Jewelry Inc., Cygnus Expositions, and National Event Management Inc.

Although an essential part of the event-planning industry, exhibition management companies are really marketing companies that create the environment in which need-satisfying exchanges can occur. Their focus is on selling exhibit space, producing an event that will keep the exhibitors happy and returning year after year, and building buyer attendance. The exhibition management companies have a need to market to two distinctly different yet inextricably linked publics. The first market that must be targeted is exhibitors who need to reach potential buyers of their products and services. The other is members of the trade or general public who have a need or desire to view, discuss, and purchase the products and services presented by the exhibitors. The trade group only needs to be informed of the dates and location of the exhibition/trade show. Direct mail, e-mail, and posting the tradeshow on social media outlets may be all that is needed for an established show. Shows appealing to the general public require extensive media advertising (social media, television, online advertising, and radio) to communicate the specifics within the geographic region. Promotional efforts like the distribution of discount coupons are common. In both cases, it is essential that the marketing effort results in a high volume of traffic at the exhibition to satisfy the needs of the exhibitors.

ASSOCIATION MANAGEMENT COMPANIES

As the name of this category implies, this type of company is contracted by an association to assume full or partial responsibility for the management of the association, based on its needs. A designated person in the association management company is identified as the main contact for the association and interacts with the board of directors and members to fulfill the association's mission. If the association is small and has limited financial resources, the contact person will most likely serve in this capacity for two or more associations. Since these organizations manage more than one association, association management companies used to be known as multi-management companies. However, confusion as to whom they targeted their services to necessitate this change.

Other employees of the association management company (AMC) support the main contact and provide services as contracted (such as membership, finance, publications, government relations, and meeting management services). With this type of arrangement, the association office is typically located within the offices of the association management company. Examples of these types of companies include SmithBucklin & Associates and the Association Management Group.

Association Management Companies
Caitlin Condie
Manager, Meetings and Expositions at Kellen

As a planner at an AMC, your role may be similar to those at stand-alone associations. The key difference is that you will work on multiple client events with varying meeting needs. As an AMC planner, you will provide full-service planning—from consulting with the volunteer committees on site selection all the way up to meeting execution. What makes working at an AMC unique from working internally at an association is that you are constantly in different phases of each of your client events and each phase of planning is just slightly different from that of your other clients. One event might be in the RFP process, while one event is just wrapping up its annual convention. Because you are working with many different clients at the same time, your days are hardly ever the same from one to the next. Challenges that arise are usually easier to handle because it is likely your other clients have already faced it or are going through the same issues.

Being a planner at an AMC has its perks—no 2 days are alike, you work on different staff teams and interact with them on almost a daily basis, and you have your own tiny network of other planners right next to you in the same trenches as you. However, an AMC can also have its challenges. When you are working on multiple clients, you typically keep a full schedule throughout the entire year without much downtime because while one client is slow, you are usually weeks out from another client's annual meeting. The AMC environment tends to be a little more fast paced and, in many situations, you are the sole meeting planner on that client's association. This may sound frightening or too much too handle for some people. But, if you are someone who thrives in a fast-paced and steady environment, enjoys working with a team of people while still wanting the responsibility and role as *the* planner for an association, an AMC could be the place for you.

MEETING-MANAGEMENT COMPANIES

These companies, also known as **third parties**, operate on a contractual basis. This is similar to association-management companies, but meeting-management companies limit their services to providing either selected or comprehensive meeting management services. They may manage all aspects of the meeting or may be focused on a specific segment of meeting planning services such as pre-meeting support, day-of support, city and venue research (also called **sourcing** in the industry), hotel negotiations and contracting, exhibit and sponsorship sales, on-site exhibit floor management, providing registration and housing services, providing lead retrieval equipment/platforms and meeting apps, marketing services, providing online meeting platforms, online moderation and coordination, or any combination of these. The meetings that these companies assist with may be held at convention centers, conference centers, special venue facilities, or hotels. Examples of meeting management companies include Conference Direct, Meeting Management Group, and Experient Inc.

If the event is onsite, in many instances, these companies make a large portion of their money from collecting 10% commission on each hotel room night booked at the hotel in return for bringing the booking to the property. A full-service third party will use some of these commissions to offset the fee charged to the client for other services provided. If the event is online, or is a direct fee for hire, the meeting management company will charge a flat fee or percentage of the overall event cost.

PROFESSIONAL CONGRESS ORGANIZERS

Outside the United States, the term *professional congress organizer (PCO)* is used to designate a meeting management company. In international destinations, a congress is defined as a conference or convention. According to the Event Industry Council (EIC) APEX Glossary, a PCO is a local supplier who can arrange, manage, and/or plan any function or service for an event. PCOs are very similar to destination-management companies in the United States. When sponsoring organizations from North America hold international events, they often engage the services of a PCO from the host region to assist them with local logistics. Some countries actually require that a domestic company be contracted to handle the meeting.

INDEPENDENT MEETING MANAGERS

Experienced meeting professionals often use their expertise and contacts to set up their own business of managing meetings, or parts of meetings, for almost any entity that has a need in the meeting and event area. This could include associations, corporations, individuals, etc. An independent meeting manager may be called to plan and run a wedding, run a golf tournament that is an integral part of a gathering, to provide on-site management, or to act in a similar way to a full-service meeting management firm and handle all logistics for a meeting. There are also times when an independent meeting planner is hired to handle last minutes crises in a meetings department at an organization. Personnel changes in the meetings department shortly before a meeting may require hiring a competent professional to pull the meeting together and bring it to a successful conclusion. The independent model works well for planners who have worked full time for an organization, gained significant knowledge and respect in the industry, and want to go out on their own and determine their own schedule. Independents are paid on a contract basis and can pick and choose for whom they want to work. The segment of the industry that individuals are associated with will dictate the type of entity that they would likely join to support their professional development. Many will join PCMA or MPI. Others will choose to join organizations like the International Live Events Association (formerly International Special Events Society), the National Association of Catering Executives, or the Association of Bridal Consultants.

Independent Meeting Planners
Melissa Whitaker, CMP
Meetings Consultant

Independent meeting planners have unique benefits that employed planners do not, such as creating their own clientele base, setting their own schedules, and being their own boss. Personally, I love working with several clients, who vary from corporate to associate to incentive, because it provides me with a variety of work so that every day looks different. Also, setting my own schedule allows me more flexibility in balancing my work and family responsibilities. Self-employment gives me the opportunity to work from home, build my own company, and direct my career accordingly.

Independent meeting planners get to choose their own work projects and what they want their particular focus to be. My work projects vary daily and include sourcing RFPs, site selection, negotiating contracts, creating budgets, preparing event specifications, planning logistics for off-site events, onsite assistance/travel directing, and more. Independent meeting planners also get to dictate if they want to travel, and if they do, how much they would like to. I travel about 30% of the time and get to experience many places that I have never been before.

In the event industry, networking is important but it is especially critical for the independent meeting planner. Networking is key to the success of my business, so I always make sure that colleagues know that I am available to help whenever they or someone they know needs assistance. Although it is up to the independent meeting planner where they want to focus their own time and energy, I have found that it is important for me to be involved in my local meeting-planning associations. These are excellent opportunities to give back to my professional community, stay on top of industry trends, and network with colleagues.

TRENDS AND BEST PRACTICES

In the earlier part of the century, the advancement of technologies allowed for more virtual interactions and meeting and event planners were worried that online conferences would replace face-to-face meetings. At the very least, planners thought it would hurt their face-to-face meetings significantly. Through substantial research over the years, it has been found that online meetings have not hurt in-person meetings; in fact, it has helped them to extend their reach to audiences who may not have been able to come and helped attendees "try out" their conference before "converting" to the face-to-face experience. Experts believe that the face-to-face meeting business will never go out of "style." Although technology now allows people to join communities online and interact more frequently, human nature dictates that people enjoy and need to get together to exchange ideas and to network.

Outside of COVID-19 specific impacts that will be discussed below, meetings and events have seen some recent trends that are still expected to continue into the near future. As a "before" and "after" review, here are the trends that were listed in the last edition of this textbook (2017). These were listed as upcoming trends at that time and have become an integral part of the meeting and event industry still to this day.

- *Budgetary constraints*
- *Shortening meetings*
- *Changing frequency of annual meetings*
- *Creating more value for their members*
- *Increasing the interactivity of meeting sessions*
- *Merging of sponsoring organizations*

- *Virtual conferences*
- *Virtual trade shows*
- *Outsourcing*
- *Focus on ROI*
- *Limiting Government Meetings/ Events*

With this in mind, what are the trends we are seeing now in the industry?

Attendee personalization. As individuals are able to mass customize their products, their delivery, and their services—events are no different. Attendees want an event that fits their lifestyle and is customized to their particular wants and needs. With event technology, this is quickly becoming a reality.

Event experience design versus traditional planning. While we all started as meeting "planners", the industry is beginning to differentiate between event coordinators who focus on logistics and event designers/strategists who can design an experience as part of an organizations overall strategy and show an ROI on that event.

More collaboration during meetings/less presentations. As we shift from the experience economy to the transformation economy, death by PowerPoint and panels is just not acceptable anymore. In a recent study, nearly 75% of meetings incorporated a workshop component. Choose an influential keynote and then get people into discussion groups.

Consolidation will dominate. Mergers and acquisitions are on the rise to include event-related organizations and suppliers. As corporations continue to get larger with more resources at their disposal, smaller corporations and competing associations will struggle to compete and will have to position themselves strategically in their market in order to thrive.

Neuroscience in event design. Neuroscientists focus on the brain and its impact on behavior and cognitive functions. Neuroscience has had a presence in marketing for a while and is now in the event spectrum—planners are using neuroscience in order to present things in the best way to encourage people to act.

Diversity and inclusion. Diversity and inclusion were trending before *Black Lives Matter* became an international movement, but now it has become essential and is well advertised. Over half of North American event websites now include information on their diversity and inclusion policies.

Embrace last minute attendees. Attendees are waiting longer and longer to make their decision to attend an event. While some of this might be because of schedule availability, other reasons could be because of financial reasons and fear of missing out on other opportunities. Event professionals should embrace last-minute attendees, reconsider early bird pricing strategies, and make sure to advertise all the way up to the event.

Hybrid events are increasing. Time has officially been recognized as the most valuable commodity on the planet and, although events might be worth it, the hassle to travel to and from an event might not be deemed essential. Hybrid events are ways to reach people who either want the in-person experience or want to attend online. Hybrid can extend the reach far beyond the meeting room walls to others around the globe.

Event technology. Event technology was already experiencing an exponential rise to include full size hologram keynotes that can be programmed to speak in any language. This is already a reality. The general publics' newfound widespread acceptance of event technology will help to accelerate this increase in offerings.

© Girts Ragelis/Shutterstock.com

HOW COVID-19 HAS IMPACTED SEGMENTS OF THE INDUSTRY

It is important to note that in the last edition of this book, the increase in virtual meetings and tradeshows was already a trend as was increasing the attendee interactivity in meeting sessions. Before COVID-19, it was cited in many associations' 2019 trends reports that hybrid and virtual events would continue to grow. COVID-19 did not cause the popularity of this phenomenon; however, what it did cause was the general publics' widespread acceptance of this format. It also made every person an instant critic of online meetings and raised the expectation for engagement. These four items have become increasingly top on the mind during and post-COVID-19.

Engagement and interactivity are a major focus. We have all sat in passive trainings, meetings, and classes. During COVID-19, we were not limited by geographic boundaries or financial constraints and were able to test-drive events from all over the world. Although it was already trending for more interactivity during meetings, COVID-19 has increased our lowest minimum acceptable product nearly overnight.

New careers. Although virtual and hybrid events were already trending, what used to be a small part of an existing job description became full-time positions that companies were hiring almost overnight. Now you can find careers as an event technologist, virtual engagement specialist, online event facilitator or moderators, or a variety of positions in an established world of online engagement activities.

Safety and security. There is a fine balance between being as safe and secure as possible without causing anxiety for your attendees. As the fear of COVID-19 and future pandemics is fresh on your attendees' minds—signage, communication, and visual cues will become particularly important.

Sitting is the new smoking. Throughout COVID-19, the world was told to stay indoors and individuals developed an entirely new appreciation for the outdoors. Walking, running, and other outdoor activities experienced a sharp increase—as did the ability for people to log in to online meetings from anywhere. Movement is key and can help attendees stay focused and energized.

SUMMARY

The types of organizations that sponsor gatherings are as diverse as the types of gatherings held and the people who attend them. Most of the population will participate in a gathering at least once in their lives. For many of them, attending a meeting, convention, exhibition, or other event will be a regular occurrence. The gatherings they will attend reflect their personal and professional interests.

People seeking meeting planning career opportunities with sponsoring organizations will have to use targeting techniques to locate them. Although these positions do exist throughout the nation, the greatest number of these positions can be found in locations where the organizations are headquartered. The metropolitan Washington, DC area is considered to be the "meetings capital" of the world, with several thousand associations located in and around the city. The federal government, also physically located in Washington, DC, employs many people in the meetings profession as they organize and hold hundreds of meetings each year. State capitals are home to many state and regional associations, in addition to agencies of state government, all of which have many meetings of their own that are held annually. Major corporations tend to be located in large cities. Although many may have offices in smaller cities and towns, their meetings are typically planned from corporate headquarters. However, it remains to be seen how the impact of COVID-19 will continue to affect large meetings as these could become more regionals. Employment opportunities with organizations and facilities that host gatherings can be found in both major cities and small towns.

With baby boomers (the largest age group in the U.S. population) approaching retirement age, it is anticipated that there will be an increasing number of employment opportunities in the coming years on both the planner and supplier sides of the meeting, exposition, event, and convention industry.

One of the main differences between corporate events and association events is the guaranteed attendee base. Typically, in corporate events, there is a set group of people who must attend (such as a sales meeting or corporate training). Association meetings are not required and therefore the organization advertises to the relevant professional community at large to secure attendees. Therefore, marketing is extremely important for these types of events.

The Engineering Association of America is a non-profit association of members who are professional engineers. This association is the longest running association focused on engineering but has recently faced sharp competition over the past decade from conferences focusing on specific segments of engineering (mechanical, electrical, etc.) and niche conferences (Women in Engineering, etc.). Due to this competition, conference attendance has decreased by a significant amount in the past 5 years. You have just been hired as the new Director of Marketing.

1. What is the first thing you would do now that you are hired?
2. What kind of marketing should the association produce for potential attendees? Existing attendees?
3. What kind of marketing would you produce for sponsors? For exhibitors? What kind of packages would you customize?
4. As you think about your attendee experience, what new experiences could you integrate onsite at your event to generate excitement and positive word of mouth?
5. Keeping in mind your target market, which social media outlets would you focus on? Why?
6. When should you begin to market their annual meeting?

KEYWORDS AND TERMS

For definitions, see https://insights.eventscouncil.org/Industry-glossary

air lift   incentive trips
associations   per diem rates
CEU   public shows
conventions   SMERFs
corporations   sourcing
exhibition   third parties
expositions   trade show
exhibition management companies

REVIEW AND DISCUSSION QUESTIONS

1. Identify the type of sponsoring organization that holds the greatest number of gatherings and the type that generates the greatest economic benefit.

2. Which type or types of sponsoring organizations have the greatest marketing challenges to ensure the success of their gatherings?

3. What changes are occurring with incentive trips to provide more value for the corporation sponsoring the gathering?

4. How do not-for-profit associations differ from for-profit organizations?

5. What types of organizations comprise the category of associations known as "SMERFs," and what similarities do they share with each other?

6. How do government procurement officers view meeting contracts from their hotel suppliers?

7. Distinguish between the trade show and the exposition.

8. What efficiencies do association management companies bring to the management and operation of small associations?

ABOUT THE CHAPTER CONTRIBUTOR

Kristin Malek, PhD, CMP, CED, DES, CHE

Dr. K, as she is known by her students, is an event management extension specialist and assistant professor in the Hospitality, Restaurant, and Tourism Management program at the University of Nebraska. Dr. Malek worked in the hospitality industry for over 10 years before joining academe and still remains active with industry groups and consulting. She teaches and researches in the area of meetings and events with a focus on experience design, engagement, hybrid and online meetings, co-creation, and ROI.

After completing internships and contract work in event management, she went on to receive her master's degree in international hospitality and tourism management from the University of South Carolina and her PhD in hospitality administration from the University of Nevada Las Vegas. Dr. K served as the executive director of events for a third-party planning company in Las Vegas where she oversaw the medical association meeting market. In this role, she managed association events greater than 1 million dollars and led a team of staff and hospitality management interns. She has been named as a Top 20 Meeting Industry Trendsetter by *Meetings Today* magazine (2016) and has been recognized as an Emerging Leader of the Year by PCMA (2018). She has achieved designations as a Certified Meeting Professional (CMP), Certified Event Designer (CED), Digital Event Strategist (DES), and Certified Hospitality Educator (CHE).

Contact information:
University of Nebraska—Lincoln
202F Leverton Hall, Lincoln NE 68583
DrKevents@unl.edu

PREVIOUS EDITION CHAPTER CONTRIBUTORS

The contributors for previous editions of the chapter were:
Nancy DeBrosse, Senior Vice President at Experient
Howard E. Reichbart, Emeritus from Northern Virginia Community College.

CHAPTER 3

DESTINATION MARKETING ORGANIZATIONS (DMOs)

© Dutchmen Photography/Shutterstock.com

CONVENTION AND VISITORS BUREAUS (CVBS)/DESTINATION MARKETING ORGANIZATIONS (DMOS) ARE FOUND THROUGHOUT THE WORLD

CHAPTER OBJECTIVES

- Articulate the roles and functions of a destination marketing organization.
- Outline the needs and opportunities a DMO can meet for a meeting professional.
- Illustrate the convention marketing and sales activities expected of a DMO.
- Describe the tools and associations available through Destination International.
- Discuss trends in the field of DMOs.
- Identify ways in which the COVID-19 pandemic is impacting DMOs.

If a destination were merely a place, a dot on a map, a bump in the road, or just another stop along the way, then the destination would not matter. Destinations matter. They are called destinations for a reason: people want or need to go there and visit. In many instances, people go to great lengths to get there. They are drawn to them. For a few, they may be the realization of some lifelong dream. By boat, car, plane, or train, they go. Why? Because contrary to the wise old proverb, it is not about the journey but about the destination. And the reasons for making the journey are as varied as the people traveling. Whether for business, convention/meeting, or leisure, they come because of the expectation of an enjoyable experience. In short, the destination must provide experiences unique enough to compel someone to travel to and spend their time and money there.

Travel and tourism enhance the quality of life for a local community by providing jobs and by bringing in tax dollars for cultural and sporting venues that cater to both tourists and locals. Tourism creates jobs at the local level in a multitude of ways. Convention facilities are often rented by groups that cater to local residents. Popular examples are home and garden shows, boat shows, car shows, golf shows, comic book expositions, and almost any show one can imagine. If sold aggressively, convention centers and similar venues can optimize their space 12 months a year.

THE ROLE AND FUNCTION OF DESTINATION MARKETING ORGANIZATIONS

WHAT IS A DESTINATION MARKETING ORGANIZATION?

A destination marketing organization (DMO) may also be known as a national tourism board, state or provincial tourism office, or convention and visitor bureau (CVB). They are often not-for-profit organizations or government entities (or a hybrid) and are charged with representing a specific destination and helping the long-term economic development of communities through a travel and tourism strategy. The DMO in each city, county, state, region, or country has a responsibility to market its destination to visitors. This includes leisure and business travelers along with meeting/event planners who can hold meetings, conventions, and trade shows in their destination. DMOs also service those groups that hold meetings in their destination with meeting preparations. DMOs entice and influence visitors to enjoy the historical, cultural, and recreational opportunities that the destination has to offer. In most instances, the DMO is the only entity charged with selling and marketing the destination brand and therefore serves everyone.

A DMO does not typically organize meetings, events, and conventions but assists meeting planners in learning about the destination and area attractions to make the best possible use of all the services and facilities the destination has to offer. The history of DMOs stretches back to 1895, when a group of businessmen in Detroit put a full-time salesman on the road to invite conventions to their city. His function expanded, and the organization for which he worked was called a convention bureau. Today, DMOs operate throughout the world and are charged with the responsibility of bringing "new revenue" to each community they represent through the attraction of visitor dollars.

Initially, DMOs existed to sell and service conventions, but as time went by, more and more of these organizations became involved in the promotion of tourism. What were originally called convention bureaus expanded their scope to include tourism and were called CVBs. This evolution and expansion of roles and functions continues today. Many CVBs use the term DMO interchangeably to better reflect their activities in selling and promoting their destinations to their wide range of customers. DMOs are synonymous with CVBs.

THE PURPOSE OF A DMO

DMOs assist in the long-term economic development of their local communities. Some DMOs are membership based, bringing together local businesses that rely on tourism and meetings for revenue. DMOs serve as the "official" contact point for their destination. Some DMOs are departments of local government, not unlike the library or highway department. This structure is most common outside the United States, where DMOs may be quasi-autonomous nongovernmental organizations (QUANGO) or may function as a division of local government called an authority. Many within the United States fall under the government tax structure of a not-for-profit organization and are classified as either "501(c)(3)" or "501(c)(6)."

For visitors, DMOs are like a key to the city. DMOs are an unbiased resource and are experts about their destination. They are a one-stop shop for local tourism interests and save visitors' and meeting professionals' time and energy. DMOs provide a full range of information about a destination and do not charge for their services.

For conventions, they are often the intermediary between the sponsoring organization and hospitality businesses. As such, the DMO may coordinate site visits, disseminate and collect **requests for proposals (RFPs)**, and develop collateral material used in event promotion. Some DMOs will also find funding to help attract large conventions and may, in some cases, provide direct financial assistance to present the most attractive proposal to the customer, if the business is valuable enough to justify the subsidy. Usually, cities compete against each other to attract business, which can mean millions of dollars to the local economy for just one event. On balance, the best financial deal usually wins the business if the competing cities' facilities are similar.

A cornerstone value of most DMOs is to offer unbiased information about a destination's services and facilities. The goal is to outsell their competition by successfully matching the customers' specific meeting needs with the facilities and services offered in the community. For example, a group of students might be budget conscious and therefore most interested in economy-priced hotels and lower-cost meeting facilities. Conversely, corporate groups tend to be attracted to the finest hotels and venues the community has to offer. A DMO's job is to determine the customer's needs and budget and provide options they will ultimately be willing to purchase. The DMO works to bring the business to the entire community and represents all equally.

IF DMOS DO NOT CHARGE FOR THEIR SERVICES, HOW DO THEY MAKE MONEY?

DMOs do not charge their clients—the leisure visitor, the business traveler, and the meeting planner—for services rendered. Instead, most DMOs are funded through a combination of a share of the hotel occupancy taxes, membership dues, and sometimes through a tourism improvement district (TID). In the United States, an improvement district is an area specifically designated in the community where any incremental increase in property taxes generated is earmarked for a specific purpose, in this case the DMO. These can come in many forms. For example, if hotels, restaurants, and other hospitality venues are added, expanded, or improved, the DMO benefits financially. The underlying concept is that these new facilities are a direct result of the marketing and promotion efforts of the DMO. Another derivation of a TID is when the hotels within that district charge an additional user fee on every occupied room night, the revenue collected oftentimes goes to the DMO for marketing purposes. If the DMO is a government agency, then funding comes from local government.

> Memphis has more than 60 tourist attractions, including Graceland, Beale Street, and the Memphis Pyramid, plus restaurants, theaters, and art museums. The Memphis Convention and Visitors Bureau takes advantage of these iconic attractions to market the city to visitors around the world.
>
> In addition to leisure attractions, the Memphis Renasant Convention Center attracts over 500,000 visitors annually to conventions, trade shows, and performing arts.
>
> The convention center completed a $200M renovation in 2020 to create a state-of-the-art facility able to attract new business to the destination. To remain competitive and fund the improvements to the convention center, the bureau, hoteliers, and the city worked together to form the first TID in Tennessee. They were able to leverage their commitment and worked with the city to simultaneously dedicate new bed tax funds for convention center improvements. The Memphis TID began on January 1, 2016, assessing $2 per occupied room per night to fund destination marketing programs. The district raised $5.3 million in annual TID funding.

ATTRACTING LEISURE TRAVELERS

Whereas hotels, attractions, and organizations, have a role in marketing a destination, the DMO is the primary tourism marketer of most destinations. Its primary objectives are to promote the destination and to increase the number of overnight guests. It leverages the community's assets and unique qualities to compel people to visit. It also leads the community in the creation of a destination brand and marketing plan.

DMOs will often group the community's attractions to market to specific demographics. For example, if the destination has a zoo, children's museum, and amusement park, the DMO will market to families (mostly moms) and provide examples of itineraries to create enjoyable family vacations. So too, they may use their city's many shopping venues, spas, and local restaurants to sell a "girls' getaway" weekend. DMOs may also market sporting events and craft beer festivals to other demographics. In short, DMOs use the most attractive grouping of destination assets to attract the largest number of leisure visitors—visitors who will spend money and return again.

MAINLY MARKETING

While some cities have built a reputation as tourist cities, such as Las Vegas and Orlando, most cities have to educate potential visitors as to the reasons why they should plan a trip.

A DMO must decide the most effective way to reach their audience and will often purchase a combination of marketing products based on their overall ad budget and research on the buying habits of their target customers. They may use traditional channels such as television, radio, newspaper, and magazines or purchase digital ads on websites like Facebook or any of the limitless offerings available to reach customers.

DMOs use public relations activities to project positive stories about the destination. An effective tactic is to invite travel press for a complimentary visit to their community and experience. The DMO will invite the travel writer for an experience (usually lasting 3 days) in their community with the intention that the journalist, blogger, or influencer will write positive stories about his or her experience. This unbiased "third party" endorsement of the destination is extremely effective in piquing the interest of their loyal readers, because these people are considered credible sources for travel information.

WEBSITE

One of the most effective marketing tools for any DMO is a smart and comprehensive website that features the best attractions and facilities the destination has to offer. The best websites feature great images, videos, and blogs that relay compelling experiences about the community. DMOs tell the story of the destination, and the most effective blogs feature engaging experiences and memorable events that make the destination attractive; they feature food, communities, nature, and interactions with real people.

WHAT A DMO CAN DO FOR MEETING PROFESSIONALS

WHAT MEETING PLANNERS NEED TO KNOW ABOUT DMOS

Many people are unaware of the existence of DMOs, and, therefore, they do not realize the wealth of information and resources they provide on a complimentary basis. The best analogy to describe what a DMO does for meeting professionals is to think of their role as being similar to a realtor. They find prospects (meeting planners) to purchase the goods and services available to them in the destination. They act as an agent for both the buyer and the seller to remove the barriers that will potentially end in a sale.

A DMO has many responsibilities. Most importantly, it serves as *the* official point of contact for convention and meeting planners, and, in most cases, where a convention center is present, the DMO controls the bookings of the center eighteen months and beyond the current date. It encourages groups to hold meetings in their destination and assists groups with meeting preparations. DMOs also provide promotional materials, giveaways, and video "teasers" to encourage attendance and establish room blocks (hotel rooms set aside for a group), among other things.

Meeting planners can access a range of services, packages, and value-added extras through a DMO. Before going into the specifics of what a DMO can do for a meeting planner, let us examine a few common misconceptions about DMOs.

> *Misconception 1:* DMOs only book hotel rooms and convention space.
>
> *Fact:* DMOs represent the gamut of visitor-related businesses, from restaurants and retail to rental cars and racetracks. Therefore, they are responsible for introducing planners to the range of meeting-related products and services the city has to offer.
>
> *Misconception 2:* DMOs only work with large groups.
>
> *Fact:* More than two-thirds of the average DMOs' efforts are devoted to meetings of fewer than 200 people. In fact, larger DMOs often have staff members specifically dedicated to small meetings, group tours, leisure tourists, and transient business travel.

Misconception 3: DMOs own and/or run the convention center.

Fact: Only 10% of DMOs run the convention center in their locations such as the Las Vegas Convention and Visitor Authority. Nevertheless, DMOs work closely with local convention centers and can assist planners in obtaining what they need from convention center staff.

Misconception 4: Planners must pay DMOs for their services.

Fact: In truth, most services of a DMO are free.

Some may question the need to work through a DMO when planning a meeting, particularly in cases where the bulk of an event takes place at one hotel or only at the convention center. However, the DMO can help a planner work with those entities and can help fill out the convention schedule (including spouse tours and pre- and post tours) with off-site activities. Since the DMO is an objective resource, it can efficiently direct planners to the products and services that will work best to accommodate the needs and budgets of their attendees.

DMOs make planning and implementing a meeting less time-consuming and more streamlined by providing direct access to the services they require. The DMO knows the inner-workings of their destination and gives meeting planners access to a range of services, packages, and value-added extras. Before a meeting begins, DMO sales managers can help locate meeting space, check hotel availability, and arrange for site inspections. DMOs can also link planners with suppliers, from motor coach companies and caterers to off-site entertainment venues that can help meet the prerequisites of any event. A DMO can act as a liaison between the planner and community officials, thus clearing the way for special permits, street closures, and so on. The DMO can offer suggestions about ways meeting attendees can maximize free time, along with helping to develop companion programs and pre- and postconvention tours.

A BUSINESS CASE FOR DMOs

How DMOs Provide Return on Investment to their communities

Based on the budget and the needs of each community, DMOs are charged with creating and effectively promoting the destination brand to potential visitors. They are the sales, marketing, and public relations firm for the entire community.

As is the case with every business, DMOs must constantly prove their worth to their stakeholders (hotels, attractions members, government). DMOs are trusted to invest the revenue they receive, in most cases through tax dollars, and are under scrutiny to show a substantial return on investment. To do this, most DMOs report in their annual meeting how they measure against key performance indicators (KPIs).

Examples of KPIs:

- Communications: media contacts, press releases, media coverage, press tours, media impressions
- Convention Sales: tradeshows attended, familiarization tours conducted, sales calls, site inspections, leads sent, definite bookings, definite room nights, definite convention attendance, lost opportunities
- Services: citywide events, welcome booth referrals, planning bulletins, registrar hours, site visits, housings, reservations processed, room nights processed
- Marketing: Web statistics, social media statistics, tracked visitors, inquiries, retail revenue, visitor satisfaction, advertising spent, ad value gained
- The KPIs that receive the most attention tend to be those associated with total industry economic impact, jobs, and local taxes paid by out-of-town visitors.

© EtiAmmos/Shutterstock.com

DMO DEPARTMENTS AND STAFF

Although departments, job titles, and responsibilities vary from one DMO to another, most with convention facilities have the following:

- president and CEO/executive director
- vice president of convention sales
- vice president of convention services
- vice president of marketing
- vice president of finance
- vice president of communications
- vice president of membership

Within each department, there are staff members who support the work of the vice president, including directors, managers, coordinators, and assistants. Some DMOs are more leisure focused and therefore have more staff support for marketing and public relations functions, whereas others with large convention facilities will also assign a larger amount of staff to selling and servicing conventions.

Some destinations have research directors, community relations directors, or government relations directors.

DMOs are very interested in engaging students in and out of college for careers in the field. Many offer a wide array of internships, primarily to college students. In many instances, these interns are first considered for entry-level positions within the organization. Be sure to check DMO websites for internship opportunities, which may exist 12 months of the year.

ACTIVITIES OF DMOS RELATIVE TO CONVENTION MARKETING AND SALES

Professionals who work in a DMO serve as the sales representative for their destination. There is an entire process that a DMO undertakes with a meeting professional to bring a meeting to its destination.

SALES PROCESSES

DMOs want to attract their share of this lucrative market and hire professional salespeople to sell their destinations. They use various sales strategies and tactics to attract conventions, tradeshows, meetings, and events. There are numerous industry events where DMO salespeople can meet potential planners to discuss their meeting requirements. An example of some of the larger not-for-profit industry shows are:

- American Bus Association
- American Society of Association Executives
- Destinations International Destinations Showcase
- International Travel Association
- National Association of Sports Commissions
- National Coalition of Black Meeting Planners
- NCAA Convention
- Professional Conference Management Association Annual Meeting
- Religious Conference Management Association

The largest 'for-profit' tradeshow in the United States, as well as in Germany, is organized by a company called IMEX, which is based in London, England. Each of their shows attracts more than 12,000 attendees.

There are numerous local, regional, and national expositions in which DMOs may choose to participate, based on the best match for their community with the type of customer who would typically attend the event. For example, a destination that does not have sporting facilities would not typically benefit from attending the NCAA Convention.

© View Apart/Shutterstock.com

Most industry events offer the DMO the opportunity to participate in a multiday tradeshow as well as many educational and networking events. The goal is to build personal relationships with existing and new customers to further the process of selling their destination.

DMO sales professionals also use traditional sales solicitation tactics (phone, email, and mail) to find new meeting planner customers. In this information age, the DMO salesperson can access customer lists and market intelligence that can streamline their efforts.

SITE REVIEW AND LEADS PROCESS

Determining whether a site or location can accommodate a meeting's requirements is critical. The DMO is the central information source for advice, on-site selection, transportation, and available local services, all with no cost or obligation to the meeting or event manager. DMO representatives have the knowledge and information to provide up-to-date data about the area as well as future planned developments.

Regardless of the meeting size, the DMO can serve as the first stop in the site review process. When a meeting planner contacts a DMO, a DMO sales manager will be assigned to assist in securing the necessary information and facts to produce a successful meeting. The DMO sales contact will gather information about preferred dates for the event and find out what facilities are available, whether there are adequate sleeping rooms and meeting rooms, and whether convention facilities are available for the entire period, including time for exhibitors to move in and out.

In order to represent all their constituents, most DMOs have a lead management process, wherein the sales contact circulates meeting specifications to facilities and lodging entities that can accommodate the requirements. Basic information required by the DMO is indicated on the convention lead sheet and distributed electronically.

The lead distribution may also be limited by establishing certain parameters, such as specifying a location downtown or near the airport. In cases such as this, the lead would be forwarded only to properties that meet the requirements identified by the customer. For example, quantity of rooms, square feet of meeting space, off-site venues for meal functions, nearby sporting facilities, or any customer requirement from big to small. If a meeting planner is familiar with the destination's properties, he or she may express interest in certain facilities by name. Then, only those facilities receive the lead.

The DMO sales contact will request that the receiving property send the information directly to the meeting planner, or the sales contact may gather the information, compile it into a package, and send it to the meeting planner. In the United States, federal antitrust laws prohibit DMOs from discussing pricing policies with hotels under consideration. All pricing discussions must take place between the meeting planner and the prospective property. A DMO sales contact may relate to a property that a meeting planner is looking for a specific price range of room rates but cannot negotiate on the meeting planner's behalf.

Many times during the sales process, the DMO sales professional interacts with the customer to ensure that the destination has provided the most attractive offer in terms of available venues, services, and cost. Some DMOs and destination venues will create specific money reserves to offer financial incentives to assist the customer in offsetting the cost of their event. These incentives are a very powerful motivator to some groups in deciding to choose one destination over another.

CONVENTION LEAD SHEET

The convention lead sheet used by DMOs will usually contain the following information:

- ✓ Name of the DMO sales contact
- ✓ Distribution date of convention lead sheet
- ✓ Name of meeting planner and title
- ✓ Name of the group or organization
- ✓ Address information for group or organization
- ✓ Email and telephone number of the meeting planner
- ✓ Total number of room nights anticipated
- ✓ Peak room nights and day of peak
- ✓ Dates for the event or meeting
- ✓ Decision date
- ✓ Total anticipated attendance

- ✓ Occupancy pattern
  - · Day
  - · Date
  - · Rooms
- ✓ Meeting space requirements
  - · Exhibit space
  - · Food functions
- ✓ History
- ✓ Competing cities
- ✓ Bedroom rate history
- ✓ Bedroom pickup history
- ✓ Meeting rotation pattern (south, north, east, west, central)
- ✓ Decision steps
- ✓ Additional information
- ✓ Name of person who prepared the sheet and date of preparation

The lead management process takes place in advance of the event. For an association, the average "horizon" or time between looking at a destination and the event taking place varies. However, with large groups and large cities, the horizon can be years and even decades in advance. For example, the Morial Convention Center in New Orleans regularly garners commitments from large groups as much as 25 years in advance of the event itself.

The DMO sales manager will communicate with the meeting planner and the facilities to ensure that all information is disseminated, received, and understood. Any additional questions will be answered, and the meeting planner will be encouraged to visit the city and visit venues/hotels being considered. The DMO can be of significant assistance during a personal site review by arranging site inspections.

SITE INSPECTIONS

A site inspection is a physical review of proposed venues and services prior to the actual program. A site inspection may be required at any point in the sales process. A site inspection by the planner may occur prior to the proposal, after the proposal, or once contracted for space. A site inspection occurring prior to the proposal is a part of the information-gathering visit by the client. Often, this is hosted by the DMO. A site inspection by the planner that occurs after the proposal has been submitted, yet prior to the customer's decision, is used to address questions regarding the execution of the submitted proposal. Finally, the planner conducts a last site inspection visit after the contract has been signed. This is often the first step in the finalization of a program or event. Site inspections can vary in time and detail.

These inspections must be carefully planned and orchestrated to show a customer the venues and services offered as well as meet the destination team, which includes community contacts. The site inspection can often be the most critical step in winning a customer's business, because this is when the DMO has an opportunity to develop a relationship with the customer and gain their confidence. Many programs have been won or lost over a seemingly simple lunch conversation during a site inspection.

DMO SERVICES FOR MEETING PROFESSIONALS

There are multiple general services that DMOs provide for meeting professionals. One category of services might be referred to as "connecting the planner and attendee to the destination." In this category, the DMO might provide hotel room counts and meeting space statistics as well as a central database of other meetings to help planners avoid conflicts and/or space shortages. The DMOs can help with meeting facility availability—information on the availability of hotels, convention centers, and other meeting facilities as well as help connect planners to their local transportation network that offers shuttle service, ground transportation, and airline information. Further, DMOs can provide access to special venues—as most DMOs have ties to city departments, personnel have the ear of local government officials. Whether an official letter of welcome from the mayor is needed or the blocking of a road for a street party, a DMO can pave the way. DMOs can also help meeting attendees maximize their free time through the creation of pre- and postconference activities, spouse tours, and special evening events. Lastly, DMOs are a liaison in destination government and/or community relations—a local resource regarding legislative, regulatory, and municipal issues that may affect a meeting or the meetings industry.

A second category of service could be labeled "information." DMOs can offer unbiased information about a wide range of destination services and facilities. They can serve as a vast information database and provide one-stop shopping, thus saving planners time, energy, and money in the development of a meeting. DMOs can also act as a liaison between the planner and the community. For example, DMOs are aware of community events with which a meeting may beneficially coincide (like festivals or sporting events). Lastly, DMOs provide destination information—information on local events, activities, sights, attractions and restaurants, and assistance with tours and event planning.

A third category of service is assistance with the meeting or event. Here, DMOs can assist in the creation of collateral material and with on-site logistics and registration. Further, the DMOs can develop pre- and postconference activities, spouse tours, and special events as well as assisting with site inspections and familiarization tours and site selection. DMOs can also provide speakers and local educational opportunities. Lastly, DMOs can provide help in securing auxiliary services: production companies, catering, security, and so on.

CHANGING SCOPE OF DMO RESPONSIBILITIES

A DMO wants clients to be happy and will work to match the meeting planner's needs with the perfect setting and services for their meeting.

DMOs have traditionally focused on success in driving hotel occupancy and number of meetings and conventions held in the destination. But the rapid growth in global tourism has caused, in some communities, a significant change in the ratio of visitors to locals. And as tourism grows, residents in many destinations are beginning to ask at what point growing tourist arrivals begin to detract from their quality of life.

Recently, there has been a shift in the roles of DMOs to transition from full-time marketers to destination managers. DMOs are working to foster stronger connections with governments and planning authorities to ensure that tourism has a seat at the table. Creating a tourism master plan is a good start, because it represents a long-term development framework for tourism (10–20 years) with emphasis on policy and strategy, planning, institutional strengthening, legislation and regulation, product development, and diversification.

DMOs are increasingly being asked to work as a community partner to help strengthen the destination's tourism infrastructure. For example, many DMOs work with the local airport authorities to increase airlift, or to work with hotel developers to build the type of property that would best enhance the city's assets.

Amateur and professional sports have become increasingly popular through the years, and many DMOs have added sports development departments or created sports commissions to capture this business. Every sport has a youth component, and destinations have found success in attracting sports tournaments to their communities. An advantage of youth sports groups is that they have their tournaments on weekends and in the summer, thus complementing the typical Monday–Thursday schedule of conventions. Baseball diamonds, swimming pools, soccer fields, and ice arenas are examples of the types of venues being offered for teams willing to travel to compete. Locals benefit because they can also use these facilities. Hotels and local restaurants and attractions benefit from this lucrative business.

Many DMOs hire a full-time research director to gather a wide variety of relevant tourism industry data, such as the following:

- Hotel occupancy, average daily rate, and revenue per available room
- Number of local tourism jobs
- Local and state taxes paid by the tourism industry
- Total direct spending relating to tourism
- Economic and social impact studies of groups, festivals, and sporting events
- Satisfaction studies of travelers to the destination

These statistics are curated and presented to local community partners, governments, and stakeholders and can effectively prove the worth of the work being done by the DMO in relation to the entire local tourism effort.

DESTINATIONS INTERNATIONAL

As the global trade association for official DMOs, **Destinations International (DI)** protects and advances the success of destination marketing worldwide.

DI's membership includes over 550 official DMOs and more than 5,700 individual members in 13 countries that command more than $2 billion in annual budgets. Membership is open to all official DMOs recognized by their respective governments, from the smallest town to the largest country, including CVBs, regional tourism boards, state and provincial tourism offices, and national tourism boards.

DI provides members with information, resources, research, networking opportunities, professional development, and certification programs.

> *Our Cause*
>
> DI protects and advances the success of destination marketing organizations worldwide.
>
> *Our Mission*
>
> DI advocates for the professionalism, effectiveness, and significance of destination marketing organizations worldwide.
>
> *Our Promise*
>
> DI is the passionate advocate and definitive resource for official destination marketing organizations and professionals worldwide.

Our Values

DI is committed to the following core values: innovation, transparency, responsiveness, and inclusiveness.

DI actively promotes DMOs worldwide, highlighting the value of using a DMO's services to the media and general public.

DI PROFESSIONAL DEVELOPMENT OFFERINGS

DI provides professional development to DMOs and their employees via an annual convention, forums, summits, sales academy, and certification.

CERTIFIED DESTINATION MANAGEMENT EXECUTIVE

DI has a certification program that is the equivalent of the Certified Meeting Planner (CMP) designation in the meeting professional community.

The **Certified Destination Management Executive** (CDME) program is recognized by the DMO industry as its highest educational achievement. The CDME program is an advanced educational program for veteran and career-minded DMO executives who are looking for senior-level professional development courses. The main goal of the CDME program is to prepare senior executives and managers of DMOs for increasing change and competition.

The focus of the program is on vision, leadership, productivity, and implementation of business strategies. Demonstrating the value of a destination team and improving personal performance through effective organizational and industry leadership are the outcomes.

PDM PROGRAM

Although the Professional in Destination Management (PDM) certificate program is not a designation, like CDME, it is recognized throughout the industry as a highly valuable skills package needed for the destination management career journey. DMO professionals who participate in the PDM Certificate Program acquire knowledge and skills necessary to be more effective and successful destination management professionals.

ACCREDITATION

DI launched the Destination Marketing Accreditation Program (DMAP) in 2006, and today more than 200 DMOs have met the rigorous standards required for industry accreditation. The DMAP standards cover a range of topics, including governance, finance, management, human resources, visitor services, group services, sales communications, membership, brand management, destination development, research/market intelligence, innovation, and stakeholder relationships. The accreditation process helps DMOs ensure they are operating using the best practices and signals to external stakeholders the professionalism of the organization.

DI RESEARCH

DI offers a wealth of research and resources that provide statistical data and information essential for calculating economic impact, budgeting and strategic planning, marketing, and promotion, and educating stakeholders. The Destination & Travel Foundation, DI's nonprofit foundation, provides destination management professionals with access to insightful, comprehensive, and industry-specific information that they can use to enhance the effectiveness of their DMO's day-to-day operations and their business planning. In addition to market intelligence on topical issues, DI also provides regular reports, such as the following:

DMO Compensation and Benefits Survey This report, conducted biannually, provides a baseline for more than 45 job position compensation levels as well as for benefits packages offered to DMO employees in the United States and Canada.

DMO Organizational and Financial Profile This survey, the most comprehensive of its type for DMOs, provides standards for a variety of operations while also allowing DMOs to compare their operations with their peers. Also conducted every 2 years, the report includes information on DMO funding sources, available facilities, tax rates, budgets, staff structure, expense categories, and reserves.

EVENT IMPACT CALCULATOR

The Event Impact Calculator measures the economic value of an event and calculates its return on investment to local taxes. Armed with this information, DMOs are better prepared to make the case to policymakers for the ongoing development and growth of the meetings sector. Updated annually, the calculator draws on 10 different data sources to provide an industry-wide standard that is also

- Credible: With minimal user inputs, DMOs can produce impact analysis based on the latest survey and economic data available.
- Localized: Each DMO receives access to a model that is uniquely developed for their destination.
- Comprehensive: The calculator measures the direct impacts of events on businesses, employment, income, and taxes.

DESTINATIONNEXT

The Destination and Travel Foundation has also commissioned several important research reports examining future trends impacting tourism and destination marketing. The **DestinationNEXT Futures Study** is designed to provide DMOs with practical actions and strategies for improving their performance and attainment of future goals.

DestinationNEXT sets out to answer the question of what tomorrow's DMO will look like and how today's DMO leaders get their organization on a path that preserves tourism benefits, secures marketplace position, and engages their community interests.

DESTINATION & TRAVEL FOUNDATION

The Destination and Travel Foundation was created in 1993 to enhance and complement DI and the destination management profession through research, education, visioning, and developing resources and partnerships for those efforts. The DI Foundation integrated with U.S. Travel Association's Foundation in 2009 to become the Destination & Travel Foundation.

The foundation is classified as a charitable organization under Section 501(c)(3) of the U.S. Internal Revenue Service Code. Therefore, donations to the foundation are tax deductible as charitable contributions.

ASSOCIATION OF AUSTRALIAN CONVENTION BUREAUX

The Association of Australian Convention Bureaux Inc (AACB) brings together city and regional bureaus and is dedicated to marketing each specific region as business events destinations to domestic and international markets. AACB uses its influence with stakeholders, including government, to support growth in business events.

The strategic priorities of the AACB are as follows:

- Growing Australia's global business events competitiveness
- Demonstrating the impact of business events through research and storytelling
- Leading a connected and vibrant business events industry
- Operating an agile, high-performing, and united organization.

TRENDS

The role and function of DMOs will continue to expand. Many are now involved in "managing" the destination. They are helping to guide the community in tourism development, tourism policy, building infrastructure, planning, and expanding convention centers, attracting hotel developers, and so on.

Some consider DMO to stand for destination **marketing** organization, whereas others consider it to stand for destination **management** organization. Furthermore, some experts in the field have suggested that an even better and more descriptive term would be Destination Marketing and Management Organizations (DMMOs).

DMMOs

The following is a synopsis of a presentation by Chris Fair of Resonance Consultancy at the European Cities Marketing Meeting in Gdansk, February 22–25, 2017

The transformation of the destination marketing organization is so profound that the organization's name itself needs to change. How should the DMMOs evolve into the future?

At this point in time, DMOs have an important choice to make as they consider how to lead their destination's success. Destination marketing organizations have traditionally been focused on and measured by their success in driving hotel occupancy and the number of meetings and conventions held in a destination. But the rapid growth in global tourism has caused the ratio of visitors to locals to change significantly in cities ranging from around the globe. As tourism grows, residents in many cities and destinations are beginning to ask at what point growing tourist arrivals begin to detract from *their* local quality of life. Savannah, Georgia, has commissioned a research study to investigate exactly this issue. Perceptions of tourism can change quickly from being a nice addition to the local economy to being a threat to the local quality of life. DMOs can go from being perceived as community boosters to community detractors. Those DMOs that do not address this issue can quickly find themselves on the wrong side of this conversation.

As destination marketing organizations think about evolving into destination marketing *and management* organizations, they need to look at all aspects of a destination's needs and overall development. DMOs currently have very little influence on city planning, policy, and programming. One step in becoming a DMMO is to foster stronger connections with government and planning authorities to make sure that tourism has a seat at the table. Creating a *tourism master plan* in partnership with the city can be a good first step in this regard. DI helps a DMO do this through their *Destination Next* initiative. Another step is developing the roles and responsibilities within the organization, with appropriate funding to support them, to ensure that the recommendations within the plan are implemented and monitored over time. Lastly, DMOs can play a more significant role in managing the guest experience within the destination. This goes beyond staffing a visitor center and should consider how tourism affects the experience of locals as well.

DMOs often evaluate visitor satisfaction with the destination but do not often engage with residents. Evolving into a DMMO means the organization needs to spend as much time communicating with, monitoring, and measuring resident satisfaction as it does with visitors.

Not many industries have been more disrupted by technology than travel, and DMOs' approach to marketing has changed significantly as a result. But little attention has been paid to leveraging technology as a marketing channel or to how technology can be used to enhance and manage visitors' experiences once they arrive at the destination. DMMOs should be modifying their existing digital channels or creating separate websites, apps, and booking systems for visitors to access on arrival so they can better manage their own experiences. Alongside, they need to deepen their connections to, and knowledge of, the visitors on the ground.

DMOs need to expand their roles within cities or destinations and position themselves as the stewards and managers of the city's brand. This applies not only to tourism but to talent attraction and investment as well. No other organization in a destination has the funding or expertise to do it, and by assuming that role, a DMO can expand its value proposition to the community it serves.

The process of building a shared vision with the community that establishes strategic direction requires considering where you want to go. Then, you need to create a plan that articulates how you will get there. Of course, the plan is just the first step. Implementing it is the hardest part, and that takes budget and staff to do so. Some DMOs have created special administrative positions within their organizations to accomplish this. Two of the titles are: chief experience officer and vice-president of destination development.

© Nucleartist/Shutterstock.com

The trend of putting destination marketing, tourism services, and convention center operation under one umbrella is likely to continue. This helps to make sales and delivery of the tourism product, especially with large citywide conventions, more efficient and "seamless."

DMOs will continue to educate the community and stakeholders about the importance and value of face-to-face meetings.

DMOs are likely to see continued threats to their budgets. Politicians often try to divert funding away from DMOs and to "more visible" endeavors such as schools. Therefore, DMOs will look for ways in which to diversify their funding.

The greatest increase in the number and scope of DMOs will likely take place in developing regions such as China and Africa.

HOW TO FIND OUT MORE ABOUT DMOS Visit http://www.destinationmarketing.org, the official website of the DI.

COVID-19: THE EFFECT ON DMOS

As the COVID-19 pandemic uprooted the tourism industry in 2020, DMOs responded in a variety of ways. As lockdowns stopped travel, DMOs adopt-

© Willy Barton/Shutterstock.com

ed strategies to encourage locals to support their local restaurants, artisans, and attractions. Many DMOs mobilized to support businesses shuttered by lockdowns and industry members impacted by layoffs and furloughs. New Orleans and Company, a DMO, hosted resources for hospitality workers and added job listings to a special page on their website.

As the summer of 2020 wore on and destinations started to open, DMOs moved to encourage activities that allowed social distancing. Some destinations, like Visit NC and Texas, showcased their commitment to safety. In Indiana, the DMO combined a program to encourage businesses to adopt safe practices with a consumer promotion, the "Hoosier Hospitality promise" was promoted by businesses that committed themselves to adhering to COVID-19 safety precautions, and the "Hoosier Hospitality Promise Pass" encouraged visitors by offering discounted travel products at participating businesses. Las Vegas encouraged convention visitors to be "Vegas Smart. Stay Smart, Stay Healthy" and even promoted itself as a work from home alternative for workers feeling trapped in their home offices. As the summer of 2020 came to an end, many embraced the US Travel Association's "Let's Go There" campaign, a program designed to encourage domestic travel.

The pandemic has had serious financial implications for DMOs. Many DMOs are funded by government funds, often from visitor taxes, that have been decimated by the lockdowns and the economic downturn. To make matters worse, many DMOs were ineligible for early rounds of government relief. Communities and policy makers are caught between the need to promote their destinations and stimulate economic activity and deep revenue shortfalls. *#Savetravel*, an advocacy campaign to support funding for economic relief in the tourism industry promoted by US Travel's Power of Travel Coalition, encouraged DMOs to encourage action to support the industry. However, until travel returns to prepandemic levels, many DMOs will continue to face reduced budgets.

SUMMARY

DMOs are an integral part of the meetings, conventions, and travel industry. For over 100 years, DMOs have been working diligently to bring meetings and conventions to their destinations and to service these meetings with a variety of free services. Over the years, DMOs have gone from being destination marketers to destination managers, becoming involved in every aspect of their destinations and therefore enriching the experience for all visitors.

The DI is the professional association for DMO employees, and it has been providing a wealth of member services to DMOs since 1914.

DMOs have been important marketing partners for tourism operators during the pandemic. Even so, DMOs face budget pressures as state and local tax revenues reduce because of the virus and the related economic downturn.

CASE STUDY PLANNING SUSTAINABLE MEETINGS IN MONTEREY, CA

Sustainability is increasingly important to meeting planners and their clients and attendees. DMOs can be critical partners in connecting planners with local organizations and resources to ensure they meet their sustainability goals.

The Monterey County Convention and Visitors Bureau (MCCVB), the DMO for Monterey California, is committed to sustainable tourism. MCCVB extends its commitment to encouraging sustainability to meeting and planners. The MCCVB "Sustainable Meeting Guide" provides 22 pages of resources to make planning a sustainable meeting in Monterrey County easy. In addition to highlighting the county's sustainability initiatives and the green credentials of hotels, attractions, and venues, their guide includes links to carbon calculators and suggestions for reducing plastic at meetings. MCCVB supplements the guide book with additional resources on their website. MMCVB also provides tips for meeting planners who want to encourage their attendees to travel more responsibly.

As more associations and corporations add corporate social responsibility (CSR) to their meeting schedules, DMOs can help planners find worthy local activities. While DMOs are known for being experts in connecting meeting planners with tourism organizations, some DMOs provide critical connections with local nonprofits. The MCCVB Sustainable Meeting Guide includes suggestions for voluntourism and other corporate responsibility projects. Some of the CSR and Voluntourism opportunities include ecosystem restoration, and swag, tchotchke, and signage repurposing for good. MCCVB also provides coordination support with local organizations that address social issues and appreciate volunteer support from volunteers.

MCCVB's support of sustainability in the meetings market is part of a larger commitment to sustainability. The MCCVB encourages tourism products in the region to adopt sustainable tourism practices. It also recognizes that visitors have a responsibility for the sustainability of the destination. MCCVB's destination marketing campaign, "Grab Life by the Moments," includes "sustainable moments," and their consumer website has resources to help travelers visit responsibly and protect the unique environment and heritage of Monterey.

© mark smith nsb/Shutterstock.com

QUESTIONS:

1. What do you think are the reasons a DMO like MCCVB would encourage sustainable tourism by their tourism operators? Why encourage visitors to travel responsibly?
2. How can DMOs support meeting and event planners in creating more sustainable events?
3. Why do DMOs provide services like connecting meeting planners with local charities?

KEYWORDS AND TERMS

For definitions, see https://insights.eventscouncil.org/Industry-glossary

Destinations International (DI)
Destination Marketing Organization (DMO)

REVIEW AND DISCUSSION QUESTIONS

1. Define the role and function of a destination marketing organization.
2. Name the different ways that DMOs can be funded.
3. Name two things that a DMO does for meeting professionals.
4. Name two things that the DI does for meeting professionals.
5. What can the DI do for DMOs?
6. How have DMOs responded to the challenges created by the pandemic.

INTERNET SITES FOR REFERENCE

http://www.destinationmarketing.org
https://www.ustravel.org/
https://aacb.org.au/
https://convention-europe.com/
https://www.europeancitiesmarketing.com/

ABOUT THE CHAPTER CONTRIBUTOR

Dr Jonathon Day is Associate Professor at Purdue University's School of Hospitality and Tourism Management. Prior to joining academia, he was a destination marketing professional with Tourism Queensland, Australia.

PREVIOUS CHAPTER CONTRIBUTORS

Craig Davis, CEO, Visit Dallas

Karen M. Gonzales, CMP, Destinations International.

CHAPTER 4

MEETING, EXPOSITIONS, EVENT, AND CONVENTION VENUES: AN EXAMINATION OF FACILITIES USED BY MEETING AND EVENT PROFESSIONALS

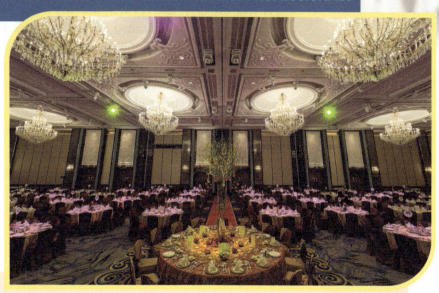

© gnohz/Shutterstock.com

CHAPTER OBJECTIVES

- Discuss the physical characteristics and financial structure of hotels.
- Identify the types of events best suited to a convention center and the reasons behind that solution.
- Discuss the space, functions, consortiums, and financing involved in using conference centers for events.
- Identify the similarities, differences, and benefits of cruise ships and other event venue options.
- Articulate the benefits of specific use facilities as event venues.
- Outline the appeal and uses of colleges and universities as event venues.
- Cover the unique needs and uses that differentiate retreat facilities from other kinds of venues.
- Discuss the expansion, use, and growth of unique and unusual venues.
- Illustrate the typical needs and obstacles specific to an outdoor event.

Meeting planners and event professionals work in a variety of facilities (throughout this chapter, the terms "meeting planner," "event professional," "planner," and "professional" are interchangeable). These facilities range in size from **hotel** suites that hold a handful of people to major convention centers and outdoor festival sites that accommodate tens of thousands. Any location where two or more people gather is a meeting/event site. Whether it is a multimillion-square-foot convention center or a local coffee shop, people will find a place to gather. The event professional's job is to match the event and the venue. Thus, the planner must determine two things about the group: (1) Who are they? and (2) Why are they here? Most events and meetings are appropriate only for a limited range of facilities. For an event to succeed, the characteristics of the event must be properly matched to the facility in which it is held. Whether the venue is the conference room at the end of a suite of offices or the flight deck of an active aircraft carrier, the goal of the meeting must fit with the choice of venue for the meeting to work.

Thus, the planner must appropriately research the group and the facilities that may fit the group's needs, understand the needs and expectations of the group, communicate the benefits offered by a facility that meet the needs of the group, and verify the arrangements between the group and the venues. Before selecting a meeting venue, the planner must complete a **needs analysis**. See Chapter 13 on Planning MEEC events for a more detailed explanation of needs analysis.

To properly explore the tremendous range of available facilities, a meeting planner must be familiar with both the physical characteristics of the venue and its financial structure. The combined impact of these two factors determines a meeting planner's relationship with the facility management and both parties' relative negotiating positions. Many other features of a facility are relevant to the success or failure of any meeting or event, but an understanding of the significance of the facility's physical form and its financial structure is vital for a meeting planner to effectively use the facility to support the meeting.

The vast majority of meetings take place in conference rooms or offices on the meeting participants' property. Typically, one room in a suite of offices is designated as a conference room, and a handful of colleagues gather to address a current issue. Whether scheduled or impromptu, these meetings rarely involve a full-time meeting planner. Yet these meetings are often organized by an employee who has meeting planning tasks included as part of their job description. As these meetings become larger and involve more people, the person who has had the position of scheduling these on-property meetings frequently plans meetings that take place outside of the company's office.

HOTELS

PHYSICAL CHARACTERISTICS

Meeting Room Spaces

Hotels have traditionally been the "go-to" location for corporate events. Any hotels that have at least one small **boardroom** are part of the meeting and events world. At one end of the meeting room spectrum is the smaller meeting room, often a boardroom that is typically focused on a few attendees and has a dedicated table and chairs. At the other end of the meeting room spectrum are the large ballrooms, which are typically more formal and elegantly appointed, and some ballrooms are able to handle several thousand guests. Because of their size and scope, ballrooms are generally planned as part of the initial construction of the facility. A common floor plan provides larger divisions flanked by smaller ones accessible from the side corridors. It is not uncommon for the ceiling to be lower in the smaller divisions than in the larger ones. This is not always obvious from printed floor plans.

In addition to boardrooms and ballrooms, larger hotels also have **breakout rooms.** The size and number of the breakout rooms can vary from hotels that have one small breakout room to hotels that have thousands of square feet of breakout room space. Breakout rooms tend to be decorated and equipped like smaller versions of the ballrooms and serve identical functions for smaller numbers of people.

Event planners are challenging hotels to rethink ballroom and breakout room configurations as the demand for traditional classroom sessions and meals is decreasing. Instead, meeting planners and attendees are looking for unique ways to engage, maximize, and create interactive meetings. Creative and welcoming space with a higher level of customization and personalization are key.

Meeting planners are looking at spaces today that were not traditionally part of the event-planning scene. Hotels are now competing with many other venues in their market for the same meeting/event business. This has challenged them to look at their space differently and innovate. Gone are the days of

Taj Lake Palace, Udaipur, Rajasthan, India, A. 5-star hotel in India.

© photooff/Shutterstock.com

just using sliding doors or air walls to subdivide a giant ballroom. Meeting planner and attendee expectations have forced hotels to focus on specific and dedicated rooms designed for different objectives, such as small group conversations, attendee reflection spaces, informal gatherings, and formal presentations. It is not uncommon to see meeting rooms that look homey and relaxing. Plain meeting rooms and boardrooms are giving way to rooms that can accommodate all the necessary technology, speaker needs, thought sessions, team sessions, and social breakouts. To emphasize their flexibility, some hotels have even gone so far as to change the names of their ballrooms and meeting rooms to coordinate with their brand image.

OTHER HOTEL MEETING SPACES

Many hotels have public spaces that can also be used for meetings and events. Pools, patios, atriums, lobbies, lawns, and gardens can all be used as meetings, expositions, events, and conventions (MEEC) locations. For example, many of the resort hotels in Las Vegas have magnificent outdoor patios and pool areas that are regularly used for events.

In addition to utilizing outdoor venues, the use of **prefunction space,** such as corridors or lobbies adjacent to meeting rooms, may also provide a location for ancillary meeting or event needs. Many hotel venues have small areas within the prefunction space where two or three attendees can connect and attendees can check emails or make phone calls before an event or during a break. Refreshment breaks, registration desks, mobile charging stations, and cocktail receptions may also be situated in these prefunction areas to provide necessary services without compromising valuable meeting rooms.

As meeting planners and attendees require more experiential events, just as with breakout rooms and ballrooms, the more unique and interesting and the more creative a hotel can be with nontraditional space, the more competitive the hotel will be against its competition.

FINANCIAL STRUCTURE

Hotels tend to be owned by major branded hotel companies or are owned and franchised by real estate investment companies that hire hotel management companies to manage the facility in accordance with corporate brand guidelines. For most hotels, meetings and events are not necessarily their primary business. The primary business of almost all hotels is the sale of sleeping room nights. In the past, a hotel's meeting space was often a loss leader, whose primary purpose was to fill what would otherwise be empty sleeping rooms, especially on **shoulder** nights when the hotel didn't have its core corporate business. While filling sleeping rooms is still very important, meetings, events, and food and beverage (F&B) are playing a more significant role in a hotel's profit and loss equation. For example, the Marriott Marquis in New York City's catering department generates annual revenue in the tens of millions of dollars. There are now many hotels that derive significant revenue from their extensive meeting spaces.

Other revenue streams where hotels may generate significant income include restaurants, bars and branded coffee kiosks that are frequented by convention attendees. A smaller percentage of revenue is also the result of **concessionaires** at the pools, beach, or spa. This dynamic changes somewhat when the hotel is associated with a theme park or casino. Casinos can be moneymaking machines and may have a significant impact on a planner's ability to negotiate. Hotels associated with theme parks have a similar effect.

NEGOTIATING YOUR EVENT

Entering the negotiation phase, the major discussion points for the meeting planner and venue to negotiate are sleeping room rates, F&B menus and costs, meeting space costs, and audiovisual (A/V) and technology costs. Although there may be other smaller concessions such as negotiating parking, transportation, or additional hotel services, these should be discussed only once the main points are agreed upon.

CHAPTER 4 MEETING, EXPOSITIONS, EVENT, AND CONVENTION VENUES: AN EXAMINATION OF FACILITIES USED BY MEETING AND EVENT PROFESSIONALS

109

ROOM RATES

In booking rooms for leisure or corporate hotel guest segments, a hotel typically works directly with the guest staying in that room. In booking meetings and events, the hotel's main customer is the meeting planner. Their needs and preferences are an important part of the sales and negotiation equation. Conventional wisdom suggests that meeting planners do not pay for meeting space in hotels. However, meeting space is expensive for hotels. The interest paid on the investment capital needed to build the hotel and the staff and materials to clean, maintain, and operate the meeting rooms are some of the most significant costs related to meeting space. These costs must be funded from somewhere. Most often, they are covered by requiring a meeting or event to commit to using a minimum number of sleeping rooms for a minimum number of nights. This is often referred to as a room block.

Sleeping room rates are often negotiated by the size of the block of rooms the meeting planner needs for the event. Usually, the bigger the block, the lower the rate. Typically associated with the room block are complimentary rooms. The industry norm is one complimentary room for every 50 rooms blocked. This could be a negotiating point to get additional complimentary rooms by negotiating the ratio to one for every 30 rooms blocked. Typically, room blocks are also linked to meeting space availability. Linking sleeping room use with meeting space availability lowers the cost of the meeting but has become a challenge for hotels based on how accurate the projection of sleeping rooms is.

Before going into the negotiation, meeting planners should do an online search of rates offered on sites like Expedia, Booking.com, and Trip Advisor for that specific hotel. Given the popularity of internet travel booking sites, many planners realize that their attendees are looking at these sites and booking lower rates than the negotiated rate. These rooms are not included in the contracted room block and cause the planner to pay **attrition** penalties for not meeting their room block numbers. There are clauses that can be added to the contract that address this issue, but they should be discussed with an attorney familiar with these issues. The planner's goal in this process is to get credit for every room night the hotel sells as a result of the meeting or event. This one issue may be the toughest part of any hotel negotiation. To avoid attrition, some associations require their attendees to book in the room block or face paying a significantly higher registration fee.

Food and Beverage

Another significant source of revenue for most hotels is F&B. The restaurants and bars in the hotel are generally designed to handle the hotel's regular leisure guests, which is likely a mix of business travelers and tourists. Many meeting planners and hotels realize that there are certain times during the meeting or event when the hotel will receive increased business in the outlets from the attendees. An example would be attendees congregating in the hotel bar before and after a meeting or event in the ballroom. During the negotiation, this ancillary business should be included as part of the F&B spend discussion.

Hotel banquet catering departments have the responsibility to create menus and catering to meet the requirements of the meeting or event. The scope and quality of hotels' banquet departments vary as much as the quality of the sleeping rooms. In a reaction to the reluctance of some meeting planners to agree to elevated sleeping room rates to guarantee meeting space, some hotels have linked banquet revenue with meeting space. Thus, a meeting planner who meets a threshold of spending in the catering department gets a break in the meeting room cost.

Other Revenue Generating Departments

Hotels derive revenue from a variety of other nonmeeting services as well. These services are also a part of the negotiation process between the meeting planner and the hotel. These types of services can enhance a meeting or event but can also add significant costs. When negotiating with the hotel, meeting planners need to understand what the added costs to the meeting or event are. Golf courses, spas, equestrian centers, and beaches all provide revenue to the hotel. Corporate meetings or conventions often plan a golf tournament for attendees.

Hotels often contract with exclusive vendors to provide services within the hotel. Service contractors, musicians/entertainment, disc jockeys, florists, and coach companies can all be contracted to the hotel as exclusive vendors of their specialized services. Commissions paid back to the hotel can be as high as 40%. Some hotels charge attrition on those services as well. The hotel's theory is that the hotel and the vendor have made an investment in the facility and equipment for the meeting planner's benefit. Should the planner elect not to use these services, the services should be paid for anyway because they were available. This is particularly common with A/V services. Hotels often require planners to use the in-house A/V department or an exclusive vendor.

CHAPTER 4 MEETING, EXPOSITIONS, EVENT, AND CONVENTION VENUES: AN EXAMINATION OF FACILITIES USED BY MEETING AND EVENT PROFESSIONALS

111

If a planner insists on using an outside company, they may have to pay a hefty fee. It is especially important to discuss these expectations early in the negotiating process to avoid confusion later. The negotiated size of the projected commission may be the determining factor.

Hotels attached to theme parks are a special case. It is not uncommon for a theme park-based hotel to include an estimate of how much money the attendees or their families will spend in the attached entertainment facilities when they decide whether or not to take a particular piece of business. Clauses relating the number of theme park passes purchased to the availability of meeting room space can appear in some contracts at these hotels. In the case of meetings planned with sufficient free time to allow the attendees to visit the theme parks, it may be easier to contract their desired meeting space. Receptions and meal functions for meeting attendees often take place in the theme park.

If the hotel is attached to a casino, it is possible for the hotel to derive more revenue from the casino than it does from the sleeping rooms. In recent years, casino hotels have come to realize that convention attendees are a good target market for their business: conference attendees come during the week, whereas the typical gambler comes on the weekend. Unlike gamblers, conference attendees do not need comps or other enticements to visit and will pay a higher price for their hotel rooms. Depending on the conference and the clientele of that event, attendees often gamble as much when not in meetings as other casino patrons.

With all of this taken into consideration, the majority of casino hotels constructed over the past decade have included significant meeting and event space. The prices charged for the sleeping rooms are fixed in advance of the guests' arrival. The potential revenue derived from the casino is limited only by the availability of credit on the guests' accounts. Meetings then become a means to bring guests to the casino, where they potentially spend more money gambling than they do on other activities. The sales team tracks this spend, and if a group fails to spend enough time and money in the casino during their meeting, the sales department may not offer reduced hotel room rates or other reduced-price concessions to that particular group in the future.

LOCAL MEETINGS AND EVENTS

Some meetings and events do not involve sleeping rooms, and many hotels are reluctant to deal with them. However, the demand for venues to hold the local social event is great enough that hotels do market to them. For the planner of a local event to get **complimentary** meeting space, a minimum amount of catering revenue would need to be guaranteed. In addition to catering revenue, hotels can also receive revenue from commissions paid by other support vendors for the privilege of working in the hotel such as **Exposition Service Contractors** (**ESC**), or A/V, the disc jockey, the florist, limo service, and the entertainers. These revenue streams are calculated in the decision to accept a piece *of social business* once all other higher revenue opportunities have been exhausted. Since a planner of a social event may overestimate F&B projections, attrition on catering revenue projections is becoming more common.

SEASONALITY

Seasonality and fluctuating occupancy levels can have a significant impact on the cost of using a facility. A hotel with a severe seasonal variation can have an off-season price that is as little as half of its peak-season price. By paying attention to a facility's seasonal occupancy patterns, meeting planners can find some true bargains. A common misconception among meeting attendees is that the incredibly cheap rate that they pay to use an exclusive resort is attributable to their planner's negotiating prowess, when it is more likely that the great rate is because of the planner's choice of a venue with extreme seasonal variations.

Aside from the typical considerations when booking meeting space in hotels, such as the size of the space available, attrition penalties for sleeping rooms and/or catering, and seasonality, planners must be aware of move-in/move-out schedules and other groups that are in-house. Depending on the size and scope of a meeting or event, it may take anywhere from a few hours to a week to set up (or tear down) the physical aspect of an event, particularly if there is an exhibition component. This time is essentially a lost opportunity for the hotel because rather than booking another group, which could generate money, the space is unavailable. Hotels may charge a rental fee for the space itself to recover some of that lost revenue, but there is no opportunity to make additional profit through catering or other revenue centers. Planners must keep this in mind and expect to negotiate move-in/move-out dates because hotels prefer to utilize their meeting space as efficiently as possible. In addition, hotels often host meetings for several different groups at any given time. In many cases, this is a nonissue, but when a corporation is promoting a new product launch or discussing proprietary information, they generally prefer that their competitors not be in the same facility.

Coordinating space is also important when groups have conflicting behavior. For instance, a significant conflict could arise if a professional organization

CHAPTER 4 MEETING, EXPOSITIONS, EVENT, AND CONVENTION VENUES: AN EXAMINATION OF FACILITIES USED BY MEETING AND EVENT PROFESSIONALS

113

giving a certification exam were placed in a meeting room adjacent to a day-long band rehearsal or if a convention alcohol provider is booked at the same time as a religious convention. These are considerations planners must be cognizant of during the negotiating and contracting process to ensure the planning and execution of their event is successful.

Meeting planners negotiating with hotels need to consider the entire financial package their business will bring to the facility. The more closely aligned the meeting's financial structure is to the needs of the hotel, the better the deal the meeting planner can get for the meeting or event. The entire financial package includes not just the revenue from the event itself but also the revenue from the sleeping rooms, restaurants, bars, and exclusive vendors. When negotiating with any meeting or event venue, meeting planners are negotiating based on not only what they will use but also what is available whether they use it or not. The availability and cost of specific amenities often drives the attendee expectations of the venue. It is important that planners match the level of their attendee expectations with the level of service provided by the hotel at a cost the meeting planner feels is reasonable.

INDUSTRY SPOTLIGHT: A PASSION FOR HOSPITALITY

Interview with Michaelene Sullivan, director of sales and marketing, Manchester Grand Hyatt San Diego

Michaelene Sullivan is the director of sales and marketing at the Manchester Grand Hyatt San Diego since 2019. The Manchester Grand Hyatt San Diego is a 1628-room convention hotel with over 320,000 square feet of flexible event space, including a 34,000-square-foot ballroom. It is conveniently located a short walk away from the San Diego Convention Center, airport, and dozens of city attractions like the USS Midway Museum and Petco Park.

Michaelene has worked her entire career for Hyatt, and she began her career as an assistant restaurant manager at the Hyatt Regency Lake Tahoe, after she received a degree in hospitality from Washing-

Michaelene Sullivan, director of sales and marketing, Manchester Grand Hyatt San Diego

ton State University. Prior to her present position, Michaelene was the director of group sales and associate director of sales at the Manchester Grand Hyatt San Diego. Prior to this, she was an associate director of sales at the Hyatt Regency O'Hare and in group sales at the Grand Hyatt in Seattle. Before moving to Seattle, Michaelene worked at the Manchester Grand Hyatt for 5 years as a group sales manager, event manager, and event concierge.

What is your most memorable event experience?

My most memorable experience was as an event manager at the Manchester Grand Hyatt. I remember planning an event for 2,000 people on the pool deck in the hotel for a corporate client. It was an amazing event with a great venue that worked perfectly with the event objectives. I remember all of the planning that went into creating and executing that event, which was not a simple task. The thing that made it the most memorable was the look on the guest faces during the event. I remember walking though the event, and all elements were going well and attendees were happy and enjoying themselves. During events thing can be hectic with many small issues to take care of; however, it was amazing to step back and look at the guests enjoying the event I helped to create.

Having worked in a variety of hotels in different roles, what do you see as the major advantages of using a hotel as an event venue?

One of the major advantages of using a hotel is the possibility of having everything under one roof. Your guest can stay in the hotel, attend meetings, and dine in the restaurants, all without leaving the property. Attendees become immersed in the hotel where they are all together, which allows for more networking opportunities. Hotels also make planning the event easier for event professionals. Hotels usually offer one contact who handles all of the event needs. This reduces the number of different individuals the event planner needs to contact to successfully execute the event. Hotels also usually do not charge organizations a venue rental fee, instead operating on an F&B minimum, which makes it a more affordable option.

Do you have any recommendations for students who are pursuing a career in the events industry?

CHAPTER 4 MEETING, EXPOSITIONS, EVENT, AND CONVENTION VENUES: AN EXAMINATION OF FACILITIES USED BY MEETING AND EVENT PROFESSIONALS

115

The best piece of advice I can give students is to keep your options open. You probably will go into your college career thinking you want to work in one segment of hospitality; I would recommend that you keep you mind open to all possibilities. I never thought I would start my career in food and beverage. However, it was a great learning experience. I learned so much and saw how all elements in a hospitality organization are interconnected and could not operate alone. Along with keeping your eyes open, I would highly recommend learning as much as you can, both in school and in your career. Gaining industry experience while you are a college student can be very beneficial when you get ready to graduate and head into the working world full-time.

CONVENTION CENTERS

Conventional wisdom has it that convention centers are huge. Many are, and the biggest continue to get bigger. Convention centers are designed to handle larger events than could be supported in a hotel. Several convention centers feature over a million square feet of meeting and exhibit space. Their very size is both their strength and their weakness. Convention centers are meeting facilities without sleeping rooms and are often little more than large bare buildings with exposed roof beams. Others are mammoth architectural marvels involving magnificent feats of engineering and awe-inspiring vistas. Table 4-1 lists the 15 largest convention centers in the world, and Table 4-2 lists the 20 largest convention centers in the United States. Table 4-3 lists the 10 hotels with the largest meeting space in the world.

Landscape of Singapore around the Marina Bay Sands Convention Center, Casino and Resort Towers at twilight.

© MOLPIX/Shutterstock.com

MEETINGS, EXPOSITIONS, EVENTS, AND CONVENTIONS

	Name	City	Square Meters	Square Footage
1	National Exhibition and Convention Center	Shanghai, China	500,000	5,382,000
2	Messegelände Hannover	Hannover, Germany	448,900	5,300,000
3	Messegelände Frankfurt	Frankfurt, Germany	366,637	3,946,500
4	Crocus Expo	Moscow, Russia	366,100	3,940,660
5	Fiera Milano	Milan, Italy	345,000	3,713,550
6	China Import & Export Fair Complex	Guangzhou, China	340,000	3,659,750
7	Kunming Dianchi Convention & Exhibition Center	Kunming, China	310,000	3,336,800
8	Koeln Messe	Cologne, Germany	284,000	3,057,000
9	Düsseldorf Messe	Dusseldorf, Germany	262,000	2,820,150
10	Paris-Nord Villepinte	Paris, France	242,082	2,605,750
11	McCormick Place	Chicago, USA	241,500	2,600,000
12	Fira Barcelona – Gran Via	Barcelona, Spain	240,000	2,584,000
13	Feria Valencia	Valencia, Spain	230,000	2,475,700
14	Paris Expo Porte de Versailles	Paris, France	216,000	2,325,000
15	Messe München	Munich, Germany	200,000	2,152,780

TABLE 4.1. Largest Convention Centers in the World (by Total Exhibition Space)

	Convention Center Name (City)	Exhibition Space	Total Exhibition & Meeting Space
1	McCormick Place (Chicago)	2,670,000	9,000,000
2	Orange County Convention Center (Orlando)	2,100,000	7,000,000
3	Georgia World Congress (Atlanta)	1,500,000	3,900,000
4	Las Vegas Convention Center	2,182,167	3,200,000
5	New Orleans Morial Convention Center	1,100,000	3,100,000
6	America's Center (St. Louis)	523,000	2,700,000
7	San Diego Convention Center	615,700	2,600,000
8	Cobo Center (Detroit)	723,500	2,400,000
9	Walter E Washington Conv. Center (Wash. DC)	703,000	2,300,000
10	Sands Expo and Convention Center (Las Vegas)	936,600	2,250,000
11	I-X Center (Cleveland)	1,000,000	2,200,000
12	Colorado Convention Center (Denver)	584,000	2,200,000

TABLE 4.2 Largest Convention Centers in the United States (by Square Foot)

CHAPTER 4 MEETING, EXPOSITIONS, EVENT, AND CONVENTION VENUES: AN EXAMINATION OF FACILITIES USED BY MEETING AND EVENT PROFESSIONALS

117

			Total Meeting Space (Sq. Ft)	Hotel Rooms
13	Mandalay Bay Convention Center (Las Vegas)		861,231	2,100,000
14	Music City Center (Nashville)		350,000	2,100,000
15	Dallas Convention Center		1,000,000	2,000,000
16	Moscone Convention Center (San Francisco)		700,000	2,000,000
17	George R. Brown Convention Center (Houston)		853,000	1,100,000
18	Jacob K. Javits Convention Center (New York City)		840,000	1,800,000
19	Greater Columbus Convention Center		447,000	1,800,000
20	Anaheim Convention Center (Anaheim, CA)		815,000	1,600,000

TABLE 4.2 Largest Convention Centers in the United States (by Square Foot) continued

	Hotels	Destination	Total Meeting Space (Sq. Ft)	Hotel Rooms
1	The Venetian & The Palazzo	Las Vegas, NV	2,250,000	7,093
2	Mandalay Bay Resort & Casino	Las Vegas, NV	2,100,000	3,215
3	Marina Bay Sands Resort & Casino	Singapore	1,300,000	2,561
4	Gaylord Opryland Resort & Convention Center	Nashville, TN	758,911	2,888
5	Wynn & Encore Las Vegas Resorts	Las Vegas, NV	560,000	2,716
6	Gaylord National Resort & Convention Center	National Harbor, MD	546,889	1,996
7	Rosen Shingle Creek Resort	Orlando, FL	524,000	1,501
8	Gaylord Rockies Resort & Convention Center	Aurora, CO	517,987	1,501
9	Gaylord Palms Resort Convention Center	Kissimmee, FL	462,296	1,416
10	Marriott Orlando World Center Resort	Orlando, FL	338,306	2,004

Table 4.3 Hotels with the Largest Total Meeting Space

Compared with hotels, convention centers are more likely to devote most of their space to **exhibit halls** and utilitarian spaces than to plush ballrooms. Common to these exhibit halls are trade shows. While hotel lobbies are designed to be comfortable and inviting, convention center lobbies are designed to facilitate the uninterrupted flow of several thousand attendees. This difference in design philosophy is evident in every phase of a convention center's operation.

Whereas discussions about convention centers in the past typically involved the number of meeting rooms and the amount of available square footage, flexibility of space is becoming more important. Customization of space, adaptability, and integrating local flavor are now essential parts of the discussion. Meeting planners and attendees are challenging the traditional approach to convention center space and trade show floors. Different configurations, different uses of space, and an expectation that all spaces be more engaging, relevant, and entertaining are the central focus. Creating hubs, education centers, interactive spaces, and tech centers is the new normal.

Just as hotels have a variety of space sizes, convention centers also have a variety of spaces. In the typical hotel, the ballrooms are the largest meeting spaces, followed by the breakout rooms. In a convention center, the exhibit halls tend to be the largest spaces, followed by the carpeted ballrooms, followed by the breakout and meeting rooms. It would not be unusual for the prefunction spaces in a convention center to be larger than the breakout rooms attached to them, unlike a typical hotel where the prefunction spaces tend to be smaller. Also, convention centers generally do not have spas or swimming pools, exercise rooms, or saunas, restaurants, or bars. Another key difference between hotels and convention centers is that whereas a hotel is open around the clock, convention centers can, and do, lock the doors at night, and the staff goes home when nothing is scheduled. In a hotel, someone is on duty at all times, whereas if someone is required to be available at odd hours in a convention center, that person must be scheduled in advance. A meeting planner using a convention center may need to plan in more detail than one who holds the same meeting in a hotel.

With well over 400 convention centers in the United States alone and more being built, meeting planners are looking for convention centers that offer

© logoboom/Shutterstock.com

The Oracle at NAB Show 2015, an annual trade show by the National Association of Broadcasters hosted at the Las Vegas Convention Center

CHAPTER 4 MEETING, EXPOSITIONS, EVENT, AND CONVENTION VENUES: AN EXAMINATION OF FACILITIES USED BY MEETING AND EVENT PROFESSIONALS

119

unique features. Differentiating is key to the success of a given convention center. Meeting planners are making two choices when selecting a convention center: space and destination. In addition, each year several convention centers expand, making the total exhibition and meeting space offered in each center a moving target.

Convention centers of the past have often been described as utilitarian and occasionally "cold" when compared with hotels. Newer convention centers have added more artistic design elements like sculptures and paintings. Many existing convention centers have been investing in complete remodels to meet the needs of the future of meetings. Common to both hotels and convention centers is the challenge of being flexible and able to create different environments based on the needs of the meeting planner and the attendee. One trend in convention centers is incorporating physical elements that engage the attendee by leveraging existing space and turning it into a new concept. An example is a "wellness stairwell" to encourage attendees to take the stairs between floors of an event. Choosing the stairs instead of the elevator is a quick way for people to add physical activity to their day.

Another trend in event space and meeting rooms are pop-up meeting rooms that can be set up or moved at a moment's notice. As meeting planner and attendee expectations for venues become more flexible, the idea of pop-up meeting rooms for last-minute meetings, executive sessions, conference calls, and so on will become a more significant part of the negotiations. One strategy that marketers are using is promoting surrounding restaurants, local tours, museums, and natural resources. Some convention centers have added services to help meeting planners create events in the local market as part of their convention center meeting and event experience.

Industry Spotlight: Associations the Overlooked Segment of the Events Industry

Interview with Colleen Bingle, meetings, exhibits, and sponsorship manager, American Academy of Pediatric Dentistry.

Colleen Bingle is the meetings, exhibits, and sponsorship manager of the American Academy of Pediatric Dentistry (AADP). After graduating from Boston College in 2013, Colleen began her career working at After School Matters, a nonprofit organization that provides programs for teens in the Chicagoland area. As retail & events specialist, she managed the After School Matters Retail Store and assisted with higher-level logistics for the Annual Gala at Navy Pier.

Colleen Bingle, meetings, exhibits, and sponsorship manager, American Academy of Pediatric Dentistry

In 2015, Colleen joined AAPD as the meetings & exhibits associate. In this role, she executes all facets of the sponsorship program, including contract renewal and relationship building for over 20 corporate companies. In addition, she handles the nearly 300 exhibitors for the 6,500-person annual session meeting. She also manages the executive retreat and board meetings.

Colleen is an active member of the Greater Midwestern Chapter of Professional Convention Management Association (PCMA), currently serving as the vice-chair of the Student Membership Committee. In addition, Colleen is the copresident of the Boston College Chicago Chapter Alumni, serving more than 6,000 alumni in the Chicago area.

As an events professional working for an association, what are some of the types of events you plan?

Most student and young professionals do not naturally think about associations as a potential workplace; however, associations provide a wide range of opportunities. As an association planner, I play a role in planning a wide range of events, from an annual convention for over 10,000 attendees to education sessions for several hundred, to small meetings. Working at an association, all events no matter the size are mission driven and provide a member opportunity. I am also the point of contact for all sponsorship opportunities and exhibitions at the annual meeting.

CHAPTER 4 MEETING, EXPOSITIONS, EVENT, AND CONVENTION VENUES: AN EXAMINATION OF FACILITIES USED BY MEETING AND EVENT PROFESSIONALS

121

What types of venues have you used during your work at the AAPD?

Typically, our national conference utilizes a convention center or large convention hotel for the majority of the meeting events, yet other venues are used to enhance the attendee experiences. Some of these include the Museum of Science and Industry in Chicago and FedEx Field in Washington D.C. When using these venues, we buy out the entire venue, meaning we are the only group using the venue at that time, allowing us to create a great experience for our attendees. For smaller-scale events, we will typically use a hotel meeting room or a boardroom at a local venue. Venue selection is typically left up to us in the meeting and events department with input from association leadership, with the most input placed on the smaller leadership events.

What are some differences you see in the various types of venues?

Having used so many different sizes and scales of facilities, there many differences, with each facility having some type of positive and negative aspects, depending on the association's needs. Conference or convention centers provide different packages to organizations than hotels provide. At convention centers, many different parties and vendors are involved, such as a general services contractor, electricians, food services providers, and audiovisual. At a hotel, there is usually one point of contact who assists with all aspects of the event needs. Hotels also usually only require one contract instead of contracting with several different vendors.

What advice would you give to a student studying hospitality?

My first piece of advice is to not limit yourself. Take advantage of any opportunity you can get your hands on. You can also gain experience through volunteering opportunities, which is ideal during your college career. If a position has certain requirements and you do not have them, don't let that limit you from applying for a job. Many skills can be taught, while other skills, such as your motivation to learn, are more valuable and not easily taught. This is something I experienced firsthand when applying to work at AAPD. Networking is also a very important in your career development, and you should take advantage of this as often as possible. Follow up with the connections you make while networking and stay in touch with them. Becoming a student member of an events association, such as PCMA, provides many different networking opportunities for students.

FINANCIAL STRUCTURE

Unlike a hotel, which is most likely part of a corporation, most convention centers are owned by government entities. Governments want the investments in convention centers to pay off and are putting more pressure on convention center profitability. Often, professional management of the convention center is contracted to a private company that specializes in managing such facilities. Many convention centers are actively supported by the local DMOs and CVBs, with some DMOs/CVBs even operating convention centers. As with everything that concerns government, the management of these facilities is ultimately accountable to the taxpayers. One controversial issue among convention center managers is whether the public sector or the private-sector companies can do a better job of managing these facilities. There are strongly held opinions on both sides of the issue. Even with all the discussion, one thing remains unchanged. The quality of a planner's event is still dependent on the planner's relationship with the individuals running the facility and how well the event is planned. Especially in a convention center, the more thorough the planning, the more successful the event. There are some convention centers that are privately owned and operated, such as the Sands Convention Center in Las Vegas.

One overlooked fact that sets convention centers apart from many other types of facilities concerns the portion of their budget spent on energy. It is not unusual for a convention center to spend more money on utilities than it does on its full-time staff. This is not a reflection of the staffing levels but rather an indication of how expensive it is to keep a large facility properly climate controlled. Hotels have significant energy bills as well, but unlike a convention center, they are not trying to climate control huge spaces with high ceilings and massive doors that stay open all day. In newly constructed convention centers, the green movement is at the forefront. Ceilings are being made of transparent materials and windows are being included to let natural sunlight come in, thus reducing costs of lighting. Thermal heat pumps are being installed to reduce heating costs. Runoff water and "brown water" is being recycled and used for irrigation.

How does a convention center make money? They are not expected to make a profit in the conventional sense but are expected to at least cover costs. Generally, the intent of the government that built the building is that the facility be an economic driver for the whole community. Therefore, the facility can take events that benefit the community as a whole with less concern for driving the demand for sleeping room nights in the surrounding hotels. This is part of the reason why convention centers, unlike hotels, will take events such as local consumer shows that generate no sleeping room nights. The convention center may be funded in part by some kind of hotel sleeping room tax.

NEGOTIATING FOR YOUR EVENT

Convention centers charge for everything they provide on a pay-per-use basis. Every square foot of the building has a price attached to it. Room rental, by the square foot per day, is the center's biggest single revenue source. Every chair, every table, and every service provided by the convention center has a price. F&B, catering services, and concessions are typically provided by an outside vendor, who then pays the convention center a percentage. Unlike hotels that often put together "packages," which include a total price for rooms, F&B, and other services, the convention center details out every cost and is specifically itemized. This itemized approach is the convention center's way of charging for services used and not charging for what is not needed.

With attendees now accustomed to personalizing everything in their lives, they are bringing those same expectations to meetings. Convention centers and catering companies need to work together to accommodate their customers. In addition to catering, there are other vendors involved in the convention centers. The financial arrangements between the vendors and the convention center vary. Some may pay a commission or a percentage based on their revenue. Others may not pay in cash but in the form of equipment owned by the vendor installed in the building. For example, in many buildings, the facility does not own the soft drink vending equipment. The soft drink company with the exclusive rights in the facility owns and services the equipment in return for a specified level of product sales.

Like a hotel, a convention center has relationships with vendors for services it does not provide internally. Such services might include parking, buses, A/V, power, data–telecom, and florists. A subject of ongoing debate in the convention center industry is whether it should have exclusive vendors forcing meeting planners to use them if they use the convention center or preferred vendors or several vendors that the convention center recommends and that meeting planners can choose from.

Traditionally, catering was the only exclusive service, but in some facilities power, rigging, A/V equipment, security, and telecom can also be exclusive vendors to the facility. Some of these relationships are the result of governmental regulations, and others are an attempt to avoid liability lawsuits. In contrast, some convention centers allow procurement of vendors that are not on the recommended list but will then charge an additional fee to the meeting planner for using a nonrecommended vendor.

Given the political climate in which most convention centers operate, combined with the size and scope of the events they support, pricing is fairly transparent. Typically, costs, services offered, and specifics on the size and scope of the facility are all either in print or on their website. With all this information readily available, it becomes the planner's responsibility to access the information and not the facility's responsibility to guide a novice planner through the process.

CONFERENCE CENTERS

A **conference** is a meeting with an agenda and set objectives designed for consultation, education, fact-finding, problem solving, and/or information exchange. Conferences have a broad spectrum of reasons for meeting, which can include auditing, budgeting, marketing and sales forecasting, product launches, strategic planning, team-building, and/or training. Conferences are usually of a shorter duration and on a smaller scale than a convention.

MEETING ROOM SPACES

Because of a conference's wide variety of uses and goals, **conference center** facilities are designed to accommodate the multiple needs of the many organizations that use their facilities. Key conference center design factors include meeting rooms, refreshment areas, restrooms, secluded seating alcoves, and an on-site business center with the conference center's staff. Conference centers are designed specifically for conference activities, with acoustics, wall surfaces, lighting, and color schemes designed to enhance attendee productivity and comfort.

Conference center meeting rooms are specifically designed to enhance learning and are often arranged in a classroom-style learning environment. The chairs are selected for comfort and alertness, such as ergonomic executive-style chairs. Tables are heavy and stable, with smooth surfaces for note-taking with

CHAPTER 4 MEETING, EXPOSITIONS, EVENT, AND CONVENTION VENUES: AN EXAMINATION OF FACILITIES USED BY MEETING AND EVENT PROFESSIONALS

125

additional room for laptops and other meeting materials. They often have electrical outlets for charging computers and smartphones. Conference centers are also known for their in-house inventory of A/V technology and full-time media technicians. This results in better equipment quality and faster response time.

Conference centers provide top service levels to accommodate their wide range of clientele who depend on an ideal meeting environment. When an organization books conference center space, a conference-meeting manager is dedicated to an organization with the full responsibility of their meeting. The conference meeting manager is involved in every aspect of the meeting, from coordinating program details, providing attentive service during the meeting, and administering the postconvention evaluation. This process provides a seamless service experience for the organization and attendees. Some conference centers are part of a corporate office complex and are used exclusively by a single corporation.

ASSOCIATIONS AND CONSORTIUMS

The **International Association of Conference Centers (IACC)** has developed a specific set of guidelines to ensure that their IACC conference centers provide high quality and consistent conference meeting facilities around the globe. These IACC guidelines ensure that conference center meeting rooms have the required lighting, technology, and sound barrier standards that organizations depend on to provide the ideal learning environment. The IACC guidelines guarantee that the facility is ideal for intense, group learning environments and managed by event professionals who have obtained certain meeting planning certifications. Some conference centers have overnight guest rooms, known as a **residential** conference centers, whereas **nonresidential** conference centers do not have guest rooms. IACC also has guidelines for a conference center's guest rooms, such as requiring a hard writing surface workspace with internet connectivity. Several major corporations run conference centers, including Aramark, Dolce, Hilton, Marriott, and Sodexo. The IACC website provides a list of their global conference centers with facility details and the services provided, making the initial search process a simple one for planners.

There are also other associations and consortiums that focus on conference centers. A consortium is an association, partnership, or union that is created by its members to expand their services to their regional, national, and international clients. Consortium members typically pay an annual fee that is used to market their consortium, which in turn brings customers to the individual members. Consortiums, like associations, typically have guidelines that all their members must follow to provide a high-quality, consistent product and service. Some conference facilities may belong to several associations and consortiums to maximize their marketing efforts.

Venues of Excellence is the United Kingdom's largest consortium of dedicated conference venues, which share the highest possible standards of conference facilities and service quality. Their standards criteria include guidelines for the conference rooms, lodging, and other services that each facility offers to ensure that organizations and their attendees have a successful conference.

The Historic Conference Centres of Europe (HCCE) presents a rich variety of professionally run conference centers, equipped with state-of-the-art technology in uniquely historic buildings in Europe. Each center has retained its character, yet has been adapted to hold the demanding and innovative functions required for conferences. Like IACC and Venues of Excellence, HCCE is a recognized quality seal in the meetings, conference, and exhibition industry.

FOOD AND BEVERAGE

The flexible dining and high service levels experienced in conference centers' restaurants and bars are intended to give attendees a high-quality

CHAPTER 4 MEETING, EXPOSITIONS, EVENT, AND CONVENTION VENUES: AN EXAMINATION OF FACILITIES USED BY MEETING AND EVENT PROFESSIONALS

127

experience. Menus are developed according to the dining environment attendees and planners' need and expectation. This often includes a wide variety of menus, including international cuisine, vibrant networking lunches, and formal award dinners.

NEGOTIATING YOUR EVENT

The major discussion points for the meeting planner and the conference center venue to negotiate are the meeting space costs, sleeping room rates (if selecting a resident conference center), F&B menus and costs, and A/V and technology options.

Many conference centers have a pricing strategy called the **complete meeting package**, which means that whatever the facility owns, the planner may use at no additional charge. This puts the facility's entire inventory of easels, projectors, microphones, and sound systems at the planner's immediate disposal. For the planner, this is a flexible way to work, eliminating the scheduling of A/V companies to provide the conference's technology needs and having to buy supplies at the last minute.

Attrition takes on a new meaning in a conference center. It is not unusual for a conference center to charge a planner a fixed price for up to a certain number of delegates. If some of the delegates do not come to the event, the planner is still responsible for the full amount of the contract. This fee is based not on the ability of the facility to resell the rooms but on 100% of the negotiated facility fee regardless of how much of the facility is used. Although the planner's tasks on-site are less intense than in a convention center, the planner's ability to predict room night use is critical.

CRUISE SHIPS

In a sense, cruise ships are floating hybrids of hotels, conference centers, and full-service resorts. Cruise ships provide a satisfying meeting experience for attendees. The quality of the planning for a cruise event has a greater impact on the success of the meeting than it does for any other type of venue. A ship moves by its own itinerary. Ensuring that all attendees' transportation arrives in time to properly accommodate the ship's schedule is key. Unlike in the case of a building, once the ship leaves port, latecomers are left behind, and getting to the next port of call is at their own additional expense.

A meeting held while the cruise is under way will have a different attendance pattern than the same meeting held when the ship is in port. The event's schedule planning is coordinated with the ship's itinerary because it can have a significant impact on a meeting's attendance. Many cruise lines have well-developed children's programs, which allow the adults to participate in their meetings while their children are kept occupied with others in their age group with interactive planned activities, giving attendees the opportunity to stay focused on their event. The children's programs on most ships are better developed and provide more opportunities than in many major resorts. Also, meeting attendees are a captive audience while the ship is sailing and less likely to miss meetings.

NEGOTIATING YOUR EVENT

In addition to finding creative uses for purpose-built facilities on existing ships, new ships are being designed and constructed with the MEEC industry in mind. Group bookings can be as small as a group of 16 guests and as large as chartering a ship for over 5,000 guests. A cruise program can be a significant saving because most of the event costs are included in the cruise fare, specifically, the accommodations, meals, entertainment, onboard activities, fitness facilities, meeting space, A/V equipment, and coffee breaks. A reserved section of the ship's main dining room is also confirmed for each group.

Royal Caribbean International has dedicated, purposely built, meeting facilities on all their ships. The seating capacities and event space configurations vary depending on the ship. The conference center rooms can accommodate 18 to 400 guests and can be configured to suit the needs of any meeting setup. A variety of room configurations including theater, classroom, boardroom, card room, or mini trade show setup can be chosen. Their conference facilities include LCD projectors, overhead projectors, slide projectors, screens, TVs, DVD players, flip charts, laser pointers, microphones, and podiums. A tech fee applies only if a group needs a technician to operate the equipment. Prepaid Wi-Fi packages can be included in a group package so that everyone can stay connected, including sharing their favorite moments on social media. Each ship has dedicated onboard group coordinators available to assist through all stages of the program, including the postconvention report. In many ways, this is no different from working with a conference center.

CHAPTER 4 MEETING, EXPOSITIONS, EVENT, AND CONVENTION VENUES: AN EXAMINATION OF FACILITIES USED BY MEETING AND EVENT PROFESSIONALS

129

There are a multitude of venues to facilitate group events. Many of the ships' features were incorporated into a ship's design to attract large groups. For example, the cruise ship's ice skating rink, theaters, and lounges can be converted into event space for a reception, general session, or meeting. The ship's outdoor spaces give planners the perfect venue for creating a spectacular evening reception under the stars.

For events that require the ultimate in privacy and customization for 3,000 to 5,500 guests, chartering an entire cruise ship is the answer. Ships are typically booked 1 to 2 years prior to the event. Chartering a smaller vessel is also an option with yachts that hold 12 to 20 passengers or European barges or river cruises for groups of around 100 to 200 attendees. Because the ship is solely for your group during the charter period, almost all aspects of the cruise can be modified. The ship's dining times, daily activities, and entertainment can be customized to better support the event's objectives. With just one group onboard, the company logo can be freely displayed throughout the ship, whether it is embossed on room keys or in desserts, creating a feeling of prestige and brand loyalty for everyone aboard the ship. The guests have exclusive use of all onboard facilities and function space, resulting in the ability to create a VIP experience with unique opportunities for attendees to learn, connect, and form relationships. Whether it is a large corporation's annual event or a poker cruise, where entire dining rooms are turned into poker tournaments, chartering a ship may be the perfect venue.

SEASONALITY

Then, there are multiple factors that will increase or decrease the group or charter cruise price. First, as a general industry rule, the newer the ship is, the more expensive the pricing is. Second, pricing is more attractive during nonpeak travel seasons, which typically include the months of January, September, October, and early December. Peak demand begins in May and runs through August, along with cruises that occur during major holiday periods, such as Christmas and New Year's Eve. High-demand cruises, particularly those to Alaska, Bermuda, and Europe, may also have a higher price. Finally, the type of stateroom selected for your group impacts the per guest price, from the least expensive inside cabin that does not have views to the outside all the way up to a wide variety of suites. Of course, when an entire ship is chartered, all guest cabins are included in the combined price.

SPECIFIC-USE FACILITIES

Theaters, **amphitheaters**, arenas, stadiums, and sports facilities can also be a great choice for large meetings and events. Spectacular and impressive events can be planned for any facility designed for public assembly. Entertainment venues range in size from huge outdoor stadiums to smaller more intimate venues. Planners who wish to use these venues can be successful if they are careful to remember that entertainment, not meetings, is the venue's primary business. Further, services considered standard in a hotel or convention center may not exist in an entertainment venue.

Busch Stadium was an unusual venue for a reception for the MPI Annual Convention. George G Fenich

FINANCIAL STRUCTURE

Most of these facilities are focused on events for the general (ticket-buying) public, and a closed event for an invited audience can be a welcome change for their staff. Even though the front-office staff might welcome the meeting planner, the planner needs to carefully determine whether sufficient house and technical staff is available to support the event. Entertainment events generally occur on evenings and weekends; therefore, staff is frequently composed of part-time employees or, in the case of those who are available during the day, retirees. The availability and demographics of the staff may or may not be an issue for any given event, but it should be discussed with the facility management prior to signing a contract.

CHAPTER 4 MEETING, EXPOSITIONS, EVENT, AND CONVENTION VENUES: AN EXAMINATION OF FACILITIES USED BY MEETING AND EVENT PROFESSIONALS

131

Like convention centers, the larger arenas and amphitheaters are often owned by government agencies or are public–private partnerships. Like convention centers, there is a significant amount of planning required when using these venues. Depending on the facility's public events schedule, long rehearsal and setup times may not be feasible. For example, if it's a facility with a resident sports team, meeting planners will have to work around the team's practice sessions and games schedules or have their event in the off-season.

Finances in a special-use facility can be a hybrid between the practices of the convention center and those of a conference center. There is generally a fixed fee for the use of the facility and a specific subset of its equipment and services. "Normal" cleanup, comparable to a public event, would likely be included in the facility rental fee. The facility may require a minimum level of staff for which there would be an hourly charge based on a minimum number of hours. All other labor, equipment, and services would be exactly like those in a convention center on a bill-per-item system.

NEGOTIATING YOUR EVENT

Among the specific-use facilities, theaters can be ideal meeting facilities. They come equipped with comfortable chairs arranged in sweeping curved rows for maximum comfort. They have built-in lighting positions and sound systems and staff members who know how to use them. If attendees are local, they probably know where the theater is and do not need directions. The stages are designed for acoustics and the seats arrayed to enhance visibility.

One issue for meeting planners to consider is how customized they need the theater to be. Moving existing equipment and adding equipment can be costly. There may also be additional charges for returning equipment to its original location.

Another issue with using the in-house equipment has to do with reliability. Many theaters, particularly educational and community theaters, are not funded to the point where their equipment can be considered properly maintained or reliable. A lighting designer, unsure of the condition of the installed equipment, would likely import his or her own rather than take a risk.

When considering catering, additional planning and costs must be considered. In many of the arenas, stadiums, and amphitheaters, they often have well-developed concessions operation but may not have more traditional types of catering. In some theaters, catering may not be an option at all. Menu selection may be challenging, depending on the scope of the meeting. Kitchen equipment for a concessions environment may not be capable of supporting the menu needs of a meeting or event, thus forcing the planner to contract with an off-site caterer.

COLLEGE AND UNIVERSITIES

"From quaint, private college galleries to Big Ten stadiums, college and university venues offer diverse meeting spaces for events of any size and budget."

There are many examples of university programs that have excellent reputations as meeting venues, including several that have well-known hospitality and tourism programs. Purdue University offers first-class conference and meeting spaces, lodging accommodations, and dining services year-round. Its Midwestern location, beautiful campus, and top-notch conference center and coordination service make it a prime spot for corporate, religious, association, and fraternal events. Another option is the UMass Amherst Hotel and Conference Center. Situated in the scenic Pioneer Valley, this venue offers full-service, year-round conference and hotel accommodations, plus summer residence hall availability. It has 32 meeting spaces, with the largest room accommodating 10,000 guests. The University of Nebraska– Lincoln has one of the largest summer conference operations of its kind in the United States. The university can accommodate up to 5,500 guests with full-service meeting and dining and overnight lodging options and offers 200 meeting spaces. The Oregon State University Conference Center is a beautiful, historic campus located in the charming city of Corvallis, in the heart of the picturesque Willamette Valley wine region and located on the west bank of the Willamette River. The university provides event attendees with state-of-the-art technology and fine event spaces, dining and catering options, and overnight stays for up to 2,000 people.

NEGOTIATING YOUR EVENT

Universities have plenty of lodging space during nonclassroom periods, such as summer breaks. But the facilities have significant differences from convention hotels or conference centers. College dorm rooms have single beds instead of doubles or queens. Most college beds are extra long, so standard linen does not fit, so using the college's linen service is recommended to provide bed linen and towels. Although some dorm rooms are singles, the majority are double

CHAPTER 4 MEETING, EXPOSITIONS, EVENT, AND CONVENTION VENUES: AN EXAMINATION OF FACILITIES USED BY MEETING AND EVENT PROFESSIONALS

133

occupancy. The process of arranging and processing roommate assignments can be a full-time job. If the meeting is large, it might be a good idea to hire an intern for this task. Another lodging difference is that dorms generally have bathrooms shared among several rooms. Although that might be appropriate for groups of high school and college athletes, it would likely not be comfortable for a meeting of professionals such as doctors or accountants. Newer and renovated dorms have elevators, but many older dorms still do not have elevator access to upper floors. Considerable savings can be realized using college campuses, particularly if the college's athletic facilities are part of the meeting plan; however, not all meetings work well in this environment.

FOOD AND BEVERAGE

University food service is a huge business often run by large corporations. This means excellent chefs with extensive backgrounds from top restaurants are now running a campus food service, making it on a par with any hotel or large convention center. These university chefs create custom menus for events, but outside staffing companies will be needed for the wait staff to give attendees the level of service.

Some universities and colleges have academic programs in hospitality, food service, and/or cuisine. They may have food labs with multiple cooking and preparation stations. These can be ideal places for food-oriented meetings, nonmeeting activities, or team building. Although some colleges are well equipped for major meetings, the staff may not be as adept at responding to immediate meeting needs of the kind expected at a full-time meeting facility. The planner using an academic facility needs to investigate and coordinate with multiple members of the institution's organizational structure.

College art museums and student centers may provide interesting and exciting locations for meetings. Art museums provide especially interesting opportunities for conversations that can enhance a networking event. All the delegates at the event will probably have opinions about the art, motivating strangers to converse. The art centers and theaters at universities have a unique attribute that many planners and the general public frequently overlook. Unlike the staff in the majority of meeting and special event venues, the venue is not just a job. It is a passion. The people who run these facilities on a daily basis take great pride in, and care deeply about, the condition of the building and its contents. Any planner who intends to use one of these facilities must understand the sensitivities involved. Equally important, they must convey this message to their own staff.

CONSORTIUMS

A great place to start searching for a college or university that may be an ideal venue for an event is to start with *Unique Venues*, a marketing and membership organization. The organization was started in the 1980s by a graduate of the University of Nevada, Las Vegas Harrah Hotel, who began helping colleges and universities market their facilities to event planners. Unique Venues represent thousands of nontraditional venues in the United States, Canada, United Kingdom, and Ireland. Their nontraditional venues include colleges and universities, arenas and stadiums, camps and retreat centers, and conference and business centers.

INDUSTRY SPOTLIGHT: USING UNIVERSITIES AND COLLEGES FOR A GLOBAL ENTREPRENEURSHIP CONFERENCE

One venue traditionally not thought of as a place to host external events is universities and colleges. One such example is the Global Consortium of Entrepreneurship Centers (GCEC) conference. The GCEC is an international organization of entrepreneurship centers that work to advance excellence in entrepreneurship through the unique roles and positions of the centers in the academic and business communities. In 2018, the GCEC conference was held in Chicago and hosted jointly by DePaul University and the Illinois Institute of Technology. The event welcomed over 600 entrepreneurship center directors and professionals to the campuses for a 3-day conference. The event planner for the conference was Kenzie Mocogni, a hospitality leadership student at DePaul University. When selecting a venue for the conference, she found that a higher educational campus was the ideal place to host the majority of the event, because it provided all of the needed rooms for the educational sessions, as well as the networking space of the conference. The vast majority of attendees came from academia and found the college campus environment familiar and comfortable. Higher education facilities also have built-in A/V equipment along with eager volunteers and student workers to help with on-site duties during events. These facilities also generally charge lower rates, allowing organizers to utilize their budget on other areas.

CHAPTER 4 MEETING, EXPOSITIONS, EVENT, AND CONVENTION VENUES: AN EXAMINATION OF FACILITIES USED BY MEETING AND EVENT PROFESSIONALS

135

Although higher education facilities provide several advantages, there are limitations with working on a university campus. Kenzie explained that higher education facilities are limited by space availability owing to the school term's teaching schedules. There can also be the challenge of ensuring that the contracted space will be private and not open to students. A final challenge is the requirement to work with the university's contract F&B services. Kenzie believes that it is also important to move attendees off the higher-education campus by utilizing other venues for receptions or other activities. This is something she accomplished by hosting one nighttime event at local entrepreneurship spaces and another evening event at the Shedd Aquarium. She sees higher education facilities as an excellent venue for the right event; however, the needs of the organization and event must align with the event goals and objectives.

RETREAT FACILITIES

Retreat facilities can help relieve workplace pressures in a relaxing and inspiring environment. Retreat facilities are more likely to be owned by a family or closely held corporation than the other facilities. Not-for-profit entities, charitable organizations, or religious groups own many of the retreat facilities.

In addition to the classroom learning typical of a conference center, retreat facilities often specialize in unique extracurricular learning opportunities. Some retreat facilities are at dude ranches; others are cabins in the woods where nature is part of the lesson plan, whereas some are attached to religious organizations where a spiritual message is incorporated into the program. Many planners, out of fear that their delegates may not appreciate the opportunities presented by the unique environment, can unjustly overlook retreat facilities.

Retreat centers are an ideal setting for hard-working corporate or nonprofit teams to discover new synergies and create lasting memories. Corporate retreats take on the atmosphere of their relaxed setting. A mountain lodge, an ocean-side hideaway, or a dude ranch can make the ideal setting for strategic planning, leadership training, and team-building sessions. Retreat venues are surprisingly affordable customizable conference services with refreshing and motivating facilities.

A Unique Guest Experience

Not all venues that can be used as a part of meetings and events may naturally be thought of as a possible event venue. However, these locations can provide a unique and extraordinary experience for attendees. One such location is the Giraffe Manor in Nairobi, Kenya. The Giraffe Manor is just one of four lodges guests can stay at from The Safari Collection, a collection of luxury accommodations in East Africa. The manor sits on 12 acres of land, is part of a 140-acre indigenous forest, and has been in operation since 1972.

Giraffe Manor, Nairobi, Kenya

One of the unique and interesting opportunities when staying at the Giraffe Manor is the ability for guests to interact directly with the Giraffes. The Giraffe Manor and the adjacent Garden Manor house a total of 12 bedrooms furnished with local and different themes for guests. Guests can wake up in the morning and have breakfast with the giraffes, which walk up to the windows in the manor. A number of activities are available to guests, which include breakfast and lunch, wine time or afternoon tea, all surrounded by the giraffes. Guests are allowed to feed the giraffes as well as view them closely on the manor's grounds; they can also receive spa treatments in the Garden Manor. Many traditional spa treatments are available, from massages to facial treatments, all using organic products inspired by ancient African healing traditions. While staying at the manor, guests have all of their F&B provided. The manor prides itself on its excellent quality of F&B.

The sanctuary is also a unique venue for corporate or incentive events, where there is a need or desire to create a one-of-a-kind experience for attendees. Such experiences allow for small groups to take the entire manor for their use during their stay. When a venue is exclusively at the disposal of a specific group, they can develop a variety of new experiences for their attendees, creating memories that last a lifetime for the attendees.

CHAPTER 4 MEETING, EXPOSITIONS, EVENT, AND CONVENTION VENUES: AN EXAMINATION OF FACILITIES USED BY MEETING AND EVENT PROFESSIONALS

137

Tower Bridge, London, England.

© Samot/Shutterstock.com

UNUSUAL VENUES

Nontraditional venues, such as hotels and convention centers, have come under increased demand for the purposes of holding MEEC gatherings. Organizations want their events to stand out from those of competitors or provide a unique experience for attendees and members. The desire to host events that are larger than life that feature unexpected experiences provide the wow factor that creates a lasting memory with attendees.

Some venues unaccustomed to this kind of business are now courting groups based on increased interest and demand. Examples include the Ngala Private Animal Reserve in Naples, Florida, and the Maryland Zoo. Because of interest from group business, both facilities have constructed venues on their properties for meeting and event rentals. The PCMA annual convention has rented out SeaWorld in Orlando, Universal Orlando, an aircraft carrier in San Diego, Chase Arena in San Francisco, the Museum of Science and Industry in Chicago, and Musicians Hall of Fame and Museum in Nashville, all for the exclusive use of their convention attendees.

Restaurants have always been a popular venue to host events, and owing to the increasing demand, many restaurants have private rooms for hosting these important events. If a group is staying at a hotel or primarily using a conference center, many planners include a meal or two off-premise at a restaurant that showcases the local cuisine. This allows for an intimate guest experience with excellent F&B options. Many restaurants have a group sales manager who can arrange for a seamless group dining experience, such as those at Lettuce Entertain You Enterprises. This often allows an event planner to have one contact who handles all event details. Group contact information can be found on most restaurants' websites along with sample group menus and prices.

There are multiple options for organizations to host their MEEC events when they have a membership to a private club, such as a city club or country club. These members-only facilities require the member to sponsor and pay for the event, but the attendees do not need to be members. Often, someone in the organization, corporation, association, or nonprofit has a membership in these clubs and acts as sponsor for the event. This sponsor works in conjunction with the organization's event planner as well as the club's event professional to design and plan the event. Their facilities run from historic urban club with luxurious conference facilities and elegant dining rooms to country clubs with sprawling golf courses, spa facilities, and multiple dining options.

Members of the military have access to several military organizations, such as the Navy Lodge, Inns of the Corp, and the Air Force Inn. The hotel-style lodges include overnight accommodations and conference facilities for active and retired military to host meetings and events. Locations are primarily available throughout the United States, typically near a military base, although there are multiple global locations.

New unique venues continue to be imagined and created each year. Multiuse venues have become very popular in recent years. One example is City Winery in Chicago. This venue is a multiuse facility with a music venue, restaurant, event space, and a working winery with over 32,000 square feet of space. With multiple event spaces, accommodating from 10 to 500 guests, City Winery can host a wide span of events, ranging from corporate and social events to concerts from world-renowned artists. Multiuse venues protect themselves by diversifying their client base to include those of all sizes and budgets, making these venues less reliant on one type of business.

In addition to utilizing unusual venues for meetings and receptions, these locations have become increasingly popular with events, especially weddings. Destination weddings occur when a couple chooses to hold their wedding in a location where neither individual resides. For instance, a couple may elect to

CHAPTER 4 MEETING, EXPOSITIONS, EVENT, AND CONVENTION VENUES: AN EXAMINATION OF FACILITIES USED BY MEETING AND EVENT PROFESSIONALS

139

hold their wedding in Paris or Bali, as opposed to their hometown. In many cases, these destination weddings take place in an unusual venue, in a famous restaurant, or on a sugar-sand beach. Beaches, botanical gardens, castles, sailboats, or theme parks are some of the many facilities that may be used for a destination wedding. Walt Disney World, in Florida, plays host to more than 2,500 weddings each year, some of which actually take place in Cinderella's castle in the Magic Kingdom. In short, almost any venue may be used to host an event when the planner is willing to be creative.

INDUSTRY SPOTLIGHT: CREATING A WILD EVENT EXPERIENCE AT THE ZOO

Meredith Schorr, Donor Relations Assistant, Lincoln Park Zoo, Chicago IL

When individuals hear they are going to the zoo, images of childhood excursions to see elephants, gorillas, and giraffes fill their heads. However, zoos across the world offer a unique and interesting venue for many different types of events. One of these is the Lincoln Park Zoo in Chicago. Meredith Schorr, a donor relations assistant at the Lincoln Park Zoo, shared her experience with the different types of events that take place outside of normal zoo operations. She explained that for most days of the year, the zoo operates just as every other zoo in the world. Yet, for several days a month, the zoo serves as the backdrop of events for corporate clients, local nonprofits, and private events. The zoo has several areas and buildings that can be used for a wide range of events. Café Bauer is a large prairie-style building on the zoo property that is attractive for wedding and social events. Events can take place in various zoo animal houses, which are popular for corporate events, while the zoo carousel provides an interactive venue for children's birthday parties. While the grounds do host many external events, they also host internal zoo events ranging from Spooky Zoo, Zoo Lights, and their grandest event, the Zoo Ball. The Zoo Ball is the largest fundraising event for the zoo and offers guests the ability to have dinner with lions in the background. The Lincoln Park Zoo is another great example of a venue that can provide that needed special venue to create a memorable guest experience at an event.

ASSOCIATIONS & CONSORTIUMS

There are multiple associations and consortiums that event planners can contact to find unique venues in most parts of the world. For example, Westminster Venue Collection is a consortium of unique venues in the United Kingdom. Their event venues include townhouses, private members' clubs, famous attractions, historic institutes, and museums. One celebrated venue is the House of Commons, home to the U.K. government. It offers a historic backdrop for an event that is experienced in hosting glittering state occasions and other high-profile events. It is available on Saturdays and when the House is not in session. Westminster Abbey, with a thousand years of royal history, is the coronation church where monarchs have been crowned amid great splendor and is another extraordinary venue in their collection.

INDUSTRY SPOTLIGHT: USING UNIQUE VENUES BY THIRD-PARTY PLANNERS

Emily Greenbaum, Event Manager, Verde Events

Emily Greenbaum is an event manager with Verde Events. Verde Events is a boutique third-party event planning company with a wide range of clients from large Fortune 500 companies to small independent firms. After graduating from DePaul with a Bachelor of Science in Hospitality Leadership and a concentration in event management, Emily began her career as an event coordinator with Verde Events and was quickly promoted to an event manager. Emily sought every opportunity and quickly gained invaluable knowledge through her behind-the-scenes and on-site experiences. She seeks to enhance any meeting and incentive program, adding that little "something" extra, no matter the budget size. On-site, clients often ask if she has a twin sister, because they tend to find her "everywhere" and thinking two steps ahead. Whether taking attendee phone calls or loading a coach, Emily always comes prepared with a smile and a positive attitude.

What types of services does Verde provide?

We provide a wide range of services for our clients, from full event planning to only managing registration for their events. This is dependent

CHAPTER 4 MEETING, EXPOSITIONS, EVENT, AND CONVENTION VENUES: AN EXAMINATION OF FACILITIES USED BY MEETING AND EVENT PROFESSIONALS

141

on the client's needs and budget. Many of our clients are corporate incentive travel clients. Besides our corporate clients, we also have several associations as clients, who we provide a variety of services for including conference registration.

What size are all of the events that you plan?

Our event size varies, but most of our clients' events range from a dozen to several hundred attendees per event. Our conference clients have thousands of attendees and potentially many different elements at the same time. Many smaller events require a high level of detail because typically these events are for an elevated level of leadership.

As a third planner, what types of events do you plan?

We have several typical events we plan. Those include incentive travel, conference planning, and board meetings, although we are open to any type of event our client needs assistance planning. The majority of our business centers around out incentive travel clients. Incentive travel is a corporate sponsored meeting or trip to reward employee efforts, such as exceeding sales goals. Incentive events are typically destination events with multiple unique experiences included in the program. This requires planners to conduct research for different opportunities for attendees. This could be exclusive events at distilleries, tile painting in Portugal, or beach barbeques in Mexico.

Do you use traditional event venues or unique venues?

We use both traditional and unique venues for our clients. It depends on the types of event we are planning for our clients, as well as their desired outcomes. We have used a variety of unique venues to enhance the guest experience and create a wow factor for our clients. While hotels and traditional venues provide an easier planning experience, many attendees want to be removed from the traditional experience, especially when working with an incentive travel client. I often use a mixture of traditional and unique venues when designing an event, especially since both have benefits for our clients.

What advice would you give to a student ready to graduate?

One of the best things I did as a student was to participate in every possible activity to gain experience. Once you are in your career, if you are asked to help with an event or project, take advantage of it, even if it means more work for you. I also believe being open and accepting feedback whenever possible greatly improve your work just as it has mine. This feedback will make you a better event professional and prepare you for your next role.

OUTDOOR EVENTS

For many, holding an event outdoors is the ideal venue. Many of these venues, however, do not have permanently installed equipment. Therefore, virtually everything needed for the event must be brought in. These venues also have little or no staff. Public parks can be beautiful venues, except that they are open to the public, making them difficult to use for a private event. If the event is a public one like an art show, a public park, with its regular traffic, can be an ideal location. But if the event is more private, especially if it involves alcohol, a public park may not be an option.

Outdoor sports arenas might be seen as easy venues because they come with bleachers and restrooms, yet they also present their own challenges. The irrigation systems for the landscaping at professional or competition fields are fragile, so driving heavy loads over them can break the piping beneath the surface. Some venues prohibit driving a vehicle heavier than a golf cart or installing a stage unless it is properly padded with plywood sheeting. Pushing heavy supplies across the grass is not likely to be approved by a venue's head of grounds either. Similar restrictions can also be found for golf courses and resorts with substantial landscaping.

OUTDOOR VENUE CHALLENGES

In addition to all the normal concerns a planner needs to organize for an event, the planner using these facilities needs to provide all the support services normally considered the responsibility of an event facility. Such services could include portable restrooms, parking, and trash removal, because most outdoor

CHAPTER 4 MEETING, EXPOSITIONS, EVENT, AND CONVENTION VENUES: AN EXAMINATION OF FACILITIES USED BY MEETING AND EVENT PROFESSIONALS

143

venues share a general lack of support and equipment. All of them have heightened challenges with logistics and catering. Access to a venue can be an issue if roads flood in the rainy season or are impassable in the winter. Even if the road is substantial enough to support the delivery trucks, it is necessary to determine whether there is a dock where supplies can be unloaded or whether a forklift is needed. If a forklift is needed, the planner must ascertain who supplies the driver as well as raise any other pertinent logistical concerns.

OUTDOOR TENTS

Tents are routinely used to create meeting venues. They fall into three categories: pole, frame, and clear span. An open-sided pole or **frame tent** set up on the grass is one of the simplest of all meeting venues. It requires little advance planning beyond making sure the tent rental people can have it set up in time. Adding tent sides and air conditioning can reduce the impact of weather. The tent may require a floor so that rain drainage flows under the floor and not over the feet of the people in the tent.

Clear span tents have a strong roof structure, and it is possible to hang lighting from its beams by using special clamps. If lighting is to be hung in a clear span tent, the lighting should be hung before the floor is put in, because many of the tent floors will not support the scissor lifts used by the lighting and décor people during setup. To hang lighting in a **pole tent** requires special brackets to attach the lights to the poles if the poles are sturdy enough to support them. Therefore, for a pole tent, supporting the lighting from the floor on boom stands or truss towers may be a better plan. Since the purpose of the tent is to create a meeting space where none previously existed, other support services such as power, water, and restrooms that may not exist, will have to be brought in.

OUTDOOR VENUE PERMITS

A challenge that frequently catches planners by surprise is obtaining permits. Many local governments require permits to use parks or even private property for special events. Failure to procure the proper permits can lead to an event being shut down at the last moment. Not only must the police and fire department be notified, but in many places the building code office must be notified too. Tents must usually be inspected by the fire department. In some areas, generators are under the purview of the fire department; in others, there is a special office that deals with electrical issues. This office may be part of the building and zoning department or part of a designated special events office. A one-time-use liquor license may be required.

TRENDS

The meetings and events industry is always evolving, with new trends appearing overnight. One of those is the demand for and use of unique venues. Planners are always looking for the newest and freshest ideas to make their events stand out from the competition, and the choice of venue is perhaps the most obvious method for accomplishing that. Attendees also expect to be "wowed" and not see the same cookie-cutter event format year after year. Rather than holding an opening reception for attendees in a convention center hall, the planner can use unexpected venues to keep the attendees guessing and prevent them from getting bored. One year the opening event could be held at Mardi Gras World in New Orleans, the next year at the Cowboys Stadium in Dallas, and the following year at the Seattle Space Needle. In each location, the attendees will have a different experience and leave feeling that their event was one of a kind.

The size and composition of convention centers continue to see significant changes. Convention center space around the globe continues to increase, with many second- and third-tier cities building new centers and/or building additions to current facilities. This expansion demonstrates the importance of meetings and events in revenue generation and growth.

Another emerging trend is the expansion of new venues owned and operated by décor, catering, and A/V companies. These existing and successful companies have determined that it is financially beneficial to add event venues to their existing portfolios. Some companies have also added catering or décor to their offerings, creating a one-stop shop for all their clients' events needs. This type of company allows a client to work with one contact for all events needs as in the case of the offerings at a hotel, i.e., event venue, décor, catering, and A/V.

Event trends have already been greatly transformed by COVID-19, and event venues are no exception. Although the exact impact the pandemic will have on the events industry is unknown, it is guaranteed that new trends will evolve over the next few years.

CHAPTER 4 MEETING, EXPOSITIONS, EVENT, AND CONVENTION VENUES: AN EXAMINATION OF FACILITIES USED BY MEETING AND EVENT PROFESSIONALS

145

COVID-19'S IMPACT ON THE MEEC INDUSTRY

UNITED STATES OF AMERICA

In January 2020, the Javits Center in New York City hosted the jovial showstopping American Kennel Club dog show, with thousands of attendees and celebrated perfectly groomed dogs. But not long after, the reality of the COVID-19 pandemic was descending on countries around the globe. In an effort to slow COVID-19's spread, many countries began halting face-to-face events, as gatherings of all sizes were banned, and business travel was put on hold to protect the health of attendees, exhibitors, and employees. Many events were rescheduled for 2021 dates or were held as a virtual experience utilizing web conferencing services. As the MEEC industry pressed the cancel button on large in-person events in countless conventions and meetings venues, suppliers transitioned their resources to serve the local populations' needs.

Three months later, in late March, that same convention center, which held the celebrated dog show, was constructed to be filled with emergency beds for the treatment of patients with COVID-19. Over 15 city, state, and federal agencies, ranging from military engineers to Javits Center carpenters, built the 1,000-bed hospital from scratch within a week, and additional wings were built in the following weeks. By the end of April, the makeshift hospital had treated almost 1,100 patients, and it was announced that it would soon close, as New York City hospitals had the capacity to handle the current levels of COVID-19 patients.

Across the country, the story was similar. The U.S. Army Corp of Engineers spent weeks scouting over 800 facilities to convert them into COVID-19 wards in response to bed shortages at hospitals to accommodate a growing number of patients as the virus began to spike at different times across the continent. Some were closed hospitals that were reopened. Other facilities were empty hotels that are getting retrofitted for patient care. The vast majority of wards were constructed in large arenas, including the McCormick Place in Chicago, the Baltimore Convention Center, the Music Center in Nashville, the Michigan Expo Center, the Santa Clara Convention Center, the Los Angeles Convention Center, and the Vancouver Convention Centre in Canada. In April 2020, the San Diego Convention Center housed more than 1,300 individuals to help ease crowding at local homeless shelters, giving individuals experiencing homelessness a fighting chance to staying healthy as the city weathered the pandemic. In mid-July and again in early August, Atlanta's convention center was turned into a makeshift field hospital. Austin's convention center was converted in mid-July.

Converting a convention center into a humanitarian effort is not a new procedure in the United States. During past hurricanes, U.S. convention centers' space has been used to help local residents over the years, particularly those in New Orleans, Houston, and throughout Florida. As hurricane season kicked into high gear in 2020, hurricane evacuees found refuge in empty convention centers. In July, the Hawaii Convention Center in Honolulu opened its doors in anticipation of Hurricane Douglas. During Hurricane Laura in late August 2020, Louisiana's governor urged citizens in evacuation zones to take shelter in empty hotel rooms throughout the state and venues in nearby states, including the Austin Convention Center.

Convention centers are designed for quick setups and dismantling for each new event. They have wide open spaces and hallways, making it easy to wheel in equipment, whether it's an event or a temporary hospital. With the urgency of COVID-19, the large open ballrooms of convention centers were being converted to accommodate thousands of patients. Their expansive space has the benefit of pooling everyone into a large room, making it easier for highly trained medical staff to be more efficient. When hospital beds are side by side, with cloth dividers and 6 feet of distance between, medical staff don't need to touch doorknobs or surfaces with walls removed, and they can quickly and easily share expensive equipment and mobilize critical medical experts. Staff can move in one direction to check on patients, like a one-way street, which helps mitigate the spread of infection. Furthermore, patients are grouped by cohorts, as sicker patients are grouped together, which helps the staff manage and prioritize care. These large venues have HVAC (heating, ventilation, and air conditioning) systems that are built to suck in fresh air and blow it onto occupants to reduce breathing in stagnant air, which is the one of the best options for diluting pathogens in the air.

Although hotels were considered for some cities as makeshift hospitals, experts quickly realized that most hotel doorways aren't even wide enough to squeeze in standard hospital beds, which made most hotel facilities unusable for mass hospital facilities. Instead, hotels became the perfect place to house noncritical patients in a private rooms with bathrooms alongside the doctors who are caring for them. Many hotels have food service and laundry facilities available on-site, which are both ideal criteria for supporting a large number of people. Furthermore, many hotel operators had no customers owing to the pandemic, and they were ready to help during the COVID-19 crisis by stepping up and

CHAPTER 4 MEETING, EXPOSITIONS, EVENT, AND CONVENTION VENUES: AN EXAMINATION OF FACILITIES USED BY MEETING AND EVENT PROFESSIONALS

147

offering their facilities for healthcare workers and patient use. Hotels in New York, Chicago, New Orleans, and San Francisco repurposed their facilities for healthcare workers and patient care during the pandemic. Near the nation's capital, The National Guard turned the Hilton Baltimore Inner Harbor Hotel into a field hospital, operated through a joint partnership with the University of Maryland Medical System and Johns Hopkins University.

Convention centers throughout the United Kingdom also turned their facilities into hospital wards, including ExCeL in London, the Manchester Central Convention Centre, the Birmingham National Exhibition Center, along with those in Europe, such as the Austria Center in Vienna and the IFEMA Convention Center in Madrid, Spain. By late April, these facilities had provided treatment to hundreds of patients, and as the numbers of cases in a host of major metropolitan areas peaked and hospitals proved that they were able to handle the capacity, many of these makeshift medical facilities were placed on standby or returned to their original purposes.

Although the large convention centers and many hotels played a part in helping deal with the COVID-19 patients and medical personnel, many MEEC venues were among the businesses that have been most severely affected by the COVID-19 pandemic. The event venues were able to operate at only a small percentage of their normal capacity, which forced many organizations to stop operations temporarily. Beginning in May 2020, some states began to allow venues to reopen but at a limited capacity. As of September 2020, many large event venues (convention centers, conference centers, and convention hotels) around the United States remain entirely closed, a good number of them unable to financially break even if they were to operate at a limited capacity.

One of the hardest hit segments of the event venue industry were small individual venues. One example is Riccardo's by the Bridge, a family-owned banquet hall in the Astoria neighborhood of Queens, New York. Riccardo's had been operating for 70 years over four generations of family ownership. After being closed during the six months period, from March to August 2020, the Riccardo family made the difficult decision to shut its doors permanently, seeing no financial way to reopen. They stated that the decision was solely because of the impact of COVID-19.

Another hard hit area of event venues were private event spaces found in restaurants. Yelp estimated that as many as 60% of restaurants have shuttered permanently because of COVID-19. Many of these restaurants were used as venues for the MEEC industry. Simon's Restaurant in Atlanta, which opened in 2017 to rave reviews from critics and guests, is one such example. The 4,500-square foot restaurant offered several private event spaces accommodating up to 125 individuals. Even as it was able to operate at limited capacity, the restaurant soon found that it was unable to sustain itself at these levels, especially without the ability to host events.

Sporting venues are another important event venue bringing together thousands of individuals to celebrate their favorite sports. Yet having thousands of cheering fans isn't safe during the COVID-19 pandemic. Therefore, all major sporting event venues were shut down in March 2020. Many professional sports associations had begun playing again by August 2020, most doing so without spectators. This is not the case for National Association for Stock Car Auto Racing (NASCAR), which made the decision to allow fans to attend their outdoor events. NASCAR began allowing fans at auto races on July 15, 2020, with only 20,000 attendees of the total capacity of 162,000 watching drivers race at Bristol Motor Speedway in Tennessee. Restrictions on fan attendance, as with all event venues, are governed and determined by either local or state governments.

PEOPLE'S REPUBLIC OF CHINA

Some countries, particularly China and South Korea, were able to get back to hosting large events in their convention centers while the rest of the globe was still overwhelmed with the pandemic. To showcase the nation's success in containing the spread of COVID-19, China continued hosting large MEEC events during summer 2020. In August 2020, the Central China International Auto Show was held in Wuhan, marking the first large-scale exhibition in Wuhan since the city lifted its 76-day lockdown on April 8 as the COVID-19 outbreak waned in the country. More than 60 car brands and 800 models took part in the city's five-day event. From August 20 to 23, Shenzhen World, the world's largest trade convention center, successfully hosted the world's largest furniture exhibition, the Shenzhen International Furniture Exhibition (SIFE). In late August 2020, the sixteenth annual Cross-Straits travel expo took place in Xiamen, China. This expo showcased China's culture and tourism bureaus and promoted their respective travel destinations to Chinese citizens with the goal of facilitating the recovery of the domestic tourism industry. The Chinese Academy of Engineering held a symposium in Beijing, in the first week of September, that included a ceremony commending role models in China's fight against COVID-19. A few days later, the China International Fair for

CHAPTER 4   MEETING, EXPOSITIONS, EVENT, AND CONVENTION VENUES: AN EXAMINATION OF FACILITIES USED BY MEETING AND EVENT PROFESSIONALS

149

Trade in Services (CIFTIS), a convention that focused on the services trade, was held in Beijing. With over 100,000 attendees, CIFTIS was the first major international economic and trade event since the outbreak.

The first show was the 2020 Hunan Auto Show, held in late April 2020, with over 60,000 attendees at the Hunan International Convention and Exhibition Center, in Changsa, China. Measures that were taken to ensure a safe experience for attendees and staff included the following:

- Attendees submitting an ID card and undergoing a health and identity check prior to arriving at the venue. Once approved, they were issued a digital link that they could use to register for the event via WeChat.
- Convention center employees dressed in full protective gear checked and verified each visitor's ID and temperature each time they entered the exhibition hall. Attendees' hands were disinfected by an automatic machine, plastic gloves were given to them to wear, and 1.5 meters' (approximately 5 feet) spacing was mandated between each other.
- All participants were obligated to wear masks throughout and urged to wash hands frequently.
- Registration was capped at 8,000 attendees daily, and once registration reached 4,000 each day, the platform was paused to assess the density of participants, before it was started again.
- The convention center was disinfected twice a day, and fresh outdoor air was pumped into the convention center through the fresh-air system.
- Two temporary medical centers were built and set up at the site, one near the show floor and one outside the building.

THE REPUBLIC OF KOREA (SOUTH KOREA)

South Korea also had great success in curtailing the spread of COVID-19 in their country, and once they felt it was safe to do so, they began hosting large-scale events. The MBC Architecture Show, held in May 2020 at the Korean Exhibition Center (KINTEX), in Goyang (near Seoul), South Korea, had over 4,500 attendees with similar protocols to those implemented in China.

The three-stage access security plan at KINTEX involves screening of visitors, who must wear masks to enter the building in the first stage. Entrances have disinfection mats, thermal imaging cameras, and facial recognition thermometers installed with ambulances on standby. In the second stage, a second body temperature measurement is performed at the entrance to the exhibition hall proper, and admission is conditional on using hand sanitizer and wearing plastic gloves. The entrance queue spaces visitors at 1.5-m intervals in the lobby. In the third stage, inside the exhibition hall, it is mandatory to wear masks and plastic gloves, and exhibitors and cafeteria employees wear face shields that cover the entire face. The exhibition hall was disinfected daily, and 100% of the air intake and air conditioning came from continuous external air. The center is playing a leading role in restarting the Korean exhibition industry, including the introduction of a virtual meeting system to support remote business meeting for exhibitors and buyers who could not visit the live exhibition.

THE REPUBLIC OF SINGAPORE

Singapore has the lowest COVID-19 fatality count globally, with under 30 deaths among the more than 57,000 people who have been infected with COVID-19 in the Southeast Asian island as of fall 2020. Their 0.05% death rate is well below the global average of around 3%. Owing to the safety of traveling there, Singapore is working to determine how to scale up to their exhibitions and conferences from 250 participants to eventually thousands of participants in a safe and financially sustainable manner in their country's venues.

The gradual resumption of business events is being positioned to help maintain the country's position as a leading MEEC hub while safeguarding the jobs and livelihoods of those working in the industry and related sectors. MEEC travelers are high-yield visitors whose spending is almost double that of leisure travelers. Unlike large nations, Singapore is a small city-state that cannot survive on its domestic market alone. To revamp the industry, the country is determining how to bring international travelers into Singapore, conduct the meeting safely, and provide them the assurance of safety as they depart Singapore. Pilot events and solutions are being designed to help Singapore lead the way as a safe, trusted, and innovative destination for MEEC events.

As this chapter is being written, the full extent that the economic impact COVID-19 will have on event venues is still unknown. Many venues remain

CHAPTER 4 MEETING, EXPOSITIONS, EVENT, AND CONVENTION VENUES: AN EXAMINATION OF FACILITIES USED BY MEETING AND EVENT PROFESSIONALS

151

closed, with many having plans to resume operations in the future. Yet the future of event venues, especially independent event venues, is uncertain and dependent on several factors, including when they can operate at full capacity and when business travel will continue.

SUMMARY

RECOMMENDATIONS FOR WORKING WITH ALL VENUES

When choosing a venue for a MEEC event, a planner should view the facilities offered through the eyes and expectations of the event attendees. Who are the attendees? What are the goals of the event? A facility without lodging might be a good fit if all the attendees are local. A remote venue might be a good option for a conference if attendees have a tendency to slip away midday when they should be in sessions. A review of the event's history is important in determining the best choice of venue for the planned MEEC event.

RESEARCH AND UNDERSTAND VENUE OPTIONS

Obtaining accurate information on the venue options is essential to planning successful meetings/events. Detailed and thorough research is the first step in the process. This first step is much easier now than it has been and promises to become even easier, as the internet and websites provide planners powerful resources to plan their events. Many of the best meeting facilities have extensive websites with detailed information. Some venues have 360-degree visual imaging that allows a planner to remotely view the facility.

A planner needs to determine whether to use the venue's technology, rent from a preferred vendor, or buy their own equipment if their needs are only the simple cost of the projector or microphone. Planners need to evaluate the proper use of their time. Is their time well spent hauling a large plastic case through airport security, or is it better spent attending to details, such as ensuring the coffee break is refreshed and lunch is ready on time? Many planners see their jobs in terms of cost containment. Although that is an important part of the job, helping guarantee the success of the meeting is the more appropriate goal. Sometimes, a penny saved is not a penny earned but a pound lost in a missed opportunity. The planner's job is to know the difference.

Weather is an issue for all events, but particularly for outdoor venues. When planning an outdoor function, an indoor backup plan or contingency plan is vital to the success of the event. A professional planner should always recognize the potential for weather to have an impact on the event and put the necessary plans in place for the worst-case scenario.

COMMUNICATION AND VERIFICATION

Once the event planner has done the research and feels a venue is a good fit, then, and only then, should the planner call the facility's sales department to start a dialogue. The most important component of working with any facility is the development of an open, honest, and trusting relationship with all parties involved. Unfortunately, there are facilities that will take advantage of that relationship, just as there are planners who do not deal honestly with their suppliers. Despite the risks involved, the attempt must be made, because the success of every event depends on the interaction between the planner and all the other parties. This relationship begins with understanding what each of the participants brings to the relationship and what each needs.

Communication begins with a set of requirements. The more accurate the requirements are, the better. It is important to note, however, that "accurate" and "detailed" are not the same thing. In a contract, the hotel needs to know how many people are coming, but they may not need the names until relatively close to the event. Accurate and timely listings of requirements are the first step in developing a successful relationship. Verification of the documentation returned by the venue is the other half of this communication. Not only should the planner provide requirements, but the venue should also reply and acknowledge that it understands them and state how it will fulfill each requirement as appropriate.

An excellent resource to use when planning an event and determining what services are needed from the venue is a needs analysis; go to the Event Industry Council website and download their request for proposal (RFP) workbook from their APEX (Accepted Practices Exchange) tab. When using the industry standards template, event planners can ensure that they are including all the details necessary for their event to be a success.

The key to working with any venue is fourfold: research, understand, communicate, and verify. Research, understand, communicate, and verify. Repeat until done! This chapter provides information that can be used by meeting planners to research and understand – the first two steps of the event planning process. The remaining steps are what separate the best planners from the rest.

CHAPTER 4 MEETING, EXPOSITIONS, EVENT, AND CONVENTION VENUES: AN EXAMINATION OF FACILITIES USED BY MEETING AND EVENT PROFESSIONALS

153

Gary McCreary serves as the vice president of Catering and Convention Operations for The Venetian and The Palazzo Hotels in Las Vegas, Nevada. Mr. McCreary was on the opening team of The Venetian and has since opened every major property for Las Vegas Sands Corp. in Macau, Singapore, and Bethlehem Pennsylvania. He oversees Banquet Operations, which generates more than $100M annually in banquet revenue.

Nearly 25 of the world's 200 largest conventions are held in The Venetian Palazzo Congress Center and the adjacent Sands Expo and Convention Center. Their 85,000-square-foot Venetian Ballroom is one of the largest obstruction-free ballrooms in the world. More than 2 million banquet meals are served each year.

The Venetian Palazzo Congress Center and adjacent Sands Expo and Convention Center have been awarded the *Meetings and Conventions* Magazine's Gold Platter Award annually, starting in 2002 as a "Best of the Best" meeting property for excellence in creativity, culinary experience, quality, and professionalism. They have also been awarded the *Meeting and Conventions* Magazine's Gold Key Award annually since 2000 for professionalism and quality. They have also been a five-time winner and 19-time nominee for the Gala Award by *Special Events Magazine.*

Mr. McCreary is a cum laude graduate from The University of North Texas, Denton, Texas, with a BA in Hotel & Restaurant Management. He was the director of Catering and then Assistant Director of Conference Management at the legendary Loews Anatole Hotel in Dallas. Mr. McCreary's was also an International Meeting Planner for the Young Presidents Organization (YPO).

Mr. McCreary was the 2016 to 2017 president of the Foundation of the National Association for Catering and Events (NACE). The Foundation of NACE is a nonprofit national organization for caterers, event planners, and event professionals that provides education, certification, and a network of resources for members in all segments of the hospitality industry. NACE's mission is to advance the catering and events industry and its professionals. NACE has grown to more than 4,000 members in over 40 chapters in North America. NACE continues to raise the standard of professionalism in the industry through education, certification, standards, ethics, and professional recognition programs. NACE remains dedicated to growing and changing with the industry's needs, providing critical resources for all its members, wherever they are in their careers and whatever their positions.

Beyond the basics of staying organized, monitoring vendors, and all of the mechanical components of running a large-scale event, Mr. McCreary draws inspiration from multiple aspects of an event to make it memorable, including history, art, and pop culture, to infuse a deeper meaning or level of passion for attendees. He was the mastermind behind the grand opening party of the Tony award-winning Jersey Boys musical at the Palazzo's Las Vegas Resort, Hotel, and Casino Congress Center. "Oh, what a night!" was both the theme and the enthusiastic response by the 1,900 celebrities and VIPs in attendance. The gala not only celebrated the launch of the popular musical but also honored the legendary musical group, the Four Seasons, and its lead singer Frankie Valli's birthday.

Guests were directed to the postperformance gala site by models in 1950s costumes. Outside the Palazzo ballroom, waiters were clad in white Eisenhower dinner jackets and served up signature cocktails themed to Four Seasons' musical hits. On entering the ballroom, guests were photographed as they walked through a series of three-dimensional, eight-foot-tall letters spelling out Jersey Boys. Anchoring the corners of the room were $1.2 million classic cars from the 1950s. The room's centerpiece was a 180-by-20-foot kabuki curtain displaying vintage footage of Valli and the Four Seasons. At the big reveal, the curtain plummeted to the floor to expose the event's true entertainment stage, where 1950s' costumed dancers came alive to the audience's cheers.

Menu design and food presentation was a modern twist on classic 1950s' fare. Passed items, including Dungeness crab canapés and pigs in a blanket, were served on trays resembling vinyl records with the Jersey Boys' logo. Sleek, stainless steel tables with minimal décor served as the delivery platform for a "no-chafing-dish" menu. Hot food items were finished to order by chefs stationed behind main service buffets, and attendants assembled plates in front of the guests. Every aspect was designed to extend the feel of a high-end diner. American Kobe beef and lobster sliders, beef and sausage meatloaf, chicken pot pie with duck confit, and Clams Casino with citrus fennel salad were served. Guests were nostalgic over the handcrafted milkshake station with penny candy that was popular during that point in history. "Working on the Jersey Boys grand opening party at the Palazzo was exciting," explained Mr. McCreary. "The event was created to fit the theme and concept of the show, and in doing so, we stretched our creative legs and had fun with the food, drink, and atmosphere."

CHAPTER 4 MEETING, EXPOSITIONS, EVENT, AND CONVENTION VENUES: AN EXAMINATION OF FACILITIES USED BY MEETING AND EVENT PROFESSIONALS

155

CASE STUDY ASSIGNMENT:

As one of the newest team members of the catering and convention services team at The Venetian & The Palazzo Resorts, which is the world's largest combined hotel event space, you have been asked to create an event for a new show that is coming to your resort. Individually, or in student teams, follow each of the case study steps.

Step 1. Go to the website for the event and convention services at your venue, The Venetian and The Palazzo Resorts: www.venetian.com/conventions.html

Review and download each section of the website so that you are aware of all of the options available at your venue: Catering Services, Meeting Planner Resources, Business Center, Audio/Visual, Corporate Event Photos, Floral Shop, Specialized Event Services (SES), and Meeting Space Floorplans.

Step 2: You are on the committee to help select the next show that is coming to the Venetian & Palazzo Resorts. Decide which show is coming and research it to get ideas for themes, décor, and menus.

Step 3: Create a broad outline of your grand opening event using the APEX guide

http://www.eventscouncil.org/APEX/RequestsforProposals.aspx

Select the document titled: Function Set-Up Order, MS Word version - without exhibits.

Step 4: Using your creative ideas for the new show grand opening event, complete the RFP for your event. Select the Venetian or Palazzo venue rooms that you feel are the best fit for the celebration. Your boss, Mr. McCreary, has high expectations of you, so be sure to come up with a creative theme, a memorable décor, and an innovative menu. He expects only the best, so use the knowledge from the chapter and online resources to create a memorable grand opening event.

Step 5: Submit your complete RFP to your professor by the due date. On a poster, include your décor ideas of the venue space and F&B menu items, along with the venue and your layout. During the class session, hang the posters on the wall. Each class member votes for their favorite poster with a sticky note with your initials on it. (You cannot vote for your own poster.)

Step 6: Discuss in class the highlights of the top voted posters. Using the best ideas from all of the posters, create a combined class concept for this case study that your class feels is up to the high standards of Mr. McCreary and his catering and convention operations team.

KEYWORDS AND TERMS

For definitions, see https://insights.eventscouncil.org/Industry-glossary

amenities	ESC
amphitheater	exhibit hall
arena	frame tent
attrition	hotel
auditorium style	local event
boardroom	needs analysis
breakout room	pole tent
classroom style	prefunction space
clear span tent	seasonality
complete meeting package	shoulder
concessionaire	sports facilities
crescent rounds	stadium
destination management company (DMC)	theater

REVIEW AND DISCUSSION QUESTIONS

1. Compare and contrast a hotel's meeting space and a convention center's meeting space. Include in the comparison the differences and/or similarities of the meeting room spaces, the financial structure, and food & beverage options.

2. What are the differences between a conference center and a convention center? Include in the comparison of the meeting room spaces the financial structure and food & beverage options.

3. How is a cruise ship similar to a hotel, convention center, and conference center? How is it different from each of these venues?

4. What are the benefits of using a college or university as a venue? What are the challenges? Does your college or university have a conference center that they market to the general public?

5. How is the financial structure of a hotel different from that of other facilities? What is a hotel's biggest source of revenue? What is a convention center's biggest revenue source?

6. Why is seasonality important to a planner when selecting a venue?

CHAPTER 4 MEETING, EXPOSITIONS, EVENT, AND CONVENTION VENUES: AN EXAMINATION OF FACILITIES USED BY MEETING AND EVENT PROFESSIONALS

157

7. What are some commonly used event space layouts? Go online and find a venue meeting-planning guide to find what different room options are available and how many guests can be held in the rooms based on the room layouts.

8. What are the benefits of using a retreat or unique venue to participants? Find one that is appealing to you. Explain what benefits this venue would bring to an event that you would plan.

9. What should be a planner's greatest concern on an outdoor event? What should a planner do about it?

10. What is the name and location of the nearest convention center near you? How much total meeting space do they have? What is one of the largest conventions or expositions that they hold each year?

ABOUT THE CHAPTER CONTRIBUTORS

Dr. Lisa Young is an associate professor in the School of Hospitality Leadership at DePaul University. She has over 20 years of experience in planning and hosting events throughout her sales and marketing career with top hospitality brands, such as Sandals Reports and Celebrity Cruises. She frequently created special events and participated in industry conventions and trade shows to introduce clients to resorts, ships, and/or destinations. Dr. Young's research interests include how special events are emerging as a strategic tool to increase revenue for resorts and how hotels utilize large citywide conferences and festivals to increase key performance metrics.

Juan Mendez has been a full-time instructor at the School of Hospitality Leadership in the Driehaus College of Business at DePaul University for the last 4 years. Prior to his current position, he was an event planner at nonprofit universities for over a decade. His primary focus was on development and fundraising events, specializing in donor recognition events.

PREVIOUS EDITION CHAPTER CONTRIBUTORS

Kathryn Hashimoto, East Carolina University
Kelly Virginia Phelan, University of Queensland
Bob Cherny, Paradise Light and Sound
Mary Jo Dolasinski, DePaul University

CHAPTER 5

EXHIBITIONS AND TRADE SHOWS

© Frank Gaertner/Shutterstock.com

Replication of a trade fair from the 1800's in Germany.

CHAPTER OBJECTIVES

- Define the different types of exhibitions
- Identify the key players of exhibition management
- Categorize the components of exhibition planning
- Identify the role of the exhibitor and the fundamentals of exhibit planning

With tens of thousands of exhibitions worldwide, the evolution of exhibitions and trade shows has turned into a thriving, ever-changing industry. This chapter provides an overview of the history and the current state of the exhibition industry and looks at it from the perspective of the show organizer and the exhibit manager.

HISTORY

Trade fairs began in biblical times and became popular in Medieval Europe and in the Middle East. These fairs served as an opportunity for craftsmen and farmers to bring their products to the center of the town or city to sell their goods as a means of survival. These were the beginnings of the "public" trade fair and featured handmade crafts, agricultural products, and other specialties. Germany and France were the first in recorded history to organize the earliest fairs. Some examples include the Leipzig Fair in 1165, the 1215 Dublin Fair, Cologne's biannual fair, beginning in 1259, and Frankfurt's Book Fair in 1445. These types of trade fairs continued through the Renaissance period until the beginning of the Industrial Revolution, when goods began to be mass produced.

Eventually, the businesses realized the value of meeting, sharing information, and providing previews of their products to potential customers. This part of the industry blossomed in the late 1800s, with many facilities being built strictly for world-class exhibitions. This buyer–seller format was termed an **exhibition** and typically took place in a large city at a facility built specifically for the exhibition. For example, the Crystal Palace in London was opened for the "Great Industrial Exhibition of All Nations," featuring 13,000 exhibits from all over the world, and attracted more than 6 million attendees. In the United States, facilities were opened in Chicago and Philadelphia to commemorate "world's fairs," which, in reality, were exhibitions highlighting the industrial advances of participating countries. In 1895, Detroit started the first joint effort to attract the exhibition business, and in 1914 the National Association of Convention Bureaus (now Destinations International—DI) was formed.

In the early and midtwentieth century, trade associations grew and saw the potential of exhibitions being held in conjunction with their annual meetings as a way to stimulate communication in the industry and expand their revenues gained from the annual meetings. The twentieth century brought exciting and trying times to the exhibition industry, with notable pauses in progress during World War I, World War II, and the Great Depression. To increase the awareness and value to exhibitions, a group of industry professionals created the National Association of Exposition Managers (which is now named the International Association of Exhibitions and Events [IAEE]) in 1978 and has members sponsoring, hosting, and organizing exhibits worldwide.

COVID-19—THE EFFECT ON EXHIBITIONS AND TRADE SHOWS

For decades, exhibitions and events around the world have been instrumental in building brands, forging partnerships, providing education, and so much more. When a pandemic crisis such as COVID-19 occurs, the effects are felt by companies in the MEEC industry, as well as brands that exhibit and attendees who attend to see the latest trends and to plan for future purchases. IAEE has continued to monitor the developments of COVID-19 and its impact on exhibitions and events.

In January 2020, The World Health Organization (WHO) published a comprehensive package of guidance documents for countries covering topics related to the management of an outbreak of new diseases. Weeks later, the Japanese Ministry of Health, Labor and Welfare informed WHO of a confirmed case of a novel coronavirus in a person who travelled to Wuhan, China. This was actually the second confirmed case detected outside of the People's Republic of China and, considering global travel patterns, additional cases in other countries were likely.

On March 11, 2020, WHO declared the COVID-19 outbreak an official pandemic. In April 2020, WHO issued guidance on considerations in adjusting public health and social measures, such as large-scale movement restrictions, commonly known as "lockdowns."

Dozens of exhibitions began cancelling in February 2020 in Asia, followed by shows in the United States as they began cancelling in mid-March 2020. Other than essential workers, many companies were forced to allow employees to work from home. In fact, many companies, including Amazon and Facebook, announced that they would allow employees to work permanently from home.

The impact on the U.S. exhibitions industry was dramatic and devastating. According to the Center for Exhibition Industry Research (CEIR), in the first quarter of 2020, 72.6% of U.S. exhibitions were forced to cancel their 2020 events. The CEIR Index tracks performance of business-to-business (B2B) exhibitions, including the number of exhibitors and attendees, the NSF (net square footage) of paid exhibit space, and organizer gross revenues decreased 15.1%. Virtually no B2B exhibitions took place in the second quarter, resulting in an historic Index drop of nearly 100%.

By comparison, the U.S. economy, as expressed by the inflation-adjusted gross domestic product (GDP), remained in positive growth territory in the first quarter, 0.3% year-over-year. In the second quarter, GDP sustained contraction, at −9.5% year-over-year, comparatively less dramatic than that suffered by the B2B exhibitions industry.

Exhibitions resumed in early May in China, the epicenter of the initial cases, with attendees returning to events, including the Hunan (China) Auto Show that drew 62,000 attendees. Countries in other parts of the world like Switzerland and the United Kingdom have considered when events can start again. In May, Germany succeeded in gaining approval from the federal government and states to allow the running of B2B exhibitions as early as June. This victory was achieved by excluding these events from the classification of mass gatherings.

The situation in the United States remains unsettled. As of the summer of 2020, the federal administration in Washington, D.C. has no national strategy for getting the virus under control, ceding those decisions to the states and local governments. Exhibitions in the United States were categorized as mass gatherings rather than controlled environments. Rules on what a mass gathering is and where exhibitions fall vary on a per state basis, making the landscape for planning for an event very uncertain and, in many instances, unviable.

Owing to varying state government restrictions in the United States on holding in-person events, organizers began adapting and demonstrating resilience by moving events that could not be held live to a digital environment. CEIR released the June pulse poll of organizers, which revealed that 79% of them cancelled one or more of their events or postponed them to 2021 or later, whereas 21% had postponed their event to a later month in 2020. Of the organizers that have postponed one or more exhibitions, 63% are going to use a hybrid model, giving participants the option of attending virtually or in-person or have a virtual event backup plan in the event the show needs to be cancelled.

One of the first industry trade shows in the United States took place on July 24, 2020, and welcomed approximately 1,000 attendees at the Orange County Convention Center, with many restrictions and safety procedures in place. The center followed the policies and procedures of the Global Biorisk Advisory Council (GBAC), a subsidiary of ISSA, the Worldwide Cleaning Industry Association because they were one of the first accredited venues to go through the newly formed program. The GBAC STAR facility accreditation program is designed for any size facility, including schools, offices, hotels, airports, assisted care facilities, stadiums, convention centers, and other public venues.

IAEE was part of the task force that was formed to assist facilities, institutions, companies, and governments in preparing for, responding to, and recovering from pandemics by being able to produce safe events. As a result of the task force work, IAEE released a white paper titled "Essential Considerations for Safely Reopening Exhibitions and Events."

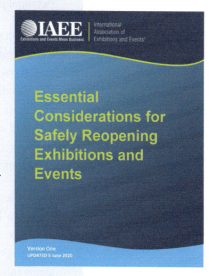

This white paper provides general information for consideration by exhibition organizers when planning for and producing an exhibition during a pandemic, and areas of content include:

- General Principles for Health & Safety Operations
- Communication, Education, & Awareness
- Exhibition & Event Operations
- Convention Centre/Venue Cleaning Prevention Measures
- Legal Considerations

IAEE partnered with GBAC to offer the GBAC-Trained Technician to the exhibitions and events industry, an individual certification available through an online course titled "Fundamentals Online Course: Cleaning & Disinfection Principles."

This course teaches professionals to prepare for, respond to, and recover from biohazards in the workplace. Participants learn infection and contamination control measures for infectious disease outbreak situations such as COVID-19.

The Go LIVE Together (GLT) Coalition was formed in Spring 2020 as an advocacy campaign leveraging the efforts of all by telling the exhibitions and business events story to U.S. legislators that exhibitions are controlled environments and can be held safely. Government restricted large gatherings, but the story to tell explained the difference between large gatherings and controlled business events. Unlike venues with fixed seating or other structures that need to be adapted to meet social distancing guidelines, the exhibitions industry can design each and every event from the outset for social distancing, and other safety measures can be deployed to reduce transmission risk consistent with guidance from Centers for Disease Control and Prevention (CDC; e.g., enhanced cleaning, provisions for personal protection equipment, reduced contact).

The Coronavirus Aid, Relief, and Economic Security (CARES) Act, the largest economic relief package in the history of the United States, was signed into law on March 27, 2020, and included major provisions to deliver economic support to travel businesses, travel workers, and their families. On June 24, 2020, the U.S. Department of Treasury released a Coronavirus Relief Fund FAQ that clarified that state and local governments may provide funds to destination marketing organizations to remarket convention facilities and the tourism industry.

With thousands of companies signing on to support GLT, funds were raised to hire a high-powered lobbying group in Washington, D.C. to advocate for moving trade shows out of the Trump Administration's Phase 5 For Re-opening the U.S. Economy for "mass gatherings" in most states (among other efforts). The Exhibitions Mean Business campaign worked with GLT, sending out timely action alerts rallying the exhibitions and events community to voice their need for relief to legislators.

Many additional resources have been created for event industry professionals to produce safe and responsible events. IAEE is a member of the Events Industry Council (EIC). EIC's mission is to serve as the global voice of the business events industry on advocacy, research, professional recognition, and standards. There are more than 30 member organizations that represent more than 103,500 individuals and 19,500 firms and properties involved in the business events industry globally. In July 2020, the EIC produced the Meeting and Event Design, Accepted Practices Guide.

This document includes several event protocol resources from various industry organizations, industry companies, and also global government entities. This information can be found on their website at www. eventscouncil.org/.

As the industry attempted to recover, the supplement provided will continue to evolve with new content.

> *The Art of the Show—An Introduction to the Study of Exposition, 5th Edition* International Association of Exhibitions and Events®, Dallas, Texas, USA

TYPES OF SHOWS AND EXHIBITIONS

TRADE SHOWS OR BUSINESS-TO-BUSINESS (B2B) SHOWS

B2B exhibitions, also known as trade fairs or trade shows, are a private event and are not open to the public. The definition of a trade fair has come so close to that of a trade show that the terms are used interchangeably. The term "trade fair" is more often used outside the United States than "trade show." Trade fairs are discussed in more detail in Chapter 15 *International Perspectives in MEEC*. Although the historical definition of exhibition is quite different from what it is today, this term has also evolved to mean a trade show or trade fair. The term **exposition** has also evolved to be similar in meaning to trade show. An association meeting may include an exposition, or expo, as the trade show segment of the association's annual gathering. In this chapter, we refer to trade shows, trade fairs, expositions, and exhibitions interchangeably.

The exhibitor is usually a manufacturer or distributor of products or services specific or complementary to those industries represented by the sponsor or organizer. Often, attendance is restricted to buyers from the industry, and business credentials are required for registration. Educational programs may or may not be a part of the exhibition program, although in recent years, educational programs have expanded as a method of attracting attendees. Sponsorship or management of the exhibition is usually either under the auspices of a trade association or has evolved to come under the sponsorship of a management company. Some exhibitions are the result of initiatives by companies and are fully intended to be profit-making ventures. Usually, exhibitions are annual events, although some occur more frequently and others less frequently. Major organizations may also have regional exhibitions that are smaller than their standard national or international event. Attendees and exhibitors may come from all over the country or world; therefore, hotel rooms and transportation may be considered in selecting the show's location.

Many organizations are considering moving to a **hosted buyer** exhibition format. At these events, attendees are prequalified as having the buying influence and/or have the authority to make a purchasing decision. These attendees have all or most of their travel expenses covered by the show management company or exhibitors/sponsors. The exhibition organizer, in return, schedules meetings between these attendees and suppliers to conduct business.

In 1988, when Ray Bloom, now the chairman of the IMEX Group, had booked space in Geneva's PalExpo for his first non-U.K. trade show, he became concerned that his target audience of incentive travel buyers might not make the cross-border trip. He turned uneasiness into positive action, however, when he decided to ask industry trade publications whether they would like to host the top buyers from their readership, paying for their travel and hotel costs. Every publication he approached (with whom he had formerly built relationships) agreed to the proposal, and suddenly there was a whole new momentum for his event and a brand-new way to make a trade show work.

What started with a handful of trade media intermediaries in Europe has grown to include a global list of more than 3,500 intermediaries for IMEX in Frankfurt and more than 25,000 intermediaries for IMEX America. Intermediaries can include hotel chains, representation and destination marketing companies, airlines, trade publications, trade associations, and more.

Not only does this three-pronged relationship create a unique experience for the hosted buyer, but the intermediaries are also able to expand their networks, develop new or strengthened business relationships, bring new value to their top clients and prospects, and explore new business opportunities and partnerships. "As a business model, once you can guarantee that the very best buyers are going to be at your show, then you have a compelling proposition for exhibitors. One follows the other," says Bloom.

Hosted buyers meeting with suppliers.

To qualify for a place on the IMEX-hosted programs, buyers must be responsible for planning, organizing, recommending, or making financial decisions for corporate meetings, conferences, seminars, exhibitions, road shows, association meetings, or incentive travel programs. In terms of reach to qualify, buyers need to place business with two "global" events in 12 months, ideally. Given the immense size of the U.S. home market, however, IMEX America also reserves a few hosted buyer places for high-level buyers who place business outside their home state but not necessarily internationally.

In return, IMEX-hosted buyers receive complimentary travel and accommodation, one-stop shopping to domestic and global destinations and suppliers, and world-class education and networking. Hosted buyers are asked to schedule up to eight appointments per day using the exclusive IMEX online scheduling tool, which gives them full freedom of choice of whom they choose to meet with. Further, these meetings can be individual appointments, open-stand presentations, or group appointments, which give hosted buyers even more freedom. This is a win-win for all, because many hosted buyers report getting a full year's worth of business done during the 3-day IMEX shows.

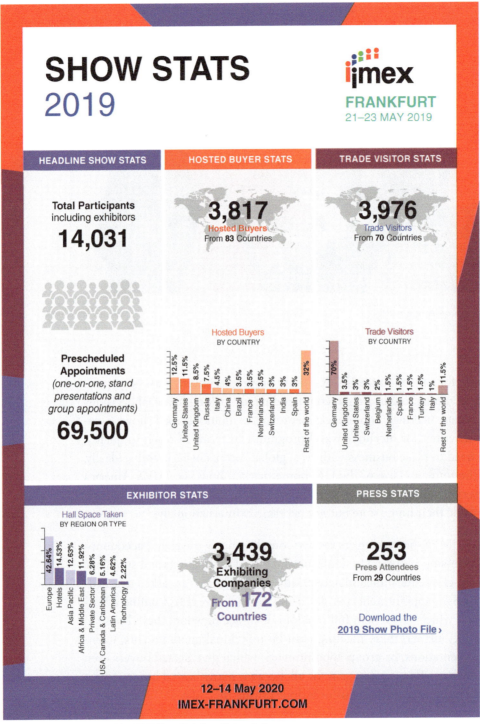

SHOW STATS
2019

imex
FRANKFURT
21–23 MAY 2019

HEADLINE SHOW STATS

Total Participants
including exhibitors
14,031

Prescheduled Appointments
(one-on-one, stand presentations and group appointments)
69,500

HOSTED BUYER STATS

3,817
Hosted Buyers
From **83** Countries

Hosted Buyers
BY COUNTRY

- Germany 12.5%
- United States 11.5%
- United Kingdom 8.5%
- Russia 7.5%
- Italy 4.5%
- China 4%
- Brazil 3.5%
- France 3.5%
- Netherlands 3.5%
- Switzerland 3%
- India 3%
- Spain 3%
- Rest of the world 32%

TRADE VISITOR STATS

3,976
Trade Visitors
From **70** Countries

Trade Visitors
BY COUNTRY

- Germany 70%
- United Kingdom 3.5%
- United States 3%
- Switzerland 3%
- Belgium 2%
- Netherlands 1.5%
- Spain 1.5%
- France 1.5%
- Turkey 1.5%
- Italy 1%
- Rest of the world 11.5%

EXHIBITOR STATS

Hall Space Taken
BY REGION OR TYPE

- Europe 42.64%
- Hotels 14.53%
- Asia Pacific 12.63%
- Africa & Middle East 11.92%
- Private Sector 6.28%
- USA, Canada & Caribbean 5.16%
- Latin America 4.62%
- Technology 2.22%

3,439
Exhibiting Companies
From **172** Countries

PRESS STATS

253
Press Attendees
From **29** Countries

Download the
2019 Show Photo File ›

12–14 May 2020
IMEX-FRANKFURT.COM

Adapted from the 2019 IMEX Frankfurt statistics. © Kendall Hunt Publishing Company

IMEX FRANKFURT, 21 to 23 May 2019 Show Stats from their website

MEETINGS, EXPOSITIONS, EVENTS, AND CONVENTIONS

A common form of marketing to potential B2B exhibitors is advertising in trade publications or targeted electronic communication. Until recently, well-established exhibitions had little trouble marketing to potential exhibitors. The exhibit halls were full, and waiting lists of exhibitors were commonplace. However, the past few years have seen many companies downsizing their exhibit space or opting to exhibit at fewer shows. Management companies have now placed a renewed focus on marketing to potential exhibitors. Exhibitions are now in competition for exhibitors, and exhibition management companies are working hard to retain existing exhibitors and attract new ones.

CONSUMER SHOW OR BUSINESS-TO-CONSUMER (B2C) SHOWS

Business-to-Consumer (**B2C) public shows,** often called consumer shows, are exhibitions that are open to the public and offer a wide variety of products for sale. This type of show is used by a consumer-based industry to bring their goods directly to their market's end user. Show management may or may not charge an admission fee, and shows open to the public are typically held on the weekend. Consumer shows are often regional in nature, with exhibitors traveling from city to city with their displays and products. They also provide excellent opportunities for companies to brand or test market new products.

Summary of Characteristics—B2B and B2C

Show Type	Attendee	Registration or Admission	Marketing	Show Days	Location
B2B Show	International and national	Preregistration, qualified buyers	Targeted Electronic Communications	Business Week (Monday–Friday)	Large markets with significant meeting space, hotel, and transportation
B2C Show	Regional or local	Ticket purchase on-site, general public	Newspapers, regional magazines, billboards, social media, and TV advertising	Weekends (Friday–Sunday)	Large or secondary markets with large parking areas

Public exhibitions also require promotion to be successful. Typically, public shows are marketed through advertisements in trade or local public media. Advertisements may offer discounts for purchasing early tickets or may promote special events or speakers that will attract the largest number of attendees. Promoting public exhibitions is a daunting task because the potential attending audience is so large that it requires a significant expense to reach them through print, radio, social media, and television advertising. Producers must be confident that their investment in promotion will result in reaching the attendance objectives. Producers must also be attentive to other events that may be occurring during the exhibition period that can affect attendance. Many B2C shows feature local and national celebrities to draw additional attention to the exhibition.

Common types of consumer shows include home and garden, travel-related, and sports-specific shows. Some examples include the following:

- *The Central Florida Home and Garden Show* hosted each spring features hundreds of exhibitors showcasing remodeling, home improvement, and outdoor gardening ideas.
- *The Kansas Sports, Boat & Travel Show* has been one of the most popular shows in the Heartland. It features exhibits in an all-terrain vehicle (ATV), hunting, fishing, camping, or the freedom of traveling in a recreation vehicle (RV). Tickets for the February event cost $7 for adults.
- *The Michigan Golf Show* hosts more than 350 exhibitors with great deals on every aspect of the golf game. This weekend show will cost adult golf lovers around $12.

CONSOLIDATION SHOWS (ALSO CALLED COMBINED OR MIXED SHOWS)

Consolidation shows are open to both industry buyers and the general public. Exhibitors are manufacturers or distributors. Hours may differ on the basis of the type of attendee, allowing trade professionals to preview the show prior to consumer buyers. Consumer electronics and the automobile industries, which have diverse audience needs, use this format to accommodate the varied industry buyers and retail consumers.

EXHIBITION MANAGEMENT: KEY PLAYERS

Regardless of the exhibition type, there are three key players that ensure that the components of the show come together to accomplish the objectives of each stakeholder—the exhibition organizer, the facility manager, and the **official service contractor (OSC)**.

EXHIBITION ORGANIZER

The **exhibition management company** (organizer) may be a trade association, a company subcontracted to the trade association, or a separate company organizing the show as a profit-making venture. The exhibition management staff member in charge of the entire exhibit area is called the exhibit manager and is responsible for all aspects of managing the show. Think of exhibition management as the "systems integrator" responsible for implementing the show, marketing it to buyers and sellers, and gathering together all the resources needed for success.

The exhibition management company must also consider the types of programs offered in addition to the event itself. Exhibition programs have evolved to encompass additional programs that serve to boost attendance. Additional programs to consider include the following:

- Educational programs
- Entertainment programs
- Availability of exhibitor demonstrations and educational/training programs
- Special sections on the show floor for emerging companies, new exhibitors, or new technologies
- Celebrity or industry-leader speakers
- Meal programs
- Continuing education units or certifications for educational programs
- Spouse and children programs
- Internet access and email centers

FACILITY MANAGER

Facilities are also needed to conduct the exhibition. Facilities range from small hotels with limited meeting space to large convention centers. Facilities also include adjacent lodging and entertainment facilities that are used by the exhibitors and visitors. The facility manager, typically known as a convention service manager or event manager, will assist the show manager in arranging the show's logistical details. Exhibition organizers consider many variables when selecting facilities, including the size of the facility, services available at the venue (telecommunications, dining, setup, and teardown times), cost, availability of service contractors, preferences of exhibitors and attendees, logistical considerations (airline services, local transportation, parking), and lodging and entertainment in the area.

Meeting and convention facilities have kept pace with the growth of the industry. From small, regional facilities to mega convention centers located in major cities, destinations have understood the benefits of attracting exhibitions and conventions to their area. Hotels and nontraditional venues are also investing in larger exhibit areas and expanding their meeting space. Many fair grounds, sports centers, and large parking lots or museums, nightclubs, and community centers are being used for expositions. These options must be considered as alternatives to convention centers and large hotels for smaller exhibitions.

OFFICIAL SERVICE CONTRACTOR

The OSC, previously referred to as a general or exhibit service contractor or decorator, provides products and services to the **exhibition management company** and the show's exhibitors. Their services are often key to the success of a show. Once selected, the OSC will provide the exhibition management and exhibitors with a list of services supplied by the contractor or other sub-contractors. Types of services the OSCs provide include the following:

- Floor plan development and design
- Aisle carpet and signage
- Custom and modular booths
- Freight handling and shipping
- Storage and warehousing
- Installation, maintenance, and dismantling labor
- Lighting, electronics, and plumbing
- Telecommunication and computer requests
- Sound and audiovisual
- Coordination with specialty contractors

Arranging and managing these services for a large show can be quite complex for the exhibition management company and exhibitors. Convention centers, management companies, and even exhibitors have become accustomed to working with various arrangements and companies. Because the service contractors operate in a very competitive environment, they have learned that customer service, fair pricing, and responsiveness to customer needs are important. This provides organizers and exhibitors with a level of comfort in relying on service contractors to take care of the problems that arise with organizing a successful show.

The OSC, in conjunction with the exhibition management company, usually develops an exhibitor service manual that encompasses all details that an exhibitor needs to plan and implement an exhibit program for the show. It also includes the forms needed to order services from the service contractors and the rules and regulations of the exhibition management company, convention center or hotel, and the local government.

Despite the controls and organization put in place by the exhibition management company and service contractors, disputes arise. When this occurs, it is important to get all parties concerned involved in achieving a successful resolution. The show manager is responsible for compliance of exhibitors, attendees, and service contractors with the show rules. See Chapter 6 for more information on service contractors.

KNOWLEDGE, SKILLS, AND ABILITIES (KSAS) OF AN EXHIBITION MANAGER

The world of event management has changed tremendously in the last few years, especially as newer technologies are emerging to make things better. Different kinds of events software help to make the event run smoothly. If an exhibition or trade show managers use technology prudently, they can gain an edge over their competitors.

One of the most important KSAs is having great interpersonal skills. An event manager must work with a team and other people to ensure the event is a success. This means that the manager should have the ability to tell and listen without any issues. It is important that the event manager understands what the client needs and then finds ways to fulfill those needs or come up with different options. Having interpersonal skills is a necessity, and managers who possess them can manage their team or communicate effectively, and it is these people who often make great event managers.

Another KSA is having a keen eye for details. It is the small things that matter. A good exhibition manager will always delve into things and look at minute details and try to get everything right. A person with a keen sense of observation will prevent small things from blowing up into big issues. Attention to detail allows them to ensure that everything is properly organized and in place for the event.

To be successful, an event manager must possess excellent leadership skills. "Leaders are born and not made." This is an old saying, and it is true for event managers as well. They will have an innate quality for leading people, and this is what shows that they were born to be an event manager. Outstanding leadership skills help guide the team toward the end goal, and that is why their events are a roaring success.

A person cannot be an effective exhibition manager without superior organizational skills. Everything in an event must be seamlessly choreographed, so that each step of the event goes off smoothly. However, although organizational skills can be learned, mastering them is difficult.

The world of exhibitions and trade shows is quite hectic and frenzied. Thus, a manager must have good time management skills. The multitasking abilities of a manager are an indication that they are tailor-made to be an event manager. They must have the ability to prioritize things at work, and this allows them to be more productive and achieve more within a limited period.

Nothing is fixed or static when organizing events. Everything is in a state of flux, and things can change at the drop of a hat. Hence, an event manager should be flexible to take these changes in stride and work accordingly. They need to be ready to face any sort of situation and be able to think on their feet. If they have always been flexible where work is concerned, they are in a position to be a successful event manager.

To be a successful event manager, one needs to do things differently. This requires innovation and creativity. If the exhibition manager is the kind of person who always thinks out of the box, they are destined to be a successful event manager. This means that problems and challenges are not an issue for them because they have an innate ability to resolve them creatively.

Event management has changed tremendously with the availability of technology, so managers need to be well-versed in using it. This will help them get things done faster and make them more efficient and productive as an event manager. Today, event managers have access to a wide range of event management software, such as event ticketing software, venue management software, and floor plan software, which makes their work easier.

CONSIDERATIONS IN MANAGING THE SHOW

LOCATION

Exhibition managers consider a number of variables when deciding on the location of the show. It is no secret that the city and venue selected to host the exhibition have a major effect on attendance. Thus, a balance must be attained between location, cost, and the ideal attendance level. Many organizations that conduct annual meetings and expositions stay in the same city year after year, and thus they can negotiate the best agreements with the local convention center and hotels and still retain the optimum attendance levels. Typically, these are association meetings that have strong educational programs and that are held at a desirable site.

However, other organizations or exhibition management companies prefer to move their exhibition from city to city each year. This strategy may help attract additional visitors. Not only is a different local attendance base able to attend inexpensively, but out-of-town visitors may be attracted by local tourist offerings as well.

Courtesy of International Association of Exhibitions and Events®

2018 bauma CONEXPO India

Organizations and exhibition management companies often survey their membership or potential attendees to assess their preferences on location. The success of convention centers in cities like Las Vegas, Chicago, Frankfurt, and Guangzhou (China) is indicative of organizations paying attention to the needs and desires of their members and potential audience. Expansion of the convention facilities in each of these cities indicates that these destinations value the revenue generated by large B2B and B2C shows.

Hotel facilities are also a factor to be considered when determining the location of the exhibition. Are the local facilities adequate for the projected attendance? Are the negotiated room rates within the budget of the typical attendee or exhibitor? What is the proximity to the exhibition site, and will local transportation need to be provided? What is the potential for labor problems to arise in the host city or at host hotels? Do the convention center and local hotels comply with government requirements?

In addition, the largest exhibitions often require substantial parking facilities and/or dedicated local ground transportation to assist visitors and exhibitors in getting from their hotels to the show site. Managers are now looking at a variety of parking and public transportation options for their ground transportation needs, such as trolleys, subways, or even bicycles, as they select meeting sites and venues. With increasing concerns about sustainability, ground transportation is becoming a key factor in the decision to select or not select a city for an event.

When determining whether dedicated ground transportation is required, consider that safety is often the key decision point. Even if hotels are within walking distance from the convention center, the conditions of the city between the hotels and the center may dictate that it is in your best interests to provide transportation. For example, in New Orleans there are many hotels within walking distance of the convention center, but in the summer, when temperature and humidity are both in the 90s, the meeting organizer is better off providing transportation. When choosing ground transportation providers, be sure to consider experience, availability, special services, insurance, condition of vehicles, labor contracts, and cost.

Housing and transportation are elements that are essential to the success of any B2B exhibition that attracts a national or international audience. A large part of any organizer's time is spent negotiating room blocks in the host city and airline and car rental discounts for attendees and exhibitors. Recently, the trend has moved toward outsourcing housing and transportation arrangements to local convention and visitor bureaus or third-party housing vendors. Regardless of how housing and transportation issues are handled, the expectation is that they will be "transparent" to the attendee or exhibitor.

Exhibition organizers must also consider the food and beverage needs and preferences of the attendees and exhibitors. Food options can range from using a concessionaire serving items such as sandwiches, pizza, drinks, and snacks to using a sophisticated caterer offering a variety of salads, entrées, and desserts. Again, food and beverage service requires much thought around budget, offerings, space to service and seat guests, and so on.

Another selection factor is the weather. Unlike B2B exhibitions to which many people come from outside the city, B2C exhibitions rely on the local and regional population for attendance. Locals and regional tourists will not venture out to a public show in the midst of a serious snowstorm or rainstorm. Thus, one episode of bad weather can drastically affect the bottom line of a show producer. The National Western Stock Show, held in Denver each January, is a good example of this. Years with extreme cold and snow greatly reduced the event's attendance. During years of unseasonably mild weather, attendance skyrockets. The solution for the National Western Stock Show has been to extend the show to a sixteen-day period, ensuring that there will be "good days" and "bad days." This has led to a more consistent overall attendance figure from year to year.

SHIPPING AND STORAGE

Once the location is chosen, the booths and other show materials need to be transported to the site. Although air freight may sometimes be used, over-the-road freight by truck is the most common method. Charges are typically per hundred pounds and are based on the distance the freight must travel.

Since an exhibitor cannot afford for the freight shipment to arrive late for an exhibition, extra time is allowed for transit. Thus, the exhibitor must arrange for temporary storage of the materials at the destination, but prior to the move-in date for the exhibition. One must also consider storage of the freight containers while the show is open. When the show closes, the whole process is reversed. Some exposition services contractors such as Global Experience Specialists (GES) or Freeman have separate divisions of their company that deal with shipping and storage.

MARKETING AND PROMOTION

Without exhibitors, the exhibition will not be successful, and, in turn, without attendees, exhibitors will not participate or return. Exhibition managers focus their attention on marketing and promotion programs that will fill the exhibition hall with both exhibitors and attendees. Regardless of the type of exhibition, attendance is the key to success. It is primarily the responsibility of the exhibition management company to target and market to the right audience. This is typically done through direct mail, advertising in trade publications, social media, the show management website, and e-marketing.

Exhibition management companies and service companies also offer additional marketing opportunities for exhibitors to consider. Exhibitors want to invest in a show because their potential customers are in attendance. Depending on their objectives for the show, exhibitors can choose to invest in several programs such as the following:

- *General Sponsorships:* These programs usually involve the company's name or logo being included or printed in the show's promotional materials or being posted in a prominent place in the exhibit hall.
- *Special Event Sponsorship:* Special events are often conducted during the exhibition, such as receptions, press conferences, or entertainment. Companies that sponsor these events have their name or logo mentioned prominently in promotional materials and throughout the event.
- *Advertising in the Show Daily:* Large shows usually have a daily newspaper available to all exhibitors and attendees each morning. It reviews the previous day's events and previews what is coming up. Exhibitors can advertise in the show daily.
- *Advertising in the Show Directory:* Almost all exhibitions provide attendees with a show directory containing information about the show and exhibitors. Advertising opportunities also exist for this show directory.
- *Promotional Items Sponsorship:* Management companies may offer sponsorship opportunities to companies for badge holders, tote bags, and other promotional items given to registered attendees. These items are given the acronym *SWAG,* which stands for *stuff we all get.*

Management companies (for B2B shows) must provide a convention program that has additional information beyond the exhibit hall to help attract visitors. Often, educational programs are provided as an incentive, or prominent industry leaders are hired to give keynote addresses that attract visitors. Contests, gifts, discount programs, and other tools to attract visitors have been commonplace. Exhibitors are also involved in helping boost attendance at shows. Usually, they are given a number of free passes to the show that can be passed on to their best customers. Exhibitors are also encouraged to sponsor or conduct special events and to promote them to their customer base.

TECHNOLOGY

Advances in technology have made managing the show, as well as exhibition itself, easier and more productive (for more information, see Chapter 12 on technology).

- Gamification is now used in exhibits to motivate and reward attendees for engaging with exhibitors and one another. Game design is a new way to participate in a fun, nontraditional way or learn about products or services of the exhibitors. Many shows offer prizes for attendees completing the game.
- The internet has had a great impact on how exhibitions are marketed to potential visitors. Most shows have sites that allow attendees to register online (B2B shows) and purchase tickets in advance (B2C shows). Attendees can view exhibitor lists, review educational programs, and even make their travel arrangements online. They can also view interactive floor plans and select educational programs and/or special events to plan their time efficiently.
- **Lead retrieval systems** are a great benefit to exhibitors. Systems are in place that enable the exhibit staff to "swipe" an attendee's card or bar-coded badge and capture all of that individual's contact information, saving many hours of entering business card data.
- R**adio frequency identification (RFID)** is now being used by convention and exhibition managers to track attendees' movement and behavior. This advanced technology is beneficial for data acquisition, lead retrieval, and reporting, but raises many issues regarding privacy and use of personal information.
- Many organizations are now introducing the option to participate at an exhibition *virtually* to save attendees travel time and costs.
- Technology is also used in promoting a company's products. Many companies now give visitors inexpensive flash drives or provide website links instead of bulky brochures. The electronic format can contain much more information and more elaborate presentations that the potential customer can view at his or her leisure.

RISK AND CRISIS MANAGEMENT

Organizing and exhibiting at a show can be a risky business. If things are not done correctly, the show can quickly become a colossal failure. Both exhibition organizers and exhibitors need to have a risk management program. A risk management plan does the following:

- Identifies all potential risks for the exhibition management and the exhibitors.
- Quantifies each risk to determine the effect it will have if it occurs.
- Provides an assessment of each risk to determine which risks to ignore, which to avoid, and which to mitigate.
- Provides risk avoidance steps to prevent the risk from occurring.
- Provides risk mitigation steps to minimize potential costs if the risk occurs.

Always keep in mind that an exhibition is a business venture that should be given every chance to succeed. Knowing how to apply risk management principles will help ensure success.

Crisis management has also become critical to exhibition organizers. A crisis is different from a risk in that it poses a critical situation that may cause danger to visitors or exhibitors. Examples of recent crises include the tsunami in Japan, the flooding in Nashville, or the volcanic ash cloud that paralyzed travel to Europe. Exhibitions that were scheduled during these incidents were either canceled or curtailed midway through the schedule. Organizing companies suffered deep losses for these events.

Every exhibition organizer should have a crisis management plan that addresses the prevention, control, and reporting of emergency situations. The plan should address the more likely types of emergencies, such as fire, foodborne illness, demonstrations, bomb threats, terrorism, and natural disasters. It should contain all procedures to be followed in the event of an emergency situation.

Consider having a crisis management team who is well versed in assessing the potential for a crisis, taking actions to prevent emergencies, and taking control should a situation occur. The crisis management team should be represented in the site selection process.

More detail on these processes can be found in Chapter 12: *Legal Issues in the MEEC Industry*.

EXHIBITOR PERSPECTIVE

If exhibitors were not successful from a business perspective, exhibitions would not exist. Exhibiting at shows is often a key part of a company's integrated marketing strategy. Companies invest a significant portion of their marketing budget into exhibitions and must see a positive return on their investment. This section of the chapter looks at the issues that face the exhibiting companies.

WHY EXHIBIT?

An exhibit booth is constructed to showcase products or services and to convey a message. It is important for a company to understand and analyze the benefits of exhibiting at a show prior to beginning the planning. Exhibiting is the only marketing medium that allows the potential buyer to experience a product or service, and therefore more money is spent on participating in exhibits than on traditional advertising or individual sales travel.

Additional reasons that companies participate in an exhibition include the following:

- Live marking
- Branding of their name in the industry
- Annual presentation of products to industry analysts
- New product rollout
- Opportunities to meet with potential and existing customers
- Opportunities to learn about customer needs
- Opportunities to meet with trade media
- Opportunities to learn about changes in industry trends and competitor products

EXHIBIT DESIGN PRINCIPLES

Although exhibit design may be limited by the rules established by the exhibit management company, the constraints of the facility, or the business culture of the host country, there are some general principles that can be discussed. These principles include selecting the right layout of the exhibit to meet your purposes; selecting the right size for your company's budget and purposes;

and making proper use of signage, lighting, and personnel. Exhibits and the space they occupy are a significant corporate investment, and attention must be given to each of these factors.

Exhibit size is a major consideration, if only because of cost. The cost of a standard booth can vary greatly on the basis of the industry, show location, and venue. The more space an exhibit occupies, the more it costs in space rental, materials, labor for setup, additional staff, and maintenance. Therefore, be sure to balance the costs with the benefits of having a larger exhibit. A larger exhibit typically means being noticed by visitors, and it creates a better impression if done well. It gives the impression that the company is in a solid financial situation and is a leader in the industry. However, the space must be used well and convey the messages that the company desires to impart to potential customers.

Companies that participate in a large number of shows will have exhibits that range in size from very small (for less important or more specialized shows) to very large (for their most important exhibitions). For example, Xerox, a company that exhibits at a variety of shows each year, has very large exhibits for information technology shows but also smaller peninsular or in-line exhibits for specialized shows or smaller, regional shows. Some companies even have two or three exhibits at the same show: a large one promoting the main theme and message they want to communicate and smaller exhibits in other halls to promote specialized products or services.

Space assignments are often based on a priority points system, in which the exhibition management company awards points based on desired space size, total dollars spent in exhibit space, number of years involved, and participation in sponsorship and advertising programs. From the organizer's perspective, this type of arrangement helps retain exhibitors and gives favor to the loyal, highest paying exhibitors.

When selecting space, the company's exhibit manager should consider the following:

- Traffic patterns within the exhibit hall
- Location of entrances
- Location of food facilities and restrooms
- Location of industry leaders
- Location of competitors

Exhibit layout is also linked to the objectives a company establishes for the exhibition. If a company's main objective is to meet as many people as possible and establish its brand in the industry, a large open exhibit is appropriate. This type of layout encourages people to enter the exhibit, and it facilitates a large amount of traffic flow. There will be a few parts of the exhibit, such as product demonstrations, that require visitors to stay for a certain period. It is the responsibility of the exhibit manager to notify the show management company if the company is hosting any celebrities, giving a loud presentation from a stage, or is hosting any special events in the booth that would draw an unusually large crowd.

Another type of layout may even purposely discourage people from entering, and parts of the exhibit may be "by invitation only." Why would a company do this? If their purpose during the show is to only meet with serious buyers or existing customers, it is important to limit visitors to only those falling in these categories. Therefore, this exhibit layout is set up to minimize traffic through the exhibit. Another strategy is to create a "closing room" within the booth space to meet with prospective buyers privately.

A standard trade show booth.

International Associations of Exhibitions and Events®

Most exhibition floor plans in the United States are based on a 10-foot by 10-foot grid or an 8-foot by 10-foot grid. This is known as the **standard booth**.

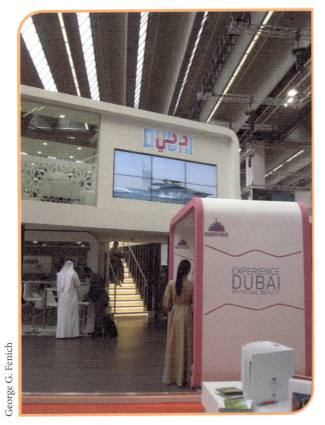

George G. Fenich

Two Story Trade Show Booth.

Typically, standard booths are set up side by side and back-to-back with an aisle running in front of the booth. Standard booths may also be used to line the inside walls of the exhibit area. Companies may combine standard booths to create an **in-line exhibit** using multiple standard booths to give greater length to the exhibit.

Island booths are created by grouping standard booths together into blocks of four, nine, or larger configurations. Island booths have aisles on four sides and can be an excellent format for medium-sized companies. **Peninsula booths** are made up of four or more standard booths back-to-back with aisles on only three sides.

Multilevel exhibits are often used by large companies to expand their exhibit space without taking up more floor space. The upper floor may be used for special purposes, such as meeting areas, private demonstration areas, or hospitality stations. Exhibitors using multilevel exhibits must be aware of each convention center's unique regulations for this type of exhibit.

As mentioned earlier, exhibitors must be aware of the location of food facilities, restrooms, entrances, and other special event areas. Each of these factors affects the traffic flow in the aisles and can either hinder or help an exhibit. Although many companies strive to be directly in front of an entrance for exposure, it may create more problems than expected because of the large amount of traffic. The exhibit staff may have difficulty discerning between serious visitors to the exhibit and those just trying to get in or out of the exhibit hall. Food service areas may create unexpected lines at mealtimes that spill into an exhibit area, essentially making that area useless for that time.

Small exhibitors face a different set of problems. If they have an in-line exhibit, their options are limited in regard to how the exhibit is organized. If they want to maximize interactions with visitors, they may "open" the exhibit by ensuring that there are no tables or other obstructions between the aisle and their staff. If, on the other hand, they want to focus interaction on serious potential customers, their approach may be to block off the inside of the exhibit as much as possible and have meeting areas within the exhibit.

Many people who pass by or through an exhibit only read the signs that the company is displaying. Signage, therefore, is important in planning the exhibit. Signs must communicate the messages that the company wants to convey clearly and quickly to visitors. Detailed itemizations of equipment specifications on signs are almost always ignored. Signs should instead focus on selling points and benefits to the user.

Lighting technology has come a long way in the past twenty years. Today, many companies use pinpoint lighting to focus visitors' attention on their products and signage. Color lighting is often used to accentuate certain parts of an exhibit to communicate a mood for the visitor. Lighting is also important for areas that will be used for discussions or meetings with potential customers.

STAFFING THE EXHIBIT

The most important part of any exhibit is the staff. A company may have an attractive, open, inviting, and informative exhibit space, but if the staff members (exhibitors) are untrained, communicate poorly, and do not dress professionally, the exhibit will communicate the wrong message to an attendee about the company and its products or services. Therefore, it is important that, whether for a large or small exhibit, the staff is well prepared and trained to promote the company and represent the product or service professionally.

Staff must be trained to "meet and greet." It is important that visitors are greeted warmly and made to feel welcome to the exhibit. Staff must also "qualify" visitors to determine whether they are potential customers or not. By asking the right questions and listening to visitors, they can easily determine whether to spend more time with them, pass them to another staff member, or politely move them through the exhibit. Time is important, especially during the busy times at a show. Qualifying visitors is an important step in focusing your staff's time.

Many companies provide product demonstrations or even elaborate productions about their products or services at the booth. This aspect must be well managed and focus the visitors' attention on the main messages the company wants to communicate.

Floor plan.

Exhibit staff must also be used wisely. All areas of the exhibit must be covered, and the right people must be in the right places. For large exhibits, greeters should be used to staff the outside of the exhibit. These people will direct visitors to the areas of their interest after initially greeting them. Technical staff may be stationed with the products displayed, being able to provide answers to the more detailed questions that a visitor may present. Corporate executives may roam the exhibit or cluster near meeting areas to enable staff to find them when needed. Often, serious customers want to be introduced to senior executives, and those executives need to be available.

Small exhibits have a special set of staff problems. Usually, the main problem they face is having enough staff to cover the busy times of the show or having too much staff for the exhibit size. Again, it is important that the right people are used to staff the exhibit and that staff assignments are planned according to the show's busiest times.

MEASURING RETURN ON INVESTMENT

In these economic times, companies must select the shows with the right buyers in attendance. Far too often, a company analyzes its **return on investment (ROI)** and cannot understand why a particular exhibition was not a success. Perhaps it exhibited at the show for years, and recently its return has dropped. This may possibly be because it has not noticed a change in the show's theme and audience; it may no longer be an appropriate venue for the company.

Calculating ROI for each show is more critical than justifying whether or not a company is participating in the right shows and using the right strategy and planning techniques. Often, however, the need to determine ROI is ignored because "we can't tell whether a sale was derived from a show lead or not" or "we don't have the data to be accurate." Avoid these excuses by determining actual expenses and revenue generated by the exhibit leads.

When calculating ROI, establish all the expenses that are a part of the show. Typical expenses include the following:

- Space rental
- Service Contractor services (electrical, computer, etc.)
- Personnel travel, including hotel and meals
- Personnel time for nonmarketing personnel
- Customer entertainment
- Preshow mailings
- Freight charges
- Photography
- Brochure printing and shipment
- Promotional items
- Training
- Postshow communications

A simple method to determine revenue from the exhibition is to set a time limit on business that was the result of leads from the show. It is easy to maintain the lead list and determine which resulted in actual business; after a certain period, however, the business may very well be the result of other activities and not participation at the show. Thus, one simple formula for measuring show ROI is to subtract expenses (listed previously) from revenue generated from the buyers at the show.

Other methods of measuring ROI include evaluating results versus objectives:

- Cost per lead (total investment divided by the total number of leads)
- Percentage of the sales goal achieved (leads gathered divided by the leads identified in objectives)
- Percentage of leads converted to sales (number of sales divided by the leads generated)

Therefore, it is important that an exhibitor continually evaluate its show program and ensure that it is exhibiting at the right shows in order to meet its potential customers. Exhibitors can use a variety of tools to measure success. Examples of these include lead retrieval data, in-booth and postevent surveys, media clips, and RFID sales tracking.

A company exhibited at a show and collected 400 qualified leads and spent a total of $75,000 to exhibit. In the next 6 months, the company tracked its sales from the show and found it generated 100 new sales totaling $175,000 in new business. The calculations of ROI based on the company's objectives for participation in the show are as follows:

- Leads generated 400 qualified leads
- Total cost to exhibit $75,000
- Sales resulting from the show 100 new sales
- Revenue resulting in show sales $175,000
- Target number of leads to gather from show 700 qualified leads
- ROI Calculations
- Revenue—Expenses $175,000 $75,000 $100,000
- Total cost per lead $75,000/400 leads $187.50 per lead
- Percentage of goal achieved = 700/400 57%
- Percentage of leads converted to sales 100/400 = 25%

The chart that follows shows a range of convention center space available to show organizers.

CONVENTION CENTER SIZE

Center	Square Feet of Exhibit Space	Meeting Rooms
McCormick Place (Chicago)	2.6 Million	173
Orange County Convention Center (Orlando, FL)	2.1 Million	74
	3.2 Million	144
Las Vegas Convention Center	566,000	83
Indiana Convention Center (Indianapolis, IN)	1 Million	21
Cox Convention Center (Oklahoma City, OK)		

TRENDS AND BEST PRACTICES

- Exhibitions have been around and will continue to be around for many decades to come. However, as times and economic conditions change, the exhibition industry must adapt in order to both survive and thrive.

- Attendance at future shows may be reduced, but it appears that the buying power of the attendee is greater. Many companies and organizations are not sending multiple representatives to shows and conferences but are sending the decision makers.
- Technology will continue to push the exhibition industry to explore new ways of conducting business. Virtual shows will advance and continue to be a supplement to, not a replacement of, the face-to-face event. The human factor is still important in business. However, there is now significant information available online, and attendees are researching companies and their products and services, prior to attending the exhibition.
- With information readily available for attendees, exhibitors will have to be creative in their booth design and activities to draw attendees into their space. The use of the booth space, décor, signage, and displays will become even more important as attendees select vendors to engage with at the show site.
- Like associations, organizations and private media firms may be forced to merge shows or events as exhibitors may only be able to participate in a limited number of B2B and B2C exhibitions during these tough economic times. This trend allows for creative business agreements, bigger and better shows, and the opportunity to be innovative in event planning.
- Some exhibitions are being downsized or even phased out and replaced with hosted buyer. This is an attractive format for both exhibition attendees and exhibitors. More and more show management organizations are seriously considering this hosted buyer format in place of the traditional trade show program.

SUMMARY

Exhibitions provide businesses with the opportunity to sell products and services to other businesses (B2B) or directly to the consumer (B2C). The exhibition organizer, the facility manager, the general contractor, and other suppliers must communicate and work together to service the show's exhibitors. Coordinating an exhibition requires the exhibition organizer to select a show venue and appropriate suppliers, to promote and market the show, to consider risks to the event, and to organize all logistics, including move in/out, shipping, and technology.

Each individual booth also requires significant coordination. Exhibitors should carefully select the exhibitions they choose to participate in and establish clear goals and objectives for each show. Planning for the exhibit operation includes staffing the booth appropriately, determining the physical layout of the space, and designing strategies to engage with booth visitors. These exhibiting opportunities are business ventures, and companies need to collect qualified leads. Following the show, the sales team should follow up with sales prospects, and the company should evaluate its ROI from each exhibition.

CASE STUDY NAMM

NATIONAL ASSOCIATION OF MUSIC MERCHANTS

SETTING THE STANDARD TO GO GREEN

For more than 30 years, the National Association of Music Merchants (NAMM) and Freeman have collaborated on The NAMM Show, the annual event that attracts more than 99,000 attendees and 1,620 exhibitors. During that time, the event has evolved to meet the diverse needs of the music merchant community.

In recent years, the community has become increasingly interested in ways to reduce the event's environmental impact. NAMM approached Freeman to look for ways that The NAMM Show could reduce waste, increase recycling, and reuse event materials to divert waste to local landfill.

Working across several departments, Freeman created a green event plan to outline the sustainability efforts that would take place before, during, and after the show. The plan, which can be adapted to events of any size in any industry, is now the standard for all Freeman clients who are interested in improving their sustainability efforts by implementing the five "R"s: rethink, reduce, reuse, recycle, repurpose.

Freeman's green event plan template included an environmental purchasing policy (e.g., preference for products containing postconsumer recycled content); a "pack in, pack out" policy for exhibitors, encouraging exhibitors to ship only the promotional materials needed and to send remainders back to their offices (instead of disposing of them on the show floor); and an online exhibitor kit, which reduced the amount of paper used and the amount of energy needed to deliver the kits.

SETTING A NEW SUSTAINABLE STANDARD

To measure the outcomes of the plan, Freeman provided NAMM with a postshow environmental performance report that included data to measure the sustainability of the event and to provide benchmarks for future events. Categories tracked included fuel used for transport and show management freight; propane usage by forklifts and boom lifts; use and reuse of carpet, graphics, and other materials (e.g., tabletop vinyl, Visqueen); and staff air travel.

"The Loft Restaurant and Lounge" is a popular networking area on the show floor that features comfortable seating areas, newsstands, charging stations, and food and beverages. In designing the area, Freeman utilized several sustainability and waste diversion best practices, including thinking through the life cycle of the materials used and potential reuse or disposal plans.

MEASURABLE, REPEATABLE SUCCESS

Since its inception, Freeman's green event plan template has guided the partnership to find innovative ways to produce an environmentally friendly event that still meets the needs of The NAMM Show's attendees and exhibitors.

Freeman innovated in many different ways, including printing interior signage on honeycomb, a direct print high-quality corrugated cardboard that is 100% recyclable. Carpet in The Loft was made of 50% recycled content and was returned to inventory for future use before eventually being recycled. Aluminum extrusions for media racks and charging stations contain 85% recycled content and are returned to inventory for future use before eventually being recycled. And mesh banners used on the exterior of the event venue are updated and can be used multiple times.

The Freeman green event plan allows clients to tap into their staff expertise and experience from other events. It is a solid foundation to build event sustainability goals now and in the future.

1. What do you think of what was done at NAMM?
2. What else could you think to do?
3. What would you NOT do?

KEYWORDS AND TERMS

For definitions, see https://insights.eventscouncil.org/Industry-glossary

B2B (Business to Business)
B2C (Business to Consumer)
exhibition
exhibition management company
exhibition organizer
exhibitor
exposition
hosted buyer
in-line booth
island booth

lead retrieval
multilevel booth
official service contractor (OSC)
peninsula booth
public show
radio frequency identification (RFID)
return on investment (ROI)
standard booth
trade fair

REVIEW AND DISCUSSION QUESTIONS

1. What is the difference between a B2B and a B2C exhibition?

2. Give some examples of services that exhibition service contractors provide to exhibitors.

3. What attributes of an exhibit layout would a company want if its major objective is branding?

4. Describe the layout of a peninsula exhibit.

5. What kinds of additional marketing opportunities do management companies typically offer?

6. Why is risk management important to an exhibition management company? To an exhibitor?

7. What factors are considered by an exhibition management company when determining the location of an exhibition?

8. What are the three phases of planning that a company exhibit manager must address?

REFERENCES

TRADE PUBLICATIONS

Art of the Show—An Introduction to the Study of Exposition, 5th edition
Convene
Exhibit Builder
Exhibitor Magazine
EXPO
Facility Manager
IdEAs
Meetings and Conventions

ABOUT THE CHAPTER CONTRIBUTOR

Marsha Flanagan, MEd is currently the vice president of Learning Experiences at the International Association of Exhibitions and Events, where she is responsible for all educational initiatives, including certification programs such as the Certified in Exhibition Management (CEM), Certified in Exhibition Management—Advanced Professional (CEM-AP), and CEM Fellow (CEM-Fellow). She is also responsible for all membership and chapter relations activities and works with various committees, executive leadership, and boards to identify member needs and design and execute member experiences. She was named one of the 25 Most Influential People in the Meetings Industry by Successful Meetings in 2017 and named to BizBash's Inaugural Top 500 in the Events Industry in 2018 and 2019.

Flanagan received her bachelor's degree from Texas Christian University and her master's degree in education from the University of Arkansas, specializing in Meeting, Tourism, and Recreation Management.

Cathy Breden, CMP, CAE, CEM, EVP, and CEO, International Association of Exhibitions and Events® and CEO of the Center for Exhibition Industry Research (CEIR).

PREVIOUS EDITION CHAPTER CONTRIBUTOR

Amanda Cecil, Ph.D, CMP, Professor, Indiana University's Department of Tourism, Conventions and Event Management

Ben McDonald, Vice President of BenchMark Learning, Inc.

CHAPTER 6

SERVICE CONTRACTORS

© pcruciatti/Shutterstock.com

SERVICE CONTACTORS ARE RESPONSIBLE FOR ERECTING TRADE SHOW BOOTHS, SIGNAGE, CARPET AND MORE.

CHAPTER OBJECTIVES

- Learn the definition of service contractors and their role in meetings, expositions, events, and conventions (MEEC)
- Understand the responsibilities of service contractors
- Become knowledgeable about the evolution of service contractors
- Understand the organization of a general services contracting company
- Learn about specialty service contractors
- Understand the relationship between service contractors and event organizers
- Discover resources in the service contractor industry
- Understand the effects of the COVID-19 on service contractors

An event producer or show manager/organizer may have all the tools at his or her fingertips to promote, sell, and execute a show or conference, but there are many pieces of knowledge, human resources, and equipment that he or she might not have. For example, while you might be a great cook, you do not make the frying pan or the spatula—you seek out experts for that. For exhibitions and events to be produced smoothly and efficiently, the producers and managers rely on professional service contractors to give the event/ show manager and the exhibitors the tools necessary to be successful. These are called **service contractors**. This chapter discusses their various roles in the process, their relationship with the organizer, and their relationship with each other.

DEFINITION OF A GENERAL SERVICES CONTRACTOR (GSC)

Depending on where you are in the world, a person who manages a trade show is known as a service contractor, show manager, event manager, or an event producer. It should also be noted that not all events and conferences have an exhibitor component. If you are going to be doing events, conferences, or trade shows outside of the United States or Canada, be sure to use your network to find the appropriate company that will help you wade through the differences of positions, cultural and business changes, language barriers, and so much more. Remember, only the United States uses feet and inches. In Canada, because much of the business is from the United States, dimensions will be given in feet and inches as well as in metric dimensions. Elsewhere in the world, be prepared for dimensions to be metric only.

SYMBOL	TO CONVERT	MULTIPLY BY	TO FIND
in	inches	25.4	millimeters
ft	feet	0.305	meters
yd	yards	0.914	meters
mi	miles	1.61	kilometers

A service contractor is anyone who provides a product or service for the exhibitor or show/event management during the actual show or conference. Service contractors can be the florist, the electrical company, the registration company, a staffing agency, and just about every service you can think of. Some service contractors are hired by the show organizers to assist with their needs, and others are hired directly by the exhibitor.

A service contractor is an outside company used by clients to provide specific products or services. Examples include exhibitor manuals, floor plans, and dance floor layouts that are generally in electronic format and may include an app. MEEC service contractors and their roles have evolved over time. Historically, they were referred to as *decorators*. This is based on their earliest primary function, which was to "decorate" the empty space of a convention center or hotel ballroom. This decorating function included pipe and drape, carpets, backdrops, booths, and furnishings.

A **general service contractor** (also called the official show contractor or exposition services contractor) is hired by the show manager to handle the general duties necessary to produce the show on-site.

> *General Service Contractor* (GSC)—An organization that provides event management and exhibitors with a wide range of services, sometimes including, but not limited to, installation and dismantling, creating and hanging signage and banners, laying carpet, **material handling**, providing booth/stand furniture, and designing and building specific client booths.

The show may have a contractor appointed by show management whose definition is:

> *Official Contractor*—An organization appointed by show management to provide services such as setup and teardown of exhibit booths and to oversee labor, drayage, and loading dock procedures. Also known as **general service contractor**.

GENERAL SERVICE CONTRACTOR RESPONSIBILITIES

Over the years, service contractors have expanded the scope of their activities to match the growing sophistication of MEEC. Today, service contractors can be, and likely are, involved in every aspect of the event from move in, to running the show, to tear down, and move out. As a result, the service contractor provides an important interface between the event organizer and other MEEC suppliers such as hotel convention services, the convention center, exhibitors, local labor, and unions. Service contractors work with the organizer to lay out trade show floors, after taking careful measurements. Service contractors are also involved before the setup of the show by sending out exhibitor kits and other information, which is typically offered electronically.

GCSs are responsible for assisting the show organizer with graphic treatments for the entrance and all signage, putting up the pipe and drape or hard wall exhibits, placing aisle carpet, and creating all the official booths, such as association centers, registration, food and beverage areas, lounges, and special areas. More importantly, the GSC offers the show organizer a valuable service by hiring and managing the labor for a particular show. They have standing contracts with unions and tradespeople and know how to hire enough labor to move a show in and out based on the requirements. It is their responsibility to move the freight in and out of the facility; manage the flow of the trucks coming in and out of the facility (creating the marshalling yard schedule and the storage of the crates and boxes during the show. This is called **material handling**. It is important to understand that material handling may be a separate services contract or included with the general services contract for the show/exhibition.

Trade show floor layout, metric measurements and Imperial systems. *Level Two, Victoria BC Conference Centre*

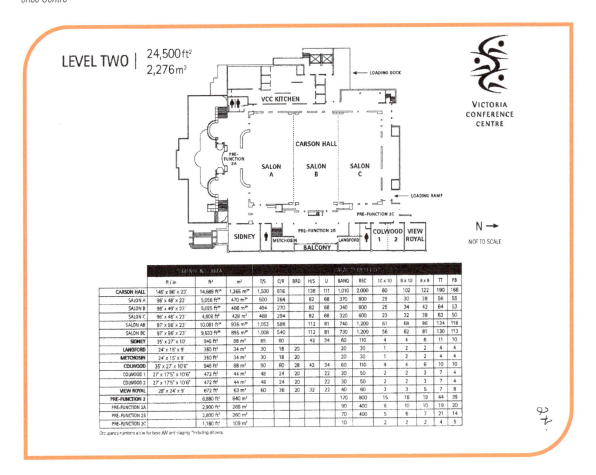

	DIMENSIONS AND AREA			CAPACITY BY USE											
	ft / in	ft²	m²	T/S	C/R	BRD	H/S	U	BANQ	REC	10 x 10	8 x 10	8 x 8	TT	PB
CARSON HALL	145' x 96' x 23'	14,689 ft²*	1,365 m²*	1,500	816		138	111	1,010	2,000	80	102	122	190	166
SALON A	96' x 48' x 23'	5,056 ft²*	470 m²*	500	264		82	68	370	600	29	30	38	56	55
SALON B	96' x 49' x 23'	5,025 ft²*	466 m²*	494	270		82	68	340	600	25	34	42	64	53
SALON C	96' x 48' x 23'	4,608 ft²	428 m²	468	294		82	68	320	600	23	32	39	63	50
SALON AB	97' x 96' x 23'	10,081 ft²*	936 m²*	1,053	588		112	81	740	1,200	61	68	86	134	118
SALON BC	97' x 96' x 23'	9,633 ft²*	895 m²*	1,008	540		112	81	730	1,200	56	62	81	130	113
SIDNEY	35' x 27' x 10'	945 ft²	88 m²	85	60		42	34	60	110	4	4	6	11	10
LANGFORD	24' x 15' x 9'	360 ft²	34 m²	30	18	20			20	30	1	2	2	4	4
METCHOSIN	24' x 15' x 9'	360 ft²	34 m²	30	18	20			20	30	1	2	2	4	4
COLWOOD	35' x 27' x 10'6"	945 ft²	88 m²	90	60	28	42	34	60	110	4	4	6	10	10
COLWOOD 1	27' x 17'5" x 10'6"	472 ft²	44 m²	48	24	20		22	30	50	2	2	3	7	4
COLWOOD 2	27' x 17'5" x 10'6"	472 ft²	44 m²	48	24	20		22	30	50	2	2	3	7	4
VIEW ROYAL	28' x 24' x 9'	672 ft²	63 m²	60	36	20	32	22	40	60	3	3	5	7	8
PRE-FUNCTION 2		6,880 ft²	640 m²						170	800	15	18	19	44	39
PRE-FUNCTION 2A		2,900 ft²	269 m²						90	400	8	10	10	19	20
PRE-FUNCTION 2B		2,800 ft²	260 m²						70	400	5	6	7	21	14
PRE-FUNCTION 2C		1,180 ft²	109 m²						10		2	2	2	4	5

Occupancy numbers allow for basic AV and staging. *Including alcoves.

Material Handling	Services performed by GSC include delivery of exhibit materials from the dock to the assigned space, removing empty crates, returning crates at the end of the event for recrating, and delivering materials back to the dock for carrier loading. It is a two-way charge, incoming and outgoing.

Material handling is the price paid for having trucks transport products. Today, the transport vehicle can be a truck or a plane, and the fee includes many aspects of the transportation service. Service contractors may charge for services like crating an exhibit in a box, using a forklift to get the box onto a small truck that takes the crate to a local warehouse or storage facility, and then putting it onto an 18-wheeler for over-the-road transport. The reverse happens at the other end, until it is unloaded at the convention center or event site. There, the service contractor will also supervise the unloading of the crate and delivery of it to the proper booth. After the crate is unpacked, the service contractor will arrange for storage of the empty crate until the show is over, and the whole process is reversed. The price for **drayage** is based on the weight, not the size of the materials or crate. The fee is based on each one hundred pounds of weight, and is thus called *hundredweight*. A "bill of lading" is completed by the shipper and delineates what the package contains, who owns it, where it is going, and any special instructions. This is the official shipping document, and authorities at checkpoints like state or provincial borders and, especially, national borders may insist on examining it.

Many GSCs have expanded into specialty areas. Thus, GSCs today may provide audiovisual and other technological equipment, security, cleaning, and more. This is done for several reasons. The first is that the GSCs are building on the relationship they have established with show organizers over years of interaction and rely on the concept of "relationship marketing." Offering a wide range of services also gives the show organizer the advantage of "one-stop shopping." By using a GSC that provides general and specialty services, the show/event organizer does not have to deal with a multitude of companies to produce the show. Also, providing an array of services allows the GSC to increase revenues and, it is hoped, profitability.

A note of caution if you are the show organizer—you must compare pricing for individual contractors versus putting all your eggs in one basket, as described earlier. What is most cost/time efficient for your event/show?

GSCs not only serve the show organizer but are also the official service contractor for exhibitors. Exhibitors can rent everything they need for their exhibit from the GSC, from a simple chair to a complete exhibit. Some GSCs will build a booth for exhibitors, store it, and ship it to other shows on behalf of the exhibitor.

The GSC adds value to his or her services by creating the **exhibitor service manual** (exhibitor services kit) along with the show organizer. The manual is electronic and often a specific application for a particular event. This manual is a compilation of all the show information, such as dates, times, rules, and regulations for both the show manager and the city. Also included are all the forms necessary for an exhibitor to have a successful show. These forms typically include order forms for carpet, furniture, utilities, setup and dismantling, and material handling. Some show organizers also include promotional opportunities to help exhibitors do preshow and on-site promotion. The service manual is most often in electronic format, included on a website, cloud technology, or as an application, allowing exhibitors to order services and products from wherever they are.

On-site, the GSC works with both the show organizer and the exhibitor to ensure a smooth move-in and move-out. He or she is often the conduit to a facility to make sure that the rules and regulations are observed. Often, he or she solves the problems of the exhibitors by finding lost freight, repairing damaged booths or crates, and cleaning the carpets and booths in the evenings.

The services provided can include the following:

To Show/Event Organizers:

- Account Management
- On-site coordination of the event
- Pipe and drape
- Entry areas
- Offices
- Registration areas
- Setup and dismantling of booths
- Planning, layout, and design of exhibit area
- Carpet
- Furniture
- Signs
- Graphics

- Backdrops
- Interface with labor and unions
- Cleaning
- Transportation services
- Material handling
- Customer Service

To Exhibitors:

- Exhibit design and construction
- Booth setup and dismantling
- Carpet
- Furniture and accessories
- Signs/signage
- Interface with labor and unions
- Rigging
- Material handling
- Exhibitor kit
- Customs brokerage when dealing internationally

Signage is an important service.

LABOR/TRADE UNIONS

Exhibition service managers as well as show/event organizers will make use of tradespeople in the community to help set up and tear down the show. Many of these tradespeople will be members of a trade union. An advantage of using members of a trade union is that the event organizer is assured that the worker has the requisite knowledge and skill to do the job assigned. A disadvantage of using trade union members is that they are restricted to doing only work of their *trade,* there are rigid regulations regarding the hours they can work, and the cost of using them is much higher than in the case of workers who are not members of a trade union.

Everyone involved in a show should be aware of the local laws and policies in the city, state/province, country in which the show/event is being held in regard to the use of unionized personnel. The primary issue is whether the community is located in a "right to work" state/province. In these states/provinces, an individual working in a specific trade is *not* required to join the trade union representing that skill. Thus, show/event organizers and participants are free to hire whom they please, regardless of whether they are union members. However, if the community is not in a right-to-work state/province, then people working in the trades such as electricians, plumbers, riggers, and porters must belong to the appropriate union. In these communities, there can be significant repercussions if the proper union members are not used. In some locales, an exhibitor cannot even carry their own materials from their automobile to the trade show booth: they must use a member of the porters' union. Prior to signing a contract, the event organizer should find out when union contracts are due for negotiations and learn whether past negotiations have been friendly or not. If a strike happened, how long before it was resolved? And should a strike be in process, who manages the work that must be done to ensure the conference/trade show setup and/or teardown is not jeopardized.

In the United States, the Taft–Hartley Act of 1947, also called the Labor Management Relations Act, gives states the right to enact Right to Work laws. This act restricts unions by prohibiting unfair labor practices, listing the rights of employers and employees who are union members, etc.

THE CASE OF EXHIBITING IN A UNIONIZED CITY

Service contractors can play a pivotal role in dealing with unionized labor. This is especially problematic because (1) the unions and rules vary throughout the United States and other countries, and (2) local labor is essential for putting together an event or trade show. The following portrays one exhibitor's interaction with unionized labor in a city in the northeastern United States. The exhibit, in its crate, was transported to the convention center in a tractor-trailer, and, according to local rules, the trailer had to be driven by a member of the Teamsters Union. On arrival at the convention center, the driver opened the back of the trailer but could do no more to facilitate removal of the crate. That required a forklift, and the forklift is considered a piece of heavy equipment, not a truck, and thus had to be operated by a member of the Heavy Equipment Operators Union. So they waited for the forklift operator, who then moved the crate to the exhibit booth and placed it on the ground. At that point, the exhibitor was eager to get set up but could do nothing until a member of the Carpenters Union arrived to take the nails out of the crate: Wood and nails are a job for a union carpenter. The crate was opened, but the exhibitor was restricted from doing anything himself that a union member should do. Thus, he waited for a member of the Porters Union to come to take the exhibit contents out of the crate. That was followed by a string of different union members who each did a separate but distinct job and would not infringe on the responsibilities or activities of a different union. So the exhibit frame that was made from pipes had to be assembled by someone from the Plumbers Union: only plumbers handle pipes. The products and cloth were assembled and laid out by a member of the Stagehands Union: after all, an exhibit is part of a "show." The sign over the booth required someone from the Heavy Equipment Operators Union to drive a bucket lift, while a member of the Riggers Union occupied the bucket to "rig" the sign. The exhibitor could not even plug his computer into the electrical outlet provided by show management—that had to be done by a member of the Electricians Union. The internet and Wi-Fi had to be set up by a member of the Communications Workers Union, and the flowers had to be "arranged" by a member of the Agricultural Union. Of course, the cleaning people, security, and other service personnel had to be members of the appropriate union. Furthermore, part of a supervisor's pay in each of these unions had to be paid by the exhibitor in proportion to the amount of time that union spent at his booth. Further complicating matters is that, unless special fees are paid, there can be significant time lapses between when one union member finishes one particular job and when the next arrives. And—oh yes—if any union rule is violated or the exhibitor tries to do something himself, all the unions will boycott that booth and refuse to work. Obviously, a service contractor who is knowledgeable about local union rules and has established an ongoing relationship with local labor can be worth his or her weight in gold to an exhibitor or show organizer.

However, unions do serve several laudable purposes. They represent a class of workers such as electricians when negotiating with management over pay scales and working conditions. Thus, they carry more clout than any single worker could possibly have. Unions also set very specific guidelines regarding termination of an employee and will provide a union member with legal counsel if necessary. In addition, they help ensure that working conditions are safe and comfortable. Lastly, they work with government agencies to help establish guidelines for the construction trades.

EVOLUTION OF SERVICE CONTRACTORS

Today, GSCs are evolving and changing to meet the needs of the client and the environment. One of the major changes has been increasing the scope of their work to center on meeting the needs of exhibitors. As is the case with the organizers of events, GSCs have come to the conclusion that it is the exhibitors who are the driving force of the trade show segment of MEEC. Furthermore, they have come to understand that exhibitors have more trade shows and vendors than ever to choose from, along with increased numbers of marketing channels through which to promote and distribute their products. Thus, both GSCs and show/event organizers are directing their attention to the needs of the exhibitor. Exhibitors are reacting to this effort by getting much more specific about their wants and needs, and they are also becoming much more discreet and selective when choosing a service contractor. Exhibitors spend huge amounts of money to participate in a trade show and thus want the best return on investment (ROI) they can get. In today's economic environment, exhibiting companies have to justify the expense of a trade show and are looking to service contractors to help with that justification and to show the value added by participating in a face-to-face show.

In the long run, service contractors must deliver quality service and products to the user, whether it is the organizer or the exhibitor. Otherwise, both constituents will seek other marketing avenues and strategies, with organizers left out in the cold. The status quo does not hold true any longer, and some companies have decided to forego trade shows in which they have participated for years. The COMDEX Show faced exactly this type of problem and has resurfaced as the Interop Show. In lieu of exhibiting at an alternative trade show, some companies are developing their own private trade shows targeted to specific markets or customers. Many are designing social media campaigns that eliminate some of the need to be face-to-face with customers.

Still another change for GSCs is that many facilities are now offering to do in-house what used to be the exclusive domain of GSCs. For example, many convention centers are now offering to provide utilities like electricity, water, steam, and gas and may no longer allow GSCs to do this. These services are exclusive to the venue, and the show organizer must use the in-house services. Venues are also offering services like cleaning, security, audiovisual, internet, and room setups. This approach is cutting into the business and revenues of service contractors. The venues are creating exclusivity of product versus suggested contractors, leaving the show/event organizer with no choice of service contractor for specific services as listed earlier.

The advent of **exhibitor-appointed contractors** (EACs), discussed later in this chapter, has cannibalized the business of the GSC. This trend began in the mid-1980s, when the U.S. courts ruled that service contractors could not have the exclusive right to control and negotiate with organized labor. Thus, an EAC from out of the area had the legal right to compete with GSCs and set up a booth for an exhibitor. EACs are a subset of GSCs that, rather than work from one city or location, work for the exhibiting company and travel throughout the country setting up and dismantling their booths. Their success is based on the long-term relationship they have built with the client company and is known as "relationship marketing." Because the EAC works for the same company over many trade shows and events, the EAC is more knowledgeable about the client company's needs and can provide better service than the broader GSC.

This competition between GSCs and EACs has encouraged the GSCs to provide more specialized, streamlined, and efficient service to exhibiting companies. For example, one GSC now provides exhibiting companies with the same service representative before the trade show opens, during the show, and after the show for reconciliation and billing. This lets the customer deal with one source for ordering of all services and products, a one-stop service desk, and a single master bill representing every product and service used. This is analogous to an individual who gets a different credit card receipt for each transaction but a single, cumulative bill at the end of the month. Several service contractors have special programs for their best customers that can provide a special customer service representative who is available twenty-four hours a day, 7 days a week, and a private service center that has a lounge, Wi-Fi, phone, copy services, and so forth. Sales representatives of service contractors are equipped with cell phones, tablets, and so on so that they can go to a booth and provide on-the-spot service. Business transactions happen in real time, on the spot. A client uses their own tablet or smartphone and transacts most business requests, ascertains freight status, and prints forms like order forms, invoice summaries, and shipping labels.

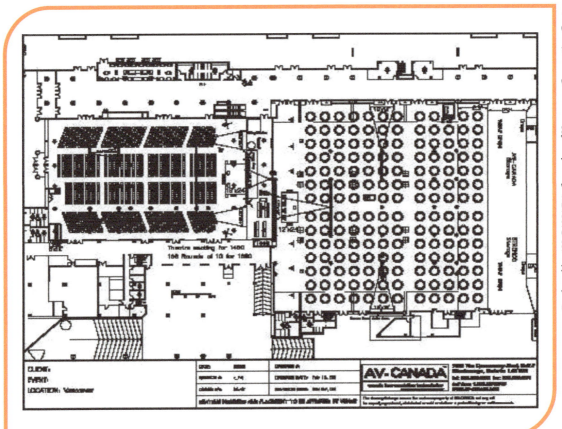

Produced by AV-CANADA: floor plan of Vancouver Convention Centre

Floor plan for Vancouver Convention Center.

GSCs are also expanding into the area of event marketing. This too is based on the desire by clients to do most of their business with someone or some company they know and trust: relationship marketing. The show/event organizer or association host may sponsor events, but corporations put on most events. As a result, many exhibitors are now responsible for corporate events outside the traditional trade show floor. The GSCs, having developed a long-term relationship with the exhibitor, are now developing corporate events programs, multievent exhibit programs, private trade shows, new product introductions, hospitality events for clients, multicity touring exhibitions, and more nontraditional promotional materials.

Technology has changed the way GSCs do business. The computer, tablet, or smartphone has improved many of the traditional tasks and activities such as updating floor plans, tracking freight, and monitoring small package deliveries. For example, as little as 15 years ago, floor plans had to be drawn by hand using drafting instruments. A simple booth change, because it affects the entire show layout, could take a week or more to redraft. Now, thanks to computer technology, changes are almost instantaneous. GSCs have proprietary software that includes floor plans and artists' drawings for every major convention facility in the United States, Canada, and beyond. Clients can now take a "virtual tour," often using 3D technology, through the venue and make floor plan changes immediately.

GSCs are also using technology to help with material handling. Technology allows tracking of all sizes of shipments to be faster and more accurate. Everything is online or in a mobile app so that when a truck enters or leaves a facility, it is in the computer system, and freight managers can go to the central computer to check the status of not only the vehicle but also its contents. Global positioning systems on many trucks allow satellite tracking of their location. This technological monitoring happens on the trade show floor, too. An exhibitor can contact the GSC and know which crates are still on the truck and which have been delivered to the booth. Small packages such as brochures can be tracked in the same fashion. Technology uses GPS tracking devices that the exhibitor has placed in each package or container to track their location, in real time, from a smartphone.

Still another use of technology embraced by GSCs is website development. They produce websites for show/event organizers that include interactive floor plans, exhibitor show information, booth reservation services, as well as personal itineraries for show attendees, using social media and mobile applications

ORGANIZATION OF A GENERAL SERVICES CONTRACTING COMPANY

Service contractors are businesses and, like most businesses, are organized into functional areas. This means that there are different departments grouped by a common activity or function that support the mission of the company. The department that controls and directs the company can be called "administration" and may include the general manager or chief executive officer, marketing, assistants, receptionists, and the like. Some of the other departments or divisions are as follows:

- *Sales:* These are typically divided or broken up into national sales and local sales or special events. Some companies also have a separate "exhibitor sales" department that takes over from national sales in dealing with exhibitors. Exhibitor sales will provide each exhibitor with an inventory of the supplies available and the cost of each item. Exhibitor sales also work to encourage exhibitors to "upgrade" ("upsell") from standard to superior quality products at a higher price. Exhibitor sales typically will have an office and full-time presence at the trade show to facilitate interaction between production and exhibitors and sell additional products and services on the trade show floor.

- *Logistics:* This handles planning, scheduling, shipping, labor relations, site inspection with show/event organizer, and preparation. This is the department that determines the flow and delivery of booth materials—with booths in the center of the hall being delivered before booths by the doors so that access is not blocked. This department may also work with the exhibit facility and lay out all the differently sized booths, aisles, food service areas, registration, and so on. Today, a multitude of software exists, and many companies have designed their own proprietary software to design exhibit floors and conference stages.
- *Material Handling and Warehousing:* This includes transportation of materials, booths, exhibits, and so on, along with their temporary storage in the host city. Material handling may include air transport, over-the-road tractor-trailers, and local transportation.
- *Event Technology:* This includes technology, special effects, reports, and so on. This department oversees the planning and subsequent installation of the output of the production department.
- *Event Services:* These include exhibitor kits, on-site coordination, and registration. The exhibitor kit tells exhibitors everything they need to know about the facility, capacities, rules, regulations, labor, and move-in and move-out times, along with the array of services provided by the service contractor. With the use of technology, this is largely handled online and saved electronically so changes can be made quickly and everyone who needs it can have access.
- *Production:* This comprises woodworking, props, backdrops, signs, electrical, lighting, metal work, and so on. For example, at Freeman in New Orleans, clients regularly request backdrops that look like the French Quarter or a swamp. They are produced on large boards like those used in theater productions.
- *Accounting and Finance:* This includes accounts receivable, accounts payable, payroll, and financial analysis.

Two of the largest U.S. GSCs are Freeman Companies and GES (Global Experience Specialists). You can learn more about various GSC companies by using a search engine and viewing their websites. The following are some examples:

The Freeman Companies are headquartered in Dallas, Texas, and have offices in the United States, Canada, the United Kingdom, China, and Singapore. Established in 1927, they are a full-service contractor for expositions, conventions, special events, and corporate meetings. The company is privately held and owned by the Freeman family and company employees.

GES is headquartered in Las Vegas and has offices in 60 countries worldwide, including the United States, Canada, and the United Kingdom. GES is a wholly owned subsidiary of Viad Corp.

The Stronco Group of Companies is an all-Canadian, privately owned company established in 1952, specializing in trade shows, conventions, special performances, and sporting events.

AV-Canada is a Canadian company specializing in digital and virtual events, audiovisual, lighting, and staging. A-V America is a subsidiary of AV-Canada. Both head offices are in Toronto, Ontario, Canada, and bring their expertise across Canada and the United States.

TYPES OF SERVICE CONTRACTORS

To this point in the chapter, discussion has been about GSCs and how they interact with the individual exhibitor and the show/event manager. Now, the focus will broaden to all the potential service contractors that help to create a successful event.

SPECIALTY SERVICE CONTRACTORS

Specialty service contractors deal with a specific area of show/event production, whereas the GSC tends to be broad and generic. Specialty service contractors can either be official contractors (appointed by show/event management) or EACs (see further on). They handle all the services to complete the production, whether it is a special event or trade show or conference or general meeting, including:

- *Audiovisual (Technology):* Services and supplies to enhance the exhibit/conference/special event through audiovisual technologies, possibly before and after the exhibit/conference/special event, including digital and virtual exhibits and conferences.

- *Business Services:* Copying, printing, faxing, and other business services.
- *Catering:* Food and beverage for show/event organizers at the conference/special event and for individual exhibitors who may want to include food and beverage in their booth or at a private client event.
- *Cleaning Services:* Cleaning of public areas of the conference/event, especially carpet along with booths, offices, and nonpublic areas.
- *Communications:* Providing the tablets, cell phones, and wired and wireless services.
- *Computers:* Rental of computers monitors and printers.
- *Consulting:* This can include pre-event planning, coordination, facilitation, layout and design of the trade show/event/conference, and booth design. Often called third-party planners or independent consultants.
- *Décor:* Basic décor company that can enhance staging, general décor theme. Can also provide florals and entertainment.
- *Electrical:* Brings electrical power to the exhibits and any other areas where power may be required.
- *Entertainment Agency:* Provides entertainment and acts as liaison between entertainer and show/event organizer.
- *Floral:* Rental of plants, flowers, and props.
- *Freight:* Shipping of exhibit materials from the company to the show and back. There are various kinds of shippers—common carrier, van lines, and airfreight.
- *Furniture:* Rental of furniture for exhibits, often fancier than in your home!
- *Internet Access and Telecommunications Equipment:* Rental of equipment and lines on the show floor or any other area required for the event/conference, including Wi-Fi and wired internet access, ensuring enough bandwidth as required. Also included are cell phones, telephones, and walkie-talkies.
- *Labor Planning and Supervision:* Expertise on local rules and regulations regarding what tradespeople to work with, union requirements, and supervision of workers on-site.
- *Lighting:* Design, rental, and lighting operators. Could be included with audiovisual supplier.
- *Material Handling:* This includes over-the-road transportation of materials for the show, transfers, and delivery of materials from a local warehouse or depot to the show site, airfreight, and returns.
- *Moderator:* A specialist who manages the dialogue between virtual attendees, on-site attendees, and the presenter. Can be a part of the audiovisual team.

- *Producer:* A specialist who acts as a producer for the event, ensuring all production is designed and delivered without any errors or omissions. Can be a part of the audiovisual team.
- *Social Media Expert:* A team or a person who is adept at social media to enhance the reach of the exhibits/conference or special event before, during, and after.
- *Staffing:* Temporary hiring of exhibit personnel, demonstration personnel, or registration.
- *Utilities:* Plumbing, air, gas, steam, electricity, and water for technical exhibits.
- *Photography:* For show/event organizers to provide publicity and to individual exhibitors.
- *Postal and Package Services:* For both organizers and exhibitors.
- *Registration Company:* A company outsourced to manage the entire registration process for an event/conference or trade show. They manage all registration processes, including database, payment, badges, and often on-site staffing.
- *Security:* Security to watch the booth during closed hours and to control the entrances when the show is open or general security for an event/conference.
- *Speaker Bureaus:* Work with show/event organizers to find ideal keynote speakers, entertainers, performers, etc. to open/close conference.
- *Translators:* Work with the show/event organizers to do simultaneous translation of speeches and presentations. They also work with exhibitors to provide communication between sales representatives and foreign attendees.

THE TRANSLATOR WHO KNEW TOO MUCH

A small American company decided that it wanted to exhibit at a trade show in Europe. One of the things it determined was that none of the sales managers who were going to staff their booth spoke any language except English. So, it was decided that a translator fluent in Spanish, Italian, and German would be hired. The translator worked so well that she was hired to provide services at another trade show a year later. At this second show, attendees asked many of the same questions asked at the first trade show. Since the questions were repetitive, the translator had learned the answers and would simply answer the attendee without translating and asking the sales managers. Response at this show was low, in spite of high attendance, and reactions to the products being displayed at the booth were poor. When the company manager did a postshow assessment, he uncovered the reason. The attendees got the impression that since a mere translator knew about the products, they must be very simplistic and not cutting edge. So, at all future trade shows, the translator was told to always translate, ask the sales managers, and never answer on her own!

Besides the standard needs listed earlier, each show has its own needs. A show in the food and beverage industry will have a contractor for ice and cold storage, whereas a show in the automotive industry might have a contractor who cleans cars.

Depending on the GSC, and what other suppliers are required, there may be times when all suppliers can be included in one-stop shopping with the GSC. Some examples of one-stop shopping are McCormick Place, Chicago, and the Metropolitan Toronto Convention Centre, Toronto. Many hotel chains, such as Marriott, also provide one-stop shopping (it is best to check with the specific hotel within the chain).

EXHIBITOR-APPOINTED SERVICE CONTRACTORS

As companies do more and more shows, their exhibits become more involved, and they often want one service supplier working with them throughout the year. Or they have a favorite vendor whom they have worked with in a city where they do many shows. This is particularly true with regard to the installation and dismantling of the exhibit. Most times, show/event organizers will allow this, assuming that a company meets the qualifications for insurance and licensing. This company is called an **exhibitor-appointed contractor (EAC)**. As an EAC, they perform the same duties as a specialty contractor but only for that exhibitor, not the show manager.

Some services may be provided only by the official service contractor and are called **exclusive services**. This decision is left up to the show/event manager, who makes that decision on the basis of the needs of the show and the rules and regulations of the facility or to ensure the smooth move-in and teardown of the show. Can you imagine what would happen if every freight company and installation company tried to move its exhibitors' freight in all at once? It would be chaos! So material handling (drayage) is a service that is often handled as an exclusive. Many facilities have very specific guidelines regarding the use of EACs. In some cases, the exhibitor must apply to the facility to use one.

Source: George G. Fenich

This simple example of rigging was used to attract attention to a booth selling chairs.

RELATIONSHIP BETWEEN CONTRACTORS AND EVENT ORGANIZERS

One of the first actions that show or event organizers take when developing an event is to hire the GSC. This partnership develops as the show develops. GSCs will often recommend cities where a show should be held, the times of the year, and the facilities that fit the event. It is important to hire this company early on.

The process for hiring service contractors is through an **RFP (request for proposal)**. The show organizer creates a list of questions and specifications for each show. Other areas of concern include knowledge of the industry, knowledge of the facility, other shows being handled in the same industry, size of the organization, and budget. On deciding which service contractor to use, acceptance of the proposed services by the organizer, and acceptance of payment amounts by the service contractor, a legal contract is entered into. This is a binding agreement. If either party fails to deliver on the terms of the contract, the case can be litigated.

As the show is developed, GSCs watch closely and may suggest how marketing themes and association logos can be used in entrance treatments and signage so that when a show comes alive, it looks and feels the way the show organizer wants it. Color schemes, visual treatments, and types of materials may all be contracted to, or suggested by, the GSC.

Specialty service contractors work with show organizers to help exhibitors save time and money. Reviewing the history of a show can tell a service contractor what types of furniture and floral and electrical needs the exhibitors have used. This permits the specialty contractors to offer money and time-saving tips to the show organizer and pass those savings on to exhibitors. All of this creates a feeling of goodwill among exhibitors who will continue to exhibit at the show.

After a time, the service contractor might come to know the show as well as the show organizer. This can be added value to the show organizer because as staff changes occur, the service contractor becomes a living historian of the show and its particular nuances.

RESOURCES IN THE SERVICE CONTRACTOR INDUSTRY

There are several national and international associations for individuals and companies in the service contractor industry. They can help the organizer find a services contractor in the city where the exhibit/conference/special event is taking place. To learn more about each association's mission, ethical principles, member responsibilities, contact information, and so on, go to their individual websites using a search engine. The following is a partial listing:

CEMA: Corporate Event Marketing Association. It advances strategic event marketing and marketing communications for senior-level event marketers and industry professionals.

HCEA: Healthcare Convention and Exhibitors Association. This is a trade association representing organizations united by a common desire to increase the effectiveness and quality of healthcare conventions and exhibitions as an educational and marketing medium.

ESCA: Exhibition Services & Contractors Association. This is an organization serving general and specialty contractors.

EDPA: Exhibit Designers & Producers Association. This is an organization serving companies engaged in the design, manufacture, transport, installation, and service of displays and exhibits primarily for the trade show industry.

EACA: Exhibitor-Appointed Contractors Association. This represents EACs and other individual show-floor professionals that provide exhibit services on the trade show floor.

IAEE: International Association of Exhibits and Events. This is an association of show organizers and the people who work for service contractors.

CAEM: Canadian Association of Exposition Management. This is a Canadian association of show organizers and the people who work for service contractors.

NACS: National Association of Consumer Shows. This is an association of public (consumer) show organizers and the suppliers who support them.

EEAA: Exhibition and Event Association of Australasia This is the peak industry association for those in the business of trade and consumer expos and events.

CEIR: Center for Exhibition Industry Research.

The example of ESCA indicates the professionalism that the various associations strive for. When looking for a show services contractor (or any contractor), be sure to check out the associations they belong to.

SO, HOW DOES IT ALL WORK?

Look at the organizational chart that follows (Figure 6-1), and you can see how the GSC could interact with the show/event organizer, the facility, the exhibitors, and the other contractors. Remember, exhibitions are like small cities, and the show organizer must provide everything a city does—from safety (security and registration) to a place to work (think of the exhibits as offices), electricity and water, and transportation (shuttle buses). It must be done in a very short period, sometimes less than a week. Communication between everyone always must be functioning properly, and often it is the GSC who provides that conduit. The coordination of all the contractors likely is the responsibility of the GSC, who is acting as the right hand of the show organizer.

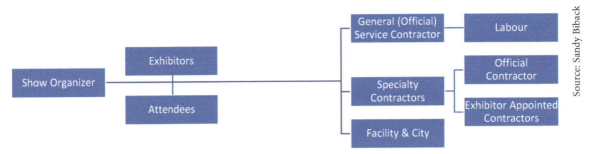

FIGURE 6-1
Relationship between show organizer and service contractors

BEST PRACTICES

Sustainability and corporate social responsibility (CSR) continue to be important when deciding on a venue. Planners are becoming more aware of their suppliers' CSR programs and the implication of their supply chains as it relates to what planners can do to create more sustainable programs. Venues play a lead role in this by designing specific policies and procedures to ensure end users and service contractors meet requirements. Metropolitan Toronto Convention Centre is an excellent example of being able to design a carbon-neutral event with clients. Contractors can play a key role in the sustainability of exhibits/conferences/special events by reducing the carbon footprint; embracing the use of recyclable materials; using products that are locally produced; working with the venues to meet the venue's guidelines with respect to low lighting usage when full lighting is not required; and working with the venues to ensure waste management policies are met. Additionally, planners, venues, and service contractors can make a conscious effort to understand the supply chain and ensure that migrant workers are paid and treated humanely and that human slavery is not used throughout the supply chain. Service contractors will develop relationships with organizers, planners, and sponsors and help produce meetings and events in multiple locations that meet CSR mandates.

As technology improves, the hybrid meeting will take more focus when a hybrid helps to meet the objectives of the exhibit/conference/special event. To that end, there will be more specialized needs from the audiovisual and/or technical service contractors, as well as bandwidth requirements. A producer and a moderator will be specialized consultants to ensure the meeting is successful and that whether an attendee is online, face-to-face, or views the event later, the attendee will be engaged. Holograms are becoming mainstream and enable exhibitors to give participants a better view of their goods and services.

Robots will do more of the heavy lifting and moving around the floor, enticing participants to go to specific booths. Drones are already making their appearance, and soon there will be rules, regulations, and policies put into place as their use becomes more prevalent. Participants can become their own robot and attend shows the participant can control, allowing them to interact with exhibitors.

With the COVID-19 pandemic, much of the conference/events/trade show world has moved to virtual, necessitating a greater involvement of technology.

CORONAVIRUS (COVID-19)—THE EFFECT ON SERVICE CONTRACTORS

CAPACITY CHART – PHYSICALLY DISTANCED
Mass Gatherings 50 and under

VICTORIA CONFERENCE CENTRE CAPACITY BY SET-UP*	ft / in	ft²	Theatre	Classroom	Office	Hollow Sq	U-Shape	TT	Booth
LECTURE THEATRE		3,700 ft²	50						
THEATRE STAGE	24' x 24'	576 ft²							
SAANICH	61' x 35' x 9'5"	2,135 ft²	21	21		14	12		
SAANICH 1	35' x 18' x 9'5"	630 ft²	12	12		8	8		
SOOKE	18' x 13' x 9'5"	234 ft²			1				
OAK BAY	50' x 37' x 9'5"	1,850 ft²	15	15		12	10		
ESQUIMALT	38' x 28' x 9'5"	1,064 ft²	8	9		8	6		
VICTORIA	24' x 16' x 9'5"	384 ft²			4				
PRE-FUNCTION 1	Ceiling ht. 9'10"	6,500 ft²						15	
PRE-FUNCTION 2		6,880 ft²						16	
VIDEOCONFERENCE	17' x 11' x 8'	187 ft²			1				
UPPER PAVILION	59' x 65'	3,875 ft²	Available upon request						
LOWER PAVILION	69' x 65'	3,741 ft²	Available upon request						
WEST COAST ROOM	Ceiling ht. 9'	980 ft²			4				
CARSON HALL	145' x 96' x 23'	14,689 ft²*	50	50		50	50		40
SALON A	96' x 48' x 23'	5,056 ft²*	40	40		26	23	Available upon request	
SALON B	96' x 49' x 23'	5,025 ft²*	40	40		26	23	Available upon request	
SALON C	96' x 48' x 23'	4,608 ft²	40	40		26	23	Available upon request	
SALON AB	97' x 96' x 23'	10,081 ft²*	50	50		40	30	Available upon request	
SALON BC	97' x 96' x 23'	9,633 ft²*	50	50		40	30	Available upon request	
SIDNEY	35' x 27' x 10'	945 ft²	8	8		6	7		
LANGFORD	24' x 15' x 9'	360 ft²			4				
METCHOSIN	24' x 15' x 9'	360 ft²			4				
COLWOOD	35' x 27' x 10'6"	945 ft²	8	8		6	7		
VIEW ROYAL	28' x 24' x 9'	672 ft²			4				

CRYSTAL GARDEN CAPACITY BY SET-UP*	ft²	Capacity	10 x 10	Tabletops
CRYSTAL GARDEN	25,000 ft²	50	42	Available upon request
UPPER LEVEL	16,196 ft²	50	Available upon request	Available upon request
LOWER LEVEL	7,632 ft²	50	Available upon request	Available upon request

* CAPACITIES SET BASED ON 6ft/2M PHYSICAL DISTANCE.
* ALL CAPACITIES ARE SUBJECT TO CHANGE.
* AV REQUIREMENTS MAY REDUCE CAPACITY, PLEASE SPEAK WITH YOUR EVENT MANAGER
* ALL EVENTS MUST OPERATE WITHIN THE ORDER OF THE PROVINCIAL HEALTH OFFICER – MASS GATHERING EVENTS

Produced by AV-CANADA: floor plan of Vancouver Convention Centre

Victoria Conference Centre, Victoria BC capacities before COVID-19 Title: Victoria Conference Centre, Victoria BC capacities, allowing 50 people mass gatherings, Post COVID-19

At the time of writing, the entire industry is reeling and trying to adapt to must-do changes in the industry. This certainly affects the planner, the venue, the trade show exhibitors, the speakers, and all service contractors. As a result of COVID-19, everyone has had to adapt immediately, often cancelling or postponing their event or shifting them online or hybrid. The biggest evolvement has been to virtual trade shows/events/conferences. At this time, venues are not being utilized, general show services contractors are no longer needed to lay down carpet, provide food and beverage, etc. In the world of virtual trade shows, technology contractors are most required. The planner, instead of seeking out the perfect venue, now seeks out the perfect technology contractor who can provide all the elements for a virtual event and trade show.

What does the future hold? At this writing, no one really knows. Will we ever return to the bricks and mortar venue? What will happen to all service contractors? Will hybrid events stay more virtual than face-to-face? How will each venue adapt to social distancing in their meeting space? Will attendees feel comfortable to be there in person? How will this impact travel? And hotels?

What we do know is that all service contractors will have to adhere to more stringent cleanliness and social distancing policies. These will be specific to each city and venue. Planners will have to ensure that detailed questions are asked at the beginning of the process.

At the time of this writing, there are more questions than answers.

SUMMARY

Service contractors are the backbone of the exhibition/event/conference industry. Their support structure, like the backbone, allows the show/event organizers and exhibitors to create an atmosphere that is smooth and efficient. Understanding the responsibilities of each contractor will allow a show/event organizer to offer the exhibitors the best possible service as well as creating a successful environment for buyers and sellers to do business in the exhibition format.

When you read this case study as it relates to The Distillery's Toronto Christmas Market, keep in mind the need to have contingency plans in place. Also, remember to ensure that all your contractors become a part of your team and are brought in as early in the process as possible. Each contractor understands its specialty and can add to the success. Each contractor will also have contingency and risk plans in place that the event organizer can add to their overall plans of the particular event or conference.

THE RELATIONSHIP BETWEEN SERVICE CONTRACTORS AND SHOW ORGANIZERS

Each year, since 2011, in a historic section of Toronto, Canada, known as The Distillery, the five-week Toronto

Distillery Christmas Market, Toronto, Ontario, Canada

Christmas Market takes place. In 2011, attendance was about 240,000; people came to enjoy food and beverage, caroling, stage performances by well-known artists, the ability to purchase unusual gifts, and to enjoy the outdoor festival. In a short time, the Market has become a tourist destination and has made a substantial economic impact on the shops of The Distillery and the City of Toronto.

By 2019, over 700,000 people attended, mostly on weekends. This has caused the Distillery District to look at traffic flow (people and transportation), safety, and several other aspects. To try to reduce the large numbers on weekends, they now charge a minimal fee on weekends, donating the proceeds to a charity. This has also resulted in more security. After the terrorist attacks in Toronto, Brussels, and around the world, the Distillery District immediately had to increase security and make major security decisions in a few hours. These were implemented overnight in 2016. Security remains a top concern each year.

When the public come, they see the Market in full swing. Most don't comprehend the 2 weeks that it took to build the Market. Working with The Distillery Special Events staff, general contractors had to work as a team to ensure it all ran smoothly. Before any of this could happen, The Distillery Special Events staff had to contract the vendors who would sell their products and contract the variety of service contractors to ensure success.

There were the builders of the huts that would sell goods, food, and beverage. There were electrical contractors required to add electricity to each hut. There were skyjacks brought in to put up the 40-foot Christmas tree and decorate it. The lighting people put up thousands of lights above the buildings. The vendors set up their wares. The entertainers had to be contracted and scheduled, both on the stage and off. The established restaurants had to ensure they were staffed appropriately and purchase enough food to handle the extra diners. The cobblestone streets had to be checked to ensure no cobblestones were loose. Extra security had to be hired. Portable toilets had to be brought in. Valet parking and parking attendants had to be hired to manage the increased car traffic. Firewood had to be delivered for the outdoor fire pits. Permits had to be obtained for the use of much of the equipment. When the market opened, 80% of the work had already been done!

Now it was time for the 10%—while guests came over the next 2 weeks. Any on-site crisis had to be dealt with so that the guests didn't know. A snowstorm meant the plows had to be ready and the salters had to quickly salt the cobblestones to ensure no one fell and injured themselves. Security had to be on the lookout for anything that could go wrong. Entertainers had to be on time. Outdoor fires had to be watched.

No sooner had it begun than it was over. Now, the remaining 10% for teardown and analysis. Again, all contractors had to work together to ensure everything was dismantled and safely taken away. Electrical and sound systems come down first. Then the center stage. As all this happens, the vendors remove their goods. Security is, as always, there 24 hours a day. Lastly, the huts come down; the wood slats are stored on tractors and taken away. Two days later, if you walked into The Distillery, you would never know a two-week Market had just taken place. Why? Because all service contractors worked as a team to design and set up the Market, to ensure safety during the Market, and to tear down efficiently.

At the time of this writing, it is not known whether the 2020 Distillery Toronto Christmas Market will take place. Much depends on the world and city status of COVID-19.

For more information about the Distillery Toronto Christmas Market, find the website using a search engine.

KEYWORDS AND TERMS

For definitions, see https://insights.eventscouncil.org/Industry-glossary

drayage

exclusive service

exhibitor service manual

exhibitor-appointed contractor

general service contractor

material handling

RFP

service contractor

specialty service contractor

REVIEW AND DISCUSSION QUESTIONS

1. What types of services do specialty contractors provide?

2. What are some of the questions that should be asked in an RFP?

3. Describe the difference between a general (official service contractor) and an exhibitor-appointed contractor.

4. How can the GSC assist the show/event organizer as it prepares for the exhibition/event/conference?

5. You are the event manager of a large conference that includes a trade show component. The trucks are ready to move and the weather sets in. Winter storms are everywhere on the route. Whom do you contact? What alternative plans can you make? What if the trucks can't get there in time to set up?

6. World pandemic strikes: How can you, the planner, adapt to a virtual trade show? What service contractors will be most important in your change to a virtual trade show?

ABOUT THE CHAPTER CONTRIBUTOR

Sandy Biback, CMP Emeritus, CMM, has been involved in the design and implementation of business events/conferences/trade shows for over 40 years. She has taught a variety of courses related to meetings and conventions in a postgraduate program at Centennial College in Toronto. She has previously taught online for the University of Nevada, Las Vegas, and George Brown College in Toronto. She has retired her company Imagination+Meeting Planners, Inc. Biback is a former active member of Professional Convention Management Association (PCMA) and Meeting Professionals International (MPI) and is a founding member and past president of the Canadian Society of Professional Event Planners (CanSPEP). She works on special projects that capture her passion to make the industry a better profession. She is the founder of Meeting Professionals Against Human Trafficking (MPAHT).

PREVIOUS CHAPTER CONTRIBUTOR

Susan L. Schwartz, CEM.

CHAPTER 7

DESTINATION MANAGEMENT COMPANIES

Alan Fyall

LONDON IS A MAJOR GLOBAL DESTINATION FOR BUSINESS TRAVEL WITH ITS FAVORABLE LOCATION IN EUROPE CONVENIENT FOR TRAVELERS FROM THE EAST AND WEST.

CHAPTER OBJECTIVES

- Define a destination management company as well as its structure and services.
- Outline a destination management company's organization.
- Describe the elements involved in the business model of destination management companies.
- Discuss strategies and tools for finding and selecting a destination management company.
- Describe at least eight best practices in destination management companies.
- Outline the expected impact of COVID-19 on destination management companies.

One of the many career opportunities that exist within the MEEC industry is providing local destination management services. These services include being a liaison between the host organization's meeting planner with suppliers such as onsite meeting management, hotel services, convention centers and bureaus, airlines, transportation, and catering. Typically, when thinking about careers in the MEEC industry, one may not always consider working in the supplier side of the business. However, services provided at the event destination play a key role in the successful planning and execution of meetings, conventions, and events. This chapter will discuss the business and services provided by destination management companies (DMCs).

DESTINATION MANAGEMENT COMPANY: DEFINITION, STRUCTURE, AND SERVICES

A **Destination Management Company** (DMC) is a professional services business that possesses extensive local knowledge, expertise, and resources. It specializes in the design and implementation of events, activities, tours, transportation, and program logistics. Depending on the company and the staff specialists in the company, DMCs offer several services, including, but are not limited to, the following: creative proposals for special events; guest tours; VIP amenities and transportation; shuttle services; onsite staffing; team-building, golf and sport outings; entertainment; décor and theme development; and onsite registration services, housing, and concierge services.

Destination management companies may also be known as **ground operator** (a term originally used for DMCs before their services in the industry expanded to what it is today) or the title of **Professional Congress Organizer** (**PCO;** a predominantly international term). PCOs are a type of DMC who are especially helpful to those planning international events. They are members of the International Association of Professional Congress Organizers (IAPCO). Destination management companies offer a critical layer of services and are hired by meeting and event professionals to provide local knowledge, experience, and resources for corporate and association gatherings. DMCs work cooperatively with transportation companies, airlines, hotels and resorts, convention centers, and other service suppliers in the delivery and implementation of MEEC activities. Successful MEEC events require comprehensive local knowledge of destination infrastructure, local laws and statutes, and regulations. Meeting and event professionals must work with local professionals who have verified and offer first-hand information about supplier availability, capabilities, and capacities gained through actual project work to ensure a successful event.

When discussing DMCs and their services, the industry denotes this as the client project, which, be it a meeting, exhibition, event, or convention, is typically referred to as a program. A program will include all activities and services provided by the DMC to the client while visiting a destination over a specified time.

SERVICES PROVIDED BY DESTINATION MANAGEMENT COMPANIES

Meeting and event professionals work closely with DMCs to provide recommendations for local destination resources that will best fit and satisfy the goals for a gathering. After these services are determined, a contract is written for the DMC to plan, set up, and deliver those services. Services typically offered by DMCs include:

- Budgeting and resource management
- Concierge services (e.g., restaurant reservations, theme park/attraction tickets, off-site tours)
- Creative itineraries
- Creative theme design
- Dining programs
- Entertainers
- Event production
- Event venue selection
- Hotel selection
- Incentive Travel
- Meeting support services
- Sightseeing and tour options
- Speakers
- Special event concepts
- Sport events (e.g., golf, tennis, fishing tournaments)
- Staffing services
- Team-building activities
- Transportation planning and delivery·
- VIP services

DMCs may make special arrangements for models or entertainers; this one in costume.

DMC services facilitate networking among attendees, celebrating accomplishments, or the introduction of new ideas and/or products. In today's competitive environment, where the impact and return on investment of meetings and events are expected to be measured, professionals rely on DMCs to provide unique and creative event concepts that will accomplish the specific goals of the event, be consistent with other activities carried out in the client's program, and stay within the client's budget. Full-service DMCs provide both meeting management support services, such as transportation arrangements, onsite staffing, and all aspects of event production, such as staging, sound, décor, and lights. DMCs often are a reliable resource for entertainment solutions, from a small trio for background music at an intimate cocktail party to the headline entertainment for large special events. Familiarity and access to local musicians and entertainers is an important criterion when selecting a DMC. In addition, DMCs often suggest and supply décor such as props, floral designs, and decorations to enhance event spaces and venues.

Transportation logistics are often a key service provided by DMCs. These services include airport "meet and greet" services, hotel transfers and baggage management, and shuttles. Moving groups of participants—large or small—is an important component of most events that require precise timing and execution, local expertise, and management responsibility. This is best provided by a professional DMC to ensure attendee comfort, convenience, and safety. In addition, many DMCs will provide customized sightseeing tours and recreational activities, such as golf and tennis tournaments.

Because of the creative element associated with meetings and events and the variety of each group's needs and expectations, the list of services that are provided by DMCs is almost limitless. It is important to note that while one client may require a DMC to manage and execute the entire event, another client may contract a DMC to provide only one or two components of the event.

DESTINATION MANAGEMENT COMPANY VERSUS DESTINATION MARKETING ORGANIZATION

The DMC business process has been compared to, and often confused with, the services provided by a **Destination Marketing Organization (DMO)**, sometimes referred to as a **Convention and Visitors Bureau (CVB).** Although they are very different organizations, there are some similarities between their services. DMOs optimize the exposure of a specific destination, leading it to develop innovative experiences for visitors and enabling the community to develop a sustainable infrastructure for tourism and travel to that particular location.

Most DMOs are quasi-government, not-for-profit organizations whose purpose is to sell their destination to tourists, business travelers, and convention visitors alike. Often funded by both tax dollars and membership fees, DMOs maintain an unbiased view of their destination's supplier and vendor members. They work with the planner to arrange site visitations, provide marketing materials about the locale, and direct planners to local suppliers of meeting services and venues. See Chapter 3 for more detailed information about DMOs.

Unlike DMOs, DMCs are for-profit businesses who can negotiate and sign supplier contracts on behalf of the meeting client. They too have an expertise of their destination and use that in-depth knowledge to recommend and eventually book the special event venue, transportation, tour guides, or restaurants on behalf of the client. DMCs provide value to their customers by representing them in the marketplace and locating a variety of products and services they may need. Ultimately, they rely on relationships with suppliers.

Today's consumers expect a destination to offer customized product and service offerings that match their expectations. The destinations that manage to maximize the satisfaction levels of customers' expectations, and support consumers throughout the buying process, will be the ones to survive and yield maximum benefits. Therefore, DMOs work with the interests of both the community at large and the private companies that provide many of these services. The key distinction between a DMO and a DMC is that while the DMO represents the destination to the client, the DMC represents the client to the destination!

BUSINESS STRUCTURE OF DMCS

Some prerequisites are essential to the destination management process:

- Staff
- Temporary "field staff"
- Office
- Technology
- Licenses and insurance
- Community contacts
- Customer contacts
- History
- Destination resources

Staffing is probably the most obvious of the prerequisites. Office staff for sales, marketing, logistics, accounting, and administrative duties are all necessary. In addition, temporary "field staff" include such positions as tour guides, greeters, and onsite supervisors. These people often work on a contract basis for each event as it arises and may be temporarily hired by other DMCs.

A strategically located office is a basic necessity for a DMC. Convenient proximity to major hotels, convention facilities, tourist attractions, and event venues is a must. In today's competitive environment, DMCs must have access to the best-possible technology. DMC clients are usually associations and major corporations that are accustomed to technology and expect to work with DMCs that are also proficient in using electronic communications. Communications equipment, office computer capabilities (including database management, customer relationship management [CRM]), imaging software, and high-speed Internet are all expected to be standard tools in today's DMC. DMCs are also known to now use computer-aided design (CAD) programs for the effective and creative design of meetings. The quick processing of information and the ability to make on-the-spot changes and produce professional documents and graphics are becoming an industry standard and a necessity for DMCs.

Given the nature of the services provided by DMCs, they must be legally insured for business liability as well as other standard coverage such as workers' compensation and automobile insurance. Each destination will have unique laws and licensing requirements for the DMC's services. Meeting and event professionals must ensure that their chosen business partners are adequately insured and knowledgeable about local ordinances that could affect the successful operation and production of their events.

As with many businesses in the service sector, DMCs compete in a relationship-driven industry. Customers and professionals will literally put their reputations and jobs on the line when selecting a DMC. DMC management and staff should have extensive community contacts among hotels, attractions, convention bureaus, airports, law enforcement, and the supplier community and must articulate their commitment to building and sustaining positive relationships with their clients. It is through the cooperation from these business partnerships, gained through repeated work experiences, that a DMC can properly service the diverse needs of its clients.

Reputation outside of the destination community—in the client community —is very important to the long-term success of a DMC. The most valuable asset a DMC has is its history of success, which is the best verification a professional can rely on when choosing a DMC partner.

Finally, the destination community must have the necessary resources to support the DMC in the execution of a well-run program or event. It must have a competitive service environment, with many suppliers that have good reputations.

THE DESTINATION MANAGEMENT COMPANY ORGANIZATION

Destination management companies come in a variety of sizes and organizational structures. Given the nature of the services that they provide, it is possible to get started in this business with little start-up funding due to their low overhead requirements and traditional low-profit margins. This section will discuss the range of organizations that operate as DMCs.

INDEPENDENT OPERATOR

Independent destination management companies are locally owned and operated by small businesses who often got their start as a "ground operator." For many years, these DMCs were the backbone of destination management and provided a limited array of targeted services such as transportation operator, tour organizer, staffing, or special event management. Today, independent DMCs are still a major factor in the industry, and many have expanded their services to compete with the larger national DMCs. The long-term success of independent DMCs is largely predicated on the ability of the owner to develop lasting relationships and goodwill by exceeding clients' expectations. Although it is relatively easy to start this business, the hours and challenges can be long and arduous.

MULTI-SERVICES OPERATOR

Destination management companies that offer multi-services are typically larger organizations rather than independent operators. Over time, these organizations establish large networks of service offerings. These multi-services suppliers must be staffed with well-trained professionals who can put together complex, diverse client programs. Often the larger multi-services operator has staff and offices in multiple destinations and can offer its clients a significant advantage in securing high-quality services at a lower cost than can typically be found with an independent operator. Examples of such organizations include Hosts Global Alliance serving over 300 destinations and Allied PRA serving over 100 domestic destinations and numerous global partners as well.

DESTINATION MANAGEMENT NETWORKS

Because local "one-destination DMCs" do not enjoy the same economy of scale that national or international DMCs do, networks of DMCs have been formed. An example of this is "The DMC Network." This group was formed in order to pool resources from individual one-city DMCs for sales and marketing purposes. Other such "DMC groups" exist primarily for the sharing of mutual sales and marketing efforts and expenses.

Destination management networks are a collection of independent destination management companies that pay a fee or commission to be affiliated with a national or regionally based organization. Destination management networks allow meeting and event professionals the peace of mind when dealing with DMCs in unfamiliar locations. This arrangement allows for smaller, independent DMCs to remain autonomous while gaining significant advantages typically afforded to the larger multi-services, multi-destination DMCs.

In some cases, particularly with DMC networks, it makes sense to employ professional representation firms to call on particular market segments. Usually, this representation is contracted for a particular geographic location, such as New York, Chicago, or London. These companies typically call on potential and existing customers in the geographic area on behalf of a DMC network. They will seek to familiarize professionals about the DMC network while uncovering leads for future business. When appropriate, these representation firms will sometimes also serve as a local liaison between the customer and a DMC partner.

BUSINESS MODEL OF DESTINATION MANAGEMENT COMPANIES

DMC clients are those who plan meetings, exhibitions, events, conventions, and **incentive travel programs.** When describing the business model of DMCs, the terms "customer," "client," and "professional" are used to describe the person, organization, or company for which the DMC is providing services. In some instances, the customer, client, and professional can be three separate entities or be the same. The **customer** is the organization that will be securing and paying for the services provided by the DMC. The **client** is the representative of the organization who is in a leadership role when making the decision to purchase DMC services. The **professional**, representing the customer organization, is the person (or persons) whom the DMC works directly with planning and coordinating programs and events.

It is important to note that those who participate in the planning of the services provided by a DMC are almost always staff of the DMC, such as a corporate sales force. It is common for DMCs to service the leisure traveler or tour groups that partner outside of the DMC organization. Increasingly, the value of DMC services is being recognized by large tour operators, and they are often contracted to assist with transportation and/or tours for large groups. A good example of this is a cruise ship that employs a DMC to manage land tours, transportation, and excursions.

A DMC may be contracted directly with an organization whose employees or members will be participating in the program, or it may contract with a third-party or independent professional meeting professional who is offering their meeting services to the participating organization/customer (see the flow chart in Figure 7-1).

Most meeting and event professionals consider the DMC as a local extension of their own office and staff while in the destination. They expect the DMC to be their "eyes and ears" in the destination, always acting on their behalf, offering unbiased, experience-based suggestions on logistics, venues, event concepts, and social program content. Professionals depend on DMCs to help them design event programs that meet their specific needs, which can vary in size, budget, length, and purpose.

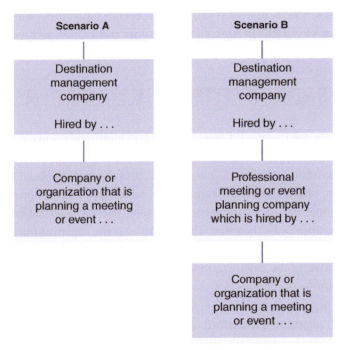

FIGURE 7-1 Sample DMC flow chart

CLIENTS

Destination management companies receive business from several categories of customers. Their contracted programs may come from corporate, association, incentive-based, or special event clients.

Corporate Accounts

Given the recent challenges facing the world economy, corporate clients organizing meetings are receiving greater scrutiny. In the past, corporate meetings holding a half-day of meetings while spending the remainder of their day on the golf course would not generate much attention. Today, just the location where the corporate meeting is being held can generate negative publicity. DMCs must be very sensitive to the constraints and attention that are facing corporate clients when planning and organizing meetings.

In addition, corporate clients are reassessing the value of holding face-to-face meetings. It is very important that DMCs focus on working with their clients to ensure that the meetings and events have a higher level of value than could be achieved by not hosting a face-to-face or "virtual" event.

The following is a list of sample event programs that DMCs work on with corporate clients:

- National sales meetings
- Training meetings
- Product introductions
- Dealer and/or customer meetings
- Team-building activities

Association Accounts

Associations are organizations that are created to support an industry, common interest, or activity. Associations can range from local, state, regional, national, and international groups. Most associations exist to provide networking and educational opportunities to their membership. In carrying out these activities, associations will hold a variety of meetings, conventions, and conferences.

In today's competitive environment, potential conference/convention attendees are being more selective as to which meetings they will attend. Attending a meeting out of town is costly in terms of both time and money. The factors involved include the return on investment (ROI) that individuals believe they will receive by attending the event. DMCs can provide considerable resources and support to help clients create events that will be offered to their membership with the highest impact. The following is a list of sample event programs that DMCs work on with association clients:

- Industry tradeshows (food, construction, aircraft, etc.)
- Professional tradeshows and conferences (for architects, doctors, teachers, etc.)
- Fraternal organizations (VFW, Lions, etc.)
- Educational conferences (medical symposia, other professional groups)
- Political conventions

INCENTIVE-BASED ORGANIZATIONS

Incentive-based meetings and events are organized to recognize and reward employees who have reached or exceeded company targets. This segment of the meetings and event market continues to experience rapid growth. Today's organizations are recognizing the value of providing rewards and recognition for employees' outstanding performance. These events can typically last between 3 and 6 days in length and can range from a modest to extravagant getaway for employees and their partners. DMCs can provide the organizing client a range of services that are customized based on the budget of the organization and the desires of the employee. The following is a list of sample event programs that DMCs work on with incentive-based clients:

- Sales incentives
- Dealer incentives
- Service manager incentives

SPECIAL EVENT CLIENTS

Local corporations, associations, for-profit, and not-for-profit organizations may also use the services of a DMC for a singular, stand-alone event such as a gala, fundraiser, anniversary celebration, walk/run challenge, or other celebratory event that needs their expertise of local resources and logistics.

DESTINATION MANAGEMENT COMPANY OPERATIONS

Unlike hotels, resorts, convention centers, and restaurants, a DMC does not require an extensive capital investment to start up and operate its business since they do not produce or manufacture any products. The DMC office is usually located in office space somewhere near the location where most meetings and events take place. Proximity to major airports can be an advantage, since so many program services involve group arrivals and departures.

Primary responsibilities and job titles for a DMC vary from company to company. Many DMCs are small, stand-alone, single-office companies that are locally owned. Other larger companies may have offices in multiple destinations with local staff fulfilling management responsibilities on all levels. (See Table 7-1 with categories of job responsibilities that follows.)

To be successful, a DMC's job tasks include finding business leads, proposing appropriate services, contracting services, organizing the group's arrival, delivering the contracted services, and following up with billing and program reconciliation. These task areas are carried out by contracting with supplier companies, hiring field staff, and assigning program staff. Field staff, who carry out such functions as tour guides, hospitality desk staff, and airport "meet and greet" staff, are usually temporarily contracted employees who are hired by a DMC only for the term of the program. It is common for field staff in a destination to work for more than one DMC as the needs arise for their services.

Management and Administration	Operations and Production
• General Manager	• Director of Operations
• Office Manager	• Director of Special Events
• Accounting Manager	• Operations Manager
• Executive Assistant	• Production Manager
• Administrative Assistant	• Transportation Manager
• Receptionist	• Staffing Manager
• Research Assistant	
	Field Staff
Sales and Marketing	• Meet and Greet Staff
• Director of Sales	• Tour Guide
• Director of Marketing	• Transportation Manager
• Director of Special Events	• Event Supervisor
• Sales Manager	• Field Supervisor
• Sales Coordinator	• Equipment Manager
• Proposal Writer	
• Research Analyst	

TABLE 7-1 Categories of DMC Job Responsibilities, with Sample Job Titles

The job titles listed earlier are examples and will vary from company to company. However, sales and promotion responsibilities, operations and production responsibilities, and management and administrative responsibilities are the basic responsibilities of all DMCs. As in most companies, the levels of authority and reporting lines do vary and are usually based on the size of the company and the qualifications of its staff. For example, a "Director of Special Events" title may appear under both the sales and marketing function and the operations and production function. The position can be either or both, depending on the company and the individual executive's area of expertise.

In many cases, DMCs do not own transportation equipment, props, décor, or other supplies that the DMC packages and sells to its customers. It is common for DMCs to buy or rent from selected suppliers and manage these products and services in the context of the larger event program. As such, the DMC becomes a "contractor" for the services of a myriad of local supplier companies.

A critical characteristic for the long-term success of DMCs is the ability to objectively recommend and select suppliers for the services contracted. A DMC's value proposition to meeting professionals depends on their ability to select the best provider for the services that meet the client's budget and program specifications. Clients must feel confident that the DMC is earning its money for the management services provided and not from some inflated financial "arrangement" made with the supplier companies.

THE SALES PROCESS

For DMCs to be successful, new business projects must be continually found and secured for the company. Business opportunities may present themselves in a variety of ways. Not all DMCs service all the clients listed earlier in the chapter. Some DMCs have created successful businesses by specializing in associations' convention business, corporate meetings, or international travel groups. Some DMCs may work with individual travelers, while others focus heavily on the domestic incentive market. However, most DMCs operate in multiple markets, which are usually determined by the nature of their destination.

In other words, the infrastructure and appeal of the destination will often dictate which of the above market segments DMCs will do business with. A destination's infrastructure such as its convention centers, convention hotels, resorts, and airport facilities all play into the equation. Other destination assets such as natural and man-made attractions play heavily into whether or not corporations will plan important meetings and/or incentive travel rewards in a location. Beaches, forests, weather, recreational facilities, fishing, arts, gambling, and theme parks all can enhance a destination's appeal.

IDENTIFYING NEW BUSINESS OPPORTUNITIES

The first stage of the sales process is to discover new business opportunities and pursue those leads. Almost all new business opportunities involve going where the customers are or where the customers do business, such as attending industry tradeshows or conferences. Some examples of these tradeshows are the American Society of Association Executives (ASAE) Annual Meeting and Exposition, IMEX America (held in Las Vegas), IMEX Frankfurt, and Holiday Showcase (held in Chicago). Sales executives representing DMCs must carefully research these tradeshows to maximize their sales and marketing resources. Knowing in advance which potential customers will attend and knowing what business opportunities they represent will ensure an increase in the DMC's prospects for creating new client relationships.

DMCs will often get **leads** on new accounts through requests by meeting and event professionals that have gone through a DMO. Once the lead has been passed on by the DMO, the DMC will communicate through direct and electronic communications and presentations. These presentations almost always exhibit the DMC's competence using examples of their past successful programs. Once it has been established that the DMC has the expertise to meet the client's needs, it will respond to the client's **request for proposal (RFP).**

Some customers, particularly corporate customers, incentive companies, and meeting management companies, will designate a "preferred" DMC in selected destinations. For DMCs, this is known as a **"house account."** Whenever house account planners require services, the chosen DMC can help without going through the often-onerous competitive bidding process. These accounts are very important and require careful maintenance. There is considerable competition for them, and competing DMCs are always active in their attempts to take over these accounts. Periodic visits to these customers and open lines of communication are vital in maintaining these relationships. In addition to continued good service, part of the successful "maintenance" of these relationships may include membership in the same industry organizations as the professionals. Attending these organizations' conferences and meetings allows DMC representatives to visit and network among existing and potential planner clients.

Sales efforts at the destination level are considered by most DMCs to be an important part of the sales plan. Creating relationships with local industry representatives who are conducting business with the same customers and planners is an efficient way for DMCs to identify new business opportunities.

For example, networking at local hospitality industry functions, such as local Hospitality Sales and Management Association International (HSMAI) monthly meetings or convention bureau "mixers," is a common practice among successful DMCs. In addition, staying abreast of industry news, people who work in the industry, and knowing changes in services and staffing within the local industry make for a well-informed DMC.

Collateral materials are essential to a comprehensive sales and marketing plan. Collateral materials include brochures, letterheads, business cards, proposal shells, and factsheets for the various activities and services offered by the DMC. In addition to these materials, a DMC will often produce a company newsletter to enhance the company's image and recognition in the industry. Increasingly, electronic media is used. That said, it is hard to replace a consultative selling approach as central to the effectiveness of a DMC is its ability to build and nurture relationships with both suppliers and clients/professionals. Ultimately, the goal is to create a long-lasting relationship.

REQUEST FOR PROPOSAL (RFP)

Typically, potential DMC customers will request that two or more DMCs bid on its program based on a set of specifications in their RFP. Each DMC will then provide detailed, creative proposals for services, which will best satisfy the client's specifications. These proposals are almost always developed with no cost with the intention to win the customer's favor, which is a major issue.

Responding to a client's RFPs often incurs a considerable cost for the DMC and requires staff time to formulate a customized proposal; therefore, DMCs must choose wisely when determining what potential business to pursue. Today, the cost for collecting and submitting bids to client's RFPs is controlled by the development of standards for submitting these RFPs electronically. The **Events Industry Council (EIC)** has been a leader in the development of these standards, and templates for the electronic formats can be found and retrieved under the **APEX** guidelines. The APEX guidelines are a type of best practices (glossary, forms, procedures) adopted by the industry for a variety of event planning components.

Destination management companies will prepare detailed proposals for services, which are based on the planner's specifications and budget. A meetings and events professional will provide the DMC with information so that the DMCs' proposed itinerary can be designed to best suit the group's purpose, demographics, psychographics, behaviors, and expectations. Initial proposals will often include more than one suggested itinerary, providing the client with several options, costs, and details about proposed services.

Once a DMC has secured the sales lead, contacted the customer, and convinced that client to consider the DMC, the DMC will be asked to provide a proposal of services. The following items must be considered and addressed in this proposal stage:

- Project specifications
- Research and development
- Creativity and innovation
- Budgets
- Response time
- Competition

As a DMC begins to determine exactly what to offer a customer, the client's project specifications become a valuable tool. A great deal of detailed information is usually included in these specifications, such as:

- Group size
- Choice of hotel, resort type
- Meeting space allotments
- Dates of service
- Types of services required
- Demographic, psychographic, and behavioral information about the attendees
- Management's goals for the meeting or event
- Approximate budget
- History regarding past successes and challenges
- Deadlines for completion and proposal submission

Armed with the client's specifications and other information, the DMC will determine what items to offer in the proposal of services that will best fit the client's expectations. The first step is often a series of creative meetings among DMC staff to discuss what might best satisfy the client specifications. After these meetings, research and development should begin. Availability of suppliers, venues, transportation, and entertainers, plus bids for services like catering, transportation equipment, and venue costs, are all reviewed and incorporated into the proposal. Costs for all items must be identified for accurate budgeting.

Creativity and innovation are usually highly valued in winning proposals. Selected programs will reflect the customer company; therefore, creativity and innovation along with a thorough and well-designed program tends to win. Response time is critical when responding to clients' proposals; however, there is a trade-off as creativity takes time, and a proposal that does not meet the clients' deadline will rarely receive the business.

A final and critical step in the proposal process is pricing. Several factors must be considered when pricing the proposal, such as:

- Total estimated costs for delivering the proposed services
- Staff time and involvement necessary before, during, and after the program
- Amount of DMC resources necessary to operate the program
- Unknown costs, which are factored into the planning and contingency stages
- Factors surrounding supplier choice and availability
- Time of the year and local business activity during a particular season
- Costs of taking staff and company capacity off the market for this customer
- Factors regarding competitive bids on the project

The following questions are the type that a DMC should ask itself prior to making a final decision on how much effort to dedicate to a given opportunity. The answers may show that ultimately the best decision is for a DMC to choose not to bid on a client's RFP.

- What is the revenue potential of the business opportunity?
- What is the value of a future relationship with the customer?
- How much proposal work will be involved in the bid?
- How many companies are bidding?
- Which competitors are bidding?
- What success rate does your company have on similar projects?
- What success rate do your competitors have?
- What time of year will the program be operating?
- What are the approximate odds of winning the program?
- How profitable will the program be?

Given the variety among proposal elements offered by the competing DMCs, a client may not choose a winning bid based solely on price. The client, in awarding the bid, may consider other important factors, such as:

- Is the proposal feasible?
- What is the perceived value of services offered?

- Will the participants appreciate the suggested program?
- Will the quality be sufficient to make the program or event a success?
- Is the DMC capable of producing the program or event in an acceptable manner?
- Is the program creative enough that it will meet the needs/appetite of the participants?

One of the changing dynamics of DMCs in recent years is their degree of legal awareness. The reason behind this is that over the years, potential clients (prospects) receive proposals but then decide not to proceed with any DMC at all. Rather, they take the information and advice and create their "own" event. Financially and ethically this can create problems, so, in response, the use of confidentiality agreements in combination with the proposal by the DMC serves as a means to protect themselves from "idea" theft and so on.

SITE INSPECTIONS

While DMCs may be involved in site inspections, they do not usually organize or sponsor them. That responsibility lies with the DMO in the locale (see Chapter 3 for more information).

PROGRAM DEVELOPMENT

The execution and civility of business transactions are supported through contractual agreements and are essential in all aspects of the meetings and events industry. Hotels, convention centers, cruise ships, airlines, and DMCs all produce contracts with their clients, which precisely spell out the details of the purchase and the obligation for both parties. Depending on the size and complexity of the program and the services provided by the DMC, contracts can vary in size.

After a program is contracted, a transition begins, moving from the active selling of the program to the operations and production of the program. Now, all suppliers contracted by the DMC are notified that the program is approved and their services are confirmed. The operations staff, who typically are different from the sales staff in larger DMCs, meet with the sales representatives to review the customer's needs, program goals, and any details that will be a factor in the successful delivery of the program.

During this phase of the business process, the participants who are actively engaged can fluctuate, requiring the DMC management to constantly monitor costs and other details. With the active involvement by the client, activities and services may be added or removed from the program during this phase. It is important that the DMC representatives are available, responsive, and note these changes. As a contracted member of the customer's team, the DMC is responsible for the destination management portion of the larger, overall customer event—therefore, the DMC must be fully cooperative and flexible. The program's project manager, either an operations or events manager, will assume primary responsibility for the entire program or event. During the setup period, each activity and service for the program is reviewed and confirmed in detail. Full-time and part-time professional program managers, supervisors, tour guides, and escorts are scheduled well in advance. In addition, during the program development phase, the event manager will put into play a system of checks and balances to ensure everything is covered in detail.

PROGRAM EXECUTION

Destination management companies require the coordination of staff and suppliers into one cohesive program of products and services. After finding the opportunity, creating proposals, earning the professional's confidence, contracting the program, and careful preparations, it is up to the operations and production staff to successfully deliver the program. At this point, everything is "on the line": The image of the customer organization, the reputation of the planner, future prospects for the DMC with the planner, the DMC's reputation in the destination, and the opportunity to profit from the contract are all at risk.

The successful execution of the client's program is very important. If the program is for a large association's convention, the members' perception of the organization is at stake. The American Medical Association, Radiological Society of North America, and the National Automobile Dealers Association are examples of associations that employ a DMC. Meeting and event professionals for these associations are orchestrating major events with thousands of participants on an ongoing basis. The participants' perception of the convention can easily be affected by the quality of the shuttle transportation to and from the convention hall, the quality of the networking events, cocktail parties, meal service, and activities like the annual golf tournament and optional sightseeing tours. All of these services are potentially the DMC's responsibility. The events must live up to the participants' expectations. The activities and tours must be entertaining and well-run. The participants are the association planner's customers, and membership renewals and future convention attendance will be affected by the quality of the program delivery.

Similar dynamics are in effect with corporate programs. Exhibiting at a tradeshow gives the exhibiting corporation an opportunity to entertain their customer through special event programs developed by their contracted DMC. Insurance companies reward top sales producers with incentive programs that effectively show the best of their workforce how the company's top executives value their contributions. Computer companies and software companies produce new product introduction events either as stand-alone events or in conjunction with industry conventions. Often, the success of these events has the future of the sponsoring companies at stake.

Through these examples, one can clearly see the tremendous pressure of running a logistically sound and high-quality program. These pressures are riding on the shoulders of the meeting and event professionals and the DMCs. The DMCs operations and production staff have one chance to deliver the program. When mistakes or missteps occur, the event cannot be rescheduled for the next day. If the bus and limousine suppliers do not provide equipment as ordered, the departure time cannot be changed. It is the reliability of execution that is the most important issue in the success of a program; price runs a distant second to reliability. However, all DMCs are not equal, and choosing the best fit for a particular program is essential. A close working relationship that fosters confidence, easy communication, and mutual understanding requires that the planner's DMC contact be readily available. Likewise, the planner must be immediately available to the DMC's operation manager throughout the course of the program.

TRANSPORTATION SERVICES

Transportation management is often a major, if not the largest, component of their business. It encompasses routing, vehicle use, staff requirements, special venue considerations, equipment staging areas, staff scheduling and briefings, maps, and signage. Transportation scenarios and requirements are usually scattered throughout the program itinerary.

Meeting and greeting guests and arranging their transportation to the hotel is only one of many services provided by a DMC with transportation coming in all shapes and sizes.

Although most DMCs do not book flights, there are a few that do. However, a DMC's largest component is ground transportation. When beginning the event process, the DMC will need to assess the travel and transportation requirements of the client by identifying the following:

- Type of event
- Size of event
- Scope of event
- Type of attendees/audience profile
- Arrival/departure service?
- Continuous or timed shuttle service?
- Transfers (from hotel to conference, etc.)
- Any mobility/disability issues?
- Bundling of transportation services?
- Special transportation needs of VIP's (limos or town cars)
- Special transportation needs of performers/entertainers (limos or town cars)
- Special transportation needs of major sponsors (limos or town cars)

DMCs are often tasked with securing or providing the appropriate transportation for the event. They will need to provide the appropriate equipment, coordinate the types of transportation, and supervise onsite transportation services. DMCs offer local transportation coordination and cater to other local travel needs, including the following:

- Group tours/chartering
- Group transfers
- Shuttle scheduling
- Special event arrangements

When a DMC sends out an RFP for transportation services, selecting a transportation provider will be extremely important in producing a successful event. Therefore, DMCs require specific information to determine the vendor's suitability, including "the size of the fleet, the condition of the vehicles, and whether the equipment is owned or subcontracted; whether or not the drivers have current commercial driver's licenses and the company has a driver drug and alcohol testing program; and if the company has its buses inspected annually, the company has the required amount of public liability insurance, and the company has notification procedures for roadside emergencies and breakdowns" (Federal Motor Carrier Administration).

After selecting a transportation company, the DMC's process is threefold. First, the DMC coordinator will need to consider the number of people who need to be transferred (travel demand), the times when transfers are required (check travel manifests/arrival times), and the types of vehicles suitable for the transfer.

Second, upon arrival/departure, a DMC may organize meet-and-greet services, special baggage handling, motor coach transfers, shuttle services and/or courtesy cars, and possibly a fleet of limousines for VIPs, entertainers, dignitaries, and so on. Oftentimes, a continuous or timed shuttle service between the airport and the conference hotels will be needed, especially if the event is a conference or convention utilizing numerous hotels for housing. The first impression a DMC makes on the attendee is the meet-and-greet and arrival transfer. Likewise, the last impression made on an attendee is the departure transfer. Dispatchers, directional staff, radios, cell phones, and signage are extremely important in making each transfer successful.

Third, during the conference, a continuous or timed shuttle service between the hotels and event venue might be required as well as to evening functions, dine-arounds, and so on. Like arrival/departure, dispatchers, directional staff, radios, cell phones, and signage are vitally important in making each transfer successful.

Traffic patterns have to be taken into consideration when planning group transfers, especially when the DMC has contracted with numerous hotels. DMCs work closely with transportation companies to review traffic patterns and route options when transferring large amounts of attendees to/from venues. Avoiding traffic congestion, construction, accidents, competing events that draw substantial traffic, rush hour, and more will not only lend itself to a smoother running event but also keep your attendees happy. Therefore, DMCs and transportation companies oftentimes have a traffic control plan in place prior to the event that addresses the above-mentioned concerns.

Last, DMCs will also charter motor coaches for remote tours, added trips before and after the conference, sightseeing tours, team-building tours, sporting events, educational programs, and off-site company events. Chartering motor coaches is safe, cost-effective, and environmentally appealing. Businesses usually prefer luxury motor coaches over public transportation or school buses. Luxury motor coaches are equipped with reclining seats, stereo music, video/TV monitors, a DVD player, Wi-Fi, outlets for devices, luggage space, a restroom, and air-conditioning.

DMCs choose the motor coach service provider based on location, reputation, insurance requirements, safety records, availability, reviews, and estimated cost. They carefully read through contracts/agreements and oftentimes negotiate on your behalf. Once they have decided upon which company to use, the tour is then created and the total cost is computed. It must be noted that costs can vary up to the tour date, mainly because of changing fuel costs and volatility of the fuel industry.

On the day of the tour, signage will be placed in the windows of each bus, name badges may be included for each guest, and tour guides/group escorts will be used to enhance the tours and keep the group on-time. Oftentimes, box lunches may be provided or stops for meals will be included, especially on longer hauls. Occasionally, shopping will be added to the excursion as well. At the end of the tour, the DMC will usually have a gift/memento of the tour to give to each guest.

Overall, transportation services can make or break an event. DMCs have the obligation to manage personalized service to attendees by means of careful planning, preparing, and delivering safe transportation services in a timely manner from the moment the attendees arrive through their departure. Being the largest component of a DMC's business, DMCs must ensure that every detail, from A to Z, is assessed and implemented so that the attendees will have a memorable event experience.

© Pavel Chepelev/Shutterstock.com

DMCs arrange ground transportation. In Thailand that includes transport by elephant.

PRODUCTION OF EVENTS

Event production is also typically a major part of a DMC's services. Events can be large or small, on a hotel property, or in a remote location. Some examples of events include the following:

- Cocktail receptions and networking events
- Breakfasts, luncheons, and dinners
- Dining events at unique venues
- Gala dinner events
- Extravagant theme parties
- Outdoor and indoor team-building events
- Guest and children's programs

Operational staff must be familiar with all the necessary municipal regulations regarding insurance, fire safety codes, permitting crowd control, and police requirements. When considering all these issues, there is no substitute for experience, and working with a DMC that has a known track record of success is very important.

Whether planning and operating sightseeing tours, a scavenger hunt, a golf tournament, or running a hospitality desk, strong organizational skills, sound preparation, and a sense of commitment and responsibility are essential traits for a professional DMC operations manager. When everything is riding on the performance of the firms, planners will often bond with the managers and become dependent on them to be their onsite consultants in the community.

Meeting and event professionals will often have to deal with onsite questions and requests for VIP arrangements with little advanced notice, and the DMC staff will support them in securing appropriate arrangements. Some examples of last-minute requests that DMCs are asked to take care of include the following:

> "Where can I send my VP of marketing and her husband for a romantic dinner? She just realized that today's their wedding anniversary!"

> "My company president is arriving early in the corporate jet. Can we get a limo to the executive airport in forty-five minutes?"

> "The boss just decided he wants a rose for all of the ladies at tonight's party."

> "Can we get Aretha Franklin to sing 'Happy Birthday' to one of our dealers during her performance at the party tonight?"

A wise person once said, "It is often the little things, the details, that separate great events from ordinary ones." Knowing someone's favorite wine, song, or dessert can turn an ordinary event into one that will be remembered forever. These are things that are not included in the contract but add special touches to an event and are great opportunities for the production staff to demonstrate their passion for service to the client. A production manager who has developed strong relationships with suppliers can often count on their suppliers to be swept up in the process and suggest ideas for program improvement on their own. Suppliers will do this because they want the event to be the best to establish an ongoing relationship with the DMC for possible future events. Planners are often pleased to be presented with options. For example, being offered confetti cannons for the dance floor area, additional accent lighting, or separate martini bars are all onsite event upgrades.

Much of an operations or production manager's day is spent confirming and reconfirming services. Constant communication with vendors and suppliers is critical to ensure that final participant counts and timing are accurate. One common task to ensure success of events is the **"advancing" of a venue**, which is when DMC staff arrives well ahead of a group to make sure that the

Alan Fyall

Sporting venues are increasingly being chosen by delegates for interesting places to meet and conduct business.

service staff and the event location are prepared and properly set up. Details such as the number of seats, room temperature, serving instructions, menu inclusions, and beverage service are all examples of items that should be verified when advancing a dinner event.

Throughout each event, operations and production managers must carefully monitor the original contracted services and all changes that occur after the original itinerary and contracts. Every addition to the program, such as changes in participant counts, times of service, and additional services, must be documented. Accurate, up-to-the-minute data on the actual services delivered must be kept for billing purposes. To avoid billing disputes, it is also important to identify that an authorized representative for the client has accepted the change or addition. Ideally, these authorizations are in writing and approved in advance by the client.

WRAP-UP AND BILLING

The final invoice for a program should mirror the contract of services agreed upon prior to the execution of the program. Actual services delivered should be outlined along with the number of participants that each charged item is based on. In most cases, items are billed either on "lot" costs or on a per-person basis. Lot costs are fixed and independent of the number of participants, such as bus tours, the price of an entertainer, or a décor package for a ballroom. Per-person pricing is based on the actual number of participants who received services, such as food and beverage at a luncheon that is billed at a fixed price per person, plus tax and gratuities.

All additions or deletions to the originally contracted services should appear on the invoice. The "grand total" for the program should be reflected along with all deposits and payments received prior to the final billing. On average, 90% of the bill is paid 30 days before the event takes place. When possible, final billing details should be reviewed and approved by the planner or representative onsite at the completion of the program, while details about the program's operation, additions, and changes are still fresh in everyone's mind. The more time that elapses between the time the program is completed and receipt of the final invoice, the more likely there will be disputes about program details, such as participant counts, times, and items, that were approved to be added to the program.

FINDING AND SELECTING A DESTINATION MANAGEMENT COMPANY

When the time comes that meeting and event professionals need to find and select a DMC, there are several steps and guidelines that are helpful in ensuring a successful outcome. When searching for DMC candidates, it is best to begin with contacting industry professionals that are managing and executing meetings and events on a regular basis. One of the best benefits of networking is to have contacts that can be called on to provide advice and guidance when searching for suppliers. If the meeting and event professional is lacking suitable connections, contacting industry groups, such as Professional Convention Management Association (PCMA), Meeting Professionals International (MPI), International Live Events Association (ILEA), and the American Society of Association Executives (ASAE), can be a valuable source. Also, the destination's CVB or DMO will have listings of DMCs that operate in and around its destination.

ASSOCIATION OF DESTINATION MANAGEMENT EXECUTIVES

An important resource in finding a DMC is the **Association of Destination Management Executives International (ADMEI)**. Founded in 1995, ADMEI is committed to the initiative that professional destination management is a critical and necessary component to every successful meeting or event. As a primary goal, ADMEI continuously seeks to identify and promote the value of destination management as a necessary resource for planners of meetings, events, and incentive travel programs. ADMEI's goals also include becoming the definitive source of information, education, and issues-based discussion of destination management for the meetings, events, incentive, and hospitality industries.

Professionals holding positions in the destination marketing field can gain an important professional designation. The designation of *Destination Management Certified Professional (DMCP)* was introduced by ADMEI in January 2000. This professional certification is only available to individuals who have qualified for an extensive examination administered by ADMEI. Applicants are screened through a detailed questionnaire, which chronicles the applicant's experience and industry education. ADMEI has also developed the Destination Management Company Accreditation (ADMC) program designed to promote professional standards and recognize those firms that demonstrate excellence in the practice of destination management and who adhere to the standards set forth by ADMEI. The ADMC designation assists the meeting planning community by identifying those DMCs that adhere to ADMC standards of practice, ethics, and industry knowledge.

Once a list of potential DMCs has been identified through references or research of the various industry associations, it is time to identify the best of the group. Factors that may be important before soliciting the RFP selection include:

- How long the company has been in business?
- What are the experience levels of the management and staff?
- What are the perceptions of the planner with the personalities of the management team?
- Is the DMC an affiliated member of any meeting and events professional organizations?
- Is the DMC adequately bonded, relative to the size and complexity of the program?
- What is the quality of the references provided by the DMC both in size of previous programs and ranking of professional providing the references?

The next step in the process is selecting a DMC that best meets the needs and budgetary guidelines. At this point, meeting and event professionals should formally notify potential DMCs by an RFP. Once the final selection has been made, it is important to begin working with the selected DMC to ensure that they have historical information related to the organization's participants that may impact the execution of the program.

BEST PRACTICES IN DMCS

The destination management industry's varied representatives are not immune to the need for change. The following is a list of eight areas that DMC operators should take seriously to enhance their leadership and stature in meeting and event management circles and beyond.

1. *Take the Lead in Green Practices.* Be proactive in initiating sustainable practices by implementing leading edge methods for leaving a smaller carbon footprint, educating other parts of the hospitality industry through professional organizational training activities and the development and distribution of training materials. In addition, DMCs should develop new partnerships to share these activities and materials with other businesses in both the private and public sector.
2. *Work Together in Consortiums.* The DMC industry will continue to see a consolidation of service organizations. It will be important for smaller, niche DMCs to bond together in consortiums to ensure that business remains in the local community and that the overall experience for meeting and event professionals is seamless from planning, execution, and payment.
3. *Identify and Develop New Business from Drive-to Markets.* Given the uncertainty of the economy and the unfriendly skies, businesses will begin to look for more local and regional sites for holding their meetings and events. This should lead DMCs to focus on developing new clients from locations that are closer to their destinations.
4. *Develop Crisis Networks.* Issues surrounding the safety and security of meeting attendees will continue to be a concern for corporations and associations. Successful DMCs will develop, implement, and execute risk management and crisis management plans and business continuity networks in partnerships with other organizations within their communities.
5. *Emphasize Standards of Conduct and Operations.* DMCs will continue to receive scrutiny about the behavior of staff used to provide client services. It will become increasingly important that DMCs implement high stan-

dards of conduct for their employees and operations. The standards and operational policies should be defined, recognized, and understood by every employee, client, and the public in general as part of an established image and reputation.

6. *Relationship Management Strategy.* Corporations and associations that conduct business and meeting travel are quickly consolidating their travel, meeting, and event expenses into a more economically efficient model. Local and niche DMCs will need to build strong, lasting relationships with meetings and event professionals to ensure that they are on the list of approved vendors. Consultative selling techniques must be used to establish strong, lasting relationships.

7. *Attentive to Competitive Forces.* Given the ubiquity of the Internet, and its convenience, successful large DMCs no longer need a continuous presence in a local market. Local, niche DMCs will need to increase the quality of customer contacts and services to meetings and events professionals and their attendees, to remain relevant in a competitive marketplace.

8. *Ethical Business Protocols.* DMCs rely heavily upon their confidential intellectual property, creative ideas, and research conducted for a specific client program. The industry's (DMCs, planners, as well as suppliers) adherence to the ADMEI Code of Ethics is vital for the continued growth and professionalism of the industry.

COVID-19: THE EFFECT ON DESTINATION MANAGEMENT COMPANIES

Without any doubt, COVID-19 has been the single-most disruptive event to negatively impact the global hospitality and tourism industry since the start of modern tourism in the 1950s. Whereas economic recessions, terrorist incidents, and natural disasters, among others, have impacted particular places, regions, or sometime nations, seldom if ever has something of this magnitude caused so much collateral damage to this industry as well as to so many others. With the path of the pandemic crossing Asia, then Europe before arriving in North America in the spring of 2020, the mass cancellation of events, be they for leisure or business, occurred almost instantly with major convention destinations such as Las Vegas and Orlando suffering devastating losses of business; and, in turn, much-needed tourist, sales, and state tax revenues. Out of any crisis or disaster, be they manmade or naturally occurring, one always has to look for the positives.

The first is that irrespective of what type of crisis or disaster has occurred previously, the hospitality, tourism, and events industry has always rebounded. Meetings, conventions, exhibitions, and tradeshows are an integral part of so many industries that projections for the future remain strong. Those destinations, and DMCs, that will succeed will be those that already have long-lasting and deeply professional relationships with their clients and customers, those that continue to understand the changing needs and expectations of the market, and perhaps most importantly in the future, those that provide a safe, clean, and healthy destination experience! Although risk and crisis management planning are already an integral part of a DMC, clearly it will be an even-more-important element moving forward. So too will be the role of technology and the innovative and creative means by which DMCs incorporate it into their destination experience. With so many people working remotely through the pandemic, whereas there may have been some resistance to the use of technology previously, it is now commonplace with video sharing and collaborative meeting technologies such as Zoom part of the new post-pandemic meeting and events agenda.

SUMMARY

The niche that DMCs provide in the MEEC industry is important for meeting and event professionals. These organizations provide a crucial service because the customer companies and organizations that sponsor meetings and events will always need access to local expertise. The depth of local destination knowledge, the local contacts and connections, the community standing, buying power, and hands-on experience with the implementation of programs and events are not readily available to organizations outside of the destination. DMCs have evolved in some interesting ways. Many of the earlier DMCs evolved from the ranks of wholesale tour operators and ground operators. These early DMCs began by specializing in tours and transportation services for visiting travel groups. In the late 1950s, the specialization in association and higher-end corporate programs demanded a wider range of services, including dining programs, expanded activities, and special events.

Today, the competitive landscape of DMCs is filled via multi-destination national DMC companies that operate networks around the world. However, just as individual one-of-a-kind hotels still prosper along with the giant hotel chains, so do unique and specialized one-destination DMCs. The services requested of DMCs by meeting and event professionals are still evolving, and destination management services have been secured as a key component for success in meetings and events industry.

Today's network of professionals who work in the destination management segment of the MEEC industry have a wide range of industry associations for support and tradeshows and conventions for marketing of their services. Chief among them is ADMEI and its DMC accreditation and executive certification programs.

Alan Fyall

Orlando, Florida, one of the busiest convention destinations in the world.

The long-term outlook for DMCs is bright, this despite the challenges posed by COVID-19. The meeting and event industry that DMCs support is robust, and many existing firms are financially sound and poised to gain market share and increase their brand recognition despite temporary threats and business slowdowns. The industry is full of opportunities for long-term successful career options for new meeting and event professionals.

CASE STUDY WORKING WITH A DMC

Natalie works for a professional association of financial managers in Chicago and has booked her conference of 1,000 participants for the late spring in San Diego. This is the first time the event or Natalie have been to that destination. To familiarize herself with the city she arranged for a site visit where she was escorted around the town by a member of the sales team of the San Diego Tourism Authority, the city's Destination Marketing Organization (DMO). They visited many hotels, attractions, special event venues, and golf courses and discussed ways in which the authority could be supportive in helping to market the conference to her membership. The DMO also provided her with a directory of member suppliers (tour and transportation companies, golf courses, décor companies, event venues other than hotels, restaurants). Prior to signing hotel contracts, she worked with the DMO in narrowing the hotel venue down to four properties where she eventually chose two to host the conference.

Now that Natalie had firm dates and a location for her program she began to think about a number of special events and activities her planning committee had recommended. As she thought about it and the additional workload involved, it became clear that she needed a partner in this endeavor. The DMO could only point her in the direction of suppliers. They were not planners, and, to be fair to all of their members, they could not negotiate contracts or recommend one supplier over another.

It was then that Natalie turned to a Destination Management Company (DMC). She referred to the DMO's membership directory, asked for recommendations from industry colleagues, and sent a request for proposal (RFP) to her top three DMC choices. Natalie was planning the following:

1. A golf tournament where she needed a golf course, transportation, awards, tournament planning, continental breakfast, lunch, and onsite supervision.
2. An adventure tour. In previous years they had done desert jeep tours, horseback riding, and swamp tours with airboats. She needed venue recommendations, transportation, a place for lunch and supervision.
3. The opening reception will be held at one of the hotels, but she needed theme décor and entertainment.
4. A historical cultural tour of the city required a planned route, bus transportation, qualified tour guides, and onsite supervision.
5. Two VIP dinners at high-end restaurants for 35 people each on two different nights. A private room was required. Floral arrangements needed to be ordered, and transportation provided.
6. Private transportation for the President, Chairman of the Board, and a keynote speaker to and from the airport.

Once the DMC's proposals arrived and after a careful review, Natalie chose to interview two of them during a site visit to San Diego. The DMCs met with Natalie, clarified the objectives and the audience for each event, and used their expertise of the city to develop a total program for the association. Rather than Natalie having to manage negotiations and contracts for each of these events and the many suppliers, she turned to a DMC as a one-stop shop. She was able to develop a trusted partnership where the DMC became her eyes and ears in San Diego. In essence, she hired an event planner for herself.

1. Did Natalie do a complete job?
2. What would you have done differently?
3. What else would you have done?

KEYWORDS AND TERMS

For definitions, see https://insights.eventscouncil.org/Industry-glossary

Association of Destination Manage-
ment Executives (ADMEI)
Advancing of a venue
APEX
Arrival manifest
Association Accounts
client project
corporate accounts
Convention and Visitor's Bureau CVB
customer
destination management company
(DMC)
destination management networks
destination marketing organization
(DMO)
Event Industry Council (EIC)

field staff
ground operator
house account
incentive-based organizations
incentive travel programs
IAPCO
leads
meet and greet
operations and production
program professional
Professional Congress Organizer
(PCO)
request for proposal (RFP)
site inspection
special event clients

REVIEW AND DISCUSSION QUESTIONS

1. What is a destination management company?

2. What services are offered by DMCs?

3. Compare and contrast the difference between a DMC and a DMO.

4. Create an organizational chart for a DMC.

5. How do DMCs generate their business leads?

6. What are the resources DMCs provide to a meeting and event professionals?

7. Describe the differences between the types of accounts that secure the services of DMCs.

8. What professional organizations support the professionals that work destination management industry?

9. List the services provided by ADMEI.

10. Describe key factors that are considered when meeting and event professionals are selecting a DMC.

11. Outline the important role, and financial contribution, that transportation plays and provides in the workings of a DMC.

ABOUT THE CHAPTER CONTRIBUTORS

Dr. Alan Fyall is the associate dean of academic affairs and visit Orlando endowed chair for tourism marketing at the Rosen College of Hospitality Management, University of Central Florida. He has published widely in the areas of tourism and destination marketing and management, including 23 books. Dr. Fyall is a former member of the Bournemouth Tourism Management Board (DMO) and has conducted numerous consulting and applied research projects for clients around the world. Alan currently teaches international tourism management and destination marketing and management.

Steve Brinkman received both his bachelor's and master's degrees in education from Illinois State University. Prior to working at UCF, he spent 24 years in the tourism and hospitality industry working in sales and marketing. He was also instrumental in developing the first commission-free group travel website, Group Travel Odyssey. Steve has sat on numerous sales and marketing boards and committees throughout his career. The most notable boards and committees included Visit Florida's International Tourism Board, Visit Orlando's Marketing Committee, the Domestic Group Travel Agency Board of Directors, the American Bus Association Marketing Advisory Committee, and co-chairman of the American Bus Association Marketplace Convention.

PREVIOUS EDITION CHAPTER CONTRIBUTORS

Brian Miller, Associate Professor at the University of Delaware.

Terry Epton, Executive Vice President, Host Global Alliance.

William R. Host, Associate Professor at the Roosevelt University in Chicago, Illinois.

CHAPTER 8

SPECIAL EVENTS MANAGEMENT

© Wedding and lifestyle/Shutterstock.com

WEDDINGS ARE "VERY SPECIAL" EVENTS

CHAPTER OBJECTIVES

- Provide an overview of the history, definition, and main components involved in special event planning.
- Outline a number of helpful special event planning tools.
- Discuss the many different considerations that go into special event marketing.
- Clarify the steps in preparing for a special event.
- Discuss the elements of a special event budget.
- Articulate the steps in breaking down a special event.
- Outline current trends, including COVID-19 trends, and best practices in special event management

HISTORY AND OVERVIEW OF SPECIAL EVENTS

A WORKING DEFINITION OF A SPECIAL EVENT

A *special event* is an umbrella term that encompasses all functions that bring people together for a unique purpose. Most events require some sort of planning on the part of the organizer. A special event, such as a city festival or fair, can mean working with **community infrastructure**, merchandising, promoting, and, in some cases, dealing with the media. The event can be as small as the local community Kiwanis picnic or as large as the Olympics. Special events are imbedded in **meetings, expositions, events, and conventions (MEEC)**, and at amusement parks, parades, **fairs, festivals, and public events**.

The Events Industry Council (EIC) glossary includes the following definition related to special events:

> *Special Event* One-time event staged for the purpose of celebration; unique activity.

> *Special Events Company* This type of company may contract to put on an entire event or only parts of one. A *special events production company* may present special effects and theatrical acts. They sometimes hire speakers as part of their contract.

A special event can bring organizations together for fundraising, establishing a city or community as a local, regional, or national destination, in order to stimulate the local economy. The event can also be an opportunity for an association or a corporation to favorably position itself with a community or with the mass consumer. Sponsoring a specific type of event can provide a marketing edge and another avenue for reaching customers. For example, Mercedes-Benz automobiles sponsor numerous PGA golf tournaments, in part because the demographics of the audience match its target clientele. It also does the same thing with the U.S. Open tennis tournament. Coors Light sponsors NASCAR races, Allstate sponsors the Sugar Bowl football game, Macy's sponsors the Thanksgiving Day parade, and the list goes on and on.

Orchestrating a special event takes more than an idea. It takes planning, understanding your target market, having basic operational knowledge, using effective communications, working with volunteers or volunteer organizations, working within a budget, promoting the event, and even creating the logistics for breaking down an event. Simply stated, the event professional needs to understand the "who, what, where, and why" of the special event.

HISTORY AND BACKGROUND

Festivals and special events have been part of human history since time immemorial. Humankind has celebrated births, weddings, and deaths throughout history and held special gatherings like the Olympics and gladiatorial combat. However, most historians credit the use of the term "special event" in modern history to a Disney "imagineer" named Robert Janni. The problem Disney faced was that the families who frequented the theme park were worn out after a day of adventure and most left by 5 p.m. each day, even though the park stayed open hours longer. In order to keep attendees at the park, he proposed producing a nightly parade called the "Main Street Electric Parade" with numerous floats decked out with lights. It was a success in keeping people in the park in the evening. When asked by a reporter what he called this parade, he replied "A Special Event." The use of special events to attract or maintain crowds is still used to this day.

USING FESTIVALS IN THE OFF-SEASON: "ROCKIN' MOUNTAINS"

The typical image of the Rocky Mountains and Colorado is one of snow-covered peaks in winter dotted with skiers. But what happens when summer rolls around and people cannot ski? What do the ski resorts do, shut down? The answer is a resounding "No!" They put on music festivals using the same facilities occupied by skiers in the winter. The setting is idyllic, with music carrying through the clean air with the awesome backdrop of mountain peaks.

This use of Colorado mountain ski facilities to host off-season musical events started in 1949, when concerts were held in the town of Aspen. At the time, it was called the Goethe Bicentennial celebration. Some of the events included the Minneapolis Symphony Orchestra playing in a tent that held 2,000 people. This special event has continued and grown into the Aspen Music Festival and School. Recently the event included more than 800 international musicians performing in over 400 events during the eight-week session. There are four major **venues**. The largest one is the Benedict Music tent that holds more than 2,000 people.

Another ski resort that has turned to musical events to attract visitors in the off-season is Telluride, Colorado. Nearly every summer weekend, the town hosts a musical event. The biggest special event is the Telluride Bluegrass Festival, which has been held for over 50 years. It runs for 4 days in June and is capped at 11,000 people per day. Telluride also hosts additional events to include a Jazz Festival, a Chamber Music Festival, and a Blues and Brews Festival.

In Winter Park just west of Denver, numerous weekends are occupied with music festivals. Concertgoers sit on the slopes and watch bands perform against the backdrop of the Continental Divide. The Winter Park Music Festival boasts a lineup of "old-school" music acts like Molly Hatchet and Cheap Trick. In July, they host the Winter Park Jazz festival for 2 days with artists covering a variety of genres. Also in July and covering two weekends is the Winter Park 30 Solshine Music Festival. This event features local artists and is presented free to the audiences.

Breckenridge also hosts a summer concert series that runs from late June until the middle of August. The event features everything from classical to rock music. They finance the event through a unique structure, raising one-fourth of its money through the Bon Appetit Series, which includes more intimate gatherings that range from country music concerts and wildflower hikes to scavenger hunts on Peak 7, tours of South Park, cabaret evenings, and Texas Hold'em tournaments.

IT ALL BEGINS WITH A RELATIONSHIP

What do these special events have in common: a wedding reception, a 5K charity run, the Macy's Thanksgiving Day parade, and a company picnic? All are very special events, though very different. And all are planned by someone who must understand the goals, the needs, and the desires of the client they are serving. The event professional has a responsibility to the client to do everything in his or her power to reach their goals, while working within the parameters of the given location, city, or facility.

How does the event professional begin to truly understand the vision of his or her client? And how does the client begin to trust the efforts of the event professional? Special events management begins and evolves by developing a very important relationship between the client and the event professional. The event professional must listen to the clients, hear their words, and see their vision. The event professional should have the capability to put that vision into a reality for the clients, given the expertise and the professionalism of the event professional.

An event professional and a client must have clear lines of communication between them. And as they talk and listen to each other, a viable plan can unfold. The event professional must always understand that the success of any event must begin with a relationship. Listen to the client, do what you say you will do, tend to the little things, and communicate without fail.

No matter what the profile of the event, each and every special event is, indeed, very special to someone, or to many. It becomes a great challenge to meet (and exceed) the expectations of your client, and this is one of the key roles of the event professional.

One very successful event that draws more than 100,000 visitors to Central Pennsylvania is the summer Central Pennsylvania Festival of the Arts™. This festival brings people to downtown State College and the University Park campus of Penn State University to celebrate the arts with its nationally recognized Sidewalk Sale and Exhibition, a gallery exhibition, and music, dance, and theatrical performances in a variety of traditional and nontraditional venues. The festival was founded in 1967 and was recently ranked first on the list of 100 Best Fine Arts and Design Shows in America by *Sunshine Artist magazine.*

THE PRESIDENTIAL INAUGURATION DAY PARADE

While the tradition of the Inaugural parade dates back to the Inauguration of George Washington, the first organized parade unfolded at the Inauguration of James Madison in 1809. Here, Madison was escorted to the Capitol by a troop of cavalry. After taking his oath of office, Madison then watched the parade of militia. In William

Henry Harrison's time, in 1841, floats were introduced to the parade. In addition, military bands, political groups, and college groups became parade participants.

As history progressed, African Americans joined Abraham Lincoln's Inaugural parade for the first time, increasing even further the number of participating groups in the parade. In 1873, President Grant reordered the events of the Inaugural Day to make the parade *after* the Inaugural Ceremony, rather than *before*. This tradition continues today.

Reviewing stands were built in 1881 for the Inauguration of President James Garfield. To combat the cold and sometimes harsh weather conditions, the grandstands became enclosed. Reviewing stands were also built for visitors.

Women became participants of the parade in 1917, and then, in 1921, President Warren Harding became the first president to ride in an automobile. This set a precedent until 1977, when President Jimmy Carter chose to walk in the parade with his wife and daughter, from the Capitol to the White House. The first televised Inaugural Parade was held in 1949 for President Harry S. Truman.

The largest parade occurred in 1953 at the Inaugural Parade of President Dwight D. Eisenhower. The parade included 73 bands, 59 floats, horses, elephants, military troops, and civilian and military vehicles. The parade lasted for over four-and-a-half hours.

The size and sophistication of the parade has developed tremendously over the last 200 years, and the Inaugural Parade has evolved into a nationally lauded special event. At the 2009 Inauguration Parade, President Barack Obama hosted 15,000 participants, including 2,000 military personnel. Forty-six bands were chosen to participate out of the 1,000 that applied. Today, millions of Americans can view the parade, whether via television viewing, Internet access, or in person. This parade has truly become a tradition of celebration for all Americans.

Today, the Armed Forces Inaugural Committee is responsible for the organization of the parade, and the Presidential Inaugural Committee is responsible for selecting all participants of the parade.

© Susan Montgomery/Shutterstock.com

Ann Arbor's South
University Art Fair

EXAMPLES OF SPECIAL EVENTS

A film festival can be a dream come true for moviegoers as they seek out famous actors who might be walking right next to them, as on the streets of Park City, Utah, during the Sundance Film Festival. Founded in 1981, the festival has grown to be the largest independent film festival in the United States, attracting tens of thousands of visitors each year to this quaint little town to view over 3,000 film submissions.

These special events came from an historical tradition that ultimately grew to attract thousands of visitors to some very remote areas. Continuing to attract visitors requires planning and planning tools, such as an understanding of the community infrastructure, merchandising and promoting the event, developing sponsorships, and working with the media. This is the art and science of special events management.

A special event is a celebration of something—that is what makes it special. Examples of special events are listed in Figure 8-1, though this list is not all-inclusive.

Civic Events
- Centennials
- Founders' Day

Mega Events
- Olympics
- America's Cup
- United Nations Assembly's
- World Expo's

Festivals and Fairs
- Marketplace of ancient days
- Community Event
- Fair = not for profit
- Festival = for profit

Expositions
- Where suppliers meet buyers
- Education
- Entertainment

Sporting Events
- Super Bowl
- World Series
- Masters Golf Tournament
- FIFA World Cup

Social lifecycle events
- Wedding
- Anniversary
- Birthday
- Reunion
- Bar Mitzvah (Bat Mitzvah)

Meetings and Conventions
- Political National Convention
- National Restaurant Association convention in Chicago
- PCMA annual conference

Retail Events
- Long-range promotional event
- Store opening

New product launches
- X-box
- Apple

Religious Events
- Papal Inauguration
- The Hajj (Mecca)
- Easter
- Kwanzaa

Corporate Events
- Holiday parties
- Annual dinner
- Company picnics
- Conferences/meetings

FIGURE 8-1
Examples of Special Events

PLANNING TOOLS FOR SPECIAL EVENTS

Special events management, like any other form of managing, requires planning tools. The first of these tools is a vision statement of your event. This vision statement should clearly identify the "who, what, when, where, and why" of the event. As the event begins to unfold, it is important to keep those involved focused on the vision. This can be accomplished by continually monitoring, evaluating, and, where possible, measuring the progress toward the outlined goals of the event (see See Chapter 13: *Planning MEEC Gatherings* and Chapter 14: *Producing Meetings and Events*).

The "who" of planning an event are those people or organizations that would like to host and organize it. In the case of the St. Patrick's Day Parade in Chicago, Illinois, it is the city that hosts and coordinates the marchers, the floats, and the bands. The "what" was a parade demonstrating Irish pride and local tradition. The "where" of the Parade is downtown Chicago, with the floats and bands marching down Michigan Avenue. The big question of "why" is one of tradition, pride, fun, and tourism. This, in turn, promotes the city and brings revenues to the local businesses. When the city decided to serve as the host of this event, it needed to incorporate the tools of special event management.

Some of the management tools that are used in staging events are as follows:

a. Flowcharts and graphs for scheduling. Look at any program for a meeting/event; there are start and end times, times for coffee breaks, a time for lunch, and a time that the meeting resumes and ends. The flowchart can be as "romantic" as a wedding ceremony **agenda**. The chart can be the order or sequence of floats for a parade, the program for a talent show, or the agenda for a weeklong international conference. A flowchart scheduling an event's activities helps guide attendees and guests and makes the execution of the event flow smoothly. **Gantt Charts** are often used for many of these tasks.

b. Clearly defined setup and breakdown **schedules**. These provide the event manager with an opportunity to determine tasks that may have been overlooked in the initial planning process.

c. Policy statements developed to guide in the decision-making process. Policy statements provide a clear understanding of commitments and what is expected to fulfill them. Some of the commitments to be considered are human resources, sponsors, security, ticketing, volunteers, and paid personnel.

© Paul Barnwell/Shutterstock.com

Detailed Gantt Chart

UNDERSTANDING COMMUNITY INFRASTRUCTURE

Another key ingredient for planning a successful event is an understanding of the infrastructure in the community where the event is to take place. This infrastructure might include the CEO of the company, politicians, prominent business leaders of the community, civic and community groups, the media, and other community leaders. Without a "buy-in" from the city leadership, a community is less inclined to be supportive. The role of business leaders in the community could be to provide sponsorships, donations, staff, or a possible workplace for the coordination of the event. Many times, community groups serve as volunteer workers for the event and are also an extension of the promotions for it.

Early on, it must be recognized whether a community or a company is truly committed to hosting any type of special event that will call on its support. This support not only includes the financial commitment but also the physical and emotional commitment it will take to manage an event from start to finish. For a promoter or special events management company to maintain a positive reputation, there needs to be a solid infrastructure in place.

SPECIAL EVENT MARKETING CONSIDERATIONS

MERCHANDISING AND PROMOTING THE SPECIAL EVENT

Merchandising and promoting a special event is another planning tool for attracting attendance and increasing the overall profitability for the event. Just because a community decides to host a craft fair or street festival does not mean that there will be the attendance necessary to meet vendors' and visitors' needs. Profit for the vendor and a memorable experience for the attendee are two main objectives for a special event. The special event requires all the promotional venues that an event management company or civic group can afford.

Understanding and utilizing the **promotional mix model** is pivotal to meet the goals of the event marketing plan. The role of promotion in special events management is the coordination of all the seller's efforts to set up channels of information and persuasion to sell or promote the event. Traditionally, the promotional mix has included four elements: advertising, sales promotion, publicity and/or public relations, and personal selling. However, this author views direct marketing and interactive media as additional elements of the promotional mix. The latter includes social media such as LinkedIn, Facebook, Twitter, and so on. Modern-day event marketers use many means to communicate with their target markets. Each element of the promotional mix is viewed as an integrated marketing communications tool. Each of these elements of the model has a distinctive role in attracting an attendee to the special event. Each takes on a variety of forms, and each has certain advantages.

PROMOTIONAL MIX

Advertising is defined as any paid form of nonpersonal communication about the event. The nonpersonal component means advertising that involves mass media (e.g., TV, radio, magazines, mobile phones, websites, and newspapers). Advertising is the best known and most widely discussed form of promotion because it is the most persuasive, especially if the event (e.g., a home and garden show) is targeted toward mass consumers. It can be used to create brand images or symbolic appeals for the brand and generate immediate responses from prospective attendees.

There are many elements of the promotional mix for special events. These include the following:

Direct marketing is a form of advertising that communicates directly with the target customer with the intent of generating a response. It is much more than direct mail or catalogs. It involves a variety of activities, including database management, direct selling, telemarketing, direct-response ads, the Internet, social media, and various broadcast and print media. The Internet has also fueled the growth of direct marketing. One of the large advantages of e-mail marketing is the ability to measure response rates.

Engagement Marketing, also called "experiential marketing," is a strategy that engages and invites consumers to be a part of a brand experience. This creates a face-to-face opportunity for the event designer. You can also cobrand as a means for increasing response. One of the more successful campaigns was Zappos "Google Cupcake Ambush" where Zappos gave away free pairs of shoes to customers who received a cupcake by trying Google's new photo app.

Interactive or Internet marketing also allows for a back-and-forth flow of information. Users can participate in and modify the form and content of the information they receive in real time. Unlike traditional forms of marketing, such as advertising, which are one-way forms of communication, this type of media allows users to perform a variety of functions. It enables users to receive and alter information and images, make inquiries, respond to questions, and make purchases. Many event attendees will go to a website to garner information about a special event such as a concert and purchase their tickets directly online. For a special event such as the Aspen Music Festival, attendees can go to the festival's official website, view the schedule, learn about the event and the surrounding area, purchase tickets, and request additional information—all forms of direct marketing. In addition to the Internet, other forms of interactive media include thumb drives, kiosks, and interactive television.

Sales promotion is generally defined as those marketing activities that use incentives or discounts to increase sales or attendance. A popular form of sales promotion is the coupon. Many events will use a two-for-one attendance coupon to stimulate attendance on slower days. In addition, merchandise is often offered when purchasing several tickets at once.

Publicity and public relations is divided into two components. Publicity is the component that is not directly paid for and doesn't have an identified sponsor. When an event planner gets the media to cover or run a favorable story on a special event, it affects an attendee's awareness, knowledge, and opinions. Publicity is considered a credible form of promotion, but it is not always under the control of the organization or host of the event. In the case of South by Southwest (SXSW), prior to the event, the organizers send out press releases highlighting the performers or acts that are participating in the event. During the event, reporters and camera crews cover the action on a daily basis. If those reporting the event have a positive experience, it will favorably affect the public's perception of the event. Unfortunately, the reverse is also true; the event professionals have little control.

Social media has exploded as a preferred strategy for promotional initiatives. Social media reaches the masses with minimal expense and relative ease of effort. This is also known as viral marketing. While there are many vehicles of social media, some of the more commonly used mediums include Facebook, Blogging, LinkedIn, Pinterest, Google+, and Twitter. Each of these mediums allows a message to be sent simultaneously to many people, projecting a controlled and positive message to the reader. In addition, the message that is sent is delivered immediately to the reader. (For more information, see Chapter 11: *Technology and the Meeting Professional.*)

There are a variety of special events that take place to promote a destination or an occasion. One example is the SXSW event held in March each year in Austin, Texas. This 9-day event is the premier gathering of music, film, and interactive professionals.

The purpose of public relations is to systematically plan and distribute information to attempt to control or manage the image and/or publicity of an event by building beneficial relationships with stakeholders and consumers. It has a broader objective than publicity because its purpose is to establish a positive image of the special event. Public relations and publicity are favored by festival and event directors because they reach the audience they are attempting to attract. Public relations can be the reason for hosting the special event altogether. Tobacco companies have used special events like a NASCAR race or tennis tournament to create a more positive image with consumers.

Personal selling is the final element of the promotional mix model, and it is a form of person-to-person communication in which a seller attempts to assist and/or persuade prospective event attendees. Typically, group tour sales are one of the best prospects for personal selling of a special event. There are several touring companies that purchase large groups of tickets for special events. Unlike advertising, personal selling involves direct contact between the buyer and seller of the event, usually through face-to-face sales. Personal selling is by far the most expensive form of promotional activity when considered in terms of the number of consumers reached. Some examples of events that group tours attend may include: the Indianapolis 500, the Kentucky Derby, or the Jazz Fest in New Orleans. Group tour organizers will meet face-to-face with event professionals or talk via the telephone to purchase tickets for an event.

BRANDING A DESTINATION

South by Southwest

South by Southwest (**SXSW**) is a group of festivals and conferences that take place every spring in Austin, Texas, and covers music, film, and interactive technologies. It began small in 1987 but has grown every year since its inception. Currently, it is the largest music festival of its kind in the world boasting over 2,200 bands on 113 stages. The film festival is focused on attracting new directors while the interactive portion is focused on emerging technology. SXSW has launched a number of new products during the, event but two of the more notable are Twitter and Foursquare. John Mayer launched his career by performing at SXSW. The film festival has launched numerous films over the years including in *The Hurt Locker*, which went on to win the Academy Award for Best Picture in 2010.

While the focus of the event has been to promote the three industries, it has also become a primary source of bringing tourism to Austin, Texas. It continues to be the single most profitable event for the City of Austin's hospitality industry. In 2019, the event created the following impact to the local economy:

- 12,800 individual hotel registrations totaling over 55,300 room nights ($1.9 million in occupancy tax revenue)
- 280,000 conference and festival participants
- A direct economic impact of $264.6 million (directly related to the local economy)
- An indirect impact of $157.1 million (increases in sales, income, and jobs associated with companies that benefit from SXSW expenditures)
- Induced impacts of $16.7 million (spending by individuals as a result of increased earnings as a result of the conference).
- Total economic impact $335.9 million

SPONSORSHIPS FOR SPECIAL EVENTS

Sponsorships help to ensure profitable success for an event. They are an innovative way for event organizers to help underwrite and defray costs. Sponsorships should be considered more than just a charitable endeavor for a company—they can be a strong marketing tool.

Event sponsors provide funds or "in-kind" contributions and receive consideration in the form of logo usage and identity with the event. Recent trends of sponsorships show rapid growth. Sponsorship can take many forms. A large corporation, for instance, may have the means to provide financial sponsorship for an event. However, mid-size and smaller organizations may need to be more creative in their sponsorship methods. A smaller organization may, for example, provide a product rather than a financial contribution. Therefore, you may not see their banner hanging at the event, but you will have their product in your hand.

Many types of special events require sponsorship to be successful. Sporting events have long been the leader in securing sponsorships for teams and athletes. However, their market share has dropped as companies begin to distribute sponsorship dollars to other events, such as city festivals and the arts. This shift in sponsorships from sports events to that of festivals and the arts over the past decade has emerged because companies are cognizant of the effective tool that a sponsorship can be for overall company marketing plans. Sponsors are beginning to recognize that festivals are now as attractive as sports at generating a return on investment (ROI).

Naples, Florida

The Annual Naples Winter Wine Festival is regarded as the nation's top charity wine auction. It is held in Naples, Florida and runs for 3 days each January.

The festival began in 2001 as a charity to benefit the Naples Children and Education Foundation and the children of Collier County, Florida. In the recent past, the live auction at the event raised more than $12.8 million. Since its debut, the annual charity wine auction event has collected over $176 million for their charity.

The event's auction rewards participants with an opportunity to bid on numerous items, including ski trips, vintage wine, hotel stays, and luxury cars. They have even auctioned off a Rolls Royce Phantom that claimed the highest bid at $780,000.

The event extends over a 3-day weekend and the excitement is non-stop. A Fund-a-Need lot raised more than $2.4 million for underserved children in need of oral healthcare and hunger relief, and a few days later, the event's online auction ended, bringing in an additional $170,275.

For the Naples Winter Wine Festival, the charity is the most important thing. The event supports children's mental health, and auction-goers get to meet some of the supported kids. The event also continues to bring new attendees each year with 40% to 50% of the attendees to the event being first-time visitors.

There are five compelling reasons why company sponsorships are an important option to consider:

1. Economic changes (both upturns and downturns)
2. Ability to target market segments
3. Ability to measure results
4. Fragmentation of the media
5. Growth of diverse population segments

Changes in the economic climate of the country will affect the goals, spending, and expectations of the sponsoring organization. In times of economic health, companies (both large and small) may be willing and able to more freely spend their promotional dollars on sponsorship. In economic downturns, however, organizations are likely to feel the necessity to account for the return they are receiving on their promotional spending. In other words, the sponsorship is seen as an investment, and the organization would like to know if, in fact, they are receiving a return on their investment. In either economic climate, sponsorships promote the intangible benefits of company visibility and overall goodwill.

When looking for sponsorships for a special event, organizers must determine if the event fits the company. Event professionals must always examine the company's goal and be sure to research the competition. Special event organizers should aid the sponsors with promotional ideas that will help them meet their goals. Promoters of an event need to ensure that sponsors get their money's worth. Remember that sponsors have internal and external audiences to whom they are appealing.

"Cross-promotional opportunities" allow the sponsor to achieve the greatest visibility possible by capitalizing on more than one promotional opportunity within one event. For example, if PepsiCo sponsored an event, then that company would likely gain notable visibility through banners, logos, and so on. However, to further capitalize on this sponsorship, PepsiCo might further request that only Pepsi products be sold at the event. They are gaining visibility through the product that is being served at the event, and they may likely be earning revenue on the product that they are serving. This sponsorship would, therefore, serve as a triple benefit to the corporation. The internal audience of a corporation is its employees, and they must also be sold on the sponsorship of the event. A company needs to provide opportunities for employee involvement. If the special event is a charitable marathon, employees may be asked to actually participate in the marathon or raise funds for the charitable cause. Those employees who participate may be featured in promotional material or press releases.

New York City Marathon

Sponsorship

The New York City Marathon boasts over 50,000 runners with more than 2 million spectators and is one of the largest live sporting events in the world, being broadcast to over 330 million viewers in more than 154 territories. Television coverage includes a live five-hour telecast on ABC channel 7 in New York, a two-hour national telecast on ESPN, and various live and highlight shows internationally.

New York Road Runners and the New York City Marathon are fortunate to have the support and commitment of sponsors and strategic partners. Their continued support makes the New York City Marathon a world-class event year after year.

Sponsors

Title Sponsor:

Tata Consultancy Services (TCS)

Additional Sponsors

Airbnb
United Airlines
New Balance
Fitbit
The Rudin Family
Foot Locker
Poland Spring
PowerBar
Gatorade
Hospital for Special Surgery
Tiffany & Co.
UPS

Selling to the external audience of the corporation (the consumer) is done in a variety of ways. First, the company might feature its logo on the event's products. The company can promote its affiliation with the special event by providing its logo for outdoor banners and specialty advertising items, such as T-shirts, caps, or sunglasses. The types of specialty products are limitless and excellent venues for advertising. The sponsoring company may wish to appoint an employee spokesperson to handle radio or television interviews.

WORKING WITH THE MEDIA FOR AN EVENT

Generating media coverage for a special event is one of the most effective methods for attracting attendance. Ideally, an event organizer wants to garner free television, radio, and print coverage. To attract the media, a promoter must understand what makes for good coverage and what does not.

When a camera crew is sent to film an event by assignment editors at a TV station, they will look for a story that can be easily illustrated with visuals captured by a camera. They also look for a vignette that can entertain viewers in 30 seconds or less. If an event organizer wants television or radio stations to cover the event, he or she needs to call it to their attention with a press release or press conference. There are no guarantees that the station or the newspaper will air the footage or print the story; however, the chances are better if a camera crew shoots footage or a reporter does an interview. Remember, special events provide ideal topics for the evening news. This can be an interview with a celebrity who will be attending the event or an advance look at an art exhibit.

Event organizers try to present the unusual to the media. In 2007, Kentucky Fried Chicken decided to unveil a redesign of the company logo for the first time in over 10 years. The logo revision included bolder colors and changing the founder Col. Harland Sanders from his customary white suit and black bow tie into a red apron against a matching red background. To unveil the logo redesign, the company decided to create an 87,000-square-foot version that could be seen from space. The logo for this event was created out of 65,000 one-foot tiles that were set up in the Las Vegas desert. The new logo was then filmed by the Google satellite and uploaded to YouTube and Google Maps, resulting in over 600,000 views.

This also resulted in the story being carried on national news broadcasts and resulted in a multitude of media coverage over the next several weeks. Promoters of special events have long recognized what TV and radio coverage can do for an event.

© CHALERMPHON SRISANG/Shutterstock.com

Kentucky Fried Chicken Logo

Here are some helpful hints for attracting television and radio coverage:

1. Early in the day is considered the best time to attract cameras and reporters. Remember, a crew must come out, film, get back to the studio, edit the film, and have the segment ready for the 5:00 or 6:00 p.m. newscast that night.
2. The best day of the week to attract news crews is Friday. That is because it is usually a quiet news day. Saturday and Sunday have even fewer distractions, but most stations do not have enough news crews working the weekend who can cover an event.
3. Giving advance notice for a special event is very helpful to assignment editors. It is nice to give about 3-day notice, with an explanation of the event via a press release and telephone follow-up. If an interview is involved, a 7-day notice is a good time allotment for coverage.

UNDERSTANDING THE TARGET MARKET FOR YOUR SPECIAL EVENT

Bringing special events to a community has not changed much over the years; however, consumers have changed. They are much more selective and sophisticated about the events they will attend. Since the cost of attending events has risen, consumers are much more discerning about how they spend their entertainment dollars. This creates a demand for quality for any special event.

Understanding your target market is one of the most important components in the overall success of the event. It is critical for the event marketer and event professional to know the participant audience. Age, gender, religion, ethnicity—all must be understood. Depending on the type of event, the event professional must understand participant restrictions (i.e., religious, dietary) and participant needs. The event must be based on the overall needs and desires of the target market.

The most valuable outcome a special event can generate for a community is positive word-of-mouth. To create this positive awareness, an organizer recognizes that the event cannot appeal to all markets. A promoter will determine the target market for the community's event.

Target marketing is defined as clearly identifying who wants to attend a certain type of event. For example, a Justin Bieber concert has been determined to appeal to a young female audience between the ages of 12 and 16. To stage a profitable concert, promoters will direct their advertising dollars to that particular targeted audience. Subsequently, all promotional items will also be geared toward that age group.

A Very Special Wedding

A couple from Texas wanted to be sure that their wedding was special, so they decided to have it in New Orleans. They were enamored with the charm of the city: moss-draped oak trees, antebellum homes, and horse-drawn carriages. They decided to invite 100 people and contacted a local destination management company (DMC) to make the arrangements. Their specification was that the DMC arrange a rehearsal dinner for 12 people and a reception for 100. Such costs as transportation to New Orleans, hotel accommodations, and the church were not part of the bid. Their stated budget for this wedding reception and dinner was $350,000. That's right—over a quarter of a million dollars or $3,500 per guest! When the event professional heard this, her reaction was twofold: (1) how could she possibly put together this event and spend that much money, and (2) if that was their proposed budget, she would try to upsell them.

The rehearsal dinner was held in a private dining room at the famous Arnaud's restaurant in the French Quarter. The real money was spent on the reception. They rented the art deco Saenger Theater for the evening, but there was a problem. Like most theaters, the floor sloped toward the stage. So, they removed all the seats and built a new floor that was level, not sloped. The interior of the theater was so beautiful that it needed little decoration. The New Orleans Police Department was contracted to close the street between the church and theater to cars so that the period ambiance would not be disturbed for the couple and their guests while being transported in their horse-drawn carriages. When the couple and their guests entered for the evening, they were greeted by models in period costume and served mint juleps while a gospel group sang. A blues band followed, and the night was topped off by not one but two sets by Jennifer Lopez who owns a home in New Orleans. The affair was catered by Emeril Lagasse and only included heavy hors d'oeuvres, not even a sit-down dinner. The ultimate cost for this event was almost $395,000, and the couple was delighted.

The planner was Nanci Easterling of Food Art, Inc.

Most communities know that a special event will have a positive economic impact on the community and the region. This has created competition to attract events. A city will commonly use inducements to lure the special event to the community. These inducements may include free entertainment space, security, parking, and even the "key to the city" to the celebrity providing the entertainment. A "city-wide" is a commonly used term for those large events or conventions that impact the entire city. City-wides are key to urban economics. When a large event or convention is hosted in a particular city, the economic effects are positive. Hotel rooms may completely sell out across the city, eateries are busy, and retail and cultural attractions may flourish due to the "city-wide."

A successful event has two vital components. One is that the community is supportive of bringing the event to the city, and second is that the event meets the consumers' need. For example, every year on Labor Day weekend, New Orleans is host to a special event called "Southern Decadence." This 3-day event, attended by over 150,000 LGBTQA+ people, generates over $150 million for the city. New Orleans is probably one of the few communities in the United States that would be supportive of bringing such an event to its city.

PREPARING FOR THE SPECIAL EVENT

Basic operations for staging an event need to be established and include the following:

- Secure a venue.
- Obtain **permits**.
  - Parade permits
  - Liquor permits
  - Sanitation permits
  - Sales permits or licenses
  - Fire safety permits
- Involve **government agencies** where necessary (i.e., if using city recreation facilities, work with the department of parks and recreation).
- Involve the health department if there will be food and beverage at the event.
- Meet all relevant parties in person so that any misconceptions are cleared up early.
- Secure all vendors and suppliers for the event.

- Recognize the complexities of dealing with the public sector. Sometimes, public agencies have a difficult time making decisions.
- Recognize the logistics that a community must contend with for certain types of special events, such as street closures for a marathon.
- Set up a security plan, which may include the security supplied by the venue and professional law enforcement. (Pay attention as to which security organization takes precedence.)
- Secure liability insurance (the most vulnerable area are those liabilities attached to liquor and liquor laws).
- Determine ticket prices if the special event involves ticketing.
- Determine ticket sale distribution if the special event involves ticketing.

The type of special event being held will determine the degree of preparedness needed. The larger the event, the more involved the checklist. Preparedness should produce a profitable and well-managed event.

SOFTWARE AND TOOLS FOR SPECIAL EVENTS

Event planners are faced with a wide variety of tasks to complete for each event, and there is a plethora of tools available to assist with these tasks. While there are too many to include here, it is important to identify the types of tools you need. Are you looking for project management help or something for attendee engagement?

One of the most common management tools is Google Drive. Planners can use the features for managing documents, folders, spreadsheets, and so on, and it is also a great tool for collaboration. While this is one option there are a number of tools to consider. If you are looking for an overall event management software, Whova makes a software that handles everything from registration, onsite check-in, attendee polling, name badge creation, and an event app.

If you typically use an Excel spreadsheet for managing tasks you might want to consider Smartsheet. This is a tool that also allows live collaboration and communication. The program has a very easy-to-use dashboard, although there is a short learning curve for new users.

Basecamp is another good management software. Although not as new as some of the others, it is still a very solid performer in the project management space.

If your event has mastered project management but lacks communication, you might want to consider a program like Slack. This tool allows users to share and discuss ideas from anywhere and is a great way to keep your team informed.

Food and beverage events require some separate tools to manage these types of events. Caterease is one of the industry leaders in this space. Ticketing is another area that planners are commonly looking for help. TicketSpice is one of the most powerful ticketing solutions available.

Floor plan design programs are also an important tool to the special event planner. AllSeated makes a program that allows the user to design floor plans, manage guests lists, and create visual seating charts.

Finally, audience engagement is the latest area that event planners are attempting to influence. EventMobi is one of the leaders in this market. They have a customizable app, built-in audience response tracking, gamification, registration, and reporting tools. While we have only touched on a small portion of the range of products available to the planner, it is clear that help is available for any task you might have in producing a special event.

GETTING A PERMIT

San Diego, California's event permitting process is fairly typical for most moderate-sized cities. The city publishes a guide to indicate to the event organizers what permits are necessary for their event. The city's website has a planning guide and access to all the forms that might be required for any event.

Events or organized activities for 75 or more people that involve street closures or include event components requiring the coordination of many city departments or other agencies such as the use of alcohol, on-site cooking, food sales, or large-scale temporary structures typically are reviewed through the Citywide Special Event Permit Process. Examples include festivals, parades, runs/walks, farmer's markets, and other planned group activities.

For an application to be considered complete, applicants must submit the following minimum information required in sections of the Citywide Special Event Permit Application in sufficient detail that the material can be understood and assessed:

- Host Organization Section (Complete)
- Event Summary Section (Complete)
- Event Infrastructure Section (All aspects that relate to the specific event)
- Operational Plan Section (All aspects that relate to the specific event)
- Site Plan/Route Map Section (Complete)
- Community Outreach Section (Complete)
- Insurance Section (Complete, including all required certificates of insurance and endorsements)
- Signature Section (Complete)
- Any required documentation relevant to the permit application processes and requirements set forth in the Special Events Planning Guide and Citywide Special
- Event Permit Application (Complete)

Applicants are responsible for obtaining all permits, authorization, and/or exemptions required by other agencies with jurisdiction for any element of the event (e.g., Alcohol Beverage Control Permits, Health Permits, California Coast Guard, California Coastal Commission approval, etc.).

https://www.sandiego.gov/sites/default/files/legacy/specialevents/pdf/planningguide.pdf

THE SPECIAL EVENT BUDGET

For any event to be considered a success, it must also be considered profitable. Profitability requires understanding the concepts of budgeting and finance as they relate to events (for more information, see See Chapter 13: *Planning MEEC Gatherings* and Chapter 14: *Producing Meetings and Events*). The basic items that make up the costs for a special event include the categories that follow.

RENTAL COSTS

Depending on the type of event, renting a facility such as a convention center or ground space to put up a tent requires payment of a daily rental charge. Convention centers usually sell the space based on a certain dollar amount per square footage used. Most facilities charge for space even on the move-in and move-out days. Multiday events can usually negotiate a discount.

There are, of course, variations to the rental cost of event space. If, for example, an association is holding a conference in a hotel, the event space may be free of charge or offered at a reduced rate if a certain number of hotel rooms are booked by the participating group. Furthermore, if the group requires food and beverage, then often the rental space is provided at a reduced rate or complimentary with the establishment of a **food and beverage minimum**.

SECURITY COSTS

Most convention centers, rental halls, and hotels provide limited security. This could mean that a guard is stationed at the front and rear entrances of the venue. Depending on the type of event, such as a rock concert performed by a band that has raucous fans, more security may be required. European Soccer (Football) matches require even more security. Actual costs will depend on the city and the amount of security needed.

PRODUCTION COSTS

These are the costs associated with staging an event. The costs vary depending on the type of special event. For example, if the special event is a large home and garden show, there are costs associated with the setup of the trade show booths. As with many home and garden shows, exhibitors bring in elaborate garden landscapes that are very time consuming and labor intensive to set up and break down. Labor costs for decorators need to be calculated to estimate the production costs based on the type and size of trade show booth. There are also electrical and water fees needed for a home and garden show, and these costs must be included in the production costs. Other production costs include signage or banners for each booth and pipe and drape fees.

LABOR COSTS

The city where the special event is being held will affect the labor costs involved in the setup and breakdown of the event. Some cities are unionized, and this can add higher costs to an event because of the higher wages. Holding an event in very strict union city means that the organizer of the event must leave more of the handling to the union crew. In some cities, the union allows the exhibitor to wheel his or her own cart with brochures and merchandise. In other cities, exhibitors cannot carry anything other than their own briefcases.

When selecting a city for an event, the role of unions has been an important influence. Most special event organizers will pass the higher costs on to the exhibitor or will increase ticket prices.

MARKETING COSTS

The costs associated with attracting attendees can make up a large portion of the budget. Here, the event organizer examines the best means of reaching the target market. Trying to reach a mass audience may mean running a series of television commercials, which can be very expensive. Most event organizers use a combination of promotions to attract the attendee. There will be elements of advertising, direct marketing, publicity and public relations, sales promotion, interactive or Internet marketing, and personal selling. All of these need to be budgeted.

TALENT COSTS

Virtually all special events use some type of talent or performers. They may include keynote speakers, band or orchestra, sports teams, vocalists, animals, and so on. While the organizer may have grandiose thoughts about the quality of the talent used, price must be considered and matched to the special event budget. The high school class reunion probably cannot afford to have Jennifer Lopez or Taylor Swift perform.

Before an event, it is essential that an event professional do a projection of all costs and revenue. These projections are essential as to whether a community will host another event. Repeat events are much easier to promote, especially when the organizers have made a profit. Before and during the event, it is critical that billing updates are completed and presented to the client on a regular (sometimes daily) basis. Any discrepancies or new costs should be handled at the point they occur. There should be no cost surprises at the end of an event.

BREAKDOWN OF THE SPECIAL EVENT

Special events have one thing in common: They all come to an end! Taking down or **breaking down** the event usually involves many steps. Once the attendees have gone, there are a variety of closing tasks that an organizer must complete.

First, the parking staff should expedite the flow of traffic away from the event. In some cases, community police can assist in traffic control.

A debriefing of staff should take place to determine what did or did not happen at the event. There may be issues pending that will need documentation. It is always best to have written reports to refer to for next year's event. Consider having the following sources add information to the report:

- *Participants:* Interview some of the participants from the event. A customer's perception and expectation is an invaluable insight.
- *Media and the Press:* Ask why it was or was not a press-worthy gathering.
- *Staff and Management:* Get a variety of staff and other management involved in the event to give feedback.
- *Vendors:* They also have a very unique perspective on how the event could be improved. Exhibitors and vendors *must* complete a survey. Because of their great perspective, exhibitors can provide some outstanding and constructive feedback for planning the next event.

The following should also be included in a final report on the event:

- Finalize the income and expense statement. Did the event break even, make a profit, or experience a loss?
- Finalize all contracts from the event. Fortunately, almost everything involved with putting together the event will have written documentation. Compare final billing with actual agreements for any discrepancies.
- Send the media a final press release on the overall success of the event. Interviews with the press could be arranged. This could be especially newsworthy if the event generated significant revenues for the community.

- Provide a written thank you for those volunteers who were involved with the event in any way. A celebration of some sort with the volunteers may be in order, especially if the event was financially and socially successful.

Once the elements of breakdown have taken place, the organizers can examine the important lessons of staging the event. What would they do or not do next year?

TRENDS AND BEST PRACTICES IN SPECIAL EVENTS

Less is the new more. Clients are seeking the simple with a "flare."

- Clients want to appear to be responsible in their spending. Excessive or over-spending is no longer the desirable trend.
- "Stylish minimalism" refers to the idea that clients still want style, flare, and innovation in the overall event but choose to uphold a conservative budgetary perception.
- Quality is paramount, at a cost that the client sees as a "value."
- Frivolous events are seen as wasteful; events should have a purpose.
- Many events are now targeted toward service or charitable causes. This provides purpose to an event. Events may be targeted toward medical concerns (i.e., cancer research, heart disease, autism awareness) or toward relief on a national or international level (Haiti Relief, Hurricane Katrina Relief, etc.).
- Clients are looking for an entire "package"—an experience. The event planner is truly planning an experience—often referred to as "experience management." Some event planners believe that a good event should captivate the audience and offer "change" every half hour.
- Going green—environmentally, event professionals are urged to consider green solutions. Earthy, environmentally friendly efforts are becoming the expectation. Interestingly, because of the perceived lack of sophistication, "eco-friendly" efforts are more likely to be incorporated into an event, rather than a primary means of service. For example, recycled coffee cups may be offered at a coffee station, along with china cups and saucers.
- Technology is key in promotional efforts. More Internet promotions are desired, as event managers are able to quantify the number of "hits" that they receive on their promotional initiative.
- Technology will also impact the meeting space. Google Glass has the opportunity to create a more personal, staged, and shared attendee experience.

- Gamification—adding games to the meeting/event mix can create a healthy competition and measurable ROI for your events.
- Every client has their own unique set of needs and wants. Every client wants the undivided attention of the event professional; their needs must be recognized throughout the entire planning and execution of the event.
- Quality, cost, and relationship are three components that must be in balance for every special event.
- While face-to-face events are still here to stay, the COVID-19 pandemic has at least temporarily shifted special events to a virtual setting. Even after the end of the pandemic, events are sure to change from prior to COVID-19.

THE IMPACT OF COVID-19 IN 2020

Live events came to a standstill in the spring of 2020 with COVID-19 spreading in the United States. Events were immediately canceled through the end of the year effectively shutting down the entire event industry. The greatest public health impact to events came with the implementation of social distancing and facial coverings. Special events that were used to holding events in a theater-style setting quickly found their venues reduced in capacity by 75% or more even if they were allowed to be "fully opened."

As the fall of 2020 approached, events began reopening, but they looked much different than prior to the pandemic. Guests were required to wear facial coverings and maintain social distance and were not allowed to warmly greet other attendees at the event. The cleaning and disinfecting procedures added a large financial load to facilities in order to even begin hosting these much smaller crowds.

While the venues are reopening, they also face the challenge of convincing their potential clients that it will be "safe" to hold their event. As of October 2020, there was a large reluctance for all groups to feel comfortable in an event setting. However, these are also times of opportunity for event planners and students who will be graduating into the industry. Those meeting planners who are able to implement COVID-19 policies and practices will be able to attract clients who are looking for reassurance. The opportunity also exists for planners who can continue to make virtual or hybrids as attractive and vibrant as a face-to-face meeting. The opportunity *is* out there.

SUMMARY

Creating a memorable event requires that an organizer meet and exceed an attendee's expectations. Recognizing that the special event could be for a meeting or convention, a parade, a festival, a fair, or an exhibit requires understanding the objectives of the event. Having the planning tools in place is the keystone for success in managing the gathering. Special events management works with and understands the community infrastructures to help support the event.

It can be costly if in advance an event professional does not decide which part of the promotional mix model of the event is used. The promotional mix model includes advertising, direct marketing, interactive or Internet marketing, sales promotion, publicity and public relations, and personal selling. Helping to defray costs by seeking sponsorships for a special event is another way to successfully market an event, and it is also an important marketing tool for the corporation sponsor. Generating publicity by working with the local and/or national media is the most effective way for attracting attendance. An organizer also needs to understand what makes for good media coverage and whether it is for print or broadcast. The target market for the special event must always be considered in terms of the objectives, promotions, and continuation of the event.

The basic operations and/or logistics for the event follow the planning and promoting. A checklist of the items that need to be handled or considered is a must for any event professional. Event professionals should also create checklists that will help develop the overall special event budget. This budget requires regular reviews of the statement of revenues and expenditures. The breakdown is the final step and includes another checklist for the closure of the event. Always remember your volunteers—without them, your event would not take place!

CASE STUDY BAD TIMING AT THE BANQUET

(Produced by G.G. Fenich and Students from East Carolina University)

Rob Clifford is the director of food and beverage at the Homey Hotel in New York, New York, which has a 10-room, 6,000-square-foot banquet/meeting facility.

Sue Collins is an event planner in New York City who has been planning a very important employee recognition/awards dinner banquet for a large, local company in the city. She has arranged to have the dinner at the Homey Hotel. The dinner will be for 450 people, served buffet-style with three separate buffets, and the total cost for the event has come to approximately $45,000.

The schedule for the evening is supposed to go as follows:

5:30 p.m.—Arrival of guests/cash bar opens

6:00 p.m.—Welcome speech given by the company president (guests mingle after welcome speech before dinner)

7:00 p.m.—Dinner (buffet is to be opened)

8:30 p.m.—Awards given

10 p.m.—Adjourn

Rob has spoken to Sue about the schedule for the night, and she has told him that they still plan on eating and want the food ready at 7 p.m.

During the welcome speech, the president of the company welcomed his employees, recognized the board of directors, and briefly talked about how the night will go. Unexpectedly at the end of his speech, around 6:15 p.m., he gives the board of directors the go-ahead to begin helping themselves to the buffet. The board of directors followed by three other groups of VIP guests sitting at reserved tables got up and proceeded to the buffet lines. The Homey Hotel hadn't planned to put their cold food out on the buffets until 6:35 p.m., followed by their hot food around 6:45 p.m. The Homey banquet staff immediately began bringing out food, but it took almost 15 minutes to get all the food ready on all three buffets. All food was brought out while the board of directors and the VIP guests were standing in line waiting.

Although Rob and the rest of the Homey staff acted quickly to this unexpected change, the president of the company was furious that the board of directors, his VIP guests, along with himself had to wait in line while food was put out and into chaffers. Because of how unhappy he was about the food, the president of the company is refusing to pay the full amount of money that he owes to Sue, and Sue is demanding a discount from the Homey Hotel food and beverage department. The Homey feels that they did their job by speaking to the event planner prior to the beginning of the event to confirm the time that the food should be out, and that it is not their fault that the president invited guests to the buffets 45 minutes prior to the scheduled time.

Do you feel that the Rob should honor the request and discount their event? Why or why not?

KEYWORDS AND TERMS

For definitions, see https://insights.eventscouncil.org/Industry-glossary

agenda
breaking down
community infrastructure
fairs, festivals, and public events
food and beverage minimums
Gantt Chart
government agencies

meetings, expositions, events, and
   conventions (MEEC)
permit
promotional mix model
schedule
venue

REVIEW AND DISCUSSION QUESTIONS

1. Discuss the types of events that a city might host.

2. What does the vision statement of an event provide for an organizer?

3. Discuss the importance of the event professionals' client relationship in event planning.

4. Discuss the types of planning tools that aid in successful event management.

5. What are the distinctive roles of the promotional mix model?

6. What are the benefits for sponsorships at a special event?

7. What are some tips for working with broadcast media?

8. What are some basic operations for staging an event?

9. Discuss costs associated with the event budget.

10. Outline the elements of breakdown for a special event.

11. Consider special event opportunities for your community. How would you offer advice as an event professional to encourage attendance?

12. What changes to events has COVID-19 caused and what opportunities does it present?

ABOUT THE CHAPTER CONTRIBUTOR

David Smiley received his M.S. degree in hospitality and tourism management from the University of Central Florida and holds a bachelor of science degree from the Pennsylvania State University in Recreation and Park Management. He is a senior lecturer in the School of Public Health at Indiana University Bloomington after serving 22 years in the industry, including 10 years with Rosen Hotels and Resorts. He also serves as the coordinator of the tourism, hospitality, and event management program in the department of health and wellness design.

PREVIOUS EDITION CHAPTER CONTRIBUTORS

Joy Dickerson, Widener University.

Cynthia Vannucci, Metropolitan State College in Denver Emeritus.

CHAPTER 9

FOOD AND BEVERAGE

MEAL FUNCTIONS CAN MAKE
OR BREAK YOUR EVENT

© Pavel L Photo and Video/Shutterstock.com

CHAPTER OBJECTIVES

- Clarify the different types and requirements of catered events.
- Discuss specific requirements and considerations related to beverage events.
- Outline items to consider when choosing, planning, and arranging rooms for an event.
- Outline important service requirements to consider when planning and producing a food or beverage event.
- Name current trends and best practices in food and beverage practices for events.
- Be knowledgeable about the effects of COVID-19 on food and beverage in meetings, expositions, events, and conventions (MEEC).

Food and beverage is an area that many event professionals typically outsource to third-party planners or in which they engage in-house contractors. It is often a mystery to many event professionals as to what is negotiable, how caterers price their services, and where caterers will make concessions.

> The Events Industry Council (EIC) glossary defines a **caterer** as: (1) a food service vendor, often used to describe a vendor who specializes in banquets and theme parties or (2) an exclusive food and beverage contractor within a facility.

The quality of the food and beverage functions can make a major impact on the overall impressions of a meeting or event. The first thing to consider when planning a catered event is to answer the question "what is the purpose?" Is it merely to satisfy hunger, a break to reenergize, to socialize and network, to present an award, to honor dignitaries, or to keep an audience entertained for the speaker?

Although many simply see food as fuel, others consider it an important component of the overall experience. From planning menus to negotiating prices, catering is one area best not left to chance. It is one of the major expenses of a meeting or event and an area where Murphy's Law prevails. Furthermore, the importance of cuisine must be emphasized. The choices and preparation of food have changed dramatically over the years—to include options of whether to go organic, ethnic, or vegetarian. It is posited that food revenue is increasing steadily owing to the increased choices and specifications of cuisine. However, beverage revenue may be in decline because sponsors of events do not want to assume liability for alcohol consumption. There are many questions that should be asked when hosting a Food and Beverage event. A list of questions to consider can be found in Figure 9-1.

CATERED EVENTS

Catered events generally have one host and one bill, and most attendees eat the same meal (exceptions would be if an attendee arranged vegetarian, gluten-free, or other special meals). A mandatory gratuity or service charge is added to the check that can typically range from 18% to 24% of the total bill, and taxes can add a further 5% to 9%. The distribution of this gratuity or service charge varies widely among venues and companies. A gratuity differs from a tip, in that a tip is voluntary and given at the discretion of the client for service over and above expectations. A gratuity is generally fully distributed to team members. A service charge includes a percentage distributed to team members

QUESTIONS TO ASK WHEN PLANNING FOR FOOD AND BEVERAGE:

1. Whom will I work with in planning the event?
2. Who will be on-site during the event?
3. When can I expect your written proposal?
4. What is your policy regarding deposits and cancellations?
5. When is the final payment due?
6. Are there other charges for setup, delivery, overtime, and so on?
7. Do you take credit cards? PayPal? Online payment?
8. When must I give you my final head count guarantee?
9. What percentage is overset above the guarantee?
10. What is the sales tax, and what are your gratuity and/or service charge policies?
11. What are the chef's best menu items?
12. What are your portion sizes?
13. Will wine be poured by the staff or placed on the tables?
14. How many staff will be working at the event?
15. What are your substitution policies for vegetarian plates and special meals?
16. Could you pass wine or champagne as guests arrive?
17. How many bartenders will be used during the cocktail hour?
18. Do you provide table numbers?
19. What size tables do you have?
20. What are the options for linen, chair covers, china, stemware, flatware, and charger plates?
21. What decorations do you provide for the banquet room, tables, buffets, and food stations?
22. Are you Americans with Disabilities Act (ADA) compliant?
23. What are your "green" initiatives?

FIGURE 9-1 Questions to ask when planning for food and beverage at your event

(which may include servers, bartenders, and sometimes the management team) and a percentage that is retained by the property. The lesson here is: when in doubt, ask. In many countries and cultures, service charges and tips do not exist.

ON-PREMISE CATERING

On-premise catering is defined as catering being done in a facility that has its own permanent kitchens and function rooms, such as a hotel, restaurant, or convention center. This means that the food is prepared and served on site. Usually, the facility would not rent the equipment but would keep permanent furniture, such as banquet style tables and chairs in their inventory. If a venue has on-premise catering, event professionals are almost always required to use this option for their food functions. In a citywide convention, one hotel is usually named the host hotel and holds most of the food functions, although some events move attendees to a variety of venues.

Most meals are catered on-premise during a meeting. Serving attendees all at once prevents strain on the restaurant outlets, keeps attendees from leaving the property, and ensures that everyone will be back on time for the following sessions.

Conference centers offer a complete meeting package, which includes meals. Breakfast, lunch, and dinner are generally available in a cafeteria-type setup at any time the group decides to break. This keeps the group from having to break just because it is noon if they are in the middle of a productive session. If more than one group is in the facility, they will each be assigned different areas of the dining room. Refreshments are usually available at any time as well, allowing breaks at appropriate times. Conference centers can also provide banquets and receptions on request.

Convention centers and stadiums usually have concession stands open. Exhibitions are increasingly holding their own opening reception or providing lunch on the show floor to attract attendees into the exhibits. Most convention centers are public entities, and the food service is contracted out to companies like ARAMARK or Sodexo. These contract food service companies often have exclusive contracts, and other vendors or caterers are not allowed to work in the facility.

The venues mentioned earlier may also have full-service restaurants on the property. If the group will use the restaurant, check the capacity and hours relative to the needs of the group. For example, The International Council on Hotel, Restaurant and Institutional Education (ICHRIE) held one of its annual conventions at a major hotel in Palm Springs, California, during late July. They attracted about 700 attendees and were virtually the only people in the 1,500-room hotel. ICHRIE felt that the five freestanding restaurants would be more than adequate to meet the dining needs of the group (dining off-site was not a practical option). This would normally be true, but, since it was low season for the hotel, they closed all but two of the restaurants, and ICHRIE convention attendees were faced with waits of over 2 hours to be seated for dinner.

OFF-PREMISE CATERING

Catered events can be held in just about any location. **Off-premise catering** requires the transportation of food to a location such as a tented area, museum, park, or attraction. Sometimes, food is prepared in a kitchen and is transported fully cooked to the event site. At other times food is partially prepared in a kitchen and is finished at the site, or everything can be prepared from scratch at the site. Mobile kitchens can be set up just about anywhere using generators and/or propane and butane as fuel to heat cooking equipment. Usually, off-premise caterers must provide their own equipment (or rent equipment), including tables, chairs, chafing dishes, plates, flatware, and glassware. As an event professional, you may be responsible for simultaneously coordinating both on-premise and off-premise catering events. In this case, a shuttle bus system should be set up to transport attendees back and forth to off-premise events, and this can be expensive.

Many excellent restaurants have banquet rooms, and bigger restaurants have banquet sales managers. Arnaud's restaurant in New Orleans has a six-person sales staff, so banquets are big business. In Las Vegas, a trend is for celebrity chefs to create their own signature restaurants within the hotel separate from the hotel's own food service operations. These restaurants, such as Spago in

© Mikhail Pogosov/Shutterstock.com

Gas Lamp District,
San Diego

the Forum Shops at Caesars Palace or Delmonico's at The Venetian, also have their own banquet sales staff. Websites such as Opentable make it easy to research what local restaurants have to offer.

For an off-premise event, the first step for an event professional would be to create a request for proposal (RFP) and send it to event managers or caterers in the area. The RFP would include basic information such as the objectives of the event, information on the company, workable dates, number of attendees, and approximate budget, as well as any special requests such as the need for a waiter-parade area. Many catering companies have online RFPs. Once the event professional has had the opportunity to review the proposals, an interview and, if possible, a site inspection would follow. During the site inspection, the event professional should look at the ambience of the space, the level of cleanliness and maintenance, and other amenities that may be required such as parking and restrooms.

In many cases, off-premise events will be outsourced through a destination management company (DMC). DMCs are familiar with the location and have relationships established with unique venues in the area. For example, in Las Vegas the Liberace Mansion is available for parties. In New Orleans, Mardi Gras World, where the parade floats are made, is an outstanding setting for a party. Just about every destination has some distinctive spaces for parties: Southfork, in Dallas, the Rock and Roll Hall of Fame, in Cleveland, the Getty Museum in Los Angeles, and so on.

DMCs also know the best caterers, decorators, shuttle companies, entertainment, and any other supplier of products or services you may require. Although DMCs charge for their services, they can often get quantity discounts because of the volume they purchase throughout the year. If there is a problem with the product or service, the DMC can usually resolve it faster because of the amount of future business that would be jeopardized.

Two of the challenges with off-premise events are transportation and weather. Shuttle buses are an additional expense for the event. Weather can spoil the best-laid plans, so contingency measures must be arranged. Backup shelter should be available, whether it is a tent or an inside function room. For example, outdoor luaus in Hawaii are frequently moved inside at the last minute because of the frequent tropical storms that arise there.

During the initial site inspection, obtain a copy of the facility's banquet menus and policies. Do they offer the type of menu items that would be appropriate for your group? Ask if they are prepared to handle custom menus if you decide not to use their standard offerings. When planning custom menus, always check the skill level of the culinary team in the kitchen and the availability of special products that may be required.

Other important considerations include the demographics of the group. Menu choices would be different for the American Truck Drivers Association as compared with the International Association of Retired Persons. The typical truck driver would probably prefer a big steak, while a retired person would likely prefer a smaller portion of chicken without heavy spices. You need to consider gender, age, ethnic background, profession, and so on.

Many meetings or events have at least one off-premise event, often the opening reception, closing gala, or a themed event. Attendees want to experience some of the flavor of the destination and often get "cabin fever" if they never leave the hotel. Events can be held at an aquarium, a museum, a winery, or a historic mansion. For example, in St. Louis, many events are held at Busch stadium, home of the world champion Cardinals baseball team. In San Diego, some large conventions actually take over the entire Gas Lamp District for an evening.

STYLE OF SERVICE

There are many ways to serve a meal, from self-service to VIP white-glove service (see Table 9-1). Although there is some disagreement on a few of the following definitions, the following entries are based on the EIC glossary. The White House protocol is also being followed in this book. The White House publishes the *Green Book*, which explains how everything is to be done for presidential protocol. However, because of confusion in the area, it is important to ensure that the event professional and the catering representative agree on what the service styles mean for the event. (Unfortunately, the *Green Book* is not available to the public, because it also includes information on presidential security.)

Continental breakfast	Typically includes an assortment of breads and pastries, juice, and coffee, although it can be upgraded with the addition of sliced fruit, yogurt, and/or cold cereals. Most are self-service with limited seating unless an additional fee for "seated continental service" is assessed. Continental breakfast is excellent for budgets, speed, and efficiency.
Full, served breakfast	The entrees are plated in the kitchen and would normally include some type of egg like Eggs Benedict, a meat like bacon or sausage, a potato item like hash browns, fruit, and coffee. When deciding on breakfast service, planners need to consult their history and guarantee accordingly because attendance is invariably lower since not everyone indulges in breakfast and many will use the time to visit the gym or to catch up on work.
Breakfast buffet	Includes a wide assortment of foods, including fruits and fruit juices, egg dishes, meats, potatoes, and breads. Buffets are good because the time food is out can be longer, allowing for latecomers to be accommodated. Buffets can be cheaper than a full, served breakfast.
Refreshment breaks	These are often beverages only but may include snacks such as cookies, bagels, or fruit. Remember that such breaks are to refresh and energize. The food and beverage selection should reflect this objective. If your breaks are put out longer, make sure the food items selected can accommodate this length and not dry out or lose quality. Refreshment breaks are often themed.
Brunch	This is a late-morning meal and includes both breakfast and lunch items. A brunch can be a buffet or a plated, served meal.
Buffet lunch	This can be a cold or hot buffet, with a variety of salads, vegetables, meats, and so on. A deli buffet may include a make-your-own sandwich area.
Box lunch	Normally, only available for carrying away from the hotel to an off-premise location. They can be eaten on a bus if there is a long ride to a destination (such as a ride from San Francisco to the Napa Valley for a day's activities) or at the destination (such as a picnic area to hear the Boston Pops Orchestra). Box lunches can also be provided to attendees at a trade show.
Full, served lunch	This is a plated lunch, usually a three-course meal that often includes a salad, a hot/cooked main course, and a dessert. A one-course cold meal is sometimes provided, such as a grilled chicken Caesar salad.
Receptions	These are networking events with limited seating, which allow for conversation and interaction during the event. Food is usually placed on stations around the room and may also include butler-style service. Beverage service is always offered at these events. Light receptions may include only dry snacks and beverages and often precede a dinner. Heavy receptions would include hot and cold appetizers, perhaps an **action station**, and are often planned to replace a dinner.
Dinner buffet	This would include a variety of salads, vegetables, entrées, desserts, and beverages. Often, meats are carved and served by attendants.

TABLE 9-1 Types of Functions

Full, served dinner	This could be a three- to five-course meal, including an appetizer, soup, salad, main course, and a dessert. Food is preplated in the kitchen and served to each guest seated at round tables in the dining room. This style of service is often referred to as American Style Service.
Off-site event	This is any event held away from the host hotel. It could be a reception at a famous landmark, such as the Queen Mary in Long Beach, or a picnic at a local beach or park.
Theme party	This is a gala event with flair. It can be a reception, buffet, or served meal. Themes can vary widely. An example would be an international theme, where different stations are set up with food from Italy, China, Japan, Mexico, Germany, and so on.

TABLE 9-1 Types of Functions (continued)

The style of service will often influence the types and varieties of foods offered. The common service styles that can be used include the following:

BUFFET

Food is attractively arranged on tables. Guests serve themselves and then take their plates to a table to sit and eat. Beverages are usually served at the tables. Buffets are generally more expensive than plated served meals because there is

© Paul Barnwell/Shutterstock.com

Dessert buffet table.

no portion control and surpluses must be built in to assure adequate supplies of each food item. However, staffing costs are lowered by 8% to 10% or more. Be sure to allow adequate space around the table for lines to form and to allow efficient replenishment by the service staff. Consider the flow and do not make guests backtrack to get an item. For example, place the salad dressings after the salad so that guests do not have to step back on the next guest to dress their salad. Provide one buffet line per 100 guests, with 120 guests being the point to break into two lines.

ATTENDED BUFFET/CAFETERIA

Guests are served by chefs or attendants. This is more elegant and provides better portion control.

COMBINATION BUFFET

Inexpensive items, such as salads, are presented buffet style, where guests help themselves. Expensive items, such as meats, are served by an attendant for portion control.

ACTION STATIONS

Sometimes referred to as "performance stations" or "exhibition cooking." **Action stations** are similar to an attended buffet, except food is freshly prepared as guests wait and watch. More flair and more interaction make action stations part entertainment. Some common action station themes include the following: pasta, quesadilla, fajita, sushi/sashimi, oyster shucking, lettuce wrap, panini, French fries, mashed potato, comfort foods, soups, espresso, pizza, s'mores, chocolate dipped fruit, grilled meats or shrimp, omelets, crepes, Caesar salad, Belgian waffles, carved meats, and flaming desserts such as Baked Alaska, crepes suzette, or bananas foster.

RECEPTION

Light foods are served buffet style or are passed on trays by servers (**butler service**). Guests usually stand and serve themselves and do not usually sit down to eat. Receptions are often referred to as "Walk and Talks." Small plates should always be included for these events, because some cost control can be managed by selecting the appropriate service pieces. Some receptions serve only finger food (food eaten with the fingers), whereas others offer fork food (food that requires a fork to eat).

Sliders are one of many food items that can be served at a reception.

FAMILY STYLE/ENGLISH SERVICE

Guests are seated, and large serving platters and bowls of food are placed on the dining table by the servers. Guests pass the food around the table. A host will often carve the meat. This is an expensive style of service. Surpluses must be built into the price to account for potentially high food costs and additional service equipment.

PLATED/AMERICAN STYLE SERVICE

Guests are seated and served food that has been preportioned and plated in the kitchen. *Food is served from the left of the guest.* The meat or entrée is placed directly in front of the guest at the 6 o'clock position. *Beverages are served from the right of the guest. When the guest has finished, both plates and glassware are removed from the right.* **American Service** is the most functional, most common, most economical, most controllable, and most efficient type of service. This type of service usually has a server–guest ratio of 1:20 or 1:30, depending on the level of the facility.

PRESET

Some foods are already on the table when guests arrive. The most common items to preset are water, butter, bread, appetizer, and/or salad. At luncheons, where time is of the essence, the dessert is often preset as well. These are all cold items that do not lose quality from sitting out for 30 to 60 minutes.

BUTLER SERVICE

At receptions, *butler service* refers to having hors d'oeuvres passed on trays and the guests helping themselves.

RUSSIAN SERVICE

(1) Banquet Russian: The food is fully prepared in the kitchen. All courses are served either from platters or from an Escoffier dish. Tureens are used for soup and special bowls for salad. The server places the proper plate in front of the guest, who is seated. After the plates are placed, the server returns with a tray of food and, moving counterclockwise around the table, serves the food from the guest's left with the right hand. With this style of service, the server controls the amount served to each guest. (2) Restaurant Russian: Guests are seated. Foods are cooked tableside on a *réchaud* (portable cooking stove) that is on a *gueridon* (tableside cart with wheels). Servers place the food on platters (usually silver), and then guests serve themselves. Service is *from the left*.

Food on a réchaud.

BANQUET FRENCH

Guests are seated. Platters of food are assembled in the kitchen. Servers take the platters to the tables and serve from the left, placing the food on the guest's plate, using two large silver forks or one fork and one spoon. Servers must be highly trained for this type of service. The use of the forks and spoons together in one hand is a skill that must be practiced. Many hotels are now permitting the use of silver salad tongs.

CART FRENCH

Less commonly used for banquets, except for small VIP functions, this style is used in fine restaurants. Guests are seated, and foods are prepared tableside using a réchaud on a gueridon. Cold foods, such as salads, are prepared on the gueridon, sans réchaud. Servers plate the finished foods directly on the guest's plate, which is then placed in front of the guest *from the right*. Bread, butter, and salad are served from the left, while beverages are served from the right. All are removed from the right.

HAND SERVICE OR CAPTAIN

Guests are seated. There is one server for every two guests. Servers wear white gloves. Foods are preplated. Each server carries two plates from the kitchen and stands behind the two guests assigned to him or her. At a signal from the room captain, all servings are set in front of all guests at the same time, synchronized. This procedure can be used for all courses, just the main course, or just the dessert. This is a very elegant and impressive style of service used mainly for VIP events because there is significant additional labor required.

A LA CARTE

Guests are given a choice of two to three entrées, with a minimum of two predetermined courses served before the entrée choice.

WAITER PARADE

An elegant touch where white-gloved servers march into the room and parade around the perimeter carrying food on trays, often to dramatic music and lighting. This is especially effective with a Flaming Baked Alaska Dessert Parade. The room lighting is dimmed, and a row of flaming trays carried by the waiters slowly encircles the room. When the entire room is encircled, the music stops and service starts. (Flaming dishes should never be brought close to a guest. After the parade, the dessert is brought to a side area, where it is sliced and served.)

Waiter Parade.

© Norberto Marques/Shutterstock.com

Mixing Service Styles

The event professional can change service styles within the meal. The whole meal does not have to conform to one type of service. For example, the appetizer can be preset, with the salads "Frenched" (dressing added after salads are placed on the table), the main course served American, with a dessert buffet.

MENUS

In times past, menus rarely changed. Today, change is necessary to keep pace with the changing tastes of the public. Most food trade journals run features on "What's Hot and What's Not." Table 9-2 lists some items that are generally always "hot," while Table 9-3 lists consumption guidelines.

Seasonal food	The use of in-season locally grown produce. These foods are served when they are at the peak of flavor, enhancing the quality of the event.
Ethnic foods	With the influx of people from other cultures into many countries of the world has come the unique cuisine of many areas of the world. The American palate has grown beyond the ethnic foods of the past, such as Italian, Chinese, and Mexican, to include the foods of many Asian countries, the Middle East, and South America.
High-quality ingredients	People may pinch pennies at the grocery store, but when they eat out at a banquet they want the best. No longer satisfied with frozen, sweetened strawberries, they want fresh Driscoll strawberries on their shortcake. They want giant Idaho baked potatoes and prime Angus beef.
Fresh ingredients	Frozen, canned, and dried foods, once seen as the newest, greatest technology, have worn out their novelty. The loss of these food's flavors during preservation has made fresh food highly prized. Fresh ingredients also mean local sourcing, with many establishments naming the specific farms products are sourced from.
New and unusual ingredients	With improvements in production, technology, and transportation, new foods have appeared in marketplaces that were previously unknown to most many people. These include artisanal breads and cheeses, heirloom tomatoes, lemon grass, Yukon Gold potatoes, purple potatoes, and blood oranges.
Safe foods	Organic foods and foods free from pollution and pesticides.
Highly creative presentations	Plate presentations are increasingly important. We eat with our eyes before anything hits our taste buds. Contemporary presentations should focus on the primary menu components, and garnishes should be minimal (based on the time food might be on display or stored in a hot box).
Excellent service Sustainable	Food served promptly (while still hot) and friendly, courteous services are important considerations in the enjoyment of a meal. For consumers, sustainability means food sourced that is healthful, protective of the environment, fair to workers, and addresses animal welfare.

TABLE 9-2 "Hot" Menu Items

FOOD CONSUMPTION GUIDELINES

Type of Reception	Type of Eaters	Number of Hors D 'Oeuvres per Person
2 hours or less (dinner following)	Light Moderate Heavy	3–4 pieces 5–7 pieces 8+ pieces
2 hours or less (no dinner)	Light Moderate Heavy	6–8 pieces 10–12 pieces 12+ pieces
2–3 hours (no dinner)	Light Moderate Heavy	8–10 pieces 10–12 pieces 16+ pieces

TABLE 9-3 Food Consumption Guidelines

The most important information in deciding how much food to order is the history of the group: Who are they? Why are they here? A pretty good determination can be made on the basis of previous years. If this is a new group, or the history is not available, then consider the demographics of the attendees.

SOME GENERAL GUIDELINES

Guests generally eat more during the first hour of a reception and may eat an average of 7 hors d'oeuvres per person during this hour. These general guidelines will vary according to the demographics of the group.

The amount of food consumed may also depend on how many square feet of space is available for guests to move around in (smaller equals less consumption).

In general, menu offerings tend to lend themselves to assembly-line production and service. Certain delicate items cannot be produced and served in quantity without sacrificing culinary quality. For example, lobster, soufflé, rare roast beef, medium-rare tuna, rare duck breast, or salmon steak are difficult to prepare and serve satisfactorily to more than a handful of guests at a time. One technology that has grown in popularity that has addressed the foregoing concern is sous vide. Sous vide cooking, which means "under vacuum," involves vacuum sealing foods in plastic, then cooking at a precise temperature in a water bath. A consistent product results, the taste is excellent because the food cooks in its own natural juices, ease of cooking is ensured because no attention is needed, and, very importantly, waste is reduced because nothing is dried out.

Menu Restrictions

Banquet servers should know the ingredients and preparation method of every item on the menu. Many attendees have allergies or are restricted from eating certain items like sugar or salt, nuts, or gluten owing to health concerns. Others do not eat certain foods because of their religious restrictions, and still others are vegetarians. The question of allergies and food restrictions should be posed as early as possible. For conventions, attendees are asked to provide information on food restrictions on the convention registration form. The caterer will never know if these food restrictions are by choice, for allergy reasons, or for religious reasons. Dietary preferences should never be thought of as optional because the guest could have severe allergies.

Guests with special diets will influence the types of foods served. Some people cannot tolerate monosodium glutamate or MSG (allergic reactions), onions and garlic (digestive problems), certain spices or peanuts (allergic reactions), sugar (diabetes), salt (high blood pressure, heart problems), fat (weight problems, high cholesterol), and wheat, rye, or barley (celiac disease). Other dietary restrictions include people who are lactose intolerant, which means they have difficulty digesting anything containing milk or milk products. Sometimes, the restrictions are not the content of the food but the frequency. Those with hypoglycemia must eat something every few hours.

According to the FDA, the eight most common food allergies are milk/dairy, egg, fish, shellfish, tree nuts, peanuts, wheat, and soy. An acute allergic reaction to a food may manifest itself as swelling of the eyelids, face, lips, tongue, larynx, or trachea. Other reactions can include difficulty breathing, hives, nausea, vomiting, diarrhea, stomach cramps, or abdominal pain. Anaphylactic shock is a severe whole-body reaction that can result in death.

Today, people have also imposed dietary restrictions on themselves in an effort to eat in a healthier fashion, including those on low-carbohydrate diets, high-fiber diets, and so on. Others choose certain dietary lifestyles to align with their beliefs. Vegetarians often make up approximately 10% to 15% of a group. There are three basic types of vegetarians: those who will not eat red meat but will eat chicken and fish, "lacto-ovo" vegetarians who will not eat anything that has to be killed but will eat animal by-products (cheese, eggs, milk, etc.), and "vegans" who will not eat anything from any animal source, including animal by-products such as honey, butter, and dairy. When in doubt, assume attendees who identify themselves as vegetarian are vegans. To serve a vegan a plate of vegetables with butter and/or cheese would not be appropriate.

Religious restrictions may also impact food and diet. For example, people who maintain a kosher diet will not eat anything that does not follow kosher guidelines, will not mix dairy products with meat products, and will keep separate china and separate kitchens for dairy and for meat. Kosher food must follow stringent rules and pass the approval of a *mashgiach*, who does not have to be a rabbi but must be recognized in the community as a person authorized to give certification for *kashruth*. Kosher food conforms to strict Judaic laws regarding the type of food that may be eaten as well as the kinds of food that can be combined during a meal. In addition to the kinds of animals considered kosher, the laws state that animals must be killed in a specific manner. In kosher service, with the exception of glass and silverware that can undergo a curing period, meat products must not be served on any plate that has ever had dairy products on it. Pork, shellfish, rabbit, and hindquarter cuts of beef and lamb are examples of foods that are not allowed for various reasons. Since these meals oftentimes have to be prepared in a specialty kitchen, they can be considerably more expensive. The conference organizer can choose to pass that cost on to the attendee or absorb the costs.

It is a good idea to have attendees fill out a form indicating whether they have menu restrictions. This information can then be communicated to the catering manager, who will ensure that the proper number and type of alternative menu items are available. At meetings of the National Association of Catering Executives, attendees are provided with complete menus of every event, along with a form in which they can indicate which meals they need to have changed.

CONTRACTS

Normally, formal catering contracts are required. Sometimes they may be forgone in place of a signed banquet event order (BEO) or a signed letter of agreement. A BEO, sometimes referred to as a function sheet, is a venue's internal communication system between departments. It is also the building block on which accounting and record keeping systems are constructed. A résumé is a summary of function room usage for a particular convention or meeting. The résumé usually includes all BEOs. It focuses on the major highlights while deferring to the pertinent BEOs for specific details. A catering contract, or letter of agreement, usually contains a combination of standard, boilerplate language, plus language specifically tailored to the event.

Food and Beverage Attrition

Most event professionals do not like **attrition** clauses, although these benefit both event professionals and venues by setting legal obligations for both sides and establishing liability limits. When a contract is signed, both parties want the food and beverage guarantee to be met. The difference is that caterers want to be certain and up-front, whereas event professionals want to wait until the last minute to give the final guarantee. If the guarantee is too high, the event professional might have to pay for it in the form of attrition.

Attrition hits the event professional in the pocketbook if the **guarantee** is not met. The event professional agrees in the contract to buy a specific number of meals or to spend a specific amount of money on group food and beverage; the caterer's obligation is to provide the service and the food. If the guarantee is not met, the event professional must pay the difference between the guarantee and the actual amount or an agreed-on percentage of the actual amount (see Chapter 10 on legal issues for more information on attrition).

BEVERAGE EVENTS

REASONS FOR A BEVERAGE EVENT

Beverage events are popular and include refreshment breaks and receptions. Beverage breaks not only provide liquid nourishment (and possibly a snack) but also allow the attendee to get up, stretch, visit the restroom, check text messages and email, call the office, check-in on social media, and possibly move into another room for the next breakout session.

Receptions are slightly different because most include alcoholic beverages and potentially more variety and quantity of food options. Reasons for receptions include the following:

Socializing: To provide a relaxed atmosphere that encourages interaction among guests.

Networking: To provide an opportunity to discuss business and develop new contacts.

Planners typically plan and purchase for only three main types of beverage functions with alcohol: cocktail receptions, hospitality suites, and poured wine service. A key consideration in finalizing a beverage menu is based on the demographics and history of the group.

CATEGORIES OF LIQUOR

The categories of alcoholic beverages offered to a customer for a catered event are liquor (distilled spirits), wine, and beer. The caterer typically offers tiers of these options, representing different price and quality levels: Well, Call, and Premium brands. The event professional will choose the tier most appropriate for their guests and the event budget.

Well Brands: These are sometimes called "house liquors." It is less expensive liquor, such as Kentucky Gentleman Bourbon. Well brands are served when someone does not "call" for a specific brand.

Call Brands: These are priced in the midrange and are generally asked for by name, such as Jim Beam Bourbon or Beefeater's Gin.

Premium Brands: These are high-quality, expensive liquors, such as Crown Royal, Chivas Regal, or Tanqueray Gin.

SPIRITS

All premium brands are available in 750ml and 1-liter bottles. One 750-ml bottle equals 20 (1 1/4-ounce) servings; a 1-liter bottle equals 27 (1 1/4-ounce) servings (see Table 9-4). Consumption will average three drinks per person during a normal reception.

		1 Ounce	1¼ Ounce	1½ Ounce
1 Liter	33.8 ounces	33	27	22
750 ml	25.3 ounces	25	20	16

TABLE 9-4 Number of Drinks per Bottle

WINE/CHAMPAGNE

All premium brands are available in 750-ml bottles and many in 1.5 liters (magnums). There are other sizes as well, such as:

- Split (187ml)
- Half bottle (375ml)
- Bottle (750ml) = five 5-ounce servings
- Magnum (1.5-liter bottle) = ten 5-ounce servings
- Double magnum (3liter)
- Jeroboam (3liter for sparkling, 4.5liter for still)
- Imperial (6liter)
- Methuselah (6liter)
- Nebuchadnezzar (15liter)

Consumption will average three glasses per person during a normal reception. Assuming that 50% of the people will order wine, you would order thirty 750-ml bottles for every 100 guests.

Champagne should be served in a flute glass instead of the classic "coupe" because there is less surface exposed to the air. This is so that the bubbles do not escape as fast, causing the champagne to go flat much sooner (see Figure 9-2).

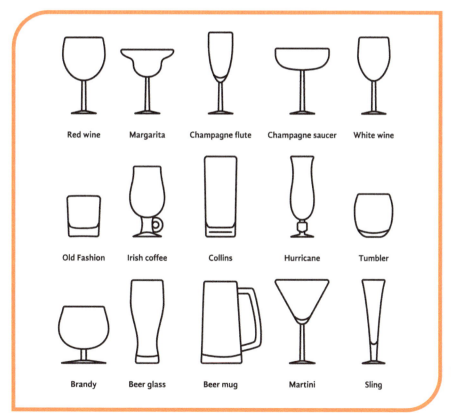

Red wine   Margarita   Champagne flute   Champagne saucer   White wine

Old Fashion   Irish coffee   Collins   Hurricane   Tumbler

Brandy   Beer glass   Beer mug   Martini   Sling

© Pranch/Shutterstock.com

FIGURE 9-2 Pack of different thin line stemware

BEER

The caterer should always offer a variety of domestic and imported choices, as well as a contemporary list of "craft" beers from small, independent, and traditional brewers (i.e., Dogfish Head 60 Minute IPA, Bell's Two Hearted Ale).

HOW BEVERAGES ARE SOLD

BY THE BOTTLE

This is common for open bars and poured wine at meal functions. The event professional pays for all of the liquor bottles that are opened. A physical inventory is taken at the beginning and end of the function to determine liquor usage. Most venues charge for each opened bottle, even if only one drink was poured from it. This method saves money but is inconvenient to monitor and calculate. The event professional will not know the final cost until the event is over. Usually, the group history will give some indication of how much consumption to expect. Open bottles may not be removed from the property. Unopened bottles may not be removed unless the venue has an off-sale liquor license. You can, however, have them delivered to a hospitality suite or to the room of a VIP to use during the meeting. This method is less and less common with the exception of wine.

BY THE DRINK

Also called "Consumption Bar," the host is charged for each individual beverage consumed during the event. Normally, the price per drink is high enough to cover all relevant expenses (limes, stirrers, napkins, etc.). Individual drink prices are set to yield a standard beverage cost percentage set by the venue. This is the amount of profit the venue expects to make from the sale of the liquor. Cost percentages range from 12% to 18% for spirits and usually around 25% for wine. The event professional will not know the final cost until the event is over.

PER PERSON

This method can be more expensive for the event professional but involves less work and aggravation. The event professional chooses a plan, such as premium liquors for 1 hour, and then tells the caterer how many people are coming ($25 per person × 500 guests = $12,500). Costs are known ahead of time, so there are no surprises. Tickets are collected from attendees at the door, and the guarantee is monitored. The key to selecting this or any other method is to know your group. Know their drinking capacity and pattern by reviewing their past history.

Charge Per Hour

This is similar to per person. This method often includes a sliding scale, with a higher cost for the first hour. This is because guests usually eat and drink more during the first hour, then level off. You must provide a firm guarantee before negotiating a per-hour charge. Or you can combine *per person, per hour*: $25 per person for the first hour, and $20 per person for the second hour, so hosting 100 guests for a two-hour reception would cost $4,500 [$25 × 100 = $2,500 (+) $20 × 100 = $2,000 (=) $4,500]. No consideration is given for those who arrive late or leave early; the fee is $45 per person regardless.

Open Bar

Also called a "Hosted Bar," this is when guests do not pay for their drinks; a host or sponsor pays for them. Guests usually drink as much as they want of what they want. Liquor consumption is higher because someone else is paying. The sponsor can be the meeting itself, an exhibitor, an external sponsor, or a similar organization. For example, at the Super Show, which features sporting goods, Nike may sponsor a bar.

Cash Bar

Also called a "No-Host Bar," guests buy their own drinks. Guests usually purchase tickets from a cashier to exchange with a bartender for a drink. At small functions, the bartender may collect and serve, eliminating the cost of a cashier. Cashiers are usually charged as extra labor but can provide better control and speed up service. This also prevents bartenders from having to handle dirty money and then handle glassware and garnishes such as lemons/limes.

Combination Bar

This is a very common format, where a host purchases tickets and gives each attendee a certain number (usually two). If the guest wants a third drink, they must purchase it themselves. This could also be set up by time—the host could pay for the first hour, and then the bar reverts to a cash bar for the rest of the time. This method provides free drinks to guests but retains control over costs and potential liability for providing unlimited drinks.

Limited Consumption Bar

This is when a cash register is used and alcohol is priced by the drink. The host establishes a dollar amount, and when the cash register reaches that amount, the bar is closed. The host may decide to reopen as a cash bar.

Calculate Total Cost to Determine the Best Option

A bottle of bourbon yields 27 14-ounce drinks. If guests are expected to drink two drinks per hour, for a one-hour reception for 1,000 people,

Purchased by the bottle, at $80 per bottle, it would cost $6,000.

Purchased by the drink, at $4.00 per drink, the same group would cost $8,000.

Purchased at $10 per person, it would cost $10,000.

So, as you can see, the hotel makes more money selling per person. Selling by the bottle is becoming less and less common.

LABOR CHARGES

Extra charges are usually levied for bartenders and/or **bar backs**, cocktail servers, cashiers, security, and **corkage** fees. These items are negotiable, depending on the value of the business. For example, if a bar sells over $500 in liquor, the bartender charge may be waived.

A "bar back" is the bartender's helper. They restock liquor, keep fresh ice filled, and make sure there are clean glasses. This is important so the bartender will not have to do it himself during service.

One of the authors attended a wedding reception at Cornell University's Statler Hall. It was a small wedding, so only one bartender was provided with no bar back. Many of the attendees were snow skiing instructors who consumed more alcohol than the typical person. Part of the way through the reception, the bar was running low on some types of liquor. Having to leave the bar to obtain the supplies, the bartender asked two males in the wedding party to cover the bar. They did, but filled each glass served with extra liquor. When the bartender returned, the bar was low on other alcohol inventory.

"Corkage" is the fee added to liquor brought into the venue, but not purchased from the venue. The venue charges this fee to cover the cost of labor, use of the glasses (which must be delivered to the room, washed, and placed back in storage), mixers, olives, lemon peels, and so forth. Corkage is not available at all properties and depends on venue policy.

Considerations for the number of bartenders include the number of bars scheduled, types of drinks, number of attendees, hours of operation, amount of bar back work, and applicable union or company human resources policies. The standard ratio is one bartender for every 100 attendees. If guests all arrive at the same time, a ratio of 75 (or down to even 50) is appropriate. At large events, with more than 1,000 attendees, a ratio of 100 is appropriate. To alleviate pressure on bartenders, ask for a few servers to pass glasses of champagne, still wines, bottled waters, or juices. This will also add an extra touch of elegance to the event. Unless the event is very small, at least one bar back is needed. Considerations for the number of bar backs include the number of bars scheduled, capacity of each bar set up, distance between bars and kitchen, ease in retrieving stock, hours of operations, number of attendees, variety of liquor stock, glasses and garnishes, and, lastly, the applicable union or company human resources policies.

HOSPITALITY SUITES

Hospitality suites are places for attendees to gather outside of the meeting events. They are normally open late in the evening, after 10:00 pm, but occasionally around the clock. Three types of hospitality suites are:

Morning: Continental breakfast
Afternoon: Snacks and sodas
Evening: Liquor and snacks

Hospitality suites can be hosted by the sponsoring organization, a chapter of the organization, an exhibitor, a nonexhibiting corporation, an allied association, or a person running for an office in the organization. Hospitality suites can be held in a client's or partner's suite on a sleeping room floor. Usually, these are handled by room service and sold by catering. Sometimes they are held in a public function room and are both sold and serviced by catering.

Some suites offer a full bar, whereas others are beer and wine only. Some have lots of food; others have only dry snacks. Some offer desserts and specialty coffees. Consider ordering more food if the attendees have had an open evening.

Watch for "underground hospitality suites," where unofficial parties pop up. In these types of hospitality suites, you only gain legal liability and lose revenue. The court case resulting from the Tailhook Scandal, in which a female was groped in a hallway at a military meeting at the Las Vegas Hilton, set a precedent that a hotel can no longer claim that it does not know what is going on within the property.

Make sure to have the appropriate alcohol licenses. There are on-sale licenses, off-sale licenses, and beer and wine licenses. Licenses also stay with the property. For example, if your hotel has a liquor license, it is not valid in the public park across the street. The caterer would need to obtain a special temporary permit. Another factor to keep in mind is that liquor laws vary from state to state, county to county, and country to country. You should always check the laws in the specific location where your event is being held. Event professionals who wish to bring their own liquor into an establishment must check local laws and be prepared to pay the establishment a per-bottle corkage fee.

EXAMPLES

In Las Vegas and New Orleans, liquor can be sold 24/7 and carried plus consumed in public places.

In California, liquor cannot be sold between 2 a.m. and 6 a.m.

In Atlanta, liquor may not be served until 11 a.m. on Sundays.

In some states, liquor may not be sold at all on Sundays.

There are generally four types of illegal liquor sales, wherever you are located:

- Sales to minors
- Sales to intoxicated persons
- Sales outside legal hours
- Sales with an improper liquor license

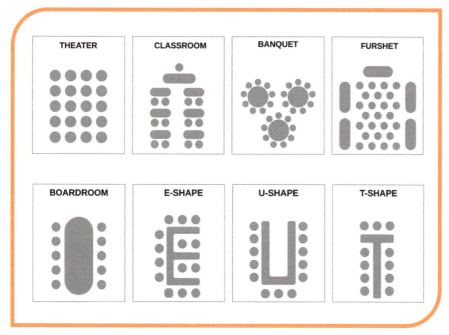

© Lantica/Shutterstock.com

FIGURE 9-3
Sample room layouts

ROOMS

ROOM SETUPS

The way the room is set up is critically important to the success of any event. The room set can affect the flow of service, the amount of food and beverage consumed, and even the mood of the guests. The ambience can make or break a meal function, whether it is a continental breakfast or a formal dinner (Figure 9-3).

Room setup includes tables, chairs, decor, and other equipment such as portable bars, stages, and audiovisual equipment. It is essential that the event professional communicate *exactly* how they want the room to be set to the banquet setup manager. This is accomplished on the **Banquet Event Order (BEO)** form and by using room layout software. These types of programs allow the placement of tables, chairs, and other equipment into a meeting room plan. Room software demos may be viewed on a number of websites, including Social Tables, Meeting Matrix, All Seated, and Room Viewer.

AISLE SPACE

Aisles allow people to move easily around the room without squeezing through chairs and disturbing seated guests. They also provide a buffer between the seating areas and the food and beverage areas. Aisles between tables and around food and beverage stations should be a bare minimum of 36 inches wide (3 feet), but 48 inches would be preferable. Also, leave a three-foot minimum aisle around the perimeter of the room. Cross aisles should be six-foot wide. Check with the local fire marshal for local rules and regulations because these vary from location to location.

PER PERSON

Remember to deduct space taken up for furniture before calculating the number of people. Include large sofas found in many hospitality suites, buffet tables, portable bars, plants, decor and props, and check-in tables. Allow 10 square feet per person at rectangular banquet tables. Allow 12.5 square feet per person at rounds (this assumes the facility is using standard 20- by 20-inch chairs). Allow 3 square feet per person for dance floors. Although these are numbers you can reference later on an internet search, it is most important to remember to always check local fire codes.

TABLESCAPES

The tabletop should be seen as a stage—it sets expectations and should reflect the theme of the event. Once seated, the focus is mainly on the table, so it is imperative that it not be overlooked.

A "wow" tablescape presentation

- The centerpiece should not block sight lines for people sitting across the table from each other. Centerpieces should be low or high with a Lucite or slender pole in the middle portion.
- The *cover* is the place setting and includes placement of flatware, china, and glassware.
- "Napery" includes all table linens, including tablecloths, overlays, napkins, and table skirting.
- Other décor may include ribbons, greenery, or other items relating to the theme of the meal.

EXAMPLES

- Trailing flower garlands or ribbons between place settings
- Different colored napkins at each cover
- Creative napkin folds at each cover
- Creative centerpieces

Large or specifically themed props for **tablescapes** can be rented from prop houses, service contractors, party stores, or be provided by the venue, hotel, or club. Other props that are small, decorative pieces can be found in many places, such as:

- Auto supply stores
- Toy or crafts stores
- Garden centers
- Ethnic food stores or import shops
- Travel agencies (destination posters)
- Sports clubs or stores
- Medical supply stores
- Military surplus stores

ROOM RENTAL CHARGES

Can they be waived? It depends on the venue. If the function is part of an event that also requires the use of sleeping rooms, it is easier to negotiate the room rental charge from the hotel. When undertaking catering events at hotels that are handled by the catering department rather than the sales department because there are no room nights involved, an event professional rarely encounters a rental fee for the space. Rather, there will be a minimum revenue requirement based on the amount of space needed for the event. The group may have to spend $50,000 in food and beverage to secure a ballroom for an event, which frequently means that guests eat *very* well.

In off-premise venues, it depends on how the venue has set up its charge/profit schedule. Most off-site venues charge a rental fee. Some charge a rental fee, some an admission fee per guest, and a few charge both and then add on catering, rentals, and service costs. The types of charges are almost always dependent on the size or projected profitability of the event. It is important to remember, however, that everything is negotiable. At several venues, it may be possible to negotiate removing the rental charge when bringing a large or highly profitable event to the property; it varies according to the venue.

SERVICE REQUIREMENTS

Labor is a major cost for catering. Most properties use a staffing guide to formalize policies in an effort to contain labor costs.

One bartender per every 100 guests is standard. If guests will arrive all at once, or you do not want long lines, you could have one bartender for every 50 or 75 guests, but there may be an additional labor charge. If a dinner involves a wine pairing for each course, or has 3 or more wines, a dedicated wine service team is commonly added.

Service is critical, and many excellent meals are ruined by poor service. Meal service levels can run from one server per eight guests to one server per forty guests. Most staffing guides allow for a ratio of 1/32, but most event professionals want 1/20 or 1/16 with either poured wine or French Service (Table 9-5).

Savvy event professionals negotiate for the following:

General
Rounds of 10: 1 server for every two tables, busser for every 6 tables
Rounds of 8: 1 server for every five tables, busser for every 8 tables

With poured wine or French Service
Rounds of 10: 2 servers for every three tables
Rounds of 8: 1 server for every two tables

Buffets
One server per thirty to forty guests
1 runner per 100 to 125 guests

French or Russian Service
Rounds of 8 or 10: 1 server per table, busser for every 3 tables

Supervision
One room captain. One section captain for every 250 guests (25 rounds of 10).

Space Requirements for Tables			
Rounds	60-inch round =	5-foot diameter =	Round of 8
	72-inch round =	6-foot diameter =	Round of 10
	66-inch round =	Compromise size	Seats 8–10
Rectangle	6-foot long	30-inch wide	Banquet 6
	8-foot long	30-inch wide	Banquet 8
Schoolroom or classroom	6- or 8-foot long	18- or 24-inch wide	
Half-moon table	Half of a roundtable		
Serpentine	¼ hollowed-out	round table	
Space Requirements for Receptions			
Minimum (tight)		5½–7 square feet per person	
Comfortably crowded		7½ square feet per person	
Ample room		10+ square feet per person	

TABLE 9-5 Space Requirements

SET OVER GUARANTEE

This is negotiable, depending on the property. It is the percentage of guests that the hotel will prepare for beyond the guarantee, in case additional, unexpected people show up. Below are **set over guarantees** at a major Las Vegas property:

Average overset is 3%, but you must look at the numbers, not just the percentages.

> <100 guests = the guarantee is the set
> 100–1,000 guests = 3% overset with a maximum of 50
> Over 1,000 guests = 3% overset

COCKTAIL SERVERS

Cocktail servers can carry only twelve to sixteen drinks per trip. Considering the time to take the order, the time to wait for the drinks at the service bar, and the time it takes to find the guest and deliver the drink, it takes at least fifteen minutes per trip to the bar. This makes it possible to serve only forty-eight to sixty-four drinks per hour. Cocktail servers are usually used only at small or VIP functions.

SERVICE TIMING

Fifteen minutes before you want to start serving, dim the lights, ring chimes, start music, open doors, and so on to get the guests to start moving to their tables.

The salad course should take fifteen to twenty minutes, depending on dressing or style of service. The main course should take thirty to forty minutes from serving to plate removal. Dessert should take twenty to thirty minutes.

A typical luncheon will last about 1 hour and 15 minutes; a typical dinner will last approximately 2 hours.

TRENDS AND BEST PRACTICES BEFORE COVID-19

Event professionals also need to stay abreast of current food trends. They do so by reading trade journals, such as *Meeting News, Successful Meetings, Convene,* or *Meetings & Conventions.* Many of the event and food trade publications, such as *Event Solutions, Special Events, Event Manager Blog, Bizbash, Meetings & Conventions, Catersource,* and *Smart Meetings* are wonderful resources as well and can be accessed online. Identified below are trends and practices that the authors identified prior to COVID-19.

- Global and sustained efforts to embrace and integrate "green" products and practices.
  - Instead of "just" recycling, there is more of a focus on reducing and repurposing.
  - Donating leftover food to local shelters and organizations for distribution to the community.
  - The use of compostable utensils and plateware.
  - Organic décor: Using cotton tablecloths instead of linen, low-cost candlescapes instead of laurels.
- Use fresh, locally/regionally sourced, sustainable foods and products.
  - Include the "story" of where their food came from (on printed menus, in presentations, etc.).
- Rethinking breakfast.
  - Some venues are allowing multiple groups to share the same breakfast buffet, thus saving cost.
  - Another trend is to consolidate breakfast and lunch into brunch, thereby making it one meal instead of two, which results in cost savings.
- Use of clean/slick/simple presentations and efficient service.
- Food flavors and options.
  - Fads are on hold. People are looking for sophisticated interpretations of familiar food.
  - Food that focuses on big/bold flavor profiles.
  - Include a signature portfolio of "house made'" items (potato chips, jams, jerky, olives, etc.).
  - Make strategic use of well-known branded products (Boars Head, Starbucks, Evian, Pellegrino).
- Food service options.
  - Food trucks continue to be popular! An interesting addition to receptions as a themed station.

- More meals are focusing on networking opportunities in lieu of a large, long, sit-down meal.
- Lunches are going to be a more "grab and go" style or small, tapas-style items.
- Dinners are often replaced by receptions.
- Consider tapas-style small plates.
  - Small plates allow attendees to taste more with every meal.
- Craft beer options and bolder options for varietal wines are being included in most bars.

COVID-19

COVID-19 struck the world in late 2019 and early 2020. It affected the entire MEEC industry, including food and beverage. Some of the same guidelines are implemented in food and beverage as elsewhere (1) social distancing (6 feet recommended), (2) everyone must wear a mask except when eating or drinking, and (3) regular washing of hands.

Some effects of COVID-19 that apply specifically to the food and beverage sector include the following:

- Self-service buffets have been discontinued.
  - Some facilities have kept the "buffet line" but have servers plate what the guest indicates and have placed plexiglass barriers between servers and guests.
- Drinks and hors d'ouvres that are passed pose a problem; most are served individually or in individually portioned containers.
- Rooms have reduced capacity; venues are trying to utilize all space to maximize attendance, so prepackaged and plated meals are being utilized more often over buffets.
- There must be a clear flow of traffic (ideally, one way) with a lot of signage.
- Chefs and all servers must wear masks.
- Food sourcing is more scrutinized to help with products' traceability.
- Increased security measures prohibiting anyone from outside (such as a supplier or delivery person) from entering the kitchen.
- All products are being washed as they come into the kitchen.
- The use of bins with a lid and pedal.
- Venues are updating the air system(s) to new sanitary standards within kitchen and eating environments.

- Investments are being made in new tables, bars, and chairs that can be easily disinfected.
- Providing masks to attendees if necessary.
- Placing individual containers or disinfectant wipes and/or hand sanitizer on each table.
- Eliminating unnecessary items on tables.
- Providing individual packets of salt and pepper.
- Serving individual bread in a separate paper bag.
- Placing dining utensils in a napkin or paper envelope.
- Working with the meeting planner to inform attendees of the sanitary measures that have been implemented.

The growing trends of food waste and sustainability over the past decade, have been, according to many professionals, undermined by COVID-19 almost overnight. The need to prepackage set amounts of food to be distributed can lead to food waste at the consumer level because attendees end up with food they would not have chosen themselves and will throw away. Many caterers have decreased the variety in their menus as the number of events dropped drastically, trying to reduce food waste within their kitchens in the hopes of being able to use their more limited bulk food purchases across different functions. The increase in individual containers for packaging food for every single meal (within all levels of catering and within venues/restaurants) that will end up being thrown away or recycled has led to many case studies and research tracking the damage this will cause to the environment. The effects of COVID-19 on these two areas in particular have yet to be fully realized.

SUMMARY

Food and beverage is an integral part of most meetings and events. Astute planning can save a tremendous amount of money. Knowing what is negotiable and how to negotiate is critical. Food and beverage functions create memories and provide a necessary service beyond being a refueling stop. Although most attendees do not specify food and beverage as a reason for attending a meeting, when asked later about a meeting they will often rave (or complain) about this particular aspect. Catered events often set the tone of the meeting and create great memories that can result in future business, not only from the event professional but also from every guest in attendance.

Food and beverage production and service must be carried out in a safe and wholesome manner. Anyone handling foods must be trained to practice safety and sanitation procedures to ensure that guests do not fall victim to accidents and food-borne illnesses. All commercial food service operations must adhere to the sanitation standards set forth by their local health districts. Certifications exist that prove adherence to safety and sanitation standards. These include sanitation guidelines developed by the National Restaurant Association Educational Foundation such as ServSafe and the Hazard Analysis and Critical Control Points (HACCP) certification; food contact equipment certified by the National Sanitation Foundation (NSF); equipment compliance by Underwriters Laboratories (UL) and the American Gas Association (AGA). The Department of Labor and the state workers' compensation agency both have relevant standards that require adherence.

1. Have you earned any of these certifications?

2. If not, will you?

3. What other food or beverage certifications can you identify?

KEYWORDS AND TERMS

For definitions, see https://insights.eventscouncil.org/Industry-glossary

action station	corkage
American Service	guarantee
attrition	on-premise catering
Banquet Event Order (BEO)	off-premise catering
bar backs	room setup
butler service	set over guarantee
catered event	tablescapes
caterer	

REVIEW AND DISCUSSION QUESTIONS

1. What is the first step for an event professional when planning for an off-premise event? List five types of functions, and give a brief description of each.

2. Describe how Family Style/English Service and Plated/American Style service differ.

3. What is the most important information to consider when deciding how much food to order for a group?

4. What is the average number of hors d'oeuvres a guest will eat during the first hour of an event?

5. What are the three categories of liquor?

6. What is the function of a hospitality suite, and what are the three types?

7. What are the important aspects of an event that are affected by how the room is set up?

8. When catering an event at a hotel, and no room nights are involved, which department handles the booking of the event?

9. Why is it imperative that the tabletop not be overlooked?

ABOUT THE CHAPTER CONTRIBUTORS

George G Fenich, Ph.D, is a professor in the School of Hospitality Leadership at East Carolina University in Greenville, North Carolina.

Kristin Malek, Ph.D, CMP, CED, DES, CHE, is an event management extension specialist and assistant professor in the Hospitality, Restaurant, and Tourism Management program at the University of Nebraska.

PREVIOUS EDITION CHAPTER CONTRIBUTORS

Donnell Bayot, Ph.D, CHE, CPCE, CFBE, is the director of academic affairs for the International School of Hospitality (TISOH) in Las Vegas, Nevada.

Gary L McCreary, CPCE, CMP, CSEP, is the vice president of catering and convention operations at The Venetian/The Palazzo Resort Hotel & Casinos in Las Vegas.

Perry Lynch, faculty at the Rosen College of Hospitality Management at the University of Central Florida.

Patti J. Shock (deceased) was the academic consultant for The International School of Hospitality and emeritus professor and chair in the Harrah College of Hotel Administration at the University of Nevada—Las Vegas.

CHAPTER 10

LEGAL ISSUES IN THE MEEC INDUSTRY

© print10/Shutterstock.com

CONTRACTS ARE A CRITICAL LEGAL FACTOR IN MEEC

CHAPTER OBJECTIVES

- Cover the most important elements of negotiation in MEEC.
- Note the specifics to consider when dealing with contracts in this industry.
- Discuss the importance of crisis preparedness and management.
- Clarify the points and impact of Americans with Disabilities Act as it pertains to MEEC.
- Articulate the legal importance of intellectual property as it has to do with this industry.
- Outline potential labor issues to consider in the industry.
- Discuss important ethical concerns to consider in MEEC.
- Outline current trends and best practices in regard to legal issues in MEEC.

Whether we like it or not, we live in a very litigious society. Thus, legal issues are becoming increasingly important, especially in the meetings, expositions, events, and conventions (MEEC) industry. There are legal aspects or issues in almost everything we do as meeting planners and organizers. Contracts are a part of virtually every event and have become increasingly complex. One reason that contracts can be so long and complex is that the parties to the contract try to eliminate as much ambiguity as possible. Ideally, contracts will be as clear as possible to the average person when they read them. We enter into negotiations regardless of whether we are the buyer (meeting organizers) or the suppliers (hotels, DMCs, caterers, audiovisual, production, etc.). We must be concerned about risks such as force majeure (emergencies, crises, or disasters), people getting injured, and failures to perform. We must also be concerned with national, state, and local laws that impact how we put on an event, whom we employ, and the entertainment we use. In this chapter, we delve into many of these issues and provide some insight into legal issues. Remember that this chapter does not take the place of consulting with an attorney who is knowledgeable about MEEC and licensed to practice in your jurisdiction. Further, legal and ethical issues vary by country. This chapter uses a U.S. framework but has broad applicability around the globe.

NEGOTIATION

Negotiation is the process by which a meeting planner and a hotel representative (or other supplier) reach an agreement on the terms and conditions that will govern their relationship before, during, and after a meeting, convention, exposition, or event.

NEGOTIATION STRATEGIES

Although many believe that the goal of a negotiation is to create a "win–win" situation, some say there can be no "win–win" because generally one or both parties must compromise on some things. The real "winner" may be the party who is better prepared entering the negotiation and has the best bargaining leverage. In this regard, hotel representatives generally have an advantage over planners, because the hotels usually know more about the planner's organization than the planner knows about the lodging industry or the specific hotel under consideration.

There are almost as many approaches to negotiating strategy as there are negotiators. One negotiator has offered these tips:

- *Do your homework.* Develop a "game plan" of the outcomes sought, and prioritize your wants and needs. Learn as much about the other side's position as you can.
- *Keep your eyes on the prize.* Do not forget the outcome sought.
- *Leave something on the table.* It may provide an opportunity to come back later and renew the negotiations.
- *Do not be the first one to make an offer.* Letting the other person make the first move sets the outside parameters for the negotiation.
- *When there is a roadblock, find a more creative path.* Thinking "outside the box" often leads to a solution.
- *Timing is everything.* Remember that time always works against the person who does not have it and that 90% of negotiation usually occurs in the last 10% of the time allocated.
- *Listen, listen, listen … and do not get emotional.* Letting emotions rule a negotiation will cause one to lose sight of what result is important.

When negotiating meeting contracts—or any contracts—it is wise to keep some general rules in mind. The following general rules will help with the negotiation of a meeting contract:

- *Go into the negotiations with a plan.* A skilled negotiator knows his or her "bottom line," that is, what is really needed, what is just wanted, and what can be given up to reach a compromise result.

© mojo cp/Shutterstock.com

- *Always go into a contract negotiation with an alternative location or service provider in mind.* Bargaining leverage is better if the other party knows you can go somewhere else with your business.
- *Be thorough.* Put everything negotiated in the contract. Develop your own contract if necessary.
- *Do not assume anything.* Meeting industry personnel change frequently, and oral agreements or assumptions can be easily forgotten or misunderstood. Put it in writing.
- *Beware of language that sounds acceptable but is not specific.* For example, what does a "tentative first option" mean? Words like "reasonable," "anticipated," and "projected" should be avoided, since they mean different things to different people.
- *Do not accept something just because it is preprinted on the contract or the proposal is given to you by the other party.* Everything is negotiable. (See Case 1. SXSW Entertainment Contract).
- *Read the small print.* For example, most contracts come with standard clauses that are copied and pasted from contract to contract, also known as "boilerplate" language. This can include indemnification of parties in the event of negligence, which can make a major difference in the resolution of liability after an accident or injury.
- *Look for mutuality in the contract's provisions.* For example, do not sign a contract in which the "hold harmless" clause protects only one of the parties. Such provisions should be applicable to both parties. And never give one party the unilateral right to do anything, such as change the location of meeting rooms without the consent of the meeting organizer.

CASE 1. SXSW ENTERTAINMENT CONTRACT

In 2017, the United States was in the wake of a change of power in the federal government. This change in power brought declarations of sweeping changes in immigration policy among many other policies. SXSW, an annual music, media, and film festival, came under fire during this time because of a controversial clause in its contract with musicians who wanted to play at the festival. The clause read in part:

> *"Foreign Artists entering the country through the Visa Waiver Program (VWP),*
> *B visa or any non-work visa may not perform at any public or unofficial shows,*
> *DAY OR NIGHT, in Austin from March 10-19, 2017. Accepting and performing at*

unofficial events (including unofficial events aside from SXSW Music dates during their visit to the United States) <u>*may result in immediate deportation, revoked passport and denied entry by US Customs Border Patrol at US ports of entry.*</u>" *(emphasis added)* (Strauss & Yoo, 2017)

One entertainer declined to participate in the event because of this language that he (and others) perceived as threatening to non-U.S. artists, despite the fact that the language had been in previous year's contracts but gone unnoticed.

SXSW, in crisis management mode after the debate over this language went public, reiterated their support of foreign artists and their stance on government issues. They claimed to have put this in the contracts as a reminder of the responsibility of the artists traveling to the U.S. and to protect SXSW in the event of "egregious acts" by foreign entertainers. Although it was too late at the time of the public backlash to go back and change all of the existing contracts, SXSW indicated that it would consider whether to modify the contract language in the future. Everything truly is negotiable.

NEGOTIATING HOTEL CONTRACTS

In addition to the general "rules" applicable to all contract negotiations, there are some special rules about hotel contracts that should also be kept in mind:

- *Understand revenue streams.* Remember that a meeting contract provides a "package" of funds to a hotel. Think in terms of overall financial benefit to the hotel (i.e., its total income from room rates, food and beverage), and allocate this to the organization's benefit.
- *Finalize details.* Never sign a contract in which major items like room rates are left to future negotiation. Future rates can always be set as a percentage of then-current "rack" or maximum increase over then-current "group" rates. This applies to rooms, catered food and beverage, audiovisual, and other expense items.
- *Specify special room rates*—such as for staff and speakers—and indicate any upgrades for them. Indicate whether these are included in the complimentary room formula, and specify what that formula is.
- *Specify when function space will be finalized.* Although it is preferable to have specific meeting and function rooms designated in the contract, a

secondary negotiation position is that they should be assigned at least 12 months prior to the meeting/event, depending on the time of the first promotional mailing. Do not permit a change in assigned meeting rooms without the approval of the meeting organizer, but be prepared to agree to alternate space or pay for original space if the group numbers decrease significantly.

- *Get changes in writing.* Do not agree to any changes that are not spelled out either in the contract or in a later addendum. If an addendum is used, make sure that it references the underlying agreement and supersedes the language in it; and if it is signed at the time of the agreement, make sure that the agreement references the addendum. Be sure that all documents are signed by individuals who are authorized to bind the parties.

NAMING NAMES

One of the most frequently overlooked yet most important parts of a hotel contract includes the names of the contracting parties. Although the meeting's organizer is listed (an independent planner should always sign as an agent for the organizer or have an authorized representative of the organizer sign), the name of the hotel is, in almost all cases, simply listed as the name on the hotel marquee, like "Sheraton Boston."

But the hotel's name is merely a trade name—that is, the name under which the property's owner or management company does business. In today's hotel environment, it may be a franchise of a national "chain" operated by a company that the planner has never heard of. For example, one of the country's largest hotel management companies is Interstate Hotels & Resorts, Inc. Included in the more than 300 hotels that it manages are properties operating under the following "chain" names: Marriott, Holiday Inn, Hilton, Sheraton, and Radisson. Thus, if a contract with one of Interstate's properties simply states that it is with the "Gaithersburg (MD) Marriott," the planner might never know that the actual contracting party is Interstate Hotels & Resorts.

Every meeting contract should contain the following provision, usually as the introductory paragraph:

"This Agreement dated _____ is between (official legal name of entity), a (name of state) (corporation) (partnership) doing business as (name of hotel) and having its principal place of business at (address of contracting party, not hotel) and (name of meeting organizer), a (name of state) (corporation) (partnership) having its principal place of business at (address of meeting organizer)."

Sleeping rooms generate the major share of hotel revenue, so this is often the biggest concern to hotels.

Catered food and beverage is also important but only if it is the "right" kind of food and beverage function, because not all functions are equal in value. For example, a seated dinner for 100 people is worth more to a hotel—in revenue and profit—than a coffee break or continental breakfast for the same number of people.

The type of entity organizing the meeting. Hotels know from experience that certain types of meeting attendees are likely to spend more at hotel food outlets (restaurants, room service, etc.) than other types of attendees who may venture outside the property for meals at more expensive restaurants. From experience, a hotel is also able to estimate the number of attendees who will not show up or who will check out early. Early departures and no-shows deprive the hotel of expected revenue.

In order for a meeting planner to successfully negotiate with a hotel, the planner should

- Understand the relative strengths and weaknesses of the meeting as a "piece of business" that the hotel may be interested in: "how much is the piece of business worth?"
- Understand how a hotel evaluates meeting business.
- Understand the competitive marketplace in which the hotel operates—for instance, its strengths, weaknesses, and occupancy patterns.
- Position the meeting in its best light, using detailed information and history of prior meetings to support this approach. The hotel may base its evaluation of a meeting, especially one it has never hosted before, on its perception of the industry or profession represented by the meeting organizer. Thus, the meeting organizer can counter any negative impressions, or play up positive ones, by providing the hotel with as much information as possible on the organizer's **meeting history**. Especially helpful is information pertaining to previous meeting room blocks and subsequent room utilization, total spending on sleeping rooms, food and beverage, equipment rental, and ancillary services like recreational activities or in-room movies.
- Many hoteliers, particularly those who have been in the industry for many years, sum up meeting negotiations with this simple maxim: "**Dates,**

Rates, and Space—*You Can Only Have Two.*" (See Exhibit 1.) By this maxim, for example, the planner can get the dates and meeting space he or she wants for a meeting, but may have to give a little on the rate. Much more than space, room rates and meeting dates are negotiable. Consider contract issues such as earning complimentary rooms for a certain number of reserved rooms, cutoff dates, rates after cutoff, attrition and cancellation clauses, meeting or exhibit space rental, comp suites, staff rates, limo service, audiovisual rates, VIP amenities, parking fees, and food and beverage provisions. In short, *everything* about a hotel (supplier) contract is negotiable. Likewise, in any other vendor or supplier contract, there are many negotiable items.

EXHIBIT 1.

Rates, Dates, and Space …You Can Only Have Two

The Cocoa Society wants to meet in Portland, Oregon, ideally the week after Memorial Day. They would like to keep their rates under $200 a night. They need 20,000 sq. ft. of meeting space. In a negotiation, they may get options like the following.

Rates	Dates	Space
$199.00/night Run of House	June 1–4	12,000 sq. ft. at a rental of $2500/day total
$199.00/night Run of House	May 15–19	20,000 sq. ft. complimentary
$289.00/night Run of House	June 1–4	20,000 sq. ft. complimentary

- Determine where the meeting organizer can be flexible. A negotiation often requires both parties to make concessions to reach an equitable, acceptable agreement. For example, if a planner understands that the meeting's space-to-rooms ratio is greater than customary, the planner can help his or her position by altering program format, eliminating 24-hour "holds" on meeting or function space that allows the hotel to sell the space in unused hours. The planner who refuses to be flexible is not likely to get the best deal. Changing arrival and departure dates to more closely fit the hotel's occupancy pattern can also lead to a successful negotiation. Moving the meeting forward or backward one or more weeks can also result in savings, especially if the preferred time coincides with a period of high sleeping room demand.

To understand how a hotel approaches a meeting negotiation, the planner must first know about the hotel. Some of the necessary information is obvious:

- The location of the hotel—is it near an airport, downtown, or close to a convention center?
- The type of hotel—is it a resort with a golf course, tennis courts, and other amenities; a "convention" hotel with a great deal of meeting space; or a small venue with limited meeting facilities?

However, some of the information that is important to know is not so obvious and may, in fact, change, depending on the time of the year. For example, it is important to know the mix between the hotel's transient business (that derived from individual business guests or tourists) and groups. Within the group sector, it is valuable to know how much business is derived from corporate, government, and association sources. It is also important to know what the hotel regards as "high" season, when room demand is highest, and "low" season, when demand is at its annual low. This information is important because it helps the planner understand the hotel's position in the negotiation process, and it may provide some helpful hints in structuring a planner's proposal to meet the hotel's needs.

Seasonal fluctuations may be driven by outside factors, such as events in the city where the hotel is located. For example, an informed planner will know that it is difficult to book rooms in New Orleans during Mardi Gras or during that city's annual Jazz Fest (in late April and early May) because hotels can sell their rooms to individual tourists at higher rates than to groups. Many hotels in Ft. Lauderdale, Florida, are heavily booked during spring break; therefore, favorable meeting rates may be difficult to obtain then.

© Jillian Cain Photography/Shutterstock.com

The arrival and departure patterns of the majority of a hotel's guests are also important for a planner to know. For example, a hotel in Las Vegas is generally difficult to book for weekend meetings, because that city attracts large numbers of individual visitors who come to spend the weekend. A hotel that caters to many individual business guests may have greater availability on Friday and Saturday nights, when business travelers are not there. A national survey indicates that, for typical hotels, occupancy is lowest on Sunday evenings and highest on Wednesdays.

Although hotels generate revenue from a variety of sources—and recently have become more sophisticated in analyzing these "profit centers"—the primary source of hotel income is sleeping room revenue; one industry research report estimates that, overall, more than 67% of all hotel revenue is generated from sleeping rooms.

Hotels set their sleeping room rates—at least the published or so-called **rack rates**—in several ways. First, the hotel wants to achieve a total return on its investment. However, since nearly 50% of all rooms in all hotels are sold at less than rack rate, hotels vary their actual rates depending on a number of supply and demand factors, including time of year (which is a function of demand).

Most hotels have adopted the concept of **yield management**, also called revenue management, pioneered by the airline industry. In this approach, hotels can vary their rates almost daily, depending on the actual and anticipated demand for rooms at a particular time. The "yield management" concept may have some negative impact on meeting planners. For example, a planner who books a meeting 15 to 18 months in advance may find that, as the meeting nears, total hotel room utilization is lower than the hotel anticipated, so the hotel, hoping to generate additional revenue, will promote special pricing that may turn out to be less than what was offered to the meeting organizer. A contractual provision prohibiting this practice—which many hotels will not agree to—or at least giving the meeting organizer credit toward its room block for rooms booked at these lower prices can help take the sting out of yield management practices.

CONTRACTS

In far too many instances, **contracts** for meetings, conventions, and trade shows, and the ancillary services provided in connection with these events, contain self-serving statements, lack specificity, and fail to reflect the total ne-

gotiation between the parties. This is understandable because neither meeting planners nor hotel sales representatives generally receive training in the law governing these agreements.

By definition, a contract is an agreement between two parties that details the intention of the parties to do (or not do) specific things. For example, at its most basic, a meetings contract says the meeting's organizer agrees to use a certain number of rooms and services and the hotel agrees to provide the rooms and services outlined.

A contract need not be called a contract but can be referred to as an "agreement," a "letter of agreement," a "memorandum of understanding," and sometimes a "letter of intent" or "proposal." The title of the document or understanding is not important—its contents are. For example, if a document called a "proposal" sets forth details of a meeting and contains the legal elements of a contract, it becomes a binding contract when signed by both parties. So, don't let the name at the top of the document mislead you.

The essential elements of a contract are:

- An **offer** by one party.
- **Acceptance** of the offer as presented by another party. This is typically done by signing the contract.

- **Consideration** (i.e., the price negotiated and paid for the agreement). Although consideration is usually expressed in monetary terms, it need not be—for example, mutual promises are often treated as consideration in a valid contract.
- **Capacity.** The parties to the contract must have legal capacity to enter into the contract. This includes both mental capacity (e.g., they must not be mentally incapacitated) and having the authority to enter into the contract.
- **Legal subject**. The contract must be for a legal subject. So a contract between parties that has all of the other legal components but that is for the payment and shipment of illegal drugs would, in fact, not be a valid contract.

Offers can be terminated prior to acceptance in one of several ways:

- At the expiration of a specified time (e.g., "This offer is only good for twenty-four hours." After twenty-four hours, the other party cannot accept it because it expired.).
- At the expiration of a reasonable period.
- On specific revocation by the offerer. In this case, however, the revocation must be communicated to the offeree to be effective.

A rejection of the offer by the offeree or the proposal of a counteroffer terminates the original offer, but a request for additional information about the offer is not construed as a rejection of the offer. For example, if an individual responds to an offer by saying, "I accept, with the following addition," that is not really an acceptance but the proposal of a counteroffer, which the original offerer must then consider and either accept or reject.

Often, a meeting contract proposal from a hotel will contain a specified termination period for the offer. These "offers" are usually couched in the phrase "tentative first option" or in a similar wording. Because the meeting organizer pays or promises nothing for this "option," it is, in reality, nothing more than a contract offer, which must be specifically accepted by the meeting planner. There is no legal obligation on the part of the hotel to keep the option or offer open for the period stated.

In a meeting context, the hotel, venue, or vendor is usually the offerer—that is, the written agreement is generally proposed, after some preliminary negotiation, by them to the planner. The meeting organizer becomes the offeree, but a counteroffer is often made.

For an offer to be accepted, the acceptance must be unequivocal and in the same terms as the offer. Any deviation from the offer's terms is not acceptance; it is a counteroffer, which kills the original offer and must then be accepted by the original offeror for a valid contract to exist.

Acceptance must be communicated to the offerer using the same means that the offeror used. In other words, if the offer is made in writing, the acceptance must be in writing. Mere silence on the part of the offeree is never construed as acceptance, and an offerer cannot impose an agreement on the other party by stating that the contract will be assumed if no response is given by a specified date.

As indicated, consideration is the price negotiated and paid for the agreement. Although consideration generally involves money paid for the other party's promise to perform certain functions—for example, money paid to a hotel for the provision of sleeping rooms, meeting space, and food and beverage functions—it could also be an exchange of mutual promises, as in a barter situation.

Consideration must be what the law regards as "sufficient," not from a monetary standpoint but from the standpoint of whether the act or return promises results in either a benefit to the promisor or a detriment to the promisee. The fairness of the agreed exchange is legally irrelevant. Thus, the law is not concerned about whether one party "overpaid" for what he or she received. One need not make an affirmative promise or payment of money; for instance, forbearance, not doing something that someone is legally entitled to do, can also be a consideration in a contract.

It is important that both promises must be legally enforceable to constitute valid *consideration*. For example, a promise to commit an illegal act is not *consideration* because the law will not require one to commit that act.

A party to a contract must have the mental *capacity* to understand what it means to enter into the agreement and what terms they are agreeing to. This mental incapacity might be attributable to mental illness, drug use, or other reasons. Society also requires that a party to a contract be of a minimum age before he or she can legally commit to contractual promises, so minors are considered to lack capacity to contract.

Even if all of the other components of a contract are present, the law will not enforce a contract if the subject of that contract is illegal.

STATUTE OF FRAUDS

Although a contract does not have to be in writing to be enforceable, every law student learns that it is better to have a written document because there can be less chance for a misunderstanding about the terms of the agreement. However, under what is called the "Statute of Frauds," some contracts must be in writing to be enforceable. This statute was first passed in England in 1677 and, in one form or another, has become a part of the law of every state in the United States, except Louisiana, where law is based on French Napoleonic code.

Among the agreements that must be in writing are contracts for the sale or lease of real estate and contracts that are not to be performed within 1 year of agreement. The latter includes contracts for meetings and other events that are to be held more than 1 year in the future. The former could also include a meeting contract, because the agreement might be construed as an organizer's "lease" of hotel space. The law requires these contracts to be in writing because they are viewed as more important documents than "ordinary" agreements. However, as indicated, planners are strongly encouraged to put all contracts in writing to avoid the possibility of misunderstanding.

A valid written contract must contain the identity of the parties, an identification or recitation of the subject matter and terms of agreement, and a statement of consideration. Often, where the consideration may not be obvious, a contract will state that it is entered into for "good and valuable consideration, the receipt and sufficiency of which are acknowledged by the parties."

When a contract is in writing, it is generally subject to the so-called "parol" evidence or "four-corners" rule of interpretation. Thus, where the written contract is intended to be the complete and final expression of the rights and duties of the parties, evidence of prior oral or written negotiations or agreements or contemporaneous oral agreements cannot be considered by a court charged with interpreting the contract. Many contracts contain what is often called an "entire agreement" clause, which specifies that the written document contains the entire agreement between the parties and supersedes all previous oral or written negotiations or agreements.

PAROL EVIDENCE

Parol evidence (or evidence of oral agreement) can be used in limited instances, especially where the plain meaning of words in the written document may be in doubt. A court will generally construe a contract most strongly against the party that prepared the written document; and if there is a conflict between printed and handwritten words or phrases, the latter will prevail.

Many contracts, especially meeting contracts, contain addenda prepared at the same time or sometimes subsequent to the signing of the contract. In cases where the terms of an addendum differ from those of the contract, the addendum generally prevails, although it is a good idea when using an addendum to specifically provide that in the event of differences, the addendum will prevail.

KEY HOTEL GROUP MEETING CONTRACT CLAUSES

Planning and executing a meeting may involve the negotiation of several contracts. Obviously, the major—and perhaps most important—agreement is the one with the hotel and/or trade show facility. However, there can also be agreements covering a myriad of ancillary services, such as temporary employees, security, audiovisual equipment, destination management (e.g., tours and local transportation), entertainment, outside food and beverage, exhibitor services or decorating, and housing bureaus. Moreover, agreements may be negotiated with "official" transportation providers like travel agencies, airlines, and rental car companies.

Attrition, cancellation, and termination provisions in a hotel are frequently confusing. If not carefully drafted, they can lead to many problems (and much expense) if a meeting organizer does not fill the room block or wishes to change his or her mind for some reason. For more information on these and other hotel group meeting contract clauses, see the Events Industry Council's Accepted Practices Exchange (APEX) *Contracts Accepted Practices* (https://insights.eventscouncil.org/Portals/0/APEX_Contracts.pdf).

ATTRITION

Attrition clauses (sometimes also referred to as *"performance clauses"*) provide for the payment of damages to the hotel when a meeting organizer fails to fully utilize the room block specified in the contract. Most hotels regard the contracted room block as a commitment by the meeting organizer to fill the number of room nights specified. However, in at least one case, a court determined that the room block did not represent a commitment by the meeting organizer; that decision was predicated, in part, on contract language that indicated that room reservations would be made by individuals and not by the meeting organizer.

A well-written attrition provision should provide the organizing entity with the ability to reduce the room block by a specified amount ("slippage") (e.g., 10%–20%) up to a specified time prior to the meeting without incurring damages. Thereafter, damages should accrue only if the organizer fails to pay for or occupy the remaining percentage (e.g., 85%–90%) of its adjusted room block. Occupancy should be measured on a cumulative room night basis, not on a night-by-night basis.

Because hotels sometimes offer rates to the general public as part of special promotional packages that are lower than those available to the meeting attendees, it is important that the meeting room **pickup** be measured by all attendance, regardless of the rate paid. This may involve some extra work on the part of the hotel and the meeting organizer, but the result could save the organization money, especially if the meeting attendance is not as expected. For example, the meeting contract could include language like the following:

> Group shall receive credit for all rooms used by attendees, regardless of the rate paid or the method of booking. Hotel shall cooperate with Group in identifying these attendees and shall charge no fee for assisting Group.

Using this language, an organization would submit its meeting registration list to the hotel and ask that the hotel match the list against those guests who are in-house at the time. An alternate approach, which many hotels reject, is to have the hotel and group sit down together with the meeting organizer's registration list and review the hotel's in-house guest list together to do the matching.

Damages triggered by the failure to meet a room block commitment should be specified in dollars, not measured by a percentage of some vague figure such as "anticipated room revenue." The latter may provide the hotel with an opportunity to include "ancillary revenue," estimated spending on such things as telephone calls, in-room movies, and the like. The specified damages should be based on the hotel's lost profit, not its lost revenue. With sleeping rooms, for example, the average industry profit margin is around 75% (a little higher for resorts, a little lower for limited service properties), so the per-room attrition fee should not exceed 75% of the group's single room rate. The industry standard for food and beverage profit is about 35%, again varying slightly by the type of property.

Because attrition damages are a type of liquidated damages, there is no requirement for the hotel to mitigate these damages by providing credit for any unused sleeping rooms the hotel is able to resell. If the meeting organizer wants credit for resold rooms, then there needs to be a clause in the contract that imposes a specific requirement on the hotel to try and resell the rooms and credit the resold rooms against the group's attrition damages. (See Exhibit 2.)

Exhibit 2.

Calculating Attrition Damages

A contract between The Cocoa Society and the Fountain Hotel initially includes the following attrition clause (it is not favorable to the Group):

Clause 1. This Agreement is therefore based on Group's use of 200 total room nights. Group agrees that if Group uses less than the room block established in this agreement, Hotel will be harmed. Hotel will allow Group 10% room block shrinkage without any liquidated damage payment. For shrinkage over and above this allowance, the Hotel will require payment from Group for each unused room night at the confirmed group average rate plus applicable tax for Group's committed room block. This payment will not be in effect with respect to any unused room nights within your committed block for any night during your stay in which all of the available rooms in the Hotel are sold.

After modification by The Cocoa Society, the clause reads as follows:

Clause 2. This Agreement is therefore based on Group's use of 200 total room nights. Group agrees that if Group uses less than the room block established in this agreement, Hotel ~~will~~ <u>may</u> be harmed. Hotel will allow Group ~~10%~~ <u>20%</u> room block shrinkage without any liquidated damage payment. For shrinkage over and above this allowance, the Hotel will require payment from Group for each unused room night at <u>75% (profit margin)</u> of the confirmed group ~~average~~ <u>Run of House</u> rate plus applicable tax for your committed room block. ~~This payment will not be in effect with respect to any unused room nights within your committed block for any night during your stay in which all of the available rooms in the Hotel are sold~~. <u>Group will receive credit against attrition damages for all room nights Hotel is able to resell. The parties understand the Hotel will resell Group rooms only after the rest of its inventory has been sold.</u>

To see how significant a few changes to an attrition clause can be in terms of financial damages, compare the calculations with Clause 1 and Clause 2. Examples assume that the Group picked up 150 room nights.

Clause 1.

200 – 150 room nights = 50 room nights unsold
Shrinkage (200 × 10%) = 20 room nights shrinkage
50 room nights unsold – 20 room nights shrinkage = 30 room nights for attrition damages
30 room nights × $235/night = US **$7,050** attrition damages

Clause 2.

200 – 150 room nights = 50 room nights unsold
Shrinkage (200 × 20%) = 40 room nights shrinkage
50 room nights unsold – 40 room nights shrinkage = 10 room nights for attrition damages
10 room nights × ($200/night × 75% profit margin) = US **$1,500** attrition damages

Attrition clauses often appear in the portion of a contract that discusses meeting room rental fees, with the contract providing that meeting room rental fees will be imposed, typically on a sliding scale basis, if the room block is not filled. If the clause appears in conjunction with meeting room rental, it should not also appear somewhere else, resulting in a double charge, and language should be inserted making it clear that the meeting room rental fee is the only charge to be imposed if the room block is not completely utilized.

CANCELLATION

This is the provision that provides for damages should the meeting be canceled for reasons other than those specified in the force majeure provision. Often, this provision in a hotel-provided agreement is one-sided. It provides damages to the hotel in the event the meeting organizer cancels. A properly drafted agreement should provide for damages in the event either party (including the hotel) cancels without a valid reason. However, as indicated previously, some contract drafters believe that damages should not be specified in the event of a hotel cancellation because it only provides the hotel with an amount that it can use to buy out of an agreement. An alternative approach is to specify what the group's damages will include if the hotel cancels. This is called an actual damages clause (as contrasted with liquidated damages, mentioned further on). This includes listing things such as increases in food and beverage costs or rooms at a substitute hotel, additional marketing materials, and site inspection trips to find a new hotel for the meeting. Although it seems like bad business for a hotel to cancel a meeting, it does happen. (See Case 2.)

The meeting organizer should not have the right to cancel solely to book the meeting in another hotel or another city or for the hotel to book another, more lucrative meeting in place of the one contracted for.

The damages triggered by a cancellation by the group are sometimes stated on a sliding scale basis, with greater damages being paid the closer to the meeting date the cancellation occurs. Damages should be expressed as "liquidated damages" or a cancellation fee, not as a penalty, because the law generally does not recognize penalty provisions in contracts. As with damages in an attrition clause, damages should be expressed in dollar amounts, not room revenue (so that sales tax can be avoided) and should be payable only if the hotel cannot resell the space.

CASE 2. SYLVANIA V. BOCA RATON RESORT & CLUB

Osram Sylvania, Inc. signed a contract with the Boca Raton Resort & Club for a national sales meeting to take place in October 2007. Sylvania had a long history with the hotel, having held 17 meetings at the hotel since 1984. Imagine Sylvania's surprise when, in 2007, the hotel cancelled the contract for the 2007 national sales meeting that had been negotiated and signed in 2004! Because the contract was signed during a recession period for the U.S., the rates Sylvania was able to negotiate in 2004 may have been more favorable than the market rates in 2007. This is why negotiating contract clauses is so important - you may think the hotel will never cancel (it is unusual), especially if you are a long-standing client, but it does happen. Sylvania never got to meet at the Boca Raton Resort & Club in 2007, but through a settlement, they did return in 2008.

Bassett, M. (2007, August 1). The seller's market strikes again. *MeetingsNet*. Retrieved from http://www.meetingsnet.com/checklists/sellers-market-strikes-again
MeetingsNet. (2007, September 21). OSI Settles Meeting Flap. *Corporate Meetings & Incentives*. Retrieved from http://www.meetingsnet.com/corporate-meetings/osi-settles-meeting-flap

FORCE MAJEURE

Sometimes called an **Impossibility** or an **Act of God** clause, this provision permits either party to terminate the contract without damages if fulfillment of the obligations imposed in the agreement is rendered illegal, impossible, or (depending on how the clause is written) impracticable by occurrences outside of the control of either party. This usually includes such things as labor strikes, severe weather, and transportation difficulties. Typical language says that performance will be excused due to circumstances beyond the control of the parties that make it "illegal or impossible" to hold or host the meeting. Sometimes the provision also uses the term "impracticable," which means that although it may not be absolutely impossible, it is functionally impossible.

Some reasons a meeting organizer may want to be able to terminate the contract without payment of damages are if the hotel ownership, management, or brand affiliation changes; if the meeting size outgrows the hotel; if the hotel's quality rating (e.g., as measured by the American Automobile Association) changes; or for reasons that make it inappropriate or impractical to hold the meeting there. The latter language should be broad enough to cover objectionable policies or laws, where a group decides not to hold a meeting in a particular location because of action taken by government. As an example, the organizer of a major shooting sports trade show—SHOT—canceled the event after the sponsoring city sued gun manufacturers who were the show's major exhibitors.

© michelmond/Shutterstock.com

Flooding is sometimes a reason for Force Majeure to be used

Because of the differences in contracts supplied by hotels, and because it is often so easy for planners, even experienced ones, to overlook key elements of a contract, many meeting organizers are developing their own "standard" contract. While many meeting organizers may be unsure of the costs involved in having a competent attorney prepare this type of document, such costs are minimal when compared with the time (and therefore expense) involved in reviewing each and every contract proposed by a hotel, whether the review is conducted by counsel or by a meeting planner or other staff member.

An organizer's development of its own contract will ensure that its needs are met and will minimize the chances of subsequent legal problems caused by a misunderstanding of the terms of the agreement.

CASE STUDY

In January 2019, the U.S. federal government shut down due to failure to come up with a federal budget. The American Astronomical Society was not a government entity, but some of its annual meeting attendees were. Out of 3,200 expected attendees, the association expected to lose 300 to 450 furloughed government worker attendees. With a loss of 10% to 15% of its attendees, the conference could likely go on, so a complete termination would not be necessary. Whether the organization considered language addressing a *partial* force majeure that excused performance damages in a situation beyond their control would be helpful in this kind of situation.

DISPUTE RESOLUTION

No matter how carefully a contract is written, disputes may occur either because the parties might disagree as to their individual rights and obligations or because one of the parties may perform less than had been promised. These controversies seldom involve precedent-setting legal issues; rather, they concern an evaluation of facts and interpretation of contract terms. When these differences arise, parties often prefer to settle them privately and informally in the kind of businesslike way that encourages continued business relationships.

Sometimes, however, such resolution is not possible. This leaves the "aggrieved" party with three options: forget the possibility of reaching a solution and walk away from the problem, go to court and sue, or resolve the dispute through other means.

Going to court can be an expensive and time-consuming proposition, with crowded court dockets delaying a decision for several months, or in some cases several years. Attorney fees can mount up quickly, especially if extensive pretrial proceedings are involved. Depending on the court's location, one of the parties may have to expend additional fees for travel expenses. Because court cases are matters of public record, potentially adverse publicity may result.

For this reason, arbitration is gaining favor as a means of settling disputes. "Arbitration" is one form of alternative dispute resolution. In arbitration, one or more arbiters are chosen to hear each party's side of the dispute and decide about the outcome. Under rules administered by the American Arbitration Association, arbitration is designed for quick, practical, and inexpensive settlements. It is, at the same time, an orderly proceeding, governed by rules of procedure and standards of conduct prescribed by law. Either party can utilize lawyers, but there are a minimum of pretrial procedures. If arbitration is chosen as the dispute mechanism procedure in the contract, the parties also generally agree that the results are binding; that is, they cannot be appealed to a court of law. The contract should also specify the location of the arbitration. Arbitration is not generally a matter of public record, so all the proceedings can remain private.

If the parties choose arbitration as a means of settling disputes, the choice should be made before disagreements arise, and language governing the arbitration option should be included in the meeting contract. If arbitration is not selected, the contract should spell out which state's law (e.g., where the meeting took place or where the meeting organizer is located) will be utilized to resolve a court dispute.

Under the American system of justice, each party to a court suit or arbitration proceeding is required to bear the costs of its own attorneys unless the agreement provides that the winning party is entitled to have the loser pay its attorneys' fees and costs.

Finally, a well-drafted contract should specify the damages to be awarded in the event of a breach by either party. Such an approach takes the decision out of the hands of a judge or an arbitrator and leaves the dispute resolver only to determine whether a breach of the agreement occurred. Damages are typically stated as "liquidated damages"; that is, damages that the parties agree in advance will be the result of a breach. Courts will generally not honor a contract provision that imposes a "penalty" on the one breaching the agreement, so that term should be avoided. As an example, a conference was held in a Las Vegas hotel, but the meeting organizer failed to pay the $57,000 master bill presented by the hotel for the meeting expenses. After multiple unsuccessful efforts to get the meeting organizer to pay the bill, the hotel decided to bill the individual attendees for a pro rata share of the master bill. After many upset attendees and much negative media, the hotel reversed its position and went back to pursuing the meeting organizer for the payment.

CRISIS PREPAREDNESS AND MANAGEMENT

WHAT IS RISK? CRISIS PREPAREDNESS?

All meetings involve an element of **risk**. *Risk* is the possibility of suffering loss or harm. *Risk management* is the process of assessing, analyzing, and mitigating the risk, or the possibility of an adverse event. Realized risks (those that actually happen) are classified on the basis of their scope and impact and may be an emergency, crisis, or disaster. Or a realized risk may just be one of the many little things that go wrong in the process of planning and managing events—a routine business incident.

Imagine that an exhibition is to be held outdoors and that during setup it rains torrentially, making it impossible to complete setup or to hold the exhibition. Inclement weather is an example of a risk. It could create a business incident (the exhibition is delayed in opening), an emergency (lightning struck a would-be exhibitor), or a crisis (the lightning struck the exhibitor materials, causing a fire that is now raging out of control). Now imagine that the wise exhibition planner has rented tents under which the exhibits can be placed so that the show can go on. That is part of crisis preparedness.

In October 2017, while the Route 91 outdoor music festival was in full swing in Las Vegas, Stephen Paddock, a lone gunman staying at the Mandalay Bay Resort and Casino, broke a window and fired down on the 22,000 event attendees, killing 59 people and injuring 500 more. No significant motive was determined. Many months of investigation followed into how the shooter could have gotten the large number of weapons he had into the hotel room and how to better secure outdoor events.

© melissamn/Shutterstock.com

CRISIS MANAGEMENT

Once the meeting professional has assessed and analyzed risks, they will have determined which crises have (1) the highest probability of occurring or (2) the greatest impact if they do occur. This is when crisis preparedness and management kicks in. Crisis management can be broken down into four stages:

1. Mitigation
2. Preparedness
3. Response
4. Recovery

The outdoor exhibition example provided earlier can be used to illustrate the steps of emergency management.

MITIGATION

Conducting a risk assessment and analysis will also help the planner determine which mitigation measures should be implemented. Examples of some common mitigation measures include:

- Contracts—signed prior to the meeting or event, contracts mitigate risk by narrowing or shifting liability to the responsible party, or they specify exactly what the monetary damage fees (e.g., attrition or cancellation) might be for underperformance of the contract.
- Insurance—the mitigation effect of insurance is that it shifts some of the liability for financial loss to the insurance company. In exchange for paying a premium, the meeting/event organizer knows that the insurance company will pay a claim for loss or damage if it falls within the boundaries of the insurance policy.
- Security—hiring security guards to provide physical security and/or monitor a property is a way of mitigating the risk of injury or loss.

In our rain example, in the *mitigation* stage, the planner would try to determine what he or she could do to mitigate the risk—that is, decrease the probability that rain would occur (and quickly realize it's hard to control the weather!). The planner would also mitigate the crisis—decrease the consequences if it did rain. Realizing that the latter was more manageable, the planner would have had a tent rental company on standby (or would have rented them just in case, if the budget allowed), contracted with a backup indoor venue and purchased event cancellation insurance in case the exhibition was rained out.

PREPAREDNESS

In the preparedness stage, the planner institutes activities like training of staff, emergency drills, and preparing documentation like a crisis plan and an incident report form. This is the stage at which people involved with the meeting—meeting organizer staff, facility staff, and vendor staff—are assigned roles for monitoring emergency indicators and gathering information that will be needed if a crisis does occur, like a list of contact information for staff and attendees.

In our rain example, the *preparedness* stage would include assigning someone to carefully monitor the weather reports on the days leading up to the exhibition.

RESPONSE

Should a crisis adversely affect a meeting or event despite the best planning, the meeting/event professional needs to have an emergency response team ready to respond. Depending on the nature of the crisis, the response may be as simple as sending an announcement to participants about a change in the program. Or it may be as complex as having to help coordinate a crisis evacuation and provide first aid to the injured. A simple response will be up to the planner's risk team. A complex response will likely require emergency professionals: firefighters to put out a fire, police to regain control of a crowd, and emergency medical professionals to administer first aid. The response must fit the crisis.

The tricky thing about response is figuring out both *when* to respond and *how*. If 2 days prior to the event dates, the weather forecast warns of a 60% chance of rain on the exhibition date, should the planner implement the rain plan? Does that mean getting the tents or just alerting exhibitors to the possible change in plans? If the planner waits until the morning of the exhibition, does that give him or her enough time to implement the rain plan? The answers to these questions really depend on the size and scope of the event as well as the nature of the plan.

RECOVERY

Recovery also depends on the nature of the crisis. If the rain in our ongoing example is so bad that the outdoor exhibition has to be cancelled, recovery would include insurance paying claims for the losses suffered by the exhibition organizer as well as the actions by the organizer to overcome any bad press.

A crisis is likely to result in loss or harm and can cause damage to property, people, or to more intangible aspects—like the organizer or planner's reputation. In the case of the outdoor exhibition, recovery might just include refunding the fees of the exhibitor or attendees who didn't attend or filing a claim with the insurance company. In the case of a full-blown disaster or crisis, however, the recovery stage can be much more serious and take a much longer time.

AMERICANS WITH DISABILITIES ACT

The U.S. **Americans with Disabilities Act (ADA)** of 1990 makes it illegal to discriminate against or fail to provide a "reasonable accommodation" for persons with disabilities. The ADA places responsibility on the owners and operators of places of public accommodation (hotels, restaurants, convention centers, retail stores, zoos, parks, etc.) to make reasonable accommodations for equal enjoyment by persons with disabilities.

A **disability** is "a physical or mental impairment that substantially limits a major life activity of an individual."

A **major life activity** under the original ADA includes performing manual tasks, walking, seeing, hearing, speaking, breathing, learning, and working. The ADA Amendment Act of 2008 modified this somewhat, as follows.

The ADA may include people with mobility, hearing, or vision limitations as well as those with "invisible disabilities" such as multiple sclerosis, epilepsy, or other conditions that may not be immediately visible.

Under Title III of the ADA, places of public accommodation (including hotels, restaurants, convention centers, and retail stores) must provide a reasonable accommodation for persons with disabilities unless doing so creates an undue hardship. The ADA Technical Assistance Manual and case law help outline what constitutes undue hardship. Just because an accommodation (such as sign language interpreters or printing large print materials) may be expensive, it does not necessarily mean it is an undue hardship.

The following is the stated purpose of ADA:

1. To provide a clear and comprehensive national mandate for the elimination of discrimination against individuals with disabilities;
2. To provide clear, strong, consistent, enforceable standards addressing discrimination against individuals with disabilities;
3. To ensure that the federal government plays a central role in enforcing the standards on behalf of individuals with disabilities; and
4. To invoke the sweep of congressional authority, including the power to enforce the Fourteenth Amendment and to regulate commerce, to address the major areas of discrimination faced day-to-day by people with disabilities. For more information on the ADA, see the U.S. government's ADA website, www.ada.gov.

The ADA Amendment Act of 2008 became effective on January 1, 2009. It was passed because the U.S. Justice Department realized that people were using the ADA more to exclude people (your disability isn't specifically listed, so you get no accommodation) rather than to include people (you fit the criteria of a person with a disability, so we will provide this accommodation for you). As a result, the definition of a person with a disability under the ADA as Amended (ADAAA) includes a nonexhaustive list of major life activities and major bodily functions. The ADAAA rules require the law to be construed broadly and inclusively, instead of narrowly, as it was under the original ADA. This means some issues like food allergies and dietary restrictions, which were deemed not to fall under the ADA in the past, are now covered. (See Case 3).

CASE 3

J.D. is a minor who went on a school trip to Colonial Williamsburg. While there, the group went to one of the Colonial Williamsburg restaurants for a meal. J.D. has a gluten sensitivity and brought his own special meal to ensure that he did not get sick from eating restaurant food with gluten in it. The restaurant's policy did not allow people to bring outside food in, and J.D. was told he would have to eat his special food outside. J.D.'s family sued for discrimination under the ADA. At the lower court level, the federal district court, the court sided with Colonial Williamsburg. The appeals court found that because J.D. had reactions to restaurant food that was supposed to be safe before, a jury might agree that he has to bring his own food and reversed to allow J.D. to go back and try to prove his ADA claim. Imagine if J.D. was a meeting attendee instead of a restaurant guest?

Title III of the ADA covers public accommodations, which applies to meeting planners and organizers as well as facilities and vendors. Meeting organizers must (1) determine the extent to which attendees have disabilities and (2) make reasonable efforts to accommodate the special needs of those attendees at no cost to the attendee. As a result, we now see sections on registration forms asking if the attendee has any special needs. An example is the attendee who is hearing impaired. The planner would have to provide a sign language interpreter, large print materials, or another accommodation that allows the person with a disability to fully participate in the meeting to the extent possible. Readers may have seen these interpreters in class or during important speeches. For those with vision impairment, the planner may have to provide documents with extra-large type or produced in Braille. Failure to accommodate attendees with disabilities can result in legal action and fines. Furthermore, the accommodations requirement is not limited to attendees but applies to employees as well.

The planner must be aware of the ramifications of the ADA and be sure that all facilities used meet the standards. The planner must also be sure that their activities and programs meet the guidelines set forth in the act. Be aware, however, that this act applies only to events and meetings in the United States. Canada, for example, does not have the equivalent of the ADA, and many of its facilities do not meet the standards put forth in the act. Accessibility and accommodation of those with disabilities vary significantly from county to county.

INTELLECTUAL PROPERTY

There are three main areas of intellectual property: patents, trademarks, and copyrights.

PATENTS

Patents are property rights for inventions. Patents allow the inventor of a device or process to protect their invention for a certain period. There are three types of patents:

© Olivier Le Moal/Shutterstock.com

- *Utility patents*—for new and useful processes, machines, articles of manufacture, or composition of matter, or any new and useful improvement thereof;
- *Design patents*—for new, original, and ornamental design for an article of manufacture; and
- *Plant patents*—for the invention or discovery of a distinct and new variety of plant.

Patents are not widely discussed in the meetings industry, although a company once made a claim that they had invented the online registration process. This company sent demands for money to associations that were using online registration for their meetings. American Society of Association Executives (ASAE) and the Center for Association Leadership got involved, and the issue ultimately went away.

TRADEMARKS

A trademark (or service mark) is a word, name, symbol, or device that is used with goods (or services) to indicate the source of the goods and to distinguish them from the goods of others. As an example, Campbell's Soup® puts their name on their cans so consumers know it is their soup. By eating different brands of soup, consumers count on a trademark to tell them what to expect. Likewise, Ritz-Carlton® puts their name on their hotels so you know where you are staying and what to expect. For more information, see the U.S. Patent & Trademark Office (www.uspto.gov).

COPYRIGHTS

Copyright is a form of protection provided to the authors of "original works of authorship," including literary, dramatic, musical, artistic, and certain other intellectual works, both published and unpublished. In the meetings industry, copyright covers event proposals, music played at events, photographs, videos, and more. Copyright protection attaches at the time the work is "fixed in a durable medium." A singer may riff and come up with an original song to sing, but until the song lyrics are written down or the music is recorded, it is not copyrightable. For more general information on copyrights, see the U.S. government's copyright website www.copyright.gov.

MUSIC COPYRIGHT

Many meetings and trade shows feature events at which music is played, either by live musicians or historically using prerecorded CDs. Music may be provided as a background (such as at a cocktail reception) or as a primary focus of attention (such as at a dinner dance or concert). At trade shows, individual exhibitors as well as the organizing entity can provide music.

Regardless of how music is provided, it is important to remember that under the federal copyright act, the music is being "performed," and, according to many court decisions, the entity organizing the event is considered to be controlling the "performance," even if that "control" means only hiring an orchestra without telling them what to play. The only recognized exemption to the "performance" rule is for music played over a single receiver (radio or TV) of a type usually found in the home.

Today, there are several performing rights organizations (PROs) that serve as intermediaries to collect the royalties for the public performance of copyrighted music for the artists, authors, composers, and publishers in their membership. Some of these include the American Society of Composers, Authors and Publishers (**ASCAP**), Broadcast Music, Inc. (**BMI**), Society of European Stage Authors and Composers (**SESAC**), SoundExchange, and Global Music Rights. These organizations exist to obtain license fees from those who "perform" copyrighted music, including radio stations, retail stores, hotels, and organizations that organize meetings, conventions, and trade shows. ASCAP, BMI, and SESAC were the original PROs. A 1979 decision of the U.S. Supreme Court conferred on ASCAP and BMI a special, limited exemption from normal antitrust law principles. This decision has enabled them to develop "blanket" licensing agreements for the various industries that utilize live or recorded music.

Following negotiations with major meeting industry organizations (such as the International Association of Exhibits and Events and the ASAE) in the late 1980s, both ASCAP and BMI developed special licensing agreements and fee structures for meetings, conventions, trade shows, and expositions. These special agreements were designed to replace earlier agreements under which hotels paid licensing fees for meetings held by others on the property. Although the negotiated agreements technically expired at the end of 1994, ASCAP and BMI have extended them on a year-to-year basis, with slight increases in licensing fees. Under court decrees, ASCAP and BMI are forbidden to grant special "deals" to individual meetings, so the agreements, which must be signed, are the same for all meetings and cannot be altered to meet the needs of a particular meeting. Failure to sign these agreements—and agreements with *both* organizations must be signed—could subject a meeting or trade show organizer to costly and embarrassing litigation for copyright infringement.

Under copyright law, an organization cannot meet its obligation by requiring the musicians performing the music or the booking agency or hotel that provided the musicians to obtain ASCAP and BMI licenses. The entity organizing the event must obtain the requisite licenses.

CASE 4. TRADEMARK INFRINGEMENT AT AN EXHIBITION

Jibbitz, Inc., the official maker of snap-on accessories for Crocs (shoes), attended the World Shoe Association trade show as an exhibitor. At the trade show, the Jibbitz exhibit staff noticed another exhibitor promoting the sale of snap-on accessories for Crocs. Because Jibbitz (as a wholly owned subsidiary of Crocs, Inc.) was the only official maker of these accessories, it filed a copyright and trademark infringement lawsuit against the other exhibitor. Jibbitz was awarded $56 million in damages.

https://www.law360.com/articles/56002/crocs-awarded-56m-in-suit-over-shoe-charms

SPEAKER/ENTERTAINMENT COPYRIGHT

An organization organizing a meeting will often want to make audio or video recordings of certain speakers or programs, either for the purpose of selling copies to meeting attendees, to those who could not attend, or for archival purposes.

Speakers or program participants have a common law copyright interest in their presentations, and the law prohibits the organizing organization from selling audio or video copies of the presentation without obtaining the written permission of the presenter. Many professional speakers who also market books or recordings of their presentations frequently refuse to provide consent to be recorded by the meeting organizer.

Permission can be obtained by having each speaker whose session is to be recorded sign a copyright waiver, a simple document acknowledging that the speaker's session is going to be recorded and giving the organizing entity permission to sell the recordings made of the speaker's presentation. If the recording is to be done by a commercial audiovisual company, a sample waiver form can usually be obtained from that company.

LABOR ISSUES

Preparation for on-site work at meetings and trade shows often involves long hours and the use of individuals on a temporary or part-time basis to provide administrative or other support. It is therefore important for organizations to understand how federal employment law requirements impact these situations.

The Federal Fair Labor Standards Act (FLSA) in the United States, adopted in 1938, is more commonly known as the law that prescribes a minimum wage for a large segment of the working population. Another major provision of the FLSA, and one frequently misunderstood, requires that all workers subject to the law's minimum wage coverage *must* receive overtime pay at the rate of 1½ times their "regular" rate of pay *unless* they are specifically exempted by the statute.

There are many common misconceptions that employers have about the FLSA's overtime provisions, including the following, all of which are not true:

- Only hourly employees (and not those paid on a regular salary basis) are eligible for overtime.
- Overtime pay can be avoided by giving employees compensatory time off instead.
- Overtime need be paid only to those who receive advance approval to work more than forty hours in a week.

Over the years, the Department of Labor regulations and court decisions have made it clear that overtime pay cannot be avoided by a promise to provide compensatory time off in another workweek, even if the employee agrees to the procedure. According to the U.S. Department of Labor, the only way so-called *comp time* is legal is if it is given in the same week that the extra hours are worked or in another week of the same pay period, and if the extra time off is sufficient to offset the amount of overtime worked (i.e., at the time-and-one-half rate).

The use of comp time is probably the most common violation of FLSA overtime pay requirements, and it occurs frequently. This is because many employees, particularly those who are paid by salary, would rather have an extra day off from work at a convenient time to deal with medical appointments, holiday shopping, or simply "attitude adjustment." Compensatory time is also frequently, but not legally, provided when a nonexempt employee works long hours in connection with a meeting or convention and is then given extra time off in some later pay period to make up for the extra work.

Overtime cannot be limited to situations where extra work is approved in advance. The law is also clear that premium pay must be paid whenever the employee works in excess of 40 hours per week—or is on call for extra work—even when the extra effort has not specifically been approved in advance. Thus, if a nonexempt employee works a few extra hours in the days prior to a meeting to complete all assignments for that meeting, the employee must be paid overtime.

Overtime pay is not limited to lower salaried employees or those paid on an hourly basis. The FLSA requires *all* employees to receive overtime unless they fall under one of the law's specific exemptions. The most generally available exemptions are the so-called white-collar exemptions for professional, executive, and administrative employees.

To determine whether an employee falls within one of these exemptions, one should review the FLSA and applicable regulations and interpretations carefully. What is explained here is simply a summary. It is also most important to remember that the exemptions apply only to those whose actual work activity falls within the definitions; job titles are meaningless in determining whether an employee is exempt.

Under modifications made to the FLSA in 2014, to qualify for white-collar exemption, an employee generally must:

1. Be salaried, meaning that they are paid a predetermined and fixed salary that is not subject to reduction because of variations in the quality or quantity of work performed (the "salary basis test");
2. Be paid more than a specified weekly salary level, which is $913 per week (the equivalent of $47,476 annually for a full-year worker) under this Final Rule (the "salary level test"); and
3. Primarily perform executive, administrative, or professional duties, as defined in the Department's regulations (the "duties test").

It is important for all employers to know which of their employees are exempt from overtime pay requirements and which are not. This is especially significant when employees are asked to work long hours at meetings or conventions, particularly those held out of town, or to "pitch in" and help complete a large project. When in doubt about overtime, an organization should review job descriptions with a competent human resources professional or experienced counsel.

ETHICS IN MEEC

The preceding part of this chapter deals with legal issues, and the event professional can look to legislation or legal advisors for assistance in dealing with them. There are many other issues, actions, or activities in MEEC that may be legal but may raise questions of ethics. Ethics guide our personal and professional lives. Furthermore, the issue of ethics has moved to center stage with the unethical practices of businesses like Enron, Tyco, Martha Stewart, and others. Ethics is addressed on the evening news and on the front page of newspapers today. The MEEC industry, by its very nature, offers a multitude of opportunities for unethical behavior or practices.

How someone responds to an issue regarding ethics is personally and culturally based. What is ethical behavior in one community or society may be considered unethical in another. Loyalty to personal friends versus an employer is another ethical consideration faced in the MEEC industry. Ethical issues and personal conduct are an important aspect of any industry, including MEEC. The topic cannot possibly be covered in a few paragraphs. Thus, readers are encouraged to seek additional sources of information on this topic.

© 3D generator/Shutterstock.com

SUPPLIER RELATIONS

Some planners feel suppliers are in it only to make money and will do anything they can to get the contract for an event. Some believe that suppliers and vendors will promise anything but may not deliver on their promises. While promising more than can be delivered or embellishing their abilities may be legal, it may not be ethical. On the other hand, many suppliers and vendors feel meeting/event professionals tend toward overstatement, for example, in estimating the number of rooms they will use in a hotel and the amount their group spends on food and beverage. This too is an ethical question. The solution to these issues is to put everything in writing, preferably in the contract.

Even with a contract, the buyer (planner or organizer) and the seller (vendor or supplier) should be as open, forthright, and honest as possible in dealing with each other. A relationship not built on trust is a fragile relationship, at best. Furthermore, given the increasing importance of relationship marketing, honest and ethical behavior can lead to future business.

Another ethical issue deals with the ownership and use of intellectual material. Destination management companies (DMCs), in particular, often complain that meeting planners submit requests for proposals (RFPs) to many suppliers and that the DMCs spend quite a bit of time, energy, and money to develop creative ideas and programs to secure the planner's business. However, there are many cases in which a planner will take the ideas developed by one DMC and have another implement them, or the planner may then do this on his or her own. Is this legal? Yes. Is it ethical? No.

Still another issue for suppliers relates to the offering of gifts. Should an event professional accept gifts and privileges from a supplier or vendor? If amenities are accepted, is there some obligation on the part of the planner to repay the supplier by steering business in the vendor's direction? When does one cross the line from ethical to unethical behavior? Is it proper to accept a Christmas gift but not proper to accept football tickets when offered? Event professionals working for the U.S. government are prohibited from accepting any gift with a value of $50 or more.

Another ethical question regards so-called familiarization or "fam" trips. Fam trips bring potential clients on an all-expenses-paid trip to a destination with the hope that they will bring their business to the community. But what if a planner or organizer is invited on a fam trip to a destination but has no intention of ever holding an MEEC gathering in that location? Should the planner accept the trip? If accepted, is there some implicit expectation that the planner *will* bring business to the locale? Although it is perfectly legal to accept a trip with no intention of bringing business to the locale, is it ethical?

The planner or organizer of a large MEEC gathering has significant clout and power based on the economic and social impact of the gathering. He or she may ask for special consideration or favors based on this power. It may be ethical to exert this influence on behalf of the group, such as when negotiating room rates, catering rates, and complimentary services. However, is it ethical for the planner or organizer to request personal favors that benefit only himself or herself? Is it ethical for the planner to accept personal favors from a supplier or community?

Examples of ethical issues and questions abound in the MEEC industry. An individual must adhere to a personal code of ethics, and many industry associations have developed their own code of ethics to which members must adhere. Colleges and universities have recognized the need to address ethics by implementing courses on the subject. The discussion of ethics in this chapter is meant to make readers aware that ethics is an important aspect of the study of the MEEC industry, but it is not meant as a comprehensive treatise.

TRENDS AND BEST PRACTICES REGARDING LEGAL ISSUES IN MEEC

- Third-party beneficiary contract issues will continue to grow in importance with the increasing number of independent meeting planners, professional congress organizers (PCOs), and the like. Where two parties have signed a contract but there are commission issues affecting a third party, the law recognizes the third party's rights to the benefit outlined in the contract.
- New and unexpected force majeure issues will continue to challenge our interpretation of existing force majeure clauses, statutes, and interpretation of case law. Not everything can be anticipated, and the force majeure clause isn't meant to be a kitchen sink clause of everything that can possibly happen.
- The protection of intellectual property becomes a greater challenge as technology makes it easier to take photos (including by drone), make copies, or "snip" a protected piece of writing that is meant to be protected.

- Who has the upper hand in negotiation—the organizer or the vendor—will depend on the economy. In a good economy where demand is strong, the supplier has the upper hand; in a weak economy, it is the organizer or buyer.
- The line between ethics and law will continue to be gray, but more organizations will formalize ethics policies to avoid public relations nightmares, especially via social media.

COVID-19

COVID-19 took the meetings industry by surprise. Not only was the way it affected meetings and events a surprise, but the way it has affected contracts and liability continues to be a surprise as the effects and after-effects of the impact of the virus unfold. Initially, the biggest issue with COVID-19 centered on whether contracted meetings should go forward as planned, whether they should be postponed, or whether they should cancel. Each of these options trigger different contract clauses, and the question became, which one(s)?

- Postponing a meeting: can be done with a contract addendum on the agreement of the parties or may be a cancellation with damages and a new agreement with some of the cancellation damages applied to the new meeting.
- Cancelling a meeting: may require use of the cancellation clause and payment of damages, or, if the circumstances are right, the force majeure clause may apply, and the contract may terminate without liability.

When certain states started to pass laws that public gatherings of more than 20 or 50 were not allowed, that made a contract for a meeting of more than that *illegal*. This triggered the force majeure clause, which causes the contract to basically self-destruct if circumstances beyond the control of the party cause it to become "illegal, impossible, or impracticable to hold the meeting or host the meeting." Unfortunately, most situations were not that clear, and instead, the parties were in a grey area, wondering if there would be such a mandate passed or if such a mandate would still be in effect once their future meeting dates arrived.

Another big concern regarding COVID-19 has been liability if meeting and events are held or hotels are open, guests or attendees come, and someone gets sick. Who, then, is liable? No one has a clear answer to that because it is so fact-specific, depending on duty of care and the due diligence put in place by the parties, but it is an issue that is sure to be litigated at some point. Some states, like Georgia, have passed laws to limit the liability of businesses that stay open during COVID-19. The Georgia COVID-19 Pandemic Business Safety Act creates a "rebuttable presumption" that a person claiming to have contracted COVID-19 at a business assumed the risk of infection if the business posted warnings that adhered to the guidelines of the law. This is, in part, to reduce the number of lawsuits that are filed against businesses.

WARNING

UNDER GEORGIA LAW, THERE IS NO LIABILITY FOR AN INJURY OR DEATH OF AN INDIVIDUAL ENTERING THESE PREMISES IF SUCH INJURY OR DEATH RESULTS FROM THE INHERENT RISKS OF CONTRACTING COVID-19. YOU ARE ASSUMING THIS RISK BY ENTERING THESE PREMISES.

Tyra Warner (2020)

SUMMARY

Legal issues are an increasingly important factor in the MEEC industry. This chapter is meant to provide insights into some of these issues, such as negotiation, contracts, statutes, labor, and intellectual property. There are other issues that were not discussed, and entire books are devoted to them. Readers are reminded to seek legal counsel whenever appropriate.

CASE STUDY. ALCOHOL AND EVENT LIABILITY

(Produced by G.G. Fenich and Students from East Carolina University)

Sydney, a recent college graduate, has just been hired by D&T Events in a midsized city. D&T houses five event planners as well as a large wait staff. The company will supply staff to serve food and alcohol; however, D&T does not actually provide the food and alcohol. Their main purpose is to plan, down to the last detail, everything that an event needs to have in order to be a success.

After going through training and working as an assistant to Madison, one of D&T's top event planners, Sydney was set to work her first big event. The event was the wedding reception of Ms. Ashley Jones to Mr. Caleb Chamberlain, a very prominent businessman well known throughout the local area. Caleb was notorious for having lavish parties and bringing in a lot of revenue for both Madison and D&T.

The arrangements for the wedding reception went off without a hitch, and Sydney felt a new-found confidence in her position as an event planner's assistant. However, about thirty minutes into the reception, Madison got a phone call and had to leave immediately to attend to a family emergency. Before Madison left, she instructed Sydney to make sure she did everything the groom asked and not to do anything that might upset him. Sydney had also been made aware before the event of Caleb's background and how important his business was to the company. Caleb's wishes were always granted, and so she passed on the information to the bartender and wait staff to make sure they were also aware of the situation.

Sydney made it most of the way through the reception alone without a problem and thought she was home free until she heard a guest being loud and boisterous. She made her way through the crowd to see who was responsible for the disturbance, only to find that the rowdy guest was none other than the best man. Sydney took notice of the fact that not only was the best man slurring his words, stumbling, and attempting to start fights with other guests but he also had two drinks in his hands. Sydney quickly went to the bartender, a D&T employee, and asked how much the best man had been served. The bartender informed her that when she tried to cut off the best man, Mr. Chamberlain came over and made it very clear that he paid a lot of money for this reception and that his best man was to have whatever he wanted. Therefore, the bartender, under direct orders from Sydney, granted Caleb's wishes and continued to serve the best man.

Being fresh out of college, Sydney remembered the Hospitality Law class that she took and the chapter about alcohol. She knew that she could be held financially liable if the best man were to injure himself or someone else after he was served too much alcohol at her event by her staff. Sydney knew the best course of action to take was to cut the best man off and ask him to leave, but she also knew how important Mr. Chamberlain's business was and how much she could hurt her company if she upset him.

1. Do you think Sydney should risk her job and Caleb's business by continuing to serve his best man, or should she do what is legal and deal with the repercussions from Madison and D&T?

2. What would you do if you were put in Sydney's situation?

KEYWORDS AND TERMS

For definitions, see https://insights.eventscouncil.org/Industry-glossary

acceptance	contract	patent
Act of God	copyright	performing rights orga-
ADA	dates, rates, and space	nization (PRO)
ASCAP	disability	pickup
attrition	force majeure	rack rates
BMI	major life activity	risk
capacity	meeting history	trademark
CGL	offer	yield management
consideration	parol evidence	

REVIEW AND DISCUSSION QUESTIONS

1. Discuss the negotiation process. What are the important points for each party to be aware of?

2. What are the five elements of a legal contract?

3. What are the most important clauses in hotel group sales contracts? Why?

4. Discuss negotiating contracts.

5. Discuss three strategies for negotiation attrition clauses.

6. What is the difference between cancellation and force majeure with regard to events?

7. Choose one type of crisis, emergency, or disaster and discuss what you should do at each of the four stages of crisis management to reduce the likelihood of occurrence or to minimize the impact.

8. What is the ADA, and how does it impact events and gatherings?

9. What are the three types of intellectual property, and give an example of something event related that might be protected under each type?

10. What are some of the labor issues unique to MEEC?

ABOUT THE CHAPTER CONTRIBUTOR

Tyra Warner (formerly Hilliard), Ph.D, JD, CMP, is the department chair of Hospitality, Tourism, & Culinary Arts at the College of Coastal Georgia. She is also an attorney who represents meeting organizers and specializes in meeting and event contracts. Published and widely quoted in academic and trade publications, Tyra's expertise is in legal and crisis preparedness issues for the meetings, events, and hospitality industries. Her 30-year meetings industry career has included management roles in hotels, travel, destination marketing, associations, catering, law, and academia. She has received national recognition for her contributions to best practices initiatives with the Events Industry Council and Meeting Professionals International. She is one of only two people in the world who are practicing attorneys, have a Ph.D in hospitality, and have earned the Certified Meeting Professional (CMP) designation.

CONTACT INFORMATION:

Tyra Warner (formerly Hilliard), Ph.D, JD, CMP
Assistant Professor and Chair
Department of Hospitality, Tourism, and Culinary Arts
College of Coastal Georgia
One College Drive
Brunswick, GA 31520
Phone: (912)279-4568
twarner@ccga.edu
http://www.ccga.edu

PREVIOUS EDITION CHAPTER CONTRIBUTOR

James M. Goldberg, PLLC.

CHAPTER 11

TECHNOLOGY AND THE MEETING PROFESSIONAL

© Mark Nazh/Shutterstock.com

VIRTUAL REALITY TECHNOLOGY

CHAPTER OBJECTIVES

- Recognize how technology historically has supported the meetings and events industry
- Understand the critical technology terms that apply to the hospitality industry
- Recognize the maturing technologies such as Mixed Reality and Artificial Intelligence in the hospitality industry
- Understand the radical changes to the meetings industry through technology applications during the pandemic

INTRODUCTION

Technology has always made a significant impact in the meetings and events industry. From its early days of automating the registration process, through the beginnings of the Internet era, and the creation of virtual (yet often limited) site inspections, and then through the proliferation of social media and conference apps as tools enhancing marketing and the conference experience, all of these changes have significantly moved our industry forward. However, with the COVID-19 pandemic upon us, the meeting industry has never seen such potentially radical changes affect our business and livelihood. As of this writing, the live event industry is on life support. Even as we move past the first wave of the pandemic, with hotels and airlines reopening for business, the events industry as we knew it is struggling to survive.

That doesn't mean that the meetings industry is never going to return or even that people still aren't meeting. What was once a tool for the industry to change and thrive, event technology can now be considered our lifeline, the bridge to the future of meetings. And while pieces of the industry will dramatically be altered forever, the need for humans to meet (and organizations to facilitate gatherings) will continue to grow, this time anchoring on the technologies that can help our industry adapt and thrive again.

Throughout the last decade, many technology leaders in the hospitality industry have continuously stated the importance of embracing technology's changes by meeting professionals. Unfortunately, some event professionals did not listen, though others embraced the new technologies and integrated it with what has worked in the past. This created a new way for the blend of technology and our face-to-face human needs to collaborate.

Accepting the integration of technology and events has traditionally been difficult in our industry. Our industry has never been at the forefront of accepting the insertion of technology in what is widely considered a "people business." Yet technology all along has done one thing exceptionally well and that is to facilitate and enhance people's ability to meet and connect. Let's look at the components of the technology that have made up our industry, and in many ways continue to do so, right through to today's "pivot to virtual" approach that is maintaining our industry's relevancy.

It is a very exciting time as we watch the integration of newer technologies into our industry and into our lives. It is clear to say that while some of these technologies will be good, others might not be. The only constant moving forward with technology and events is change.

VIRTUAL SITE SELECTION AND RESEARCH

Back in the day (albeit many, many thousands of days ago), planners would have huge encyclopedic books that listed critical information about facilities for meeting professionals. This all changed in the 1990s with searchable CD-ROMs and the Internet. As hotels and DMOs saw the value in replacing their traditional marketing with these tools, the planner's research palette expanded exponentially. The site selection and research component of the present day is now not only about hotels and physical conference spaces but also the capabilities and limitations of the virtual spaces that are now essential to the continuation of meetings and events in 2020.

ONLINE RFPS

As the worldwide web developed in the mid-late 1990s, one of the first tools available were those allowing the planner to create an efficient online RFP (Request for Proposal, which is the tool many planners use to distribute information to hotels about potential meetings). This was available both through Convention and Visitors Bureau websites as well as hotel and third-party planning sites. While the model has evolved over time from a fee-based RFP to a free approach, the concept remains the same—allow the planner to input their specs easily and allow the web to be the conduit for distributing the information to potential cities and hotels.

Without a required industry standardization, each RFP can be different, which costs the planner time in completing each one as required. Planners still need to determine which vehicle (CVB-based, hotel-based, or third-party-based) is best to distribute their meeting specs. This lack of standardization has and will continue to plague our industry. While some could argue it shows each event's uniqueness and the importance of a professional planning team to understand each meeting's fundamental objectives, it can still be considered an inefficient use of time. Some planners skip the RFP forms for this reason and simply email their already written-up specs directly to sales representatives. Either way you look at it, technology is saving significant time in helping planners distribute their meeting requirements.

VIRTUAL TOURS

Recent industry statistics have estimated that over one-half of all meetings are booked without a formal site inspection. This number continued to grow into 2020 until physical meetings came to a crashing halt. While there is no substitution for visiting a hotel, the web's visual capabilities have allowed planners to at least get a sense of a facility if time or budgetary restrictions prevented their in-person site inspection.

The concept of a virtual site inspection has evolved over the years, from its early beginnings utilizing only pictures of meeting rooms. This morphed into videos and 360-degree panoramic tours of meeting spaces and sleeping rooms that are now facing ongoing development into the use of virtual and augmented reality site inspections.

As we move beyond the current pandemic, the importance of virtual site visits will grow exponentially. Hybrid meetings will likely be a large part of this decade's meeting palette, especially in the early half of the 2020s. It is likely that physical site inspections will be further reduced until all travel safety and protocols are in place. The effective virtual tour, which can also help showcase how a hybrid meeting can be organized, is becoming even more essential.

More than a decade ago, a virtual world named Second Life had the techy part of our industry buzzing about the future of site selection and other services. Starwood Hotels' brand Aloft was developed during that time and used Second Life to showcase design ideas to their potential customers. However, Second Life was way ahead of its time (and the processing power of computers needed to run it) and never completely took off. With the developing VR and AR devices available and on the horizon, it wouldn't be surprising if we soon saw some progressive properties embracing those tools. How the industry embraces truly virtual and hybrid conferences will also be defined by the underlying technologies that support their "site visit" and event management.

MEETING INDUSTRY PORTALS AND INFORMATION RESOURCES

While less elegant, but still enormously useful, industry information portals continue to thrive. While search engines are incredibly useful for general research, our industry has a great deal of information at the fingertips of the savvy web user, who can find resources and tools at their disposal in a few clicks. While there are many sites that have great information, I am only stating here those where registration (or paid subscription) is not a requirement of entry. All of these communities are welcoming and accepting of students and industry professionals in training.

Any discussion of information portals for the hospitality industry begins with the website of Corbin Ball (http://www.corbinball.com). From his homepage, linking onto his favorite's page presents the viewer with nearly 3,000 industry-related websites, organized categorically. Corbin keeps the site updated frequently and has plenty of additional information of value for the meeting professional.

Liz King Caruso's techsytalk (http://techsytalk.com) is both a great tech resource and portal for planners and is also one of the industry's top tech conferences. While this event did not run for a few years, 2020 has seen the rebirth of the techsytalk event. Liz was one of the first people to showcase to the industry how to run a successful all-virtual conference in the early stages of COVID-19.

While perhaps not a true portal, another not-to-miss site is the Event Manager blog (http://www.eventmanagerblog.com/). This site is filled with great articles and meeting planner resources. Julius Solaris has created this page as another critical tech resource for our industry.

Social media is always a place rich in information, especially if the person knows how to separate solid content from noise. Our industry has some great go-to Facebook communities where the industry is helping one another with information about our industry. Liz King has created a community around techsytalk. Tracy Stuckrath, a pioneer in the area of understanding the importance of food safety for attendees at events, has created the wildly successful "Eating at a Meeting" Facebook community. And in the area of supporting the return of live events, the "Facebook Live Events Coalition" has over 20,000 people following the posts.

If you're looking for a nontraditional destination, the Unique Venues (https://www.uniquevenues.com/) site is your friend. College campuses, cruise ships, and business offices are all part of this rich resource for planners. They also offer a great blog and traditional magazine. Unique Venues was also one of the most successful organizations providing content to their constituency through the use of successful virtual meetings in the early stages of the pandemic.

Through Google Groups (http://groups.google.com), the Meeting Industry Forum and the Meetings Community (MeCo) continue to be an ongoing dialogue for planners and suppliers to exchange ideas and best practices. Many of its users love that no sales or marketing is allowed in this space.

MARKETING AND COMMUNICATIONS

As more and more new events are created, the amount of work to market your brand and your conference is more important than ever. The best marketing tool you have is the completion of a successful conference that meets and exceeds the needs of its audience. As many will say, getting people to the event is becoming more and more of a challenge. Most planners and suppliers would agree that the decision process of their customer occurs later and later in the selling cycle; people don't confirm attendance months and months ahead of time anymore. This makes marketing a critical part of the successful planner's toolbox, with technology being the primary (sometimes sole) distribution medium for these efforts. How this will change when live events return (frequently becoming hybrid) is anyone's guess, but it can be expected that the decision-making cycle will become even shorter.

It is clear that a critical, if not overwhelming, part of the marketing process today occurs through social media channels. We will discuss those components in the next section of this chapter, which is dedicated to social media.

WEBSITES AND STRATEGIC COMMUNICATIONS

Historically, it used to be all about one-way communications—information was sent from the event organizers to the (potential) attendees. This has evolved in the past decade as websites and then social networks have become synonymous with real-time communication. The model of event marketing has now become a two-way communication model.

Websites are still an important part of the communication conversation. Not only do event organizers need to integrate a two-way communication model, they still must serve the purpose of efficiently providing critical information to the conference goers. The best online event models have both successful social media strategies and an event website that is easy to find, navigate, and make purchases from.

In this decade, one thing that needs to be understood by all event marketers is that a primary focus of all of their marketing and communications needs to be targeted to mobile devices. As we are squarely in a mobile-first world (moving rapidly to a voice-reliant, mobile-first world), the importance of the large-screen website has become overshadowed to how effectively the content is accessible on smaller screens.

EVENT WEBSITES

The event website is to today what the conference marketing brochure was to a generation ago. This is the go-to place to provide information, create interest, and, hopefully, get people to register for your conference.

The best websites integrate a two-way strategy (interactive communications and/or a live social stream, with clear links to all social channels essential). Having an event website that can allow people to find out everything they need to know about the event is of critical importance. The core rules of a successful conference website include:

- Clear, easy-to-find information.
- The 5 Ws about the conference (who, what, where, when, and why)
- Easy access through any device (smartphone, tablet, laptop/desktop, with a potential eye on engaging content through wearable devices and through voice access)
- The ability to make the sale (in our industry, which would be the payment process on the registration form).

With the greater usage of WYSIWYG (what you see is what you get) website development tools (such as Wix, SquareSpace, and many others), the ability to create basic web presences at little to no cost is available for most groups. It is important to note that larger meetings with more sophisticated needs will still need a higher degree of customization and development.

A frequent issue with event organizers is not getting information on the website early enough. While there is no definitive required timeframe for information to be advertised, it is a common industry practice that if you are running an annual event that you have information about next year's meeting ready to go live the day this year's meeting concludes. If people are pleased with the conference, it makes sense to encourage and allow them to register for next year when their memories are still vivid from the past event. Many planners do not establish their website as early as they should. Even if the sales cycle has become shorter, as previously discussed, the planner should have the information up and ready for when the attendees would like to purchase.

MOBILE WEBSITES

As we have already mentioned, the web strategy must include a clear focus on mobile access of information. Unfortunately, some planners (and suppliers) still focus most of their website efforts as if the desktop/laptop platform is the only device a user could access their site from. In the past 5 years, mobile usage has surpassed traditional computer usage. This means that a well-designed website could be considered of secondary importance to a well-designed mobile site. In fact, many people would make the argument that a mobile website and an effective use of social channels is all a planner needs these days. The phrase "Responsive Web Design" has been used to identify a website that optimizes itself for whichever platform (desktop, tablet, or phone) is being used to access the site. While this does make sure that the content is clear on each of the screens, it doesn't embrace the fact that mobile and desktop users often have different needs when they're searching for content.

The critical question that planners need to ask themselves (and discuss with their web designers if they're not doing that themselves) is what content is most important for the mobile user. It should always include easy access to registration and other critical event information that is not bogged down with slower-loading videos and resources hogging up the channel. The planner can't assume that the user is on a device using exceptional bandwidth; they may be on their cellular signal, but the planner needs to be sure that the content gets to their potential customer efficiently. The 6-second rule is still a good tool for the planners to use. If the page doesn't load on a mobile device in 6 seconds or less, they may want to reconsider what is being sent to the mobile device and trim accordingly.

E-BLASTS

Thirty years ago, Jane Planner could (and would) send out as many direct mail pieces as she could. She would do so as frequently as her budget would allow, since she knew that the more information that landed on the desk of the buyer, the greater the likelihood that they might attend the function.

Twenty years ago, Jane would have taken advantage of email as her primary marketing tool. And, if she uses it correctly, she still can reap great benefits from a well-orchestrated e-blast strategy.

Now, however, the rules have changed. We are so inundated with spam email (some experts have estimated the percentage of spam we receive as high as 85% of our daily email), that multiple, unsolicited emails are having the inverse effect. People are tuning out all communications with that sender. Or, even worse, the email is just landing in their recipients Promotions or Spam folder.

Instead of just blasting the audience with email after email, Jane Planner may be wise to heed a different set of marketing rules to best promote her conference to her audience.

- *Opt-in*—Just because you have obtained an email address, it is not an open invitation to commence spamming. The Federal Trade Commission's CAN-SPAM act of 2009 (https://www.ftc.gov/tips-advice/business-center/guidance/can-spam-act-compliance-guide-business) forces all businesses, including the event's business, to comply with proper rules about email marketing. In fact, the technology-savvy (and proper) approach would be to establish a dialogue and confirm that the recipient wants to be included in future mailings.
- *GDPR (General Data Protection Regulation)*—In 2018, European Union (EU) countries began implementing this regulation, designed to require opt-in for all email marketing, with heavy financial penalties assessed to any company violating this rule. Even though it is a European rule, its reach is global, as the rule applies to any individual living in one of the EU countries. Through early 2020, the GDPR led to over 160,000 data breach notifications, with a single fine of over 50 million Euros assessed to Google.
- *Don't Overdo It*—Once you've received the okay to email, don't begin a barrage of mindless communications. The end result of too many emails from a single person or organization is the tuning out of all of them (or worse, having the emails automatically placed in the recipient's promotions or spam folder!). We get hit with far too many communication messages on a daily basis, so we're looking for ways to reduce the number on which we need to focus. Better to spend time on creating useful messages, sent occasionally, rather than mindless reminders, sent repetitively.
- *WIIFM (Technology-Version)*—What's in It for Me? From the perspective of your customer—why would they want to read your emails? If all you are doing is sending information about the conference, it will look just like a continuous hard sell. Since this is a marketing medium (as well as one that can finalize the sale), use the technology to create a dialogue of important information for your customer. Give them

educational information. Inform them of useful tools to help them become better at their job. You can also tell them about your conference's benefits but that information is better received in an environment of trust than one of constant sales.

- *Keep It Simple*—Don't write a novel in every email. Over the past generation, where we have become accustomed to sound bites, we must understand that people don't have time to read lengthy pieces (you can always give access to that but allow them to venture down that path). Keep your messages easy to read and as short as possible. Videos attract more attention than photos, which are more seen than plain text. If you are providing any links—make sure they work.
- *Make It Visually Appealing*—As we discuss in a moment, we tend to respond more to pictures than to words and more to videos than to images. Not losing this approach is certain to create more success in your email marketing.

VIDEO MARKETING

We have become the video generation. The success of YouTube, Instagram, and more recently TikTok makes it essential for planners to send as much content out through short-form videos as they do through email blasts. It would not be surprising if, by the end of this decade, video marketing is used more (and more effectively) by planners and suppliers than any text-based option.

ROOM DESIGN SOFTWARE

Another level of more efficient communications is how the planner shares information with the facility to ensure that their wants are translated into the actions of the facility. Conference Resumes and Run of Show documents create a very effective flow chart of what has to happen and at what time. As a side note, use of a standard database is very good at helping create a professional-looking Event Resume, though most planners still use Excel.

However, certain aspects of your event (themed parties, banquets, or just unique setups) are not as efficiently communicated by the written word. In these cases, planners have traditionally used CAD (computer aided design) room design software to enhance their communications. Our industry now has many versions of this type of software. They tend to be simple to use but can range in price. Two of the top providers of these floorplan programs are Social Tables (https://www.socialtables.com/) and All Seated (http://www.all-seated.com/). Some work better for meetings, others focus on special events. Social Tables is a premium model, while All Seated is free for planners to use. They both have 3D room tour capabilities. Many facilities have used these 3D room tours to showcase their space virtually on their website.

SELLING THE SHOW FLOOR

Another way technology is enhancing event communications and marketing is assisting the tradeshow manager in selling the show floor. Traditional exhibit sales were focused on a document called the Exhibit Prospectus, along with a generic layout of the show floor. Almost every tradeshow now uses some kind of virtual enhancement to the tradeshow-floor-selling process. These sites also include a downloadable version of the Exhibit Prospectus as well as other information of use for the exhibitor.

By posting the tradeshow floor diagram on the web, the tradeshow manager can now offer potential buyers a better look at where they might want their booth. Advantages of this include updated layouts (as the tradeshow floor diagram is frequently modified when exhibitors buy space) as well as helping the buyer locate a floor space that either is near, or far away, from their competitors (depending on their approach). The use of colors to represent booths can help differentiate which ones are available and the ones where premium costs apply.

When large-scale tradeshows come back into the picture is certainly an unknown at this time. We will discuss virtual tradeshows some more in the webinars and virtual events section.

ONLINE REGISTRATION

Online registration is a mature technology in our industry that is perhaps only surpassed by the site selection/RFP process. With this said, it is interesting to note that all meetings still do not use online registration. Many meetings, especially internal meetings, where attendance is mandatory, do not wish to incur the expense of establishing a professional online registration presence.

These events prefer to use more traditional, or even email, approaches to handling meeting registration. In this virtually pivoted age, online registration for virtual events can even be handled easily within the virtual platform itself (e.g., Zoom's webinar functionality supporting online registration).

With this said, there are still a number of issues that confront planners when establishing the online registration process. The largest one for many planners is the integration of data. If we conceptually agree that even in the best of circumstances, 100% of the attendees will not use an online service, then the planner's challenge is to make sure that when they integrate the data, there are no inaccuracies or duplication of records. Ensuring that the online service can properly export into whichever tool you are using to maintain the remaining records (such as Excel) is a critical question to ask when considering companies to use.

Another issue that is raised by organizations using online services is in the added, unexpected expenses. One particular area of concern is in the creation of additional reports. The planner has two approaches to offset this issue. One is understanding all of the reports they might require and having this discussion negotiated into the purchase package. The other, more technology-savvy approach is to learn how to use the report-writing feature. Many online registration services use the product SAP Crystal Reports to generate reports for the client.

Regarding online resources that can perform the online registration service, there are too many to mention. Research using an industry portal such as the aforementioned Corbin Ball site (http://www.corbinball.com) and his industry favorites will give the user a plethora of options from which to choose.

SOCIAL MEDIA

Has social media overtaken websites as the critical go-to information tool for events? For many people, that would be a stretch to believe (for others, not so much). If nothing else, the combination of a well-designed website (both mobile- and desktop-optimized) and the use of multiple social channels enhances the marketing and communication efforts of the planner. Can a planner even imagine holding an event without, at the very least, a Facebook page (and possibly an event-specific Facebook page) being part of their communication strategy?

PRIMARY SOCIAL CHANNELS

The past decade has seen the ascension and dominance of social media services. Social networks have always been at the root of this industry's success. A conference gathering about a specific topic (such as the Annual Widget Convention) is nothing more than a large social network of Widget professionals gathering to learn and share from one another.

The only difference is that now the social network is online as well as face-to-face. This has only expanded exponentially in this pandemic era. The applications created over the past decade have enabled real-time communication in this area. Facebook, Instagram, Twitter, YouTube, and LinkedIn are currently the dominant general social channels used by planners, with tools such as Snapchat and TikTok showing their value for events where the audience demographics is aligned with using the newer technologies.

- Facebook's event pages, viral marketing, and social interaction make it a great platform for communication (and marketing) to occur about the meeting. A good Facebook event page can help to create buzz for an event, especially when supported by an active community (as always, the planner needs to understand their own group to see what works best). The social channel with the largest community, Facebook is an essential part of the marketing strategy for all groups.
- Instagram, owned by Facebook, is the ultimate visual tool, as photos and videos are its sole domain. While incredibly popular, it is surprising that in 2020 many planners still did not use Instagram as a tool to promote and/or enhance their event. It's hashtag-centric approach also plays very well for using it for conferences and events. As we, as a society, continue to obsess about food photography—it is a very useful tool to help promote that aspect of a special event or meal.
- Twitter has tried to keep pace with Facebook, but while it has a very engaged audience, the user numbers are far below Facebook. For many savvy social uses, Twitter's true benefit is in its ability to curate content from its stream by its users. Whether using hashtags or lists, these features can turn the noise of social media into nuance. Twitter walls, especially for larger conferences and events, became largely used by major events in the last decade. These tools allowed the posts that use the conference hashtag to be aggregated and exclusively shown.
- YouTube, owned by Google, is the number one video channel available. Any savvy planner will create a YouTube channel that contains the

various videos they want to use to promote and highlight their event. Monetization of YouTube channels have become more regulated by Google rules, so many planners will host their videos on other video channels such as Vimeo (http://www.vimeo.com). YouTube, like Facebook, supports 360 videos, which will be discussed in the section on mixed reality.

- LinkedIn is considered more of a business network than a social network. However, it is also more of an individual networking tool. While they have groups (which are a great tool), there is no place to promote an event directly. The Senior Planners Industry Network (SPIN) is one of many vibrant meeting communities on LinkedIn.

By no means are these three services the only social networks available for the planner. TikTok and Twitch (which is more focused on the gaming community) are two examples of social channels that might make sense for the right audience with event planners. Customizable networks (some free, some premium) are in favor with many groups. The benefits of a customized network are just what it seems to be—to be able to design the layout and content to meet the specific event needs. One such service is Pathable (www.pathable.com), which helps create dialogue and networking between attendees before, during, and after an event, especially when integrated within the conference Event App (which Pathable can also provide).

LIVE STREAMING

Since the inception of Meerkat in February 2015, livestreaming has become a standard of communications for everyone. Facebook Live, YouTube, and Instagram Live are arguably the most widely used and the most active aspect of their respective channels. For the events industry, livestreaming can evoke different responses among planners. Those in favor of it highlight how easily it can extend the meeting to those who cannot attend, while those against it focus on the fact that people can easily broadcast content for which they do not have the rights or permissions.

No matter which side of the livestreaming debate you are on, it has become a frequently used tool within social channels. Both Facebook and YouTube have made it simple to broadcast live and post to their services (with a one-click approach from within any Zoom meeting). There's no disputing that the value of video on social channels far exceeds any other type of post, so the conversation about livestreaming in meetings has only begun. The pandemic of 2020 has only increased the amount of livestreaming to social channels seen in the events industry (and in all industries).

BLOGGING

A blog, or web log, is an online diary that is posted to the web. Now considered an "older school" social channel, blogs are still an effective way to impart information to your customers and followers. Blogging inherently is a two-way medium, as any successful blog will allow for people to respond and further the discussion on the posted topic.

The concept of a blog in the marketing of a conference is simple—create a dialogue between the organizers and their audience. Since blogs have a built-in comment functionality, it is a two-way communications tool that can greatly help organizers get a pulse of what is on the minds of their attendees. Savvy planners have used bloggers outside of their organization to help them share content to those not in attendance. Whether these types of bloggers will continue to be sought after in our post-pandemic rebound is yet to be determined.

While blogs are an easy point of entry into social media, and a great way to enhance your web presence, it is surprising how few planners and suppliers maintain and update blogs on a regular basis. To some extent, the explosion of the overall use of Facebook and Twitter are in part to blame. Still, planners would be wise to create and update a blog to help enhance their event communications. As mentioned earlier, Julius Solaris' Event Manager's Blog (http://www.eventmanagerblog.com/) is a great example of a successful industry blog.

PODCASTING

Like blogging, podcasts originated many years ago, though they have steadily increased in popularity. In 2019, there were nearly 1,000,000 active podcasts with hundreds of millions of listeners worldwide. While podcasts are often used to listen to a variety of education and entertainment shows, their use within the meeting industry is still nominal.

The event podcast is essentially an extension of what planners have been doing for many years. A generation ago, planners would audio-tape sessions and then distribute (sell) the tapes to those who couldn't attend. Podcasts can do that by digitizing the recording. However, as our attention spans have gotten shorter (and with the proliferation of free podcasts online), the event podcast may find itself to be more of a marketing tool than revenue stream. Still, it provides a great way to extend the event to those who could not attend.

Popular podcast listening platforms include Apple Podcast, Spotify, PodBean, and many other platforms. As we move more into the age of personal AI devices (e.g., Google Home and Amazon Alexa), podcasts can also be listened to on these devices and may explain continued growth in this platform over the more traditional blogging.

HASHTAGS

No conversation about social media is complete without a discussion on the importance of hashtags. Hashtags are a keyword or phrase that helps target social posts to an interested audience. Though some users think of hashtags as "cool"—hashtags are a search term and should be treated as such. Hashtags drive two social services primarily—Twitter and Instagram—although you will see them used extensively in nearly all social channels.

In the world of Twitter, the hashtag establishes and feeds a threaded conversation that everyone can view and join in. Some events establish a single hashtag for their event, sending out information before and during the event through Twitter. This also provides attendees an opportunity to be part of the dialogue. With larger, more technology-savvy groups, some events have multiple hashtags, allowing for more focused dialogues to occur.

While hashtags in Twitter are part of any successful post, it can be said that in Instagram, it's all (and only) about the hashtags. There is no limit on the number of hashtags usable in an Instagram post. Many top-notch Instagram users believe 15 to 20 or more hashtags on a post is the way to maximize reach.

Hashtags allow for the content curation necessary for open channels to streamline content to those interested. In our industry, hashtags aren't only the domain of conferences, but they are a great way to curate and receive content about our industry at large. The hashtag #eventprofs is one of the top respected meeting industry tags in use. The hashtag search tool Hashtagify. me (http://hashtagify.me/) allows users to see which hashtags are used alongside ones they already know about. This is a great way to find more relevant hashtags about your industry. While Hashtagify used to be free, it has become a premium tool, showcasing the importance of understanding critical hashtags.

SOCIAL SELLING

The marriage of event marketing and social channels isn't complete without mentioning the use of advertising within the social channels (and, of course, in Google as well). Paid social media is an often underutilized tool to get past the noise of the social channels and deliver content onto the screens of potential attendees.

Targeted ads (prevalent on Facebook), often referred to as Re-Targeting, allow organizations to identify target demographics (e.g., 35–44 year olds in New York and Connecticut who are interested in Widgets) and serve ads onto the users' Facebook pages. Since Facebook heavily curates the content that people see (no, you don't see the posts from everyone you are following), they have forced businesses to consider ads, or an option of paid boosted posts, to hopefully ensure your message is seen by those you want to see it.

Outside of Facebook, most other social channels accept paid placement. Promoted Tweets is a tool on Twitter allowing the event organizer to increase the amount of people who see their posts. Like Facebook, it comes with targeting tools. Both Instagram and LinkedIn have ad functionality within their channels.

For all social channels, the cost of ads tends to be much less expensive than more traditional advertising. Following the successful Google model, these reasonably priced tools can certainly help the technology-savvy planner to promote their conference without depleting their marketing budget.

EVENT APPS

Is the printed program guide dead? Depends (as always) on who you ask, but the proliferation of event-specific apps has allowed planners to drive all event content directly to the attendee's mobile devices. Clearly, this is a more ecologically sustainable approach to content distribution as events and event apps have become an industry standard.

Content within the event app is a decision that the planner makes (often based on budget restrictions) but consistently these apps include sections labeled program, maps, local information, social media, and a tab that involves gamification concepts, among a variety of other options that can enhance the attendee's experience. By making the social posts part of the app, the event app can help drive social posts about the event. This enhances event marketing and awareness.

Some of the top industry providers of event apps include Crowd Compass (http://www.crowdcompass.com), EventMobi (http://www.eventmobi.com/), and Cvents' Double Dutch (http://doubledutch.me/). With the increased indexing of content located on mobile devices by Google, event organizations need to consider the value of an organization-level app as well as event apps, in order to stay relevant digitally.

In 2019, a group of entrepreneurs created an app creation tool called Glide (https://go.glideapps.com), which uses the ubiquitous Google Sheet as the database and a no-coding-necessary drag-and-drop interface to allow anyone to create apps. A number of their templates support the creation of apps for meetings and events. While the meeting industry (an industry that is not typically an early adopted of technology) has not embraced this tool significantly, it would appear likely that this tool, or similar ones that transfer the creation of apps to the everyday user, will gain in value as the 2020's progress.

DESKTOP AND MOBILE TOOLS

While there are dozens of industry-specific software packages on the market, the clear leader in our industry is still the basic MS Office Suite. With Word, Excel, and PowerPoint, the meeting professional has the tools on their desktop to manage all components of any event. For some planners, these tools are too feature-rich and outdated in some ways. Online collaborative office-based tools, such as Google Drive (https://drive.google.com), provide more than enough functionality, with better collaboration tools for documents. Google Drive's hidden gem, Google Forms, allows planners to create surveys, evaluations, and questionnaires through their service at no cost.

Other programs have increasing popularity in our industry, to include Slack and Microsoft Teams. These are designed to facilitate better communications through a combination of minimizing emails and maximizing direct and group messaging options. Both services have infrastructures of add-on communities to enhance productivity. As our current work environment is greatly remote, these tools should see more and more usage among distributed work teams.

General packages like Microsoft and Google often do not fill every need. Many planners, especially in organizations with non-centralized meeting departments, need tools that allow information to be shared across the organization. The industry has a number of tools that foster better information centralization.

At the core of this need to centralize information is the ability for organizations to get a handle on the amount of purchasing leverage they have. The individual planning a small meeting within a large organization is at a disadvantage in terms of negotiation, unless they can combine their hotel room contracting with others within the organization. This is where third-party software tools can have a significant advantage over the Microsoft or Google options. While more expensive, they frequently provide exceptional cross-organization value by allowing organizations to bundle their purchasing needs. Naturally, it is important to state that the pandemic has, at least temporarily, halted the use of these industry-specific tools due to the decrease of face-to-face event planning that is taking place. It will be interesting to see what develops when we move beyond this current situation.

APEX

The Events Industry Council (formerly known as the Convention Industry Council), the organization that manages the Certified Meeting Professional (CMP) examination, has been at the forefront of establishing the **APEX— Accepted Practices Exchange** for our industry. The essential concept of APEX is to make the industry more efficient by creating a set of standards that all parties within the industry would accept. As it relates to technology, APEX has created white papers and information on event bandwidth, RFPs, and, more recently COVID-19 resources, among many more tools. A great link to learn more about APEX can be found at the Event Industry Council website (http://www.eventscouncil.org/).

VIRTUAL TRADESHOWS

A few years ago, virtual tradeshows were often marketed as the next big thing. At its most basic concept, a virtual tradeshow can be an online tradeshow floor plan with hyperlinks to the sites of the exhibitors for the attendees to visit. Virtual tradeshows proclaimed that they could also be a virtual experience in itself, with the attendee virtually "walking" through the event and clicking on information (or in some cases, actually chatting with sales reps). While companies are still creating these virtual experiences, as of now, they have mostly lost the steam and interest of most groups. In 2020, as COVID-19 puts much of the events industry on hold, planners are looking to virtual meeting providers that can support virtual tradeshows as part of the virtual meeting experience for their attendees. It is likely that a reemergence of better-designed virtual tradeshow tools will become part of the planner's virtual toolbox for their events.

ONSITE EVENT TECH INFRASTRUCTURE

The meeting professional understands the importance of negotiations with hotels. From rates, dates, and space to every other aspect of the event, the planner can have a productive give and take with the hotel to create a win-win event. However, many planners are fearful about or unaware of event technology. They leave out any discussion of technology needs during this part of the planning and negotiation process. This can be a very expensive omission. The technology-savvy planner, however, understands enough about the technologies that support their event that they know what the need to plan for (even negotiate) during the initial stages of planning.

BANDWIDTH

Bandwidth is the amount of information that can pass through a communications line. The more bandwidth you have, the more information (number of emails, hits to a social networking site) can occur simultaneously. Bandwidth can be an expensive proposition for planners, especially when they are holding their meetings at convention centers instead of hotels.

Planners need to think about issues of bandwidth. While you would think in 2020 this particular matter would not be an issue anymore, nothing could be further from the truth. The technology-savvy planner will think about how their attendees will want to use technology to enhance their meeting experience. While Jane Planner may not be able to implement all of these technologies, she can identify which ones are most critical (and useful) to successfully implement everyone's goals, thereby allowing the technology to play a spectacular supporting role in the success of the conference.

How much bandwidth is needed at an event? Here is where the planner may need help, and it can come from their own internal Information Technology (IT) personnel if they understand and plan for their onsite needs. Here is a partial list of tasks where the planner needs to use bandwidth (and understand how much they need) at the event:

- Registration networking (for the planner)
- Any provided computers or Internet cafes—these were very popular in the teens but are no longer as essential in the age of smart devices and widespread connectivity
- HQ office and press room bandwidth for office communications
- Speaker Internet access for presentations
- Attendee bandwidth for interactive elements
- Livestreaming for sessions and events
- Social channel content distribution
- Hybrid meetings

Hybrid meetings might be considered by some a questionable inclusion in this list. However, not only will the hybrid meetings of this coming decade require bandwidth for the dissemination of content to the non-live audience, but as it becomes a more interactive medium, the likelihood of the live attendees following the virtual stream in real time could be a significant bandwidth requirement.

So, how much bandwidth will you need? That depends on the answers to those, and other, questions. Having that dialogue with your IT staff (or a third-party organization with whom you contract to support your onsite technology setup) before the contract is signed will enable you to ensure that the facility can meet your needs and allow you to negotiate costs to a more reasonable level. (While it is possible to find a bandwidth calculator through Google, this is not a trusted resource for event professionals as the likelihood that the needs and demands of post-pandemic technology will make the current bandwidth estimation models obsolete.)

And as we enter into this decade's pivot to virtual/hybrid meetings, the bandwidth requirements at events will only continue to soar. It has yet to be determined whether Wi-Fi (either provided by the hotel or brought in by third-party organizations) or the burgeoning 5G cellular technologies will be the constant provider of Internet connectivity at events.

WIRED VERSUS WIRELESS

Most attendees will want to access their email wherever they go in the hotel. With the proliferation of 4G/4G LTE mobile phones (such as the iPhone, Samsung phones, and Google Pixel) and the establishment of 5G networks, attendees can use their mobile device to access the Internet. One key question to ask is whether the meeting space will have a strong cellular signal. Is the event space below ground (lacking service) or in an international destination where the attendee might not be able to use their devices?

The invention of and slow rollout of 5G wireless capabilities in the United States and around the world will likely foster further technological progress in various areas. This could potentially minimize the need for expensive Wi-Fi to be purchased from venues for events. However, the monetization of 5G is going to be a strong consideration in its ultimate roll-out and whether costs to customers (and planners) will be lower than for Wi-Fi remains to be seen.

A facility that allows for the attendees' computer to pick up a wireless signal, whether it is in their guest room or in the public space, is still an important service to provide. Some guestrooms could also provide wired access, but today, wireless is the standard. Wireless connectivity in guestrooms has improved considerably in the last decade, but as demand always seems to outpace supply, hotels were continuing to struggle to provide connectivity for their ever-digitally-connected guest.

The wireless standard is an engineering specification named 80211. This spec, adopted in the late 1990s, defines how a wireless interface between clients and access points is constructed. However, there are a number of types of 80211. Each one provides a different amount of potential bandwidth to the user. It is important to talk to your IT department about the limitations and capabilities of each of these types (e.g., 802.11n, 802.11ac, and the latest, 802.11ax). To make it even more confusing to the average person, the WiFi Alliance that manages the naming of these specs is changing their names. For example, 802.11ac is now known as WiFi5; 802.11n is now known as WiFi4; and the latest standard, 802.11ax will now be known as WiFi6. It's no wonder you need a friend in the IT department!

If you ask many speakers who require high speed access for the success of their presentation, they will respond by stating that they prefer hardwired Internet (an Ethernet cable attached to their computer, as opposed to going wireless). As our industry progresses to create a more seamless broadband experience, wireless will be the standard. However, a good planner will at least have a hardwired backup in case the wireless signal is not an adequate solution. Planners should also make sure that the bandwidth streaming to the speaker is dedicated for their device(s) and not part of the shared bandwidth that the attendees are using; otherwise, a busy online audience can negatively impact the needs of the speaker.

DIGITAL RECORDING AND STREAMING MEDIA

The General Session is a critical part of any annual meeting or conference. The marketing success of many conferences depends on the quality (and often name recognition) of the keynotes who establish the tone of a conference. However, there are many people who cannot attend your conference and would like to watch/hear the talk either in real time or on an archived basis. The organization can extend their keynotes (as well as other meeting components) to those who cannot attend by streaming it over the Internet. Livestreaming of events is here to stay.

If you have never done this at a meeting, be aware that a lot of extra coordination and support is required, especially with video content. You will need to have cameras and good room lighting (and video/audio engineers) in the session to ensure the recorded material is of good quality. You will need a company to digitize the video into a format that can be electronically distributed. You will need to determine whether the event should be streamed live (always a riskier proposition) or archived. And you will need to determine whether people have free access to it or if the organization will charge a fee for people to virtually attend? Or, you could have a single person with a phone and one of the previously mentioned livestreaming apps stand up and provide real-time content at no cost (though clearly not at the same quality). These are all decisions that should be made before the event begins.

While learning about the technical side, the planner must also understand a great deal about their audience and what they might want to view online. Age and demographics certainly play a role in whether an entire session should be digitized, or if a highlights approach is best for their group. The adage "Know Your Group" applies to all aspects of meeting planning, even the technology side.

DRONES

One of the latest technologies being utilized for meetings and events is in the use of drones to provide aerial photography of the event. A drone is an unmanned aircraft that can be maneuvered by remote control. These have been used for years by the military for aerial reconnaissance, but drones have now fallen into the mainstream user base. While they are heavily regulated by the Federal Aviation Administration (don't think of flying it indoors, even in a high-ceilinged convention center), many technology-savvy photographers are offering drones and drone photography as part of their package of services.

ATTENDEE INTERACTION AND COMMUNICATIONS

Paper badges with just identifying information on them are so last decade—at least that's what many people believe today. Technology has moved the name badge from a simple identification tool to one that can interact with a variety of planner tech tools as well as ultimately being able to actually interact with other badges.

BEACONS

A beacon is a Bluetooth-based tool that broadcasts small bits of information directly to a Bluetooth-enabled device such as your smartphone. The content that is broadcast is typically location specific and specifically targeted for that individual. Within meetings and events, beacon technology can interface with phones or even "Smart Badges" (badges that have tiny beacon receivers within). This allows event organizers to pass along content, recognize attendance for CE credits, promote sponsors, or any other creative uses.

Two-way beacon technology is the next wave of utilization for this technology. Typically, these are included in a wearable tool, such as on a lanyard around the attendee's neck, and sends and receives data directly to the wearable device. Planners tend to avoid using the attendee's phone for these devices, as many attendees keep Bluetooth off for a variety of reasons. This opens up a wide-ranging possibility of wearable social media integration and communications between wearable devices. If you really want to think long term, there is potential that these tools could potentially be integrated with Augmented Reality to provide floating information above the attendee's head that could facilitate networking.

NFC AND RFID

These two acronyms are at the core of many of the interactive technologies available onsite at conferences. NFC stands for Near Field Communications, which is a short-range, high-frequency wireless technology allowing for information exchange between certain devices. RFID stands for Radio Frequency Identification tags (readers) that can be used to access these signals. We are very used to RFID tags—any of us living in a city with tolls from bridges or tunnels can obtain RFID tags (known by a variety of names, including EZPass, SmartPass, and others) to quickly pay these fees. RFID can also be used to inventory products in a company's warehouse, enabling them to better track their products. RFIDs and NFCs are finding a use in our industry as well; currently, they are used mainly in interactive nametags.

LEAD RETRIEVAL SYSTEMS

Tradeshows and exhibitors have used Lead Retrieval Systems for many years to capture potential customer information from those who have visited their booths on the show floor. The process begins with the meeting organizer asking questions during the registration process that will help identify information of importance to the exhibitor. These questions often include the attendees purchasing responsibility and nature of the products and services in which they may have interest. The information is coded into their profile, which is assigned a bar code, QR code, or coded into an RFID chip. From the 199s through today, many groups still use a simple bar code on the badge (or even a credit card–based system) that can contain this information.

When the attendee enters the tradeshow floor and interacts with an exhibitor, the exhibit staff member can ask to scan the badge with their lead retrieval device (these are typically rented to the exhibitor for the duration of the show by a vendor who is supporting the meeting). Once scanned, this information now resides in their handheld lead-retrieval device. At the end of the day, the exhibitor can download this information to their spreadsheet or database and have customized thank you notes emailed to the attendee before their work for the day is complete (not to mention excellent information about their prospective clients).

The planner's job in this process is to identify and select a system or service that can support the lead-retrieval process. Since exhibitors require this level of information to determine whether exhibiting at a function will potentially help their business, lead-retrieval systems are primarily used for tradeshows. However, these systems have also been used to help facilitate attendee surveying using automated kiosks around the event.

Also available to the planner is what is known as a reverse lead-retrieval system. Instead of the exhibitor scanning the planner's badge, the planner uses a handheld device to scan information positioned in the booth of the exhibitor. This is rarely used, and when it is, it is frequently for much larger shows.

AUDIENCE RESPONSE SYSTEMS AND SPEAKER INTERACTION

Audience Response Systems (ARS) have come a long way in the past decade. Historically, ARS were handheld devices given to audience members so that they could interact with questions from the front of the room. Smartphones, and the apps created for them, have all but made the separate device unnecessary while still allowing for significant interactivity.

Historically, ARS systems had been an expensive proposition for the planner to implement, but today's technologies have made it a more affordable and necessary part of many meetings. One such service is Poll Everywhere (www.polleverywhere.com), which uses SMS (texting) in addition to web and

Twitter voting that interfaces with a real-time web-based poll. The audience members respond to a question broadcast on the screen, and the data are instantaneously updated and posted for all to see. Many event apps have built in the ARS technology to make it more controllable by event organizers.

Twitter has also been frequently used to help facilitate interactivity during a session, whether it's for providing an audience chat discussion or for sending messages and questions directly to a speaker. SMS (through texting of questions to a session moderator) is another way that these technologies have created a better real-time connection between a speaker and the audience.

This technology allows the meeting organizer and speaker to gain instant information (demographic or otherwise) about attendees and can be used to create highly customized content and set the direction of educational sessions.

POST-CONFERENCE TECHNOLOGY APPLICATIONS

Technology has served a clear purpose in the marketing and running of the meeting. However, it continues to be a useful tool once the meeting is completed. From the post-conference evaluation process to creating digital highlights (which weave into the marketing for the next conference), there is more to review regarding technology applications in our industry.

EVALUATIONS AND SURVEYS

Many organizers have moved the meeting evaluation process from a paper-based process onsite to a post-conference approach online. While there is much debate over whether post-conference evaluations provide a significant enough sample size (physical, onsite evaluations always have a higher rate of return) its mainstream usage cannot be ignored.

Regardless of one's position, it is a system in use by many planners. Web-based tools such as Survey Monkey (https://www.surveymonkey.com/) are becoming increasingly popular for this process. Web-based services not only distribute evaluations but also run analytics on the data collected and provide the planner with an easy-to-read analysis of the questions they posed to the attendees. Many integrated online solutions for meeting professionals include event survey functionality.

Earlier in this chapter we discussed the Google Drive tool known as Google Forms. As a free alternative, this tool can also become a survey distribution tool at no cost to the planner. This service also automatically builds the back-end database of the survey, so that all of the responses go directly into a spreadsheet that can be analyzed by the planner. Currently, Google Forms does not do any automatic analytics or reports for the planner to simply download.

As artificial intelligence (AI) weaves into all digital tools and services, AI-based surveying tools are becoming more popular, allowing the conference organizer to have the AI analyze larger amounts of data and find relevant trends and information. The aforementioned Survey Monkey is now incorporating AI analytics into their services. Companies such as Qualtrics (https://www.qualtrics.com/core-xm/survey-software/) and Response AI (https://response-ai.com/products/) are also at the forefront of this movement. Needless to say, AI-based services tend to be a more expensive proposition than the tools that aren't using that functionality.

This process should not be limited to conference evaluations. Any meeting professional who is involved in the programming process understands that learning about the needs of their audience is one of the best tools to identify program elements that create greater value for the attendee. The online survey, independent of the conference evaluation, can be of significant support to that process.

MARKETING THE MEDIA

The essence of post-conference technology is to extend the event past the physical start and end times. A conference is no longer bound to a Monday-to-Thursday timeframe (and in our current environment, many digital-only conferences are extending the event over multiple weeks). It can begin with attendees networking months prior to the opening session by using tools focused on pre-event networking previously discussed. After the conference, the planner can provide content to those who were not able to attend (or even those who wish to view it again).

As the planner decides whether to video or livestream activities at their conference, the wheels are placed in motion to consider how they will deliver this information. Issues of cost and delivery are a significant part of the conversation. Regarding cost, will the planner charge for virtual attendance? In the immediate COVID-19 environment, organizations are significantly struggling with the concept of how much to charge in a time of such high unemployment. Regarding content storage, services such as AWS (Amazon Web Services) are the gold standard.

As for delivery, especially in a live environment, the planner needs to make certain that they have the servers and technology (including bandwidth) available so that whoever wishes to log on and view the event can do so without the signal degrading or breaking up. This clearly is not a function of the planner but, rather, a function of their IT department (whether internal or external). As we've said before, the planner's best marketing tool is the success of their previous event. The digitization and distribution of this content is then an absolutely critical tool for not only generating revenue from this year's event but also continuing to attract attendees in future years.

MIXED REALITY

The newest of the game-changing technology in meetings and events falls in the category of mixed reality. In that category stands two tools that are just finding their way into our industry: Augmented Reality (AR) and Virtual Reality (VR). To say that these are potentially game-changing tools for our industry is an understatement. However, being a new technology, its current usage is limited

© lassedesignen/Shutterstock.com

Virtual Reality Glasses

with the early tech adopters finding different ways to integrate it successfully. Many technology observers feel that this limited usage of AR and VR will be addressed as more Apple products come into this space. In 2020, it has been confirmed that Apple is working on products, including AR glasses, that will integrate into their ecosystem, with a targeted release in 2021 to 2022.

AUGMENTED REALITY

Many experts expect that AR will be the most useful tool specific to meeting and events moving forward. Augmented Reality is the ability to see content that is not visible to the naked eye. By looking through a device (phone, tablet) or through a wearable (headset or glasses), the user will see and interact with content that is visible only to them, often dropped into the "real" world. We can't talk about AR without mentioning the 2016 breakout AR tool that was Pokemon Go. Many people thought it was the silliest app, but before you completely dismiss it, process these numbers. By the end of 2019, over 1 billion cumulative downloads of the app have been registered with user spending approaching $1 billion dollars.

Many people still think of Augmented Reality as QR codes where you point your device and content comes to life. The difference between AR and QR codes is that instead of a bar code, the object that can be scanned is anything. In 2009, a company named Layar created the first augmented reality browser, allowing users to use their mobile devices (supported with built-in GPS and camera) to display real-time information on top of live images. A few progressive hotel companies followed suite by adding an augmented element to their traditional magazine advertisements, providing users with "second screen" content for their audience. A simpler use for planners is to elevate their traditional session signage at meetings to have an augmented video accessible, so when the attendee hovers their phone over the sign, they can watch a short video clip of the session or speaker in action.

The inevitable changing nature of tech products (and inherent financial instability as it tries to create and monetize a user base) makes it not surprising that Layar is no longer on the market. However, user-friendly AR tools such as Roar (https://theroar.io) and ZapWorks (https://zap.works) allow for the planner (or just the everyday tech user) to be a creator of simple, inexpensive AR tools. The real challenge here isn't the technology; it is in the creativity of the person to figure out what connects best with its customers.

VIRTUAL REALITY/360 VIDEOS

VR is an immersive experience with the user wearing goggles to see content in 360 degrees. The user doesn't see anything other than what is projected inside the wearable device. VR devices are used to fit into three categories: phone-based, computer-based, and stand-alone. However, in the past few years we have seen the near elimination of the phone-based devices, as the cost and technical superiority of the other two genres have made the phone-based devices obsolete. Computer-based (Oculus Rift, HTC Vive) systems are powerful tools, as the goggles are attached to a powerful PC. The stand-alone headset (completely untethered) market is currently dominated by the Oculus Quest, which has already bypassed its first stand-alone product, the Oculus Go, as the best of breed. HTC Vive is also making stand-alone devices as are other companies.

For our industry VR has many uses. Special events where attendees can try on the goggles and experience content (such as multimedia, photos, videos, even games) is one point of usage. In fact, integration of VR into event gamification can greatly enhance the user's experience. In the late teens, a number of hotels and CVBs were using virtual reality to promote destinations at tradeshows and on sales calls. How it will be used post-pandemic is anyone's guess, but the use of 360 video in both VR and web-based applications makes it likely that the usage will continue to grow. Both Facebook and YouTube support 360 content on their pages.

As technologies mature, price comes down and quality increases. That is definitely the case in the 360-camera market. Products such as the Insta360 (https://www.insta360.com/) are allowing everyone to become a creator in this area as the prices are lower than many higher-end cameras. These products come with basic editing software and higher-end editing tools. This could include Adobe Premiere Pro which has allowed users to incorporate 360 videos into their editing functionality. The value of 360 cameras, even without the goggles, is significant as these videos can be placed on destination's websites or social channels.

ARTIFICIAL INTELLIGENCE AND BIG DATA

As a society currently in 2020, we create as much data in 2 days as we had previously from the beginning of time through 2003. Think about that for a second. The number of videos, pictures, posts, and comments we make and upload on an ongoing basis has helped coin the phrase Big Data. Of course, Big Data is meaningless unless we can find a way to interpret this information and make it useful to our organization. Massive computing capabilities, once the domain of massively sized computer systems, are now available in our home office that can segment information and analyze it as long as the users ask the right questions and interpret it without bias.

The hotel industry has seen and capitalized on the power of this. They have been able to use digital tools to learn more about their customers wants and needs, which provides them the ability to deliver what they want in a timely manner. The more data they get (and properly interpret), the more useful the information. Hence, hotels (as should planners) love people using their property app, with location and Bluetooth services turned on. Every point of data becomes a piece of an information puzzle that's getting easier to complete.

However, on the planner side, there are still only a few groups (mainly those with larger tradeshows and conferences) who have begun to understand and harness the power of Big Data. Yet the same is true for planners as it is for hoteliers. The more you know about your customers, the better you should be able to serve them.

ARTIFICIAL INTELLIGENCE

Even though we still may not be aware of it, we are using artificial intelligence (AI) tools regularly. Ever have Netflix tell you that people who like a certain movie also watched these films? Or have Amazon suggest similar products to those you are viewing or have purchased? These are everyday examples of AI in use. Do you have an Alexa or Google Home in your residence? You are using AI-based devices. When coupled with the Big Data we just discussed, today's AI can use recursive learning techniques to better understand the data and learn from how it connects with people.

One use of AI in meetings is in the integration with chatbots, to create automated responses to user questions from websites and event apps. By definition, a chatbot is a computer program that is trained to have conversations with humans, using natural language.

For many planners, one of the most time-consuming activities leading up to the event is in answering a steady stream of questions from the attendees, which often involves the same question many times. "When does registration begin?" "Who's delivering the Tuesday keynote?" "At which hotel is the convention located?" These are all examples of queries that a chatbot, using AI, could (and are) answering. For groups already using chatbots, nearly all of them will say that the number one question the chatbot is asked is, "What is the WiFi password?"

Some enterprising individuals have begun to realize that the home AI interface (Alexa and Google Home) are ripe for opportunities for their organization to make their customized content (perhaps gamified) available to the home user who asks a simple question. In a more DIY-based functionality (such as the previously mentioned Glide Apps), creating custom content for voice interfaces is no longer the sole domain of the code warriors. Amazon's Skill Blueprint (https://blueprints.amazon.com/) provides the everyday average person with the ability to create these interactive components.

In the past few years, a startup named Wordly (https://wordly.ai) has entered our industry's conversation supporting language translation at events. The first AI-based translation tool designed specifically for our industry, its simplicity and multiple simultaneous translations (all driven by each users' preference) is making a large presence in international conferences and may transform the older approach to event language translation.

Zoom, which has become the go-to tool for virtual meetings, has a large range of AI services, both that connect internally to their functionality and allow Zoom to be connected with other services (e.g., Microsoft Teams). Zoom has a complete list of AI-based integrations with their service (https://zoom.ai/integrations).

VIRTUAL AND HYBRID MEETINGS

Even though face-to-face is still what most people want and strive for (both for their networking and education), COVID-19 has completely changed the meeting industry, at least for the time being, and very possibly forever. Even the best crystal balls are foggy when it comes to understanding what the live event industry may look like by the middle of this decade. In this pivot to virtual, tools such as online meetings (including webinars) and hybrid meetings currently provide the primary way our industry operates.

ONLINE MEETINGS AND WEBINARS

If one company could state that the pandemic was essential for them in a positive way, it very likely would be Zoom. A combination of ease of functionality and being in the right place at the right time, Zoom became the default tool for the majority of meetings to occur in 2020. While not without its flaws, Zoom provided a simple interface, more stable connectivity, reasonable pricing (freemium model), and other features that made sure that we not only used it but that we began to despise it (as humans frequently do when they get too much of a good thing).

The creation of a successful online meeting or webinar is very different than a live event. All-day online events are rarely successful (who's going to sit at their desk all day to actively view a meeting?). Short-burst training (15–20 minutes) can be as effective, if not more so, than 60–90 minute sessions. The speaker, who is getting no visual or audio cues from the audience, must be able to keep their audience engaged. Q&A tends to be relegated to a specified timeframe following the session, or more successfully, limited to the Q&A and Chat functionality of the platform (unless you want 100 people speaking at the same time!).

There are many meeting and webinar providers outside of Zoom that a planner can use. The planner should make certain that the service they use is priced properly for their needs. Additional questions include how the service handles the audio (through the computer or the phone), the maximum capacity of the virtual event (and do note that platforms such as Zoom differentiate meetings from webinars), does the service provide interactive tools such as chat and polling, and how easy is it for the event organizers and speaker to switch the view from the platform being used to their desktop, so they can showcase their applications and browser.

LARGE-SCALE VIRTUAL MEETINGS

The purpose of Zoom and similar platforms (Adobe Connect, Bluejeans, etc.) is to hold a single meeting. Many event planners now need more than that. What if we wanted to hold multiple simultaneous sessions? What about a virtual tradeshow? What if we wanted to provide a single landing page for attendees so they could choose which aspect of the meeting they want to attend? This is where more sophisticated event industry virtual meeting tools are rushing to fill the gap.

It became clear to many in our industry at the start of the pandemic that these services, while useful, were not ready for the demand and sophistication required/desired by the planners. In speaking with many of the owners of these companies, one would hear the same comments. First, they weren't staffed adequately for the number of requests (many of them were not taking new clients for months), and second, their infrastructure needed a serious upgrade.

In this area of large-scale virtual events and meetings, one size does not even come close to fitting everyone's needs. Strengths and missed opportunities abound within all of the available products (as they work diligently to upgrade what they can provide). Still, the event planner needing a more robust event could and should look at these products to see if they can meet their modified event objectives. Some players to consider include MAP Digital (https://www.inxpo.com), Pathable (https://pathable.com), Hubb.Me (https://www.hubb.me), and INXPO (https://www.inxpo.com/).

HYBRID MEETINGS

If done well, a hybrid meeting successfully extends the reach of your live events to those who cannot attend. As the name indicates, a hybrid meeting combines a live event with a remote component. Successful hybrid events do not just show home attendees a video of what's happening at the event; they are designed to deliver unique and enriching experiences for both the live and remote audiences. This involves a delicate balance of paying attention to the needs of both audiences in the creation and delivery of these types of sessions.

There are a host of examples of types of hybrid meetings. From town halls to technical trainings, as long as you can satisfy both your live and remote audiences, you have the potential for a successful event. These events are not the least expensive option, as they require A/V and content delivery tools that will engage the remote audience in real time as well as the live audience's experience.

We are at the precipice of the age of hybrid meetings. Shortcoming and limitations on both the planner's side (including how to create and execute compelling content and interactivity for both audiences) and the supplier's side (creating a virtual environment that looks and feels live even for the virtual participant) are a few of the challenges that need to be addressed and overcome before we can see truly successfully hybrid meetings.

THE ROARING TECH TWENTIES

If there ever was a decade that has begun with more questions than answers about its future, it is the 2020s, or what I like to call the Roaring Tech Twenties. We are in a time when the future of meetings is unknown other than the fact that change is inevitable. We are in a time where new technologies continue to be developed while older ones mature and begin to deliver on their technological promises.

One hundred years ago, the decade known as the Roaring Twenties (1920s) is the perfect match for now. A worldwide pandemic was upon us. Technological advances were changing the nature of business. Business never could go back to what it once was before these tech tools became adopted. Which ones? Commercial radio stations, sound movie films, and the early stages of commercial aviation, just to name a few.

So which technologies are likely to define this decade? It will likely be a combination of ones we have not heard about yet and those technologies that find a sweet spot in our lives, both at work and at home. Since it is really hard to discuss the not-yet-created ones, here are some technologies (some of which have been already mentioned) that planners, suppliers, and everyone should be watching.

- **5G**—This game-changing cellular technology will redefine the speeds that we get over our devices without the use of WiFi. This will impact the further development of the autonomous vehicle (discussed separately). WiFi at hotels and conferences may (and should) never be the same. As its rollout has begun (though much slower and more limited than the phone companies want you to think), 5G has the capability to eliminate the need for WiFi, and create wide-reaching, seemingly unlimited bandwidth for all users. The only catches we see are in the monetization discussion, as well as in the ability of this tech to truly help everyone, and not just those more financially fortunate. In fact, we need to be aware of the economic divide that digital tools are enhancing.
- **Mixed Reality**—How will AR and VR be integrated into events and all aspects of our lives? With the previously mentioned Apple involvement (with wearable AR glasses) now inevitable, it will be interesting to see when one of these tools will have its "killer app" moment in our industry. It is a matter of when, not if. As some point, AR technology could become synonymous with wearable technologies.
- **Autonomous Vehicles/AI**—Since we've already discussed AI, let's focus on one of its byproducts, the autonomous car. For our industry, what

if we considered it as the autonomous, driver-less shuttle bus. In 2019, most planners wouldn't even consider having a driver-less approach to their group ground transportation. With the maturation of the technology, plus the development and implementation of 5G, the safety and abilities of non-driver transportation may well meet and exceed those of human-driven vehicles. A controversial point? Perhaps. But maybe only controversial in 2019/2020 and not in 2025.

- **Blockchain**—More defined by the tool that is primarily using it, Crypto-currency, the use of blockchain in our industry could become a part of us in specific areas. This could include security of online data and registration as well as the automated digital enforcement of contracts. Way too many obstacles are still in the way for this to become a standard, but as blockchain technology grows in industries such as the financial industry, it would be wise to keep an eye on it.

- **3D Printing**—This technology has a large footprint, but not yet in the meetings industry other than niche usage as customized giveaways at events. Could 3D printing of food, which has been explored for well over a decade, become a frontier we cross in this decade?

- **Virtual/Hybrid Meetings**—We are already in the era of the virtual meeting. The pandemic and Zoom are the defining components. What will come next, when some sort of live meetings begin again, is how the live and virtual worlds will seamlessly integrate. Watch for companies that will attempt to blur the line between the two worlds. Is it possible the hybrid event will be the dominant approach to our industry in 10 years? It is.

SUMMARY

You think the technology has changed fast up until now? You have not seen anything yet. Consider this a perfect storm when the opportunity for change has blossomed due to the uncertainty of our lives. In the lower-tech events community, these changes can and probably will have significant ramifications. How the tech will be used, what type of meetings (live, virtual, hybrid) will come to dominate the industry, and how the virtual component impacts the livelihood of organizations and individuals who were inextricably tied into its success, are all questions that are completely unknown in the middle of 2020. What we do know from experience and history is that successful movement is always forward and not backward, so the industry professional of this decade needs to be sure to have the technical awareness and skill sets that society is going to require.

It is an exciting time to be in our industry, don't you agree?

CRITICAL TERMS

For definitions, see https://insights.eventscouncil.org/Industry-glossary

3D Printing	Blogging	Portal
5G	Chatbots	RFID
APEX	Industry Council	RFP
Artificial Intelligence	Hybrid Meetings	Room Design Software
Audience Response Systems	Interactive Nametags	Social Media
	Lead Retrieval	Twitter
Augmented Reality	Mixed Reality	Virtual Reality
Autonomous Vehicles	NFC	Virtual Tradeshows
Big Data	Online Meetings	Webinars
Blockchain	Podcasting	80211

ABOUT THE CHAPTER CONTRIBUTORS

James Spellos is the president of a company called Meeting U located in New York City. The website is "meeting-u.com". He is a consultant and frequent speaker on technology issues in the MEEC industry.

Kathryn Hashimoto, PhD, is an emeritus member of the faculty in the School of Hospitality Leadership at East Carolina University.

PREVIOUS EDITION CHAPTER CONTRIBUTORS

Dennis Rudd, EdD and Kathleen Taylor Brown of Robert Morris College

CHAPTER 12

SUSTAINABLE MEETINGS AND EVENTS

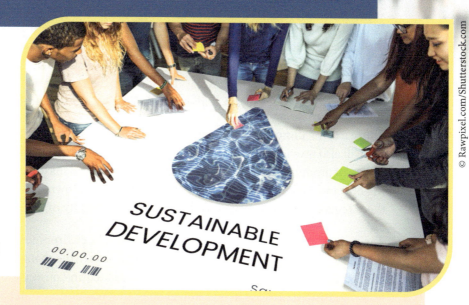

© Rawpixel.com/Shutterstock.com

SUSTAINABILITY IS A CRITICAL ELEMENT OF THE MEEC INDUSTRY

CHAPTER OBJECTIVES

- Define sustainable meetings
- Describe best practices in sustainable meetings
- Outline sustainable event standards and guidelines
- Describe the benefits of sustainable meetings and events
- Identify sustainable trends in the MEEC industry

Innovative Rooftop Garden Debuts at Los Angeles Convention Center

Los Angeles (February 21, 2018)

The Los Angeles Convention Center (LACC), managed by AEG Facilities, revealed its new 9,500-square-foot rooftop garden in January. The project began taking shape in April 2017 and features various citrus trees, herbs, vegetables, and seasonal flowers above the South Hall lobby.

"Sustainability and innovation are core values at AEG Facilities, and at the Los Angeles Convention Center we take this to heart," says Brad Gessner, senior vice president and general manager at the LACC. "The idea for the rooftop garden has been developing over the past few years, and we are thrilled with this addition to our facility."

This garden will not only contribute to the green efforts of Downtown Los Angeles but will also provide produce for LACC's in-house caterer Levy Restaurants. Currently 90% of produce at the LACC is locally sourced; Levy plans to build on this by utilizing oregano, chili peppers, citrus, lettuce, and carrots grown in the garden and using them regularly in their recipes to showcase the originality of the convention center.

The rooftop garden is an addition to more than 30 environmentally friendly practices and procedures implemented at the LACC under the management of AEG Facilities. These various implementations have resulted in conservation of energy and water, consistent increase in waste diversion rates, responsible purchasing of in-house goods, and the demonstration of leadership to local real estate and broad convention center communities.

About the Los Angeles Convention Center

The LACC is renowned internationally as a prime site for conventions, trade shows, and exhibitions. Owned by the City of Los Angeles and professionally managed by AEG Facilities, the LACC attracts over 2.5 million visitors annually. The facility is an integral economic component of the Southern California area, generating economic benefits through attendees' direct and indirect spending and sustaining over 12,500 local jobs. The LACC also remains an enduring symbol of environmental sustainability and social responsibility and is proud to be an LEED® Gold-certified facility; the venue was recertified on the Gold level in 2015, making the LACC the first convention center of its size in the United States to receive LEED® EB:O+M Gold recertification. For more information, please visit lacclink.com.

INTRODUCTION TO GREEN AND SUSTAINABLE MEETINGS

Green meetings are defined in a variety of ways, but the term "green" is now commonly used to describe a meeting's environmental practices. In other words, how "green" a meeting is is usually determined by policies such as recycling, using energy-efficient lighting, or serving pitchers of water as opposed to bottled water. The emphasis on protecting the "environment" is often a key indicator for green meetings.

Green meetings refer to those that have been designed to curb harmful effects on the environment (e.g., minimizing waste, minimizing use of single-use plastic). While taking the current state of the environment into consideration, it is not usually associated with the overall impact on future generations, or the triple bottom line.

The industry started referring to green meetings roughly 10 to 12 years ago, when the idea of being green was becoming popular in the lodging arena. The green meeting movement is now evolving to include efforts that impact the people side of meetings and events. This includes taking care of employees working the meetings and events, attendees, and also those who are impacted in the community where one may occur—all while also making a profit. This "triple" threat is often referred to as the Triple Bottom Line, or sustainability.

© Alison Hancock/Shutterstock.com

Rooftop Garden

© YuRi Photolife/Shutterstock.com

Rooftop Garden

While sometimes used interchangeably, the terms "green meetings" and "sustainable meetings" have different meanings.

The term sustainable meetings is more encompassing and includes implementing and executing a plan to save resources while improving the performance of a meeting or event. This term suggests that the impact that a meeting has on the environment, society, and the economy has been taken into consideration. According to the United Nations Environment Programme's (UNEP's) *Green Meeting Guide*, published in 2009, a green or sustainable meeting or event is one that is designed, organized, and implemented in a way that minimizes environmental impacts and leaves a positive legacy for the host community. The Events Industry Council takes the view that the demand sustainability places on our society and industry to achieve it requires everyone to be part of the solution. By working together, they believe we can all create sustainability and sustainable development within the framework of the events and meetings that occur in our communities. In addition, they emphasize that meeting professionals should source materials that are both environmentally *and* socially responsible.

The widely recognized Brundtland Report, created after the 1983 World Commission on Environment and Development, defines **sustainability** as "development which meets the needs of the present without compromising the ability of future generations to meet their own needs." This definition is one of the most often cited and focuses on three aspects of sustainable development—economic development, social development, and environmental protection. These three aspects, or pillars, as many people refer to them, are often called the three P's of sustainability—profit, planet, and people—all of which are interconnected; none can exist without the others.

TIDBIT

Coordinated primarily by the World Wildlife Fund, **Earth Hour** began in Australia in 2007 to help curb the effects of global warming and conserve energy by encouraging people to turn off their lights for one hour, from 8:30 pm to 9:30 pm, toward the end of March. In 2020, 190 countries and territories supported Earth Hour virtually amid the COVID-19 outbreak and generated over 3 billion social media impressions around the world.

The movement toward sustainable meetings within the MEEC industry is impacting all areas of meeting planning. As more planners strive to minimize their events' environmental impacts, suppliers are also working to make their products and services more earth friendly. Meeting professionals are actively learning the ins and outs of executing sustainable meetings, and meeting suppliers are jumping on board accordingly. When meeting professionals begin planning more sustainable meetings, the ripple effect has an impact on all parties involved.

WHY DO IT?

THE TRIPLE BOTTOM LINE

Perhaps answering the question "why?" includes more than a single answer could report. Some experts consider the "triple bottom line" as a more accurate measure of a company's accomplishments and a better answer to the question. The triple bottom line takes into consideration people (social impact), planet (environmental impact), and profit (economic impact); this expands the concept of success to include environmental and social accomplishments in addition to financial. Research suggests that many forward-thinking organizations, associations, and companies are applying the triple bottom line concept because they measure success and report to stakeholders.

PROFIT (ECONOMIC IMPACT)

Economic sustainability refers to a meeting's ability to efficiently and responsibly use resources to ensure all financial obligations are met over time. In the MEEC industry, this is important for both the meeting planner and for the company or organization holding/requesting the meeting. This makes good business sense, and companies that choose to do so are reporting higher gross profit margins, higher return on sales, higher return on assets, and a stronger cash flow than their less sustainable competitors. Examples of economic sustainability include return on investment (ROI), fair trade, local economy, growth, and business performance. Once a company has made the commitment to become more sustainable within its own organization, it is easier to apply the same principles to their meetings and events.

Taking small steps to become sustainable can make an enormous difference to a company's bottom line. For example, one large event eliminated the use of bottled water and saved $1.5 million at an event attended by 40,000 people over a five-day period. Reusing name badge holders saved another group more than $1,500 in just one year. In addition to the monetary savings to these groups, the amount of waste deposited into a landfill was also reduced dramatically. Oracle's sustainability efforts during their annual OpenWorld event saved the company $1.7 million over the past 5 years. Among their many green efforts, they saved $420,000 solely by reevaluating their signage policies. Their signage is now made from lighter, reusable materials and is sourced from local companies.

PLANET (ENVIRONMENTAL IMPACT)

Many efforts that are related to the economic impacts and savings of sustainability are directly related to the environmental efforts associated with those cost savings, thus highlighting the interconnectedness of the triple bottom line. It is difficult to have one without the others. Perhaps the easiest piece of the triple bottom line to grasp is the focus on environmental sustainability. In fact, it is how most in the industry would describe or define sustainability; participating in and encouraging actions that help our meetings and events reduce the negative impact they may have on the environment. The MEEC industry professionals can address environmental issues and impacts of their meetings in many ways. For example, they can reduce the amount of printed material such as program guides, maps of a venue, or exhibition material they use for a meeting. This, by the way, will also save on cost! Many groups have eliminated the old practice of automatically printing conference and meeting programs for each attendee. Instead, they take advantage of technology to encourage attendees to use applications (apps) via their mobile devices. Event apps have evolved over the years to include daily schedules, speaker and exhibitor information, social medial tools, calendars, and options for personal customization and have become very user friendly. All this information would typically be presented in a paper program guide.

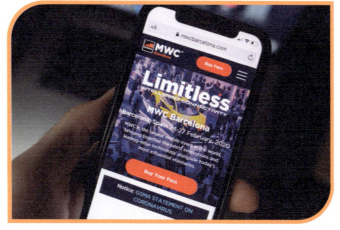

Buying a pass for, and engaging a conference utilizing a smart device and app.

Carbon Offsets

Large trade shows or conventions also incorporate the option for attendees to purchase carbon offsets as a way to diminish their environmental impact. It is inevitable that attendees need to use some form of transportation (e.g., airplane, car, train) in order to attend a meeting, which produces emissions that are not good for the environment. In fact, transportation is the largest contributor to an event's environmental footprint, accounting for 90% of the emissions produced by an event with travelers around the world. A **carbon offset** is meant to reduce the carbon dioxide or greenhouse gases produced when we travel—it compensates for the emission and is meant to balance or cancel them out. Officially, a carbon offset "reduces or offsets carbon emissions through the funding of activities and projects that improve the environment." If, for example, someone flies from Phoenix to New York round-trip for a meeting or event, the trip will produce approximately 806 pounds of carbon per person, assuming the flight is full. The impact will be greater with an emptier plane. The purchase of a carbon offset helps to minimize that impact by funding projects that help reduce carbon and other greenhouse gas emissions. Some projects include planting trees, investing in renewable energy sources such as windmills, or alternative fuels. This is an option that meeting professionals are now offering their attendees who can choose to voluntarily purchase those carbon offsets. The costs for such programs vary. This is not the most preferred method for reducing the impact on the environment, but it is an available option that is better than doing nothing.

PEOPLE (SOCIAL IMPACT)

In addition to the plant and profit factors of sustainability, it also encompass-es people. People include those who attend meetings and events, those who work them, those who organize them, and those in the communities with-in which they are held. This is "realized by equitably meeting the needs of all people affected by the planning or activation of an event." The question that meeting planners must ask themselves is how their events impact both their own employees and those attending and those in the local communities where the events are held. Is that impact a positive one?

To provide a framework for this idea of work with and for people, many com-panies have adopted the concept of **corporate social responsibility** (CSR). The concept has been around since the 1950s and has been referred to in many different ways (e.g., corporate responsibility, corporate accountability, corporate ethics, corporate citizenship, corporate sustainability, and responsi-ble business). According to the World Business Council for Sustainable Devel-opment, CSR is the "continuing commitment by business to behave ethically and contribute to economic development while improving the quality of life of the work force and their families as well as a local community and society at large." This is right in line with the people side of sustainability. Another ap-propriate definition is from *Simply CSR*, which states that CSR is "a long-term approach to business that addresses the needs of communities, people, and their employers. CSR provides frameworks for a successful enterprise that is harmonious with its surroundings. It is an opportunity to generate honest, authentic good-news stories that a business and its community can be proud of." At the center of CSR is the people and doing the right thing for them.

How does this translate into action in the MEEC industry specifically? Inter-nally, employees who work in organizations that support sustainable efforts could be healthier for working in an office that is naturally lighted or better ventilated for energy savings. They may be encouraged to take the stairs or ride their bike to work, contributing to personal health. In addition to health reasons, employees like to be a part of a good culture. Encouraging employees to become participants in sustainable efforts often means encouraging them to live a healthier and more active lifestyle; this leads to happier and more productive individuals in the workforce. This also has tremendous potential for contributing to the bottom line of the company. Examples of such programs might include paid-time-off to volunteer at a local charity or one-for-one matching donations to a charity of an employee's choice.

Externally, meeting and event attendees are also positively impacted by sustainable efforts and participating in reduce, reuse, and recycle programs. Popular programs include those activities that get them out into the communities or, at the very least, help to raise funds for local charities. The rising expectation is to not provide attendees with the same-old meeting experience but instead familiarize them with the local city that they are visiting and how their impact of being there affects that city and its' residents.

These types of activities can take many formats. Some organizations encourage attendees to become actively involved in a project while attending an event, while others may simply ask for donations or make donations on behalf of the entire organization. The following are some examples:

Oracle—During Oracle's annual OpenWorld conference, they partner with local agencies and charities to donate a variety of options. For example, in one year they donated 1,135 pounds of event furniture to a local chapter of Habitat for Humanity; 1,268 pounds of backpacks, socks, toiletry sacks, and office supplies; 1,621 pounds of food; and 150 pounds of lightly used soaps and room amenities.

Clean the World—Clean the World is a third-party company that partners with hotels to recycle soap and partially used toiletries. At events, attendees can take a few minutes out of their day to put toiletries into bags to create small toiletry kits that are then given to the local homeless or other shelters in need.

Tee it Up for the Troops—This is an organized run at the annual Club Management Association of America's World Conference and Business Club Expo, with all proceeds donated to this charitable organization. The run sells out every year.

Food Runners—Anyone holding a meeting or event in San Francisco can donate leftover food to Food Runners, who then distribute it to feeding programs throughout the city. They typically deliver 17 tons of food per week, which is enough for 20,000 meals per week in San Francisco.

BENEFITS OF SUSTAINABILITY

In an industry as hectic as the meetings and events industry, where every detail is important, it is easy to understand why planners, suppliers, vendors, and facility managers want to streamline wherever possible. So why should industry professionals take on the extra challenge of becoming more sustainable? Because doing the right thing is the right thing to do.

ENHANCED BRAND IMAGE

Planning or executing a sustainable event is good business. This is especially important for those large corporate and association events that occur around the world. If attendees are aware of the good that event organizers are doing for both the planet and the people, it will improve the organization's image and repeat attendance. It will also make attendees feel good about attending, especially if they know they can do so and still minimize their impact on the environment and help local communities.

DIFFERENTIATION

A challenge for some in the MEEC industry is keeping their meeting and events interesting and pertinent to attendees—some of whom attend the same events every year. Sustainability offers a point of differentiation from one year to the next and can thus give attendees something new to look forward to.

COST SAVINGS

Reducing waste, conserving energy, sourcing local food, or eliminating the use of bottled water lead to cost savings.

RAISE AWARENESS

The MEEC industry has a tremendous opportunity to educate attendees every time they incorporate a sustainable practice into a meeting or event. Attendees of events hail from around the world, and they may not be familiar with such practices or the benefits they can bring. This may encourage people to make decisions to minimize their own footprint on the environment, for example, and take those practices back to their own businesses or personal lives.

SOCIAL BENEFITS

If planned and implemented carefully, the meeting can benefit the local region through providing jobs, benefiting regional suppliers, promoting better working conditions and act as a catalyst for encouraging environmental best practice across the region (UNEP, Green Meeting Guide).

SUSTAINABLE MEETING STANDARDS AND GUIDELINES

The MEEC industry is moving quickly toward the real possibility of sustainable meetings becoming the norm of the future. Evidence that corroborates this theory lies in the number of guidelines and certifications that are currently available. These types of standards help identify, unify, and contain these efforts.

SUSTAINABLE MEETING STANDARDS

In 2019, the Events Industry Council (EIC), along with 100 industry practitioners, revised the internationally accepted industry standards (formerly known as the Accepted Industry Practices Exchange and the American National Standards Institute (ANSI)-certified environmentally sustainable event standards). The new standards are referred to as the *Events Industry Council Sustainable Event Standards* and cover seven individual sectors of the MEEC industry:

1. Event organizer
2. Accommodations
3. Audiovisual and production
4. Destination
5. Exhibitions
6. Food and Beverage
7. Venue

Exhibit 1: Events Industry Council Sustainable Event Standards

The event organizers are assessed on internal practices, climate action, supply chain management, accommodations, venue, food and beverage, destination, audiovisual and production, and exhibitions if any of those elements are a part of their event. Suppliers are assessed on organizational management, air quality management, community, climate action, water, energy and waste management, marketing and communications, and supply chain management.

For detailed information on these standards, see the Events Industry Council website.

Sustainable Development
Goals

UNITED NATIONS SUSTAINABLE DEVELOPMENT GOALS

The United Nations (UN) crafted the 2030 Agenda for Sustainable Development, which was adopted by all UN members in 2015. It "provides a shared blueprint for peace and prosperity for people and the planet, now and into the future." It is an urgent call to action to work together globally to fulfill the 17 Sustainable Development Goals (SDGs) that are at the core of their agenda. The Events Industry Council has also adopted the goals as the base on which they built their four principles of event sustainability.

ISO 20121

ISO 20121 is an international management system designed to help MEEC organizations improve the sustainability of their events as they relate to products, services, and related activities. It is the international version of a British standard established in 2007, and was specifically created to coincide with the 2012 London Olympics. ISO 20121 was designed to address all areas of the MEEC industry. Successful implementation of the standard will allow corresponding organizations to seek certification through an independent accrediting body. Although ISO 20121 and the EIC Sustainable Event Standards represent two different approaches to defining a sustainable event, they are designed to work independently or in collaboration with one another.

GES Achieves Environmental Sustainability Recertification

Global Experience Specialists (GES) became the first general service contractor to be certified to an international sustainability standard for the meetings and event industry in 2015 and has since become recertified at Level 2 of the Accepted Practices Exchange/ American Society for Testing and Materials (APEX /ASTM) Environmentally Sustainable Event Standards, now known as the EIC Sustainable Event Standards. The certification pertains to the Evaluation and Selection of Exhibits for Environmentally Sustainable Meetings, Events, Trade Shows, and Conferences.

GES has a long and ongoing commitment to sustainable practices. Its operations in the United Kingdom are ISO 20121 certified, a complex and challenging international standard accreditation that takes a management systems approach to running more sustainable events (GMIC, 2017).

In addition to the EIC Sustainable Event Standards and ISO 20121, there are many eco-friendly, third-party certifications that are recognized within the MEEC industry. The following is a list of the various certifications or awards that apply primarily to the suppliers to the MEEC industry.

A. Accommodations/Venues
- Green Key Global's Green Key Meetings
- Audubon Green Lodging Program
- Green Globe
- Leadership in Energy and Environmental Design (LEED)
- Energy Star Qualified Buildings
- ISO 20121
- Green Seal

B. Catering/Food and Beverage
- Marine Stewardship Council (MSC)
- Fair Trade Certified
- USDA Certified Organic
- Green Restaurant Association
- Rainforest Alliance Certification

C. Printing/Promotional/Gifts
- Forest Stewardship Council (FSC)
- The Programme for the Endorsement of Forest Certification (PEFC)
- The Sustainable Forestry Initiative(r) (SFI)
- American Tree Farm System (ATFS)
- Waterless Printing Association

Although not all the meeting industry certifications are noted here, the list of these certifications continues to change. New certifications are added, some are blended together, and some have simply outlived their usefulness and have been replaced by a more meaningful certification. From a meeting professional's perspective, it is important to gain a thorough understanding of what is required for each certification that is claimed. Planners must do their homework and verify that the certification in question is of value. They all have individualized requirements, but the overall goal is to bring a level of quality to the ever-evolving practice of incorporating environmentally friendly applications. Due diligence on the part of the meeting professional will ensure that there is no misrepresentation to the attendees of the meeting and will also help guarantee that the sustainable goals for the meeting will be met.

GREENWASHING

The aforementioned certifications can help meeting professionals identify those companies that are embracing sustainability. As consumers become more and more aware of sustainable practices, companies are responding by incorporating more efforts into their business standards. As these companies compete for consumers, many become too eager to tout their sustainable campaigns, achievement, or standards. As awareness grows, it is becoming more difficult for even the consumer to distinguish between those companies that are actually implementing sustainable practices and those that are **greenwashing**.

The term greenwashing refers to any misrepresentation by a company that leads the consumer to believe that its policies and products are environmentally responsible, when its claims are false, misleading, or cannot be verified. Greenwashing is also used to identify the practice of companies spending more money on the campaign to notify customers of their environmentally friendly efforts than on the efforts themselves.

The actual practice of greenwashing began in the mid-1960s when companies were eager to be seen as part of the environmental movement that was taking shape. As these practices continued to evolve, they eventually became known as "greenwashing." This term was first used in an essay written by environmentalist Jay Westerveld, in 1968, which reviewed the practice of placing a card on the pillow in each hotel room explaining that the hotel encourages reuse of guest towels for environmental responsibility. On closer examination of this practice, Westerveld surmised that, in most cases, hotels were making little effort to reduce energy waste with their programs and were using the practices simply to increase profits.

Being knowledgeable about sustainability standards is one way for planners to educate themselves and their clients. A back-of-the-house tour should be part of the due-diligence process of the meeting professional and can be very helpful in validating (or not validating) the green claims being stated by any given company. If a claim was made by the participating venue, for example, that recycling opportunities were readily available and would be made available for all attendees, evidence of this should be apparent during the back-of-the-house tour. The event professional should be able to observe where the recycled material is stored and the process that takes place once it is removed from the event space. If the venue has made claims that local produce is used for all meals, evidence of this could be apparent during this tour as well. Lastly, planners must practice being green within their departments and companies so that they can be an advocate and lead by example. Although there are numerous checklists available that can be used to assist meeting professionals with planning a green meeting, the checklist included at the end of this chapter is a good place to start. Once a planner is aware of the obstacles greenwashing can present, it is easier to identify those areas of concern and proceed in a positive manner with the planning of a green meeting.

CREATING A PROCESS FOR SUSTAINABLE PRACTICES

According to recent studies, more than half of all meeting professionals are considering environmental practices as they plan their conferences. No longer is it possible to limit considerations to sleeping rooms. At all major events held by Meeting Professionals International (MPI), for example, the board of directors purposefully considers the seven areas of sustainable meetings as defined by the Events Industry Council's standards.

Planning, managing, and evaluating a sustainable meeting used to be thought of as difficult and expensive, when, in reality, it may be as simple as paying attention to the decisions that are made regarding company policies. Here are some simple steps professionals can follow to make their next meeting more sustainable, as suggested by the Events Industry Council:

Step 1: Create a plan (management system approach) for identifying your event's sustainability objectives. This plan should include how you will achieve your objectives and what the key performance indicators are to track the success of your plan. Identify specific activities (such as a certain percentage of waste diversion, percentage of local or organic meals, etc.), metrics for tracking, and outcomes you want to achieve for each objective identified and who is responsible for the end results.

Step 2: Engage internal stakeholders in supporting your plan. Establish or create a sustainable meeting policy for your team/department/meeting. Ideally, this policy will reflect the internal values of your company/organization to ensure that it is supported by your event efforts.

Step 3: Engage vendors in supporting your plan. Make the "ask" of your current vendors at cost savings or cost neutral pricing. Include language in your request for proposal (RFP) process and contracts that includes vendors reporting back to you with the data you need to track your performance. (The first year can be your benchmark year to evaluate and grow in future years.)

Step 4: Track your performance. Just as we monitor our event budgets, we need to monitor and track the performance of our sustainability action plans. Post event—ensure accurate reports so you can build on them for future years and use them in your site selection process.

Step 5: Communicate the results, celebrate the success. Although continuous improvement is always our goal as sustainability professionals, be sure to pause, breathe, and share the success of your action plan with attendees, vendors, media, and the industry. The more you can quantify your results in human scale terms (amount of $$ saved, number of trees, amount of CO_2 kept out of the atmosphere), the more engaged you and your stakeholders will be for your plan the following year.

Step 6: Be innovative and have fun! This step may not technically be on the environmental management action plan; however, it is important for us as meeting professionals to enjoy what we are doing. Our goal is to create rewarding experiences for our attendees. So, if it is aligned with your

© Elena Schweitzer/Shutterstock.com

organization, be creative and include a yoga break, human-powered energy stations, or networking events that have purpose in the local community. Remember to allow for some outdoor or nonscheduled activity time. Your attendees will appreciate your efforts to take care of their sustainable needs.

BEST ENVIRONMENTAL PRACTICES

Now that best sustainable practices have been established, the following are some specific actions that meeting professionals can take to incorporate those best environmental practices into their meetings:

Use Technology: Take advantage of technology to reduce the need for paper. With easy-to-use apps or registration companies, there is virtually no need to produce printed materials. To cut down on travel costs, utilize podcasting, webinars, and video streaming. In doing so, event professionals may find an increase in attendance because they are making it easier for more people to attend.

Choose a Local Destination: Ninety percent of an event's carbon footprint comes from air travel. Whenever possible, event professionals should choose a destination close to where participants live to reduce the distance that must be traveled to attend. If air travel is necessary, event professionals should choose a venue or hotel that is close to the airport or within walking distance of off-site events. Research public transportation options in the host city.

Reduce, Reuse, and Recycle: Proper recycling bins should be added to the event supplies list, and the staff should be trained in the proper ways to recycle. Venues should be asked to provide visible and accessible recycling services for paper, metal, plastic, and glass. Banquet managers should be asked about composting options or giveaway programs and also the option of using real china for meals. If this is not possible, choose disposable plates made from renewable resources that will biodegrade in a landfill. Collect name badge holders and lanyards for use the next year.

Volume Up: Encourage food and beverage providers to serve sugar, creamer, and other condiments in bulk dispensers rather than individual packets. Find hotels that use dispensers for shampoo and lotions rather than small bottles. Request water stations as opposed to bottled water. Give attendees a water bottle for their personal use throughout the meeting (this also provides a sponsorship opportunity).

Eat Local: Speak with the banquet manager about using local fruits and vegetables that are in season. Include more vegetarian meals, because they require less carbon energy to prepare. Obtain an accurate headcount prior to finalizing the food to order so that food waste can be minimized.

Decorate with Nature: Use local flower, plants, and succulents to decorate your tables, and leave them in pots so that you can use them as gifts or prizes. This

© denira/Shutterstock.com

Decorating with nature.

ensures that they are not wasted once the meeting is over. Some cities have local charities that will collect flowers at the end of an event and donate them to churches or assisted living facilities around their city.

Use Paper Wisely: If print materials are necessary, use chlorine-free, recycled paper and vegetable-based inks. Print on both sides of the paper, and print materials for a participant only if requested. Use "print-on-demand" stations rather than printing copies for each attendee.

Save Energy: Look for venues and hotels that practice energy efficiency and have policies in place for doing so. Coordinate with the venue to ensure that lights, audiovisual equipment, and air-conditioning in meeting spaces will be turned off when not in use. Remind attendees to conserve energy in the guest rooms by turning off lights when they leave and not leaving electronics plugged in and powered on unnecessarily.

Inform Everyone: Tell participants, speakers, suppliers, vendors, and the media about your sustainability efforts and your expectations from them as event partners. Communication is the key in encouraging and securing active participation from all involved parties. For example, in the speaker contract, green expectations should be made very clear so that speakers do not arrive with printed handouts when electronic versions of the handouts are expected.

Repurposing: Companies will repurpose items such as meeting banners into useful and creative things like messenger bags, wallets, tote bags, and laptop sleeves.

EVALUATION OF SUSTAINABLE EFFORTS

If you can measure it, you can manage it. This is a common mantra in many sectors of the business world. It applies equally well to sustainable meetings and sustainable efforts. It is important for meeting professionals and companies to set clear goals at the beginning so that it is possible to measure the success or failure of an event. Fortunately, because of the growing interest in conducting green meetings, a few tools have been created to help in the measurement/evaluation process.

MEETGREEN® CALCULATOR 2.0

Measuring the impact of sustainable efforts can be challenging. To address this challenge, *MeetGreen* has developed a calculator that is a comprehensive tool used for benchmarking sustainable aspects of an event, regardless of size. The tool allows event professionals to "capture valuable information throughout the event planning process to make it easy to see … accomplishments and where improvements can be made." The tool assesses event management practices and measurable outcomes in 14 key categories to audit the environmental impact of conference activities. The MeetGreen Calculator integrates aspects of the ISO 20121 and EIC Sustainable Event Standards.

SUSTAINABLE MEETING PROFESSIONAL

MPI offers a Sustainable Event Strategist Certification.

The program teaches planners how to view the event planning process through the lens of sustainability. They learn tactical best practices for reducing the environmental impact of events and explore how to create a culture of sustainable decision-making throughout the planning process using the EIC Sustainable Event Standards and ISO 20121.

The following three examples provide insights into sustainable efforts in practice.

GRAND CAROLINA RESORT AND SPA

The resort was chosen to host 1,000 delegates over 6 days. Although it was not particularly "green" at the outset, management responded to the client's greening requirements by altering standard operating procedures and implementing capital improvements, such as installing solar panels. Delegates joined in the effort by reducing their own consumption while on-site.

For the duration of the event, data was collected each day on utility usage and waste generation and reported the following morning at general sessions. Total consumption was compared with the average of a similar convention held the previous year. The results were impressive: Total electricity consumption had been reduced by 21%, water use by 48%, and solid waste by 34%. The greening measures were estimated to save the resort over $1 million per year.

As the need for measurable outcomes continues to grow and companies look for ROI on green strategies, the ability to measure sustainability factors will become increasingly important. Look for new and more sophisticated tools that track carbon, energy, and water footprints and overall conference achievements. Newer tools will work hand in hand with established tools such as paper savings calculators and the MeetGreen Calculator.

A Look into the Oregon Convention Center's first-of-its-kind Waste Diversion Policy

As one of the most sustainable convention centers in the world, Portland's LEED® Platinum-certified Oregon Convention Center (OCC) is a proven leader in environmentally responsible practices. OCC is dedicated not only to minimizing the footprint of its facility, but also to setting a new standard in sustainability for the entire convention industry to follow.

It will not come as a surprise that the convention industry generates a tremendous amount of waste, particularly from the decisions of event organizers. From banners to cardboard boxes, events require numerous materials that are typically left behind at convention centers and end up in landfills.

In 2015, OCC introduced a first-of-its-kind Waste Diversion Policy to reduce event waste, encourage innovation, and promote reuse. The creation of this policy did not come without its own set of challenges. Without any industry examples to reference, OCC started from scratch, conducting in-depth research and discussions with internal staff and external partners to begin crafting a strategic approach.

Today, the Waste Diversion Policy is fully integrated into OCC's contracts and operations, from beginning to end. A point of particular pride for OCC is the donation aspect of its Waste Diversion Policy. Many items left over after a convention can be donated, so OCC partners with local nonprofit organizations in need of those materials. For example, in conjunction with its catering partner, Pacificwild, OCC donates tens of thousands of meals each year to the nonprofit social services organization, Blanchet House. Another partnership with local nonprofit FreeGeek allows used electronics to be recycled after an event. Through its partnerships with local nonprofit organizations, OCC has donated over 120,000 pounds of reusable goods and 46,600 meals to address food scarcity in the Portland area.

OCC has an ambitious long-term goal of reaching at least an 80 percent diversion rate. Currently, 94% of events hosted at the OCC are in compliance with its Waste Diversion Policy. In the past year, OCC has recycled more than 400 tons of materials and diverted 122 tons of food scraps away from the landfill by composting.

The OCC is owned by Metro and managed by the Metro Exposition and Recreation Commission. OCC hosts groups from around the world and brings millions of dollars into the Portland and Oregon economy.

FREEMAN

Since Freeman was founded as a family-owned company in 1927, one of its core values has centered on ethical business conduct and a strong commitment to the well-being of their employees, communities, industry, and environment. Today, the Freeman family and Freeman employees continue that legacy every day through a variety of activities, programs, and, most of all, a spirit of caring.

In fiscal year 2018:

- More than $700,000 in goods and services donated to charities

- Employees volunteered 5,010 hours to organizations

- 229 individual programs or events held in 2017 to 2018

Organizations they have worked with include American Heart Association, local schools and school districts, local food banks, Veteran's Stand Down, Boys & Girls Club, BL Duke, Goodwill, Salvation Army, and blood donation drives.

TRENDS AND BEST PRACTICES

The following are some of the best practices in MEEC sustainability.

- Increasing numbers of planners will have sustainable meeting policies that will extend to suppliers.
- Sustainable meeting practices will continue to be incorporated into increasing numbers of events.
- Increasing numbers of groups will have meeting and event policies associating all three factors of sustainability—people, profit, planet.
- Many national governments and large corporations are likely to demand that the meetings and events they organize and sponsor incorporate sustainable elements.
- There will be increasing "accountability" and planners will be required to "prove" their meetings and events are sustainable.
- There will continue to be an increased focus on cost versus benefits of sustainability. Being able to document and calculate the true cost of sustainability versus the true benefits will be crucial.
- Some sustainable activities that are now voluntary will become legal requirements.
- Educational training and certification programs for providers of sustainable events will become more abundant.

CORONAVIRUS 2020 AND SUSTAINABLE EVENTS

According to Shawna McKinley, a sustainability consultant and event planner, sustainability practices at events due to COVID-19 will change. In some cases, they will get easier with low-carbon online event platforms, but in others it will be more difficult, especially as waste and chemical use for cleaning rises. McKinley advises event planners to consider taking the following measures:

- Embrace virtual events, because they are not only safer, but more sustainable and inclusive as well
- Use virtual event components to lessen the carbon impact of in-person events
- Minimize the disposables at events and double-check that materials can be recycled

- Source locally and plan to accommodate local vendor limitations in producing food and beverage to scale
- Ensure workers are protected from chemical exposures while cleaning

Even once COVID-19 is under control, these recommendations are still important ones to consider for sustainable practices.

SUMMARY

This chapter summarizes the most recent developments in the MEEC industry as related to sustainability. Sustainability is not a fad but a fact of life in the twenty-first century. The challenge is how to incorporate sustainability into meetings and events and show how those efforts impact the bottom line, the environment, and the people, while also providing attendees with a good experience.

Now that you have completed this chapter, you should be competent in the following Meeting and Business Event Competency Standards:

**MEETING AND BUSINESS COMPETENCY STANDARDS (MBECS)—
SKILL 2: DEVELOP SUSTAINABILITY PLAN FOR MEETING OR EVENT**

	Subskills	Skills (standards)
A2.012	Implement sustainability management plan	
A2.02	Demonstrate environmental responsibility	

(Produced by G.G. Fenich and Students from East Carolina University)

Nick Saltmarsh is the new general manager at a very nice boutique hotel in Charleston, SC, called the HarbourView Inn. With the recent push to go green in South Carolina, Nick was aware that, as a new general manager coming in, he would have to get the ball rolling on this going green issue and really push the subject. When Nick first started managing the Harbour View Inn, there was next to nothing being done in the way of going green. When Nick chose to hold a staff meeting, he informed the employees that this was going to have to be a team effort and that everyone would have to be on board to make the necessary changes to actually be certified as a green property.

During the staff meeting, Nick held a discussion and everyone brainstormed what their departments could do to put a stop to waste. The housekeeping, front desk, and restaurant were the main culprits for significant waste. The front desk needed to stop the ridiculously excessive waste of paper and start shredding and recycling it. The restaurant had always thrown containers, cardboard boxes, and packaging straight into the trash can, and they were now going to recycle all of that. The housekeeping staff was going to attempt to reuse untouched items, and the front desk agents made recycling cards for each room that explained that if guests hung their towels up it would be a sign that they did not need new towels to preserve water. They also posted something similar for the bedding.

As far as the meeting rooms go, everything mentioned previously played a part on the meeting space because the restaurant caters the meetings and the housekeepers clean the rooms. The paper wall hangs ended up being transferred into dry erase boards so that less paper would be wasted, and the lights were changed to LED lights to conserve energy. Most of the guests that hold meetings at their property will be staying in the hotel too, so this created going green awareness.

Nick realizes that at first the Harborview Inn may take a hit financially but that in the long run the property will gain the respect of clients and save money on energy preservation. The HarbourView Inn just received their certification for the South Carolina Green Hospitality Alliance, which puts them one step ahead of most properties with meetings competition in Charleston.

The HarbourView Inn has been implementing the greening of their property for about a year now, but they still have a long way to go. There is so much that can be done to help the environment, and yet in our industry it is very hard not to waste just because of the nature of the business.

1. What do you think the HarbourView Inn's next step should be in their conquest to continue to become more sustainable?

KEYWORDS AND TERMS

For definitions, see https://insights.eventscouncil.org/Industry-glossary

carbon footprint calculator   greenwashing
carbon offset   sustainability
corporate social responsibility (CSR)   sustainable meeting
green meeting   triple bottom line

REVIEW AND DISCUSSION QUESTIONS

1. Discuss the economic advantages of a sustainable event.

2. How does a meeting manager evaluate sustainable efforts?

3. Explain the difference between the terms "green meetings" and "sustainable meetings," and give examples for each that supports your answer.

4. Describe how an event planner can ensure that a venue is not greenwashing.

5. What is corporate social responsibility (CSR)? What role does CSR play in the MEEC industry?

6. What is the Triple Bottom Line, as applied to the MEEC industry?

7. Define sustainability.

8. Describe best practices for incorporating sustainability into your meeting or event.

RECOMMENDED WEBSITES

Events Industry Council—http://www.eventscouncil.org/

Events Industry Council Centre for Sustainability & Social Impact—https://www.eventscouncil.org/Sustainability/CSE

UN Sustainable Development Goals—https://sdgs.un.org/goals

ISO 20121—http://www.iso20121.org/

MeetGreen—https://meetgreen.com/

Sustainable Event Professional Certificate Program—https://www.eventscouncil.org/Sustainability/SEPC

Terrapass—https://www.terrapass.com/

ABOUT THE CHAPTER CONTRIBUTOR

Michelle Millar, Ph.D, is an associate professor and department chair at the University of San Francisco's School of Management, in the Department of Hospitality Management. Dr. Millar teaches Meeting and Event Management, Corporate Event Management, Introduction to the Hospitality Industry, and Sustainable Business. She is a certified hospitality educator, who earned her master's degree at Temple University and her Ph.D from the University of Nevada, Las Vegas.

Green Event Checklist
15 THINGS YOU CAN DO TODAY

1 Ask for recycling at the facility

2 Ask for a towel reuse program at the hotel

3 Request no bottled water be served

4 Ask for all condiments and beverages to be served in bulk

5 Request leftover food be donated

6 Request water glasses not be pre-filled at banquets

7 Request china and linens for meals, no disposables

8 Ask if there is electronic signage in the meeting venue

9 Ask about sustainable local food

10 Reuse signage and create using sustainable material

11 Reduce printed material and use recycled content where possible

12 Reduce conference swag and use a sustainable source for any swag

13 Minimize packaging on all purchased products

14 Find a donation stream for leftover materials (think of end use when making purchases)

15 Communicate sustainability efforts and options to attendees

CHAPTER 13

PLANNING MEEC GATHERINGS

© r.classen/Shutterstock.com

CHAPTER OBJECTIVES

- Discuss the importance and process of setting goals and objectives when planning Meetings, Expositions, Events, and Conventions (MEEC) gatherings.
- List the considerations to keep in mind during the site selection planning process.
- Articulate the areas of concern when program-planning for an event.
- Outline the many logistical considerations to keep in mind when planning a MEEC gathering.
- Discuss the main considerations in direct and indirect marketing and promotion that a MEEC professional must consider when planning a gathering.

A meeting/event professional may be familiar with all the elements of the MEEC industry. However, it takes good planning, organizing, directing, and control to put these diverse elements together and "make it work." To accomplish this, the organizer needs to understand the group and its wants and needs: Who are they? Why are they here? Then objectives can be set that will guide the program delivery to meet these wants and needs while staying within budget constraints. It should be noted that the focus of this chapter is meant as a broad overview of planning a MEEC event. There are two other textbooks available that go into more detail. They are meant to be read in sequence: The first one addresses *Planning and Management of Meetings, Expositions, Events, and Conventions*, and the second focuses on *Production and Logistics in Meetings, Expositions, Events, and Conventions*. The reader is reminded that the "process" and steps of planning are the same for any event, whether it is for business or for leisure/recreation/entertainment.

NEEDS ANALYSIS

As part of setting objectives for a meeting, a needs analysis must be undertaken. A **needs analysis** is a method of determining the expectations for a particular meeting. A needs analysis can be as simple as asking senior management what they want to accomplish at a meeting and then designing the event around those expectations. It should be remembered that the needs of corporate and association meeting attendees are very different (see Chapter 2). The first step is to know the attendees by asking the question "Who are they?" A meeting/event professional must collect demographic information of both past and prospective attendees. This is much easier for an annual event, such as an association meeting or corporate management meeting. The meeting/event professional keeps a detailed **group history** of who attended the meeting, their likes and dislikes, and all pertinent information that can be used to improve future meetings. Questions to consider include the following:

What is the age and gender of past attendees?

- What is their level of expertise—beginner, intermediate, advanced?
- What is their position within the organization's hierarchy—new employee, junior management, or senior management?
- How is the content best delivered? Only face-to-face? Hybrid? Virtual only?

- What hotel amenities are preferred—indoor pools, spas, tennis courts, exercise rooms, wireless Internet access?
- Are there specific dietary restrictions for attendees (i.e., Kosher, Muslim, vegetarian, and low-carb, low-sugar, gluten-free food cooked keeping in mind specific medical conditions or health issues, such as allergies, diabetes, or celiac disease)?
- Who is paying the expenses? Most people are more cost-conscious if they are paying out of their own pocket rather than on a company expense account.
- Will meeting attendees bring guests or children to the event?
- Are networking opportunities important?
- How far are attendees willing to travel to attend the meeting?
- Will international guests who require interpreters attend?
- Are special accommodations needed for people with disabilities?
- What are the educational outcomes expected at the meeting?

Some of this information can be answered by questions on the event registration form. Other information can be obtained through association membership or company records. Most meeting/event professionals do some type of evaluation after an event to provide feedback that can be used to improve the next meeting. This is covered later in this chapter.

In the assessment of the event process, the event professional should also outline the event **stakeholders**. A stakeholder is one who has a stake in an enterprise. Typical event stakeholders are the producing organization of the event, decision-makers, sponsors, exhibitors (if the event has exhibitors), organization membership (if the event is for an association or other membership organization), beneficiaries (if the event is to promote a cause or is a benefit event), and various types of participants such as attendees, speakers, presenters, volunteers, and performers. Some event professionals prioritize these stakeholders and their needs through the planning process.

SETTING GOALS AND OBJECTIVES

DETERMINING THE MEETING AND EVENT GOAL(S)

The first thing a meeting/event professional needs to determine is (1) who is the group and (2) what is the objective of this event? These simple questions are the basis of much of the planning process.

A meeting *goal* defines the purpose of the MEEC gathering and provides a clear direction for the organization. It simply clarifies "why the organization exists and why the event is happening."

An *objective* is defined as something strived for or to be accomplished. All meetings and events should begin with clear, concise, and measurable objectives. Objectives are the basis for virtually all components of the planning process, regardless of the type of event to be managed, for example, corporate meetings, association meetings, special events, exhibitions (formerly referred to as tradeshows), or virtual meetings held via the Internet. The objective of the meeting will impact site selection, food and beverage (F&B) requirements, transportation issues, communication channels, and especially program content.

Most people attend meetings for three reasons: education, networking, and to conduct business. Some people participate in association **annual meetings** for the networking and educational offerings. Others may attend primarily to develop business relationships and to generate leads or make sales. If the meeting/event professional does not design the program content and scheduling to accommodate these objectives, then the attendees may become dissatisfied.

Another key point is that program planning, especially for association meetings, begins months or years before the actual event. The average meeting attendee does not understand how much effort goes into planning even simple events, let alone something as complex as an association's annual meeting and tradeshow/exhibition. As with much of the hospitality industry, the real work goes on behind the scenes, and unless something goes wrong, the attendees are blissfully unaware of the planning process and the coordination and cooperation necessary to produce an event.

Good meeting objectives should focus on the attendees. What will make the attendees want to attend the meeting? What will be their **return on investment (ROI)**? What makes the event more desirable than that of a competitor? The following are some of the key meeting planning components that are directly affected by the meeting objectives.

Developing *SMART* Objectives

Once the meeting/event professional has determined the needs of the attendees and the sponsoring organization, objectives must be written in a clear and concise format so that all parties involved in the planning process understand and are focused on common goals. A common method of writing effective meeting objectives is to use the **SMART** approach. Each letter of the SMART approach reminds the meeting/event professional of critical components of a well-written objective.

After the meeting/event goals have been determined, for each goal develop one or many SMART objectives necessary to determine whether the goal has been accomplished.

EXAMPLE GOAL: IMPROVE EVENT ATTENDEE REGISTRATION PROFITS

So, how would a meeting/event professional do that? They could increase attendee registration revenue, decrease attendee-related expenses, or both. Let's write one of the SMART objectives that would determine whether the goal was accomplished and focus on revenue.

Specific: Only one major concept is covered per objective. For example, instead of stating *make the event more profitable,* state *generate more event revenue.*

Measurable: Must be able to quantify or measure that objectives have or have not been achieved. For example, instead of stating *generate more revenue*, state *generate 100% more revenue.*

Achievable: Is it possible to accomplish the objective? So, instead of stating *generate 100% more revenue,* state *generate 30% more revenue.*

Relevant: Is the objective a relevant way to determine whether the goal is accomplished? For example, instead of stating *generate 30% more revenue,* state *generate 30% more revenue from attendee registrations.*

Time-related: The objective should include when the objective must be completed or be time-bound. So, instead of stating *generate 30% more revenue from attendee registrations,* state *generate 30% more revenue than last year from attendee registrations in the 6 months that registration is open.*

It is also good to begin meeting objectives with an action verb (e.g., *achieve, promote, understand, design*) and include cost factors if applicable. In addition, for each objective make sure to identify the person or department responsible for achieving the objectives. Designing well-written meeting objectives is a very important activity for the meeting/event professional. Objectives serve as signals to keep the planning process focused and on track. At the end of the meeting, the meeting/event professional can communicate to management what objectives were achieved or exceeded or what was not achieved and why. Incentives or individual or team performance review(s) may focus on whether or not these objectives were met or exceeded. If objectives are met, it helps demonstrate the ROI that the meeting/event professional provides to the organization. If objectives are not met, then management can focus on new ways to achieve the outcome for the next meeting.

MEETING GOAL: INCREASE REVENUE FOR THE ANNUAL MEETING

SMART Objective: The Meetings Department of the International Association of Real Estate Agents will "generate attendance of 7,500 people at the 2021 annual meeting to be held in Orlando, Florida, USA."

MEETING GOAL: HOST SUCCESSFUL SALES TRAINING EVENT

SMART Objective: The Brettco Pharmaceutical Corporation will "execute a two-day 2021 sales training conference for 12 regional sales managers to launch five new products where total meeting costs do not exceed $15,000."

Site Selection

The site selection process can begin after meeting objectives are developed. The meeting goals and objectives will guide the meeting/event professional in deciding the physical location for the event, type of facility to use, transportation options, and many other meeting components. Depending on the type of meeting, site selection may take place days, weeks, months, or years before the actual event. For major conventions, a city is usually selected 3 to 10 years in advance. Some large associations, such as the American Library Association, have determined meeting sites (cities) decades into the future. However, small corporate meetings usually have a much shorter lead time of a few weeks or months.

The association meeting professional is usually not the final decision-maker when it comes to which city will be selected to host a convention. Typically, determining the actual site selection is a group decision made by a volunteer committee, with much input from the board of directors and the association staff. The meeting professional will review numerous reference materials, talk with other meeting/event professionals, and may make recommendations but usually does not personally make the final decision. The corporate meeting/event professional may have more influence over site selection, especially for smaller meetings. But, for larger corporate meetings, the CEO or chairman of the board may make the decision. Sometimes, locations are chosen because of the availability of recreational activities like golf, shopping, or spa, not because the meeting facilities are outstanding. It differs with each organization.

Large travel expos such as IMEX in Frankfurt, Germany, or IMEX America held in Las Vegas, Nevada, are also great opportunities for meeting/event professionals to gather information about possible locations for their meetings and events. They employ a "hosted buyer" strategy where the exhibitors pay for the travel expenses of the meeting/event professionals (buyers) in return for guaranteed appointments (see Chapter 5, "Exhibitions," for more information on IMEX and the hosted buyer concept).

Other factors to consider in site selection are the rotation of locations and the location of the majority of the attendees. In the United States, the meeting/event professional may want to "rotate" their conventions and hold a major convention in the East (Boston) the first year, the South (New Orleans) the next year, the West (San Francisco) the third year, and the Midwest (Chicago) the fourth year. This allows attendees to enjoy a wide variety of meeting locations, and attendees who live on one side of the country are not always traveling many hours and through several time zones to attend the meeting. But if most of the attendees live on the East Coast, it may be preferable to hold the meeting in a city conveniently located there. However, some conventions, such as the National Association of Broadcasters, MAGIC Marketplace, International Builder's Show, or the Consumer Electronics Show, are so large that they are extremely limited to their choice of cities due to the amount of sleeping rooms, meeting, and exhibition space required.

Cost is another consideration. In addition to the costs incurred by the meeting/event professional for meeting space and other essentials, the cost to the attendee should be considered. Some cities, mostly first-tier cities, are notoriously expensive for people to visit (the average daily rate [ADR] in New York City is over $250 per night plus tax). It all depends on what is important to the attendees—cost or location. Another option is to hold a meeting in a first-tier city at a first-class property in the off-season or during slow periods, such as around major holidays. Most hotels discount prices when business is slow. As witnessed by the global economic downturn that began in 2008, most hotels had to reduce their rates to attract a shrinking volume of MEEC gatherings. As economies and the willingness to spend money on travel continue to improve, rates for many services have continued, and will continue, to rise.

The mode of travel is another factor in site selection. How will the attendees get to the location? Air? Road? Rail? In recent years, most major airline carriers have been struggling to survive, resulting in a number of mergers and acquisitions in the industry. Many people are still cautious about flying due to terrorism threats, the ordeal of getting through security at airports, packed airplanes, additional baggage fees, food charges, government-imposed travel restrictions, and a host of other challenges that make air travel distasteful. The availability of flights (**air lift**) can also be an important consideration in site selection. Cities with the greatest number of flights include Chicago, Atlanta, Dallas, and New York. Some cities that are convention destinations (have a convention center) and have no air lift include Anchorage, Alaska; Huntington, West Virginia; Davenport, Iowa; and Wheeling, West Virginia.

The type of hotel or meeting facility is another major consideration. There are a variety of choices, including metropolitan hotels, suburban hotels, airport hotels, resort hotels, and casino hotels. In addition, there are facilities especially designed to hold meetings called "conference centers." The International Association of Conference Centers is an association in which the member facilities must meet a list of over 30 criteria to be considered an approved conference center. Visit their website for more information. Other options are full-service convention centers, cruise ships, and university campuses. These facilities are discussed at length in Chapter 4.

Meeting space requirements are also critical in the site selection process. How many meeting or banquet rooms will be needed? How much space will staff offices, registration, and pre-function areas require? Floor plans with room dimensions are readily available in the facilities' sales brochures or on their websites. Good diagrams will also provide ceiling heights, seating capacities, entrances and exits, and location of columns and other obstructions. Most major hotel chain websites will provide direct links to their hotels and their specification information.

Once the meeting objectives are clearly defined and the basic location and logistics are drafted, the meeting professional creates a **Request for Proposal (RFP)**. The RFP is a written description of all the major needs for the meeting.

The Events Industry Council (EIC), a federation of over 30 MEEC industry associations, has created a standardized format that may be used. It is copyright-free. It is important to note that an RFP can be used for the selection of other suppliers for providing services such as audiovisual arrangement, transportation, special event venues, registration contractor, and virtual event platforms.

After the completion of the RFP, it is disseminated to hotel properties and convention facilities that may be interested in submitting a bid for that meeting. Typically, the meeting/event professional can submit the RFP via the Internet directly to preferred hotels and the Destination Marketing Organization (DMO) or Convention and Visitor Bureaus (CVBs) of desirable cities for distribution to all properties or can submit it to the DI website. Planners can also opt to send their RFP to national hotel chains, such as Marriott or Hyatt, directly. The RFP also serves to allow hotels to examine the potential economic impact of the meeting and decide whether or not to create a bid for it. DI offers members an economic impact calculator. If the group has limited resources and can only afford an $89 room rate, then major luxury hotels may not be interested in the business. However, smaller properties or hotels in second-tier cities may be very interested in hosting the event. If a meeting facility decides to submit a proposal, then the sales department will review the meeting specifications and create a response.

NEW COVID-19 CONSIDERATIONS TO ADD TO RFP:

- Cancellation and Termination (Act of God, Force Majeure) Clause requirements
- Commitment to adhering to federal/state/local health and sanitation mandates or guidelines from government, health organizations, or industry best practices/standards
- Request an outline of current facility upgrades and operational procedures undertaken to ensure maximum health and safety of event attendees—describe what the guest experience will be and how it is affected based on these procedures

Once the meeting/event professional has reviewed the proposals and conducted any necessary site visits (in-person or through virtual site visit methods), then the negotiations between the meeting/event professional and the sales department at a facility can begin. This process can be quite complex, and careful records of all communications, concessions, and financial expectations should be well documented.

> Freeman used drones and their PLATOUR Application to do this virtual site tour of the Omni Dallas. Here is the link: https://www.youtube.com/watch?v=FHS0oy2Vpb4

Familiarization or FAM trips are another method of promoting a destination or particular facility to a meeting/event professional. Fam trips are a no-cost or low-cost trip for the meeting/event professional to personally review sites for their suitability for a meeting/event. These trips may be arranged by the local DMO or CVB or by the hotel directly. During the fam trip, the hotel or convention facility tries to impress the meeting/event professional by showcasing its property, amenities, services, and overall quality. Throughout the visit, the meeting/event professional should visit all F&B outlets, visit recreational areas, see a variety of sleeping rooms, check all meeting spaces, monitor the efficiency of the front desk and other personnel, note the cleanliness and overall appearance of the facility, and if possible meet with key hotel personnel. A seasoned meeting/event professional always has a long list of questions to ask. A lot goes into the selection of hotel.

EVENT BUDGETING

Budgetary issues are usually the next major consideration in planning a meeting/event. How much will it cost to produce the event? Who will pay? How much will attendees be charged for registration, if anything? What types of F&B events are planned, and what will be served? Will meals be provided free or at an additional cost to the attendee? What additional revenue streams are available to produce and promote the meeting? Are sponsorships possible? If the event is being held for the first time, the meeting/event professional will have to do a lot of estimation of expenses and potential revenues. An event that is repeated benefits by having some historical data to compare and project costs. The basis for a meeting budget can be developed by establishing financial goals, identifying expenses, and identifying revenue sources.

ESTABLISH FINANCIAL GOALS

Financial goals are important and should be easily measurable. They may be set by the meeting/event professional, association management, or by corporate mandate. Basically, what are the financial expectations of the event? Not every meeting/event is planned for profit. For example, an awards ceremony held by a company to honor top achievers represents a cost to the company. Similarly, a corporate sales meeting may not have a profit motive. The ultimate goal of the meeting may be to determine how to increase business and thus "profit," but the meeting itself is not a profit generator; it is an expense for the company. On the other hand, most association meetings rely heavily on conventions to produce operating revenue for the association (see Chapter 2 for more details). For most associations, the annual meeting (and often the accompanying tradeshow) is the second highest revenue producer after membership dues. The financial goal for an annual meeting may be based on increases or decreases in membership, general economic trends, political climate, competing events, location of the event, and many other influences. For any event, there are three possible financial goals:

- *Break-even:* Revenues collected from all activities cover the expenses. No profit is expected.
- *Make profit:* Revenues collected exceed expenses.
- *Deficit:* Expenses exceed revenues.

IDENTIFY EXPENSES AND REVENUE SOURCES

It is suggested that expenses be categorized by their different functions:

- *Fixed costs* are expenses incurred regardless of the number of attendees, such as meeting room rental or audiovisual equipment.
- *Variable costs* are those expenses that can vary based on the number of attendees (e.g., F&B).
- *Indirect costs* should be listed as overhead or administrative line items in a program budget. These are expenses of the organization not directly related to the meeting, such as staff salaries, overhead, or equipment repair.

Expenses will vary according to the overall objectives of the meeting and will be impacted by location, season, type of facility, services selected, and other factors. For example, a gallon of Starbucks coffee in San Francisco at a luxury hotel may cost $90 or more. A gallon of coffee at a moderate-priced hotel in Oklahoma City may only cost $25 or less. There are many areas of expense to host a meeting to include:

- Meeting space
- Food and beverage
- Audiovisual
- Shuttle service
- Production
- Speakers
- Internet
- Temporary staff
- Staff travel   General Service Contractor (exhibitions)
- Volunteers
- Décor/Rentals
- Signage
- Security
- Insurance
- Licenses and Permits
- Marketing
- Registration System/Services
- Event Tech/Apps/Virtual Platforms

There are many ways to fund meetings and events. Corporations include meeting costs in their operating budgets. The corporate meeting/event professional must work within the constraints of what is budgeted. Associations usually have to be a bit more creative in finding capital to plan and execute an event. Associations must justify the cost of the meeting with the expected ROI of the attendee. It can be quite expensive to attend some association meetings. Consider a hypothetical example of one person attending an association annual meeting: transportation ($500), accommodations for three nights ($700), F&B ($300), registration fee ($500), and miscellaneous ($200), for a total of $2,200. Depending on the city and association, this amount could easily double. It is a complex process to create an exceptional and affordable event. If the registration fee is too high, people will not attend. If it is too low, the organization may not achieve revenue expectations. But there are more possible sources of funding available other than registration fees. These include the following:

- Corporate or association funding
- Private funding from individuals

- Exhibitor fees (if incorporating a tradeshow/exhibition)
- Sponsorships
- Selling logo merchandise
- Advertising fees, such as banners or ads in the convention program
- Local, state, or national government assistance
- Selling banner ads or links on the official website or on social media platforms
- Renting membership contact lists for marketing purposes
- Establishing "official partnerships" with other companies to promote their products for a fee or percentage of their revenues
- Contributions in cash or in-kind (services or products)

Estimating expenses and revenues can be accomplished by first calculating a break-even analysis. The simple way of doing this is to determine the total all of your expenses (e.g., $300,000) and then recognizing you will need at least that same amount (e.g., $300,000) in revenue to have a break-even—$0—no profit or loss.

However, a meeting/event professional is not often asked to consider break-even so simply. Instead, leadership will often ask: How many attendees do we need to break-even, or what do we need our registration fee to be in order to break-even?

A couple of simple formulas help us to answer these more specific questions:

How many attendees do we need to break-even?

For this, you need to know total fixed costs, variable costs per attendee, and an idea of what the attendee registration fee will be.

Total Fixed Costs / (Registration Fee – Per-Attendee Variable Costs)

What do we need our registration fee to be in order to break-even?

If instead you are trying to determine what you should charge for attendee registration, you need to know total fixed costs, variable costs per attendee, and an estimation of how many attendees will come to the event.

(Total Fixed Costs/Estimated Number of Attendees) + Per-Attendee Variable Costs

PROGRAM PLANNING

Once the basic objectives of the meeting have been identified, the site selected, and the budget set, the meeting program can be developed in detail. Some major concerns involved in this process are: Is the programming to be designed in a way that facilitates communication between departments within a corporation? Is the programming geared toward training new employees in the use of a particular computer system? Is the programming geared to educate the members of a professional association and lead toward a certification? To address these concerns, the meeting/event professional must consider several factors, including the following:

- Program type
- Content, including track and level
- Session scheduling
- Speaker arrangements
- Refreshment breaks and meal functions
- Ancillary events
- Evaluation procedures

Putting together a good meeting program requires the meeting professional to select appropriate program types, understand the content appropriate and interesting to attendees, and scheduling the different formats into a master agenda.

PROGRAM TYPES

Each type of program or session is designed for a specific purpose, which may range from providing information to all attendees, discussion of current events in small groups, hands-on training, and panel discussions. The following are typical descriptions of the major program types and formats.

A **general or plenary session** is primarily used as a platform to communicate with all conference attendees at one time in one location. Typically, the general session is what kicks off the meeting and includes welcoming remarks from management or association leadership; outlines the purpose or objectives of the meeting; introduces prominent officials; and recognizes major sponsors or others who helped plan the event, ceremonial duties, and other important matters of general interest. General sessions can last between 1 and 1.5 hours.

Often, an important industry leader or a recognizable personality will give a **keynote address** that will help set the tone for the rest of the meeting. For a corporate meeting, this may be the CEO or the chairman of the board. An association may elect to hire a professional speaker in a particular subject area, such as business forecasting, political analysis, leadership and change, technology, or a topic that would be motivational to the audience. Many meeting/event professionals use highly recognizable political, sports, and entertainment personalities. At a recent association convention, the famous former basketball player Magic Johnson was the keynote speaker. Other associations have hired former presidents as keynote speakers. These individuals are hired not because of their personal knowledge of the association and the various professions it represents but as a "hook" to attract people to come to the meeting. As a note, it is not uncommon to spend $75,000 to $100,000 or more (plus travel expenses) to hire a well-known sports or entertainment figure to speak at a general session. General sessions may also be held at the end of a convention to provide closure and summarize what was accomplished during the meeting or as a venue for presenting awards and recognizing sponsors. Attendance at closing general sessions is typically smaller than with opening sessions as people make travel plans to return home early.

A **concurrent session** or breakout session is a professional development or career enhancement session presented by a credentialed speaker who provides education on a specific topic in a conference-style format. Alternately, several speakers may form a panel to provide a variety of viewpoints on the topic at hand. Group discussions at individual tables may also be incorporated. They typically last between 30 and 90 minutes.

Workshops are more intimate sessions that offer a more interactive learning experience in smaller groups. Participants may learn about the latest trends, challenges, and technologies of a specific field. These sessions are often presented by experienced members or peers of the association and may involve lectures, role-playing, simulation, problem-solving, or group work. Workshop sessions usually serve groups of 150 or fewer attendees. These are the mainstay of any convention, and dozens or even hundreds of workshops may be offered throughout the course of the event, depending on the size of the meeting. A large association, such as the American Library Association, has more than 1,000 workshop sessions at its annual convention. Workshops typically last from 50 minutes to an hour.

Small team works on a project

Roundtables and discussion groups are small, interactive sessions designed to cover specific topics of interest. Basically, 8 to 12 attendees convene around a large round table, and a facilitator guides discussion about the topic at hand. Typically, several roundtable discussions will take place in one location, such as a large meeting room or ballroom. Attendees are free to join or leave a particular discussion group as desired. Roundtables can also be useful for continued and more intimate conversation with workshop speakers. The role of the facilitator is to keep the discussion on track and not allow any one attendee to monopolize the conversation. Roundtable discussion groups may also employ a **subject-matter expert** to inform and moderate the group.

Poster sessions are another more intimate presentation method often used in academic or medical conferences. Rather than utilizing a variety of meeting rooms to accommodate speakers, panels or display boards are provided for presenters to display charts, photographs, a synopsis of their research, and so on for viewing. The presenter is scheduled to be at their display board at an appointed time so that interested attendees may visit informally and discuss the presentation.

General or Plenary Session	High-level broad, motivational topics; shorter session
Concurrent or Breakout Session	Ankle-deep, more information, mid-high-level topics; shorter session
Workshop	Deep-dive, hands-on, very specific; longer session
Roundtables	Collaborative, peer-to-peer learning of application of a specific topic
Poster Sessions	Very deep dive into a specific topic and the research performed/outcomes related to the topic

Types of sessions

PROGRAM CONTENT

The average attendee will only be able to sit through three to six sessions on any given day. It is critical that the attendee be as well-informed as possible about what each session will offer and the appropriateness of the session to their objectives for attending the meeting. For association meetings, programming objectives are developed months in advance and used extensively in marketing the convention to potential attendees. Program content is not a "one-size-fits-all" proposition. The content must be specifically designed to match the needs of the audience. A presentation on "Basic Accounting 101" might be good for a junior manager but totally inappropriate for the chief financial officer. A good way to communicate to attendees how to select which programs to attend is to create tracks and levels. **Track** refers to classifying programs under specific topics, such as computer skills, professional development, marketing, personal growth, legal issues, certification courses, or financial issues. A variety of workshops can be developed that concentrate on these specific areas. **Levels** refer to the skill level—beginning, intermediate, or advanced—the program is designed for. Thus, the speaker who is assigned a session can develop content specifically tailored for a particular audience. Attendees can also determine if a session meets their level of expertise. Most programs offer multiple tracks and levels of content.

The following is an example of typical description of a session.

Workshop 14: Effective Marketing through Social Media and
E-Mail Marketing:
Frank Wise, PhD
3:30 p.m. to 4:45 p.m. (1530–1645)
Room 314

With over 132 billion e-mail messages sent daily and billions of users on thousands of social media platforms, how can your company develop an effective marketing strategy to capitalize on these technologies? What are the most effective options to do so?

Attend this session to:

- Discover the top 10 steps in developing effective electronic media marketing messages.
- Discuss a variety of delivery platforms.
- Enhance your own effectiveness with social media.

Track: Marketing

Level: Intermediate

SESSION SCHEDULING

The meeting/event professional must orchestrate every minute of every day to ensure that the meeting runs smoothly and punctually. Each day's agenda should be an exciting variety of activities that will stimulate attendees and make them want to attend the next meeting. One of the biggest mistakes meeting/event professionals make is double-booking events over the same time period. If a meeting/event professional schedules workshops from 8:00 a.m. to 1:00 p.m. and the tee time for the celebrity golf match at 12:30 p.m., then they stand to lose any of the attendees who want to attend the golfing event. Tradeshows/exhibitions are another challenge. If workshops are scheduled at the same time that the tradeshow floor is open, attendees must choose between the two options. If attendees choose to attend the education sessions, the exhibitors will not get the traffic they expect. Conversely, if attendees go to the tradeshow rather than attend sessions, there may be empty meeting rooms and frustrated speakers.

Another major issue is allowing enough time for people to do what comes naturally. Do not expect to move 5,000 people from a general session into breakout sessions on the other side of the convention center in 10 minutes. Plan thoughtfully. Allow sufficient time for people to use the restroom; check their e-mail, text messages, or voicemail; say "hello" to an old friend; and comfortably walk to their next workshop. If these delays are not planned for in advance, then there may be attendees disrupting workshop sessions by coming in late—or worse—by skipping sessions.

Some recent trends in scheduling include: micro-sessions, time for self-care, incorporating outdoor activities, CSR projects, and so on.

The following is a description of the schedule for an association meeting.

EXAMPLE OF AN ASSOCIATION MEETING SCHEDULE

While no two conventions are the same, the following timeline provides a good idea of a typical meetings flow.

Day 1
8:00 a.m. Staff office and pressroom area setup
    Exhibition setup begins
    Preconvention meeting with facility staff
    Registration setup

Day 2
8:00 a.m. Association board meeting
    Registration opens
    Staff office opens
    Exhibition setup continues
    Set up for preconvention workshops
1:00–4:00 p.m. Preconvention workshops (with break)
    Various committee meetings
    Program planning committee finalizes
        duties for meeting

5:00 p.m. Private reception for board members and VIPs
7:00–9:30 p.m. Opening reception

Day 3
6:30 a.m. Staff meeting
8:00 a.m. Registration opens
    Coffee service begins
9:00 a.m. General session
10:30 a.m. Break
10:45 a.m. Concurrent workshops
12:00 p.m. Registration closes
12:00–1:30 p.m. Lunch
1:30–3:00 p.m. Exhibition open
3:00–4:30 p.m. Closing session
    Pack up staff office
    Pressroom closed
5:00 p.m. Post-conference Meetings

LOGISTICAL CONSIDERATIONS

REGISTRATION

To attend most conventions or exhibitions, some type of registration is typically required. Even weddings require an R.S.V.P. Registration is the process of gathering all pertinent information and fees necessary for an individual to attend the meeting. It is much more than merely collecting money. Registration data are a valuable asset to any association or organization that is sponsoring an event. Registration begins several weeks or even months prior to the event and usually lasts right up to the final day. Discounts are often provided to attendees who register in advance. They are offered an **early-bird rate** incentive to pay fees early. The association can then use that money to pay deposits or bills coming due. By registering early, the meeting/event professional can determine if registration numbers are at anticipated levels. Also, this income allows for a positive **cash flow** so that advance deposits and expenses can be paid. If not, it can increase marketing or negotiate with the hotel or meeting facilities about lowering expectations and financial commitments that may have been promised.

Data collected on the registration form may include name, title, occupation, address, e-mail, phone, fax, membership category, desired workshop sessions, social functions, optional events, method of payment, special medical or dietary needs, and a liability waiver. A recent addition has been to ask attendees where they are staying while at the convention and their length of stay so that the impact of the meeting can be determined. Some organizations inquire about the size of the company, number of employees, or financial responsibility of the attendee (such as whether they make or recommend purchase decisions). These registration data can be used before, during, and after the meeting.

Prior to the meeting, the data can be given or sold to exhibitors or advertisers so that they can promote their company, products, and services before the actual event. It may also be used to market to potential attendees who have not committed to attending. Advertising "we have 7,500 qualified buyers attending this year's convention" may entice more companies to register or exhibit. Preregistration data can also help the meeting/event professional monitor interest in special events or particular workshops that may be popular. If a particular workshop is getting a lot of interest, then the meeting/event professional can move it to a larger room or increase seating.

During the meeting, registration data can be used as a promotional tool for the press to gain media attention for the organization, sponsors, and exhibitors. It can also help the local DMO in justifying the costs of marketing and soliciting groups to come to their city. Hard facts, such as using 3,000 rooms and 200,000 square feet of meeting space, are music to the ears of hospitality companies. For the attendees, technology now allows them to automatically access via smartphone or computer who is at a particular meeting and save the list for future use.

After the meeting, registration data can be used to update association membership records and solicit new members or can be sold to interested parties. Most important, the data can be used to help the meeting/event professional with logistics and to promote the next meeting. A close study of registration data gives the organization a better view of who is attending its meeting and if there are any trends apparent in key areas such as attendees' gender, age, education, or their organizational position and title.

REGISTRATION FEES

There may be a wide range of pricing structures for a single meeting. For association meetings, members typically receive a discount on the cost of registration. This helps encourage people to become members of the association. But not all members will pay the same price. For example, in 2018, the Professional Convention Management Association (PCMA) charged professional members (meeting/event professionals) $1,095; suppliers (hotel salespeople, CVBs), $1,295; university faculty, $525; and student members, $275. These are the early-bird preregistration prices available until about six weeks prior to the convention. After the **cutoff date** for preregistration, all prices increased by $50 to $100. Additional fees of $200 were added if the registrant did not stay in the room block at a host hotel. All attendees, regardless of how much they pay, receive the same opportunities for education and networking and are invited to the scheduled meals, breaks, and receptions. However, additional activities, such as golf, tours, or special entertainment functions, may incur a separate cost.

For some events like the Exhibitor Show, an annual tradeshow for people in the exhibition industry, registration fees are priced based on what the attendee wants to attend. Entrance to the tradeshow is free, but education sessions may cost $295 or more per workshop. Additional events, such as dinners and receptions, may be purchased separately. All-inclusive registrations at the Exhibitor Show are also an option with full registration and attendance to all education programs costing well over $1,500. Allowing attendees to select event activities a la carte has the benefit of a custom schedule and attendee price point based on the attendee's needs and budget. However, it may mean lost revenue to the event and an attendee who is not able to add/adjust their event activities onsite, missing out.

Associations usually offer substantial registration discounts to their members. The "nonmember" rate to attend may well exceed the difference between the cost of membership and the member rate, making it desirable to join the association. This is a clever way for associations to increase their membership base and provides an opportunity to promote other products and services to the new members. Registration fees are often waived for members of the press, speakers, and local dignitaries. Complimentary registrations must be monitored closely because there may be costs involved if the meeting has F&B or if other events are available.

Corporate events for internal stakeholders/attendees do not typically have a registration cost for the attendee. However, there are some exceptions. Many companies, like Do It Best (hardware stores) or McDonalds, invite their franchise store owners to attend training and recognition events. In these instances, the franchisee is expected to pay a registration fee and cover the expenses of their travel to engage.

HOUSING

Not all meetings require housing (overnight arrangements) for attendees, exhibitors, sponsors, suppliers, speakers, or staff. But if housing is needed, there are basically four methods of handling housing for attendees:

1. Attendees arrange for their own room. Lists of hotels may be provided, but the meeting owner makes no prior arrangements regarding price negotiations or availability.
2. A group rate is negotiated by the meeting/event professional at one or more properties, and attendees respond directly to the reservations department of their choice.
3. The meeting host handles all housing, and attendees book rooms through them. Then the meeting host provides the hotel with a **rooming list** of confirmed guests.

4. A third-party **housing bureau** (outsourced company) handles all arrangements either for a fee or is paid by the DMO. The meeting owner will pay the third-party to manage the entire process.

Having attendees make their own hotel reservations is the easiest method. It totally removes that responsibility from the meeting/event professional and the contract liability from the meeting organization. However, the hotel facility is going to base its pricing to host the event on the total revenues it anticipates from the group. Sleeping rooms represent the largest amount of potential revenue and profits for the hotel. If rooms are not blocked (set aside for the group), it is most likely that a premium will be charged to the organization for renting meeting space and other services (such as food and beverage, audio-visual equipment, etc.). The room block is a key negotiation tool for the meeting/event professional.

The last three options require that the meeting/event professional establish a rate for the attendees. The room rate will reflect prior negotiations with the sales department in which the total value of the meeting to the facility is considered. A certain number of rooms will be reserved, called a "block," and rooms are subtracted from this inventory as attendees request them. This can be a gamble for the meeting/event professional. As with F&B events, the meeting/event professional must estimate how many people will be attending. If the meeting/event professional blocks 100 rooms and only 75 rooms are used by the group, then they may be held responsible for part, if not all, of the cost of those unused rooms. The difference between rooms blocked and rooms "picked up" (actually used) is called **attrition** (for more information on attrition, see Chapter 10).

A serious challenge to meeting/event professionals these days is attendees booking rooms outside the block. That is, the attendee opts to bypass the hotels for which the meeting/event professional negotiated special pricing and find other accommodations or even less expensive accommodations within the host hotels. If the host hotel charges $199 per day and a smaller and less luxurious hotel down the street is charging $99, a certain percentage of the attendees will book the alternative property for the lower price. Sometimes, by calling the hotel directly or by using a discount hotel broker on the Internet, attendees can get better prices in the same hotel for less than what the meeting/event professional negotiated. If large numbers of attendees do this, then the meeting/event professional is going to get stuck paying for a lot of unused rooms. One method of reducing this potentially expensive problem is to establish review dates in the hotel contract, whereby the meeting/event professional can reduce (or increase) the **room block** by a certain percentage at a certain time. Other methods include incentives and penalties to attendees based on whether they booked their room in the block. Incentives could include drawings for room discounts, VIP experiences, access to speakers, or discounts on the next year's event. Penalties, which can be difficult to enforce, could require an attendee to pay a higher registration fee if they are not booking a room in the block. This would need to be verified for delayed credit card charges and needs very clear policies stated and accepted in registration materials. The closer to the actual meeting dates, the less likely the hotel will allow a reduction in room block. The hotel must have time to try to sell any unused rooms and recoup any losses. A hotel room is a perishable commodity if it is not sold each day; the potential revenue is lost forever.

Having attendees call or reserve rooms online directly with the hotel is a good option. The attendees should benefit by the negotiated room rate, and the hotel handles the reservation processing directly. The meeting/event professional will need minimal involvement. For larger meetings where multiple properties are used, it is advisable to provide a range of hotel prices to accommodate the budgets of all the attendees.

REGISTRATION AND HOUSING COMPANIES

Several companies have evolved that specialize in handling both conference registration and housing. Examples include companies such as ConferenceDirect and Experient.

Outsourcing the housing process to a third-party vendor or DMO is most prevalent with medium and large meetings. Some groups, such as the National Association of Broadcasters or Consumer Electronics Show, are so large that they require most of the hotel rooms in the host city. Housing for a so-called *citywide* meeting is best left to professionals who have the most current technology and are well-equipped to handle thousands of housing requests. The housing bureau may charge a fee per transaction. This cost may be paid by the sponsoring organization, or, in some cases, the local DMO will absorb some or all of the costs. Indeed, many DMOs and even hotels operate their own housing bureaus as a service to meeting/event professionals. Third parties may manage or assist with registration components. The scope of their services can range from only using their registration platform, to managing all preregistration, to being onsite to supervise and assist with the registration process.

Handling attendee reservations in-house is possible, but it is easiest with small groups. If the event is a small, high-profile event, the meeting/event professional can have attendees reserve rooms with the organization, and a **rooming list** will be created to give to the hotel. The rooming list should include type of room, ADA requests, smoking or nonsmoking, arrival and departure dates, names of additional guests in the room, and special requests. Handling reservations in-house can be quite time-consuming and may require additional staffing. Alternatively, a housing bureau can be of great assistance.

REFRESHMENT BREAKS AND MEAL FUNCTIONS

As with scheduling workshops, it is important to provide time for attendees to eat and relax throughout the day. F&B functions should be thoughtfully planned, as they are important yet expensive. However, it may be more productive to feed attendees than have them wandering around a convention center or leaving the property to find something to eat. Refreshment breaks provide the opportunity to catch up with old friends, make new business contacts, network, and grab a quick bite or reenergize with a cup of coffee or tea. Breaks and meals are excellent sponsorship opportunities and companies gain attendee recognition. Additional information on Food and Beverage can be found in Chapter 9.

SPEAKER ARRANGEMENTS

For large conventions, it is almost impossible for the meeting/event professional to independently arrange for all the different sessions and speakers. The meeting department often works together with the education department to develop the educational content of the meeting. In addition, a program committee comprising industry leaders and those with special interests in education will volunteer to assist the meeting/event professional. These volunteers will work diligently to arrange what topics are appropriate for sessions and who the likely speakers might be. It is the job of the committee to be the gatekeeper of educational content. Subcommittees may be created to focus on finding a general session speaker, workshops, concurrent sessions, student member events, and so on.

Most associations cannot afford to pay all of the speakers at a large convention and use volunteer speakers. A moderate-sized convention of 2,500 people may have 100 or more sessions offered at a three-day event. Remuneration for speakers may range from providing no assistance at all to paying a speaker fee and all expenses, such as the case with a paid general-session speaker.

BENEFITS OF USING VOLUNTEER SPEAKERS

- Reduces expenses (the person may already have budgeted to attend the meeting, so no housing or transportation costs are required)
- They are knowledgeable about important industry topics
- Popular industry leaders may increase attendance at sessions
- Builds relationships between speaker and event sponsor

CHALLENGES OF USING VOLUNTEER SPEAKERS

- May not adequately prepare for presentation
- May not be a good presenter, even if they are knowledgeable about topic
- May have a personal agenda; may use the session to promote self or company

A more expensive but often more reliable source of speakers is to contact a *professional speaker* from a speaker bureau. A **speaker bureau** is a professional talent broker who can help find the perfect speaker to match your event objectives and your budget. Typically, a speaker bureau has a stable of qualified professionals who can talk on whatever topic you desire. Fees and other amenities range from the affordable to the outrageous. If you are a small Midwestern association of county clerks, you are not going to be able to afford a world-

© Rawpixel.com/Shutterstock.com

Keynote speakers can be paid or volunteer, but all should be under a contract

MEETINGS, EXPOSITIONS, EVENTS, AND CONVENTIONS

famous athlete as your keynote speaker at your annual meeting. However, you might be able to afford a gold medal Olympian from the 1990s who can talk about teamwork and determination for a bargain price of $4,000.

Providing popular, highly paid, and sought-after speakers will most likely increase attendance at your meeting. The smart way to provide such talent is to have the costs of the speaker sponsored by a key exhibitor or leader in the industry. The general session is a high-profile event, and it may be cost-effective for a company to fund the keynote speaker to promote itself to a maximum number of attendees. For example, a $30,000 speaker for a group of 5,000 attendees is only $6 per attendee. That may be less expensive than designing and distributing a traditional mailing!

Another source for speakers is local dignitaries, industry leaders, and university professors. As they are local, you will not incur transportation and lodging costs. In addition, their services are often free or very affordable. The local DMO or university can assist you in finding people who are willing to assist you. A small gift or honorarium is customary to thank these individuals for their time and effort.

Speaker guidelines should be developed to inform the speakers (paid and nonpaid) of the logistics required to speak at an event as well as to clearly define the expectations of the organization. Speaker guidelines vary from one group to the next, but most should include the following:

- Background information about the association
- Date and location of meeting
- Special events or activities the speaker may attend
- Date, time, and location of speaker's room for presentation
- Presentation topic and duration
- Demographics and estimated number of attendees for the session
- Room set and audiovisual equipment requests and availability
- Request for short biography
- Names of other speakers, if applicable
- Remuneration policy
- Dress code
- Location of **speaker-ready room**, where the speaker can practice or relax prior to speaking
- Instructions for preparing abstracts or submitting final papers (typically for academic conferences)
- Instructions for having handouts available

- Transportation and lodging information
- Maps and diagrams of hotel or facility
- Deadlines for all materials that must be returned
- Hints for speaking to the group (i.e., attendees are very informal; attendees like time for questions and answers at the end of session)

It is not uncommon to include a variety of contractual agreements that must be signed by the speaker. These include:

A **presenter contract** is a written agreement between the presenter and the sponsor to provide a presentation on a specific topic at a specific time. A contract should be used regardless of whether the speaker will be paid or not. The contract will verify, in writing, expenses that will be covered, the relationship between the two parties, promotional material needed to advertise the session, deadlines for audiovisual and handout materials, disclosure statements pertaining to any potential conflict of interest, selling or promoting products or services, penalties for failure to perform the presentation, and allowable conditions for termination of the contract.

If the session will be recorded in any digital format and made available on a website or online video platform, the speaker must be informed and must sign a *recording, Internet authorization and/or waiver.* Some speakers do not want their presentation materials to be accessed on the Internet, where their content may be easily copied and used by others. Selling digital recordings of programs is an additional revenue stream for associations. Since attendees are limited in the number of sessions they can attend each day, by purchasing recordings of missed sessions, they can have the information from the sessions they missed.

AUDIOVISUAL EQUIPMENT

Most hotels and meeting facilities do not allow meeting/event professionals to provide their own audiovisual equipment, such as LCD projectors, television monitors, and media players. The rental and servicing of this equipment is a significant revenue stream for facilities. Audiovisual equipment is extremely expensive to rent. In many instances, it costs as much to rent the equipment as it does to buy it. A 40-inch television, which may be purchased at a discount store for $350, may cost the meeting/event professional that amount in rental fees *each day*!

Thus, controlling audiovisual costs is very important. The event professional may wish to inform speakers that only an LCD projector and laptop computer are available. Thus, the speaker can craft their presentation to the media available. Another good idea is to provide speakers with a template to use in preparing overheads and handouts. You can request that all slides and handouts be developed with a certain font, such as Arial or Times New Roman, and dictate the text and background colors that should be used. Also provide a crisp logo for the organization or event. This will provide some uniformity in the "look" of your meeting. In addition, some organization may implement strict deadlines for content review and approval.

To reduce expenses and conserve resources, most groups have opted to put all handouts on an event app, cloud service (dropbox), or flash drive and make it available free or for a nominal charge. Likewise, some groups will post all the handouts on their company website rather than distribute it at the meeting. Others will provide "print on demand" stations for those attendees who desire hardcopy. If handouts will be used, remember to request a master copy well in advance of the meeting.

MARKETING AND PROMOTION
(adapted from *Planning and Management of MEEC* by Fenich)

Plan an event and people will come. Right? Not necessarily. The costliest mistake in event management is not having an audience. No amount of lavish decoration, fine food, effective room design, engaging speakers, energetic entertainment, flawless audiovisual, or elaborate staging will compensate for an event that few attend. Despite all efforts to coordinate and manage a well-run event, if the intended audience does not attend or if the attendance numbers are too low, the event will not be deemed a success. It is impossible to underestimate the importance of event marketing and event communications.

Marketing is much more than just communication. The use of marketing principles goes all the way back to the creation of a new event, identification of the audience (**target market**) for the event, and determination of how the event will be positioned to serve that audience's needs. From there, the marketing mix, or 4Ps of marketing, further develops our event design and strategy through Product, Price, Place, and Promotion. We address the first three with questions specific to the meeting/event industry:

Product
- What does the target market want from the event? What need is met?
- What event features meet those needs?
- What does the event look like? How will it be experienced?
- What should the look/feel be?
- How is it different from competitors?

Price
- What is the value of the event to the attendee?
- Is the attendee price-sensitive?
- What discounts should be offered?
- How will the price compare with competitors?
- What price generates a profit?

Place
- Where/when will the event be? Is that good for attendees?
- How and when will potential attendees register?

For the final P, Promotion, this is where the communication plan comes together. It outlines when, where, and how the event will be communicated out to potential attendees. The promotional mix is the blend of communication channels that will be used to share event information. Meeting/event professionals often do not have enough human or financial resources to promote their event through every channel. So, decisions must be made as to which are the best channels to use to reach the target market for event attendees, exhibitors, or sponsors. Lots of options exist, and some may even be blended; these include:

The promotional mix as applied to events

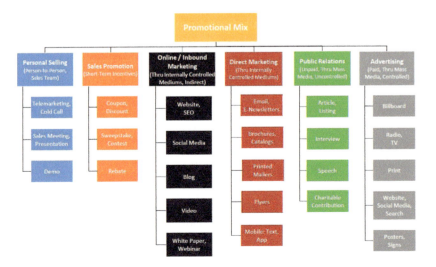

Some events and meetings have minimal promotional channels used. For example, a corporate sales meeting, where employee attendance is mandatory, might only require an email notification. Social events, such as a wedding, birthday party, or an anniversary, may only need printed or emailed invitations. Events that depend on attendee registration, exhibitor engagement, and sponsorship dollars require more extensive promotion in order to guarantee an audience.

In some organizations, event marketing efforts might be handled by an entire team of event professionals. They might also hire contractors who specialize in marketing, public relations, and promotional campaigns. In contrast, there are some organizations where an event professional has the sole responsibility for all event marketing efforts. In either case, it makes sense for the event professional to be involved in all of the marketing activities and efforts to ensure that the event objectives are clearly represented and that there is a consistency in the meeting/event look, design, and theme concepts.

TYPES OF PROMOTION FOR EVENTS

PERSONAL SELLING

Personal selling includes three main promotional channels: phone calls (telemarketing or cold calling), presentations, and demos. These channels are most commonly executed by the sales professionals within the team supporting a meeting/event. They are most commonly used to convince exhibitors or sponsors (groups with larger costs related to their event participation) to engage in the event in some or many ways.

SALES PROMOTIONS

All sales promotion channels are focused on highlighting a special deal, rate, or game to excite and incentivize attendees to register. These channels are often combined with other channels. For example, an event might offer a discount code through their social media event page to engage their followers and draw new social media followers, while getting them to register for the event.

ONLINE/INBOUND MARKETING

The content delivered through online/inbound marketing channels are completely controlled by the organization hosting the event. However, the reader/

viewer is coming to this content by their own choice. These channels might include the organization or event: website, social media accounts, blog, or YouTube channel. Some associations even have digital magazines and resources for their members that could include event promotional content. These channels are considered "inbound" because the potential attendee or viewer chooses to come to the website, social media page, or channel on their own seeking information. They do so because they enjoy engaging with the organization for entertainment or information purposes already. While they are visiting, it is a perfect opportunity to promote/highlight an upcoming event that the organization is hosting. Quality content that is not overly selling in nature is crucial for success in these channels.

DIRECT MARKETING

Unlike inbound marketing where the reader comes to you, in direct marketing you are pushing information straight to the reader. The content of the communication is controlled completely by the organization and delivered directly to the target market (potential attendees) through a variety of channels, such as email, e-newsletters, brochures or catalogs, printed mailers, digital or printed flyers, and mobile communications via text or an app. In this area, printed materials (e.g., save the dates, invitations, reminders) can be very expensive to produce and mail. With smaller groups or VIPs, however, the impact of a hardcopy piece or package can go a long way to creating excitement around an event. Digital options are less expensive and easier to reach a wide audience, but in order to cut through the overwhelming number of email and digital communications the content should be short, exciting, customized, and drive the target audience to the website for more information. The frequency of digital communication is critical. If they are sent too often, readers will stop engaging and may even opt out of receiving future communication. Opt-out options, by law, must be included in these communications. These laws differ across countries and should be explored to ensure adherence.

PUBLIC RELATIONS

Public relations is defined as the effective management of relationships and communications in order to influence behaviors and achieve objectives. As it relates to the meetings/events industry, public relations can be defined as the "presentation of an event via the media or other outlets, stressing the benefits and desirability of such event" (CIC, 2011). All events involve public relations strategies, some at a smaller scale and others at a bigger scale.

Meeting/event professionals have to consider multiple public relations strategies to address media engagement before, during, and after the event. This is discussed in much more detail in the next chapter. In addition, there are different groups of media that need to be considered. While most meetings/events have topic-based industry or trade media to communicate with, many also need to consider the engagement of local, state, and event national major news media if the content of the meeting/event is of importance to any public groups.

When pursuing public relations as a function of the promotional mix, it is critical to remember that the meeting/event professional does not control the way the media reports on the meeting/event. They are responsible for providing members of the media with the event information, highlighting newsworthy content, and access to spokespeople to try to deliver the desired message, but the media controls the final communication to their audiences. While public relations is an unpaid promotional effort, there can still be costs associated to the organization that the meeting/event professional should include in the event budget. These costs include items such as a dedicated staff person, hiring a PR consultant or firm, development of media materials, and support of media engagement onsite at the event.

ADVERTISING

An advertisement is a public notice. In most cases, advertising refers to paid forms of commercial advertisements (also called "ads"). The most common forms of commercial advertising are print media ads, such as newspapers and magazines; broadcast media ads, such as television and radio commercials; and online media, such as ads on websites and on search engines and ads on social networking sites and web video commercials. Commercial advertising may also take many other forms from billboards, to mobile-phone screens, bus stop benches, aerial banners and balloons, human wearing signs (called human billboards), bus and subway train signs, and much more.

Because advertising can be expensive, event professionals want to target their advertising dollars to the people most likely to attend the event. Ads might be placed in relevant trade magazines, journals, or publications in order to provide exposure not only for the event but also for the organization. For example, if an event was targeted to an audience of event professionals, a few professional trade journals where the event might be advertised are: *Convene, Successful Meetings or Meetings and Conventions Magazine.* If the event had a target audience of bankers, the event might be advertised in the American Bankers' Association publication, *ABA Banking Journal.*

Some media outlets will offer trade-out advertising in exchange for a service that the event organization can provide. For example, an event manager for a large exhibition might trade exhibit space to a publishing company in exchange for an advertisement in their publication. A radio or television station might be willing to become an event sponsor to give them marketing exposure at the event in exchange for free advertisements on their radio or television station.

COVID-19

The coronavirus has had many effects on the planning and producing of MEEC events. Most events scheduled to occur in 2020 and early 2021 were either cancelled or postponed. A significant number of events were changed to be "virtual" or "hybrid," and many events in the future are already being planned in a hybrid format in case a last-minute switch is necessary. New pricing models and registration fees are being examined and analyzed. Planning has thus become much more complex. While many in the industry are hoping for a quick return to the pre-COVID "normal," the industry has already gone on record to say that they foresee hybrid events becoming the new normal.

SUMMARY AND BEST PRACTICES

Planning a meeting/event is a long process that often requires input from many people or committees. Setting event goals and clearly defined objectives is the first essential step in creating effective program content and managing logistics. The objectives will impact site or city selection, type of facility used, and the services required. The meeting/event professional must also understand the motivations of the attendees: Why should they attend? Is attendance voluntary or mandated by management? Planning a corporate event can be a very different process compared to planning involved in conducting an association event. Education has replaced recreation as the driving force for most meetings.

Once the objectives are clear, a needs analysis should be conducted to further guide the meeting/event professional in selecting appropriate meeting space, speakers, and amenities that are expected from the attendees. The demographics of attendees must also be considered. Meetings and conventions represent enormous economic potential for cities. In the site selection process, the RFP is the announcement of what is required by the meeting/event professional. DMOs and individual hotels must evaluate the potential of the meeting and respond accordingly. Interested properties may invite the meeting/event professional for a fam trip to visit the property.

Education and networking are the most important elements for most meetings. However, people like to be entertained as well as educated, so the meeting/event professional must attend to all the needs of the attendees and provide both. The format of the education sessions and the setup of the meeting space should be appropriate to the objectives of the meeting. Program content should be designed with both a track and level that will target the majority of the attendees. Housing and registration are important components in implementing the plan for a meeting/event. Both paid and voluntary speakers can be utilized—each has positives and negatives. Care must be taken to ensure that speakers are adequately prepared to address the group and are contractually obligated to perform. Finally, ancillary activities like shopping trips, tours, childcare, and other services that enhance an attendees' meeting experience should be planned thoughtfully so as not to interfere with the scheduled programming.

Because of the complexity of the meeting planning process, this chapter can only highlight some of the planning activities involved. There are two books that provide more detail on the planning and production aspects of MEEC. They are *Planning and Management of Meetings, Expositions, Events and Conventions* and *Production and Logistics in Meetings, Expositions, Events and Conventions*, both by Fenich.

CASE STUDY USING 'VIRTUAL' TECHNOLOGY TO ENHANCE A MEETING

(Produced by G.G. Fenich and Students from East Carolina University)

The Governance Institute is a member organization serving health care system directors, executives, and physicians. This organization offers annual conferences that provide valuable tools that greatly benefit their members. Members are encouraged to attend, and in the past years these conferences have been a success. This year's conference will take place at the Mountain View Resort and Spa located in Boulder, Colorado. Amy Foote, who is the head meeting planner for The Governance Institute is experiencing a major decline in attendance for this year's conference. With this challenge Amy and her team of event planners must come up with new ways to market the event and increase attendance.

With the conference only being 2 months away, Amy decided her team needed to come up with a solution to this problem and increase attendance. The team researched many options and scenarios. With so many new technologies, Amy questions if a virtual component tied into the onsite event could replicate the conference experience. With this in mind, Amy and her team developed a virtual conference that will be held during the Boulder conference. This would be the first virtual conference Amy has ever planned, and she wants it to be a success. The virtual conference would stream live presentations from all keynote speakers through webcasts and offer online networking with other virtual attendees. There would also be panel discussions featuring question and answer sessions with speakers and virtual booths from participating sponsors.

A major concern Amy has is how to market this event. She does not want to take away attendance from the actual event. Amy decides only to offer it to members who had declined in advance, and they would not start marketing this event until after most members had registered and booked their travel arrangements. They started to promote the virtual conference 2 weeks before the live conference took place. Email invitations were sent out that accompanied an online registration. These emails included introduction to the virtual conference concept, program of the online sessions, descriptions of the interactive forms, and a link to the website.

With all the planning and research, it is finally time to go live with the conference. On the day of the event Amy and her team monitored online activity through laptops at the Boulder conference. Her virtual team welcomed attendees, announced session schedules, answered questions, and provided feedback while moderating chat sessions. After reviewing surveys and feedback from attendees, the virtual conference was considered a success. It nearly doubled the total attendance with 300 virtual attendees who attended the online conference and 600 prospects registered to attend. Amy and her team will continue to implement virtual conference options when planning future conferences.

1. What do you think of the job Amy did?
2. What else could she have done?
3. What could she have done better?
4. Was it fair to attendees who arranged for and paid to attend in person NOT to be given the opportunity to participate virtually?

KEYWORDS AND TERMS

For definitions, see https://insights.eventscouncil.org/Industry-glossary

annual meeting	housing bureau	room block
attrition	keynote address	rooming list
cash flow	level	SMART
concurrent sessions	needs analysis	speaker bureau
cutoff date	plenary session	speaker-ready room
early-bird rate	Request for Proposal	stakeholder
fam trip	(RFP)	track
general session	return on investment	
group history	(ROI)	

REVIEW AND DISCUSSION QUESTIONS

1. What is the difference between a meeting goal and a SMART objective?

2. What is the purpose of using program formats, levels, and tracks in designing effective meeting programming?

3. What are the benefits and challenges of using volunteer speakers compared to paid speakers?

4. What are the benefits and limitations of outsourcing components of a meeting, such as housing or registration?

5. How can meeting/event professionals use registration data before, during, and after a convention?

6. How does preregistration assist the meeting/event professional in planning a meeting?

7. Describe the four different methods of housing.

8. Think of a MEEC event you have attended. Who was the target audience? What marketing strategies did the organizer utilize?

ABOUT THE CHAPTER CONTRIBUTORS

Amanda Cecil, PhD, is a professor in the Department of Tourism, Event, and Sport Management at Indiana University (IUPUI). Her teaching and research focuses on event tourism and business travel.

Erica Shonkwiler, MBA, is a lecturer in the Department of Tourism, Event, and Sport Management at Indiana University (IUPUI). Her teaching and scholarship focuses on event design and management.

PRODUCING MEETINGS AND EVENTS

© vlaru/Shutterstock.com

ERECTING TRADE SHOW BOOTHS IS A MAJOR COMPONENT OF THE MEEC INDUSTRY

CHAPTER OBJECTIVES

- Discuss the basic requirements of producing an on-site meeting or event.
- Outline strategies and considerations for managing the on-site team.
- Discuss the various considerations and specifics that go into on-site communications.
- Cover the specific considerations to keep in mind when planning and executing public relations when producing an event.
- Articulate the reasons and important elements of preconvention meetings.
- Specify the elements needed for a successful postconvention review.

Producing meetings and events is part of the sequential process of planning and producing. "Producing" or production and logistics is often thought of as what happens "on-site." In large convention hotels, planning is accomplished by the sales team, whereas production is accomplished by convention services. These are two completely different departments with completely different teams.

ON-SITE MANAGEMENT

There are various areas that must be carefully managed on-site for every event. These include registration, housing, food and beverage, speakers and entertainers, audiovisuals, and **ancillary** events. Managing each area requires a skillful approach to ensure the logistics are flawless, costs are contained, and strategic goals and outcomes are being achieved. The following explains each key area.

REGISTRATION AND HOUSING

Like the front desk of a hotel, the registration area is the first experience an attendee has with a meeting, convention, or exhibition. A slow or inefficient registration process can set the tone for the entire meeting. The registration area should be heavily staffed the first day and should remain open throughout the event. If international guests are expected, registration materials may need to be translated, and interpreters may be necessary to facilitate a smooth check-in. If an exhibition is involved, having a separate area for exhibitor registration is a good idea.

Registration is one of the areas often outsourced by the meeting/event professional, especially for large events. It is a complex process that requires much training on the part of the registration attendants. Some hotels or convention centers have arrangements with temporary agencies that provide staff that do registration on a regular basis. Some registration management companies handle housing as well.

The registration area should be well designed, and attendees should not have long waits to check in or ask a question. Electronic kiosks are increasingly being utilized to make registration more efficient. If a significant problem with one's registration or an entire group's registration is identified, a full-time staff

© drserg/Shutterstock.com

member should be available to meet with the individual or representative of the group. It is advisable to create a private meeting room or hospitality area near the registration area for this purpose.

Additionally, questions and concerns about housing should be addressed at the registration area. If someone there cannot assist, then registration staff should direct attendees to the appropriate resource to solve housing concerns. If the attendee or guest has concerns about accommodation or a concern with the service at the hotel property, he/she should be directed to the key contact at the hotel. If it is not resolved, the meeting planner or third-party representative should intervene.

It is important to note that final registration and housing reports should be requested prior to leaving the event location. These reports include critical information needed for future negotiations with hotels, venues, and suppliers. Additionally, these reports should be discussed at all strategic follow-up meetings.

FOOD AND BEVERAGE

At this point, all food and beverage orders, room location and design, food providers are determined and permits purchased. Most facilities will send a **banquet event order (BEO)** for each individual function, in which food and beverage will be provided. This document outlines food and beverage quantities, timing, and logistical specifics, staffing needs, and service type. Once on-site, the planner should meet with the catering manager or CSM to review each BEO and ensure that anything that is incorrect or needs to be updated is addressed.

One important consideration that must be finalized is the **guarantee** for each event. This is the contracted number of meals or items that the organization will pay for, regardless of attendance. Planners may be required to submit the guarantee between 48 hours and 2 weeks before the event, depending on the size of the group and the complexity of the menu. This process can dramatically affect the budget if the event professional overorders and can be a source of embarrassment to the host if not enough food and/or beverage is provided. Knowing their event history and projected attendance is imperative to correctly make the guarantee.

Other areas to follow through with on-site include ensuring all vendors and the organization have the proper permits and licenses to operate, evaluating the space prior to the event to confirm appropriate room set-ups, discussing service expectations with the banquet or food and beverage (F&B) captain, and reviewing all policies and procedures for food safety and liability issues, especially if serving alcohol. Chapter 9 goes into detail on food and beverage logistical details and considerations.

FUNCTION ROOM LAYOUTS

A consideration when selecting a venue for an event is how the room will be arranged. Specific factors influence the room layout, such as the number of people, type of meeting, attendee learning styles, audiovisual and technology needs, speaker tables, refreshment tables, and physical room attributes and/or obstacles. The traditional layouts include auditorium/theater, banquet, reception, classroom, cocktail, boardroom, hollow square, exhibit, conference, and U-shape. Most venues can give planners a rendering of how each room can be arranged using each layout (Figure 14-1).

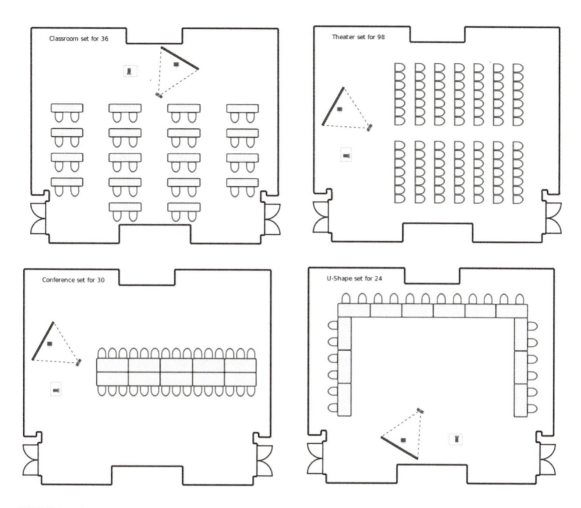

FIGURE 14-1 Traditional venue layouts

AUDITORIUM OR THEATER STYLE

Probably the most common seating arrangement in meetings is an auditorium or theater design. An **auditorium-style** room setup is particularly useful when there is no need for attendees to interact with one another during the course of the session. This format is used to maximize the number of seats in a room. In this instance, chairs are arranged in rows facing the same direction. Most commonly, those rows will face the head of the room, which may be designated by a stage, head table, lectern, or screen. A speaker or panel will generally run the meeting, often lecturing to attendees, who may be taking notes on the basis of the information the speaker is conveying.

Classroom Style

Sometimes, meetings may require tables for attendees to use for completing tests, taking notes, using their electronic devices, or interacting with other attendees to solve presented problems. **Classroom style** is the most common setup used for these types of meetings. In classroom meeting setups, chairs are arranged in a similar manner as in an auditorium but with tables provided for each row of chairs. These tables are generally six or eight feet long and 18 inches deep. If the design is intended for attendees to be sitting on each side of the table, then 30-inch-deep tables (or two 18-inch tables placed back to back) are used to allow sufficient space. In this room setup, the tables are draped, with pads of paper and pencils/pens at each place setting.

Like auditorium room sets, classrooms may be modified as needed. Sometimes, classrooms are arranged diagonally toward the head table, or even perpendicular to the front of the room. Perpendicular room sets are challenging because it often necessitates a significant number of attendees to have their backs toward the speaker at the front of the room. If the purpose of the session is to work with table partners, this may not be problematic, but a perpendicular classroom setup is seldom wise when attendees need to be focused on the individual on stage.

Rounds

Round tables are sometimes used for meetings but utilized most often for food functions. In smaller breakout sessions, or those meetings requiring a lot of interaction between attendees, round tables facilitate and encourage communication. All the individuals at the table can easily see their table companions and are seated sufficiently close to one another to allow collaboration.

Many meeting venues use six-foot rounds (i.e., 72 inches in diameter) or, less often, five-foot rounds (i.e., 60 inches in diameter). The size of the rounds is important because the diameter dictates how many individuals can fit comfortably. Five-foot rounds can accommodate six to eight individuals, whereas six-foot rounds may seat eight to ten.

In the previous image, six-foot rounds were used to seat eight guests each. An alternative to full rounds is the **crescent round**. Crescent rounds may use full-sized round tables but will not have seats all the way around the table. This is designed so that no one is seated with their backs to the head table and everyone at the table would have a clear view of the speaker.

A variation on rounds that serves the same function is a sunburst setup. In a sunburst, rectangle tables can be used or a combination of rectangles and rounds to create a more diverse look of the total space, while still supporting interaction at tables. The use of the rectangles creates the feel of attendees gathering around the dinner table at home and can foster a more intimate and trendy feeling (Figure 14-2).

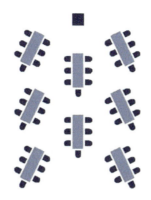

FIGURE 14-2 Additional seating layouts
Sunburst for 56

Nontraditional Room Setup

With the changes in expectations from attendees and meeting planners to create interactive meeting spaces, multiple new concepts have resulted in creative room layouts. New designs include creating hubs for small groups to be connected. Casual layouts with soft seating like couches and buffets served at action stations are just the beginning of the future of meetings. Meeting/event professionals should also consider the diversity of attendee learning styles when determining the room setup. Blended setups are often being used to allow attendees to choose the comforts and seating that best fit their needs— for example, countertop level tables where attendees can stand while taking notes or use stools set up at the back of the room to help those that need to move, stand, or struggle to sit still for long periods. Then there are traditional rounds or classroom-style tables set in the middle of the room for those that prefer traditional style seating. Lastly, at the front of the room, soft couches, benches, bean bags, and/or coffee tables for those that desire more comfortable options. In this example, one meeting room for an educational session provides options to accommodate multiple learning types and physical needs of attendees while imparting a unique and engaging look to the room. Many of these unique setups require special furniture to be rented, which is available at additional cost from many venue vendors. Therefore, a venue's setup can be laid out according to the unique vision of the event planner or client.

COMMON ISSUES FACED ON-SITE

Regardless of where an event is held, there are some issues that all events have in common. Many of these issues are based on logistics, such as transporting delegates from the airport. The following list includes issues that are common to most, if not all, meetings.

OBSTACLES

Perhaps a planner's greatest challenge is to overcome the obstacles in the way of the delegates' ability to be successful as a result of the meeting. The facility can present many obstacles that a planner will need to overcome. An example of such an obstacle would be an understaffed or undersized registration desk. Another would be inadequate parking space for the delegates who drive. Yet another would be a noise ordinance that prohibits loading out between the hours of 10:00 p.m. and 6:00 a.m. Physical obstacles are not limited to disability considerations. There are also questions of how the delegates will get from their rooms to the gala dinner in their formal gowns if it is raining and whether the buses transporting guests to the off-site venue can get to the actual door of the venue.

POWER

Most outdoor special events and many events in smaller indoor venues have power requirements that exceed the power available. A generator usually provides this power, and generators are expensive. Properly anticipating the power needs is even more important in this type of event than one in a traditional meeting venue. With a generator, the planner will pay not only the daily cost to rent the generator but a fuel charge as well. The fuel consumption is determined by two factors: how long the generator runs and how much power is actually drawn from it. The fuel cost will be a multiple of the cost per gallon of the fuel, the time the generator runs, and the power consumption. The planner has control over two of the three elements in this equation.

For any meeting or special event using video or name entertainment, more than a few trade show booths or large scenic units will have special power requirements. Power is expensive. The power to run the sound system can be more expensive than the rental of the equipment. Many convention centers offer a discount if the power is requested early. The technical vendors can calculate power requirements fairly easily. If the discount for requesting power early is 30%, which is a fairly common discount, it would make sense to order 10% to 15% more power than estimated. In this way, ample power is available for less than it would have cost to place the power order after all the detailed requirements had been calculated.

Power charges are not based on consumption but rather on the maximum amount of power deliverable at any one time. To meter the actual power consumption and charge accordingly is illegal in many states. This would make the facility a utility company and subject to rate regulations. Generator use is charged based not on power consumption but on fuel consumption. A generator that is idling uses fuel even if it is supplying no power. Turning a generator off when it is not needed will save money.

Event professionals involved in events around the globe must be very conscious of local differences. The base voltage may vary: 110 volts in North America versus 220 volts in much of the rest of the world. The style of electrical outlet and corresponding plugs vary widely with more than 10 different configurations.

RIGGING

Plaster ceilings are a production rigger's worst nightmare. Precast concrete roofs with no steel underneath run a close second. Any event involving more than a few hundred people or video image magnification should involve lighting suspended from the ceiling. Unless the facility is unusually well equipped for lighting from ceiling positions, lighting must be accomplished by hanging

© TZIDO SUN/Shutterstock.com

Lighting Rigging

trusses, and hanging trusses involves rigging. Theaters are generally adequately equipped for lighting without hanging trusses, but not necessarily hotels.

The hotel's contracted rigging company will require access to all floor plans not less than two weeks in advance of the event. While two weeks' lead time on a floor plan should be simple for an event contracted a year in advance, generating an accurate floor plan turns out to be a challenge many planners cannot accommodate. In some jurisdictions, the fire marshal, building code inspector, or safety officer can refuse to allow a show to be hung without a detailed hanging plan. Having to cancel a show at the last minute for failing to submit paperwork can be a career-ending mistake.

Most facilities contract rigging to an outside company for liability protection. This is in addition to the normal reasons one would outsource any task that the facility management may not have enough experience to properly supervise. Given that the rigger's normal job description involves hanging "live loads" over the heads of the general public, they take their work seriously. This is intended to keep people safe and is not meant to impede the event. Adequate advance notification of schedules and requirements can help ensure that the event venue is hung properly and on schedule.

Floors

It is not safe to assume that just because the building has a ground level loading door big enough to drive a tractor-trailer through, once it fits through the door, the floor will support it. Even though the floor may be made of four inches of steel-reinforced concrete on the ground, the utility boxes in the floor may not be so well designed. One Orlando area facility dug up and re-poured the concrete around several floor pockets because the constant forklift traffic drove them into the ground. It is also not safe to assume that a certain size scissor lift can be brought into the ballroom. For events where these issues are relevant, as part of the site inspection, the planner must ask about the floor load because the information is rarely readily available.

Ballrooms are carpeted, and many hotels insist that plastic sheeting be placed over the ballroom carpet during the move-in and move-out process. If the facility has such a requirement, it is important that the Event Services Contractor (**ESC**) and all technical vendors know about it in advance. The requirement to cover the floor with "Polytack" or one of several similar products is becoming more common. Failure to submit a proper floor plan to the people who apply the floor covering or failure to properly schedule the installation can result in expensive delays.

Many academic theaters have polished wood floors on the stages. Nailing or screwing into them is not recommended and is generally a fast way to be refused the use of the venue in the future. These floors are not designed for heavy loads such as scissor lifts or forklifts. Staffing and equipment requirements may need to be adjusted to compensate.

ACCESS

It is not only the delegates who must be able to find the venue and its entrance, but also the technical support and catering people who need to gain access. The design of the loading access can have a significant impact on an event's finances. There is a facility in South Florida where the only loading access to the ballroom is to back a truck along a sea wall for a hundred yards. A 21-foot truck will not make the corner; a 17-foot truck will. The closest a tractor-trailer can park is a quarter mile away. For an event here, technical support equipment shipped on a tractor-trailer would need to be unloaded off-site and the equipment trucked into the loading dock using a smaller truck at considerable additional expense. There is another facility on Florida's west coast where the loading access to the ballrooms is via an open-sided elevator with no top attached at the outside of the building. In this part of Florida, it rains almost every afternoon in the summer. A load scheduled for 4:00 p.m. in July is almost guaranteed to have a problem.

The presence of truck height docks is not enough to guarantee smooth loading. Some facilities, including the WDW Dolphin and the Gaylord Palms, have elevators from the docks to the ballroom. Access to the theater at the Orange County Convention Center involves two elevators and a push down the hall between them. The number and location of the docks is significant. The Morial Convention Center in New Orleans is all on one level, with loading docks lining one entire side of the building.

For even more "common issues" in producing meetings and events, there is an entire book in this series called *Production and Logistics in Meeting, Expositions, Events, and Conventions* by Fenich.

SPEAKERS AND ENTERTAINERS

For a large meeting with multiple speakers and entertainers, keeping track of who is where and what is going on is a monumental task. Recruiting volunteers or hiring temporary staff to assist will make a big difference. The worst thing that can happen is to have a speaker fail to show up for the meeting without the event professional realizing it. Likewise, most speakers and entertainers expect some sort of recognition for their time and effort. They may have specialized needs and contractual expectations to be addressed on-site. This is especially true of musicians.

The planner, facility manager, and speaker/entertainer must work together once everyone is on-site for a rehearsal. At this time, the speaker or entertainer should practice his or her presentation on the stage (or in the room) with audiovisual, lighting, music, etc. Adjustments to the session should be made if appropriate. This is the time for all questions to be answered by the speaker or entertainer or support personnel.

A new trend is to preselect sessions or activities with speakers and entertainers of interest so that attendees come better prepared for a large event. Social media such as Facebook, Twitter, LinkedIn, Pinterest, Google+, Tumblr, and blogs can be utilized months in advance for people to begin discussions on a topic. The speaker may facilitate discussion and will design the actual presentation on the basis of what has transpired online. Similarly, some speakers will use this intelligence to assess the attendees' level of knowledge of the group. After the session, attendees can be reassessed, and the amount of learning that occurred may be measured.

ON-SITE AUDIOVISUAL

Managing the technology needs and design of a program on-site requires a well-planned approach. Meeting planners are no longer looking for only flip charts and projectors but sophisticated technology options, including plasma screens, digital signage, LCD projectors, and intelligent lighting.

A critical piece in planning for and managing the audiovisual needs of the event is selecting a key supplier. The AV provider may or may not be in-house. Some planners opt to travel with their own preferred AV supplier, who is familiar with the event and the organization. The purpose of the partnership is for the supplier to assist the organization in communicating a message(s). Selection of equipment is not the focus; achieving your meeting goals and outcomes is the focus. Sound, lighting, staging, and other equipment needs should be discussed in that context.

During the planning process, key individuals will assemble a **production schedule**. This will provide an overview of the production of each function starting at the installation of equipment to the dismantling of the stage or room setup. This timeline serves as a detailed, step-by-step plan for all parties to follow on-site. It is customary for a production or technical director to be assigned to an event to oversee all technical aspects of the meeting and lead the team of skilled professionals. It is his/her responsibility to ensure the objectives are met, safety and security standards are followed, and the program runs smoothly.

Chapter 11 goes into additional detail on event technology and on-site management.

ANCILLARY EVENTS

There are a variety of activities that may be incorporated before, during, and after the actual scheduled program. Many event sponsors and/or exhibitors offer corporate hospitality offers to event attendees that could include golf outings, exclusive dinners, or tickets to sports or cultural events in the area. Additionally, in today's hectic business environment, many people try to squeeze a short vacation into their meeting schedule. We are increasingly seeing husbands, wives, significant others, and children attending meetings as guests. Some meeting attendees tack on a few extra days at the beginning or end of the scheduled meeting to spend some quality time with their family and friends. Likewise, while the meeting attendee is attending workshops and trade shows, the guests want something to keep them occupied. Tours, shopping excursions, cultural events, sport events, dinners, museums, festivals, and theatrical shows are all popular diversions. Every city, no matter how small, has something of interest to explore. The key is not to let these ancillary activities interfere with your overall program objectives. **Ancillary activities** should not be more attractive than the program. Ancillary activities must be provided, and it is important that they are appropriate to the age, gender, and interests of the guests.

If possible, limit participation in planning ancillary activities for two reasons: additional effort and liability issues. As a meeting/event professional, you need to concentrate on what is going on in the meeting facility. You do not want to worry about whether the bus to the mall is on time. If possible, outsource the management of ancillary activities to a local **Destination Management Company (DMC)**. A DMC is a company that specializes in arranging activities and is an expert on the local area (see Chapter 7 on DMCs, for more information). Likewise, if something should happen and people are injured at an event that you arranged, you do not want to worry about liability issues. If childcare is offered by the sponsoring organization, for example, additional insurance may be needed to protect the organization from any liability issues. Childcare is definitely a service that must be outsourced to a professional childcare service. Special licensing is needed to ensure the safety and security of children.

The safest strategy is to provide a list of local activities and the website address of the DMO. Let the attendees plan their own activities. Be warned: When holding meetings in popular resort locations like Orlando or Las Vegas, the "attractions" available can quickly become "distractions" for the attendees. It is not uncommon to lose a few attendees in Las Vegas when the call of the slot machines is louder than an hour-long workshop on a dry topic.

MEETING AND EVENT SPECIFICATION GUIDE

One of the challenges in the meeting and events profession is that, historically, there were few standardized policies, procedures, and terminology. To begin a codification of definitions and standardized practices, an industrywide task force called the **APEX Initiative** was created. As mentioned in Chapter 1, APEX stands for Accepted Practices Exchange, and one of its first accomplishments was the development of accepted practices in regard to terminology. The committee found that many terms were used interchangeably to describe the document used by a meeting/event professional to communicate specific requirements for a function. Some of these terms included "catering event order," "meeting résumé," "event specifications guide," "staging guide operations manual," "production schedule," "room specs," "schedule of services," "working agenda," "specifications sheet," and "group résumé." After a considerable amount of effort and input from all types of meeting/event professionals, hotel convention service managers (CSMs), DMCs, exhibit managers, and DMOs, the panel created a format that greatly facilitated the communication between meeting/event professionals and the entities that service their meetings.

The panel developed the term **Event Specification Guide,** which is defined as "a comprehensive document that outlines the complete requirements and instructions for an event." This document is typically authored by the event/meeting professional and is shared with all appropriate vendors as a vehicle to communicate the expectations of services for a project. The industry-accepted practice is to use the APEX ESG, which can be found at the Events Industry Council website.

The ESG is a three-part document that includes the following:

1. **The Narrative:** general overview of the meeting or event
2. **Function Schedules:** timetable outlining all functions that compose the overall meeting or event
3. **Function Setup Orders:** specifications for each separate function that is part of the overall meeting or event. This is used by the facility to inform setup crews, technicians, catering and banquet staff, and all other staff regarding what is required for each event.

There is also a standardized timetable for communication between the meeting/event professional and the facility and service providers. Although these guidelines may differ depending on the size, timing, and complexity of the individual event, they do provide a useful general format.

The ESG contains quite a bit of detailed information. Both the meeting/event professional and the catering/convention services staff and key suppliers will need access to a copy. If any changes are made, they should be recorded in all copies. Fortunately, as technology and connectivity improve, this document will be easier to maintain and update. What was once a five-pound, three-ring binder full of paper forms has been reduced to an app on a mobile device. Changes to the ESG can be made easily and accessed by the appropriate people. What is certain for all meetings is that changes to the ESG are unavoidable. In fact, one of the chief responsibilities of a good meeting/event professional is to react and manage change—often unexpected change.

Size of Event	Submit ESG in Advance (weeks)	Receive Return from Facility and Vendors (weeks)
1–500	4	2
501–999	6	4
1000+	8	6

CONTROLLING COSTS

To stay within budget and reach the financial objectives, it is important to exercise cost control measures. Cost control measures are tools for monitoring the budget. A large event for thousands of people may be managed by only a few meeting planning staff. The opportunities for costly mistakes are rampant. The most important factor is to make sure that the facility understands which person from the sponsoring organization has the authority to make additions or changes to what has been ordered. Typically, the CEO and the meeting planning staff are the only ones who have this "**signing authority**." For example, an association board member may have an expensive dinner in the hotel restaurant and say "put it on the association's bill." The restaurant cannot do so without the approval of a person who has signing authority. This helps keep unexpected expenses to a minimum. A review of your expenses should be conducted on a daily basis and disputes addressed each day. Following the event, the invoices or cost projections should be discussed to avoid conflicts after leaving the event destination.

MANAGING THE ON-SITE TEAM

The organization will need to determine how to staff their meeting/event using full-time employees, temporary staff, and/or volunteers. All staff, regardless of the type, need to be trained, supervised, motivated, and evaluated. The size of the team will depend on the size and complexity of the event. Again, determining staffing types and service levels should be reflective of the meeting's goals and objectives. It is also important to ensure staffing needs are budgeted and appropriate resources allocated to ensure the team is ready on-site. An orientation for employees, temporary staff, and volunteers should take place on-site and/or virtually, followed by a tour of the meeting space and the opportunity to answer any questions of the team. Additionally, a handbook should be distributed to all team members that details information on the event, roles and responsibilities of the team, key contact list, answers to frequently asked questions, maps of the facilities, and additional important information.

EMPLOYEES

The planning team should carefully determine which organizational employees should travel to the event and how they will be utilized on-site. Full-time staff should serve as supervisors across a variety of areas to include registration, educational sessions, and the exhibition or trade show. These individuals are already trained on the needs of the attendees, the type of group and their needs, the culture of the organization, and the expectations set by the leadership of the group. They should serve as a source of information for temporary staff and volunteers, assist with training and supervision and serve as role models.

The organization will need to budget for the travel of employees. In most cases, air travel, ground transportation, hotel accommodations, and meals must be covered. The organization should have a clear travel policy in place and clearly communicate whether other expenses such as dry cleaning, phone or internet expenses, parking at the airport will be covered. Depending on the location of the event, these expenses can add up quickly, so the organization will need to conduct a cost-benefit analysis to determine which employees they will need on-site.

Notably, not all roles can simply be covered by a temporary employee or volunteer. The organization must remember that key on-site positions should be staffed with employees. These areas include overseeing registration, important high-profile functions, production of the general sessions, logistics of the exhibition, or food and beverage guarantees. These areas can affect the outcomes of the meeting and have significant budget implications.

TEMPORARY STAFF

Using temporary staff is a good alternative for roles that require specialized training (such as registration software, accounting, or security). Facilities may require that organizations use temporary staff for areas focused on safety and security. Medical and security personnel, if required, are typically local, hourly staff, or contractors that are familiar with the facility and local services (hospitals, medical clinics, etc.).

During an event, temporary staff will represent the organization to attendees, and guests may appear to be employees of the organization hosting the meeting. Therefore, it is imperative that they are trained on the service expectations of the group, briefed on the makeup and needs of the attendees, supervised by employees that share the goals and objectives of the meeting, advised on policies and procedures, and evaluated on their performance. The role of temporary staff members should be clearly defined to avoid conflicts in different scenarios. For instance, the contracted staff will need to know if they can issue a refund to an attendee (registration) or if they have the authority to remove an exhibitor for inappropriate behavior (security). Communication between temporary staff and key employees is vital to the success of the event.

The destination management organization (DMO) or facility can recommend staffing agencies that provide temporary employees. As mentioned previously, these workers should not replace employees in key roles but provide specialized service roles to support the operations of the event. Planners can contract with agencies or individuals to provide support and save money on travel expenses.

VOLUNTEERS

Most events rely heavily on volunteers. A volunteer is someone who is giving his/her time and expertise to assist with the operation of an event at no charge. Again, volunteers should not be used in roles that require specialized services (such as security) or replace employees in key roles at the meeting. However, they can be utilized in many ways, including greeting at main entry points of a facility, providing directions or destination/facility information to attendees, assisting in the registration area with distribution of badges or materials, or monitoring educational sessions.

It is important to note that volunteers still need to be trained, supervised, and evaluated. Like temporary employees, they will need to be informed on the history, goals, and objectives of the organization; given detailed profile information on attendees and guests; provided with clear role expectations; instructed on their level of authority; given a key contact for questions or to direct someone who needs further assistance, or even something as simple as directed on what to wear or the hours they are expected to work. Volunteers can be recruited from many sources, including: (a) members of the association or organization assisting for reduced registration rates or simply to "give back," (b) local professionals interested in assisting the specific event, (c) community members who are retired and interested in serving the destination, or even (d) college students looking for professional experience. The destination marketing organization (DMO) or local contacts can provide options for recruiting volunteers.

Volunteers are not paid an hourly wage, but there are expenses associated with volunteers. Planners will need to consider and communicate if they are providing uniforms, meals, reimbursement for parking, or other related expenses. There should be no confusion on what is provided and what is not provided for volunteers. Also, planners should communicate whether there is a minimum number of hours volunteers are expected to work. For instance, volunteers may be required to commit to two shifts of four hours each. This will help justify training and providing basic services to volunteers.

Another consideration is motivating volunteers. Organizations want to retain their volunteers for future events, so ensuring they have a meaningful experience is important. There should also be a recognition of the volunteers, either during or after the event, to show appreciation of their time and expertise. A simple certificate or small gift or thank-you after the event can go a long way. Some organizations host volunteer appreciation events and even designate a "volunteer of the year" award.

ON-SITE COMMUNICATIONS

PERSONAL COMMUNICATIONS

The event professional must bear in mind that they will always be involved in personal types of communication. Personal communication falls under two techniques, formal and informal. Although these techniques are self-explanatory, the event professional and their constituents must be aware of when and how to use each. Formal communication occurs in business settings, when interacting with officials and dignitaries, etc. Informal communication occurs within groups of peers in nonbusiness settings. It is critical that the correct technique be used in the setting where it is demanded (Figure 14-3).

Written	Verbal	Visual	Behavioral
Training manual	Briefings	Photographs	Videos
Memo	Meetings	Displays	Working practices
Letters	Radio conversations	Models	Role modeling
E-mail	One-to-one discussions	Demonstrations	Nonverbal communication
Handbooks	Instruction	Printed slogans	Social networking
Staff newsletters	Telephone conversations	Posters	
Reports	Training	Videos	
Information bulletins	Word-of-mouth messages	Internet	
Checklists			

FIGURE 14-3. Communication Strategies

Here are some guidelines for improving communication within the event team.

Establish the Level of Priority—It is important to establish the level of priority immediately. Emergency situations are, of course, the highest risk for any event, and communication about an incident or potential incident should be given top priority.

Identify the Receiver—By identifying the receiver, the event professional will be able to match their message to the receiver's needs, thus demonstrating empathy. The message will also reach the correct target.

Know the Objective—Clarity in communication is often linked to the development of an action objective. If the event professional knows what they want to achieve, they will be able to express themselves more easily and clearly. Stating a problem and its ramifications is often only the first stage. By indicating what needs to be done, the event professional can more easily achieve the objective and reach an agreed outcome.

Review the Message in Your Head—In preparing to send a message, the event professional should structure the given communication effectively. It is also useful to review the receiver's likely response.

Communicate in the Language of the Other Person—If examples and illustrations are used that the receiver will understand, the message will be more easily comprehended.

Clarify the Message—If the receiver appears from his or her nonverbal behavior not to understand the message, clarification is essential.

Do Not React Defensively to a Critical Response—Asking questions can help the event professional to understand why the receiver had responded defensively. The event professional can be assured they have reached a common understanding.

USE OF TECHNOLOGY

DETERMINE AND ACQUIRE COMMUNICATION EQUIPMENT AND RESOURCES

The event professional must be knowledgeable about communication equipment and resources; what is needed and where to get it—who can supply it. This is done while being cognizant of the budget. The event professional must set realistic concepts and expectations and not put forth "pipe dreams" that the client cannot afford. The event professional must analyze event needs, taking into consideration the type and size of site/venue along with users, attendees, staff, and volunteers.

The following strategies can help to develop effective communications between users:

- Identify specific information needs of group members.
- Use simple words in the language of the conference and/or host country.
- Allocate buddies or partners to develop subteams.
- Use graphics to impart information.
- Rotate roles.
- Provide all users with opportunities to participate in the group.
- Develop groups' rituals and a group identity.

Special communication equipment and resources might need to be dedicated to emergency personnel. Emergency personnel need dependable, battery-powered communication devices. They may also require nonpowered devices such as semaphores, reflective batons, and even signs to help them communicate with and direct others during emergencies. The event professional should also assess the adequacy of emergency lighting and illuminated directional signage (battery-powered exit signs) in any venue being used. This "signage" is a form of communication equipment.

Communication with the attendees will most often utilize written and/or digital text such as the event program, list of activities, signs indicating what is happening in a given place and when. During presentations, AV equipment such as microphones and amplified sound along with projection equipment will be used. For more extravagant events' special effects lighting, signage, etc. will be used. Public address systems may also come into play.

DETERMINE TECHNOLOGY APPROPRIATE FOR MEETING/CONVENTION/EVENT

Mobile communication—Reducing waste and the focus on sustainability has required event professionals to plan and execute on-site communication in the most efficient and effective way. As technology evolved, the primary thrust and also challenge for the event professional is in moving content onto mobile platforms. With the explosion of smartphones and tablet computers designed for mobility, stakeholders are expecting communication to be available and easily accessible on these devices.

The effectiveness of mobile communication devices comes from the increasing gravitation toward meeting enhancing, online, and social networking tools such as Twitter.

- More demands from meeting professionals for innovative technology such as polling tools.
- A broadening scope of event technologies such as request for proposal (RFP) and bidding software.
- Demands from delegates and speakers—especially younger ones who have grown up in a digital world for increasing the use of sophisticated multimedia and other technologies that facilitate the flow of ideas between them and their audiences.
- The growing prominence of mobile applications.
- The growing adoption of events that combine in-person and virtual aspects.
- Given the extensive use of the internet, it is critical that the meeting/event professional ascertain that the facility has sufficient bandwidth to handle the traffic the event will generate.

TYPES OF EQUIPMENT

- Smartphone—The primary piece of communication equipment used by event professionals and their attendees is the smartphone. Most larger events will create an app that contains all the critical information about the event. Texting is used regularly. Sometimes, people will actually call each other. It is important to note that organizations may need to rent smartphones, in view of employee privacy issues.
- PA System—Public address systems are used to communicate with large groups of people. They are usually "hardwired' and thus not affected by intensity of usage. The event professional should ascertain that the PA systems in venues they are using have backup power supplies that enable the PA system to be used during emergencies.
- Walkie talkies—These are two-way radios that provide secure, reliable, and instant communication between event professionals.
- Hard land line—A hard land line may be needed for the operational and/or media room. This would be critical in times of crisis and if there is a loss of cell phone service.
- Computers—Computers and their equivalent are the backbone of modern communications. Thus, having a firm grasp of desktop publishing software (i.e., Microsoft Office Suites) is an invaluable skill for an event

professional and essential for good written communication. The event professional should consider where their information is stored, besides on the device itself. One alternative is external storage, often using a USB port. A newer alternative is Web storage, often referred to as "cloud computing." Here, information is stored on a remote server and accessed via the internet. The obvious advantage is that the data or information can be accessed from anywhere and by anyone with an access code. The downside is that it is dependent on internet access.

Monitor On-Site Communications

The last aspect of on-site communication at meetings and events is to *monitor*. The event professional must keep track and be up to date on what is being communicated, when it is being communicated, and how it is being communicated. All established policies, protocols, and hierarchies must be adhered to. Equipment must be on hand when needed and in good working order. If any of the foregoing are not correct, the event professional must make adjustments and corrections. The event professional is the one ultimately responsible for every aspect of the meeting/event.

One critical area of this is monitoring is responding on social media accounts. Although many meetings/events still offer a dedicated phone number where attendees can call with questions on their way to the event and during it, younger generations do not prefer this type of communication. Instead, they are more likely to post a question to the event, host organization, or even CEO on their social media platforms privately or publicly. There is a clear and measured expectation that social media communications from attendees will be responded to quickly and adequately. Also, social media posts can be one of the fastest and easiest ways to get announcements out to attendees quickly. Meeting/event professionals need to ensure that there are dedicated staff or volunteers monitoring social media platforms and that they have been provided with the necessary talking points and answers to frequently asked questions needed to respond.

PUBLIC RELATIONS

WHAT IS PUBLIC RELATIONS?

Public relations is defined as the effective management of relationships and communications in order to influence behaviors and achieve objectives. As it relates to the meetings/events industry, public relations can be defined as the "presentation of an event via the media or other outlets, stressing the benefits and desirability of such event" (CIC, 2011). All events involve public relations strategies, some at a smaller scale and others at a bigger scale.

Public relations activities involve much more than media relations. They include all communications and the development of relations with all event *publics,* from attendees to sponsors, speakers, the community where the event is being held, the government, and the organization members and leadership, and so on. It also involves the management of a crisis or unexpected situation in a way that the event image remains positive and therefore attractive for constituents.

Professional relationships, just like friendships, grow and strengthen with time and collaboration. In that sense, the relationships built today with the community, the media, organization members, attendees, sponsors, vendors, and other people involved in the execution of the event plan will likely last for years. Cultivating these relationships helps to make the organization and their events smoother, and probably more successful, each year.

DEVELOP AND MANAGE MEDIA RELATIONS

Media will play a key role in the publicity plan, because they will be responsible for generating the publicity we look for. The catch is that we cannot control whether they will support our event or not. Nevertheless, we can help them make the decision of supporting us by developing positive (and hopefully long-lasting) relations with them.

The first thing to know when working with media is that writers and editors specialize in different areas. Therefore, the contact person that is in charge of an event may not be the same as the one that writes about political events and so forth. It is important that we establish a relationship with the right person.

In other words, the editor in charge of political events will cover your event only if it is of interest to his audience and if it relates to his or her area of expertise. If you send your communications to any editor, without knowing their area of expertise, the communication will likely be ignored. Depending on the event, media may be all over you, wanting to get the latest news minute by minute, or just not interested at all. Different strategies can be used to keep them informed and interested.

NEWS RELEASES

A news release or press release is a story, written in third person, that helps communicate important information to the media so that they can write or talk about a particular event. During the event planning process, a series of these releases can be sent to the media to start generating interest and build excitement. The release can be sent alone by email or distributed as part of a full press kit.

When writing a news release, the event professional should:

1. Think like a reporter—Reporters receive hundreds of these communications and will not pay attention to them unless they are provided with something that can really make their jobs easier, such as a story that can attract their audience. Unless that is achieved, reporters will likely ignore the event professional, not return their calls, and will not make the decision to cover the event.
2. Develop the story from the reporter's perspective—When we write, sometimes we assume that others know everything we do, and that is not correct. It is likely that reporters do not recognize the event name when they get the release, and even if they do, they will not know the details, because they have not been part of the planning process.
3. Make sure to include all of the relevant and important details.
    a. What is the event all about?
    b. When will the event take place?
    c. Where will it take place?
    d. Why is this newsworthy?
    e. Who will be there?
4. Get to the point and provide unique information—Sometimes including a quote from a well-recognized industry leader can be attractive to the media. Twisting the story to touch people's hearts is almost always a winning formula.

5. Make sure the message sent is clear, easy to understand, and accurate.
6. Write persuasively, but do not lie—Lying is not ethical and will put the event professional in a difficult position sooner or later.
7. Make sure the communication does not have grammatical errors—Sending communications with errors makes an event professional look unprofessional.

Once the news release is written, it needs to be distributed. To do so:

- Have a database containing the names and contact information of media outlets that should be approached. The database should contain, at a minimum, the name of the reporter or editor, area of expertise, email, phone number, and the way they prefer to receive communications. Obtaining this information can be time consuming and frustrating. Therefore, the event professional should collect this information ahead of time and have it ready when they want to send the communication.
- Send communications soon after writing the release so that the information contained in it is still new when the media gets it.
- Use the proper way to communicate with media. If they prefer fax, then use it.
- Address communications to the correct person.
- Follow up by phone the day after sending communications, to make sure they received the news release. This will give the event professional an idea if they are interested in covering the event and will give an opportunity to answer questions. Reporters are usually very busy and will not necessarily answer all the voice mails they receive. Practice patience and, most importantly, be respectful and professional.
- Check the media outlets approached to see if they have written an editorial or have announced the event. That is another way to assess the effectiveness of the plan.

ATTRACT AND ACCOMMODATE MEDIA

Unfortunately, it would be impossible for the media to cover every single event in town. Therefore, the event professional's job is to make enough noise to get their attention. Doing it requires only one little thing… providing them with something that is newsworthy.

The best way to attract media attention is to build interest by creating a series of stories and events that surround the main event. These activities must be outlined in the event plan. For instance, when an event professional is bringing a citywide convention to a city, they may calculate the economic impact the convention will have on the local economy and communicate that to the local media. This is certainly interesting for the local community and may be a good way of getting their support. If the event is supporting a local charity, they can also develop a story based on that fact and that could generate interest among potential attendees or sponsors and so forth.

Once the event professional has attracted the media, they must be ready to answer all their inquiries and accommodate all their needs. To that end they must have someone on staff assigned to answer media inquiries immediately. Voice mails and emails must be returned within 24 hours, remembering that there is media coverage every day, including holidays. Some of the things the media will expect from event professionals on-site are:

- Have a media registration area, separated from attendee registration.
- Have someone on staff assigned to accommodate media needs. That person should receive members of the media during registration and introduce himself or herself as their facilitator, for whatever need they might have.
- Provide media with complimentary tickets to enter the event, and give them preferential access to special events, speakers, and sponsors.
- Prepare a media or press room with access to computers, internet (Wi-Fi), phone, fax, electric outlets where they can connect their electronic devices, tables and chairs where they can sit and write their stories, and a small table in a quiet place to conduct interviews. It is always nice to provide refreshments in the media room.
- Have someone ready to provide media with the latest, most accurate news as quickly as possible.

Once the event is over, a news release should be sent to media communicating the event's most important outcomes. It is a good idea to include some good quality pictures the media can use in their publications. Always remember that for event professionals to be able to publish an image, they must have permission, not only from the photographer but also from the individuals portrayed in the picture.

If people have been reading and listening about a specific event for months, it is likely that they are interested in the outcomes. When promoting a fundraising event, the event professional should inform everyone of the amount of money raised and what it will be used for. That will help build credibility, which will, in turn, make the path smoother when pursuing media attention and community support in the future.

Saying thank you is always advisable, not only to the media but to all constituents too. To that end, writing thank you letters or emails may help enhance relationships with supporters and may even ensure getting their support once again in the future.

Table 14-1 provides some tips to accommodate and manage media before, during, and after the event.

Before the Event
• Editors and reporters focus on different industries. Make sure to communicate with the right person.
• Use their preferred way of communication.
• Follow up by phone after sending a news release.
• Build interest by creating stories around the event.
• Treat media with respect and professionalism.
• Follow protocols and make media aware of them.
• Appoint someone to be the contact person for all media inquiries.
• Answer media inquiries immediately
• Invite media to the event and provide them with complimentary tickets
During the Event
• Have a media registration area, separated from attendee registration.
• Make sure someone is available on staff to accommodate media needs and provide latest news.
• Have a pressroom equipped with Internet, phone, fax, computer access, electric outlets, etc.
• Have a quiet place available to conduct interviews
• Provide access to speakers, sponsors, and other VIPs.
• Provide preferential access to special events.
After the Event
• Send a press release with event's most important outcomes.
• Send pictures to reporters and editors.
• Call supporters and thank them for their help.

TABLE 14-1: Tips to Accommodate and Manage Media Before, During, and After the Event

Public relations activities involve much more than media relations; they include all communications and the development of relations with all event publics. Public relations are a fundamental element of the event's marketing plan and will help control people's perceptions regarding an event.

MEDIA OUTLETS

Various traditional and advanced media, including podcasting, mobile advertising, YouTube, and social media, can reach mass target consumers. The meetings, expositions, events, and conventions (MEEC) industries can utilize media outlets through internet technology by broadcasting their messages effortlessly as long as the message content is well developed and properly worded in advance. Messages may be created by independent producers and can be distributed with an affordable budget when social media and channels can be joined and clicked by the public easily. For example, podcasting could be downloaded by one click to a mobile device. The created messages could be heard and watched through video or audio files, be attached into a blog's file exchange, or generate followers and Facebook's "like" link. Podcasting could be a very good return on investment in terms of being capable of generating a high volume of listeners.

More and more groups have used social media to provide daily communications and activity news announcements. Many companies have benefited from the power of "word of mouth" when the advertisements are posted on Facebook or linked to websites. The Facebook site has generated its own sense of community. Blogs are also seen as the place where individuals can share their thoughts and event activities freely with global participation from others. Interactions among members can also stimulate the popularity of social media and enhance the visibility of advertisement and promotional activities. Customers also rely on other customers' product or service reviews. However, the accountability of reviews has been questioned because "fake" customers posted some reviews. More and more on-line brokers only give access of "customers'" reviews to real customers who purchased or booked products, services, and participating events through the particular broker's site (e.g., Expedia).

SELECT AND MANAGE SPOKESPERSONS

Not everyone can verbalize a message properly or remain calm and professional during a crisis. To that end, it is important to select a spokesperson that will be responsible for communicating with the media on behalf of the event. Some organizations decide to find someone in-house to manage this, whereas others prefer to outsource it. Depending on the scope of the event, the person selected could be the president of the host organization or a public relations manager appointed to handle all event communications. In other instances, the organization chooses a celebrity speaker or someone renowned to manage communications, in the hope that this person will become a magnet for people and the media. For example, if the event professional is planning a national culinary fest, they may select a nationally renowned chef to be the spokesperson. The host organization's executive director may also serve as the spokesperson for a nonprofit event, whereas the president of the Olympic Committee may be appropriate for the Olympic Games. In any case, the person in charge should

- Be knowledgeable and available to speak about any situation or detail of the event when needed.
- Understand the message that is to be sent and the image it is meant to portray.
- Review the "talking points" scripted by the communication specialist.
- Have a proper image that is aligned with the hosting organization and the event.
- Be a good communicator, capable of clearly communicating an idea verbally or in writing, and able to control his facial expressions and remain calm before any situation.
- Have the right combination of knowledge and character to establish a healthy relationship with the media.

If the person selected as the spokesperson is not involved in the planning of the event, event professionals must meet with him/her regularly to inform him/her of what has been going on and the way the organization would like to handle it.

PRECONVENTION MEETINGS

A day or two prior to the actual beginning of a meeting, the meeting/event professional should partake in a pre-convention **(precon)** meeting. This is a gathering of all critical people representing all departments within the facility and other outside vendors or suppliers who will be part of the team. In addition to the CSM, who is the primary contact for the meeting/event professional, the following representatives may be requested to attend the meeting: catering or banquet manager or F&B director; audiovisual representative; sales manager; accounting manager; front desk manager; bell staff or concierge; housekeeping manager; security manager; engineering manager;

switchboard manager; recreation manager; and all outside service providers, such as transportation, special events, and decorators. Often, the general manager of the facility will stop by, be introduced, and welcome the meeting/event professional. The precon meeting allows the meeting/event professional to meet and visually connect with all the various people servicing the event. In most cases, this will be the first time the meeting/event professional meets many of these people. Each representative is introduced, and any changes or additions of duties in their respective departments are reviewed. After the individual departments have been discussed, the meeting/event professional should release each person to return to his or her duties.

The ESG is reviewed page by page with the CSM. All changes are made, guarantees are confirmed, and last-minute instructions are conveyed. The precon is basically the last time the meeting/event professional has the opportunity to make any major changes without disrupting the facility. Once an event is in progress, it is very difficult and potentially costly to make major changes. If the meeting/event professional decides one hour before a session that the room should be set with only chairs rather than with tables and chairs as listed on the function sheet or BEO, it can cause havoc. Additional staff may be needed to remove the tables, and the meeting/event professional may be charged for the labor. Sometimes, the last-minute request of a meeting/event professional cannot be fulfilled. If fifty tables are requested just prior to an event, the hotel may not have them available or may not have scheduled staff for setup.

POSTCONVENTION REVIEW

At the conclusion of a major meeting, the meeting/event professional will create a written postconvention report to record all key events and should include all vendor reports and data from the meeting. This is used for planning the next meeting. It also serves as a "report card" for the facility and the meeting manager. It will include what went right as well as what went wrong. Then, a postconvention (postcon) meeting is held. It is smaller than the precon and may include the planning staff, the CSM, the F&B director, the audiovisual manager, and a representative from the accounting department. This is the time to address any discrepancies in billing, service failures, and problems or to praise facility staff for a job well done. Most major meetings will have a postcon; smaller meetings may not. If the organization is returning to the destination or venue the following year, it is important to openly discuss "lessons learned" on both sides to ensure the issues are addressed and corrected. However, if the event will move to a different city, it is a time to recap the event and note improvements.

EVALUATION

Creating and implementing most meetings is a team effort. All meeting/event professionals should conduct an evaluation after each meeting to obtain feedback from the attendees, exhibitors, facility staff, outsourced contractors, and anyone else involved in the event. Individual sessions may be evaluated to determine whether speakers did a good job and whether the education was appropriate. Overall, evaluations may collect data on such things as the comfort of the hotel, ease of transportation to the location, desirability of location, quality of F&B, special events and networking opportunities, and number and quality of exhibitors at a trade show or convention. This information may be collected by a written questionnaire after the event as well as by telephone, association or corporate website, or Web-based collection methods. One of the fastest and least expensive is to broadcast an email with a link to the electronic questionnaire. Many software packages are available that will design, distribute, collect data, and tabulate results. The data concerning speakers and logistics will assist the meeting/event professional and program planning committee to improve the programming for subsequent years.

The use of electronic **audience response systems** (ARS) has gained popularity as a way to engage session participants. ARS allow meeting/event professionals to survey a variety of stakeholders via handheld devices or an event app accessed from a smartphone that transmits information to the meeting/event professional in real time. This allows the meeting/event professional to adjust while it is still going on and can provide valuable data for future events.

Evaluations can be time-consuming and expensive to design and implement. Unfortunately, some of the data collected by meeting/event professionals are often filed away and not used appropriately—especially if the results are negative toward the event. No board of directors or CEO wants to hear that the site they selected to hold a meeting did not meet attendees' expectations. However, negative comments may ultimately turn into a favorable marketing tool. A good evaluation form is simple and concise, and can be completed in a minimal amount of time. A good source for questions can be to review your event goals and objectives. If the meeting is an annual event, it is important to ask similar questions each year so that data may be collected and analyzed over time.

Timing is also an issue with administering individual session or event evaluations. If data is collected on-site during or immediately after an event, it may increase the response rate. The meeting/event professional can remind attendees to complete and return evaluations before moving on to the next session/event. Other meeting/event professionals prefer to wait a few days to ask for feedback. This gives the attendee time to digest what actually occurred at the meeting and form an objective opinion when not clouded by the excitement of the event.

The process of evaluating the overall meeting should begin in the early stages of meeting planning and tie in with the meeting objectives. Questions consist of the registration process, housing options, overall functionality of the meeting space, selection of the food and beverage options, and so on. Costs for development, dissemination, analysis, and reporting should be included in the meeting budget. The evaluation serves as a valuable component of a meeting's history by recording what worked or did not work for a particular event. It is a cyclical process whereby the overall evaluation results feed directly into next year's meeting objectives. Committees plan most large meetings. Evaluation results are how information is passed from one committee to the next.

COVID-19

COVID-19 struck the world in late 2019 and 2020 and had a significant impact on the MEEC industry. In terms of producing MEECs, it caused many to be postponed or canceled. Further restrictions were placed on face-to-face gatherings that included how far apart participants needed to be (social distancing), reduced room capacity, elimination of buffets for eating, hotel suspending service, limited dining opportunities, and more. A significant number of planned face-to-face gatherings were moved on-line to "virtual gatherings." The degree of MEEC disruption varied across localities. Further, the restrictions keep changing. Thus, there is no agreement and what MEECs will look like in the future. Hopefully, a vaccine will be developed and COVID-19 conquered.

SUMMARY AND BEST PRACTICES

Producing a meeting or event requires a skilled team to execute the meeting plan. Each area of the event—registration, food and beverage, audiovisual, housing, speakers and entertainers, and ancillary events—must be carefully managed on-site. The event specification guide contains all the details of each function and important information for the on-site team to review. The event team, consisting of staff members, temporary and contracted staff, and volunteers, assumes many roles to execute the meeting plan. Communicating with the team, the attendees, and the general public requires an intentional strategy, skilled professionals, and dedicated resources. Before, during, and after the meeting, the team should meet to discuss successes, concerns, lessons learned, and improvements to the event plan.

Because of the complexity of the meeting production process, this chapter can only highlight some of the activities involved. There is a book, *Production and Logistics in Meetings, Expositions, Events and Conventions,* that provides more detail on the production aspects of MEEC..

CASE STUDY DILEMMAS FOR THE NEW EVENT PLANNER

(Produced by G.G. Fenich and Students from East Carolina University)

Jack is the director of Meeting and Events of The Almedia in Florida. This beautiful 500-room hotel is located right on the beach and features many luxurious amenities. The property includes three meeting rooms, two ballrooms, and ample amounts of outdoor space for events. The scenic outdoor area is very popular for weddings and receptions.

Chloe, the new meeting and event planner, is getting ready to produce her first event on her own. It will be a reception for V Pharmaceuticals with an estimated 100 attendees. The event is scheduled to begin outside at four o'clock on a Friday. Chloe has been working with Mr. Vladimir from V Pharmaceuticals for months and assures Jack that everything will run smoothly.

The event planning process was smooth, but on the day of the event everything seemed to go wrong. Chloe got to work late because she was stuck in traffic. Although she arrived in time, this did not put her in a good mood. When she got there, she checked her email and saw an email from V Pharmaceuticals. The email was sent the previous night and they wanted to change their number of attendees from 100 to 200. Her contact, Mr. Vladimir, apologized for not letting her know sooner but hoped that she could handle the changes. Frantic, Chloe immediately called the hotel restaurant to let them know of the changes. They planned to serve a lot of seafood and were worried about having enough. Chloe immediately got on the phone with their seafood distributers and inquired about getting more. They informed her they did not have all of the items she needed but could provide her with some alternatives. Chloe had a bit of an attitude from earlier and the changes, but eventually agreed to change the menu.

After the phone calls, Chloe went outside to check on the new enlarged setup. Mr. V had requested a plate meal; Chloe was outwardly enraged when she a saw a buffet style set up for the food. She screamed at the staff to fix it and follow the directions they were given. Chloe also noticed that the flowers and decorations were not properly set up. She screamed at the staff again. As things were progressing behind schedule, Chloe found out that one of the servers called out of work. That was the last straw. Chloe continued to yell at everyone within earshot of some guests.

By three-thirty, everything was set up as planned and all the food was almost ready. All of the guests soon arrived and the event went great. The attendees had no idea about the problems Chloe had had earlier in the day. Chloe planned everything for the event, but she did not think of what might go wrong. She was not prepared for some of these problems and had not had experience or known how to deal with them. Chloe reflected on the day and realized she acted very unprofessionally. If she wanted to continue in the event business, she would have to learn to prepare for anything and be able to handle the unexpected.

1. How would you have handled each problem?

2. How should Chloe prepare for the future and the unexpected problems that may arise?

KEYWORDS AND TERMS

For definitions, see https://insights.eventscouncil.org/Industry-glossary

Ancillary activities
APEX
Audience response system
Banquet Event Order (BEO)
Destination Management Company
    (DMC)
Event Specification Guide (ESG)

Guarantee
Precon
Postevent report
Production schedule
Public relations
Signing

REVIEW AND DISCUSSION QUESTIONS

1. What is the difference between the food and beverage projection and the final guarantee?

2. Describe the benefit of the meeting planner managing ancillary events.

3. What roles should volunteers and temporary (paid) staff be assigned on-site? What roles is it critical that a full-time staff member performs?

4. How has technology advanced to better communicate with attendees or the public?

5. Articulate the key principles of a good press release.

6. What is the primary purpose of the preconference meeting? What is the primary purpose of the postconference meeting?

ABOUT THE CHAPTER CONTRIBUTORS

Amanda Cecil, Ph.D, is an associate professor in the Department of Tourism, Conventions, and Event Management at Indiana University. Her teaching and research focus on event tourism and business travel.

Erica Shonkwiler, MBA, is a lecturer in the Department of Tourism, Event, and Sport Management at Indiana University (IUPUI). Her teaching and scholarship focus on event design and management.

PREVIOUS CHAPTER CONTRIBUTOR

Curtis Love, Ph.D, emeritus associate professor at the William F. Harrah Hotel College at the University of Las Vegas.

CHAPTER 15

INTERNATIONAL ASPECTS IN MEEC

MEEC EVENTS ARE HELD AROUND THE GLOBE. THIS IS FRANKFURT, GERMANY, WHERE IMEX IS HELD

© Sean Pavone/Shutterstock.com

CHAPTER OBJECTIVES

- Articulate ways in which MEEC varies around the globe.
- Discuss ownership, sponsorship, and management models important for international meetings and gatherings.
- Recognize important international meeting and trade fair associations.
- Name some specific considerations that are necessary to think through for successful international MEEC events.

The growth of international communications and travel has brought about impressive changes in how the world does business. Thirty years ago, only the largest companies were considered "international." Today, there are few large companies that do not have an international presence.

Consequently, the meetings, expositions, events, and conventions (MEEC) industries have expanded internationally. In this chapter, we will look at how the international scope of MEEC has evolved and how it differs in various parts of the world.

The Union of International Fairs (UFI) publishes regular, and impressive, statistics about the international **trade fair** industry. In the 23rd edition of their Global Exhibition Barometer, released in July 2019, UFI reported that 32,000 exhibitions are held annually, attracting 4.5 million exhibitors and welcoming 303 million visitors. UFI values the global exhibition industry at nearly $325 billion in terms of its total global economic impact.

International meetings also contribute greatly to employment, creating more than 3.2 million jobs worldwide. Regardless of the location, the purpose of international meetings and exhibitions remain the same—communicating, learning, networking, trading, and marketing.

HOW MEEC VARIES AROUND THE GLOBE

Despite similarities of purpose, cultural and business influences have created different models for MEEC happenings in various parts of the world. Chinese incentive travel, for example, can be very large indeed: Tien's Group took 6,400 of their employees on a 4-day visit to France to celebrate the 20th anniversary of the company. Highlights included a private viewing of the Louvre Museum in Paris. They also formed a human-made phrase on a beach in Nice, which at the time was verified by the Guinness World of Records as the largest of its kind. It read "Tien's Dream Is Nice in the Côte d'Azur." The cost of the incentive trip was estimated at $18 million.

The legendary Stratos brand-activation experience, organized by the Austrian multinational Red Bull, is another example of a truly global international business event. After 5 years of planning with a staff of 300, including 70 scientists and engineers, Felix Baumgartner jumped from the stratosphere in 2012, at 128,100 feet of altitude (or four times higher than most passenger jets fly) and set a new speed world record at 833.9 miles per hour. The freefall took place in New Mexico but was televised by 40 TV stations from around the world and, very importantly, it became a livestream sensation on the YouTube. It was watched by 8 million followers. All of this was to prove that "Red Bull Gives You Wings."

This chapter will focus primarily on conventions and exhibitions as they have experienced exponential and sustained growth over the past decades. When reviewing 50 years of international association meeting data, the International Congress and Convention Association (ICCA), looking at aggregated figures for each five-year period, concluded that the number of regularly occurring, internationally rotating association meetings has been increasing by 100% every 10 years and has been doing so consistently for the last half century, showing no signs of a slowdown. This trend peaked in 2019 when, on its website, the organization declared the "highest ever recorded annual figure in its yearly statistics" counting 317 additional congresses over and above the "record-breaking figures" of the previous year. The same situation appears to be true for trade fairs. Kai Hattendorf, Managing Director of UFI, the global association for tradeshow stakeholders, comments on data from the body's Global Exhibition Barometer in 2019 by saying that "the data proves that exhibitions are not just resilient, but show a consistently strong performance and growth opportunities in many core markets around the world."

This chapter examines the types of exhibitions and conventions held in Europe, Asia, Australia, Africa, and the Middle East, with a discussion of how they differ in scope and operation and what areas of the world are embracing events as a primary method of marketing or communication. Included at the end of this chapter is a short list of international trade fair and meetings organizations.

One of the many buildings where the Canton Fair is held in Guangzhou china.

© GuoZhongHua/Shutterstock.com

The World's Largest Fairs

The Canton Fair

The China Import and Export Fair, also known as the Canton Fair, has been held in Guangzhou every spring and autumn since 1957. In spring 2019, the exhibition attracted over 195,000 buyers from more than 200 countries and regions as well as 25,000 exhibitors. Trading turnover negotiated at the fair reached almost $30 billion. In response to COVID-19, the fair went online in its June 2020 edition (see final section in this chapter for further information).

Hannover Messe (Fair)

In 2019, the Hannover Messe organizers, Deutsche Messe, stated that 6,500 international exhibitors met with over 215,000 visitors. Of these, almost 40% were international visitors, especially from the United States and China. The show, which occupied 227,000 square meters of floor space (over 2.4 million sq. ft.), reported that 6.5 million business contacts were made over the 5 days of the show. It is important to note that the organizers also held some 1,400 lectures and panels on topics around industrial technology. Combining exhibition floors and conferences is a growing trend, called the "ConFex" trend by UFI's CEO Kai Hattendorf, who points out that attendees come for knowledge acquisition especially regarding innovation in their industry sector and not just for negotiating the purchase of goods and services. In 2020, the conference element of the fair was spun into the successful Hannover Messe Digital Days in July, after the physical element of the fair had to be cancelled due to COVID-19. The final section of this chapter will discuss the Digital Days in detail.

The fair focuses on core industrial technology in:

- Industrial Automation
- Energy
- Digital Factory
- Industrial Supply
- Research and Technology

George G. Fenich

EUROPE

The trade fair industry's roots are in Europe. During the Middle Ages, the concept began with farmers and craftsmen bringing their products and wares to the town center to connect with their customers. Although the wars of last century had temporarily devastated the European industry, today Europe is the focal point of international trade fairs and exhibitions.

There are two primary reasons for this. The first is location—Europe has always been the crossroads of the world. International hub airports in Frankfurt, London, Amsterdam, Paris, and Madrid enable visitors and cargo to arrive easily from all parts of the world. In addition, a superlative network of rail transportation within Europe enables many cities to be within speedy reach of one another. For example, the Eurostar train links London to Paris and Brussels within 2 hours and to Amsterdam in just under 4 hours. The second reason for the growth of trade fairs is Europe's industrial base. With reconstruction help from the United States, Europe recovered its manufacturing and distribution base within a few decades of World War II. With the help of their governments, European industrial centers developed excellent trade fair facilities.

Germany is usually thought of as the center of industry and trade fairs in Europe. Spending by international visitors to Germany on business travel has reached over 53 billion Euros (more than $62 billion) per year, and 4 of the world's 10 largest exhibition centers can be found in Germany (Hanover, Frankfurt, Cologne, and Dusseldorf).

THE LARGEST EXHIBITION VENUE

Hannover Fairgrounds is the world's largest exhibition site. It features almost 11 million sq. ft. of exhibit space in 27 exhibit halls and an open-air display area. The site includes a convention center with 35 conference rooms, 42 restaurants seating a total of 14,000 people, parking facilities for 50,000 vehicles, banks, laundry, a pharmacy, and Münchner Halle—the world's largest trade fair beer hall. Hannover Fairgrounds offers separate units that provide partitioned areas with their own infrastructure, which helps several events run concurrently. More important, the regional government and the management company have worked together to establish excellent transportation and lodging facilities.

Report from CeBIT

CeBIT, the world's biggest high-tech fair in terms of visitors, has historically attracted around 200,000 visitors. Over 3,000 companies from 70 countries participated in CeBIT 2017. Germany's chancellor attended as did Japan's prime minister.

For 2018, the show had plans to transform itself into "Europe's Number 1 platform and festival for digital technology," according to a Deutsche Messe spokesperson. It moved to June to enable activities around its theme to take place in an open-air "campus-style setup" and deliberately aimed to appeal to Generation Y attendees, with a mixture of entertainment, product demonstrations, dialogue, and "party-style get-togethers." Unfortunately, these plans were not enough to counter a decrease in visitor and exhibitor numbers, due, ironically, to an increase in the use of digital tools to conduct business. According to some sources, this decline was also due to the destination's inability to keep pace with the rapid growth in numbers in earlier years, especially in accommodation and hospitality services.

CEBIT trade fair, Hanover

© flowgraph/Shutterstock.com

In the United Kingdom in 2018, over 9 million visitors attended more than 1,000 exhibitions, generating 11 billion pounds in spending. Top exhibitions included the Farnborough International Air Show, International Spring Fair (Birmingham), World Travel Market (London), and London Fashion Week.

Italy is another focus of international trade fair activity. Milan is the fashion trade fair center of the world. Other important centers are located in Bologna and Verona. In Spain, trade fair activity is concentrated around Barcelona, Valencia, and Madrid. The Benelux nations (*Belgium*, *Netherlands*, and *Luxembourg*) also have a strong trade fair program. Excellent facilities exist in Amsterdam, Rotterdam, Brussels, and at Schiphol Airport. Paris, too, hosts numerous international events throughout the year. It is probably true to say that the growth of the European Union, its common currency—the Euro, and the removal of trade barriers and tariffs has helped the European trade fair and exhibition industry to grow.

Perhaps, the greatest growth of trade fairs in Europe is occurring in the countries of Eastern Europe. New facilities have come up in Zagreb, Belgrade, Warsaw, Moscow, and in St. Petersburg, where the ExpoForum center was launched in 2014. In recent years, other large Russian cities such as Kazan, Yekaterinburg, Kaliningrad, and Perm have also successfully hosted a variety of international and domestic business events.

© DrimaFilm/Shutterstock.com

London Fashion Week

Previous research highlights the rise of Sochi, a resort town on the Black Sea that has recorded a rapid increase in business travel due to the 2014 Winter Olympic Games. Development of infrastructure for these games led to a modern transportation system, the building of new world-class hotels, and investment by large international hotel chains. It also included building modern facilities to host exhibitions, congresses, and conferences. During the Olympics, visitors were able to buy a 72-hour visa on arrival and were allowed to explore the area, which generated a lot of word-of-mouth. Sochi is also on the Formula One circuit and was one of the host cities for the FIFA World Cup in 2018.

Europe also hosts many international association meetings. In fact, in its 2019 statistics of international association meetings, ICCA (The International Congress and Convention Association) reports that 14 of the top 20 destinations hosting the highest number of international association meetings globally are European cities. In 2019, Paris maintained its place as the top destination for international association meetings.

The European Society of Cardiology (ESC) Congress

One of these international association meetings is the ESC congress. The ESC is a not-for-profit medical federation of national cardiology associations and individual members from around the world and represents more than 100,000 cardiology professionals. Its mission is "to reduce the burden of cardiovascular disease." They organize 15 international meetings on different cardiology topics. Their main event, the ESC Congress, is the world's largest cardiovascular event, and it has been held annually since 1962. It takes place over a period of 5 days in late August or early September and changes its location every year.

The duration and complexity of their planning cycle can be viewed as typical for a large medical convention. It begins with the creation of the Request for Proposal multiple years before the event and ends with a "postmortem" reporting on the convention just held. Historically, the destination selection process usually starts 3 years before the convention, and the format of the event begins to take shape approximately 18 months before the event day, when the layouts of the lecture and exhibition rooms are sketched out and the scientific program and abstract policy are determined. This is followed by a focus on operational logistics and supplier selection around 10 months prior and, a couple of months later, the development of the scientific program and marketing for the event.

In 2016, the congress was held in Rome, and the figures were staggering: a record 33,000 health professionals and stakeholders (clinicians, scientists, epidemiologists, nurses, technicians, health care industry executives, opinion leaders, media representatives, and policymakers) from more than 140 countries attended the congress. They discussed topics arranged in themed scientific villages at the Fiera di Roma exhibition and conference center. The congress also featured an exhibition where over 200 companies displayed their goods and services, spread out over almost 120,000 sq. ft.. The event closed with a historic address by Pope Francis.

The statistics below show that international meetings now make increasing use of technological tools to communicate even more widely. The audience was not limited to onsite participants at the ESC Congress as the events had a virtual reach:

- Over 100+ resources were consulted on ESC Congress 365 (the ESC Congress scientific content platform) between its launch in January 2013 and September 2016.
- Over 66,000 resources were consulted during the 5 days of ESC Congress, including more than 35,000 presentation slide sets.

The congress changes venues within Europe every year: Previous destinations have been the Fira Gran Via 2 in Barcelona, the ExCeL center in London, and the RAI in Amsterdam. The above information was adapted from documents kindly provided by the ESC management.

© hydebrink/Shutterstock.com

Paris, France—September 1, 2019: Congress of the European Society of Cardiology at the Porte de Versailles Convention Center in Paris

ASIA

The growth of trade fairs and exhibitions in Asia over the past 15 years has been astonishing. New facilities and government promotions have taken the industry from its infancy to world class in little more than a decade. Traditionally, Asian trade fairs focus on technology, consumer electronics, and food. However, all types of manufacturing and service industries are also represented. Asian trade fairs and exhibitions are either sponsored by trade organizations, such as the world trade centers, or by individual governments.

Taiwan and Singapore have been leading the way for Asian trade fairs and exhibitions. Taiwan has excellent facilities and routinely sponsors trade fairs in the semiconductor, consumer electronics, and food industries. Taiwan is also an important exhibitor at trade fairs and exhibitions in North America and Europe.

Singapore is a major "destination" city and consequently attracts many visitors to its textile, fashion, food, and electronics trade fairs. It has multiple facilities, all linked to excellent shopping and entertainment complexes. In addition, Singapore is attractive because it provides first-rate transportation facilities with a world-class airport. It also helps that the government of Singapore is very active in promoting their destination to attract exhibitions. Enterprise Singapore, formerly known as International Enterprise Singapore, engages the Singapore Exhibition and Convention Bureau (SECB) to market Singapore as an international exhibition city. It provides financial and marketing support for trade fairs organized by both Singaporean and international organizers.

China

The growth in Asia's foremost economy, China, is nothing short of extraordinary. Business events in China, the world's second largest economy, have benefited greatly from the major sporting events and expos hosted there, especially because of the infrastructure development and skills enhancement. The Olympics were held in Beijing in 2008, and the expo took place in Shanghai in 2010. In 2022, China will host both the Winter Olympics (in Beijing) and the Asian Games (in Hangzhou). In addition, the corporate hospitality at these events has brought an increase in corporate meetings held in China and encouraged the establishment of event service companies in China. The hosting of important political meetings such as APEC and G20 summits (in 2014 and 2016, respectively) has also raised China's awareness as a meeting destination.

Exhibitions are well established in China, as they are an extension of trading. Corporate meetings and incentives are newer concepts, and association conventions are not as easily understood since associations are mainly managed by the Chinese government. Overall, the government plays an important role in Chinese business life. In fact, all international events held in China must be approved both by Central Government and the provincial government or the relevant ministry. All large international congresses with a high proportion of international participants have to be approved by the Central Government and the State Council.

Convention and Exhibition Industries in China

In 1978, only six international conventions and exhibitions were held in China, and China took part in only 21 exhibitions abroad. The first exhibition company in China (SIEC) was established in 1984. Today, the quantities and scales of exhibitions in China have increased hundred-fold and penetrated into all fields of the national economy. Consequently, each industry has its own international professional exhibitions. According to UFI, in December 2018 there were almost 62 million sq. ft. of indoor exhibition space in China's main venues, roughly 17% of the world's total. In this respect, China is now second in the world after the United States. China is also now the world's largest business travel market, ahead of the United States (2nd place) according to the Global Business Travel Association (GBTA). In 2017, Chinese business travelers spent a total of $346 billion during those trips. Beijing and Shanghai make up a significant amount of room supply and meeting space in the country. Hotel construction has been robust in secondary markets, including Macau, Guangzhou, Shenzhen, Sanya, and Wuhan, and many top-tier hotel offerings are increasingly available to MEEC buyers in these markets (Table 15-1).

Destination	Convention Center Space (sq. ft.)	Major Airport(s)	Total Number of Hotels	Total Number of Sleeping Rooms
Beijing	3,429,965	PEK	703	120,521
Guangzhou	1,371,147	CAN	343	66,885
Hong Kong/ Shenzhen	5,000,000	HKG	483	140,580
Macau	1,143,573	MFM	60	31,652
Shanghai	42,761,208	PVG	657	124,618
		SHA		

Source. Adapted from CVENT website; accessed August 24, 2020.

Table 15-1 Hotel Capacity in Major Chinese Cities

Five convention and exhibition economic belts—the Yangtze River Delta, Zhujiang Delta, Bohai Bay Area, and Northeast and Central China—have been built on the mainland, although many tradeshows have reached as far west as Chengdu, Sichuan Province; Chongqing City; and Xi'an, Shaanxi Province. As far as the scales and impacts of exhibition projects go, the three cities of Beijing, Shanghai, and Guangzhou are the most important in the Chinese convention and exhibition industry. As one form of economic concentration, some cities have grown into regional centers, such as Dalian, Shenzhen, Chengdu, Hangzhou, Nanjing, Ningbo, Suzhou, Qingdao, Xiamen, Xi'an, Wuhan, Nanning, Kunming, and Chongqing.

Both Hong Kong and Macau, which are Special Administrative Regions of China, have an important place in international MEEC. As a free port with a major international airport hub, Hong Kong has been ranked in CVENT's Top Meeting Destinations in Asia Pacific for several years. Hong Kong's main venues are the Hong Kong Convention and Exhibition Center, the Asia World Expo, and the Hong Kong International Trade and Exhibition Center. Macau, on the other hand, is a favorite incentive destination, and its many casinos attract numerous international travelers to the "Vegas of the East." Similar to elsewhere in China, the government also plays an important role in Hong Kong. For example, its visa-free scheme allows travelers from 170 countries to visit Hong Kong visa-free for periods ranging from 7 to 180 days.

It is probably true that even though the Chinese exhibition and meetings industry is developing very rapidly, organizing an event in China is administratively and legally a complex affair. The UFI Special Interest Group on China identified some key points to consider for international organizers wanting to hold an event in China. These are:

- Need to understand local regulations and licensing requirements
- Importance of a local partner
- Rise of e-commerce and online competitors
- Rising labor costs
- Challenge to find skilled and professional managers

However, Chinese companies and the government are becoming increasingly aware of the need for greater internationalization. For example, the China Convention and Exhibition Society (CCES) and China Association for Exhibition Centers (CAEC) have partnered with international organizations to train and promote their members. Outside of the major convention cities, many Chinese cities have begun to realize the importance of meetings, which can contribute to the balanced development of the convention and exhibition industries.

Incentive Travel in China

Incentive travel is a newer business in the Chinese tourism industry but has huge potential. With more and more Chinese organizations and companies making use of incentive travel, many of the traditional travel agencies in China (such as Ctrip, Tuniu, and JD) have changed their business models or have started to offer new services. Economic success has generated an increase in incentive travel—Chinese companies hold incentives more frequently and travel to more destinations and with a higher number of employees. This trend is expected to increase in the next few years, and, correspondingly, the number of small corporate meetings being held is also on the rise. These are mainly commissioned by pharmaceutical/medical, IT, direct selling, automotive, and financial companies.

Some professional tradeshows represent the incentive events sector. The largest is the China Incentive Business Travel and Meetings Exhibition (CIBTM) and the Incentive Travel and Convention Meeting IT and CM China. The first international exhibition in China dedicated to business travel, incentives, and conferences, CIBTM was launched in 2005. Both shows offer exhibitors the opportunity to meet qualified buyers with an interest in different business travel products and services.

With plenty of tourism resources, competitive prices, and a good tourism image, China is expected to become one of the most popular incentive travel destinations in the world. Many countries such as Australia, the Netherlands, and Egypt are enhancing marketing to business customers and residents in China.

THAILAND

Thailand is a major center for clothing and textile tradeshows, food and agribusiness tradeshows, and automotive and engineering fairs. Excellent transportation facilities in Bangkok make it easy for visitors to arrive from around the world. The IMPACT Exhibition and Convention Centre is Thailand's largest, with a total indoor space of over 1.5 million sq. ft. across 5 venues. Its IMPACT Challenger conference venue boasted three interconnected halls with a combined column-free space of more than 645,000 sq. ft.—which was the world's largest column-free hall. Since its opening in 1999, IMPACT Exhibition and Convention Center has hosted more than 8,000 events with over 100 million visitors from all over the world. On its website, the company states its ambition to become one of "Asia's Top 5 Venues." Recent projects include the development of IMPACT Lakefront on the adjacent Muang Thong Thani Lake, which provides open-air venue space for corporate and private events.

KOREA

COEX, Kintex, and Songdo Convensia are Korea's three main exhibition centers. All three are situated in or right near the capital of Seoul and host a variety of events (exhibitions and meetings). COEX is not just an events venue with almost 5 million sq. ft. of floor space; it also hosts Asia's largest underground mall, three five-star hotels, office blocks, a department store, and a subway station. Kintex (or Korea International Exhibition Center) is in Goyang City. Its exhibition and meeting space were expanded in 2011 to almost 1.2 million sq. ft. of floor space. It is run as a partnership between the Korean national government investment agency and regional and municipal administrations. Songdo Convensia, situated next to Korea's main international airport, Incheon, is operated by the local tourism organization.

INDIA

The world's second most populous country, India, has become an economic powerhouse. Research in 2018 pointed out that "India [was] to remain the fastest growing major economy amidst heightened concerns over global trade war and oil price concerns" (Sharma, 2018). By 2025, 99% of India's workforce could be counted as skilled, and it was set to become the youngest nation in the world, with an average age of 29. The Indian Exhibition Industry Association (IEIA), which commissioned the study, estimated the Indian exhibition sector in 2018 to be worth 649 billion Indian Rupees (or $8.8 billion) in economic impact. What is interesting to note is that the Indian government, similar to what we will see later in this chapter with Australia, identified main industry sectors to support and the exhibition calendar reflects these sectors. In India, the government's initiative called "Make in India" aims to transform India into a global design and manufacturing hub.

Sharma (2018) identified the following trends in the Indian exhibition industry:

- Shift in focus from general events to specialized exhibitions
- Increasing emphasis on quality of participants, better services
- Industry consolidation through acquisition of local organizers
- Incorporation of technology/digitalization
- Introduction of global events
- Rise in international participation for exhibitions as well as visitors (~15% share) Source: Adapted from Sharma, 2018.

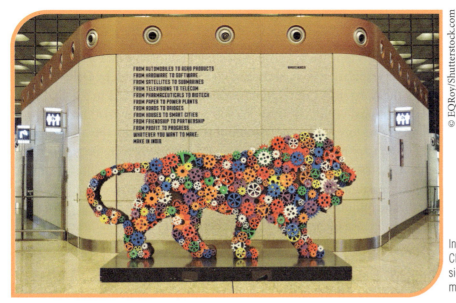

Indian lion logo at Chennai airport. The cogs signify India's strength in manufacturing

The MEEC activity in India tends to be centered on a number of important business cities in the country, namely New Delhi, Mumbai, Bangalore, Hyderabad, Chennai, and Goa. Due to ongoing foreign direct investments within the "Make in India" sectors, the country is also becoming a booming market for outbound MEEC trips. One DPI Research study compiled in 2018 goes as far as predicting that the "India Outbound Meetings, Incentives, Conferences and Exhibitions (MICE) tourism market is expected to reach nine billion US dollars by 2025."

OTHER ASIAN COUNTRIES

Other countries nurturing trade fair programs with government involvement and support include Vietnam, Malaysia, and Indonesia. In these countries, the facilities are usually owned and operated by the government, and promotional activities are sponsored by various government agencies. Vietnam has taken a strong position in clothing and food trade fairs. In Indonesia, the ministry of tourism and creative economy recently appointed a deputy of tourism products and events. They aim to improve foreign earnings by increasing the number of business events in Indonesia.

AUSTRALIA

Australia has a long track record of hosting high-profile international events, especially association congresses and incentives. Research by Deloitte on behalf of the Australian Convention Bureau established that 1 in 5 dollars spent by international visitors in Australia was spent by an international visitor attending some form of business event. It is also clear from this study that the MEEC industry in Australia has aligned itself strongly with the government's economic strategy by concentrating on the so-called five pillars: manufacturing innovation, advanced services, agriculture exports, education and research, and mining exports. Research has shown that over 78% of participants who attend these international business events are related to one of these five pillars.

Australia's major cities such as Melbourne, Brisbane, Perth, and Adelaide, all have internationally renowned conference and exhibition centers—the Brisbane Convention and Exhibition Centre (BCEC) was awarded the 2016 AIPC Apex Award for the "Best Client-Rated Convention Centre." In Sydney, the ICC (International Convention Centre) opened in Darling Harbour and describes itself as Asia Pacific's premier integrated convention, exhibition, and entertainment precinct. It offers exhibition capacity of 376,000 square feet, 86,000 square feet of total meeting space, an external event deck on the waterfront of 54,000 square feet, a theatre with a seating capacity of 8,000, and an adjacent headquarters hotel with 590 rooms.

The Image of the Sydney Opera House in Australia is known around the world. It is actually an event center putting on not only operas but also orchestra recitals, theater, meeting, and other special events

© Alan L Meakin/Shutterstock.com

AFRICA

Home to 16% of the world population, Africa's economy is quickly developing. The agreement establishing the vast African Continental Free Trade Agreement (AfCFTA) entered into force in May 2019 for the 24 signatory countries. Trading under the AfCFTA was due to commence in July 2020; however, as a result of the COVID-19 global pandemic, this date has been postponed. It has been indicated that the new date for operationalization is January 2021. Similar to its European equivalent, this agreement aims to create a single, continent-wide market for goods and services and facilitate the movement of capital and persons more easily. This would facilitate and promote business travel and events both within and outside of Africa utilizing strategic relationships and support from global trading partners.

The leading economies in Africa in terms of highest GDP in 2019 included the following, and their growth rate is rank-ordered as follows:

1. Nigeria
2. South Africa
3. Egypt
4. Algeria
5. Morocco
6. Angola
7. Ethiopia

The MEEC industry is developing rapidly within Africa, for corporate as well as association events. In 2015, the African Society of Association Executives (AfSAE) was successfully founded. Four new conventions centers opened their doors in 2016:

- Calabar, Nigeria: Calabar International Convention Centre—377,000 sq. ft., with a total capacity for accommodating 5,000 delegates.
- Algiers, Algeria: Centre International Conference d'Alger—2,900,000 sq. ft., with an auditorium that can accommodate 6,000.
- Cape Town, South Africa: Century City Conference Centre—on a precinct that combines residential, commercial, and leisure components and offers 20 floor spaces with a combined capacity to accommodate 1,900 participants.
- Cape Town's foremost venue—the Cape Town International Convention Centre expanded in 2017 to offer an extra 10,000 sq. m. of multipurpose space.

- Kigali, Rwanda: Kigali Convention Centre—auditorium for 2,500 and onsite hotel with 292 rooms.

Africa is the only "growing continent" that is home to some of the world's fastest growing economies. With its rapidly growing population and continuing urbanization, it expects to achieve a substantial improvement of life expectancy and a serious increase in disposable income per capita. This development is captured in the specialist exhibition for the MEEC industry in Africa—Meetings Africa. Organized since 2004 by South African Tourism, Meetings Africa is a pan-African show, which in 2019 attracted 343 exhibitors from 86 countries.

The MEEC industry in Africa is therefore seeing significant growth, particularly in South Africa. Since the early 1990s, South Africa has become an increasingly important player not only on the continent but also worldwide. This culminated in the highly successful hosting of the FIFA World Cup in 2010. The International Congress and Convention Association recently ranked South Africa as 38th among the top meeting destinations worldwide. In the African context, however, the country is far ahead of its competitor countries. The closest African rivals, Morocco and Rwanda, occupy 57th and 64th positions, respectively. Cape Town is the most popular urban meeting destination in Africa. The city hosted the first Africa Travel Week in April 2014, when three large travel and meeting–related fairs were held at the Cape Town International Convention Centre (CTICC). The World Tourism Market Africa, IBTM Africa, and the International Luxury Travel Show Africa attracted almost 4,500 leisure, luxury travel, and meeting planning professionals. Africa Travel Week has since grown to host eight related travel and tourism shows in 2019, as well as offering the virtual ATW Connect insight hub.

Traditionally, the MEEC industry in South Africa has concentrated around hotel venues and game lodges, but considerable development has taken place in the creation of large multipurpose conference and exhibition facilities. In South Africa, three cities dominate the MEEC industry—Cape Town, Durban, and Johannesburg. To support the development of MEEC in South Africa, the Tourism Grading Council of South Africa launched a star grading system for meetings and exhibition venues, which is considered the first initiative of its type in the world. The FIFA World Cup also left behind a nationwide legacy of improvements in telecommunications and broadcast technology and public transport as well as a highly positive reputation for the country as a successful destination for major events.

A large number of domestic trade fairs and conventions dominate the South African industry, predominantly around Johannesburg, although all of South Africa is growing rapidly as a major destination for trade fairs. The list of major venues in South Africa includes the Tshwane Events Centre (Pretoria Showgrounds). Upcoming cities in the MEEC industry in South Africa include Bloemfontein, Port Elizabeth, and Pretoria. The South African Tourism event, Indaba, is an annual event that has been held in Durban since 1997. This event is one of the largest tourism marketing events on the African continent. In its 2019 edition, Travel Indaba attracted more than 6,500 attendees, including over 1,000 exhibitors and 1,500 visitors from across the world.

MIDDLE EAST

Trade fairs and exhibitions in the Middle East are most prominent in Dubai and Abu Dhabi in the United Arab Emirates. This is due to excellent government promotions, new facilities, and ease of travel access. Both Dubai and Abu Dhabi have international airports with service to every continent. This "crossroads" concept, as well as the fact that exhibition facilities are located at or near the international airports, is emphasized heavily in promotional materials. For example, both Dubai and Abu Dhabi strongly promote the duty-free zones near their airports and the extensive duty-free shopping available at their facilities. In addition, the regional market for consumer goods is very strong.

Dubai was set to hold the World Expo in 2020, being the first Middle Eastern nation selected to host this prestigious event. Due to COVID-19, the event was postponed to 2021. It was expected that the expo would attract more than 25 million visitors and positively impact UAE's GDP by $23 billion between 2015 and 2021 and create 277,000 new jobs. A new convention center in Al Jaddaf near Dubai Creek was part of the run-up to the expo and provides 592,000 sq. ft. of event space. In 2016, Dubai welcomed three new world-class venues, suitable mostly for corporate conferences, team-building, and incentive trips: Dubai Opera, Dubai Parks and Resorts, and IMG Worlds of Adventure.

It is also fair to say that Qatar has been working very hard to attract both exhibition and meeting planners. The Qatar National Convention Centre, which opened in 2011, was built according to U.S. Green Building Council's Leadership in Energy and Environment Design (LEED) gold-certification standards. In August 2016, the Oman Convention and Exhibition Centre (OCEC) opened its doors with the Oman 2016 event, one of the largest building and construction exhibitions in the Middle East.

Across the entire Middle East region, new hotel properties continue to be built.

LATIN AMERICA

The large population base of Latin America makes it well suited for trade fairs and exhibitions. Until recently, most of the Latin American trade fairs and exhibitions have been regional. However, new facilities and promotional efforts have set the stage for growth in international exhibitions. New facilities in Sao Paulo, Brazil, and Mexico City are hubs for this activity. The Las Americas Exhibition Center in Mexico City provides the latest in technology to support exhibitors and attendees. In addition, the center is built within an entertainment complex that includes a horseracing track, restaurants, hotels, and a shopping center.

Brazil was in the limelight between 2010 and 2020, hosting both the World Cup in 2014 and the Olympic Summer Games in 2016. It is estimated that the 2014 World Cup contributed over $60 billion to the country and created 3.63 million jobs. The event also helped change Brazil's reputation as being famous for just soccer and samba to that of an innovative country with proven research and development capabilities, a robust economy, and modern cities.

Table 15-2 shows a list of international top cities for meetings and events, according to the 2020 American Express Global Meetings and Event Forecast report.

	Top Cities Based on Meetings and Events Activity			
	Europe	Asia	Australia & Oceania	Central/ South America
1	London, England	Singapore	Sydney, Australia	Nassau, The Bahamas
2	Berlin, Germany	Bangkok, Thailand	Melbourne, Australia	Playa del Carmen, Mexico
3	Barcelona, Spain	Hong Kong, China	Brisbane, Australia	Cancun, Mexico
4	Paris, France	Kuala Lumpur, Malaysia	Gold Coast, Australia	Punta Cana, Dominican Republic
5	Amsterdam, Netherlands	Shanghai, China	Perth, Australia	San Juan, Puerto Rico
6	Madrid, Spain	Tokyo, Japan	Auckland, New Zealand	Cabo San Lucas, Mexico
7	Frankfurt, Germany	Seoul, South Korea	Adelaide, Australia	San Jose del Cabo, Mexico
8	Rome, Italy	Beijing, China	Queenstown, New Zealand	Montego Bay, Jamaica
9	Prague, Czech Republic	Bali, Indonesia	Cairns, Australia	Mexico City, Mexico
10	Munich, Germany	Mumbai, India	Nadi, Fiji	Grand Cayman, Cayman Islands

Compiled from American Express, 2020 Global Meetings and Events Forecast

Table 15-2 Top International MEEC Cities

OWNERSHIP, SPONSORSHIP, AND MANAGEMENT MODELS

In the United States, many tradeshows are adjuncts to association meetings and are owned by the association. Others may be sponsored by private, entrepreneurial companies and operated on a for-profit basis. Ownership and management are usually accomplished by two companies working toward the success of the show. Other service companies support the industry by helping both the tradeshow management company and exhibitors.

This model is not always followed for trade fairs and exhibitions in other parts of the world. While there are very important commercial tradeshow-organizing companies (especially in the United Kingdom), in other countries, such as Germany and Italy, it is the owners of venues that organize the fairs in addition to renting the space. Often governments, in collaboration with organizing companies, plan and operate the trade fairs. For example, the government of China plays a major role in the sponsorship of most trade fairs held in Beijing, Hong Kong, and Shanghai.

PROFESSIONAL CONGRESS ORGANIZER

Although not a popular term in the United States, the Professional Congress Organizer (PCO) is an important title representing a service provider for organizers and sponsors or large congresses around the world. The PCO represents the client in dealing with the DMO, DMC, hotel, restaurant, transportation company, and other suppliers. The PCO will negotiate with vendors on behalf of the client. PCOs also tend to be more familiar with international issues like customs, taxation, and government regulations. The PCO may even handle financial transactions, letters of credit, and foreign bank accounts. PCOs are often involved in the content of shows and with speakers, entertainers, and performers (SEPs). PCOs have their own association called the International Association of Professional Congress Organizers (IAPCO).

GLOBAL COMMERCIAL EXHIBITION ORGANIZING COMPANIES

There is a leaderboard of global commercial exhibition–organizing companies. The companies are truly global trade fair–organizing companies that operate across the world in all main markets. These companies include: Informa Markets, Reed Exhibitions, Comexposium, and Messe Frankfurt Clarion Events.

IMPORTANT INTERNATIONAL MEETING AND TRADE FAIR ASSOCIATIONS

THE INTERNATIONAL CONGRESS AND CONVENTION ASSOCIATION

The International Congress and Convention Association (ICCA) is the global community for the world's meetings industry. It is the only association that comprises a membership representing the main specialists in handling, transporting, and accommodating international events.

ICCA's network of over 1,000 suppliers to the international meetings industry spans the globe with members in almost 100 countries. ICCA tracks over 18,000 regularly occurring association meetings that rotate between at least three countries. Access to this data and association clients is the primary reason why companies and organizations belong to the ICCA. ICCA's head office is based in the Netherlands, with regional offices located in Malaysia, South Africa, the UAE, the United States, and Uruguay.

International meeting planners can rely on the ICCA network to find solutions for all their event objectives, as ICCA members represent the top destinations worldwide, and are seen as the most experienced specialist suppliers. Speaking on the occasion of ICCA's 50th anniversary in 2013, Martin Sirk, then CEO of ICCA, said: "What the long-term data tell us is a story that is dramatic. What is shown is an incredible picture of growth and dynamism, and a trend that justifies even more investment by destinations and suppliers into the international association market, in anticipation of what the future holds."

AIPC

AIPC (Association International de Palais de Congrès or International Association of Convention Centers) represents a global network of more than 185 convention centers in 60 countries. Its mission is to encourage, support, and recognize excellence in convention center management, based on the diverse experience and expertise of its international membership, through a wide range of educational, research, networking, and standards programs to achieve this. AIPC members are purpose-built facilities whose primary purpose is to accommodate and service meetings, conventions, congresses, and exhibitions. They provide numerous services some of which are listed as follows:

- Conducting industry research and analysis
- Preparing and publishing technical publications
- Carrying out training, educational, and professional development activities
- Maintaining a global marketing and communications presence for members
- Facilitating member networking and information exchange forums
- Maintaining performance standards including the AIPC Quality Standards program and the AIPC/Ipsos Economic Impact Tool
- Recognizing management excellence through awards programs such as the AIPC Apex Award, an award made in recognition of the highest client rating received by a convention center and the AIPC Innovation Award
- Supporting and carrying out advocacy initiatives to promote the value of the industry to key audiences.
  Adapted from Introducing AIPC, http://www.aipc.org/index.asp?id=5

UFI—THE GLOBAL ASSOCIATION OF THE EXHIBITION INDUSTRY

UFI (Union des Foires Internationales) is the association of the world's leading tradeshow organizers and fairground owners. This group also includes major national and international exhibition associations and selected partners of exhibition industry. UFI's main goal is to represent, promote, and support the business interests of its members and the exhibition industry. The association represents some 50,000 employees working in the exhibition industry from 84 countries around the world.

Over 930 international trade fairs carry the UFI-approved label, a quality guarantee for visitors and exhibitors alike. UFI members continue to provide the international business community with a unique marketing medium aimed at developing outstanding face-to-face business opportunities.

Adapted from the UFI website, http://www.ufi.org/about/

INTERNATIONAL MEEC CONSIDERATIONS

LESSONS TO BE LEARNED

It is important for trade fair, event, and exhibition managers to learn the reasons for success in different aspects of the international marketplace. For example, North American tradeshow managers and destination representatives can learn from their European colleagues in three areas:

- Infrastructure excellence: Public transportation systems in Europe provide excellent support of trade fairs and exhibitions.
- Logistics: International trade fair organizers are, by necessity, experts in logistics. Because the lifeblood of many international shows is the international exhibitor, many have specialized departments devoted to helping exhibitors overcome obstacles for exhibiting in their countries. Shipping and storage procedures are simplified and expedited by these agencies to help make exhibiting in their countries as easy as possible.
- Support Organizations: In America, many tradeshows are sponsored and organized by associations. In other parts of the world, trade fairs and exhibitions are sponsored and organized by trade promotion organizations, such as the world trade centers or government agencies.

METHODS OF EXHIBITING

There are many differences between exhibiting at an American tradeshow and at an international trade fair or exhibition. These differences need to be a part of the basic research before initiating an international trade fair program.

Typically, companies have choices in how they will exhibit at an international trade fair or exhibition. The U.S. government sponsors U.S. pavilions at many trade fairs, and a U.S. company can work through the government to be part of the U.S. exhibit. If a company does decide to be a part of the exhibit, the U.S. Department of Commerce can provide significant help. Another option is to exhibit under the auspices of another company that is organizing a pavilion. Like U.S. government sponsorship, a private company may be the main interface, and contractual arrangements are made with it. Companies should fully investigate this type of situation to ensure that the organizing company has a strong reputation and has experience working in the host country and especially in the desired trade fair.

Joint ventures can also be formed between companies, particularly when one has experience exhibiting at a certain trade fair. In this case, it is important that companies be sure that their products or services do not compete with each other. This type of arrangement works best when the two companies' products complement each other. It is thus an excellent way for a company to enter the international trade fair marketplace and gain valuable experience.

"Going it alone" is another option for companies entering the international trade fair arena. Many large companies choose this route because they have the budget and staff to support the complexities of international exhibiting. Smaller companies must ensure that they have a clear understanding of all the requirements, costs, and scheduling should they decide to go it alone like big companies do. For example, smaller companies must factor in all the personnel time and costs involved in verifying that all tasks are completed. Assuming that the preparation time for an international tradeshow is the same as that for a domestic tradeshow can be a very costly mistake.

TERMINOLOGY

In many parts of the world, an exhibit is not called an exhibit—or even a booth. Rather, it is called a **stand**. And this is only the beginning of the differences in terminology. Depending on where the trade fair is being held and who is managing it, participating companies must be familiar with those differences.

For example, in Germany the following terms must be understood:

- **Ausstellung:** Consumer show
- **Kongress:** Meeting or convention
- **Gesellschaft:** Company or society
- **GmBH:** Limited liability company
- **Messe:** Trade fair
- **Messegelaende:** Fair site

And in the United Kingdom:

- **PLC:** Public limited company
- **Trade Exhibition:** Tradeshow
- **Delegate:** Attendee at conference
- **Accommodation:** Housing
- **Value-Added Tax**: This is usually included in the price of shop goods, but sometimes it will be listed as an additional item on quotes and invoices for services rendered by suppliers. The 2020 VAT rate in the United Kingdom is 20%, and the country has processes for allowing international event organizers to reclaim the tax on genuine business expenses.

CONTRACTUAL AND PROCEDURAL ISSUES

In addition to terminology differences, contractual and procedural differences abound. Labor rules in the United States are very different from those in Europe or Asia. In Asia, there are few unions or jurisdictional issues. Exhibitors have much more freedom in what they can do within their exhibit. In Europe, although there are unions, they are much more flexible than many in the United States.

Companies should not assume that setup or logistical contracts read the same as those in their home country. Substantial differences exist from country to country and from trade fair to trade fair. Companies should read each contract closely and adhere to all the requirements. If something is not understood, it should be brought to the attention of show management immediately.

CUSTOMS CLEARANCE

Exhibition organizers at international shows provide access to experienced international freight forwarders, who also act as custom brokers, to ensure that everything is in order and arrives on time. The freight forwarders are knowledgeable about the customs regulations for the host country and act to ensure that exhibitors know of every requirement and deadline.

Typically, goods can be temporarily imported to an international show site without having to pay duties or taxes, using either a **carnet** or a **trade fair bond**. A carnet can be very complicated to obtain, and a hefty bond must often be established. However, most trade fair venues offer trade fair bonds, which are simple to arrange. Again, the international freight forwarders are the point of contact for trade fair bonds. Be sure to inquire about host-country rules on giveaways and promotional materials. In some countries, a duty is charged when the value is above a certain limit; in others, a duty is not charged for materials used for this purpose.

PROTOCOL

Business etiquette refers to the rules that allow people to comprehend what is suitable in any situation. It is the responsibility of an event organizer working internationally to research the business customs of the host country in which they are holding their event. Staff should then be thoroughly trained on these differences before departing for the trade fair or other events. Always remember that what is acceptable in one country may very well be offensive in the next country or at another trade fair. Language is one of the most obvious differences; although English is normally the "official" language of international business, it is not safe to assume that all attendees or suppliers speak English. The wise company will ensure that at least some of the staff is bilingual, particularly in the host country's language. In addition, different cultures are more, or less, direct when passing on information. Hall (1976) categorized communication behavior as low-context when, as in Scandinavia and North America, people spell out information explicitly. In contrast, information may have to be deduced from the context and nonverbal clues, as in Chinese and Arabic, which are high-context cultures.

Staff members will be greeting people from many countries to their international event. It is imperative that they be familiar with the appropriate greetings for different cultures and forms of address. Although most event stakeholders will not be offended if protocol is not strictly followed, it does give them a positive impression if their cultural standards are observed. Culture can be defined as the collective programming of the mind that distinguishes the members of one group or category of people from others. In 1980, the Dutch academic Geert Hofstede first identified six dimensions regarding international culture, four of which are particularly important for conducting international business. They are explained as follows with examples of how business etiquette should be adapted accordingly.

IDENTITY (INDIVIDUALISM VERSUS COLLECTIVISM)

This dimension deals with the position of the individual in society—while in collectivist countries people see themselves primarily as belonging to powerful groups (such as an extended family) and work hard to maintain group harmony, individualist societies value independence and individuals are expected to speak their own minds.

In collectivist countries, such as China, it is very important to invest time to build strong, mutually beneficial relationships, also known as guanxi. It is rude to say a blunt "no" in negotiations, since this will hurt the group harmony. When negotiating in China, always give many alternatives so that the Chinese negotiators have room to negate several options with dignity. Also, always keep the same negotiating team throughout the process.

Hierarchy (Power Distance)

This refers to the degree in which less powerful members of a society or an institution (like the family) are happy to accept inequalities in the distribution of authority. A high level of power distance indicates that a particular society expects top-down authority as their norm.

In the Netherlands, a country with low power distance, avoid giving an impression of superiority. Egalitarianism is a central tenet of Dutch society. Everyone in a Dutch company, from the boss to menial laborers, is considered valuable and worthy of respect.

The United States has traditionally been a low-power-distance country.

When interacting with French business contacts, never use first names or the informal 'tu' until you are told to do so. France is a country with relatively high power distance, and it is important that you respect the hierarchy of employees within the same company.

Age and rank are very important in Korea, so it is usually easiest to establish a relationship with a businessperson of your own age.

Gender association (Masculinity versus Femininity)

This dimension denotes societies as being more achievement-oriented or more care-oriented, reflecting the predominance of presumed masculine versus feminine values, respectively.

Japan is the country that scores highest in masculinity dimension. Japanese are known for their work ethos and high competitiveness. For example, when doing business with Japanese stakeholders, you will need to be careful in your selection and presentation of business gifts. If a Japanese person gives you a gift, do not throw away the wrapping or tear it up as it is considered part of the gift.

The United States also has a high score of masculinity, according to Hofstede.

Truth (Uncertainty Avoidance)

This factor refers to the degree in which a society can tolerate ambiguity. Are people looking for the one, absolute truth (high uncertainty avoidance) or are they happy to live in a less structured or even unstructured environment (low uncertainty avoidance)?

Meetings in high-uncertainty-avoidance countries such as Germany and Greece should be planned well in advance. These countries also tend to have a large number of official rules and legal regulations regarding contracts and import/export barriers. The United States, in contrast, scores below average on uncertainty avoidance.

In addition to the dimensions listed above, other elements should be considered when doing business internationally. Food and drink often play a more important role than in the United States. In many parts of Asia, lengthy business dinners with many toasts to the hosts and VIP guests are a vital part in forming a lasting business relationship. In Japan, the host will always treat when you are taken out. Allow your host to order for you. Be enthusiastic while eating and express your gratitude and delight freely afterward. In Russia, everyone at a dinner is expected to consume vodka—by the shot and not sipped. Furthermore, with each shot a different guest gives a toast—with toasts becoming more and more lengthy with every drink. At a business meeting in Saudi Arabia, coffee is often served toward the end of the meeting as an indication that the meeting is about to end.

Differences in the perception of punctuality also exist. Therefore, a meeting should absolutely start on time in Switzerland or Germany, but people in India or Nigeria may see event project milestones as flexible.

There are also marked differences in how much "personal space" people from different cultures might expect and how close people could be to each other before feeling uncomfortable. Anglo-Saxons tend to occupy the largest area of personal space, followed by Asians, whereas Mediterranean's and Latin Americans have been found to use the shortest distance. In many countries, there is little public contact between the sexes, apart from handshakes. Do not kiss or hug a person of the opposite sex in public—even if it is your spouse. On the other hand, in some countries contact is permitted between people of the same sex that is often seen as platonic. Men may hold hands with men and even walk with arms around each other, which is interpreted as nothing but friendship.

- When giving gifts in Switzerland, avoid giving knives—it is considered bad luck.
- In many Asian countries, it is not appreciated to pat people on the shoulder or initiate any physical contact.
- In China avoid the colors blue, black, and white for gift wraps, as they are associated with disease, funerals, and death, respectively.
- You should not give chrysanthemums in Spain or France or carnations in Germany, where they are used for funerals.
- In most Arabic countries, the left hand is considered dirty, so you should never eat or accept anything with this hand. Be sure when giving gifts or promotional materials that you do so with the right hand.
- The number 8 is the luckiest number in China, as its pronunciation is close to a word meaning "to make a fortune," whereas the pronunciation for the number 4 sounds like "death."
- You would present your card using both hands, where your name is facing your Japanese colleague directly in such a manner that it can be read immediately. Handle cards very carefully and do not put them in your pocket or wallet. Never write on a person's business card in their presence.

Last, there are some symbols/colors/numbers and gestures to avoid:

In the United States, the hand gesture where the thumb and forefinger are forming a circle with the other three fingers raised is considered the "OK" sign.

- In Brazil, it is considered a vulgar or obscene gesture.
- In Greece and Russia, it is considered impolite.
- In Japan, it signifies money.
- In southern France, it means zero or worthless.

In the United States, waving the hand back and forth is a means of saying hello.

- In Greece, it is called the *moutza* and is a serious insult. The closer the hand is to the face of the other, the more threatening it is.
- In Peru, waving the whole hand back and forth can signal "no."

In most of the world, making a fist with the thumb raised means "OK." In Australia, Greece, or the Middle East it is a rude gesture.

These are simply a few of the cultural issues that foreign businesspeople must face. Before traveling to any country, it is wise to consult as many sources as possible to learn the appropriate business and social behaviors for the culture. Take the time to learn the appropriate behavior in the host country and the greeting expectations for potential visitors to the trade fair.

The following are aspects of international trade fairs that are different from the U.S. exhibitions. Keep in mind that these are generalizations and do not apply to all situations.

- Hospitality events are generally held on the exhibit floor, with many companies providing food and beverages as a matter of course in their exhibit.
- Height restrictions may be nonexistent. Many large exhibits may be two or three levels.
- Rules on smoking in the exhibit hall may not exist, and many exhibitors and attendees may smoke in the exhibits.
- Some trade fair–organizing companies may not offer "lead retrieval" systems that U.S. companies are accustomed to. It is always wise for a company to bring its own method of capturing leads.
- International trade fairs are not only often longer in duration than U.S. tradeshows but remain open on weekends as well. Although in Europe the show may run from 9 a.m. to 6 p.m., in Brazil or other Latin American countries it is common for trade fairs to open at 2 p.m. and run until 10 or 11 p.m. at night.
- Be aware that most of the world outside the United States uses the metric system. Voltages may differ, and exhibitors may need plug-in adaptors or transformers.

Other Considerations

- Visas may be required for entry and exit.
- Items that Americans take for granted may have to be declared upon entry to a country. For example, brochures and written materials must be declared and taxes paid on them.
- Many international destinations require payment of departure taxes.
- Most countries require that payment be made to ensure that goods exhibited at a tradeshow are exported and not sold within the country. A freight handling company can arrange a bond as security.
- AND many more! When in doubt, ask.

CORONAVIRUS AND ITS EFFECT ON INTERNATIONAL ASPECTS IN MEEC

The chapter you have just finished reading is based on research and observations from 2019 or earlier years, that is, on pre-COVID business models and practices. COVID-19 is a highly contagious virus that can trigger severe respiratory problems in humans. It has caused a worldwide pandemic, with stark consequences for international business, travel, and events. Scientists believe that the pathogen causing COVID-19 thrives in close-contact situations, like choir practices, church gatherings, and social events, where the so-called super spreaders can infect dozens of people. To stop or slow down its spread, the WHO recommends countries to enforce strict quarantine measures in disease clusters and demand self-isolation for travelers from particularly affected areas when arriving in new, less affected destinations. While physical distancing (i.e., maintaining a distance of at least 6 feet between individuals) is now encouraged in most countries around the globe, the effect on the MEEC sector in the short term has been nothing short of catastrophic. Obviously MEEC is among the industries that suffers most from such a vicious disease, as the activity has traditionally relied extensively on face-to-face experiences to facilitate participants' objectives of networking, idea exchange, and trading. International MEEC business suffered in particular as airlines cancelled flights and routes due to a huge drop in passenger numbers, because governments around the world issued travel advisories and encouraged people to stay at home. In April 2020, at the peak of the first wave of the epidemic in the Northern Hemisphere, air travel intelligence company OAG reports in their press release that "Some five million more scheduled seats were removed by airlines around the world for operation in the coming weeks…. In the last four weeks, some 58 million seats have been taken out of the market each week as airlines seek to find a way through the COVID-19 crisis that is crippling the aviation industry."

Examples of 2020 versions of high-profile events cancelled or postponed by the COVID-19 outbreak include the Tokyo Olympics, The World Expo 2020 in Dubai, the Mobile World Congress (world's largest mobile phone showcase), and ITB, the world's largest travel trade fair. Thankfully, we live in an era where technology is sophisticated enough to step in to mitigate some of the effects. In this chapter, we already mentioned the MEEC sector's trend toward an increase in information and communication technology (ICT)–enabled totally virtual events and/or hybrid events. These include the now-almost-ubiquitous smaller business meetings on Zoom to the delivery of an entire congress like the ESC annual showcase entirely online (described below in more detail). Another example is CEBIT, the technology show. CEBIT in fact shows how MEEC events have to keep adapting to prevailing macro environmental conditions. As already pointed out before in this chapter, CEBIT was cancelled in 2019 because of the decline in attendance and integrated into the Hannover Messe of that year in a new format to appeal to millennial visitors.

ESC CONGRESS 2020—THE DIGITAL EXPERIENCE

Due to COVID-19 concerns and worldwide travel restrictions, the ESC decided to hold their annual congress in 2020 as a virtual event. In an effort to support healthcare professionals around the world further, the society chose, exceptionally for 2020, to offer complimentary registration to the entirely online event.

Mirroring previous face-to-face events, participants could choose from live studio speeches with hotlines for questions, an on-demand playlist of recorded presentations, and interact with peers in related forums and industry-specific Q&A panels. To encourage deeper discussion in specialist disciplines, the ESC organized all congress sessions into separate channels or tracks by topic. In the on-demand program, which will stay available for some time after the congress, users can contact abstract presenters, rate presentations, and discuss presentations with other participants.

In addition, all abstracts presented at ESC Congress 2020—The Digital Experience will be published in the *European Heart Journal* (Supplement, Vol. 41, October 2020), which is important to the continuing medical education requirements of physicians and to substantiating credentials for medical researchers.

To communicate with its members and the congress participants, the ESC also uses the following social media platforms with a variety of hashtags: Facebook, Twitter, LinkedIn, and Instagram.

CANTON FAIR

In a similar vein the world's largest trade exhibition, the Canton Fair, moved its 127th edition entirely online in June 2020. Using tools such as livestreaming, exhibitor and exhibit search functionality, messaging, and virtual events, buyers and exhibitors could trade remotely.

HANNOVER MESSE

This industrial manufacturing trade event did not take place in 2020. However, in the organizers' news release Jochen Köckler, Chairman of the Board of Management, Deutsche Messe AG was keen to state, "We firmly believe that nothing can replace direct, person-to-person contact and we are already looking forward to the time after Corona, but especially in times of crisis, we must be flexible and act pragmatically. As organizers of the world's most important industrial trade fair, we want to offer orientation and sustain economic life during the crisis. We are doing that with our new digital offering. Next year, they will then present themselves with the latest products and solutions for Industry 4.0 and the energy system of the future" ("No Hannover Messe in 2020"; *Hannover Messe News*, March 26, 2020).

Replacing the physical exhibition, the Messe presented their conference content during the so-called Digital Days over two days in July 2020. This program featured approximately 200 speakers and 100 partner companies and attracted more than 10,000 participants. A program of the event can be downloaded from https://www.hannovermesse.digital/projects/dmag/hm20/data/program_digital_days_14_7_2020_EN.pdf

UFI GLOBAL CONGRESS 2020

UFI opted for a slightly different way to deliver their annual congress in 2020.

The organization offered a glocalized (a mixture between global and local) event that took place in different destinations as well as online during the course of one week:

- In Dubai, UAE (Sunday, November 15–Monday, November 16)
- In Basel, Switzerland (Wednesday, November 18–Friday, November 20)
- In Hong Kong (exact dates to be confirmed at the time of writing)
- Online (Sunday, November 15–Friday, November 20)

This event provided a networking platform to meet face-to-face AND digitally—onsite and online. The "glocalised congress" will in fact allow would-be participants to attend one or more destination(s) of their choice in person as well as being connected digitally. Alternatively, it was possible just to log in online.

SUMMARY AND BEST PRACTICES

The growth of international trade fairs and exhibitions and international meetings has been phenomenal over the past few decades. Europe, the historical home of trade fairs, continues its stronghold on the world's largest trade fairs and those with the most significant economic impact. Asia has made great strides by building state-of-the-art facilities and promoting its efforts throughout the world. The Middle East, Africa, and Latin America all have strong efforts under way to capture a larger piece of the international trade fair, exhibition, and convention market.

Worldwide communications, easy travel access, and open markets have been a boon to the international event industry. Few large companies can afford **not** to be in the international marketplace today. What was once the playground of only the world's largest companies is now a necessity for most companies of any size. Trade fairs and exhibitions are the easiest method for these companies to enter the marketplace and meet their potential customers.

Exhibiting at international trade fairs is not easy. Cultural and business differences present a new set of challenges for the exhibitor, along with more complex logistics and travel procedures. Companies must seriously analyze all factors before committing to an international trade fair program.

CASE STUDY MAKING ALTERNATE PLANS BECAUSE OF A VOLCANO

(Produced by G.G. Fenich and Students from East Carolina University)

Steve has worked for the Courier Hotel in London as a meeting planner for 4 years. During his time there, he has brought in a lot of business to the hotel and is seen as being great with potential clients. After many years of negotiation, he finally brings in Contech Financial for their yearly convention of all their sales reps from around the world. During this convention, Contech will use all the meeting space located at the Courier as well as use the in-house bar and catering for all meals, so Steve is looking for a rather large profit from this event.

One week prior to the event a volcano erupts in Iceland, putting ash into the sky and grounding all air traffic across much of Europe. With there being so little time before the start of the conference, Steve is worried about the event canceling. Usually Steve would not worry too much because he would still get money from the group if they canceled. However, in talking with Contech, he was reminded of the Act of God clause that was put into the contract, meaning that if this volcano caused air travel to be stopped, the meeting could be canceled at no charge.

After several calls to the local airports, Steve finds out that every airport near London expects to not resume any flights for at least a week, and probably more: after the dates of the Contech meeting. Steve finally finds out that an airport across the English Channel expects to resume international flights in 2 days since it was not being affected by the ash as much as England. Steve comes up with a plan to shuttle people across the English Channel from this airport in order to still accommodate their meeting.

Steve contacts Contech and lets them know of the new plan and tells them exactly how much extra the shuttle will cost. The company grows angry over the fact that Steve is requiring them to pay for the shuttle, which will add a few thousand more pounds onto their already large bill for the meeting. Contech tells Steve that unless the Courier Hotel picks up the bill for the shuttle the company will have to cancel the meeting as they are already at budget.

1. Should Steve agree to have the Courier pick up the bill for the shuttle?

2. Was it wrong of Steve to suggest that Contech should pick up the bill for the shuttle in the first place, considering that the company already had an out in their contract?

3. Steve has obviously gotten Contech upset about the shuttle. What could Steve do to assure that they not only do not cancel this event but make sure that they return for future events?

4. Is the attrition clause in the contract enforceable since many of Contech's employees may not be able to change their flight plans?

5. Will the extra cost for the shuttle offset airline costs that attendees would incur if the meeting was cancelled?

KEYWORDS AND TERMS

For definitions, see https://insights.eventscouncil.org/Industry-glossary

Ausstellung	Messe
Carnet	Messegelaende
Gesellschaft	PLC
GmBH	trade exhibition
International Congress and	trade fair
Convention Association	trade fair bond
Kongress	stand

REVIEW AND DISCUSSION QUESTIONS

1. List some ways that international trade fairs may differ from U.S. trade-shows.

2. What are two reasons for Europe's strength in the international trade fair industry?

3. What is the purpose of UFI, AIPC, or ICCA?

4. What are some of the complexities that a company must consider before taking part in an international event in China?

5. Before proceeding with your exhibition or conference outside of North America, list at least five pieces of knowledge you will require before moving ahead. Where will you get the information from?

ABOUT THE CHAPTER CONTRIBUTORS

Mady Keup is a part-time professor (postsecondary education) at Algonquin College in Ottawa, Canada, and a former course director for the master of science programs in strategic event management and tourism management and in international hospitality management at SKEMA Business School in France. Mady was the head of the London Convention Bureau (now London & Partners) for 5 years, and she is an MPI (Meeting Professionals International)–accredited trainer and an instructor for destination sales training in Europe and the Middle East on behalf of Destination Marketing Association International (DMAI). Mady has travelled extensively for consultancy and training in Europe, the Middle East, and North America.

The section on China is based on a previous contribution by

Jenny Salsbury, CEO, at IMC Convention Solutions, formerly senior director, international, China National Convention Centre.

Dr. Chunlei Wang, associate professor in the Department of Event Management, School of Tourism and Event Management, Shanghai University of International Business and Economics, Shanghai.

The section on South Africa is largely based on the contribution by

Uwe P. Hermann, a faculty member and researcher in the Department of Tourism Management, Tshwane University of Technology, Pretoria, South Africa.

PREVIOUS EDITION CHAPTER CONTRIBUTOR

Sandy Biback, CMP, CMM, lecturer of meetings and conventions.

CHAPTER 16

PUTTING IT ALL TOGETHER

© Businessvector/Shutterstock.com

MEEC EVENTS ARE LIKE PUZZLES—EVENTUALLY THEY HAVE TO BE PUT TOGETHER

CHAPTER OBJECTIVES

- List items needed to understand the event's organizing association.
- Articulate the event's goals.
- Articulate specific items to consider when determining the event's budget.
- Discuss the elements to keep in mind considering the event's income.
- Specify the necessary components involved in the request for proposal.
- Discuss the main considerations for conducting the first site inspection.
- Outline the important steps in destination selection.
- Articulate the importance of and the considerations necessary for the second site inspection.
- Discuss the part played by the marketing committee.
- Cover the steps involved in the creation of the conference program.
- Outline the importance of partnerships.
- Clarify the considerations involved in handling the event's contract.
- Specify the events and sequencing determined by the meeting timeline.
- Discuss the important items to consider after the meeting.
- Identify changes in the way meetings are planned due to COVID-19.

Many books contain a concluding chapter that repeats and summarizes the elements of the earlier chapters. In this textbook, a fictitious case study of a citywide convention serves the same purpose. The goal of this case study is to bring together all the previous chapters. Throughout this text, you have read about the tasks associated with meeting/event planning. Through this case study, you will learn more about topics from the previous chapters, and how they apply to a citywide annual conference for 3,000 attendees. The objective of this case study is to help you understand the various tasks a planner or event professional (these terms will be used interchangeably through the chapter) must complete for a meeting, exposition, event, or convention (MEEC) to be successful. In addition, this case study will help the reader understand the complexities of the budget and timetable, as well as the many people with whom an event professional must communicate.

CASE STUDY

This case study uses a three-year planning timetable for one citywide conference. The meeting planning cycle is continuous, and it is important to understand that two of the key skills an event professional must possess are the abilities to organize and to multitask. Event professionals typically work on three to five meetings or events simultaneously, each in different stages of development.

As you review the budget portion of the case study, it is important to understand that many variables, including the time of year the meeting is held, the planner's ability to negotiate, the value of the business to the facility, and the trade-offs, will affect the budget. This budget is broad and was created to highlight the many details the planner must consider.

THE ASSOCIATION

As a meeting or event planner, it is important to understand your audience—the attendees of the event. For association meeting planners, this is critical as they market the conference to association members and to potential members. The meeting planner must also communicate information about members of his or her association to suppliers for the convention. The better a supplier understands the audience of the meeting planner, the better the supplier can serve them. For example, if a hotel knows that most of the people attending a meeting are women, the hotel might add products that women use, such as hand cream or shower caps, to room amenities.

The American Small Animal Association (ASAA) is an example of a (fictitious) typical association in the United States. The ASAA is an 8,000-member nonprofit association whose members are veterinarians from throughout the United States who specialize in care for small animals. Funding for the organization is derived from membership dues, publication advertisement, and the annual conference that generates 40% of the association income.

The ASAA was founded 25 years ago by a group of veterinarians who saw the need to update research and to network with other veterinarians specializing in small animal care. Over 60% of the organization's membership operates independently owned veterinary clinics; the remainder of the association members are suppliers to the veterinary industry. The suppliers include pharmaceutical companies, prescription food companies, and product suppliers. Although the number of women members is increasing, 60% of the members are male; 55% Caucasian; 30% African American; and 15% a mix of Latino, Asian, and Native American. It is important to know the makeup of the organization so that the event can meet its wants and needs. The planner or organizer must ask two questions: Who is the group? Why are its members here?

An executive committee and a board of directors operate the ASAA, while the executive director and seven committee members oversee the day-to-day operations of the association. Members of the board of directors are elected from seven established regions and serve two-year terms. All board elections take place during the annual meeting and are announced during the final night. Sue Rodriguez is the director of meetings for the ASAA and is a full-time employee. Sue is one of the five full-time employees and is responsible for coordinating the seven regional meetings and the annual conference; she reports directly to the executive director. Planning for the annual conference begins 3 years in advance of the meeting date. For the past 5 years, attendance at the annual conference has increased 5% per year; and last year, 37% of the membership attended the meeting. This increase is attributed to the success of the trade show portion of the conference that was added 5 years ago.

Logo for the (fictitious) American Small Animal Association.

Source: Kristin Malek

GOALS

To begin preparation for the annual conference, Sue reviews past annual conference evaluations from attendees and members of the board of directors. The board of directors wanted to save money by cutting down on the cost related to networking activities, but the members indicated how important it is to have time to meet other professionals from around the country. The board also would like to see the money collected from this conference increased by 10% because other than membership dues, the annual conference is the largest revenue source for the association. Last year, the ASAA created the Small Animal Preventive Disease Certificate (SAPDC). During the annual convention, veterinarians earn twenty-five continuing education units (CEUs) and learn about the preventive medicines that can be used to save the lives of small animals. Additionally, the board of directors requested that a **Corporate Social Responsibility (CSR)** segment be included in the annual conference. Once a destination is selected for the annual meeting, Sue will work with the local community to identify not-for-profit organizations that need help.

To help focus her thoughts, Sue reads the ASAA mission statement: The mission of the ASAA is to provide an educational forum for members to exchange ideas and develop ways to ensure the health of small animals. This mission is accomplished by providing quality education for its members, offering assistance to new veterinarian clinics, and providing a forum for members to meet and to assist each other with emerging technologies.

To help Sue measure **return on investment (ROI)**, she creates operational and educational objectives. The operational objective is to increase meeting profits by 5% over last year's conference and the educational objective is to increase the number of attendees enrolled in SAPDC classes by 10%. The conference objective, "to host a four-day educational conference for veterinarians and suppliers to the veterinary industry that will result in a 10% increase in attendance and 5% increase in profit from last year's conference" is share with Sue's team and all conference partners.

BUDGET

To create the budget (see Tables 16-1 and 16-2), Sue reviews past meeting budgets. For her expenses, she includes the cost of marketing materials, the convention center, host hotel, decorator, audiovisual equipment, speakers, entertainment, and staff. In addition, Sue must consider operational objectives for the meeting. To locate income sources, Sue looks at past meeting **sponsors** and exhibitors. This year, marketing will include increased social media and solicitation of technology sponsors to offset the cost of WiFi.

Budget	Income	Registration
		3,000 attendees
Members		1,680 attendees
early (at 60% = 1,008 people)	$600 p/p	$604,800
late (at 40% = 672 people)	$800 p/p	$537,600
Nonmembers		600 attendees
early (at 50% = 300 people)	$700 p/p	$210,000
late (at 50% = 300 people)	$900 p/p	$270,000
Student (at 5% = 120 people)	$200 p/p	$24,000
Speakers (100 people)	$300 p/p	$30,000
Exhibitors	Included in exhibit fee	
Registration Total		**$1,676,400**
SAPDC (500 people)	$200 p/p	100,000
Exhibitors	$3,500 p/exhibit	$1,750,000
Sponsors (500 exhibitions)		$150,000
Bookstore		$10,000
Other		$5,000
Total income		**$3,691,400**
Expenses		2,081,188
Net income		**$1,610,212**

TABLE 16-1 Budget Income

The hotel budget will include meeting room rental, food and beverage, staff sleeping rooms, and service charges and gratuities. In creating the budget, Sue knows that she will have some negotiation opportunities based on the ASAA sleeping and meeting room usage ratios. The better that the ASAA's use of meeting rooms to sleeping rooms will match the hotel's ideal sleeping room to meeting room ratio, the better the rate that can be negotiated. To assist in managing the hotel blocks, Sue uses a housing bureau.

The convention center expenses will include the cost of space for meeting rooms, exhibit hall, electricity, Internet connection, garbage pickup, security, and staffing for coffee and food stations. To maximize dollars, Sue plans the majority of her educational events at the convention center. This not only enables her to use the daily rate for the rooms at the convention center but also is a selling point for exhibitors who want attendees near the trade show.

Sue will need to identify a **general services contractor (GSC)** to provide decorations and to set up the trade show. She will also need to assess audiovisual needs for both the hotel and convention center. The GSC will provide staging for the reception, general session, trade show, and awards night, and the **audiovisual (AV) company** will provide sound and light. To provide an accurate quote, the GSC must be given information on carpeting requests, number of trade show booths, estimated freight use, and types of staging needed for the opening session, general session, and awards dinner. The AV company will need to know the sound and lighting needs for each venue and the type of production for the general session, opening reception, and awards dinner. The general session will be sent via Webcast to members who are unable to attend, so Sue lists this as a separate expense (see Table 16-2).

Budget	Expenses
Convention Center	$450,000
Host Hotel	$312,643
GSC	$102,245
Signage	$80,000
Audiovisual	$220,000
Webcasting	$60,000
Pressroom	$30,000
Transportation	$50,000
Off-Site Venue	$75,000
Golf Event	$20,000
Marketing Committee	$190,000
Program Committee	$20,000
Speakers	$82,000
Entertainment	$30,000
Security	$180,000
Insurance	$100,000
Special Services	$5,000
Printing	$10,000
Temporary Staff	$67,200
Gifts	$20,000
Site Visits	$2,100
Other	$5,000
Total Expenses	$2,081,188

TABLE 16-2 Budget Expenses

To budget transportation, Sue looks at past budgets to determine how many attendees used the shuttle service for airport transfers, but she knows this expense will vary greatly depending on the existing transportation options in a given city. At this point, she includes full shuttle service for each day of the conference, VIP transportation, and transportation to the off-site events and the golf tournament. In addition to ground transportation, Sue's transportation budget includes air transportation for staff and VIPs as well as freight shipping.

To allocate funds for marketing, Sue reviews the cost history. This year she plans to spend less on hard items like brochures and direct mail pieces and more on electronic marketing, social media, and bloggers.

Of the speakers for the ASAA, 75% are members presenting research papers. To encourage members to make presentations, the ASAA offers presenters a 50% discount on the early registration fee. Most of the money allocated for speakers actually is used for a keynote speaker and entertainment. To locate the keynote speaker and entertainment, Sue uses a speaker's bureau; the speaker's bureau's fee is included in this expense item.

In order to have a smooth meeting, Sue will need to hire temporary staff. This budget item includes the cost for registration personnel, staff for on-site assembly of attendee packets, room monitors, and staff to distribute evaluations and carry out other duties. Sue will need to bring in temporary staff one day prior to the meeting for training and will pay staff for their time.

Security is an ongoing expense that the ASAA must include in its budget. Because the ASAA is increasing its involvement in new research for small animals and this new research is both confidential and controversial, more security will be needed.

Insurance is another expense that is increasing. Sue includes insurance to cover attrition and loss of revenue due to acts of God, terrorism, and liability. To cover expenses for attendees with special needs, Sue includes a special services item in the budget, which will be used for members who identify themselves as needing translators, written material to be published in Braille, sign language interpreters, special accommodations for Seeing Eye dogs, and so on.

When Sue creates the budgets, she contacts city officials where the meeting will be held. As a nonprofit organization, the ASAA is exempt from most city and state taxes, but she must file the documents to ensure the exemption. Furthermore, Sue will need to bring forms proving that the ASAA is a not-for-profit organization; the forms will also be filed with suppliers.

Sue includes some expenses in the budget even though she knows that these expenses will be picked up by sponsors. Each year, Sue has no problem finding a company to sponsor tote bags given to all attendees, transportation, the meal for the opening reception, and the entertainment for the VIP dinner. It is important that Sue includes these items in the budget to document these expenses.

To allow for unexpected expenses, Sue creates an "Other" expense category, which is used to cover additional expenses that do not occur every year or that are not planned for. For example, if the cost of shipping increases, this contingency would be covered.

INCOME

The income (see Table 16-1) will offset the expenses for the meeting. Estimated expenses for this meeting are $2,019,188. To reach the financial objectives and make a profit, Sue must not only pay all expenses but also build in a profit.

In determining the income, Sue starts with income generated from the registration fees. She first takes the expected attendance of 3,000 and subtracts 500 exhibitors whose registration fee is included in the exhibitor fee and then subtracts the 100 speakers who will pay a reduced registration. The ASAA has three registration fee categories: members, nonmembers, and students. Convention history shows that 70% are members, 25% nonmembers, and 5% students. To reduce attrition fees, Sue creates an early registration fee and a late fee for members and nonmembers. Typically, 60% of the members and 50% of the nonmembers will register early. Sue estimates that if registration alone will cover expenses, she must charge $629 per person. With this in mind, Sue's registration fee structure is $600 for an early member, $700 for an early nonmember, $800 for a late member, and $900 for a late nonmember. Students only pay $200, thus encouraging them to join when they are employed in the field. Sue estimates her registration income to be $1,676,400.

Following the income generated from registration fees, the exhibitors are the largest single source of income for the ASAA. It will cost the ASAA approximately $15 per square foot to rent the convention space, GSC, and audiovisual equipment. The ASAA will sell this trade show space for $35 per square foot. History shows a steady 10% increase in exhibitors per year; at the last conference, about 450 companies ordered booths. Sue estimates exhibitor income for this year to be $1,750,000 (500 exhibitors spending $3,500 each for a ten-foot by ten-foot booth).

Other sources of income that Sue will include in the budget are rebates generated from hotel rooms, the transportation company, and the GSC. Rather than accept commissions for these items, the ASAA negotiates a rebate per room per night that becomes an income stream. There is a small amount of money raised by the sale of the bookstore products, including books, shirts, and branded products.

Last year, 454 people took classes to earn the Small Animal Preventive Disease Certificate (SAPDC). Anticipating that she will reach her goal of a 10% increase in the number of attendees who will take the class, Sue estimates that 500 people will earn the certification this year. The $200 fee will remain the same as last year to encourage attendance. This is an additional cost that is not included in the registration fee.

REQUEST FOR PROPOSAL

Once the meeting objectives are laid out and a budget determined, Sue creates a **request for proposal (RFP)**. In creating the RFP, Sue wants to include accurate information to help hotels and cities submit good proposals. She includes meeting specifications on the ASAA and explains that the RFP is sent three years prior to the annual conference date. Although most RFPs are submitted electronically, Sue creates a hard copy and uses it as a guide to help her send consistent information to vendors. After the venues and destinations respond to the RFP, Sue reviews the information with Dave Rogers, Executive Director, and Elizabeth Rice, a board member serving as the convention chair. Sue, Dave and Elizabeth will choose two cities to visit to conduct an initial site inspection. After the initial site inspections to all selected cities are complete, a decision will be made, and Sue and Dave will conduct a second site inspection to the chosen city to begin contract negotiations. To avoid any bias, the ASAA will pick up the cost of the site inspection with the understanding that when a city is selected; the host city will rebate the cost of the site inspection.

The RFP will include a list of cities under consideration and the preferred dates. Although the dates may vary between the months of March and April, the days of the week must be Thursday to Sunday. The annual conference is held around the country, primarily in large cities near places where members of the board of directors reside.

Sue's RFP includes a detailed grid of her meeting room needs. She includes special requests; for example, her classroom sets require two chairs per six-foot table and a water station with recyclable water cups set in the back of the room. Attendees are encouraged to use the water bottles that were included in their welcome packet. She also includes a food and beverage summary that notes special dietary needs of attendees. Her meeting room grid includes the event, number of attendees, and room set.

The ASAA prefers to use no more than five hotels in a given city. A grid is created requesting the number of suites, single rooms, and double rooms that the ASAA anticipates using at each hotel. In considering a city, Sue looks for downtown hotel properties that offer a wide range of room prices, but the hotels need to be in close proximity to each other. The host hotel must be willing to block a minimum of 900 rooms; in addition to the sleeping room block, the host hotel will be the site of the opening night reception and breakout rooms for special-interest groups. A detailed history, in the form of a grid of the last three years, is included in the RFP. The history grid shows the peak room nights, meeting room block, sleeping room block, pickup for the host hotel and the room block, and pickup at each of the non-host hotels. She also includes a food and beverage section showing reported use. The ASAA reports a 10% increase in meeting attendees per year over the last two years and has an attrition rate of only 2%.

The final portion of the RFP is a two-page questionnaire for the hotel to complete and submit with the proposal. Questions include green initiatives, comp room policy, deposit policy, definition of "sold out," attrition policy, master accounts, split folios, shuttle service availability, tax rate, nonprofit tax policy, service charges, gratuity distribution, Internet connection and fees, phone charges, and fitness facilities fees. Sue also includes questions how the hotel handles "in conjunction with" (ICWs) and exhibitor room blocks and whether the hotel will work to create priority housing for members over nonmembers. Sue found that this form provides a quick way for her to compare hotels.

Using the RFP link on the destination marketing organization (DMO)/**convention and visitors bureau (CVB)** website, Sue enters meeting information and attaches a questionnaire for the DMO to complete. The questionnaire includes questions regarding state, local, and hotel room taxes as well as holidays, union contracts, special venues, DMO services, and citywide events or holidays that take place during the ASAA meeting dates.

FIRST SITE INSPECTIONS—EXPLORING TWO POSSIBLE CONFERENCE LOCATIONS

Sue, Dave, and Elizabeth have reviewed the proposals and identified two cities with available dates to host the ASAA citywide: Chicago and Dallas. Sue calls the DMOs in those cities to arrange to spend three days in each city and explains to them that the team plans to conduct a detailed site inspection to look for hotels, off-site venues, and golf courses. She sends the site inspection form that the team will use to evaluate the city and properties, explaining that the team will stay at the hotels under consideration as host properties and will conduct short tours of non-host hotels under consideration. For the non-host properties, the team only needs to meet with the hotel sales contact, see a standard room, and tour the outlets.

DAY ONE

Mark Tester, Vice President of sales, Chicago CVB, meets Sue, Dave, and Elizabeth at Chicago's O'Hare airport. On arrival, Mark gives a driving tour of downtown, passing by all the hotels under consideration. They have lunch at the Chicago Museum of Art, where they are joined by Kesha Evans, owner of Windy City, a **destination management company (DMC)**. Kesha explains the various services she can provide, including transportation and arrangements for off-site events, spouse tours, and private dining. Tom Delaney, Catering Manager at the Chicago Museum of Art, introduces himself and takes the group on a tour of the private function areas of the museum and recommends the best area for an off-site event. He opens his tablet to show visuals of the many meeting set-ups and décor options. He gives Sue a sales packet with sample menus and pricing and says that he will send an email with a link with more detailed information.

After lunch, Mark takes the inspection team to the Hyatt Regency McCormick Place to meet with its sales manager, Bob Taylor, and its general manager, Larry Rose. They tour the property, looking at sleeping rooms, suites, singles, and doubles as well as the meeting rooms and ballrooms for possible locations for the opening reception, special-interest group meetings, and available outlets. After the tour, they meet in one of the conference rooms to discuss available dates, rates, and available bandwidth.

Then Sue, Dave, and Elizabeth meet at 6:00 pm in the hotel restaurant for dinner. During dinner, they make observations, noting how the guests are treated, what the quality of the food is, the time food is served, and whether the wait staff are attentive. They order different entrées to sample the many types of food their attendees might order if they stay at this hotel. After dinner, Sue walks the meeting space, looking into the meeting rooms to see how the rooms are set.

DAY TWO

At 8:30 am, Mark meets the team members who have already eaten breakfast and checked out of the hotel. Mark has arranged for a 9:00 am meeting with Randy Moses, Senior Sales Manager of McCormick Place Convention Center. Randy gives a tour of the facility, taking time to show them what he sees as the best locations for their functions, loading docks, and shuttle drop-off and pickup, as well as the areas where sponsored items such as banners are allowed. Sue asks about available dates, food and beverage concession hours, Internet/WiFi charges, taxes, union rules, and contract renewal dates. Randy provides this information and discusses the security and the medical and emergency procedure guidelines. Both Mark and Randy explain to Sue, Dave, and Elizabeth how the DMO and convention center work as a team to help market the Chicago meeting to attendees. They discuss marketing options, including pre-mailers, email, social media, and on-site promotions the year prior to coming to the host city.

For lunch, Mark takes the group to the Golden Princess, a luxury yacht owned by ABC Charters, a company that provides dinner tours of Lake Michigan. Rich Cunningham, General Manager of ABC Charters, meets with them. Today, they are having a special lunch for meeting planners to sample the menu and enjoy a mini-charter experience. The president of Chicago DMC Services, Deborah Adams, explains her services and has videos on her tablet that show other off-site locations Sue may want to consider.

The afternoon is spent making contacts and touring the hotels under consideration. Mark arranges thirty-minute tours of each non-host hotel and explains to the hotel sales contact that they only want to see sleeping rooms and restaurant areas. By 4:00 pm, Sue, Dave, and Elizabeth are ready to check into the Hyatt Regency Chicago, the second hotel under consideration as the headquarters hotel. Rachel Monroe introduces herself as the Association Sales Manager and begins the tour. She is excited about a new ballroom that was recently added and explains how the ballroom could be used for the opening reception. After the tour, Richard Moore, the General Manager, joins the group to look at available dates and rates. Sue, Dave, and Elizabeth take an hour break and meet in the restaurant for dinner. During dinner, they review all notes from the past 2 days. After dinner, Sue takes her tour of the meeting rooms.

DAY THREE

The team checks out early and waits in the hotel lobby. As they check email, they notice a line forming as people check out of the hotel. They take mental notes, observing how long the checkout time is and how courteous the employees are at the front desk and bell stand. Mark arrives at the hotel and takes the group to the first stop, Harborside International Golf Center, a four-star course only twelve miles from downtown Chicago. The group meets with the special events manager of the Harborside to discuss the optional golf outing that is part of the ASAA event. The tournament is held Thursday afternoon, prior to the opening reception. Mark takes the group to one more golf course and on two more hotel site inspections before they depart for the airport. Sue, Dave, and Elizabeth thank Mark for his time and inform him that they will be touring Dallas next month and plan to decide in 2 months. After the Dallas site inspection, the ASAA will make its decision and will contact the bureau regarding that decision.

One month later, Sue, Dave, and Elizabeth go to Dallas for another three-day site inspection. Patty Brown, the Sales Manager of Visit Dallas the DMO, arranges for the group to meet with staff from the hotels, the convention center, and the off-site locations. Patty points out all the changes in Dallas including the Omni Dallas Hotel that is attached to the Dallas Convention Center.

DESTINATION SELECTION

After both site inspections conclude, the inspection team reviews their notes. Due to the conflict of dates with other industry meetings, they decide to meet on St. Patrick's Day. In evaluating Chicago, they are concerned about room availability, the renewal dates for some union contracts, and the fact that the cost to hold the meeting in Chicago is 25% more than in Dallas. This increase in cost might be offset by the number of attendees who prefer to meet in Chicago over Dallas, but this meeting will attract more attendees seeking the SAPDC—thus location will not be as much of an issue. Dallas is selected for the annual conference. Sue calls Mark from the Chicago CVB expressing their concerns and explains why Dallas was selected. Sue reminds Mark that they have not held a meeting in Chicago in 5 years and would like to look there again in the future.

SECOND SITE INSPECTION; FINALIZING DETAILS OF THE CONFERENCE

DAY ONE

Sue sends Patty Brown, at the Visit Dallas DMO, a letter of intent to hold the conferences in Dallas and contacts her to help arrange a second site inspection. This second site inspection will include only Sue and Dave and will be for 3 days. The goal is to finalize non-host properties, select off-site venues and a golf course, select the DMC and transportation company, begin contract negotiations, and select an organization for the CSR project. When Sue and Dave arrive in Dallas, they rent a car and take a self-guided tour of the city. They check in at the Omni Hotel Dallas, the location of the headquarters hotel for the meeting.

At the Omni Hotel Dallas in downtown Dallas, Sue and Dave meet with Loretta Jones, Global Director of Sales and Vicki Wall, the **convention services manager (CSM)**. Once the contract is signed, Sue will work with the CSM for the remainder of the meeting. During this meeting, Sue and Loretta will begin negotiations for sleeping rooms, meeting rooms, shuttle service, and so on.

After the meeting with the hotel staff, Sue meets Sonja Miller, Sales Manager of the Dallas Convention Center; Erika Bondy, CMP, Senior Event Coordinator; and Bill Baker, Director of Catering. Once the contract is signed, Sue will work with Erika on all her meeting details and with Bill on meeting food and beverage requirements. Today, Sue begins negotiating rates with the Dallas Convention Center. At the meeting, she will review her needs and see what is the best win-win situation for her attendees and the convention center.

Sue and Dave have lunch at the Dallas Museum of Art and meet with the Catering Sales Manager, Cindy Hartman, to review rates for having the VIP dinner in the restaurant. Carolyn Petty, president of EMC (a DMC), joins Sue and Dave for lunch to discuss what the DMC can provide for the ASAA meeting, including gift baskets and general transportation needs.

In the afternoon, Patty has arranged for Sue to meet with two of the non-host hotels under consideration in the city for sleeping room space. At each hotel, Sue meets the sales manager to negotiate the rates and amenities. For dinner, Patty takes Sue and Dave to a small Mexican restaurant that is a favorite of

Registration Company trains temporary staff prior to the opening of the conference

the locals. At dinner, Patty discusses the services that Visit Dallas can assist with, including registration personnel, marketing, social media packages to promote the meeting, leads for suppliers, transportation, Internet services, and on-site concierge to help attendees with local dining and sightseeing activities. She will staff a promotional booth at the meeting prior to the one in Dallas.

DAY TWO

The morning is spent touring and re-establishing contact with the remainder of hotels that will provide sleeping rooms. Sue and Dave have lunch at the Perot Museum of Nature and because they are looking for a fun site for the VIP meeting. They meet with Nicole Benson, Event Sales Manager, for a tour and a discussion of possible dining options. Although this is an option, it might be too casual for the group. Nicole brings her tablet to show pictures of events held at the museum, and Sue's concerns dissipate.

In the afternoon, Sue and Dave tour two golf courses. For each course, Sue makes contacts, has the event sales manager take them on a nine-hole tour, and begins discussing rates. Sue pays attention to where the group might meet before and after the tournament to determine if there is an area where the group might meet as they finish playing golf.

DAY THREE

Sue and Dave begin the day meeting the GSC contact, Jack Boyd, Account Executive for the Freeman Companies, the GSC and Mark Lee, Director of Sales, PSAV, Dallas, an AV company. Jack, Mark, Dave, and Sue meet first at the Dallas Convention Center and then at the Omni Dallas Hotel to discuss GSC and audiovisual equipment needs. They tour each venue, discussing specific staging, setup, WiFi, and other needs for each event.

The last stop of the day is to the Dallas SPCA to meet with Iris Henderson, Volunteer Coordinator. In researching a site for the meeting CSR, Sue learned about the Dallas SPCA and their program for groups to donate time sanitizing the animal shelter.

MARKETING COMMITTEE

ASAA has both an in-house marketing department and an outside advertising agency, and they work together to create the marketing campaign for the annual conference. After Sue returns home from the second site inspection, she meets with George Day, the ASAA Director of Marketing, and Julie Love, the Account Manager for Idea Maker, Inc., an advertising company. George and Julie share the results of a member survey, which reported that members are using Facebook, LinkedIn, and Twitter. They explain to Sue the importance of integrating social media in the marketing plan. Sue discusses the convention location and the meeting objectives and also explains how important promoting the new SAPDC is for this conference. After 2 weeks, Sue meets with George and Julie again. Julie brings theme ideas and visuals for the marketing pieces. After reviewing several themes, "Power of Prevention" is selected. It is decided that three marketing tools will be used. A four-color, postcard-size mailer will be developed as a teaser and mailed to all past conference attendees and targeted to potential members. This teaser will also be used as an advertisement that will be placed in industry newsletters digital magazines. The second piece will be an email announcement sent to all association members with a link to the convention website that will include a convention agenda giving dates, times, and speakers; a program-at-a-glance grid; current sponsors; and convention and housing registration forms. The final approach is the social media campaign that will include posts on Facebook, LinkedIn, Instagram, and Twitter. Working with popular convention speakers, the marketing committee will post information on Facebook and

LinkedIn and will Tweet about the conference activities. In addition, YouTube videos will be added to the conference website to generate excitement and encourage early registration and bloggers will be hired to write about and post their conference experiences. This year, in an effort to use less paper, a one sheet program will be created with the location of exhibitors in the trade show and a summary of the conference activities. After registering for the conference, attendees will download the conference app that includes information on the program, speakers, educational sessions, location of exhibitors, and detailed information on their products. Additionally, the app will have a section for attendees to interact with each other and include an electronic game that will encourage attendees to network and meet exhibitors.

George is excited about the app and explains to Sue and David that the game developed for the app will be used to highlight key sponsors thus adding a new revenue source to the conference.

During each conference, a new board of directors is introduced, awards are given, and important announcements must be made. Sue, George, and Dave meet to discuss the types of presentations that will be made and the scripts that George and his team will write. Sue is responsible for arranging rehearsal time for each presentation.

The marketing committee is responsible for creating press releases that will be sent to professional publications. For each conference, a new piece of research is featured, and the marketing committee works to promote this research to the public.

CREATION OF THE CONFERENCE PROGRAM

When Sue returns from the Dallas site inspection, she meets with the program committee to begin creating the educational content of the meeting. Serving on the program committee is Doug Walker, Board Member and chair of the SAPDC; Dan Dearing, Chairman of the board of directors of the Program Committee for the Power of Prevention annual convention; and his appointed committee members Liz Stewart and Mark Collins, along with Donna Smith, ASAA Administrative Assistant. These five people and Sue will work together to create the content of the meeting.

Sue begins the meeting by giving each committee member an option to receive a hard copy or electronic notebook with responsibilities of the committee members, past convention notes, and the meeting theme, the "Power of Prevention." Sue wants to make sure that the committee members understand the objective of the meeting: to increase the number of member attendees taking the SAPDC by 10% by offering a four-day conference that is focused on education that will increase meeting profits by 5%. The committee agrees to follow the same meeting agenda as in the past: opening reception, general session, concurrent sessions, awards dinner, and a **poster session** that is located in the middle of the trade show. The conference will include an ASAA VIP dinner, a golf tournament, and a total of 120 60-minute education sessions in two days. The one change in the schedule is to add two 4-hour segments for the SAPDC class. The committee will locate speakers for SAPDC classes and all breakout sessions. ASAA members will present 100 of the 120 educational sessions. To help the program committee, a separate committee—called the paper review committee is created that will issue the call for papers, grade and evaluate papers, and inform the program committee of its final selection for presentations and poster session. Sue will use a speaker's bureau for the opening reception, general session, awards dinner, ASAA VIP dinner, and all entertainment. Sue reviews the timeline with the committee. Using abstract management software, the paper review committee will begin the call for papers one year prior to the meeting; 6 months prior, the paper review committee will provide the program committee with the final selection, and the program committee will make initial contact with presenters and speakers. The committee will recommend speakers for all sessions. Once speakers and backup speakers have been identified, Sue will send out invitation letters, in which she will ask the speaker to sign a commitment sheet, outline the audiovisual options and will require the speaker to provide an abstract of the presentation and his or her biography and photo.

The committee will be responsible for contacting all the speakers and following up with those not responding. There will also be a point person for all speaker questions. Once speakers have been selected, Sue's role is to collect information, assign time slots, and correspond with the speakers, including letters of acceptance and a reminder letter.

One key feature in the conference is the exhibitors. Jill Kochan, ASAA staff, is the ASAA trade show manager for the conference. Jill is responsible for all communications with the exhibitors and the GSC as they set up the trade show. Jill will work closely with Sue to communicate exhibitor needs and will meet with the GSC to create specifications for the exhibitor prospectus.

The newly formed CSR Committee will work with the Dallas SPCA on a program that will give attendees an opportunity to volunteer at the new shelter during the conference. In addition, the committee will work with marketing to create an announcement to encourage attendees to bring items to the conference that will be donated to the SPCA. To thank ASAA for their help, the SPCA will put on a "puppy pet" in the lobby on the first day of the conference.

PARTNERSHIPS

As Sue prepares for this meeting, she knows the importance of her meeting partners. Throughout the conference, Sue depends on many companies to provide excellent service and to create a memorable experience for the ASAA members. She reviews her contact list, looking at the many companies she will partner with for the upcoming conference.

Although most housing bureaus can provide a complete housing package, including hotel selection, negotiation, and contract, Sue prefers to work with the housing bureau after she has selected the hotels. Once the selections have been made, the housing bureau will manage the hotel room block. The housing bureau will create a website for attendees to book rooms online and a downloadable form for attendees to complete, scan, and email. Once an attendee selects a hotel, the housing bureau will send a confirmation letter. One of the best aspects about Sue's partnership with the housing bureau is room block management: Rather than call all the hotels being used, Sue calls the housing bureau for monthly, weekly, and daily rooming reports as needed and depends on the housing bureau to manage the exhibitor room block.

Sue likes to partner with a local DMC for the annual conference. For this conference, Sue uses the DMC for arranging the airport meet and greet, hotel transfers, VIP transportation, and shuttle service from hotels to the convention center. The DMC made all logistical arrangements for the VIP dinner, which allowed Sue to concentrate on VIP invitations and content of the event. Sue also appreciates the fact that a DMC normally has access to many motor coach suppliers because transportation is always an area of concern for Sue. Once, in Washington, DC, Sue contracted with a motor coach company, and one of the motor coaches broke down with all her attendees in it. The company had no backup motor coaches, so her attendees waited almost an hour to be rescued and taken to the event.

For key speakers and entertainment, Sue uses a speaker's bureau because she does not have the time to research the many speakers and entertainers who could speak to ASAA members. The speaker's bureau will make recommendations on the best speakers and entertainers; and once Sue makes her selection, the speaker's bureau will handle all arrangements. It will ensure that the speakers are at the meeting on time and if something happens, the speaker's bureau can quickly arrange for a backup speaker.

Sue selects an online registration company to create the meeting registration site and collect registration fees. The designated registration company will accept registrations electronically, automatically send attendees a confirmation letter that contains a link to the housing bureau, and stores the registrations for easy retrieval to create name badges. The company that Sue selects offers on-site registration services, staffing, and financial reports. This provides attendees a consistent registration experience and the meeting planner quick access to reports to monitor registration activity and income.

Sponsors are important partners for the ASAA conference. Sue will work with all the sponsors to ensure that they receive exposure to members in exchange for their financial and/or in-kind support. Sue realizes that without annual conference sponsors, the ASAA would not reach its financial objectives for the convention.

The ASAA has always included meeting security for attendees' safety and exhibitor products, but for this conference Sue will increase security. An animal rights association contacted the ASAA and plans to protest a new test being conducted on laboratory rats. Sue realized that she must allow this group to protest, but she wants to ensure that they protest peacefully and do not disturb meeting attendees.

Key partners in making the conference a success are the GSC providing the decorations and the AV company supplying the electronic equipment. Sue considers the GSC as the partner that brings the theme to life, so the decorations must wow attendees visually. Sue recognizes the important role the GSC plays in keeping the exhibitors happy in addition to pleasing the conference attendees. This is important to the ASAA, as the exhibitors generate 44% of the revenue for the conference.

Sue loves to work with the AV company because this partner is crucial for every meeting event. Without proper projection and sound, the attendees would not be able to learn. Sue works closely with its staff during the meeting. One burned-out light bulb or malfunctioning microphone can ruin a breakout session.

To keep things running efficiently at the conference, Sue hires temporary staff and builds a partnership early with these people. They will be part of the team and will represent the ASAA during the conference.

CONTRACTS

Sue has a contract for each convention partner and every service provider. Each contract specifies the exact services that are expected and the penalties if the expectations are not met. Early in Sue's career, she worked with an association that signed a contract that did not include a realistic attrition clause. The association did not meet its room block and paid the hotel over $50,000 for unused rooms. At least one year out, Sue reviews each contract carefully. Long before the meeting begins, Sue will have contracts finalized with the host hotel, housing bureau, registration company, airlines, off-site venue, golf course, speaker's bureau, security, AV company, DMC, GSC, and many others.

MEETING TIMELINE

ONE YEAR TO SIX MONTHS COUNTDOWN

Sue looks at her **meeting timeline** and realizes that she is twelve months away from the Power of Prevention annual conference. She takes out her meeting resume and reviews all contracts. She meets with George and Julie from the marketing committee to review electronic and hard copy marketing pieces. If Sue and her team miss an educational session or a grammatical error, then that is the way it will be printed. If the mistake is important enough, the marketing piece will be reprinted, and the expenses added to the cost of the conference. Fortunately, with the electronic pieces, changes can quickly be made with minimal expense.

She arranges a meeting with Doug and Dan from the program committee to select the speakers for the convention. Once selected, Sue sends out the acceptance email to the speakers. In her message, Sue requests that the speaker confirm his or her commitment by sending an electronic speaker biography, digital photo, presentation abstract, and audiovisual needs form. Sue makes a point to contact the speaker's bureau to check the status of the motivational speaker and entertainment. She requests that all audiovisual needs are identified 8 months prior to the meeting. By doing this, Sue can have a more accurate budget item for the equipment.

Sue secures 10 sponsors for the meeting, including Small Vets Pluss, a company that supplies the vaccines for small animals, for the tote bags; Houver Pharmaceutical, a small-animal antibiotic producer, for transportation; LabSmlab, a provider of medical instruments used in animal surgery, for the opening night reception; Mix-a-vet, developer of special food for small animals, to sponsor the conference app and Smalco, a pet store featuring small-animal products. Small Vets Pluss will cosponsor the VIP entertainment and the awards dinner. Sue will contact each sponsor to confirm the commitment and sign the contract. In her conversation, Sue reminds sponsors that she needs to have them return a form with the exact spelling of their company name and the design of their signage or logo in a form that can be used on mobile applications.

The trade show floor plan for the Dallas conference was created and approved fourteen months prior to the Dallas meeting. Exhibit space for the Power of Prevention conference was sold on-site at the ASAA conference prior to Dallas—the ASAA has an 87% exhibitor retention. Nine months out, the GSC updates the floor plan and emails electronic exhibitor links to potential exhibitors. The ASAA uses exhibition software to create an electronic floor plan, manage booth sales, exhibitor registration, and provide financial reports to monitor sales.

In addition to the trade show, Sue works with the GSC in finalizing the setup for the opening reception, general session, and awards dinner. She determines where the media center and the registration area will be located. Sue depends on the GSC to recommend the best location to place sponsor banners, gobos, and signage. Most convention centers have strict rules regarding banner and signage placement, and GSCs that work with convention centers frequently know the rules and have great ideas on how sponsors can be recognized.

SIX MONTHS TO DAY OF THE MEETING

Fast forward to the six-month countdown for the Power of Prevention conference. The marketing committee writes and sends press releases and increases Facebook, Instagram, LinkedIn posts, and other social media promotions.

Early registration forms begin to arrive within weeks after being sent. In reviewing the registration forms, Sue notices that three of the attendees indicated that they have mobility disabilities and will need special accommodations. In compliance with the Americans with Disabilities Act (ADA), Sue will work with all meeting partners to ensure that these attendees are able to fully participate in the conference. She needs to arrange for handicapped rooms and notes that the meeting rooms will need to be set with aisles to accommodate these attendees.

Sue receives the menus from the hotel catering manager and selects the meals. She focuses on selecting menus that will appeal to all the attendees. The evaluations from last years' conference indicate that attendees wanted more healthy and vegetarian options.

She contacts the host hotel and convention center to get the names of the meeting rooms that will be used for the Power of Prevention conference. It is important for Sue to get the name of the location of the meeting rooms so that this information can be added to the convention program and app. Hotels and convention centers rarely want to give this information out early, as they do not want to commit to a particular meeting room that might be sold to another planner, so good communication and flexibility are important.

Sue works with the DMC to review the menu and with the GSC for the VIP dinner at the Perot Museum of Nature and Science. The dinner will be in a room that overlooks downtown Dallas and the evening will include a private tour of the museum and the opportunity to create a new virtual species of bird and test its ability to fly. Sue contacts Larry Grant, the Event Organizer at Tenison Golf Course, to finalize tournament rules. It looks like this will be a great year for this event—thirty people are already registered for this event. Sue gives Larry the names and handicaps.

During this time, Sue will also contact the DMC to finalize shuttle routes to all events, enabling her to begin ordering signage for transportation. Sue learns each year how even highly educated people get lost at meetings—it baffles her that veterinarians cannot read the location material in their program and on the app; Sue must clearly list all the events, their locations, and the shuttle service times. Signage is very important in the total conference experience.

MONTH FIVE

Five months prior to the event, Sue sends out reminders to all speakers, and she works with the marketing committee to finalize and send the marketing brochure and update social media promotions. After some quiet time to proofread the meeting material, she creates a detailed work schedule for staff, temporary employees, and volunteers. Sue orders meeting name badges and meeting supplies and then calls the security company to review her needs.

MONTHS FOUR AND THREE

During the fourth and third months prior to the event, Sue monitors registration on a weekly basis. At the third month, Sue reviews registration and adjusts her room block (she negotiated this option in her hotel contract as a way to control attrition).

Sue looks at her initial room block (see Table 16-3) and compares it with current hotel registrations. Convention history shows that 60% of the people register early, indicating that in a perfect world, the host property would have 600 rooms reserved. In looking at the actual hotel registrations, Sue notices that all rooms have been filled at the Hyatt Regency Downtown Dallas, but she is unable to get additional rooms so will need to close reservations for the Hyatt Regency. The Hilton Anatole and W Hotel are right on schedule and will require no changes. The Holiday Inn has 50 rooms less than what it should be; Sue reduces the block by 40% and is now obligated for 60 rooms rather than 100. She has the opposite problem with the Omni Dallas Hotel, the host hotel—the host property is 100 rooms over what she expects, so she conservatively increases the block by 5% and is obligated for 954 rooms.

Hotel	Omni Hotel Dallas	Hyatt Regency Downtown Dallas	Hilton Anatole	W Hotel	Holiday Inn
Initial Room Block	900	800	1,000	200	100
90-Day Room Block Review	700	500	500	150	50
Room Block Adjustment	Over—will add 54 rooms	No change	On Schedule	On schedule	Under—will remove 40 rooms
New Room Block	954	800	1,000	200	60

TABLE 16-3 ASAA Hotel Room Blocks

In addition to the room block adjustments, she has received calls from the convention center needing to move the location of several meeting rooms and calls from speakers needing to cancel. These changes affect the information in the one-page printed program, the website, and the conference app, so it must be revised. She sees this as a time of many changes, but these changes are all part of Sue's job. The work she did a year ago is paying off. To handle the speaker cancellations, she contacts the program committee to see who they have planned as a backup speaker.

MONTH TWO

At two months out, Sue arranges another trip to Dallas. Patty, CSM of the Dallas CVB, arranges for Sue to meet with all the key contacts to make the Power of Prevention conference a success. Vicki, the Director of CSM at the Omni Hotel Dallas, meets with Sue to conduct a property walk-through, and he will introduce Sue to the catering manager to review the menu, the accounts receivable contract to explain the bill review process, the front desk manager to confirm pre-key guests and the check-in and checkout process, and the director of security and medical staff to review emergency procedures. The CSM explains that he is the hotel contact and will assist Sue in providing information needed from the hotel, from room pickup to bill review. Vicki and Sue will work closely together.

At the Dallas Convention Center, Sue will meet with Erika Bondy, Senior Event Coordinator, to conduct a walk-through and invites the GSC and the AV contacts to join her. By doing this, Sue has many eyes looking for potential problems that might occur. She will also spend time with the catering manager to review the menu for the lunch and awards dinner.

Sue meets with the DMC representative to walk through hotel transportation routes and finalize menus, decorations, and entertainment for the VIP dinner at the Perot Museum of Nature and Science. Sue then meets with the event coordinator at the Tenison Golf Course to update the player list and review pairings.

When Sue returns from Dallas, she works with marketing to make updates to the app and sends the one-page paper program to the printer. She also ships materials to the convention site; works with the marketing committee on the final scripts; and reviews her staging guide that has all her contacts, the timeline, contracts, menus, and notes for her to review.

MONTH ONE

One month prior to the event, Sue continues weekly monitoring of the registrations and sends reminder emails to all the speakers. She works with the advertising firm to approve press releases to announce research findings that will be presented at the Power of Prevention conference; she also works with the staff to finalize work schedules, marketing, scripts, and rehearsal times. Sue will create a checklist and pack her convention material. She is a good planner and has thought about backup plans for her activities. For example, if the golf tournament is rained out, the group will spend the afternoon on a sports tour of Cowboy Stadium.

Sue likens the month before the meeting to a tennis match. Emergencies— which feel like 5 to 10 tennis balls coming across the net at her at the same time—can hit her, so Sue knows she must be ready with her racket in hand to successfully hit those balls back over the net and be ready for the next barrage of balls.

PRE-MEETING ACTIVITIES

Three days prior to the event, Sue and her staff arrive in Dallas to set up the meeting headquarters. She is happy to see that all her convention material has arrived safely. Sue meets all contacts to finalize meeting plans and arranges a walk-through of the host hotel and the convention center with her staff, temporary employees, and volunteers. The host hotel arranges a pre-con meeting where everyone working on the meeting will get together and review the meeting resume for any changes or concerns.

Sue monitors the setup of all meeting events and conducts on-site troubleshooting. Something always needs to be changed; it might be a sponsor sign with an error that needs to be redone by calling the GSC or a more complicated situation like the space for the registration being too small. This is a time of constant problem solving.

Sue joins George and the marketing staff as they rehearse for the general session, set up the pressroom, and conduct a press conference. George takes time to review the press list with Sue because she needs to know the names of press attendees to ensure that when they arrive, someone from the ASAA staff can quickly assist them. Good publicity can ensure the success of future conferences.

MEETING DAY ACTIVITIES

The meeting begins, and Sue is busy working with the staff to ensure all meeting rooms are set up properly and that all speaker materials and evaluations are ready. Her role is to work behind the scenes to make the attendees' experience perfect. She is the first one to arrive on-site and will be the last person to leave. The day is filled with questions that she must clarify or problems that need to be solved. This is the time that Sue is excited—the time when she sees all her hard work become a reality. She uses the contacts she made to quickly solve problems. For example, the equipment in one of the rooms is not working, so she calls the AV company and the problem is quickly solved. At the beginning of each day, Sue meets with the hotel CSM and the accounts receivable department to conduct a bill review. She also checks with the housing bureau to follow up on a comparison of the ASAA registration with the in-house guest list to ensure that the ASAA attendees are properly coded to the ASAA block, which helps with future event accommodations.

A special ASAA exhibitor headquarters office opens at the convention center. Jill, the ASAA's trade show manager, will remain in this office to handle any problems that might occur during the trade show and to accept exhibitor bookings for next year's ASAA conference.

AFTER THE MEETING

IMMEDIATE POST-MEETING ACTIVITIES

A tired Sue sips coffee and takes a moment to review the successes and the areas of opportunity of the Power of Prevention conference. Before leaving Dallas, Sue will facilitate a post-con meeting to evaluate this year's conference, where people who attended the pre-con meeting will be present to discuss the conference and answer questions: What were the problems? What could be done to improve this situation for future conventions? She will work with the hotel and vendors to reconcile registration numbers, review all pickups, and estimate ancillary business.

Planning a convention is a team event. Sue takes time to thank all speakers, sponsors, committee members, and facilitators for helping with the conference—she also rewards her staff by giving them a free day in Dallas to relax.

Since Sue works with small animals, she often jokes that her job is like "pulling a rabbit out of a hat."

TWO-MONTH POST-MEETING ACTIVITIES

After the statistics and evaluations have been reviewed, Sue begins her report to the executive director and to the board of directors regarding conference ROI. It is important after each conference that an evaluation is conducted. In creating this conference, Sue and her team set the convention objectives: to increase the number of attendees taking the SAPDC by 10% by offering a four-day conference that is focused on education and networking that will increase conference profits by 5%. What is the point of having a convention if the success is not measured? Part of the meeting planner's job is to demonstrate how a convention or meeting helps achieve organizational goals. By establishing objectives and reviewing ROI, a planner can show his or her role in supporting company objectives and the bottom line.

Sue is excited about the Power of Prevention convention. The industry press gave excellent pre-meeting coverage, with over $50,000 tracked as nonpaid advertising. The marketing committee decision to purchase push-ads on Facebook and hire bloggers for the meeting also contributed to the success of the meeting. Sue believes this third-party endorsement increased attendance. She also credits the marketing committee for adding the exhibitor Scavenger Hunt to the conference App. Ten sponsorships were sold to exhibitors at $1,000 each resulting in $10,000 additional sponsorship revenue and both the attendees and exhibitors enjoyed the experience. The attendees loved playing

Attendees participate in App scavenger

the game and competing with each other and the exhibitors who purchased the Scavenger Hunt sponsorship enjoyed the increased traffic to their booth. The meeting objectives were met: 500 people took the classes for SAPDC (a 10% increase from the 454 who took SAPDC classes last year), and meeting profits grew from $1,598,512 to 1,678,437 (a 5% increase).

Sue finishes her report and takes a call from the Orlando Convention Center, the location for next year's annual conference. She is twelve months away from the conference and is receiving the names of the meeting rooms that will be used. The meeting cycle continues.

COVID-19: THE EFFECT ON PUTTING IT ALL TOGETHER

In 2020, the MEEC industry faced its biggest challenge, COVID-19. This global pandemic required the industry to rethink how it does business.

This section focuses on what the meeting planner must do to address these changes. Some things like the need to understand the attendee's needs and wants and to set measurable objectives are the same. The delivery is different and, as the business community becomes more comfortable with digital events, the more attractive hybrid meetings become.

Converting a live event/meeting to a digital or hybrid is more than having a speaker present in front of a video camera, it is a completely new format that requires planners to carefully think about the attendee experience before, during, and after the event. It requires creativity to overcome digital barriers and enable attendees both at the event and who participate digitally to feel connected. Meeting planners are not television producers; while the expectation is that each meeting looks like a television production with smooth transitions from the plenary session to sponsor videos to speakers, in reality, the meeting will not be a success without the feeling of connection and engagement.

In the Small Animal Association (SAA) Case Study, Sue and her Board of Directors decide on a hybrid event. The event will be 3 days and 2 nights using three hotels for the room block. A total of 32 education sessions will be offered and half will be delivered both live and online. Day 1—Attendees will arrive and check into the hotel. The board of directors will meet that evening. Day 2—Attendees will have breakfast on their own then meet in the ballroom for the general session that will be aired live and digital. Following the general session, the first round of eight (8) 45-minute concurrent educational sessions will be offered followed by a 30-minute break for the rooms to be cleaned before attendees return for the second round of eight (8) 45-minute educational sessions. Each session will be closely monitored so that each room follows the allowable safe social distance protocol. After the morning educational session, the trade show (live and virtual) will be open for 5 hours and attendees will have the option to pick up a pre-packaged lunch and dine in a designated area on the show floor or take their lunch to their rooms and/or attend a third round of (8) 55-minute concurrent sessions. The last concurrent sessions will include a 10-minute pre-recorded message from the President of the SAA with closing remarks. Dinner will be on their own and Day 3—Attendees will depart.

The trade show, prior to COVID-19, was the leading income generator of the SAA conference. After COVID-19, most trade shows canceled or the number of exhibitors decreased substantially. Although the number of onsite exhibitors is expected to decrease, the SAA will offer a new virtual exhibition option to gain new exhibitors and as a value-add to those onsite. To persuade both onsite and remote exhibitors, the SAA will keep the virtual trade show open for 6 months after the conference thus enabling companies to continue to engage with the veterinarians after the event.

Attendance at the hybrid event will decrease for the live face-to-face portion and increase for the remote attendees. The number of onsite attendees will depend on the recommendation of the Centers for Disease Control (CDC), the destination COVID-19 risk alert levels, and the corporate guidelines for business travel. By providing a digital experience, attendees may join from any location around the world. Although going digital saves attendees time and money, experts say that it can never replace the live experience.

BUDGET

EXPENSES

The cost of a digital or hybrid event is offset by the reduction in room nights and food and beverage costs. In the Pre-COVID-19 meeting, the SAA utilized five hotels for four nights. Post-COVID-19, only three hotels plus the convention center will be used and the length of the meeting will be reduced to two nights with one full day of education and a trade show.

Costs that will decrease are the host hotel, food and beverage, the general service contractor, signage, transportation, printing, press room, temporary staff, site visits, and onsite security. Expenses that will remain the same or increase are the convention center, audiovisual, webcasting, marketing and programs, speakers, entertainment, and gifts.

New expenses include social media services and digital production. According to sources at the time of the writing, digital events start at $15,000 for a production team to live stream, pre-record, and upload pre-recorded content for a one-day event that includes a general session and concurrent sessions. The price will increase to $50,000 to $100,000 for a multi-day interactive customized digital program that incorporates the creation of sponsorship ads, polling, and gamification. The more customized an event, the more it will cost.

INCOME

The income structure for the SAA will change. Once expenses are identified and both the live and digital attendance is estimated, a break-even analysis can be made to determine the break-even cost for the event and new registration fees can be determined for both the digital and live attendee.

Digital/hybrid events afford more sponsorship opportunities to increase revenue. Corporate digital commercials and messages can run during session breaks, posted in the chat box, included in social media posts, and more.

REQUEST FOR PROPOSAL (RFP)

New sections will be added to the venue RFP and a separate RFP created to select a digital provider.

Changes and additions to the Venue RFP include:

- The requirements of the meeting and to clearly explain if the event is 100% digital or hybrid.
- Meeting space requirements; meetings will need more space to host fewer attendees. For example, a six (6) foot table once sat up to three people, to practice social distancing, the table now sits one person.
- Food and beverage requirements; buffets and self-serve foods like hors d'oeuvres, coffee stations, and refreshment breaks are no longer an option. The CDC discourages the sharing of items that are difficult to clean, sanitize, or disinfect. The planner will require that the hotel create attractive pre-packaged options for attendees to grab and go.
- Request for disclosure of other groups meeting at the hotel; although this has always been a recommended practice, in a post COVID-19 environment, groups will not only be concerned with competitors but also the bandwidth they will use.
- Bandwidth capabilities and the cost to add additional coverage if needed.
- Safety practices both in the front and back of the house.

Digital Provider RFP:

Hybrid meetings require an RFP to select a digital provider. The RFP must include information on the dates, times, the number and length of the sessions, type of AV needed in each session, the number of presenters in each session and if they will be pre-recorded or live or both, and how many attendees are expected to see the show simultaneously.

One section of the digital RFP will focus on the expectations of the attendee experience and addresses the planners wish list. For example, does the planner want a managed webinar with dedicated technical support? Will the conference content be available to attendees after the event and, if so, for how long? Will the planner want the vendor to house data? This information is needed to give vendors an understanding of the planner's needs and wants.

SITE INSPECTIONS

Pre COVID-19, the planner would make multiple trips to the destination before and after the location was selected. Post COVID-19, meeting professionals are relying on viewing the cities under consideration and available hotels online through video. Once the selection is narrowed, the planner will contact representatives at the DMO and hotels to set up virtual/digital site inspections.

Before the final selection is made, the meeting planner will travel to the destination to finalize the space and technology. Nothing replaces the ability to see a space to understand how the meeting will be experienced by the attendee.

MARKETING

The marketing department now works with an advertising agency and a social media company. The social media company is responsible for scheduling and deploying the messages on multiple platforms and the advertising agency looks for ways to increase revenue and sponsorships. In addition to meeting branding and promotion, the marketing team now uses data collection to customize the message for each audience.

CONTRACTS

New contracts are written to address the legal and financial risk of the host organization. Terms like "duty of care" will be revised to ensure that all attendees are safe. Cancellation clauses will be tied to government mandates regarding the standards for a venue or event to operate. Planners need to closely review Force Majeure clauses to determine under what conditions their meeting can operate. Statements that identify sponsor and venue responsibilities is important. Should the venue or the planner offer face masks and other personal protective equipment to attendees?

MEETING TIMELINE

The time to plan a digital or hybrid event could take longer than a live event. When planning a hybrid meeting, time must be allocated for both the live and the digital component.

Additions to a live event timeline include:

- Monthly communications with the DMO/CVB and hotels to discuss any state-ordered requirements that would affect the meeting. These requirements include wearing a mask, social distancing, and quarantines.
- Dates for speakers to submit pre-recorded videos (normally 6–8 weeks before the meeting).
- Speaker video production—once the speaker videos are received, they will be edited to ensure quality and branding.
- Technical rehearsals are normally held a few weeks in advance, then again, a few days before the meeting. A rehearsal the day before or on the day of the meeting works for live meetings, but not digital.
- Social media posts for all of the days before the conference, during the conference, and after the conference. The branding and message must be creative and engaging.
- Pre-mailing to VIP, speakers, and attendees.
- Sponsor video production.
- Day-of script.

The timeline for the trade show could increase as dates are set to create the digital part of the show.

CONFERENCE PROGRAM

SPEAKER SELECTION AND PREPARATIONS

Not all speakers are effective in both digital and live formats. The speaker selection committee will need to review recordings of speaker digital and live performances. Once speakers are selected, they will be sent a tool kit with instructions on how to record and submit the video as well as the guidelines on what to wear and preferred background and lighting. This will ensure quality and create consistent branding for the meeting. Companies like PSAV offer to send the speaker tool kits and live support to ensure that the speaker will produce a quality video.

DIGITAL ADVANTAGE

One of the key advantages of hosting a digital or hybrid meeting is the ease of gathering data on each attendee. Analytical reports can be reviewed that track the number of attendees in each session, time spent in the session, and attendees' demographic and geographic data including age, education background, zip code, and more. Event statistics can analyze how much money each attendee spent and product selection.

Marketing analytics can be reviewed to determine attendees' web browser selection, use of social media platforms, and which message produced the best response. This information can be reviewed daily to make immediate changes to the marketing campaign and customize messages to attendees.

If organized correctly, attendee engagement for the digital event can increase. The speaker who used polls and surveys and during the presentation can get immediate feedback and ensure that attendee needs are met.

RETURN ON INVESTMENT (ROI)

Whether the conference is live, digital, or hybrid, there must be a ROI for the attendees, exhibitors, and sponsors. Data analytics offer multiple ways to collect and review data to determine ROI and event success. Once this data is collected and analyzed, it must be reported to all stakeholders. The hybrid meeting will only continue if they, like 100% live events, can demonstrate the ability to fulfill meeting objectives.

SUMMARY

In this chapter, you have learned about the process of creating a citywide meeting. This is a large task for one person and requires many partners to make the conference or event successful. Through this case study, you have been able to see the life of a meeting planner and have looked at the many tasks leading up to the conference. The chapter began with creating conference objectives and budgets, and it ended with evaluating ROI to determine the success of the meeting.

KEYWORDS AND TERMS

For definitions, see https://insights.eventscouncil.org/Industry-glossary

audiovisual (AV) company
convention services manager (CSM)
destination marketing organization
    (DMC)/convention and visitor
    bureau (CVB)
corporate social responsibility (CSR)
destination management company
    (DMC)

general services contractor (GSC)
meeting timeline
poster session
request for proposal (RFP)
return on investment (ROI)
sponsor

REVIEW AND DISCUSSION QUESTIONS

1. Who is the group in this chapter? Why are they here?

2. What is the SAPDC and what is the value to the attendees and to the organization?

3. What are the steps that Sue goes through to plan this meeting?

4. Who does Sue work with on her staff?

5. Who does Sue work within the city where the meeting is being held? Which suppliers or vendors?

6. What does Sue do after the meeting is over?

7. What changes did Sue make to meetings due to COVID-19?

ABOUT THE CHAPTER CONTRIBUTOR

M. T. Hickman, CMP, CSECP, is the lead faculty and head of the Hospitality, Exhibitions and Event Management, Dallas College—Richland Campus in Dallas, Texas. She began her career at the Irving, Texas, CVB, where she worked in many departments, including tourism sales, convention sales, and special events. Over the years, she has worked as director of marketing for the National Business Association and as a proposal writer for WorldTravel

Partners. She is active in the meeting and exposition planning associations, including MPI, PCMA, IMEX, and IAEE.

PREVIOUS EDITION CHAPTER CONTRIBUTORS

Roy T. Benear, Vice President, Exhibits + Specialty Events—PSAV

Laura Jordan, CMP, CTA, Meetings & Events Manager, OsteoMed, LLC

Patty Stern, Chief Creative Officer, PattyStern.Com Creative Marketing & Event Concepts

David Gisler, (Retired) Director of Sales and Training, Total Show University, Freeman Companies

Bitsy Burns, CMP, (Retired) Director of Operations, Southwest Veterinary Symposium

Erin Donahue, Global Account Director at Trump Hotels

Patty Towell, Sales Manager, San Antonio Convention and Visitor Bureau

Dana Rhoden Dana Rhoden, CMP, CMM, Marketing and Recruitment at CityVet

INDEX

C

E

H

I

Microsoft, 393

Middle East

MEEC, international aspects in, 535–536

trade fairs and exhibitions in, 535

Mixed reality, 403–404, 410

augmented reality, 404

virtual reality/360 videos, 405

Mixing service styles, 307–308

Mobile charging stations, 108

Mobile communication, 501

Mobile devices, 380

Mobile kitchens, 299

Monitor on-site communications, 503

Multilevel exhibits, 184

Multi-services operator, 230

Multiuse facility, 139

Music copyright, 362–363

N

NACS. *See* National Association of Consumer Shows (NACS)

NAICS codes. *See* North American Industry Classification System (NAICS) codes

National Association of Broadcasters, 119

National Association of Consumer Shows (NACS), 215

National Association of Convention Bureaus, 160

National Association of Exposition Managers, 161

National Western Stock Show, 177

Natural attractions, 8

Natural Products Expo East, 34–39

Needs analysis, 106, 444–445

Negotiation

contracts, 337–338

naming names, 338–342

strategies, 334–337

Negotiator, 335

News releases, 505–506

New York City Marathon, 275–276

Nonresidential conference centers, 127

Nontraditional destination, 379

Nontraditional room setup, 487–488

North American Industry Classication System (NAICS) codes, 8

O

Objective, 446

OCEC. *See* Oman Convention and Exhibition Centre (OCEC)

Offcial contractor, 197

Offer, 343

Official service contractor (OSC), 170, 172–173

Off-premise events, 300

Oman Convention and Exhibition Centre (OCEC), 535–536

"One-size-fits-all" proposition, 459

One-way communications, 380

Online/inbound marketing, 473–474

Online meetings, 408

creation of, 408

Online RFPS, 377

On-site audiovisual, 492–493

On-site communication, 503

equipment and resources, 500–503

meeting/convention/event, 501–502

monitor on-site communications, 503

personal communications, 499–500

use of technology

equipment, 502–503

equipment and resources, 500–501

meeting/convention/event, 501–502

monitor on-site communications, 503

Onsite event tech infrastructure, 394

On-site management

ancillary events, 493–494

common issues

access, 491

floors, 490–491

obstacles, 488

power, 488–489

rigging, 489–490

controlling costs, 495–496

S